Christ Jesus, the Way

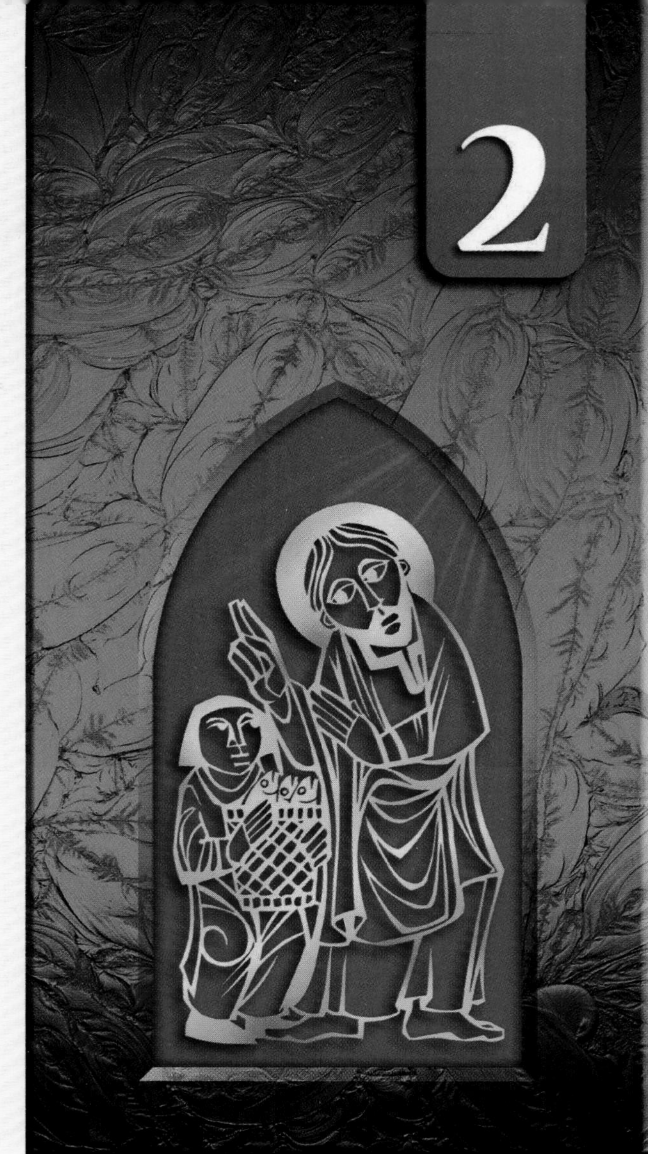

School Teacher's Edition

General Editors
Sister Catherine Dooley, O.P.
Rev. Berard Marthaler, OFM Conv.
Rev. Gerard P. Weber

Consulting Editors
Monsignor Thomas McDade, Ph.D.
Irene Murphy
David Michael Thomas, Ph.D.

Benziger
Woodland Hills, California

The Ad Hoc Committee to Oversee the Use of the Catechism, United States Conference of Catholic Bishops, has found the doctrinal content of the student editions of *Christ Jesus, the Way* to be in conformity with the *Catechism of the Catholic Church.*

Credits
Total Parish Catechesis: William Huebsch
Educational Consultants: Anne Battes Kirby, Barbara Kay Bowie, Judy Deckers
Consultants: Clare Collela; Rev. John Gallen, SJ, Ph.D. (Liturgy); Dr. Peter Gilmour, Ph.D.; Rev. Robert Hater, Ph.D.; Sr. Ann Laszok, CSBM (Eastern Catholics); Sister Eva Marie Lumas, SSS; Rev. Ronald Nuzzi, Ph.D.; Daniel Pierson; Rev. Peter Phan, Ph.D.; Art Zannoni (Sacred Scripture)
Contributors: Christina DeCamp, Silvia DeVillers, Sandy Lauzon, Camille Liscinsky, Joanne McPortland, Yvette Nelson, Catherine M. Odell, Dee Ready, Charles Savitskas, Margaret Savitskas, Susan Stark, Helen Whitaker
Mission Education: Maryknoll Fathers, Brothers, and Sisters
Liturgical Catechesis: Sr. Catherine Dooley, OP (General Editor); Maria Elena Cardena; Silvia DeVillers; Sr. Miriam Malone, SNJM; Ret Siefferman; Joan Vos
Editorial Management/Teachers' Editions: Maureen A. Kelly and The Mazer Corporation
Music Editors: Gary Daigle, Jaime Cortez
Video: Dr. Thomas Boomershine, Ph.D.; Amelia Cooper

Design: Bill Smith Studios, Monotype Composition
Production: Monotype Composition
Cover Design: Robert Hyre and Logan Design
Cover Art: Br. Stephen Erspamer, SM
International Photography: Maryknoll Magazine
Teachers' Editions
Design: Bill Smith Studios
Additional Design: The Mazer Corporation
Production: The Mazer Corporation

Nihil Obstat: Sister Karen Wilhelmy, CSJ, Censor Deputatus
Imprimatur: † Roger Cardinal Mahony, Archbishop of Los Angeles, September 25, 2001
The nihil obstat and imprimatur are official declarations that the work contains nothing contrary to Faith and Morals. It is not implied thereby that those who have granted the nihil obstat and imprimatur agree with the contents, statements, or opinions expressed.

Send all inquiries to:
Benziger
21600 Oxnard St. Suite 500
Woodland Hills, CA 91367

ISBN 0-07-821729-6 (School Student Text)
ISBN 0-07-821730-X (Teacher's Edition)
ISBN 0-07-821754-7 (*Celebrate* Student Edition)
ISBN 0-07-821763-6 (*Celebrate* Catechist's Guide)
ISBN 0-07-821735-0 (*Home*)
ISBN 0-07-821799-7 (Music CD)
ISBN 0-07-821737-7 (Interactive Lesson Planner)
Printed in the United States of America
1 2 3 4 5 6 7 8 9 073 06 05 04 03 02 01

Contents

Faith Formation

A Little Catechism

Core Lessons

Contents

Glossary and Index

Catechetical Toolbox

0-07-821721-0 0-07-821730-X 0-07-821739-3 0-07-821748-2 0-07-821757-1 0-07-821766-0

Christ Jesus, the Way

esus said, "Do not let your hearts be troubled. You have faith in God; have faith also in me. In my Father's house there are many dwelling places. If there were not, would I have told you that I am going to prepare a place for you? And if I go and prepare a place for you, I will come back again and take you to myself, so that where I am you also may be. Where [I] am going you know the way."

Thomas said to him, "Master, we do not know where you are going; how can we know the way?"

Jesus said to him, "I am the way . . ."

John 14:1–6

he Word of God, incarnate in Jesus of Nazareth, Son of the Blessed Virgin Mary, is the Word of the Father who speaks to the world through his Spirit. Jesus constantly refers to the Father, of whom he knows he is the only Son, and to the Holy Spirit, by whom he knows he is anointed. *Jesus is "the Way" that leads to the innermost mystery of God.*

General Directory for Catechesis, 99

"
e holy, for I, the Lord your God, am holy" *(Leviticus 19:2)*. This is a forceful reminder to all Christians how important is the doctrine of the universal call to holiness in the Church. "I am the Way, the Truth, and the Life" *(John 14:6)*. With these words, Jesus presents himself as the one path that leads to holiness. But a specific knowledge of this way comes chiefly through the Word of God which the Church proclaims in her preaching. Therefore, the Church in America must give a clear priority to prayerful reflection on Sacred Scripture by all the faithful.

The Church in America, 31–32

t is not a matter of inventing a new program. The program already exists: it is the plan found in the Gospel and in the living Tradition; it is the same as ever. It has its center in Christ himself, who is to be known, loved, and imitated—so that in him, all may live the life of the Trinity, and with him transform history until its fulfillment in the heavenly Jerusalem.

At the Beginning of a New Millennium, 29

Overview

- Mission Statement
- Knowledge, Love, Service
- A Little Catechism

Benziger welcomes you to *Christ Jesus, the Way,* a new basic catechetical curriculum that provides a complete and comprehensive religious formation program for grades K–6. *Christ Jesus, the Way* builds on the foundation formed by *To Teach as Jesus Did* and *Catechesi Tradendae*. The content of *Christ Jesus, the Way* is taken from the Sacred Scripture, the living Word of God, and from the *Catechism of the Catholic Church*. The series takes its mandate and its sense of urgency from the *General Directory for Catechesis*. *Christ Jesus, the Way* takes its spirit of joy and renewal from Pope John Paul II's Apostolic Letter, *At the Beginning of the New Millennium*. Finally, the series answers the call for evangelization, inculturation, and holiness from the Apostolic Exhortation, *The Church in America*.

Mission Statement

It is the purpose and mission of *Christ Jesus, the Way* to provide parishes and Catholic schools with the very best in contemporary catechesis for elementary-school children. In its development, the material has been guided by a biblical faith, a fidelity to the doctrine of the Church, and an authentic vision of the Gospel. *Christ Jesus, the Way* is also the cornerstone of total parish catechesis in which all members of the local faith community can participate as a teaching and learning community.

Knowledge, Love, Service

For scores of years, the first catechism question youngsters faced was simple and basic: "Who made you?" The answer was straightforward: "God made me!" "Why did God make you?" asked the follow-up question. The chorus of young voices responded, "God made me to know him, to love him, to serve him, and to be happy with him in this world and the next!"

Christ Jesus, the Way returns to that simple formula, recognizing that human beings share a common origin—creation by God. Each human being shares a common destiny—returning to God. The path between creation and final destiny is a three-part journey of holiness.

The Journey of Holiness	
A Journey of Knowledge	Learning about and spreading the Good News
A Journey of Love	Adoration, prayer, worship, and care for others
A Journey of Service	Seeing Christ in those who are hungry, thirsty, naked, sick, or imprisoned, and in those who need to hear the Gospel message of hope

Each lesson of *Christ Jesus, the Way* weaves together knowledge, love, and service in a seamless garment of instruction, formation, and example. Each lesson of *Christ Jesus, the Way* introduces a witness—a real person of faith who has successfully brought together in his or her life the key elements of knowledge, love, and service.

A Little Catechism

In addition, each grade level of *Christ Jesus, the Way* contains *Know, Love, Serve: A Little Catechism*. This catechism provides summaries of Church doctrine and explanations of seasons and feasts. This section also contains special devotions to the saints, tips on living a Christian life, and prayers that every child should know, and examples of loving service.

Ministry of Catechesis

Catechesis is an educational ministry. Those who teach religion are ministers as well as teachers, and the whole parish is the catechist. Whether religious instruction takes place in parish programs or in parochial schools, it needs to include three important aspects of catechetical ministry.

1. Parents are a child's first catechists. Faith is first handed on by the parents.
2. Parochial school teachers and parish catechists *support* and *extend* the parents' role.
3. Parish and school catechetical programs make connections between the home and the parish, between family life and parish life, and between family gatherings and the Sunday Eucharistic assembly.

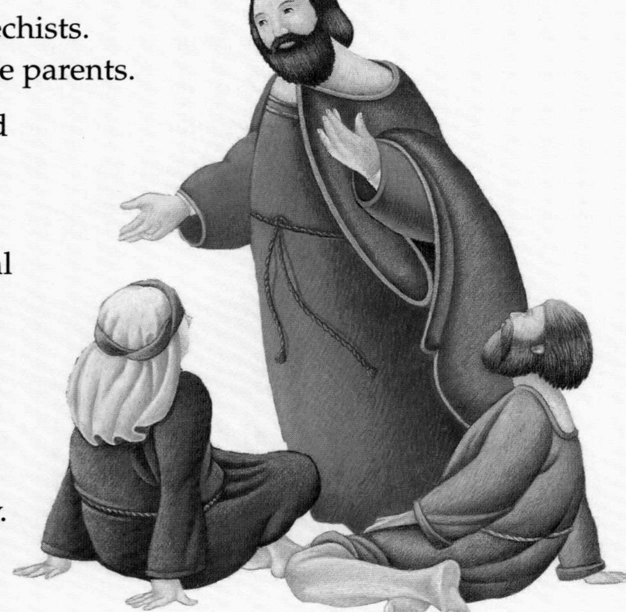

Developmental Catechesis

The General Directory for Catechesis (143) stresses the gradual nature of God's revelation and the developmental learning of the children. Just as life gradually unfolds for a young child, so too do the mysteries of creation, of the Word become flesh, of Redemption, and of life in the Holy Spirit.

Christ Jesus, the Way is developmental in all its aspects. As a result, the series meets important catechetical objectives:

1. **Christ—the Center and Focus:** The series offers a contemporary and realistic vision of Jesus Christ in the world today. "The Incarnate Word is the fulfillment of the yearning present in all. It is the mystery of grace and source of all holiness" (John Paul II, *Tertio Millennio Adveniente*, 22).
2. **Religious Literacy:** The series develops religious literacy in the learner. This literacy is built by using a process of initiation—inviting the learner to share more and more in the history, language, celebrations, and traditions of Catholic Christianity.
3. **Religious Imagination:** *Christ Jesus, the Way* engages the whole learner in the process of catechesis. It strives to inspire religious imagination and to help the learner express faith in creative, even artistic, ways.
4. **Lived Christianity:** People who follow Jesus try with all their hearts and souls to live good lives. *Christ Jesus, the Way* teaches that faith leads to action.

Catechetical Method

Christ Jesus, the Way is organized into a series of age-appropriate, developmental, and self-contained sessions. The series does not espouse any single method of catechesis. It cultivates a diversity of methods to ensure that revelation will be proclaimed in the words, actions, sentiments, and culture of the learner. (GDC, 148)

- **Inductive and Deductive:** Because catechesis is an event of grace, *Christ Jesus, the Way* fosters an encounter with Jesus Christ. The program is inductive in that it presents biblical events, liturgical acts, events in the life of the Church, and events of daily life so as to discern the meaning these might have. The program is also deductive in that it explains and describes truths by teaching general principles and the authentic doctrine of the Church (GDC, 150).
- **Human Experience:** The program recognizes that human experience arouses interest, raises questions, causes hope and anxiety, and gives rise to reflections and judgments. Human experience is part of every lesson in *Christ Jesus, the Way* (GDC, 152).
- **Memorization:** Memory has its place in catechesis. Whenever memorization is called for in *Christ Jesus, the Way*, it involves communal support and cooperation among the children. This approach helps children know and treasure the basic prayers and formulas of the faith (GDC, 154).
- **Activity and Creativity:** *Christ Jesus, the Way* is based on the foundational principle that good catechesis actively engages the learner and taps his or her religious imagination and creativity. Throughout the series, participants are called to prayer, to participation in the sacraments and liturgy, and to involvement in activities and projects of apostolic witness and social concern (GDC, 157).
- **Group Activity:** *Christ Jesus, the Way* fosters an experience of community and a form of participation in ecclesial life through its emphasis on the actions and collaboration of the group. Catechists are encouraged to gather for support and learning. Families are shown the importance of being together. In each catechetical session, children are involved in group activity, dialog, and sharing (GDC, 158–159).
- **Media:** *Christ Jesus, the Way* blends a wide variety of print and electronic media throughout the series. Electronic media and resources are included in every teaching edition (GDC, 160–162).

Catechetical Content

The content of *Christ Jesus, the Way* has two sources: Sacred Scripture—the living Word of God—and the *Catechism of the Catholic Church*—the compendium of what the Catholic Church believes and teaches. All the stories, activities, lessons, conversations, exercises, tests, reviews, and celebrations of *Christ Jesus, the Way* are designed to teach Scripture and the *Catechism*. In addition, the program strives to articulate those elements of the *Catechism* that the United States Conference of Catholic Bishops considers to be of particular importance in the formation of faith in children.

Children's Catechesis

Christ Jesus, the Way begins with the catechesis of children from kindergarten to grade six. Benziger recognizes that the catechesis of adults is a *primary focus* of the catechetical mission. It also recognizes that the product of catechesis is an adult believer of mature faith (GDC, 172–176). There is, however, in the Church in general and in the Church in the United States in particular, a great tradition of starting early. This tradition recognizes that the childhood years are an important time in the formation of adult believers.

Catechist Formation

Christ Jesus, the Way provides help for those who participate in the ministry of catechesis. Most catechists are volunteers. Often teachers in parochial schools feel inadequate when it comes to religious education—the ministry of catechesis. Therefore, *Christ Jesus, the Way* contains a thorough and consistent catechist formation.

- **The Catechist/Teacher Resource:** In each lesson of each grade of the teaching editions, there is a resource containing information and reflection on the Word of God, and the *Catechism of the Catholic Church*.
- **Background and Preparation:** The resources and suggestions provide ongoing support that helps the catechist experience the joys and successes of this ministry and deal with its frustrations.
- **Helpful and Simple Tone:** The lesson plans, directions, background essays, and other materials are written in a simple, direct style. Religious vocabulary and the common language of the faith are explained for the catechist.
- **Catechetical Toolbox:** Available in each teaching edition of *Christ Jesus, the Way*, as well as online, is a special section containing tools and skills that can help each catechist attain a certain proficiency in the ministry to which he or she has been called.

Families of Faith

Christ Jesus, the Way acknowledges the primary role of the parents and the extended family in catechesis. In addition, *Christ Jesus, the Way* helps parents and families grow in faith and share that faith with one another. The program provides weekly opportunities—in the text—to help families share faith. In addition, *Christ Jesus, the Way* provides a faith-sharing book that helps families talk about the faith, participate in the life of the parish, and celebrate the seasons and feasts that are great sources of faith formation.

Total Parish Catechesis

Every component of *Christ Jesus, the Way* has the entire parish in mind. This new program leads children, catechists, families, and other adults to active participation in the Eucharistic community. In addition, *Christ Jesus, the Way* provides adult catechetical experiences connected to every lesson in the program. These experiences are provided on a CD-ROM and online. The online lessons will be updated regularly to make sure that the adult catechesis is grounded in current events. *Christ Jesus, the Way* can provide catechetical ministry for the entire parish.

Worship and Prayer

Christ Jesus, the Way is the first catechetical series to provide a worship book for the children's liturgical formation and catechesis. Each grade level has an edition of *Celebrate*—a series of twelve worship services that help the children learn to celebrate the sacred mysteries, pray the liturgy of the hours, remember the lives of the saints, and participate in the Eucharist. In addition, the entire program is filled with opportunities for prayer and worship in all its creative forms. *Christ Jesus, the Way* stresses poetic imagination, creativity, simplicity, and clarity in all its worship.

The Maryknoll Connection

At the very heart of catechesis is the evangelical mission. Catechesis is part of the missionary mandate of Jesus. It is the responsibility of God's People to preach the Good News to all—to plant the seed of the Good News on good soil.

The need to fulfill this mandate gave birth to an alliance unprecedented in the development of catechetical materials. Benziger has become a partner with Maryknoll—that unique missionary organization founded in the United States and dedicated to the worldwide spread of the Good News. The priests, brothers, sisters, and lay people of Maryknoll radiate from their New York headquarters a Gospel presence throughout the world. The experiences of Maryknoll are woven into every grade level of *Christ Jesus, the Way*. These experiences reinforce the missionary vocation of every baptized person. The experiences also foster a sense of evangelization. The experiences bring to life the commitment to social justice. In addition, the Maryknoll experiences till the soil so that, should the Holy Spirit so decide, the seed of priestly, religious, and lay vocations can also be sown in young people.

Maryknoll and *Christ Jesus, the Way*

The Maryknoll connection is found in the series in four specific ways:

At Each Grade Level	The Little Catechism that begins the student text contains specific stories and activities for mission education and social justice.
In Each Unit	Each unit opener features pictures from the Maryknoll archive. These pictures show how the Good News is preached in and out of season. The pictures show the faces of children of "every tribe and nation." And they show why the Church's mission is a mission of social justice and peace.
Through Projects	Each unit has at least one project or activity taken from the pages of *Maryknoll Magazine*—one of the best resources available anywhere for mission education.
Throughout the Program	Scattered throughout the program are pictures, examples, and models of evangelization, of global Christianity, and of a real and personal hunger for justice, peace, and care for the earth.

Tapestry of Themes

On a tapestry, richly colored threads are woven in and out, over and under, to provide the striking beauty that is the whole. *Christ Jesus, the Way* provides a rich tapestry of themes—truths and traditions of the faith that weave in and out of every lesson. The weaving of these themes into all the lessons of the series ensures that the child hears over and over again the mystery of Jesus Christ, the Son of God, and of the Blessed Trinity—Father, Son, and Holy Spirit. The sources of the threads in this tapestry of themes include the *Gospel of Life*, *The Coming of the Third Millennium*, and *At the Beginning of a New Millennium*.

Description Themes

Holiness The series calls each learner to a high standard of Christian living and provides "training in holiness" adapted to the children's needs.

Prayer The series tutors the children in the art of prayer. A variety of prayer experiences is presented at every grade level and in every lesson. Each child is given a worship book of his or her own. Throughout the series the children are also shown that the spirit of prayer and devotion is a great gift.

Creation and the Incarnation This series stresses that God communicates his love through creation. Each chapter anchors Catholic life and teaching in the other great Word God uttered—Christ Jesus, the Word Incarnate.

Grace In every grade, the series teaches the children that by baptism they share God's life. They learn to rely on God's grace and to cooperate with the gift of grace.

Listening to and Proclaiming God's Word The series cultivates in the children a love for Sacred Scripture—especially the Gospels. It stresses that a spirit of holiness and prayer is impossible without a love for God's Word. It is important to hear and read God's Word, but it is also important to proclaim the Word to others.

The Sunday Eucharist The series teaches the children that Sunday is the Day of the Lord and that the Sunday Mass is the center of that day. The children also learn the richness of the Mass and develop attitudes that infuse that celebration. They are imbued with a consciousness of Christ's Real Presence.

The Sacrament of Reconciliation The series teaches that a key to holiness is the regular and frequent celebration of the sacrament of Penance and Reconciliation. The children learn that God and the Sacrament of Reconciliation bring them face to face with the merciful Christ.

The Spirituality of Community The series teaches that Christianity is communal—beginning with the life and mystery of the Trinity. The children learn to see God in the faces of the people around them. They grow in the awareness that there can be no strangers in the Church, no outcasts at the table.

Diversity of Vocation The series teaches that everyone has gifts to share as part of the Body of Christ. The children see the many ways to live out their baptismal covenant. The series includes a strong emphasis on vocations to the priesthood, to the religious life, and to a life of dedicated service.

Ecumenical Commitment The series teaches the children to respect and honor the religious traditions of others. The children also learn to pray and to work so that all may be one.

The Primacy of Charity The series teaches that charity leads to service. The children learn that no one can be excluded from their love and that charity extends to a hunger and a thirst for justice.

Mary The series weaves devotion to the Blessed Mother into every level. The children learn to see Mary as Mother and Model of the Church and as their own Mother.

A Guided Tour

Three-in-One

Christ Jesus, the Way is three separate and complete programs that cover common content for different learning situations—(1) Parish Edition (2) School Edition (3) Bilingual Edition (for programs conducted mostly in Spanish).

Celebration and Worship

Liturgical catechesis is an integral feature of *Christ Jesus, the Way*. This catechesis is found throughout the program. In addition, each grade level has its own full-color worship book, *Celebrate*. The worship book contains a liturgical calendar, instructions for the children, and twelve celebrations. *Celebrate* also contains a guide that provides backgrounds, scripts for the services, and strategies for planning and celebrating the worship services. A Spanish-language worship book, *Celebremos*, is provided for each grade.

Christ Jesus, the Way provides music for each grade level. The music has been selected from the wide range of music readily available for parish programs for worship and celebration. Lyrics are provided in English and in Spanish.

Home and Family Catechesis

Each lesson in the series is connected to the home and the family. At each grade level, there is a family faith-sharing book called *Home*. These books contain a summary of the content in the Student Edition and four seasonal sections. The seasonal material provides a wealth of activities, that will help households foster a religious family life.

Christ Jesus, the Way Online

Benziger forms a full-time partnership with the parishes that adopt *Christ Jesus, the Way*. With the adoption of the series, each parish gets three online services that support and facilitate Total Parish Catechesis.

Word	Table	Home
Resources for principals, teachers, and pastors; for in service and teacher training	Liturgical formation and planning, resources for Christian Initiation, lectionary catechesis	Online guidance in Christian parenting, faith formation at home, and movie and television reviews

The School Edition

Christ Jesus, the Way offers everything necessary for a complete and rich catechetical experience for parochial school. It provides enough material for a daily religion period.

For the Student

The essential student experience involves three books. For best results, a parish should choose to use all three.

1. **Student Text:** The student text has three parts—all essential elements of the instructional program:
   a. Know, Love, Serve: A Little Catechism
   b. Twenty-four core lessons organized into six units
   c. A Bilingual Glossary
2. ***Celebrate*:** A separate worship book that makes classroom liturgical catechesis an integral part of the experience
3. ***Home*:** A take-home component that helps families share faith all year long

For the Teacher

The teacher resources include:

1. **The Teacher's Edition:** This book contains everything necessary for five daily religion periods at point of use. It also provides all the background and preparation the teacher needs.
   a. Faith Formation
   b. Strategies for A Little Catechism
   c. Helps in planning and scheduling
   d. Simple and clear lesson plans
   e. Blackline resource
   f. Catechetical Toolbox
2. ***Celebrate*—Catechist's Guide:** This book provides everything the teacher needs to conduct the worship services in the *Celebrate* book.
   a. Liturgical background
   b. Planning aids
   c. Complete scripts for the services
   d. Reproducible materials to enrich the celebrations
3. **Interactive Lesson Planner:** This CD-ROM contains the following features.
   a. Automated Scheduling
   b. Activities and resources
   c. Test Generator
   d. Sheet music and lyrics
   e. Lessons for adults
   f. Materials for social justice
4. **Music:** This CD contains music for the entire program—lessons and worship services.

There is also online support for teachers.

Lesson Process

Each chapter of *Christ Jesus, the Way* follows a simple process that reflects Jesus' own method of proclaiming the reign of God:

1. **Invitation:** "Come and see!"
2. **Discovery:** "Learn of me!"
3. **Living:** "Abide in my love!"

Each chapter provides a Review and Explore page that reinforces the lessons. A Home and Family page extends the lessons into the home. These two pages can be removed from the book and sent home each week. Finally, each chapter ends with a project page—The Church Today—that reinforces the lesson content.

Getting Ready

Christ Jesus, the Way is easy to use.

1. **Look over all the components.** Get a feel for what you will be experiencing throughout the year.
2. **Explore the section called A Little Catechism** at the front of the student text. You will find it a familiar look at the Catholic faith.
3. **Become familiar with the Teacher's Edition.** It will be your constant companion throughout the year.
4. **Read through the student material.** You will find inspiration for the entire year in the friendly, graphic approach to traditional Catholic teaching. Enjoy the stories of Jesus, the People of God, and all the wonders of the faith.

Teacher Resource Center

Your Teacher's Edition provides you with two pages called the Teacher's Resource Center. These pages provide the following.

1. **Faith Formation:** Doctrinal and scriptural foundation for the chapter
2. **Check the Catechism:** A direct link to the *Catechism of the Catholic Church*
3. **Background:** A reflection on the purpose of the lesson
   - Vocabulary Preview—new words to know
   - Scripture—the passages that form the heart of the lesson
   - Related Resources—books, music, and videos providing support for the lesson
4. **Faith Summary:** A capsulated view of the lesson content
5. **Growth and Development:** What you need to know about the children you teach
6. **A Teacher's Prayer**

Teacher Organizer

The Teacher Organizer has everything needed for the five days of lessons:

1. **Planning Guide:** Everything needed for the first four days is laid out in detail
   - Objectives
   - Preparation
   - Materials
   - Optional Activities
2. **Chapter Goals:** A reminder of the teacher's goals for the children
3. **Learning Objectives:** The expected outcomes
4. **Day 5 Alternatives:** Choices for the last day of the week
   - Prayer
   - Review and Explore
   - Home and Family
   - The Church Today
   - The chapter resource and test
5. **Quick Check:** An evaluation tool for the teacher
6. **Correlation to other materials**

In the Classroom

All you need to do in the classroom is follow the lesson plan that guides you through each week's sessions.

An easy to use Lesson Plan

Christ Jesus, the Way provides the clearest, most concise, and easiest to follow lesson plan. It concentrates on using the textbook effectively.

1. **A simple classroom plan:** Follow the step-by-step plan across the top of the page. You will work with the page. You will never be tangled up in a complicated verbatim script.
2. **Large Student Page:** *Christ Jesus, the Way* gives you the largest view of the student page.
3. **Constant Help:** The margins contain a wealth of tips for more effective lessons.
4. **White Space:** Every page has room for you to add your own notes—to personalize the lesson.

Remember: Simplicity and clarity are the secrets to catechetical success!

Catechetical Toolbox

Christ Jesus, the Way provides a wealth of helpful hints, reminders, strategies, planning, arts and crafts ideas, and much more in the Catechetical Toolbox. This toolbox will help you build even more effective learning experiences for the children you teach.

Special Features

Throughout your book, you will find special features that will enrich your teaching experience, provide valuable information, give teaching tips, define vocabulary, offer alternatives, detail scriptural background, give answers to exercises and reviews, and help with difficult teaching situations.

TEACHING TIP
Ask the children to repeat the chapter's Scripture verse several times to help remember it. You can them remember by ge bodies involved. For ir the children might cre or more hand, arm, or movements for the ve might also create you simple melody and sir verse to the children. have them sing it bacl
OPTIONS
For Children Who Learr by Manipulating Objec
Provide blocks and other materials, and invite the ren to create a three nsional representati ion. Or provide clay, aterials, and a large board box, and invite ren to create a class ma of creation. Phot hildren's work, and s ictures with the pare
VOCABULARY
Presider Refers to the ordained minister who leads the assembly in worship. Presiders are bishops, priests, or deacons. Lay people are commissioned to carry out other roles related to worship, such as extraordinary minister of the Eucharist, musician, or acolyte (altar server).
Homily A homily, or sermon, refers to the spoken instruction about and interpretation of the Scriptures.
BIBLE BASICS
Emphasize that Abraham is the father of all believers. Tell the students that he is also the father of all the people of Israel. Remind the students much of the Old Testa tells the story of Abra family. Introduce them Concordance and help find entries under Abr Have them look up at references to Abrahar help them write the pa their own words.
ANSWER KEY
Respond
1. The Bible is God's message written in human words. It contains stories about faith, hope, and love.
2. Creation is a sign of God's love for us, and it should be treated with respect.
3. The followers of Jesus obey the Ten Commandments to strengthen their relationship with God and others.
IDEAS THAT WORK
Create a Dilemma Box Have the students write about their real-life dilemmas. Keep the box containing the written responses on your desk to ensure privacy. Read and restate the dilemmas to confidentiality. Use the s to engage the students his week and in the weeks. This continuing grounds religion in the metimes troublesome fourth graders.

There are two features of particular importance.

- On the unit opening page is a summary of the Storykeepers video segment that supports the unit.
- On each Review and Explore page is a guide for the use of Know, Love, Serve: A Little Catechism.

The icons will alert you to these special features.

The Story Keepers

Annunciation
In the story of the Annunciation, the angel Gabriel tells Mary that she will conceive and give birth to God's Son and will name him Jesus. Helena tells this story to the children while they are traveling in a wagon during the night. View the clip, tell the story, and lead activities suggested in the guide.

A Little Catechism

Invite the children to open their religion books to *A Little Catechism.* Choose one or more of the selections below for memory work or reinforcement. You will find your copy of the catechism on pages 23–43 of this Teacher's Edition.

1. Review with the children that Jesus, Mary, and Joseph are the Holy Family.
2. Turn to the Things to Remember section, and review the questions about the Holy family.

Know Love Serve

Teaching Second Graders

Whether you have taught for years or are a first-time catechist, it is important to have a perspective on the work you will be doing this year.

Know the Child

The pedagogy of God is the gradual revelation of himself to his people. You are participating in that pedagogy. Gradual revelation depends on your knowledge of the developmental stage of the children you are teaching.

Characteristics

If you keep the following characteristics in mind, you will find relating to a second-grade child natural and enriching.

1. Second-grade children have an active interest in knowing how things are made, especially living creatures. Questions regarding what, why, and how will come up often.
2. Seven year olds have a fairly well developed sense of right and wrong and of their power to choose.
3. Group involvement and approval are important. Second graders are even capable of empathizing with others, although acting unselfishly is still difficult.
4. Children at this age learn concepts best through concrete experience. An emphasis on stories, activities, and song in learning is especially effective.
5. Second graders are still limited by a short attention span. Repetition and review are helpful, and simple memorization tasks are enjoyed.
6. Second graders are eager for adult approval. They find criticism and correction from adults especially difficult to handle.

Growth in Faith

Aware for the first time of many new feelings and freedoms, children of this age need direction and positive reinforcement to aid their development in Christian values and behavior. The effects of their personal choices must be pointed out, with an emphasis on how these affect their relationship with God and others. The value of prayer and sacrament in deepening their relation with God needs to be taught, as well as a basic intellectual understanding of their significance. Since children of this age rely on example for instruction, they can be taught how to listen and to cooperate with others. Overall, you, as the catechist, help the children foster responsibility, self-discipline, and a sense of loving security in their relationship with God.

Doctrinal Content

Grade two of *Christ Jesus, the Way* has as its theme story, Jesus feeding the crowds (see Luke 9:11–17). The theme is demonstrated throughout the year by taking a closer look at the celebration of the Eucharist. While Jesus was on earth, he provided food for the Apostles and the large crowds that followed him. In that same spirit, God's people are able to share in a meal with Jesus still today. In Holy Communion, God's people become one with Jesus and the Church, nourished by the presence of Jesus. Grade two invites the children to understand the Eucharist and to discover other ways to be nourished by their friendship with Jesus.

Here is the core doctrinal content of grade two in *Christ Jesus, the Way*.

Knowledge

Scripture

- The Good News of Jesus
- Moses and the Ten Commandments
- The Great Commandment
- The parables of Jesus
- The Holy Spirit

Doctrine

- The Bible is God's Word.
- God created all creatures and the world they share.
- Humans are created in God's image.
- The gospels tell the Good News of Jesus.
- Through Baptism Catholics become children of God.
- God gives the Ten Commandments to help people make good choices.
- The Holy Spirit, the Helper, gives special gifts.
- God forgives all who ask forgiveness in the sacrament of Reconciliation.
- Jesus is present in the Eucharist.
- The Church is sent to spread God's love around the world.

Love

Christian Life

- God's goodness can be shown in actions and words.
- Christians show love and respect for those around them.
- Followers of Jesus gather celebrate, remember, and share.
- Christians forgive others and ask for forgiveness.
- Christians treat all people with kindness.

Prayer and Worship

- Sign of the Cross
- The Lord's Prayer
- The Hail Mary
- The Glory Be
- Act of Contrition
- Ways to talk to God
- The sacraments
- Seasons and Feasts
- The parts of the Mass

Service

Moral Living

- Jesus wants his followers to live the Golden Rule.
- Christians listen to their conscience to choose what is right.
- God's Word, the Ten Commandments, and Church teachings are guides for living.
- God calls everyone to do good and avoid evil.
- Christians serve God by obeying his law.

Living for Others

- Missionaries help people all over the world.
- Christians show the light of Christ to others.
- The Church strives to heal people.
- Jesus sends everyone to do God's work on earth.

Celebrate

An essential element of all religious education is liturgical catechesis. *Christ Jesus, the Way* has a unique component for prayer and worship—the *Celebrate* book. The chart on this page will help you plan your use of *Celebrate* throughout the year. The chart contains page references to the Student Edition (SE) and the Catechist's Edition (CE) of *Celebrate*.

Season	Title	When	Description	SE	CE
Advent	Come, Lord Jesus	During the season of Advent	We wait and prepare for Jesus' coming	6	8
	Ave Maria	Any feast of Mary or anytime during the year	We celebrate and honor Mary, the mother of God	8	12
Christmas	Peace to God's People!	During the Christmas season	The song of the angels proclaims the birth of Christ	10	16
	Celebrating Family	The feast of the Holy Family or anytime during the year	We are one in the Body of Christ	12	20
Lent	Out of Darkness	During the season of Lent	Living in the light of Christ	14	24
Easter	I Believe!	During the Easter season	Renewing our baptismal promises	16	28
Pentacost	Come, Holy Spirit	The week before/after Pentecost, fifty days after Easter	The Holy Spirit is poured out on all members of the church	18	32
Ordinary Time	We Are the Body of Christ	The week before/after Pentecost, fifty days after Easter	We are a Eucharistic People	20	36
	Triumph of the Cross	September 14 or anytime during the year	We glory in the cross of our Lord Jesus Christ	22	40
	Blessed Marie Rose	October 6—Feast of Blessed Marie Rose Durocher	Honoring the names of Jesus and Mary	24	44
	Saints of God	November 1—Feast of All Saints	Honoring the Communion of Saints	26	48
	Lord, Have Mercy	Anytime during the year	The Lord is kind and merciful	28	52

0-07-821721-0, 0-07-821730-X, 0-07-821739-3, 0-07-821748-2, 0-07-821757-1, 0-07-821766-0

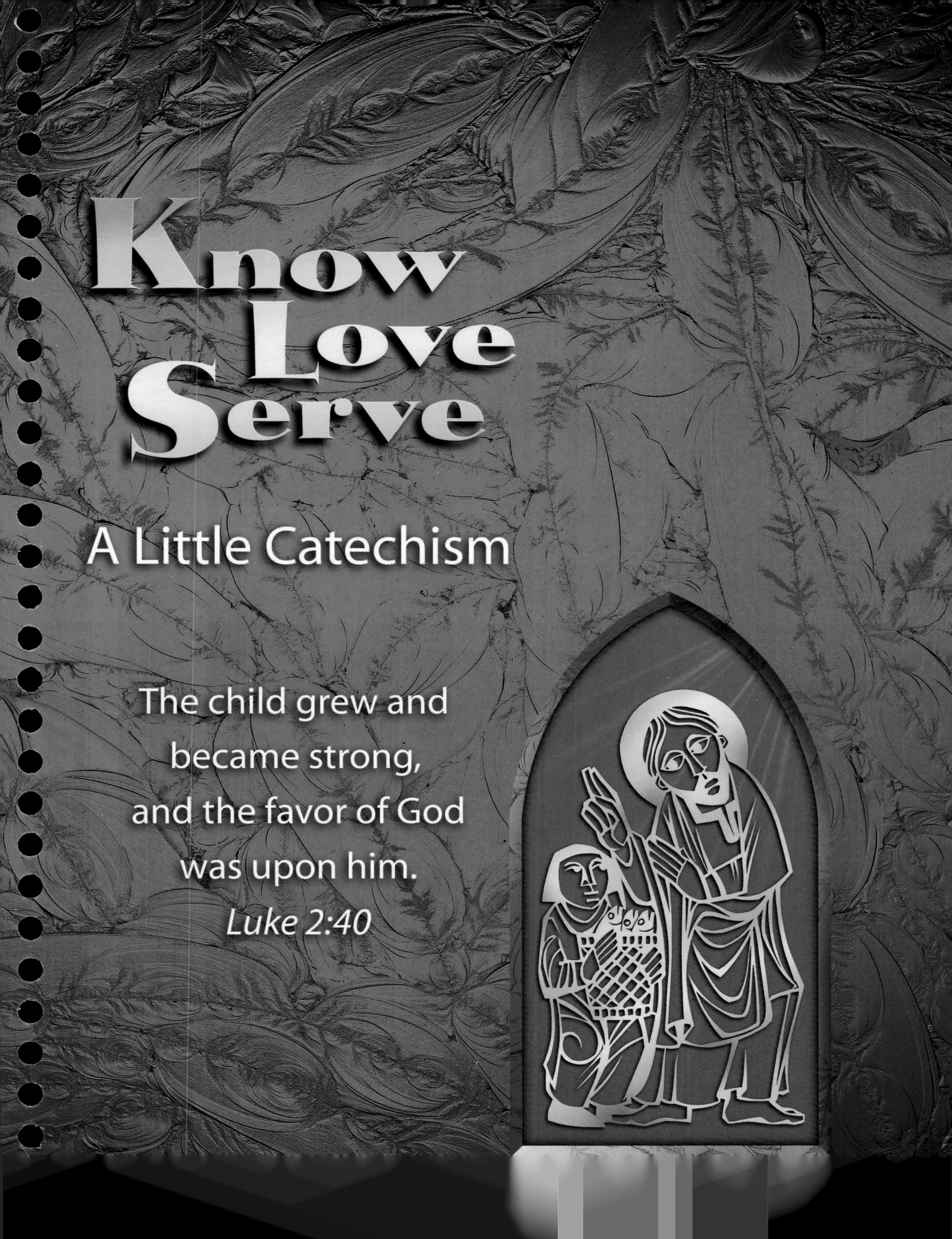
Know
Love
Serve
A Little Catechism
The child grew and
became strong,
and the favor of God
was upon him.
Luke 2:40

Plan a Welcome Lesson

It is a good idea to use pages 8–9 in the student text to provide a welcoming experience for the children. It need not be a full period, but it will set the tone for the whole year.

1 Pass Out the Books

Make a great ceremony of giving each child his or her religion book. Have the books attractively displayed at a child's eye level, and hand them out individually. Take this opportunity to get to know each child by name. This book is not an ordinary text book like reading or arithmetic. It is a key to the child's life of faith. Let the children page through the books.

2 Welcome!

Get the class's attention and read the first paragraph to the children. Ask what answer they would give to Father Albert's question. After a few children have responded, return to the story to find out what Thomas said. Tell the children that all year long you will be learning how to know, love and serve God, so that you can be happy with God now and forever.

A Little Catechism

This little catechism is a book within a book. It will be a constant companion for you and for your class. It is organized according to the classic notions of knowledge, love, and service. You will not be marching through the section. Rather, you will be dipping into it, going through parts as a reward at the end of a lesson. Everything in this section is correlated to each of the chapters. Watch for this feature on the Review and Explore page of each chapter.

1. **On each page you will find suggestions for using the material. You may use all of the suggestions or none of them.**
2. **At the end of the year, *A Little Catechism* should be given to the children as a permanent record of their year.**

Know Love Serve

Welcome!

Father Albert looked at the boy in the first row. The boy was so eager to learn. He wanted to learn everything he could. Father Albert was teaching about God. "Why did God make you?" Father Albert asked.

It seemed that the boy always had his hand in the air. "Me, Father," he would say. "Call on me."

"All right, Thomas," Father Albert said, "give us the answer."

"God made me to know him," Thomas replied. He waited a moment and went on. "God also wants me to love him and to serve him, too." After another moment, Thomas added, "And God wants me to be happy with him in this world and forever."

The boy was Thomas Aquinas. He grew up to be a great teacher. He became a Dominican priest. He wrote and taught his whole life. Millions of people learned about Jesus from the words Thomas wrote.

Your Book

Your religion book will help you learn about your faith. The book has three parts. This first part is a catechism that teaches you what to remember. The second part has your lessons. You will learn more and more each week. The third part is a list of words to know.

Lord, be in my heart and on my lips that I may learn about you and tell others how wonderful you are.

3 The Holy Family
Reinforce children's knowledge of the Holy Family and its relationships once again. The figures of the creche at Christmastime are helpful visual aids for this teaching. Don't compare all families to the Holy Family. The notion of Mary being "your mother, too" is not too difficult for this age. Don't over-explain that notion.

4 The Ten Commandments
This version uses traditional wording and the Catholic numbering of the commandments. The children can become familiar with the commandments without understanding all the vocabulary at this stage. Emphasize that God gives rules for people to follow, and introduce the idea that the first three commandments are ways to show our love for God, and the last seven are ways to show our love for people.

The Trinity

The Trinity is God the Father, God the Son, and God the Holy Spirit. There is only one God. But God is three Persons. You can say, "I believe in God—Father, Son, and Holy Spirit."

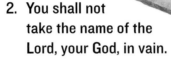

The Holy Family

Jesus, Mary, and Joseph are the Holy Family. Jesus is the Son of God who became a human being. Joseph is the foster father of Jesus and the husband of Mary. Mary is the mother of Jesus. Mary is your mother, too.

The Ten Commandments

1. I am the Lord, your God. You shall not have other gods besides me.
2. You shall not take the name of the Lord, your God, in vain.
3. Remember to keep holy the Sabbath day.
4. Honor your father and your mother.
5. You shall not kill.
6. You shall not commit adultery.
7. You shall not steal.
8. You shall not bear false witness against your neighbor.
9. You shall not covet your neighbor's wife.
10. You shall not covet anything that belongs to your neighbor.

IDEAS THAT WORK

Through the ages, people have used numbers to help them remember the truths of faith. Make use of numbers in art projects and memory games to reinforce the children's learning. To visualize the Ten Commandments, for example, the children could trace their ten fingers on paper, or build a pyramid of colored squares (four at the base, then three, two, and one), and label each one.

5 Signs and Symbols

The Catholic faith embodies a sacramental tradition—one that uses the physical universe as both a catechism and a prayer book. Each year the children will learn more about the signs and symbols that are an important part of Church theology and practice.

Each of these reminders lends itself to art projects. Remember how important arts and crafts are to learners of this age. They never tire of expressing themselves and what they are learning.

6 Important Questions

This section gives the children some encapsulated doctrines of the Catholic Church. The opening paragraph describes the importance of these questions and answers. Read the introduction to the children. Take time to encourage them in their learning.

Signs and Symbols

Catholics use signs and symbols to remember the wonders of the faith. Here are a few signs for you to use to help you remember.

1. **Wheat and Grapes**
   Sometimes in church, you see a picture of wheat and grapes. The picture reminds you of the Eucharist. Bread and wine are made from wheat and grapes. Jesus changed bread and wine into his Body and Blood.

2. **Fish and Bread**
   Pictures of fish and bread help you remember how Jesus fed thousands of people. Jesus feeds God's Family at the Eucharist.

3. **Palms and Ashes**
   Blessed palm branches remind you that Jesus is Savior and Lord. Palms are burned to make the ashes used on Ash Wednesday. The ashes remind you to put God first in your life.

Important Questions

The questions and answers below will help you remember what you learn all year long. When the year is over, you should know all these answers by heart.

1. **What is the Good News?**
   The Good News is that God loves everyone and sent his Son to save all people.
2. **Who is invited to the kingdom of God?**
   Everyone is invited to the kingdom of God.
3. **What are the sacraments?**
   The sacraments are signs and celebrations given by Jesus. The sacraments give grace.
4. **What is the sacrament of God's loving forgiveness?**
   Penance, or Reconciliation, is the sacrament of God's forgiveness.
5. **What is one way to serve God?**
   One way to serve God is to serve others.

The children will learn the answers as they come up in the text. Keep track of those that the children have learned, and use these questions as a review every once in a while. You can also make large flash cards for a quick group drill.

6. **What did God give the Ten Commandments?**
   The Ten Commandments are God's Law. They show how to love God and how to love others.
7. **What is the Great Commandment?**
   Love God above all things and love your neighbor as yourself.
8. **What is sin?**
   Sin is choosing to do wrong. Sin hurts one's friendship with God.
9. **What helps you know what is wrong?**
   God's Law, the teaching of the Church, and my conscience help me know what is wrong.
10. **What is the community of the followers of Jesus called?**
    The followers of Jesus are called the Church.
11. **What is the prayer Jesus taught?**
    Jesus gave the Lord's Prayer—the Our Father.
12. **What meal is remembered during Mass?**
    The Mass remembers Jesus' Last Supper.
13. **What is the Eucharist?**
    The Eucharist is the Body and Blood of Jesus Christ.
14. **Is Communion bread just like any ordinary bread?**
    No, Communion bread is Jesus.
15. **What mission do you receive at the end of Mass?**
    I am sent to love and to serve the Lord.
16. **What is celebrated on Easter?**
    Jesus' death and resurrection are celebrated on Easter.
17. **What is celebrated on Pentecost?**
    Pentecost celebrates the coming of the Holy Spirit.
18. **How do you follow Jesus?**
    I follow Jesus when I witness to him through what I say and do.

TEACHING TIP

Memorization has its place in catechesis. It is important that children are comfortable with the basic prayers and formulas of faith. Items to be memorized should be repeated orally by the class. Children catch the rhythm and cadence of language by hearing it spoken. The rhythm of a spoken phrase (and sometimes rhyme) helps the memory to retain it.

7 The Sacraments

It is important that the children begin to discover the importance and sacredness of the sacraments. The image of the door opening up to God's treasures will build their anticipation and curiosity. It is not important for second graders to know all the details of each sacrament. It is enough that they know the names and one main point about each.

Go through the list of seven, one at a time. Read the name, read the description, and let the children comment or ask questions. Talk about the pictures. Go through the list again. Say the name. Ask the children to supply the description.

LEARNING TO PRAY

Young children have a natural love for ritual, and will readily pick up habits and patterns of gathering, working, playing and praying. Consider incorporating some of the symbols of the foundational sacrament, Baptism, into your classroom prayer ritual. For example, the children could bless themselves with holy water as they come into the prayer corner. One child could open the Bible on the table and another light a candle. A moment of silence before a shared song or spoken prayer can also become part of the children's prayer ritual.

The Sacraments

The seven sacraments are like seven doors that open up God's treasures for you. There is always something new to learn about the sacraments.

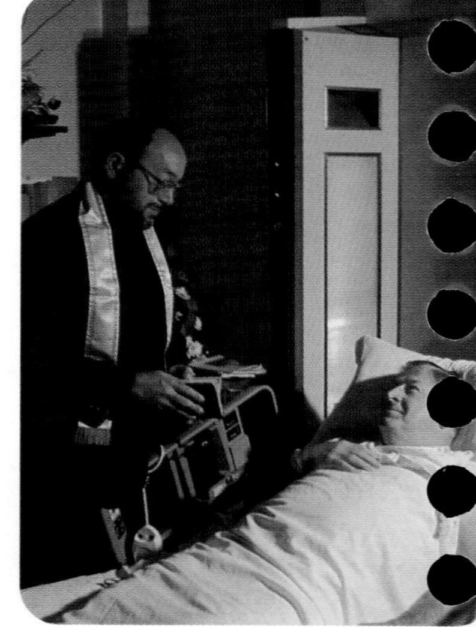

1. **Baptism**
   You become one of God's own children.
2. **Confirmation**
   You receive the gift of the Holy Spirit.
3. **Eucharist**
   You receive the Body and Blood of Jesus.
4. **Reconciliation**
   The priest gives you God's forgiveness—pardon and peace.
5. **Anointing of the Sick**
   The priest blesses those who are sick and marks them with holy oil.
6. **Marriage**
   A man and a woman promise to love each other, to be together always, and to raise their children in God's love.
7. **Holy Orders**
   The Church ordains bishops, priests, and deacons.

Introduction

The Love section of *A Little Catechism* includes matters of the heart—prayers and ways of praying, seasons and feasts, Mary, and the Mass. Children learn over and over again that prayer is a conversation with a God who loves them very much and who wants them to love him in return. At some point, read the opening paragraph to the children.

❶ Sign of the Cross

Go over the hand motions of this introduction to prayer. Explain that Catholics begin and end most prayers with the sign of the cross. Have them make the motions silently, then do it again while speaking the words. Ask them who the three persons are in whose name we make this sign (the Trinity).

❷ Hail Mary

Tell the story of how Mary met Elizabeth, and explain that the first part of the prayer consists of Elizabeth's joyful greeting to Mary. The second part of the prayer asks Mary to pray for us. Pray this prayer together from time to time.

Love

In a community, everyone is needed. Everyone has much love to give. You are important to your community. God's community is called the Church. The Church needs all the love you have to give. You show your love for God in prayer and in celebration.

Prayers to Learn by Heart

Sign of the Cross

In the name of the Father,
and of the Son,
and of the Holy Spirit.
Amen.

Glory Be to the Father

Glory be to the Father,
and to the Son,
and to the Holy Spirit:
As it was in the beginning,
is now and ever shall be,
world without end.
Amen.

Hail Mary

Hail Mary, full of grace:
The Lord is with thee.
Blessed art thou among women,
and blessed is the fruit
of thy womb, Jesus.
Holy Mary, Mother of God,
pray for us sinners, now
and at the hour of our death.
Amen.

3 Glory Be to the Father
This doxology on student page 15 is a frequent element of liturgical prayer, in praise of the Trinity. It also occurs in the Rosary. If you know a musical setting of this prayer, teach the children to sing it.

4 Act of Contrition
Explain that this is a prayer we use in the Sacrament of Penance to say "I am sorry" to God for whatever wrong we have done. Go over each line, and point out the characteristics of someone who sincerely prays this prayer: heartfelt sorrow for doing wrong; deep love for God. Have the children memorize the prayer gradually. Add a new sentence each time you review it.

5 The Lord's Prayer
Use this prayer frequently throughout the year. Explain that Jesus himself taught this prayer to his followers. By the end of the year the children should know this prayer by heart.

Act of Contrition

O my God, I am sorry for my sins with all my heart. In choosing to do wrong and failing to do good, I have sinned against you whom I should love above all things. I firmly intend, with the help of your grace, to do penance, to sin no more, and to avoid whatever leads me to sin. Jesus Christ suffered and died for us. In his name, dear God, forgive me. Amen.

Short Prayers

Jesus, I believe in you, I hope in you, and I love you.

Jesus, I am sorry for the wrong things I have done.

The Lord's Prayer

Our Father, who art in heaven,
hallowed be thy name.
Thy kingdom come; thy will be done
on earth as it is in heaven.
Give us this day our daily bread,
and forgive us our trespasses
as we forgive those
who trespass against us.
And lead us not into temptation,
but deliver us from evil.
Amen.

Morning Prayer

I give to you, my God, this day,
all I do, think, or say.

Blessing before Meals

Bless us, O Lord,
and these, your gifts,
which we are about to receive
from your bounty,
through Christ our Lord.
Amen.

6 Short Prayers
The first of these is an act of faith, hope and love; the second, a short prayer of sorrow for sin. Encourage the children to add their own words to these prayers, expressing praise and love for God. Hold off on petitions at this point. It is important for the children to learn that prayer is not always about asking for things.

7 Talking to God
Read the text to the children. Ask the children about how, where, when, why, and with whom they pray. Give a personal example of how you talk to God in your own words. Focus on the second item. Ask the children for examples of a quiet time when they can talk to God. Focus on the third item. Invite examples, and add some of your own.

8 Prayer Tips
Go over the list with the children. Some of these ideas may be new to them. Invite them to try them during the weeks ahead. You are planting seeds. Come back to this list from time to time and ask the children to share their experiences of prayer.

Talking to God

God loves you, and God wants you to love in return. When you love God with your whole heart, mind, soul, and strength, you will find happiness. So, when you pray—

1. Talk to God with your whole heart and mind.
2. Find quiet time to talk to God.
3. Tell God what's on your mind anytime at all.

Prayer Tips

Here are some prayer helps for you.

- Tell God stories.
- Ask God questions.
- Pray like Mary, who always said yes to God.
- Keep alert at Mass.
- Pray by singing, standing, kneeling, and sharing the sign of peace at Mass.
- Visit Jesus in the Blessed Sacrament.
- Pray by asking God for what you need.
- Ask God to be part of your fun times, too.

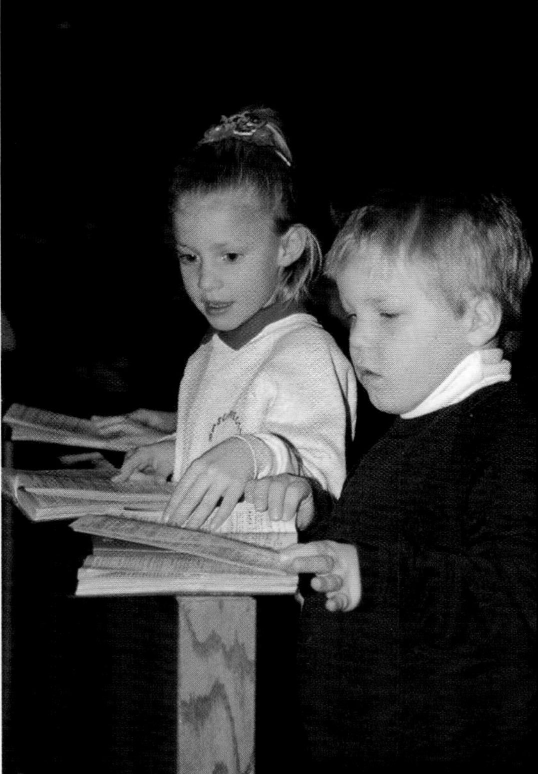

TEACHING TIP

Prayer inviting God "to be part of your fun times" is a much greater opportunity than adults may imagine. Studies have shown that children laugh far more frequently than adults — an average of 400 times a day. Show the children a picture of Jesus smiling. Encourage the children to share joyful moments with God. Make a list of happy times when the children especially want God to be present, and hang it up in your classroom.

Seasons and Feasts

The material on these pages can be handled as special lessons on points in the liturgical year.

All Saints Suggestions

While the popularity of Halloween remains constant, the children need to learn about the Church feast of All Saints, on November first. Read the first paragraph to the children. Ask them to name some of the saints they know. Read the next two paragraphs. Choose either the patron saint of the parish church, or another popular saint, and find out what the children already know about him or her. Tell a story about that person's life and share a picture, explaining any symbols that may be included. Read the last paragraph. Remind the children that All Saints Day is a holy day for Catholics, so we go to Mass on that day.

Seasons and Feasts

All Saints

On November 1, the Church remembers all the men and women who followed Jesus, were faithful to him, and are now happy with him in heaven. They are called the saints.

Saint Paul taught that all Christians belong to the Communion of Saints. Some of the Communion of Saints are already in heaven with God. Some are waiting in what the Church calls purgatory. They will soon join the saints in heaven.

You are part of that community on earth. You are following Jesus so that you can be happy with him and with the saints forever.

Remember the saints. Learn about the saints. Talk about the saints. Their example will help you. Celebrate the feast of All Saints with all your heart.

I have called you friends, because I have told you everything I have learned from my Father.

John 15:15

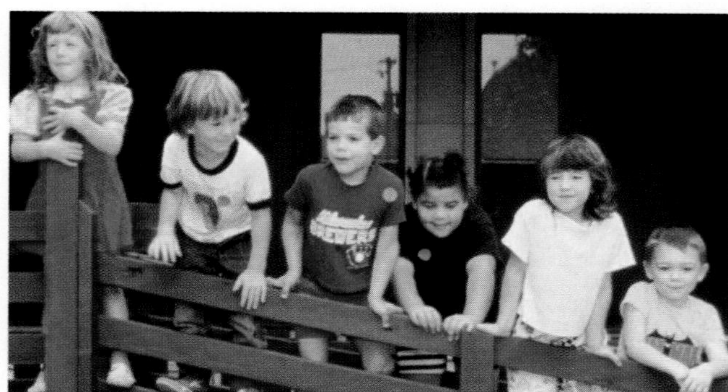

Advent Suggestions

Set aside some time near the first Sunday of Advent for this lesson. Have the children open their books and look at the picture. Ask them what the people are doing. If you have an Advent wreath in the classroom, point out the greenery and the candles. You may want to ask them to describe the Advent wreath they see in church at this time of year as well.

Tell the children that you are going to read to them about a very important person in the Bible: John the Baptist. Read the first two paragraphs. Direct their attention to the box at the top of the page, and have them read the quotation together several times. Explain that this was John's message.

Read the next two paragraphs. Distribute art materials and help the children to complete the exercise. Hang their posters around the room or have them take them home as a reminder of Advent.

Advent

Prepare
the way of
the Lord!
Matthew 3:3

John the Baptist was a cousin of Jesus. He told people that the Savior was coming. He got people ready to know and to love Jesus.

During the season of Advent, you will hear some of the words John said. He said that every valley would be filled up, and every mountain made low. He said the crooked would be made straight, and the rough places smooth.

Advent is a time to get ready for Christmas. The most important part of Advent is remembering that Christmas celebrates the coming of Christ.

Make a sign for yourself. Put some of Saint John's words on the sign. Remember to get ready for the coming of Jesus.

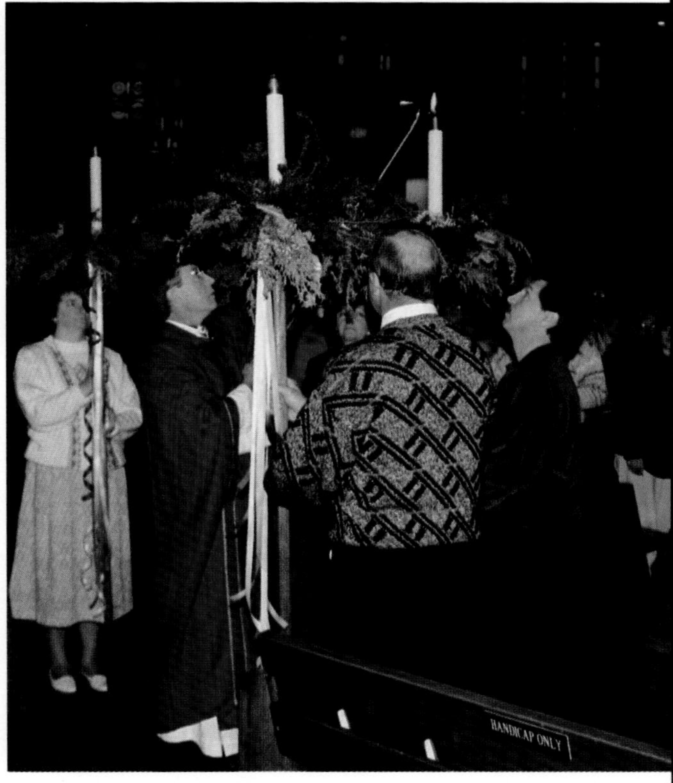

Christmas Suggestions

Christmas is a season filled with catechetical opportunities but it can be easy to miss the Yuletide message. It is a good idea, therefore, to take some time to focus on the more spiritual aspects of the feast.

Read the quotation from Luke's Gospel in the box at the top of the page. Explain that this was the message that angels brought to shepherds when Jesus was born. Allow them to supply whatever details of the story they remember. Read the first two paragraphs of the text with the children. Ask them to name some things at Christmas that remind them of Jesus, and why.

The third paragraph issues a caution, and invites the children to work on good behavior during Christmas time. Without belaboring the negative, you can help the children to have a better Christmas by acting out of their best selves. Read the rest of the text, down to the prayer. Have the children read the prayer aloud with you. Complete the lesson with a craft project that the children will take home.

IDEAS THAT WORK

There are many arts and crafts available for the Christmas season. Choose one of the suggestions from the text they just read, such as making their own manger set. Children get very, very fidgety right before Christmas. Getting them to work on a large project with lots of materials will help them to remain focused on the lesson. It will also serve to keep them from jumping out of their seats.

Christmas

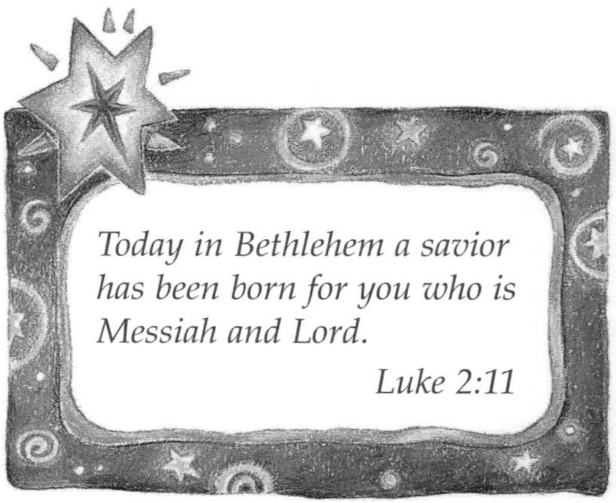

Today in Bethlehem a savior has been born for you who is Messiah and Lord.

Luke 2:11

Christmas is a wonderful time of the year. Music is playing. Everything is covered with red and green. There are decorated trees and lights everywhere.

Christmas is a happy time because it celebrates the birth of Jesus. Everything about Christmas should remind you of Jesus.

Sometimes, Christmas can become a selfish time—a time to think about presents and toys. A follower of Jesus tries to remember to be very kind during Christmas. Remember to obey your parents. Remember to share what you have with others.

Make yourself a special reminder that will help you think of others during the Christmas holiday. You can make a sign. You can make a manger set. You can hang a special ornament on the tree.

Every day during the Christmas season, say a Christmas prayer.

Gracious God, you are the giver of gifts. You gave us the greatest of gifts—Jesus, your Son. Thank you for thinking so much of us. Help us be gift-givers like you. Amen.

Have a merry Christmas!

Lent Suggestions

Shortly before Ash Wednesday, have the children open their books to page 21, and read the first paragraph of the text. Ask the children if they know what this period of forty days is called. *(Lent)* Arrange for the class to take on a commitment for Lent that they can work on each week (such as prayer for a specific need, or contributing to a particular work of charity). Or they can make a Lenten calendar and mark each week with a sticker for a good deed or prayer intention that they have focused on during that week.

Near the end of Lent, return to this page and review the items in Holy Week. Talk about the pictures. *(Palm Sunday, Holy Thursday, Easter Vigil)* Read each item, pausing for the children to ask questions. Then repeat the description, and have the children read the concluding sentence (in quotation marks) together, as an acclamation.

Springtime

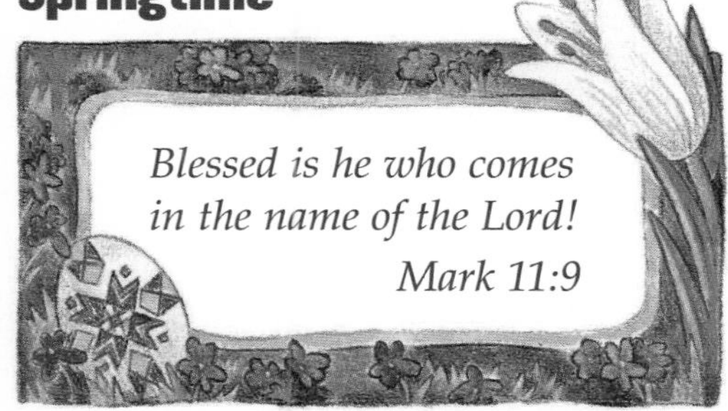

Blessed is he who comes
in the name of the Lord!
Mark 11:9

For forty days in the spring of the year, the followers of Jesus try to be better and better. They remember what is important. They try to grow in God's love.

At the end of that time, they pray and think about the week when Jesus died.

1. **Palm Sunday:** A day to remember Jesus entering the holy city of Jerusalem. "Hosanna!"
2. **Holy Thursday:** A day to remember Jesus' love and the Last Supper when Jesus shared his Body and Blood. "The Body of Christ. Amen!"
3. **Good Friday:** A day to remember that Jesus suffered and died on the cross to save all from sin. "Lord, remember me!"
4. **Easter Vigil:** A time to celebrate the resurrection and to remember your baptism. "Alleluia!"

Christ has died!
Christ is risen!
Christ will come again!

TEACHING TIP

The liturgies of Holy Week, with all their rich symbols, pageantry and processions, can be very powerful religious experiences for children. Encourage families to take their children to these celebrations. When you discuss these liturgies in the classroom, foster a sense of anticipation and awe. Share with the children your own excitement and favorite elements. These are our high holy days—the center and high point of the whole liturgical year. The children are only beginning to learn about them, but they will catch from you a sense of their wonder and sacredness.

Easter Suggestions

Use this section near the end of the Easter season. It presents Ascension and Pentecost as they are described in Luke's Gospel and the Acts of the Apostles, and connects them with feasts of the Church today.

Read the text to the children. Ask how the people felt when they received the Holy Spirit on the first Pentecost. *(joyful, generous, brave, not lonely)*

Explain that whenever we are unhappy or afraid or lonely, we too can pray to the Holy Spirit to strengthen us. Have the children read together the quotation from Luke's gospel in the box in the middle of the page. Talk about the flame illustration. Have them cut out flame-shapes, and write the quotation on them.

More about the Mass

Each year the children will learn more and more about the Mass. These items are not about the mechanics but about the meaning of the Mass. They will reinforce the lessons. Do not try to digest all of them at once. Devise a way to return to this topic at intervals throughout the year. This list can also be used as a review.

IDEAS THAT WORK

Construct a large, colorful box, and label it "More About the Mass." Inside have strips of colored paper, upon which each of these items is printed in large letters. Whenever it is time to learn more about the Mass, select one child to pick a slip from the box and read it to the class. The slip can then be displayed on a bulletin board, as you first talk about the statement, and then do an activity that will help the children understand and internalize its meaning. Some of these might be art projects, such as making chains of paper dolls to illustrate that "The Mass reminds people that all are brothers and sisters." Or they might involve practicing a liturgical gesture, such as offering the Sign of Peace.

Come, Holy Spirit

After Jesus rose from the dead, he returned to be with his Father. Jesus' return is celebrated on the feast of the Ascension. But Jesus did not leave his friends all alone. Jesus sent the Holy Spirit.

On the day the Holy Spirit came, Peter spoke to all the people. "Join us," Peter said, "and be baptized in the name of Jesus. You will receive the Holy Spirit, too."

Many, many people were baptized that very day. All who believed shared everything they had. The day the Holy Spirit came is remembered at the feast of Pentecost. It is a Sunday of great joy. Everything is decorated in red. People rejoice in the Holy Spirit.

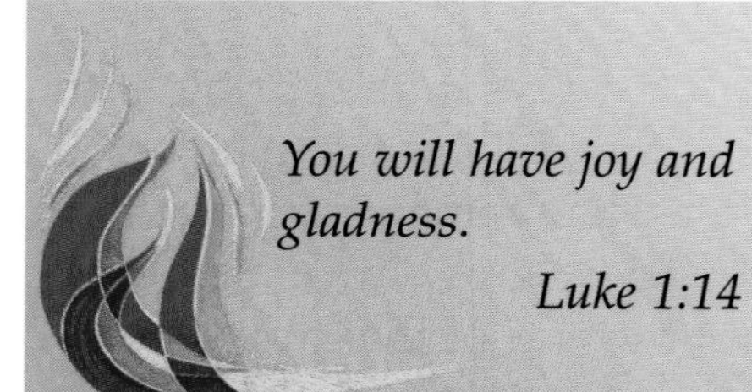

You will have joy and gladness.

Luke 1:14

MORE ABOUT THE MASS

God's People Gather for Mass

The Mass keeps the members of the Church faithful.

It reminds people that all are brothers and sisters.

It helps the members care for one another.

It asks all to reach out.

Jesus is with all who gather.

Jesus is with you in the Word of God.

Jesus is with you in the Eucharist—in his Body and Blood.

All are asked to be at peace with one another.

Introduction

The Serve section of *A Little Catechism* includes matters that relate to seeing Christ in others, to doing for others in Jesus' name, to social justice, and to spreading the Good News. This section includes stories from the world-wide mission outreach of Maryknoll.

1 Opening Text

Read the paragraph to the children. Let them tell you the many ways they serve others. Don't worry about repetition.

2 Called to Serve

Read the story to the class. Have them look at the picture while you do so. Ask the children to say in their own words what Jesus is asking his followers to do. Have the children give examples of how they too can follow this teaching of Jesus. Offer an example of your own.

Serve

You are a member of the Family of God. Members of God's Family always try to put God first. One way to put God first is to serve other people. Jesus told his friends, "Whatever you do for others, you do for me."

Called to Serve

One day, Jesus called his Apostles together. "Friends," Jesus said to them, "you know how powerful people act. They act high and mighty. They boss people around. You must never act that way."

The Apostles looked at one another. Jesus then said, "If you want to be number one, you must serve others. I did not come to be served. I came to serve others. I will even give my life for others. You must be willing to serve like that."

Based on *Matthew 20:25–28*

3 Saint Katharine Drexel

Recall with the children what they learned earlier about saints (see page 18). Tell them the story of Saint Katherine Drexel, using the text and pausing to point out the pictures as you read. Have them compose a prayer to Saint Katherine, asking her to help them grow up to be good and faithful servants in Jesus' name, as she did.

If there is time, you might also invite the children to pick someone they know who serves others, and to draw a picture of that person surrounded by all the people that he or she has helped. Then have them connect the people with lines that form a "web of care" expressing God's love.

Saint Katharine Drexel

The Drexel family lived in Philadelphia. They were very rich. Katharine and her two sisters had everything any children could want. They had friends, lots of clothes and toys, parties, and parents who loved them.

But there were two things eight-year-old Katharine wanted for Christmas. She wanted a box of chocolates, and she wanted to receive Jesus Christ in Holy Communion.

As she grew up, Katharine loved Jesus more and more. To be more like Jesus, she gave away all her money to help the poor. She started a group of sisters to teach and to care for people who were not well treated.

Bob Borton/Courtesy of the Sisters of the Blessed Sacrament

Katharine opened schools for American Indians and for African Americans. Her group is called the Sisters of the Blessed Sacrament.

One remembrance her sisters keep is a pair of her old worn-out shoes. The rich girl grew up to wear out her shoes serving others.

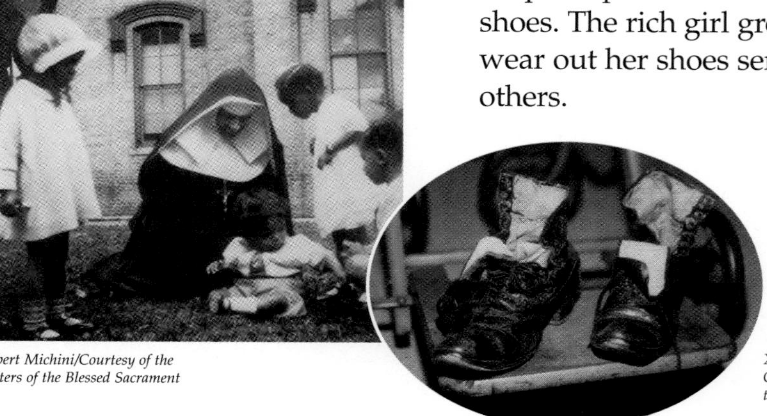

Albert Michini/Courtesy of the Sisters of the Blessed Sacrament

Xavier Photographs/ Courtesy of the Sisters of the Blessed Sacrament

Note: The next two stories are taken from the pages of *Maryknoll Magazine.* They are true stories that show that the Catholic Church is a worldwide church. It reminds the children that they have brothers and sisters around the world. You can use these in connection with a lesson, or simply as a refreshing change of pace.

4 Suggestions

Point out Cambodia on a world map or globe, showing the distance between Ting Vi's home and yours. Gather the children for a story, and emphasize that this is a true story. Read the text to the children. Let them ask questions and give their reactions to the story and the picture. Tell the children that the story is from their missionary friends at Maryknoll.

The Boy and the Buffalo

My name is Ting Vi. I live in the village of Malik in Cambodia. I live in a longhouse with my big family, which is really ten families. Our house is set on poles. That keeps it safe from flood waters. It lets cool air come through, too. Our pigs and chickens live underneath.

I go to school at the other end of the village every day. I can't read or write yet, but I am learning. My job at home is to bring water from the well, find firewood, and take care of the animals. I take good care of our buffalo. The buffalo helps us plow the fields.

There are some Christian people living in our village. They are kind. They go out of their way to help me and my family.

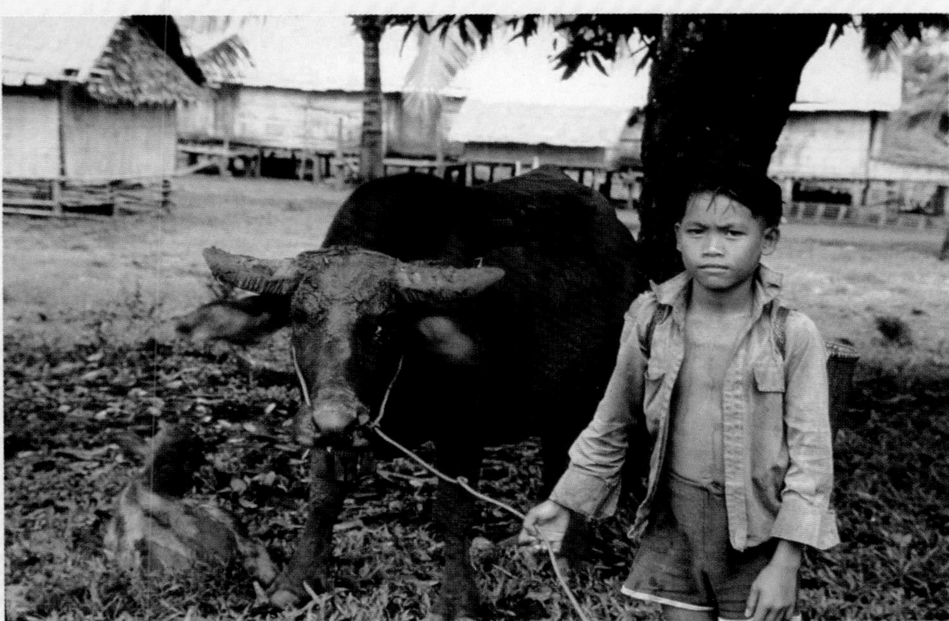

5 Suggestions

Point out Tanzania on a world map or globe, showing the distance between Tanzania and your home. Gather the children for a story. Read the text. Have them look at the pictures. Let them ask questions and give their reactions to the story and the pictures. Show them a set of rosary beads, and let them handle them. Ask them why we should pray for people such as they read about in Tanzania.

LEARNING TO PRAY

Encourage the children to ask someone from their families to teach them about the rosary at home. You can reinforce this learning by praying the Our Father, the Hail Mary, and the Glory Be to the Father from time to time in the classroom. October 7 is the day the Church honors Our Lady of the Rosary, and many parishes encourage praying the rosary throughout the month of October. If possible, provide inexpensive rosaries for the children to use in class—but not to wear as jewelry!

Mary's Love Beads

Far away in the African country of Tanzania, life is very, very hard. There have been many wars and much sickness. The Watatulu people wander from place to place taking care of flocks and looking for food.

Beads are an important sign for the Watatulu people. A string of beads around a baby's neck shows a mother's love. A bracelet of beads can show how much a man loves a woman.

You have a string of beads, too. Catholics often use beads to say a special prayer. The beads and prayer are called the rosary. The rosary helps you remember Mary's love. You remember the love her Son, Jesus, has for you. You might call this great prayer Mary's love beads.

When you pray the rosary, you can remember the people in Africa. You can pray for them. Praying for others is a way to serve.

Ask someone to teach you how to use Mary's love beads.

From your friends at Maryknoll

6 Suggestions

You can use this page at any time of the year. Feel free to return to it more than once, to enrich the children's prayer and reinforce their understanding of Mary.

Have the children open their books to student page 27, and look at the picture. Ask them what they notice about the picture. Read the text.

Have them read together the prayer of Mary in the box at the bottom of the page.

Have them copy the prayer, or paste a printed copy, onto one side of a colored strip of construction paper to use as a bookmark in their religion book. On the other side, have them draw a picture of Mary with the child Jesus. Provide materials for them to decorate the bookmark freely with bright colors, stickers, and yarn tassels.

Mary's Joy

Mary is the mother of Jesus. Mary is your mother, too. She wants you to have the joy of following Jesus. She wants you to have the joy of serving others, too.

An angel told Mary she was going to be the Mother of God. Mary said yes to the news. Then Mary visited her cousin Elizabeth. She said a prayer at Elizabeth's house. You can say that same prayer every day.

The prayer will help you follow Jesus your whole life long. It will help you remember to love others. It will help you serve others, too.

My soul sings of the
greatness of the Lord.
My spirit rejoices in God
my savior.
Luke 1:46

Unit 1

We are God's children now.

1 John 3:2

Chapter

0-07-821721-0, 0-07-821730-X, 0-07-821739-3, 0-07-821748-2, 0-07-821757-1, 0-07-821766-0

God Loves Me

The Story Keepers

Annunciation
In the story of the Annunciation, the angel Gabriel tells Mary that she will conceive and give birth to God's Son and will name him Jesus. Helena tells this story to the children while they are traveling in a wagon during the night. View the clip, tell the story, and lead activities suggested in the guide.

Albania  From Maryknoll

TEACHER RESOURCE CENTER

Faith Formation

CHECK THE CATECHISM

In paragraph 295 the *Catechism of the Catholic Church* reminds us that God created the world out of wisdom and love. Paragraph 293 states a fundamental truth of the Catholic faith: the world was created for God's glory. For other insights into the nature of God's gift of creation, see paragraphs 288, 290, and 293.

In God's Image

God created man in his image; in the divine image he created him; male and female he created them.

Genesis 1:27

God created the world and everything in it out of love. God wants all creatures to share in his life, wisdom, and goodness. As human beings, we are God's most precious creation. Each of us is made in God's image and likeness. It is the divine image deep within everyone of us that calls us to value and respect all human life. Besides being created in his image, each of us is uniquely blessed by God with specific gifts that contribute to the wonder and glory of God's creation.

What are some of your gifts?

God's Creative Love Surrounds Us

The world and everything in it was created by God, and as the story of creation in Genesis 1:12 states, "God saw how good it was." Each of us contributes to the goodness of God's creation by first becoming aware of our own goodness. We reveal God's goodness to others as we encounter each other in loving service. It is important to ponder, reflect, and give thanks for the abundant gifts God has given us.

How do your gifts reflect the presence of God in your life?

Background

Creating the Environment

The theme of this unit is God's love. The first few times you meet with the children, the most important thing you can do is emphasize an environment that reflects God's love and goodness. Without that emphasis, it will be very difficult for children to be open to God's message of love for them. The goodness you show to the children will be God's goodness.

This lesson focuses on God's goodness as shown in creation. You will help the children see that they are the best part of God's creation. In their goodness, they image God. Give them opportunities to express this goodness. Showing God's goodness is a concept that will be reinforced and expanded throughout the year.

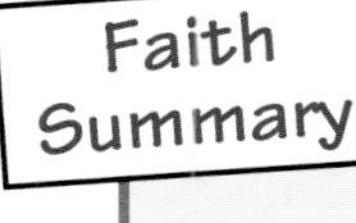

- God made all creation good.
- In creation we come to know the Creator.
- We use our gifts to show God's goodness.

Growth and Development

It is helpful to remember two characteristics of second graders as you teach this lesson:

- ***Second graders may enter a new school year with some apprehension.*** To second-grade children, summer vacation lasts a long time. They may forget all that was good about school and religion classes.
- ***Second graders want to know what to expect.*** They have to adjust to being back at school. Welcome the children warmly. Take the time to review expectations. Get the children excited about all they will be able to do by the end of the year. Give them hints about all that they will learn in religion class.

A Teacher's Prayer

Creator God, you have filled the world with your goodness. Let the children I teach see your goodness in me. May each child know your love through my words and actions. Amen.

Vocabulary Preview

creation
image

Scripture

Psalm 8:5: created by God
Genesis 1:1–27: creation
Luke 12:27–29: God will provide
Psalm 8: gifts of creation
Psalm 98:1: Praise the Lord.

Related Resources

Video

"Genesis"(Vision Video, 1-800-523-0226 or www.catholicvideo.com). This video addresses all of the major theological themes in the biblical book of Genesis. (Adult, 93 minutes)

Books

Haidle, Helen. *Field Guide to Bible Promises* (Zondervan, 1-800-727-1309 or www.zonderkidz.com). This book helps children learn about the promises God makes in the Bible. (Children)

Brian Wildsmith. *Saint Francis* (Eerdmans Press, 1-800-253-7521 or www.eerdmans.com). The children will enjoy seeing the use of gold leaf and finding the angel in every illustration. (Children)

TEACHER ORGANIZER

Planning Guide

The basic content for each chapter is divided into four class sessions. There are a number of options for the fifth session. Extension, review, and testing are options described under Day 5 Alternatives. The Quick Check box will help you evaluate the week's lessons.

Chapter Goals

In this chapter, the students will learn about

- ❑ God's goodness
- ❑ God's gifts
- ❑ Ways to show God's goodness

	DAY 1 · INVITATION	DAY 2 · DISCOVERY	DAY 3 · DISCOVERY
OBJECTIVES	**The students will be able to** • See that God created all that is good • Creatively express their part in God's circle of life • Use words associated with God as Creator	**The students will be able to** • Identify gifts of others • Identify a personal gift	**The students will be able to** • Identify ways to show God's goodness • Creatively express ways to show God's goodness
PREPARATION	• Plan some simple, fun actions for the introduction • Make copies of the resource master on page 62	• Read through the story • Plan the introduction to the lesson	• Read through pages 34–35 • Begin to observe the musical and visual-spatial learners
MATERIALS	• Drawing supplies • Magazines and writing paper • The last poem in *God Made Me Most Wonderfully*	• Drawing supplies	• Drawing supplies • A fairly large mirror, label, a couple of pencils, and writing paper
OPTIONAL ACTIVITIES	• Curriculum Challenge Make three vocabulary cards	• Teaching Tip Make a chart of classroom tasks or a poster showing classroom rules • Options Have writing and drawing materials for the students writing the faith statements	• Vocabulary Teach the word "image"

Learning Objectives

By the end of this chapter, the students should be able to

- ❑ Know that each person can reflect God's goodness
- ❑ Identify a personal gift
- ❑ Use a gift to show God's goodness

DAY 4 · LIVING

The students will be able to

- Creatively review the beauty of God's creation
- Participate in a psalm of praise

- Make a sample mobile
- Gather the art supplies to make mobiles
- Prepare a prayer area
- On the board, write the question listed on student page 30 as Do You Know?

- Sample mobile
- Art supplies, scissors, string, and a small branch or hanger for each student
- Ink pads with washable ink
- Wet paper towels

DAY 5 · ALTERNATIVES

There are a number of alternatives to help you plan Day 5.

Prayer Experience

Use The Circle of Life prayer experience on either Day 4 or Day 5. Follow the suggestions on page 58 for leading the prayer.

Review and Explore

Follow the suggestions on page 59 for teaching the page. You will need drawing and writing supplies.

Home and Family

Send the page home with the students.

The Church Today

This page provides a class project. Use it if time allows. You will need large cardboard boxes, poster board, and drawing supplies.

Chapter Test

The chapter test appears as a resource master on page 63.

Quick Check

Do this evaluation as soon as you finish each chapter.

Did I follow my lesson plan?

How can I tell that I met the learning objectives for the lesson?

What activities did the children enjoy most?

How could I improve this lesson?

Benziger on the Web
For more ideas, visit us at **www.benziger.glencoe.com**

Interactive Lesson Planner
Your ILP provides more help in preparing to teach this chapter.

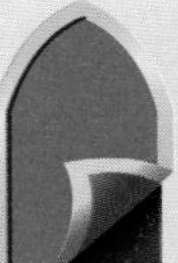

Celebrate
Turn to page 22 of this book. Check for seasonal celebrations.

Lesson Plan · Day 1
Along with the children, do some simple, fun actions: hop on one foot; smile and shake hands, pretend to ride a horse. End by saying, "God made us wonderfully!" Or, read and act out the last poem in the book *God Made Me Most Wonderfully.*

1 Talk about the Creator
Say to the children that God is the Creator, or Maker, of all that is good in the world. Direct attention to the picture, and share the first sentence. Have children call out some of the good things God created. Make a quick list on the chalkboard; comment now and then on the wonderfulness of a specific creation. Read student page 30.

2 God's World
Say that all God made is called creation. Write *creation* on the chalkboard, and have the children repeat it. Ask the children to imagine being in any part of God's creation. Where would they go? Each child may write a response on the page. Have a few volunteers share their responses and tell why they chose them.

TEACHING TIP
At the beginning of the lesson, you ask the children to name good things God created. Some children may mention manufactured items, such as computers. If so, say that God created people so wonderfully they have the brains to make things like computers.

RESOURCE MASTERS
The resource master on page 62 is a drawing and coloring activity on God's gifts of creation. You may let the children do the activity when they have free time during the day, or you may send the page home.

You crowned us with glory and honor.
Psalm 8:6

Do You Know?
◆ How are you made in God's image?

God's World

Nothing at All

Once there was nothing—nothing at all. There were no stars, no mountains, and not even any wiggly worms or slippery fish. There were no lions or bears, no dogs or cats, no hamsters or gerbils.

There were no people either. No mothers were holding babies. No big sisters were teasing little brothers.

God didn't like the empty world. He wanted to share his great love. God decided to do something about it.

3 Circle of Life

Share the information from Genesis given on student page 31. Then, have a few rows of children start at the top left of the circle and say each item aloud. "God created the ______." The other rows may respond to each item by saying, "This is good!"

4 Complete the Circle

See whether anyone can guess the best part of God's creation. Then tell the children that God made each of them. They are the best part of God's creation. Ask the children to add themselves to the circle of life. Allow a few minutes for drawing.

5 Celebrate

Suggest praising God for creation. Have the children stand and hold their arms up, palms facing in. Beginning with the words "Creator God," say the chapter's Scripture verse. Have the children repeat the verse after you. The tone of your voice will help the children understand the meaning of the verse.

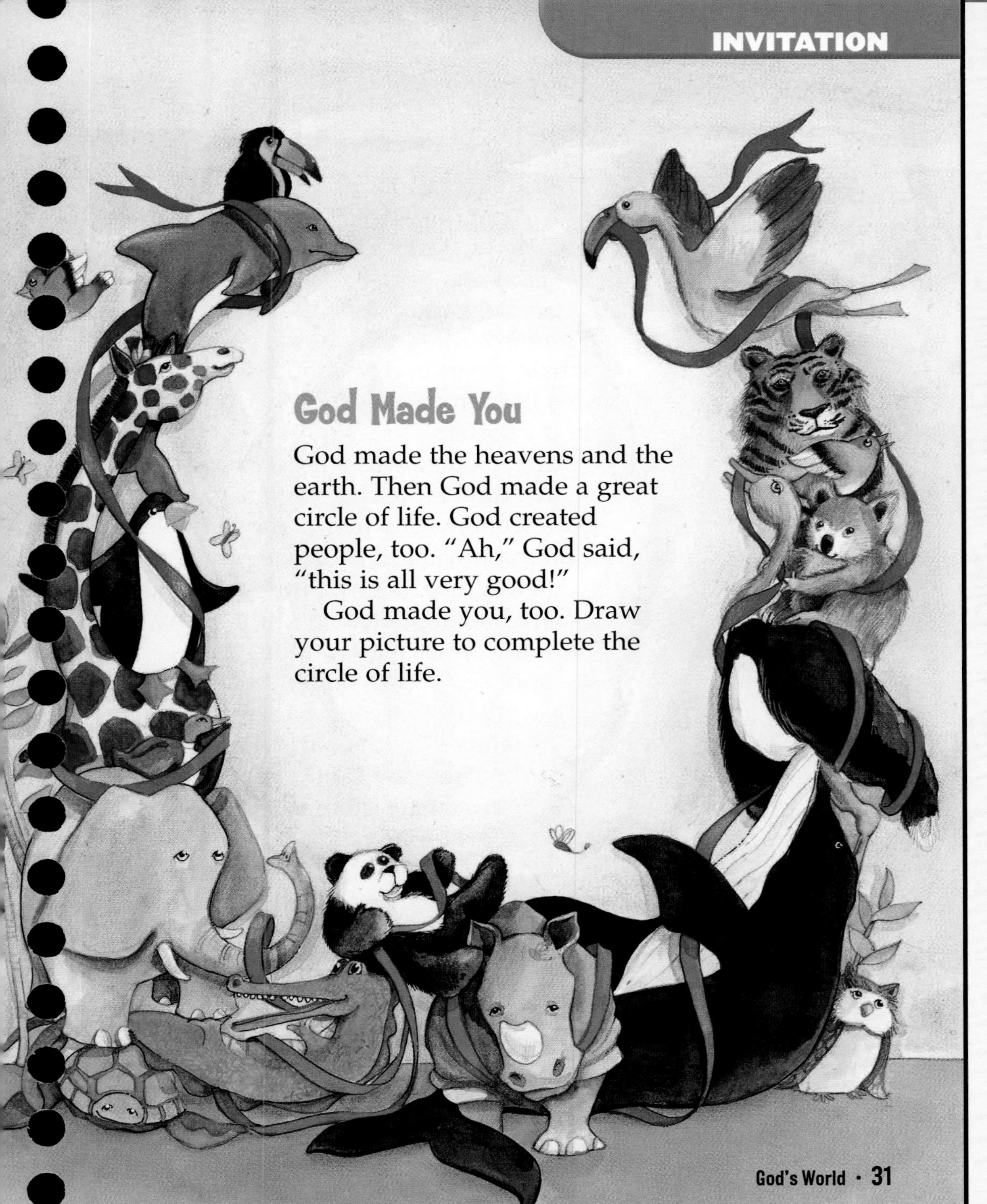

INVITATION
God Made You
God made the heavens and the earth. Then God made a great circle of life. God created people, too. "Ah," God said, "this is all very good!"
God made you, too. Draw your picture to complete the circle of life.
God's World · 31

VIRTUE FAITH GRACE

VOCABULARY

The more children use words, the more they understand them. Since many religious terms refer to abstract ideas, they need to be used frequently and accurately for the children to understand them. During the lesson, the children say, "God created the ______" to associate God as the Creator. Try to find other ways for the children to use the words Creator, created, and creation.

MATH ART SOCIAL STUDIES

CURRICULUM CHALLENGE

Language Arts Make vocabulary word cards for *God the Creator, created,* and *creation.* Display the word cards in an area of your room that focuses on writing. You may wish to have the children use magazines or drawing material to create rebus sentences that include the new vocabulary. For example, a child may write, "God created the [picture of the stars] and the [picture of the sun]."

Lesson Plan · Day 2

Use a team sport, such as soccer or baseball, to talk about the different parts the players play. Let children act out those parts. Spend just a few minutes on this introduction.

1 The Class Play

The story on student pages 32–33 is about a second-grade class putting on a play. Assign children to say, not read, the lines of Carrie, Danny, Ramon, Jenny, and Sara. Tell the class that you will point to each child when it is his or her time to speak.

2 Focus

You may wish to gather the children around you. Focus them on good listening. Tell the children that they will hear a story about Mrs. Gomez and her second-grade class, who are planning a play. Ask the children to listen for the part that tells about a girl named Jenny.

TEACHING TIP

The theme of inclusion is found throughout this book. From now on, there are many simple ways that you may incorporate and reinforce the theme. You may wish to make a chart of tasks that need to be done in the classroom and title it *We all play a part.* Or you and the children may come up with simple rules for the year. List the rules and label them with a statement like this: We all play a part in making this classroom a good place to be.

This We Believe!

God created the world and you. Everything God made is good.

Room for Everyone

Mrs. Gomez clapped her hands. "Attention, class!" she said. "We are putting on a play. The name of the play is *The Whale and the Mouse.*"

Carrie wanted to make scenery. Ramon wanted to play the part of the whale. Everybody had ideas—everyone except Jenny. She just bit her lip and sat in the corner.

Mrs. Gomez was a little worried about Jenny. But before she could say anything, Sara went over to Jenny. She said, "Jenny, don't you want to be in the play?"

"I do!" said Jenny. "But I am so shy."

Sara had an idea. She said, "Jenny, being shy is a good thing for a mouse." Jenny smiled.

"Mrs. Gomez," Sara asked, "can Jenny play the part of the mouse?"

"Yes, she can!" replied the teacher. "There is room for everyone."

What do you like to do? Tell about it.

3 Room for Everyone

While the children listen, read the story with enthusiasm. Point to each child when it is time for him or her to speak. At the end of student page 32, stop reading and ask the question at the bottom of the page.

4 All Play a Part

Complete the story. Have the child playing Jenny say the lines that are her thoughts on the page. Ask this child how Jenny may have felt once she found a part to play. Let volunteers suggest what gift from God Jenny had. Read the This We Believe! feature.

5 Room for You

Tell the children that God has given them a part to play in everyday life. Their part is to show God's goodness. Read the material on student page 33.

Read the directions for the activity. Organize the activity into short scenes, with volunteers playing each part. The rest of the class may give a loud "Hooray" or "Oh, no" in reponse.

Room for You

You are made in God's own image. When God made you, he said, "Ah, this child is very good."

You are an important part of creation. You have a part to play, too. You can show God's goodness to others.

ACTIVITY — SHOW GOODNESS

Look at the pictures and read the words. Put a happy face near a picture that shows goodness. Put a sad face near a picture that does not. In the empty space, tell how you can show God's goodness.

1. Kevin hit his little brother.

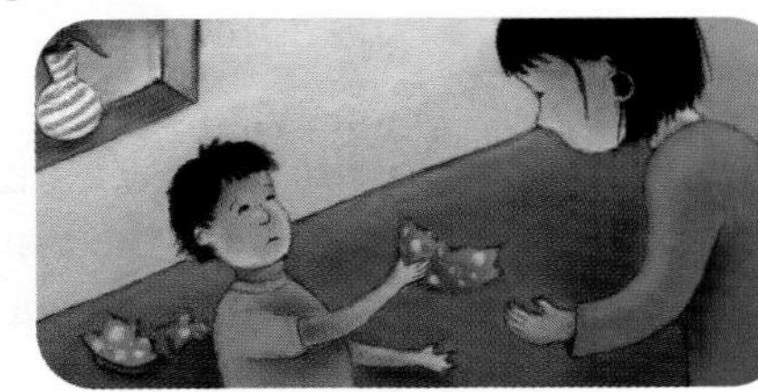

2. Manuel told the truth about breaking the vase.

3. Selena gives everyone a chance to play.

CURRICULUM CHALLENGE

Science Using a science lesson, you may be able to continue the theme of "all playing a part." If you are studying animals, point out how parents and extended family members play different roles in caring for and raising their offspring. If you are studying living things, such as flowers, help the children see how the parts of a plant work together to help the plant live.

OPTIONS

For Young Artists You may wish to place emphasis on the This We Believe! feature. One of these important statements of faith appears in every chapter. Each week a different child may copy the sentences, illustrate them, and place them in your prayer area for all to read.

Lesson Plan · Day 3

See who can summarize the story "Room for Everyone." Recall that the second grade children all played a part to make "The Whale and the Mouse" a hit.

❶ Everyday Goodness

Tell the children that they will not only experience God's goodness through the love and good actions of others but also through the beautiful creation that surrounds them. Read the material on student page 34. Call the children's attention to the pictures. What do they see as proof of God's love? *(animals, friends)*

❷ Activity

Ask the children to look out the window. What do they see as proof of God's love? *(sun, clouds, rain, birds, trees)* Have the children close their eyes and "see" the proof of God's love at home and at school. Ask them to share their answers. Read the directions for the activity, and allow the children time to complete it on their own.

VIRTUE FAITH GRACE **VOCABULARY**

Image To reinforce an understanding of the word *image,* set up a fairly large mirror somewhere in the room. On or near the mirror write this question: *What image do you see?* Have a sheet of lined paper available for the children to write their answers.

Everyday Goodness

God's People believe that God made everything. They tell the story of creation over and over. The story of creation is found in the Bible.

In the Bible, you will find many, many stories about God and God's People. You will find that God loves you very much.

Look at the pictures. Talk about how much God loves you. Talk about the everyday goodness you see around you.

ACTIVITY — GOOD GIFTS

On the blue star, write or draw a gift that God has given you. On the red star, write a gift that God has given to a friend of yours. Share your work.

3 The Father's Love

Ask the children to think about many things in God's creation. Make a list on the chalkboard. *(trees, kittens, dogs, birds, etc. . . .)* Discuss some ways that God takes care of this part of his creation. Tell the children that Jesus told many stories of God's love. Jesus told how God would always give his people what they needed. Read the Scripture story on student page 35.

4 God Loves Me

Add the word *Me* to the list created for step 3. Talk about how God has taken care of their needs. *(parent or caregiver, food, friends, teachers)* Emphasize the difference between what they *need* and what they may *want.*

The Father's Love

Jesus wanted his friends to know how much God the Father loved them. So he told them to look at the world God made.

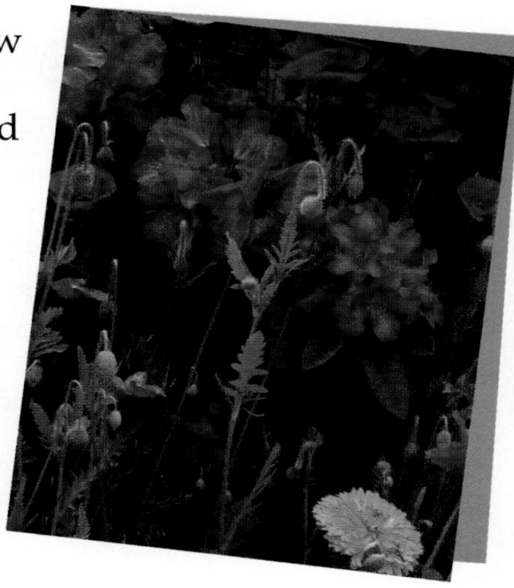

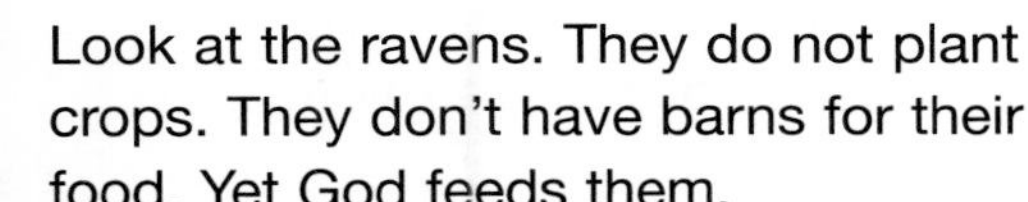

Look at the ravens. They do not plant crops. They don't have barns for their food. Yet God feeds them.

Look at how the flowers grow. They do not work or make fine clothes. But I tell you; not even King Solomon was dressed like one of these beautiful flowers.

If God your Father takes such good care of flowers and birds, he will take care of you, too. Do not be afraid any longer, little ones. Your Father is going to give you his kingdom.

Based on *Luke 12:27–29*

What do you see in God's good world that reminds you of his love for you?

TEACHING TIP

The need to show God's goodness is a faith response. You can help reinforce their good behavior with the words, "I can see God's goodness in the way you [mention the specific action you observed]."

OPTIONS

For Musical Learners Some children learn best through musical expression. These children may make up lines to the tune of "The More We Get Together." They may sing, "The more we show God's goodness, the happier we'll be." The children may also make up verses with actions that tell how to show God's goodness, such as "We share what we have."

Lesson Plan · Day 4

Hide the sample mobile. Give the children a clue to guess the art project: Tell the children that today they will hang out in God's good world.

1 Creation Stories

Tell the children that it is their turn to write creation stories of their own. Pass out writing paper. Read the directions for the activity. Allow children time to write their stories. Encourage them to add illustrations. This can be done in class if time permits or at home. Display their stories if possible.

CREATION STORIES

Make up a story about the goodness of God's creation. When you have finished your story, you can share it with the class. You can act it out if you like.

The list below will give you some ideas.

1. Tell about somebody who cares for God's creation.
2. Tell about someone who shares his or her gifts with others.
3. Tell about somebody who is kind and loving.
4. Tell about somebody who teaches others about God's love.

Remember that you can tell any story you want. Make sure that the story tells about God's good world.

2 God's Good World
Gather the children and ask who created the world. Then briefly talk with the children about the ways they enjoy the beauty of God's world.

3 A Reminder
Let the children determine the steps needed to make the mobile. Those who wish may work in a group. Ask for suggestions for good ways to work in a group, such as taking turns using the materials. Spend some time with each group (or individuals) to give positive feedback and help.

A REMINDER

Talk about the things you like best about the world God made. Talk about crunchy leaves and gusty wind. Talk about blue lakes and tall trees. Talk about snowflakes and puppy dogs.

Now make a reminder of God's great love for you.
1. Draw three or four little pictures of God's gifts.
2. Cut out the pictures.
3. Attach the pictures to a coat hanger.
4. Hang your reminder where you will see it every day.

TEACHING TIP

Art Projects It is good to have a sample on hand of any art project that you do. Have all of the needed supplies in an easily accessible place. If the children work at tables, place supplies on each table. Have space ready to display the finished work. For today's lesson, if the children will not take their mobiles home, have ready the means for hanging them.

Prayer
If you have a prayer area, gather there. Tell the children to think about all the special gifts from God.

1 Thumbprints
Recall that everyone has a part to play in God's circle of life. God has given everyone gifts. Have each child carefully make a thumbprint in a circle on the page and then add his or her thumbprint to one another's pages. Spend just a short time doing so, and have wet towels on hand for clean-up.

2 The Circle of Life
Prepare to pray. Say that all the second-grade children are needed to pray to God. The prayer you will say is from the Bible. It is a happy prayer that praises God. Practice the lines. Display the mobiles near the prayer area. Gather and pray.

LEARNING TO PRAY

Talk with the children about how to pray with respect. What should they think about when they pray? How should they stand or sit? Where should they look? What are some differences between praying and playing? What are some similarities? You may want to focus on one aspect of prayer at a time (such as quietness, posture, focusing on God, and so on) until the children learn it.

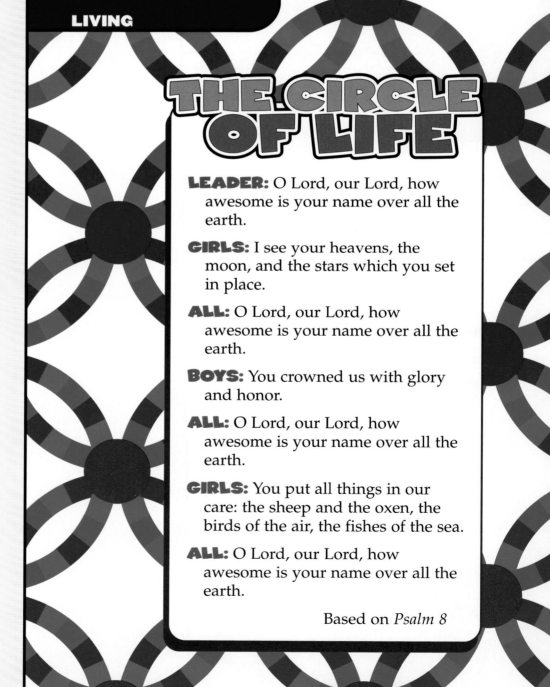

THE CIRCLE OF LIFE

LEADER: O Lord, our Lord, how awesome is your name over all the earth.

GIRLS: I see your heavens, the moon, and the stars which you set in place.

ALL: O Lord, our Lord, how awesome is your name over all the earth.

BOYS: You crowned us with glory and honor.

ALL: O Lord, our Lord, how awesome is your name over all the earth.

GIRLS: You put all things in our care: the sheep and the oxen, the birds of the air, the fishes of the sea.

ALL: O Lord, our Lord, how awesome is your name over all the earth.

Based on *Psalm 8*

1 Know
Direct the children's attention to the two panels in the Know section. Say that this section shows what the children learned in Chapter 1. Let the children point to each panel and read the words aloud. Then, point to the Do You Know? question you have written on the chalkboard. Say that the children are now ready to answer it.

2 Love and Serve
The children will need time to draw. They may draw a picture for a friend, as explained in the Love section. After the drawing, have the children do the Serve activity.

3 God's Friends
After the drawing and writing are completed, hold up a student book and direct attention to the drawing of Saint Francis of Assisi. Tell the children about him. See whether any children have seen statues or pictures of Saint Francis.

CHAPTER 1 REVIEW and EXPLORE

Know

God made you in his image.
You show God's goodness to others.

Love

Make a drawing of something wonderful in God's world. On the drawing, write the name of a friend or family member. Give the drawing to the person you name. Tell him or her about God's good world.

Serve

How did you show today that you are made in God's image? Write or draw your answer.

GOD'S FRIENDS

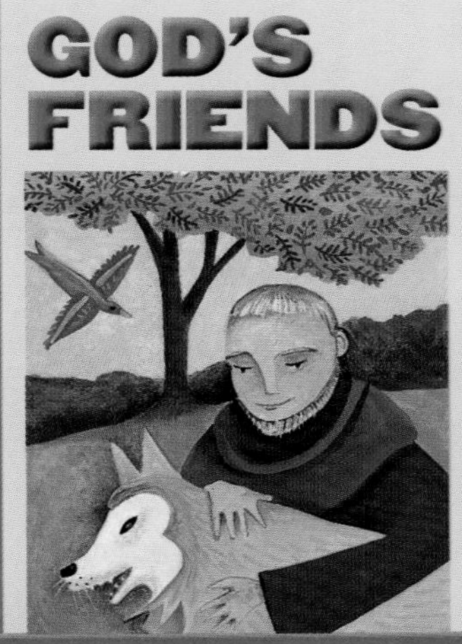

Saint Francis of Assisi

Francis saw God's goodness everywhere. He said the sun was like his brother, and the moon was like his sister. Some people put a statue of Francis in their yards. It reminds them to care for living things, just as Francis did.

A Little Catechism

Invite the children to open their religion books to Part I, page 7, *A Little Catechism*. Choose one or more of the selections below for memory work or reinforcement. You will find your copy of the catechism on pages 23–43 of this Teacher's Edition.

1. Introduce *A Little Catechism* by reading the section called Your Book.
2. Read the story in the Welcome section aloud. Ask the children, "Who made all things?" *(God made all things.)*
3. Together, pray the morning prayer: "I give to you, my God, this day, all I do, think, or say." Conclude by making the Sign of the Cross.

Know Love Serve

Note The activities on this page provide ways for the children to share their learning with their families. The activities are related to the week's theme.

1 Introduce

Have the children look at the page. Say that this is a page they can do at home. Then, have the children look at the illustration of the Creation Scrapbook. Explain how to do the activity. Ask for ideas as to how the children can get their families to help them do the page.

2 Pray Together

You may ask the children to stand and hold up their arms in praise. All together pray the verse from Psalm 98. If you wish, invite volunteers to say something God has created and use the verse as a response.

IDEAS THAT WORK

Family involvement is essential in building faith. Keep the families aware of the religious concepts their children are learning. You may be able to arrange a time for families to view the religion books (perhaps after Sunday Masses). You may wish to send home a note with the Home and Family page for Chapter I. Briefly describe the purpose of the page. Say that the suggested ideas are simple and quick to do and that not all of them need to be done. Encourage the family to pick a time to say the prayer together.

Online for Families

Remind the children to check the Benziger Web site this week with their families.
www.benziger.glencoe.com

Dear Family,

I have just finished chapter 1. I have learned that God made me in his image. I learned that there is room for everyone in God's world. Help me show God's goodness to others.

On your own

Make a creation scrapbook. Fold and cut two sheets of paper to make a little book. On each page, put pictures or words about God's world and the people in it. Share your scrapbook with others.

With your family

Some evening, talk about all the ways your family shows God's goodness. Talk about what it means to be made in God's image.

Lord, you have done wonderful things.

GO ONLINE!
http://www.benziger.glencoe.com

1 Talk About
Ask the children to read aloud the title of the page. Say that this page tells ways the Catholic Church shows God's goodness. Then say that the world is a gift from God. The Church teaches that people should care for God's world. People should not waste what God has given.

2 Make Collection Boxes
Lead the children in decorating collection boxes for the school or parish. Explain the purpose of the boxes. Then ask the children to suggest what jobs need to be done to complete the project. List on the chalkboard the jobs and the volunteers who will do them. Emphasize the fact that all will have a part to play in making the boxes.

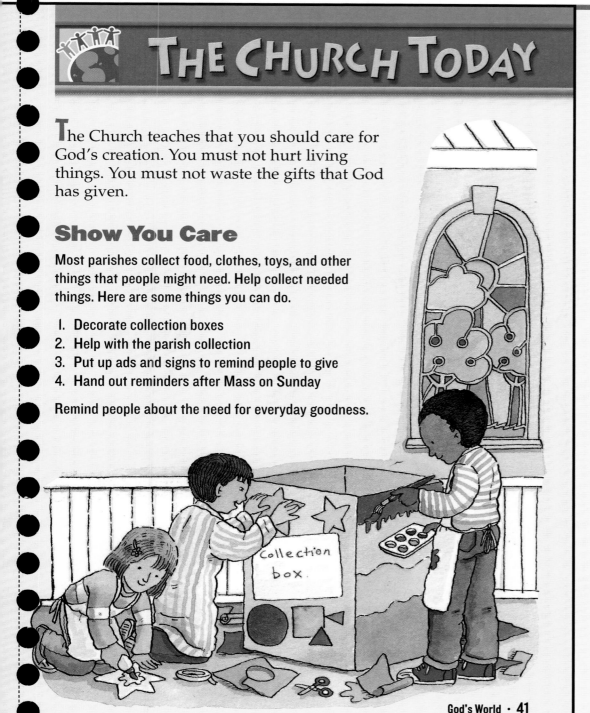

THE CHURCH TODAY

The Church teaches that you should care for God's creation. You must not hurt living things. You must not waste the gifts that God has given.

Show You Care

Most parishes collect food, clothes, toys, and other things that people might need. Help collect needed things. Here are some things you can do.

1. Decorate collection boxes
2. Help with the parish collection
3. Put up ads and signs to remind people to give
4. Hand out reminders after Mass on Sunday

Remind people about the need for everyday goodness.

TEACHING TIP

Many hands are needed to carry out the project. Here are job suggestions that may help you get all of the children involved:

- Decide how to decorate the boxes.
- Name the project.
- Decorate the boxes.
- Pick places to put the boxes.
- Talk to the principal or pastor about the project.
- Place the boxes.
- Collect the items.
- Make signs that explain the project.

ANSWER KEY

This is the answer key for the chapter test on page 63.

A. 1. b 2. a 3. a

B. 1. b 2. c 3. a

C. 1. R 2. R

Name ______________________________

God Made All Things Good

Circle all the living things that God made. Draw more of God's gifts.

Name ______________________________

Chapter 1 Test

A. Circle the word that best finishes each sentence.

1. Everything God created is
a. tall.
b. good.

2. When you are kind, you
a. show God's goodness.
b. are part of creation.

3. God created
a. the world.
b. buildings.

B. Draw a line to match the parts that go together.

1. God is called	**a.** the circle of life.
2. People and plants are	**b.** the Creator.
3. Creation is part of	**c.** God's creation.

C. Write R if the sentence is right. Write W if the sentence is wrong.

_____ **1.** God made you.

_____ **2.** God wants you to care for living things.

CHAPTER 2 God's Son

TEACHER RESOURCE CENTER

Faith Formation

The Living God

In a way, it is almost unthinkable that God would ever become a human being. But God did. God became fully human in the person of Jesus of Nazareth. We call this the mystery of Incarnation. The unthinkable became reality: God came into the world as a human person, to reveal to his followers who God is. Jesus, the "Image of the invisible God," (Colossians 1:15) shows through his life, death, and resurrection what it means to be the Son of God. As we come to know and follow Jesus, we grow in our understanding of who God is.

How does God come alive for you when you read the stories of Jesus?

Jesus Heals and Reconciles

The Gospels reveal Jesus' love for the outcast, the poor, and the sick. God's loving-kindness and compassion are mirrored in the life of Jesus. Jesus teaches the forgiveness of God in parables such as "The Prodigal Son" *(Luke 15:11-32)*. Jesus describes what it means to be a neighbor in the story of "The Good Samaritan" *(Luke 10:25-36)*. Jesus brings sight to the blind *(John 9)* and feeds the hungry *(Matthew 15:32–38)*. Jesus, the image of the invisible God, reveals God again and again in these Gospel passages.

What can you do this week to follow Jesus' example?

CHECK THE CATECHISM

The *Catechism of the Catholic Church* explains the tradition that underpins the Church's understanding of Jesus as Son of God. Paragraphs 442–443 teach that acknowledging Christ's divine sonship is at the center of the apostolic faith. See paragraphs 424, 444–445 for more on this topic.

Background

Jesus Shows God's Love

This week the students will learn that Jesus, the Son of God, was sent to model God's love. The students will learn about Jesus, and therefore, God, through Bible stories. It is your role to help make Jesus personable to the students. You may talk about the stories from two aspects, Jesus as God and as man. For example, the students will hear about Jesus healing the man born blind. You may say that Jesus was able to do so because he is the Son of God. Then lead the students to discover what this action tells about Jesus—that he cared, that he was willing to help others, that he did not ignore people in need, that he was gentle. Helping the students uncover these human aspects of Jesus will help them to discover ways to model him.

Faith Summary

- **Jesus is the Son of God, one with the Father.**
- **Jesus was sent to show God's love.**
- **Jesus showed love to everyone.**

Growth and Development

It is helpful to remember two characteristics of second graders as you teach this lesson:

- ***Second graders have a developing sense of history.*** When Jesus lived is difficult for them to understand and is not very important.
- ***Second graders tend to view things as black and white, right and wrong.*** Be aware of this as you teach about Jesus.

A Teacher's Prayer

Jesus, you lived among the people
and were a model of what is possible.
Peace is possible. Love is possible. Forgiveness
is possible. Bless me with the courage
of my convictions. Amen.

Vocabulary Preview

Son of God

Scripture

Matthew 3:17: My Beloved Son
John 9:1–7: Jesus heals a blind man.
Matthew 14:13–21: Jesus feeds the crowd.
Luke 5:27–32: Jesus forgives a sinner.
Luke 17:11–19: Jesus heals the lepers.

Related Resources

Video

"What Catholics Believe About Jesus Christ" (Liguori Publications, 1-800-325-9521 or www.liguori.org). This video is a basic overview of the Church's teachings about Jesus as contained in both Scripture and tradition. (Adult, 30 minutes)

Book

Jesus for Children (Twenty-Third Publications, 1-800-321-0411 or www.twentythirdpublications.com). In this book, the life of Jesus is faithfully retold from Scripture in contemporary language. (Children)

TEACHER ORGANIZER

Planning Guide

The basic content for each chapter is divided into four class sessions. There are a number of options for the fifth session. Extension, review, and testing are options described under Day 5 Alternatives. The Quick Check box will help you evaluate the week's lessons.

Chapter Goals

In this chapter, the students will learn about

- ❏ Jesus, the Son of God
- ❏ Ways Jesus showed God's love
- ❏ God's care and forgiveness

	DAY 1 · INVITATION	DAY 2 · DISCOVERY	DAY 3 · DISCOVERY
OBJECTIVES	**The students will be able to** • See that people have ways to stay close • Identify ways to show love to those far away	**The students will be able to** • Retell Bible stories about Jesus, the Son of God • Interpret Bible stories about Jesus showing God's love • Explore ways to show God's love	**The students will be able to** • Determine Jesus' teaching in a Bible story • Apply the teaching to personal life
PREPARATION	• Read through the story	• Read through the Bible stories and the feature Bible Basics	• Make copies of the activity resource master on page 80 • Read through the Bible story and determine how you will help the children understand its message
MATERIALS	• Pencils	• Pencils	• Pencils • Copies of the resource master, drawing supplies
OPTIONAL ACTIVITIES	• **In The Media** Set aside some time to do a survey regarding the children's use of computers and e-mail		• **Ideas That Work** Have blank index cards, one for each child, and drawing supplies for making prayer cards

Learning Objectives

By the end of this chapter, the students should be able to

- ❏ Identify Jesus as the Son of God
- ❏ Identify ways Jesus showed God's love
- ❏ Discover personal ways to show God's love

DAY 4 • LIVING

The students will be able to

- Share what they know about Jesus
- Pray to Jesus to follow him

- Be ready to play and sing
- Decide how you will form the groups: see Ideas That Work
- Observe which children learn by doing

- Music
- Crayons or colored pencils, pencils

- **Ideas That Work** Get items for forming groups

DAY 5 • ALTERNATIVES

There are a number of alternatives to help you plan Day 5.

Prayer Experience
Use A Litany on either Day 4 or Day 5. Follow the suggestions on the Lesson Plan.

Review and Explore
Follow the suggestions on page 77 for teaching the page. If you using Ideas That Work, from page 76, prepare the newspaper.

Home and Family
Send the page home with the students.

The Church Today
Putting on a puppet show is a class project. You will need art materials to make puppets, scenery, and invitations. You may choose to use an art class to do the project.

Chapter Test
The chapter test appears as a resource master on page 81.

Quick Check

Do this evaluation as soon as you finish each chapter.

Did I follow my lesson plan?

How can I tell that I met the learning objectives for the lesson?

What activities did the children enjoy most?

How could I improve this lesson?

Benziger on the Web
For more ideas, visit us at **www.benziger.glencoe.com**

Interactive Lesson Planner
Your ILP provides more help in preparing to teach this chapter.

Celebrate
Turn to page 22 of this book. Check for seasonal celebrations.

Lesson Plan · Day 1

Have the children read aloud the chapter title, the chapter's Scripture verse, and the Do You Know? question. Let volunteers make guesses as to what the chapter covers. Then skim through the pages, and find visual clues that support (or refute) the guesses. At the end of the week, come back to this question to see how the children's knowledge has developed.

1 Keeping in Touch

Say that you are going to read a story about Jake and Karen, two children who do not live with their dad. Ask the children to follow along in their books and listen for ways Jake and Karen's dad keeps close to them. Then, read the story. Ask for ways that the family stays close.

2 Activity

Ask the children to think quietly about someone they do not see often. They may then write an e-mail message in the space. You need not be concerned with accurate spelling.

IDEAS THAT WORK

Some children find it difficult to begin an assignment. Be aware of those students. You may need to approach them and quietly and gently lead them to come up with the first idea to put down on a page.

This is my beloved Son. I am well pleased with him.

Matthew 3:17

Do You Know?

◆ How did Jesus show God's love to others?

God's Son

Keeping in Touch

Jake and Karen's dad lives far away. They don't see him often. He does call, and he sends cards. Jake and Karen put his cards on the refrigerator door. Their dad sends presents, too. But Jake and Karen like it best when the computer says, "You've got mail!" They like keeping in touch.

Send a make-believe e-mail message to someone far away.

To:

From:

Message:

3 A Real Letter

Talk about the common ways that people keep in touch. *(telephone, e-mail)* Say that people who love one another cannot always be together. Even though people cannot see each other in person, they find ways to stay close and to share news. Have the children read the story. Ask questions such as: Why do the children miss Uncle David? Are the children excited to hear Uncle David's letter? Do you think the children will write a letter to Uncle David?

A Real Letter

Sometimes it is hard to keep in touch. Now, listen to a story.

When Shari, Selma, and Sarah got home from school, Mom gathered them in the living room. We got a *real* letter from Grandma King.

"Why didn't she just call?" asked Shari.

"Why didn't she send an e-mail?" asked Selma.

"Sometimes, Mom answered, "Grandma just wants to put her thoughts on paper. When she was a girl, it cost a lot of money to make a call. And there was no e-mail at all."

"Grandma does write good letters," said Sarah. "They are funny and interesting, too."

They read Grandma King's letter together. It was a newsy letter. At the bottom of the letter were X's and O's—hugs and kisses.

When they were through, Selma had an idea. "Let's write a letter back," she suggested.

"What a great idea," they all agreed.

How do the members of your family keep in touch?

IN THE MEDIA

See how many children have access to e-mail and to the Internet. See how many use their access and how often they use it. Find out how many children use a computer to play games. See what kind of games they play. The more you know about the children you teach, the more you will know how to teach them.

Lesson Plan · Day 2
See who can recall the previous lesson: Some people do not see each other very often. They find ways to show their love.

1 Review
We cannot see God, but we know God's love. Review the ways we know that God loves us: We see God's love in creation. We know God's love in Baptism.

2 Jesus Is God's Son
Write on the board: *Jesus is the Son of God.* Say that God sent Jesus to show how much God loves us. Jesus showed God's love in what he said and did. Next, have everyone read aloud This We Believe! Then, lead the children through each Bible story. One story at a time, guide the children to discover what Jesus did to show God's love.

BIBLE BASICS

- Do not expect too much of the children's ability to interpret Bible stories. There are age-appropriate lessons throughout the book showing how to discover the message of a story.
- Do not let Biblical language interfere with age-appropriate interpretation. For example, even though they do not know the meaning of Sabbath, the children will know how Jesus showed God's love to the blind man.
- As often as possible, have one focus. For example, in today's lesson, focus on the love Jesus shows. What the children need to understand are these beliefs: Jesus is the Son of God. In Jesus we know the love of the Father.

Jesus Is God's Son

God sent Jesus to keep in touch with people—to save them from sin and death. Jesus is the Son of God. Jesus is truly God and truly man. Jesus showed God's love. Listen to some stories about Jesus.

"My heart is sad, because the crowd is hungry."
"Go, wash your eyes."

The Blind Man

Jesus met a blind man on the road. The man asked Jesus for help. Jesus rubbed clay on the blind man's eyes. When the blind man washed his eyes, he could see.

Based on *John 9:1–7*

The Hungry Crowd

A large crowd had been listening to Jesus. The people were very hungry. Jesus told his friends to feed the crowd. They had only a few loaves of bread and a couple of fish. Jesus blessed the bread and the fish. His friends passed the food out. Everyone had enough to eat. And there were baskets of food left over.

Based on *Matthew 14:13–21*

3 Show God's Love
If you wish, use these prompts to help the children write a sentence about ways to show God's love: (1) When someone is not feeling well, I can . . . (2) When someone makes me upset, I can . . . (3) When someone is in need, I can . . .

4 Activity
Have the children point to each of the three Bible stories and say aloud a one-sentence summary of the story. Say that in each story Jesus showed God's love. Some children may want to do the activity on their own, and others may want to have a partner. After a few minutes, have the children share some of their answers.

THIS WE BELIEVE!

Jesus is God's Son. Jesus shows God's love to everyone.

Forgiveness

Jesus was at a party. Some of the people were angry at Jesus because he had a party with sinners. Jesus said, "Yes, I am here with sinners. I have come here to heal and to forgive them. When sinners turn their hearts to God, it is time to celebrate!"

Based on *Luke 5:27–32*

ACTIVITY — LEARN FROM THE SON

In your own words, write what you learned about God the Father from the stories about Jesus. (If you want to, you can draw a picture instead.)

VIRTUE FAITH GRACE VOCABULARY

Son of God Jesus is the only Son of God. This title used for Jesus signifies his unique relationship to the Father.

Lesson Plan · Day 3

Review the three things learned from Jesus about God's love. God heals, God forgives, and God gives you what you need.

1 Recall

State that Jesus *said things* that showed God's love. In pairs, have the children look back at the stories on student pages 44–45, and find words of Jesus that prove the statement. Then, say that Jesus *showed* God's love. Again, have the children look back and suggest actions of proof.

2 The Ten Lepers

See the Teaching Tip. Gather the children, and ask them to listen to how the people treated Jesus. Read or tell the Bible story. Ask whether there are any questions.

Ask volunteers to act out the Bible story in their own words. This will help the children understand the story, and figure out its message.

TEACHING TIP

Before you present a Bible story, anticipate what difficulties the children may have in understanding it. For example, in the story of the ten lepers, the children will need to know about leprosy ahead of time. You will probably have to lead them to discover the meaning of the phrases "made well" and "your faith has served you."

The Lepers

One day Jesus was traveling. On the road he met ten lepers. Lepers are people who have a very, very serious sickness.

The ten lepers called out to Jesus, "Master, save us!"

Jesus said, "Go and show yourself to the priests."

On the way, all ten lepers were made well. They were so excited that they went off singing and dancing—all except one. That leper came back. He praised God and thanked Jesus! Jesus said, "Ten lepers were made well, but only you came back to say thank you. Go, your faith has served you."

Based on *Luke 17:11–19*

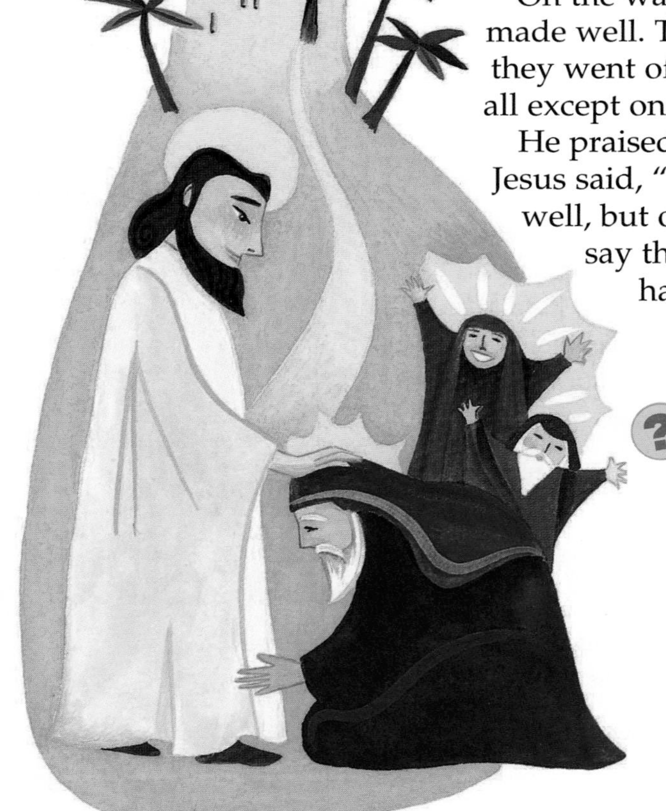

What does the story of the ten lepers tell about Jesus? about keeping in touch with God?

3 Learn from Jesus

Ask: If someone wanted to know about you, whom could they talk to? Allow children to respond. Why did they choose that person? Say that God wanted everyone to know about him, and that is why he sent his son Jesus. When you get to know Jesus, you get to know his Father. Read the material on student page 47. Lead the children though each of the Jesus facts.

4 Activity

Tell the children that they are going to get a chance to write their own prayer to Jesus. Ask them to keep in mind all that Jesus has taught them about God and his love for them. Allow the children time to complete the activity.

Learn from Jesus

God wanted everyone to know about him. So God sent Jesus. One time the Apostle Philip asked Jesus to show him the Father. Jesus told Philip that when he saw Jesus, he saw the Father, too.

When you listen to the stories about Jesus, you learn about God:

- Jesus is God's only Son.
- Jesus is the Savior and the Lord.
- Jesus shows you that God listens.
- Jesus shows you that God forgives.
- Jesus teaches you to love God.
- Jesus is always with you.

ACTIVITY CALL ON JESUS

Write a three line prayer—a very short one. Keep the prayer in your pocket and say it often during the day.

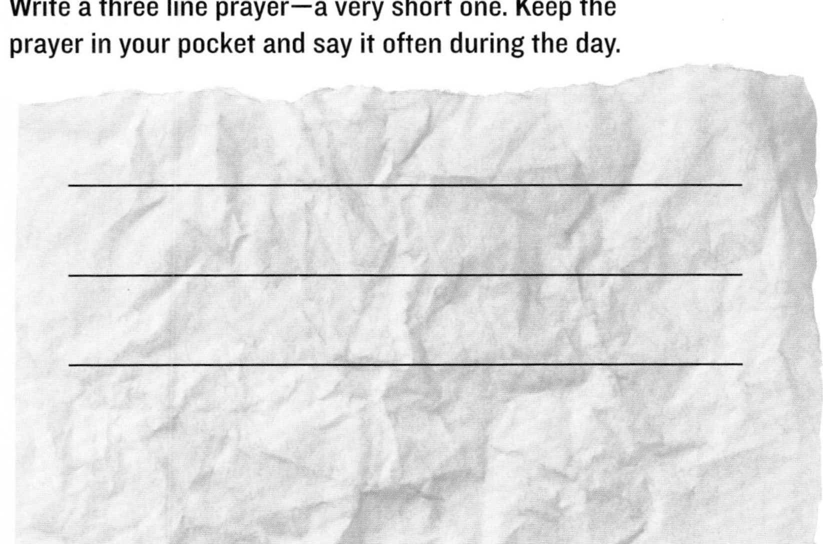

RESOURCE MASTERS

The resource master on page 80 is a drawing activity about Jesus showing God's love. Use the page when it best suits your schedule.

IDEAS THAT WORK

Have each child transfer the prayer he or she wrote for the activity on student page 47 to a small note card. They may decorate the cards and keep them in their pockets. You may wish to transfer the children's completed prayers to the prayer area. Choose one of the children's prayers and pray it out loud at prayer time. You may also wish to take the children's prayer cards and create a bulletin board entitled "We Call on Jesus."

Lesson Plan · Day 4

Say that one way to show God's love is to follow Jesus.

1 Follow Jesus

Tell the children that they will have to think of one thing that they remember about Jesus. But they are going to do it in a fun new way. Review the directions for the circle game. Add that the child in the middle will have his or her eyes closed and his or her arm and pointing finger out. Whoever the child is pointing to when the music stops will share something about Jesus.

The song is sung to the melody of "Frère Jacques." Practice the song. Then find a large space, join hands and make one or two circles.

IDEAS THAT WORK

Here is a way to form children into groups.

- Pick an item to distribute, such as jellybeans, stickers, or strips of colored paper.
- Decide how many groups will work best.
- Have as many different varieties of the item you chose as you have groups (for six groups have six flavors of jellybeans).
- Have one item per child.
- The children pick an item. Those having like items form a group.

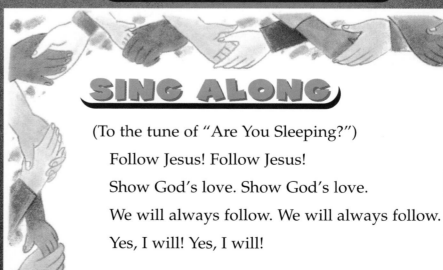

FOLLOW JESUS

Play a circle game.

1. Join hands and form a circle.
2. One of you stands in the circle.
3. Sing the song below and march around.
4. When the music stops, the child closest to the person in the middle has to share something about God's Son.
5. Give everybody a turn to be in the middle.

SING ALONG

(To the tune of "Are You Sleeping?")

Follow Jesus! Follow Jesus!
Show God's love. Show God's love.
We will always follow. We will always follow.
Yes, I will! Yes, I will!

② Jesus is Lord

Review the directions for the activity. Allow the children time to complete the activity. Ask for volunteers to share their three facts about God the Father.

LIVING

JESUS IS LORD!

Look at the outline of Jesus. With crayons or colored pencils, finish the picture of Jesus. Then, around the picture, write or draw three things Jesus teaches you about God the Father. Share your picture with the class.

OPTIONS

For Those Who Learn by Doing

You may have some students who find it difficult to express themselves in writing. If so, have them form one group. Rather than write, they may think of ways to show God's love and act them out. Give the group a little guidance when needed—how to stay focused and how to make the message clear.

Prayer

Gather in the prayer area. Help the children pronounce the title for the prayer. Explain to children that a litany is an asking prayer.

1 A Litany

A prayer leader will pray a line and the students will respond with "Jesus, hear us!" after each line is read. Ask the children to practice the response. Choose a prayer leader and gather for prayer.

IDEAS THAT WORK

Ask the children about the different ways that we receive information (newspapers, television, radio). Use a newspaper format for the Serve activity. Ahead of time, prepare an 8 1/2 x 11 sheet of paper divided into two sections entitled "Have You Heard?" and "Have You Seen?" The title for your newspaper can be the *Good News Gazette.* The children can review what they have learned in a fun way.

A LITANY

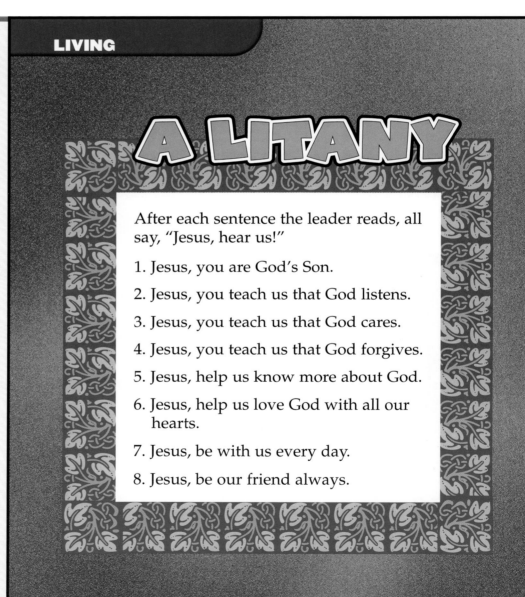

After each sentence the leader reads, all say, "Jesus, hear us!"

1. Jesus, you are God's Son.
2. Jesus, you teach us that God listens.
3. Jesus, you teach us that God cares.
4. Jesus, you teach us that God forgives.
5. Jesus, help us know more about God.
6. Jesus, help us love God with all our hearts.
7. Jesus, be with us every day.
8. Jesus, be our friend always.

1 Know
Direct attention to the picture of Jesus and have everyone read the words aloud.

2 Love and Serve
Have the children do the Love section. Give a time limit. Those who wish may share their prayers. Do the Serve activity as a class. Make everyone feel comfortable about suggesting words and actions. Agree on two statements and actions and post them.

3 God's Friends
Call attention to the illustration of Blessed Damien. Using the text, tell about him. Talk with the children: How do you know that Damien listened to the people? How did he show he cared?

Know

Jesus is God's Son.

God listens.
God cares.
God forgives.

Love

Keep in touch with God. In the space, write a short prayer to thank God for sending his Son, Jesus. Say the prayer every day for a week.

Serve

Share what you know. How can you share what you learned about God's Son with someone else? Talk about what you can say. Talk about what you can do.

CHAPTER 2
REVIEW and EXPLORE

GOD'S FRIENDS

Blessed Damien

Damien was a priest. He showed God's love to people who were very sick. They were forced to live on an island with no one to care for them. They were sad and alone. Damien made them feel cared for and wanted.

A Little Catechism

Invite the children to open their religion books to *A Little Catechism.* Choose one or more of the selections below for memory work or reinforcement. You will find your copy of the catechism on pages 23–43 of this Teacher's Edition.

1. With the children, read statements 1, 2, 6, 7, and 9 on page 10. Review the many gifts that Jesus brings.
2. Read about the celebration of Jesus' birth on page 20. Encourage the children to say the Christmas prayer during the Christmas season.

Know Love Serve

Note The activities on this page provide ways for the children to share their learning with their families. The activities are related to the week's theme.

1 Introduce
Direct attention to the On Your Own section. Explain the activity. Let the children share ideas for carrying it out. Then, explain the next activity. Let the children share ways they encourage their families to share stories.

2 Pray Together
Use the prayer in the prayer burst to end the day.

TEACHING TIP

Make family involvement as easy as possible. Make copies of the stories as found in the student text. Staple a copy to each Home and Family page.

Online for Families
Remind the children to check the Benziger Web site this week with their families.
www.benziger.glencoe.com

Dear Family,

I have just finished chapter 2. I learned that Jesus is the Son of God. Jesus showed that God listens and cares and forgives, too. Help me remember Jesus. Tell me what you know about Jesus.

On your own

Make a sign to remind you that God listens and cares and forgives. Put the sign where you will see it every day.

With your family

Take some time to tell Jesus stories. Share what you know about Jesus. Everybody can tell a favorite story about Jesus. You can start with the stories in this chapter. Let everybody have a chance to tell a story.

Jesus, Son of God, help us forgive, listen, and care.

GO ONLINE!
http://www.benziger.glencoe.com

1 Preparation
Share that the Catholic Church tells Bible stories about Jesus to show people how to live good lives. The children can do this work of the Church. They can create a puppet show to tell about Jesus.

2 The Project
Have the children determine what jobs will be needed to make the puppet show. Be sure that everyone has a part.

THE CHURCH TODAY

Those who follow Jesus never get tired of hearing and telling stories about God's Son. There are many ways to share all you know about Jesus. Working together, you can have fun sharing what you know.

A Puppet Show

1. Pick one or more of the stories of Jesus.
2. Make simple puppets—one for each character in the story.
3. You can make props, too.
4. Practice your show.
5. Put on the show. You might even be able to share your puppet show with another class.

CURRICULUM CHALLENGE

Making the puppets, the scenery, and the invitations can be your art lesson for the week. Ahead of time decide what kind of puppets will be made (sock? stick? paper bag?). Think of some guidelines for making the puppets, the scenery, and the invitations. Help the children feel that every role is important. Together they will make a great puppet show.

ANSWER KEY

This is the answer key for the chapter test on page 81.

A. 1. R 2. R 3. R

B. 1. c 2. a 3. b

C. 1. a 2. a

Name ______________________________

Jesus Showed God's Love

Pretend that Jesus is in the room with you. Draw what Jesus would say or do to show God's love.

Name ____

Chapter 2 Test

A. Write R if the sentence is right. Write W if the sentence is wrong.

_____ **1.** Jesus is the Creator.

_____ **2.** Jesus said and did things that showed God's love.

_____ **3.** Jesus is the Son of God.

B. Draw a line to match the parts that go together.

1. Jesus healed — **a.** a sinner.

2. Jesus forgave — **b.** the hungry.

3. Jesus fed — **c.** a blind man.

C. Circle the letters that tell ways you can show God's love.

1. You can forgive a friend.

One way to forgive is to

a. ask your friend to play.

b. pick another friend.

2. You can care.

One way to care is to

a. smile at someone who is sad.

b. call the sad person a name.

TEACHER RESOURCE CENTER

Faith Formation

Understanding the Bible

The Bible has been described as "the Word of God in the words of people of faith." Sacred Scriptures tell the stories of salvation history. These stories were told and written by those whose encounters with God resulted in a profound faith response. The Bible is a collection of books, written in many languages over a period of thousands of years under the inspiration of the Holy Spirit. The Old Testament tells us the story of God's Chosen People Israel and their experiences of the saving power of God. In the New Testament, the Gospels present the message of the life, death, and resurrection of Jesus Christ, the Son of God. Other parts of the New Testament (the letters, Acts of the Apostles, and Revelation) describe the faith development of the early Church.

Which of the many Scripture stories is your favorite?

Praying the Bible

Sacred Scriptures contain many levels of meaning. A quick reading of a passage may inspire us, but more is required if we are to understand the significance of a Scripture passage. It is important to learn as much as possible about when, where, why, and for whom the passage was written. It is also vital that prayer be a part of all Scripture study.

Invite the Holy Spirit to guide you when you read and pray the Bible. Ask questions like these: What does this passage tell me about God? What is God asking of me? How is God comforting me? Whom am I being called to forgive?

Do I regularly pray with the Scriptures?

CHECK THE CATECHISM

Article Three in Part One of the *Catechism of the Catholic Church* focuses on Sacred Scripture. Look especially at paragraphs 101–114 for helpful instruction and insight about how the Scriptures are the inspired Word of God.

Background

The Bible

Students love stories. They learn from stories because stories stay with them. If students really like a story or have been moved by it, they will not forget it. The story takes root and lives in them. The thoughts and emotions that go along with a story become a reference point for the way students look at life.

The stories Jesus told his followers changed the way they looked at life. In turn, the stories they told about Jesus—his miracles and his death and resurrection—continue to change the way people look at life. Remembering what Jesus said and did to show God's love is a way the students can hold on to the Good News. The Good News will take root and become a reference point for faithfully living the Christian life.

Faith Summary

- The Bible is the Word of God.
- In the Bible we come to know God and how God wants us to live.
- The Gospels teach about Jesus.

Growth and Development

It is helpful to remember two characteristics of second graders as you teach this lesson:

- ***Second graders love stories.*** Bible stories, although written in adult language, are a wonderful way to connect the students to their faith. Put special preparation into the Bible stories you will share.
- ***Second graders are becoming capable readers.*** Several ideas in this book will show how you can help the students listen to, retell, and discover age-appropriate messages in Bible stories.

A Teacher's Prayer

Thank you, Jesus, for the stories you give us that inspire us and guide us through life. Help me tell your stories to the students in a way that leaves them the same memories of joy, love, and excitement that the stories created in your first followers. Amen.

Vocabulary Preview

Bible
Gospels

Scripture

Luke 11:28: the Word of God
Matthew 21:28–31: story of Two Sons

Related Resources

Video

"Parables for Children" (Twenty-Third Publications, 1-800-321-0411 or www.twentythirdpublications.com). This 12-video set helps children understand the Gospel stories of Jesus. (Children, 8–11 minutes each)

Book

Glavich, Mary Kathleen. *Acting out the Gospels* (Twenty-Third Publications, 1-800-321-0411 or www.twentythirdpublications com). These easy-to-perform plays can be incorporated into any lesson on Sacred Scripture. (Children)

TEACHER ORGANIZER

Planning Guide

The basic content for each chapter is divided into four class sessions. There are a number of options for the fifth session. Extension, review, and testing are options described under Day 5 Alternatives. The Quick Check box will help you evaluate the week's lessons.

Chapter Goals

In this chapter, the students will learn about

- ❑ The Bible as the Word of God
- ❑ The Gospels of Jesus
- ❑ Messages in the Bible

	DAY 1 · INVITATION	DAY 2 · DISCOVERY	DAY 3 · DISCOVERY
OBJECTIVES	**The students will be able to** • Understand the term Good News • Discover ways to share good news • Share good news about Jesus	**The students will be able to** • Understand that stories give messages • Discover the message of a story	**The students will be able to** • Identify the Bible as the Word of God • Identify the Gospels as stories about Jesus • Understand that Bible stories have messages
PREPARATION	• Think of prompts for the song • Have a child make a rainbow for tomorrow	• Be ready to tell or read the story • Read through Ideas That Work	• Be ready to share the information on pages 58–59 • Make copies of the resource master on page 98
MATERIALS	• Walkie-talkies or telephones • Bowl, slips of paper with one noun written on each slip	• Paper rainbow	• Variety of Catholic Bibles and a children's Bible • Drawing supplies • Egg carton, slips of paper containing Bible questions or trivia, button
OPTIONAL ACTIVITIES	• Curriculum Challenge Make up a conversation	• Ideas That Work Retell a story	• Ideas That Work Answer questions about the Bible • Resource Masters Solve a word puzzle

Learning Objectives

By the end of the chapter, the students should be able to

- ❑ Discuss how God speaks to us in the Bible
- ❑ Identify the Gospels as stories about Jesus
- ❑ Discover the message in a Bible story

DAY 4 · LIVING

The students will be able to

- Differentiate Bible stories from other stories
- Discover a Gospel message
- Explain ways to be Good News
- Celebrate God's love

- Drawing supplies
- Plant, class picture, holy water, image of Jesus

- Ideas That Work Pantomime a prayer

DAY 5 · ALTERNATIVES

There are a number of alternatives to help you plan Day 5.

Prayer Experience
Use the prayer service Celebrate Good News on either Day 4 or Day 5. Follow the suggestions on the Lesson Plan. Follow the suggestions on page 94 for leading the prayer.

Review and Explore
Follow the suggestions on page 95 for teaching the page. If you will give the chapter test on Day 5, assign this page as homework the night before.

Home and Family
Send this page home, if possible. You may also assign one or more activities as class work or homework.

The Church Today
This page provides a class or group project that may be started in class following the chapter test and completed outside of class.

Chapter Test
The chapter test appears as a resource master on page 99.

Quick Check

Do this evaluation as soon as you finish each chapter.

Did I follow my lesson plan?

How can I tell that I met the learning objectives for the lesson?

What activities did the children enjoy most?

How could I improve this lesson?

Benziger on the Web
For more ideas, visit us at www.benziger.glencoe.com

Interactive Lesson Planner
Your ILP provides more help in preparing to teach this chapter.

Celebrate
Turn to page 22 of this book. Check for seasonal celebrations.

Lesson Plan · Day 1

Call attention to the chapter title, and read aloud the chapter's Scripture verse, "Blessed are the people who hear the Word of God and live by it." Point out that although we do not see God, he speaks to us in the Bible. That is Good News! Illustrate this concept by sharing some good news about anything relating to school.

1 What's Up?

Use the walkie-talkies you brought to class, and have the children share good news. Ask questions like these: Why do you want to share good news? To whom do you like to tell good news? How do you feel when you share good news? Read aloud the material on student pages 54–55.

2 Share News

There are many ways to share good news and messages. Ask the children to think of some of these ways. Next, ask volunteers to pantomime ways of sharing good news. Have the rest of the class guess what ways the volunteers are miming.

TEACHING TIP

Today's lesson may involve children with various learning strengths. Musical learners may lead the singing. Kinesthetic learners may be encouraged to pantomime. Pantomiming is also valuable for shy and introverted students because it allows them to participate without saying a word. Your encouraging smile and a whispered idea may be all they need to perform.

INVITATION 3

Blessed are the people who hear the Word of God and live by it.

From *Luke 11:28*

Do You Know?

◆ What is the Bible?

God's Word

WHAT'S UP!

Everybody want's to know what's happening. Mark and Louis use their walkie-talkies to tell each other what's up. Mark's dad uses a cell phone to get the news. Louis's grandpa watches television news. Everybody in the family listens to the radio.

Some people find out what's up from computers and the Internet. Every day, millions and millions of words are printed in newspapers and books. Just think about your public library. There are so many books nobody could read them all.

? How do you find out what's up?

3 Activity
Organize the children in groups of four. Tell them to follow the directions on the page. Allow time for writing the message, and then ask the fourth person from each group to share the group's message with the class.

SPREAD THE NEWS

News spreads like wild fire. Everybody wants to know what is going on. Sometimes people greet one another by saying "What's happening?" or "What's up?"

You want to share good news about you, too. If you get a good mark in spelling, you want *everybody* to know about it.

God wants to share the news of his great love. God wants everybody to know about it.

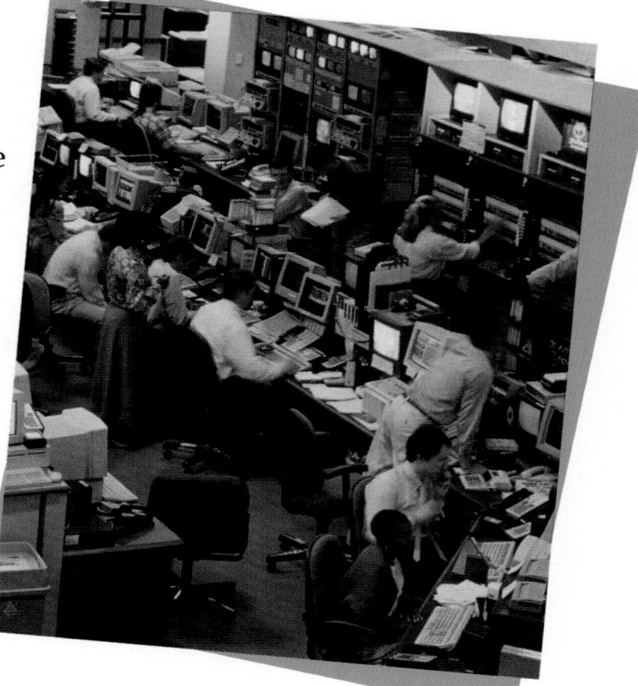

Pass it On

Play a little game. Write a bit of news in the space. Then sit in a circle. The first person passes on his or her news by whispering it to the child next to him or her. Each child passes on the news. The last child says the news out loud. What happened to the news?

CURRICULUM CHALLENGE

Language Arts Connect to a writing activity. Let the children use the walkie-talkies and then write their conversations. As an alternative, have a bowl containing slips of paper, each slip listing a person or a thing. Each child chooses two slips and makes up a conversation between the two nouns. Auditory learners may speak their conversations into a recorder.

Lesson Plan · Day 2

Recall that people share messages. Then have the children guess the answer to this riddle: "I give messages, too. I have a beginning, a middle, and an end. What am I?" *(a story)*

1 Prepare

Tell the children that they will hear a story about the sun and the rain. Have three children pantomime the story. They will play the sun, the rain, and Mother Nature. Divide the rest of the class into two groups. The first group will say the lines of the sun, and the other group will say the lines of the rain. Signal the appropriate group members when it is their turn to speak.

2 The Sun and the Rain

Read aloud or tell the story with feeling. Emphasize the verbs so that those pantomiming will hear them as prompts for their actions. At the end of the story, let a child carry in the rainbow that was made ahead of time.

TEACHING TIP

Your class will need Bibles. If parish classes have begun, the grade two catechist will also need Bibles. Perhaps you can reach the catechist and make arrangements to share the Bibles.

IDEAS THAT WORK

Here is a technique to use for retelling: Divide an area of the chalkboard into four parts labeled *Somebody, Wanted, But,* and *So.* Lead the class into retelling the story by using the four words as prompts. For example, the story may be retold in this way: The rain and the sun both wanted to be best at making things grow. Mother Nature separated them, but without each other, the sun and the rain could not make anything grow. So the sun and rain apologized and agreed to work together.

DISCOVERY

Sun and Rain

There are many ways to share the news. Sometimes people tell stories. The stories are good to hear, but tucked into the stories are important lessons.

Once upon a time, Sun and Rain were arguing. They both wanted to show who was most important. "I am the most important being in the world!" said Sun. "I make the world bright and warm. I make everything grow!"

"Ha!" responded Rain. "I make the world cool and wet. I make everything grow! Therefore, I am most important."

Mother Nature grew very tired of the spat. She got a little twinkle in her eye. She had an idea. She banished Sun to one side of the earth and Rain to the other.

56 · God Loves Me

3 Retell
Lead the children to retell the story. Developing this important skill will help them understand the more difficult stories found in the Bible. See Ideas That Work.

4 Discover
Help the children relate to the story. Ask: Do people ever act the way the sun and the rain did? Give an example. Could this be a story about a mother and her children?

5 Activity
Explain the activity. After all have written the message, the children may say it aloud.

Day after day Sun beat down on his side of the earth. Soon the land became parched and cracked. Nothing grew.

Day after day, Rain poured down on her side of the earth. Soon the land was flooded and cold. Nothing grew.

Both Sun and Rain knew something was quite wrong. They went to Mother Nature. "We are very sorry," they said. "Now we know that we are both important."

Mother Nature was so happy she danced for joy.

Find the story's hidden message. Cross out every *B, M,* and *P.*

MBBMWORKPBM
PPTOGETHERM
BPMALWAYSMB

CURRICULUM CHALLENGE

Reading Use retelling techniques to help children discover the main points (the plot) of a story. The more the children develop the skill of retelling, the more likely it is that they will apply it to understanding Bible stories.

Lesson Plan · Day 3

Recall that stories have messages that need to be discovered. Ask volunteers to say aloud the message of the story, The Sun and the Rain.

❶ The Bible

Explain that God speaks to us in the Bible, which means that its messages must be very important.

❷ God's Library

Share the information as you would tell a story. Have the children locate the word *Gospels.* Show the Bibles you brought. Tell the children that the Bible is the Word of God, so it must be handled with care and respect. To help the children understand the difference between the Bible and the Gospels, show the Gospel stories in each of the Bibles. Then, let the children find the Gospels in the Bibles provided.

BIBLE BASICS

The children will learn reverence for the Bible by the way it is treated in the classroom. Have a Bible in your prayer area; if possible, place the Bible on a stand. Have a children's Bible there, too. Whenever you use the Bible, handle it reverently.

IDEAS THAT WORK

Check the students' recall of the Bible stories they have studied so far. On a strip of paper, write a Bible question or name a Bible person, place, or thing for the children to identify. Place a strip in each section of an egg carton. Put a button in an egg carton and close the lid. Have a child shake the egg carton and lift the lid. The child then answers the question or identifies the person on which the button has landed.

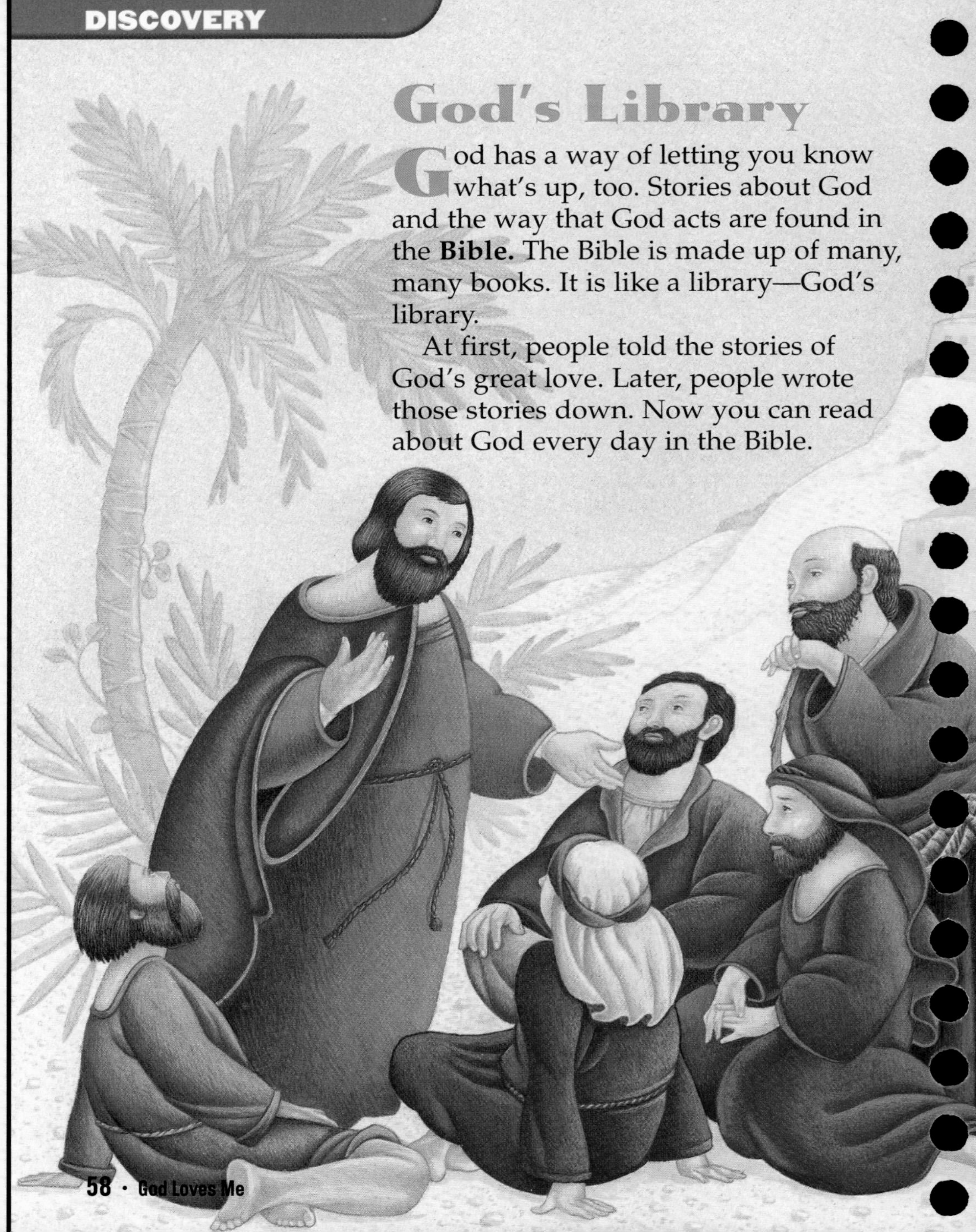

DISCOVERY

God's Library

God has a way of letting you know what's up, too. Stories about God and the way that God acts are found in the **Bible.** The Bible is made up of many, many books. It is like a library—God's library.

At first, people told the stories of God's great love. Later, people wrote those stories down. Now you can read about God every day in the Bible.

58 · God Loves Me

3 Activity
Allow time for the children to decorate the Bible covers. Then read aloud This We Believe! Ask whether the children have any questions.

The stories about Jesus are found in four books in the Bible. These books are called the **Gospels.** The word *gospel* means "good news."

Jesus came to tell about God's kingdom. He wanted everyone to love one another. Jesus taught by word and by action. Jesus told good stories, too.

Jesus told people how much God loves them. He told people that God would care for them. He told people that they would be with God forever and ever.

Now that is really good news!

The Bible is the Word of God.

ACTIVITY GOOD-NEWS BIBLE

Decorate the Bible. Show that the Bible tells the Good News.

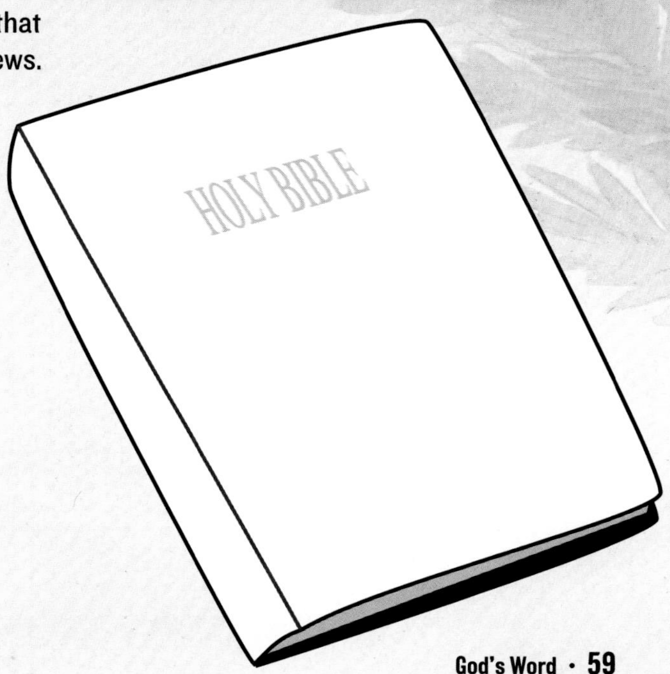

VOCABULARY

Bible The Word of God written by humans. The Bible is also called Scripture.

Gospels The Good News of Jesus' life and teachings.

RESOURCE MASTERS

You may wish to use the resource master on page 98, a fun word game about the Bible.

Lesson Plan · Day 4
Remind the children that Bible stories have messages, just as other stories do. Ask what makes Bible stories different from other stories. *(God speaks to us in Bible stories; they tell about God's love and God's People; the messages tell us how to live.)*

1 Getting Help
Let the children talk about ways they look for help. You may suggest certain situations, such as help with homework, help in making friends, or help in making an important decision. After the children have talked among themselves, ask volunteers to share their responses. Write them on the chalkboard.

2 God the Helper
Acknowledge the listed responses. Then tell the children that God is always with us. We can look to God for help. God gave us the Bible to help us know how to live good lives. The Gospel stories contain the Good News of Jesus and his messages for us.

TEACHING TIP

Religion is a subject area that requires you to impart some information that the children cannot discover on their own. Religion is also something that is personal and experienced. Whenever possible, try to share the information rather than read it.

GOSPEL LIVING

Read the Gospel story below. When you have finished, talk about the story. In the space, show what message there is for you. Write or draw how this story can help you follow Jesus.

A man had two sons. He came to the first one and asked him to go to work in the vineyard. "No, I will not," said the son. But later he was sorry and went to work anyway.

The man asked his second son. "Sure, I will go right now," said the second son. But he never went.

Which boy did what the father wanted?

Based on *Matthew 21:28–31*

A MESSAGE FOR ME

3 Gospel Living
Tell the children to listen to the Bible story, The Story of Two Sons. After reading the story, use the retelling technique on pages 88–89 to guide the children in restating the story. Then, lead the children to discover the message: Who are some people who ask for your help? Tell some ways you feel about doing chores. Can this Bible story be about a mother and her children? A teacher and her students?

4 Activity
Working in pairs, the children can answer these two questions and write their responses on the page: What is Jesus saying about obeying? What is Jesus saying about telling the truth? Walk around the room and read the responses, giving guidance as needed.

5 Be Good News!
Have the children read aloud the introduction. They may work in pairs to plan their actions. Challenge the students to think of something no one else will think of. Set a time limit for planning.

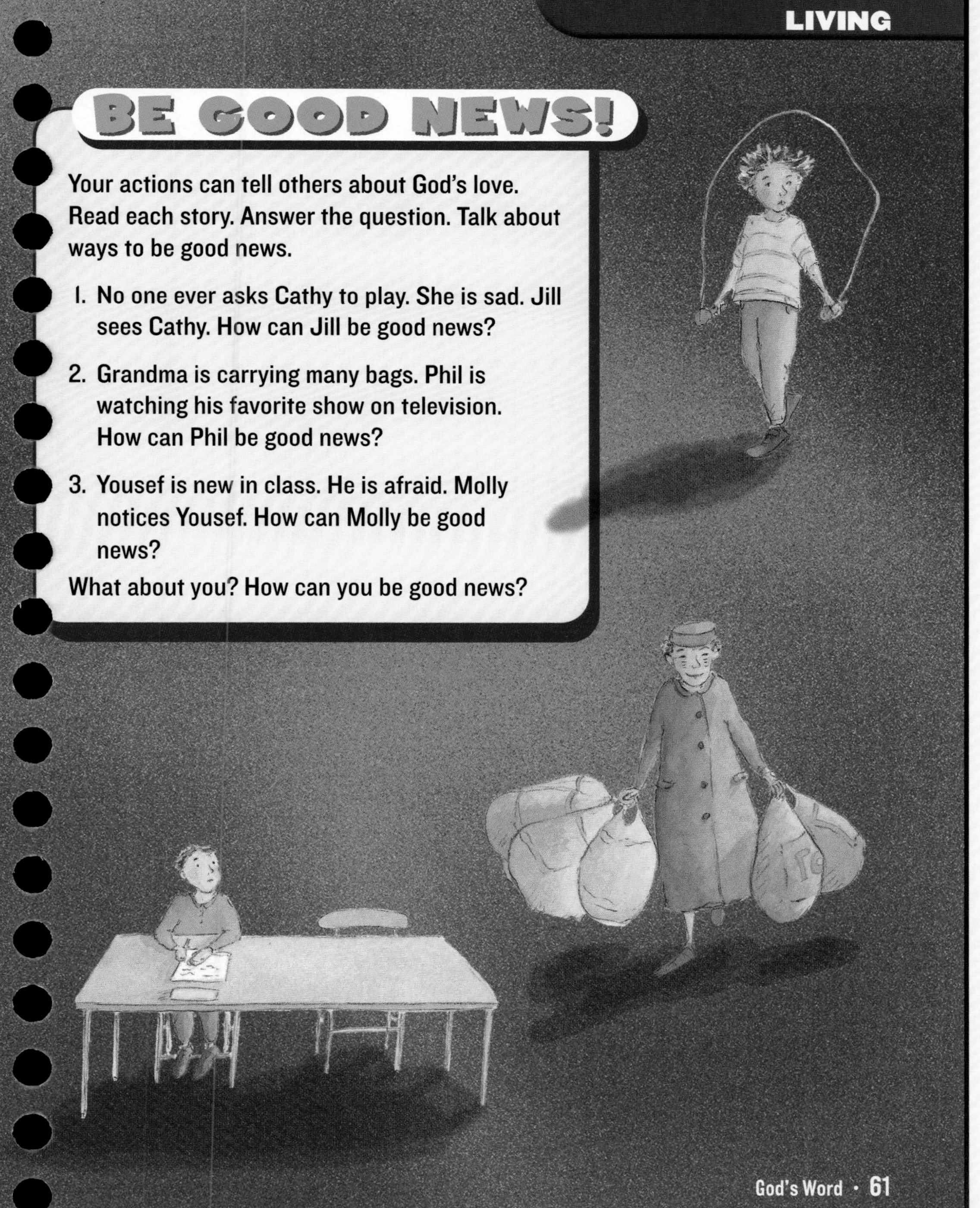

LIVING
BE GOOD NEWS!
Your actions can tell others about God's love. Read each story. Answer the question. Talk about ways to be good news.
1. No one ever asks Cathy to play. She is sad. Jill sees Cathy. How can Jill be good news?
2. Grandma is carrying many bags. Phil is watching his favorite show on television. How can Phil be good news?
3. Yousef is new in class. He is afraid. Molly notices Yousef. How can Molly be good news?
What about you? How can you be good news?
God's Word • 61

TEACHING TIP

The prayer experience on student page 62 summarizes Unit I. Ahead of time, you may wish to enlist the children's help in acquiring the objects that will be placed on the prayer table. Keep track of volunteers so that throughout the year, all will have an opportunity to help in the planning.

Prayer

The prayer experience is an essential part of the chapter. This prayer will help the children remember the Good News.

1 Prepare for Prayer

Prepare the children for prayer. Lead the prayer yourself, or choose a good reader to lead.

2 Celebrate Good News

Tell the children that they will conclude the lesson by remembering the Good News that Jesus brought to the world. Say the prayer. You may want to add some variety to prayer time by using the suggestion in Ideas That Work.

IDEAS THAT WORK

Encourage the children's creativity by asking them to create some simple gestures or pantomimes for each line in the prayer. Ask for two volunteers to pantomime each line. Situate the pairs around the room. As each line is spoken, one pair will pantomime that line. The class prays the response.

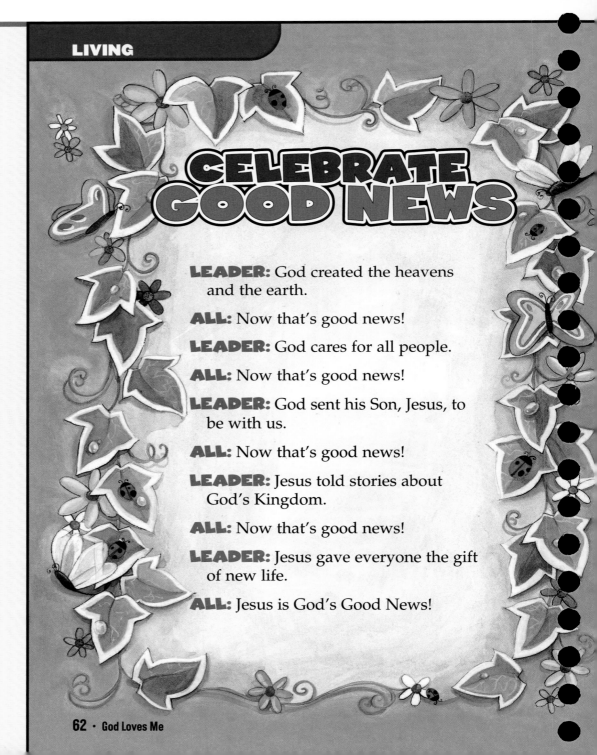

CELEBRATE GOOD NEWS

LEADER: God created the heavens and the earth.

ALL: Now that's good news!

LEADER: God cares for all people.

ALL: Now that's good news!

LEADER: God sent his Son, Jesus, to be with us.

ALL: Now that's good news!

LEADER: Jesus told stories about God's Kingdom.

ALL: Now that's good news!

LEADER: Jesus gave everyone the gift of new life.

ALL: Jesus is God's Good News!

1 Know
Use the graphic organizer to review the content of the chapter. Emphasize concepts you want the students to remember. Ask whether there are any questions. Volunteers may wish to name a favorite Bible story.

2 Love and Serve
Talk about the term *Good News*. Allow the children to complete the Love activity. Talk about how the children could be Good News to others. Have them complete the Serve activity.

3 God's Friends
Tell the children that Jesus had a cousin named John, whom people called John the Baptist. Show the illustration and share the information.

Know

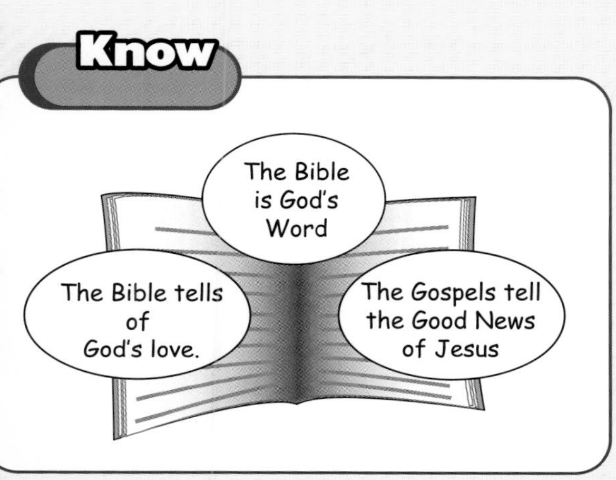
The Bible is God's Word
The Bible tells of God's love.
The Gospels tell the Good News of Jesus

Love

In the space, write one reason why Jesus is God's Good News.

Serve

Sometimes you can turn bad news into good news. Think about somebody you know who is sad or lonely or afraid. How can you help that person turn the bad news into good news?

CHAPTER 3 REVIEW and EXPLORE

GOD'S FRIENDS

Saint John the Baptist

John was a cousin of Jesus. He told people that Jesus was coming. He told them to listen to the Good News Jesus had to tell. He told people to be sorry for their sins. John baptized people with water, too.

A Little Catechism

Invite the children to open their religion books to *A Little Catechism.* Choose one or more of the selections below for memory work or reinforcement. You will find your copy of the catechism on pages 23–43 of this Teacher's Edition.

1. Invite the children to read the scripture stories on pages 9 and 23. Remind the children that the Bible contains many stories of God's love.
2. Together with the children, read the Prayer Tips on page 17.

Know Love Serve

Note The activities on this page provide ways for the children to share their learning with their families. The activities are related to the week's theme.

1 Introduce
Let volunteers share their experiences with the last lesson's Home and Family page. Then, have the children read silently the On Your Own activity. Talk about the different people the children can give their bookmarks to.

2 Pray Together
Create some prayer actions for the prayer. Encourage the children to teach these actions to their families. Ask the children to explain why these actions may help them pray.

The signing of the forehead, lips, and heart is done at Mass right before the reading of the Gospel. This is a custom that dates back hundreds of years. It is a way of saying "May God's Word be in my mind, on my lips, and in my heart."

Online for Families
Remind the children to check the Benziger Web site this week with their families.
www.benziger.glencoe.com

Dear Family,

I have just finished chapter 3. I learned that the Bible is God's Word. I learned about the Gospels, too. I learned that Jesus brought the Good News to people. Help me by sharing stories from the Bible.

On your own

Make Bible bookmarks. On strips of paper, print "The Bible is God's Word!" or "Listen to the Good News!" Give the bookmarks you make as little gifts.

With your family

Make sure that your family has a Bible. Put the Bible in a special place. Put a candle or some flowers near the Bible. Before going to bed, say a night prayer near your family Bible.

May the Word of God be in my mind, on my lips, and in my heart.

GO ONLINE!
http://www.benziger.glencoe.com

1 Discuss
Share the introductory information. Then, read a simplified version of the Gospel for the coming Sunday. Have the children retell the story. They may work in pairs and use the technique *Somebody, Wanted, But,* and *So.* Walk around the room to see that the children are getting the basic story line. They need not write it.

2 Project
Allow time for each student to draw a picture of the story and label the picture with a name. All may share their work.

3 Pray
Guide the children in coming up with one sentence that tells what Jesus is asking of them. Include their sentences in the prayer.

THE CHURCH TODAY

Every Sunday, you hear the Bible read at Mass. At every Mass, there is a reading of the Gospel. It can help you get ready for Sunday.

1. Read the Gospel story for the coming Sunday. (Your teacher will help you find it.)
2. Talk about what you hear.
3. In the space, draw a picture that will help you remember the Sunday Gospel.
4. Give your family a preview of Sunday's Gospel.

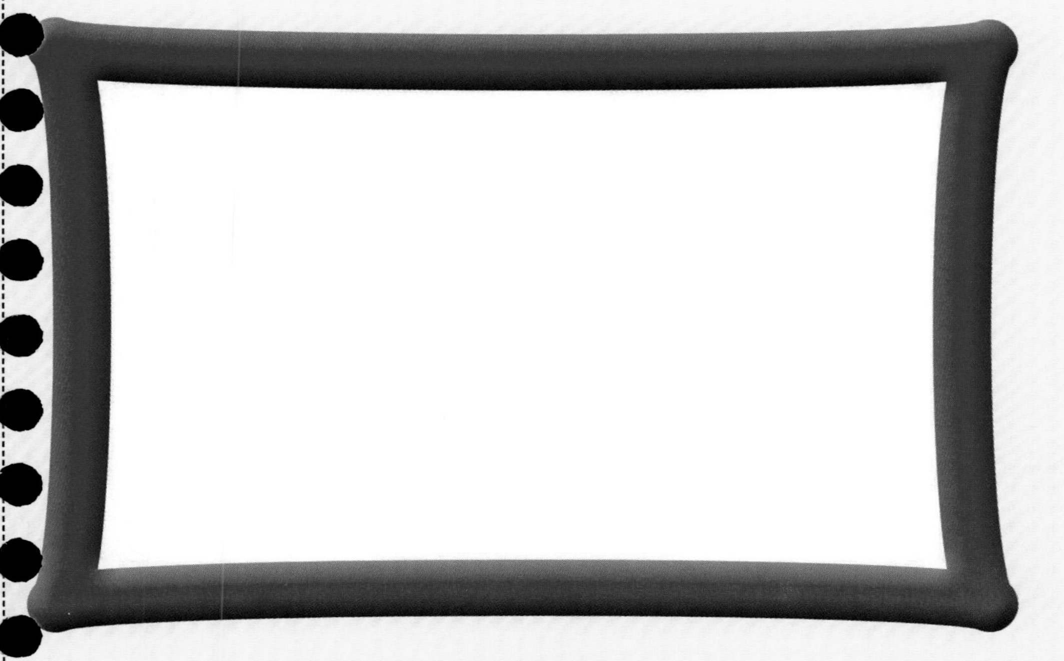

BIBLE BASICS

Bible stories, particularly the parables of Jesus, can be read over and over again; a new message may be discovered each time. Your role is to guide the children in determining a message that is age-appropriate—something they can understand and apply to their lives.

ANSWER KEY

This is the answer key for the chapter test on page 99.

A. 1, 2, 3

B. 1. a 2. b 3. a

C. 2.

D. Accept all reasonable answers.

Name ___________________________

The Bible

The Catholic Church has another name for the Bible.

Follow the clues. Write the name on the line.

BTWOBRD MIOBBF IMGTBTOID

1. What letter sounds like a bug that makes honey? Cross it out.
2. What letter is found on small, round chocolate candy? Cross it out.
3. What letter names a drink that is served hot or cold? Cross it out.
4. What letter names something you see with? Cross it out.

Write on these lines the letters that remain.

__________ __________ __________

Name ______________________________

Chapter 3 Test

A. Circle three sentences that tell about the Bible.

1. The Bible helps you know about God's love.

2. The Bible has stories about Jesus.

3. The stories about Jesus are called Gospels.

4. The Bible is too old to read.

B. Circle the words that best finish each sentence.

1. You can share good news by
a. asking someone to play.
b. lying just a little.

2. Catholics call the Bible
a. Books of God.
b. the Word of God.

3. Bible stories can teach you
a. how to love God.
b. how to make money.

C. The Bible is called the Word of God because

1. There are many, many words in the Bible.

2. God speaks to you in the Bible.

D. Tell a Bible story that you know.

God's Children

TEACHER RESOURCE CENTER

Faith Formation

Belonging to God's Family

When we experience a baptism in the parish, it is clear why it has been called the "sacrament of belonging." We see that those who are baptized are called by God to join with others in the Christian community and to go forth as disciples of Jesus. Promises are made: to reject sin and to accept the faith of the Church. When infants are baptized, parents and godparents speak for them. Older children and adults participate fully in preparing for and celebrating their own baptisms. All the baptized are surrounded by the support of the Catholic Christian community in living out their baptismal promises.

Your baptism brought you into the Family of God. What does this mean to you today?

CHECK THE CATECHISM

Belonging is not the only thing which Baptism celebrates. Other images and meanings are also described in the *Catechism of the Catholic Church.* For further understanding of the sacrament of Baptism, see paragraphs 1213–1284.

Signs of Belonging

Water, oil, and light are significant signs of God's presence in the baptismal rite. The waters of Baptism recall the death and resurrection of Jesus, as those to be baptized die to sin and rise to new life of faith in Jesus. The oil, or chrism, strengthens and renews the baptismal promises. Burning candles signify the light of Jesus Christ that now shines forth in the lives of the baptized. These sacramental signs help to express God's grace, the presence of the Holy Spirit that enables all members of God's Family to respond in love to God's love.

How does your Christian community support you as you live out your baptismal promises every day?

Background

God's Love in Baptism

Chapter 4 focuses on the love God shows in Baptism. Through no fault of their own, some of the children you teach may not be baptized. Teach the lesson as if all have received the sacrament. Let your tone of voice and your manner of presentation say to the children that Baptism is an important sacrament that changes our lives. Baptism is presented through a story. God's love, as experienced in the signs of God's presence, is emphasized.

Some children may be eager to share their own experiences with Baptism. Encourage them to do so. Their sharing helps to further emphasize the importance of the sacrament.

Faith Summary

- God is our heavenly Father.
- In Baptism our sins are forgiven.
- In Baptism we become children of God and receive God's grace.

Growth and Development

It is helpful to remember two characteristics of second graders as you teach this lesson:

- ***Second graders usually want to share information.*** It is their way of being noticed and accepted. You may have to gently help them direct their sharing and to steer them away from revealing information that is too personal.
- ***Second graders should not be forced to answer or give information.*** Those who find it difficult to respond may be asked questions of a non-threatening nature.

A Teacher's Prayer

God our Father, you are present with the children and me. Bless my efforts to teach them. Bless them with a growing awareness that they are your children, filled with your life and love. Amen.

Vocabulary Preview

Baptism
grace
children of God

Scripture

1 John 3:2: God's children
1 Corinthians 1:4: Grace in Jesus
Matthew 5:16: Let your light shine.

Related Resources

Video

"Baptism: Sacrament of Belonging" (St. Anthony Messenger Press, 1-800-488-0488 or www.AmericanCatholic.org). This video clearly explains how Baptism is the sacrament that has us belong to the church. (Children, 15 minutes)

Book

Sullivan, Mary Anne Getty. *God Speaks to Us in Water Stories* (Liturgical Press, 1-800-858-5450 or www.litpress.org). This book shows how God connects with humans through one of the most powerful metaphors in the Bible—water. (Children)

TEACHER ORGANIZER

Planning Guide

The basic content for each chapter is divided into four class sessions. There are a number of options for the fifth session. Extension, review, and testing are options described under Day 5 Alternatives. The Quick Check box will help you evaluate the week's lessons.

Chapter Goals

In this chapter, the students will learn about

- ❏ God, their heavenly Father
- ❏ Baptism as a sign of God's love
- ❏ Grace, God's goodness

	DAY 1 · INVITATION	DAY 2 · DISCOVERY	DAY 3 · DISCOVERY
OBJECTIVES	**The students will be able to** • Share ways to be close to someone • Determine ways to show acts of love	**The students will be able to** • See that Baptism makes them children of God • Identify signs of Baptism	**The students will be able to** • See that grace is a gift of Baptism • Connect acts of love with showing God's grace • Become familiar with calling God, Father
PREPARATION	• Make copies of the resource master on page 116 • Write the Do You Know? question on the chalkboard	• Prepare the Baptism of Matthew story	• Know the information on grace • Know how to sign the three words on page 70 • Make three vocabulary cards: grace, Baptism, children of God
MATERIALS	• Pencils • Drawing supplies • Copies of the resource master, scissors, glue	• Baptismal candle, holy oil, and holy water (will also be used in Day 3) • Three index cards per child	• Three vocabulary cards • Pencils
OPTIONAL ACTIVITIES	• Resource Masters Cut and paste ways to show love in a family	• Ideas That Work Get a copy of *Welcoming Babies* by Margy Burns Knight • Vocabulary Do a simple vocabulary writing exercise	• Options Make arrangements for kinesthetic learners to sign the words *God the Father* for first graders

Learning Objectives

By the end of this chapter, the students should be able to

- ❑ Tell about the sacrament of Baptism
- ❑ Identify actions that show God's grace
- ❑ Profess baptismal promises

DAY 4 · LIVING

The students will be able to

- Apply words of Jesus to their life
- Profess baptismal promises
- Discover ways to be holy

- Write the guessing game on the board
- Find out the regulations for use of candles in the classroom

- Crayons
- Candle

- **Options** With a sheet and a light, set up a pantomiming area for visual-spatial learners

DAY 5 · ALTERNATIVES

There are a number of alternatives to help you plan Day 5.

Prayer Experience
Use the Profession of Faith prayer experience on either Day 4 or Day 5. Follow the suggestions on page 112 for leading the prayer.

Review and Explore
Follow the suggestions on page 113 for teaching the page. You will need drawing and writing supplies.

Home and Family
Send the page home with the students.

The Church Today
This page provides the students an opportunity to create a symbol of their love for God the Father.

Chapter Test
The chapter test appears as a resource master on page 117.

Quick Check

Do this evaluation as soon as you finish each chapter.

Did I follow my lesson plan?

How can I tell that I met the learning objectives for the lesson?

What activities did the children enjoy most?

How could I improve this lesson?

Benziger on the Web
For more ideas, visit us at www.benziger.glencoe.com

Interactive Lesson Planner
Your ILP provides more help in preparing to teach this chapter.

Celebrate
Turn to page 22 of this book. Check for seasonal celebrations.

Lesson Plan · Day 1

You may want to begin each chapter by writing the Do You Know? question on the board. Let a few volunteers suggest answers. At the end of the week, come back to this question to see how the children's knowledge has developed.

1 A Nickname

Let everyone read the title of Chapter 4. Say that you are going to tell a little story about a boy named Chet and his Grandpa. Ask the children to listen for a way Chet and Grandpa show each other love. Read or tell the story. Ask how Chet and his Grandpa show love.

2 Names

Let volunteers share their special names and how the names make them feel. Ask each child to write his or her special name on a nametag and place it on the desktop.

RESOURCE MASTERS

The resource master on page 116 is a cut and paste activity about ways to show love in a family. Scissors and glue will be needed if the activity will be done in class.

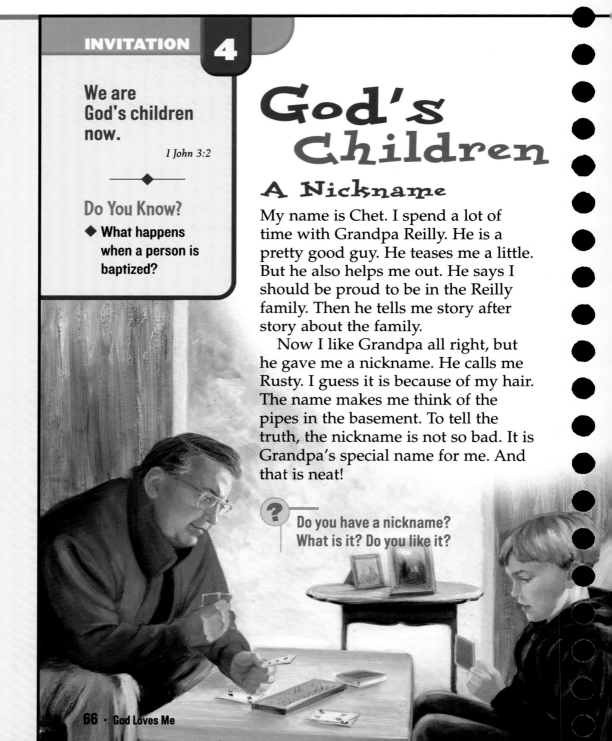

We are God's children now.

1 John 3:2

Do You Know?

◆ What happens when a person is baptized?

God's Children

A Nickname

My name is Chet. I spend a lot of time with Grandpa Reilly. He is a pretty good guy. He teases me a little. But he also helps me out. He says I should be proud to be in the Reilly family. Then he tells me story after story about the family.

Now I like Grandpa all right, but he gave me a nickname. He calls me Rusty. I guess it is because of my hair. The name makes me think of the pipes in the basement. To tell the truth, the nickname is not so bad. It is Grandpa's special name for me. And that is neat!

? Do you have a nickname? What is it? Do you like it?

3 In A Family

Say that being in a family means being close. Having special names for one another is one way to be close. Doing acts of love is another way. Direct attention to the pictures on page 67. Talk about the ways the family members are showing love.

4 Activity

Ask the children to think of one way that they show love to their families. They may draw the way in the space. Walk around and give prompts to those who may not be able to think of a way.

In A Family

People in a family care for one another. Sometimes they tease and call one another silly names. Sometimes they laugh and play together. Sometimes they are very busy with school and work and chores.

In a family, people care for one another. Members of a family do what they have to do to make sure everyone is safe, warm, and has food to eat.

Look at the pictures. Tell what is happening in each picture. How are the people in the pictures showing love in the family.

On the sign, tell how you show love to the members of your family.

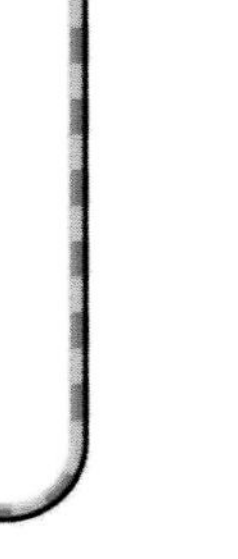

IDEAS THAT WORK

If time permits you may wish to conclude the lesson by reading *The Relatives Came* by Cynthia Rylant. This is a story about a family reunion with family members coming from miles around. They celebrate being part of a family not so much rich in material things, but rich in love.

Lesson Plan · Day 2
Show and identify the holy water, the candle, and holy oil. Say that the items are used during Baptism. The holy water, candle, and holy oil show God's love for us. Ask the children to listen to the story to learn how.

1 Preparation
Recall the story of Chet and his Grandpa. Say that today the children will hear a story about the baptism of Chet's brother, Matthew. Give three index cards to each child. Ask the children to write a W (for water) on one card, a C (for candle) on another, and O (for oil) on the third.

2 Child of God
Ask the children to listen to the story about Matthew's Baptism. Focus the children on listening. When they hear about the water, they are to hold up the W card. When they hear about the oil, they hold up the O card, and when they hear about the candle, they hold up the C card.

IDEAS THAT WORK

Whenever you tell a story or read one, focus the children. Give them a fact to listen for or a question to answer. Or have them respond during the story, such as raising a hand or holding up a card.

Child of God

Listen to the story of the day Chet's brother Matt became a child of God.

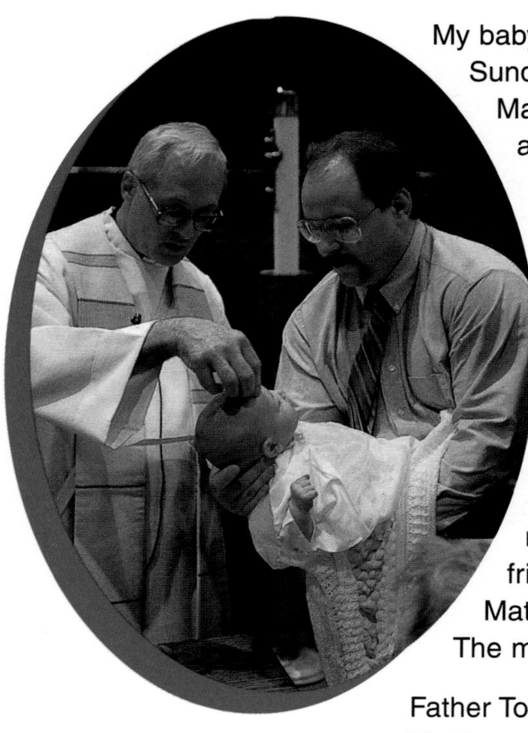

My baby brother, Buster, was baptized last Sunday. His name is not really Buster. It is Matthew—Matt for short. It's Grandpa again. Every time Grandpa sees the baby, he says, "How you doing, Buster?" I hope that name doesn't stick!

I would like to tell you about the baptism. I don't remember my baptism. Do you remember yours? Anyhow, Father Tom said to Matt, "Matthew, I claim you for Christ with the sign of his cross." Mom likes the name Matthew. One of Jesus' close friends was named Matthew. She said Matt would be marked as God's own. The mark will last forever.

Father Tom asked my parents and Matt's godparents some questions about faith. Then he poured water over Matt's head. He said, "I baptize you in the name of the Father, and of the Son, and of the Holy Spirit." Father Tom rubbed oil on Matt's head, too. He told Matt he was born again of water and the Holy Spirit. He told Matt he was free of Original Sin—in fact all sin.

3 A Warm Welcome
Say that God loves us very much. God shows this love in Baptism. Baptism takes away our sins and makes us children of God. Baptism is a day to celebrate. Baptism is like a birthday because the baptized person is born into God's Family.

4 Activity
Ask the children to recall the different ways in which water, oil, a garment, and light were used in the story. Have the children complete the activity.

Matt got a white garment, and Dad lit a little candle from the Easter candle. Dad told us later that Matt had a new life of grace. Matt was going to shine with the light of Christ, too.

All the people at the baptism were very happy. We had a party. Everybody told stories. We are proud to be members of the Catholic family.

Christians are baptized in the name of the Father, and of the Son, and of the Holy Spirit.

ACTIVITY: REMEMBER WHAT HAPPENS

In each box, draw a little picture to help you remember what happens at Baptism.

Water	Oil
Garment	Light

VOCABULARY

Children of God Through a simple writing exercise you can help the children understand this concept. Ask the children to write their name and complete the sentence with the names of their parent(s)or guardian(s): ________ is a child of ________. Then they are to write their name and the words "is a child of God."

Lesson Plan · Day 3

Ask the children to look around the room and tell what signs they see that show second grade children use the room (second-grade books, the identification on the door, and so on).

1 Signs of God

Show the water, oil, and candle and recall that they are used at Baptism. Say that the water, the candle, and the oil are all signs of God. They show that God is there at Baptism. The water, the oil, and the candle are signs that can be seen, heard, smelled, and touched.

2 A Gift of Grace

Say that there is one sign of God's love that is not so easy to see. Grace is a sign of Baptism and a sign of God's love. Grace is God's goodness in you. You receive God's grace at Baptism. Grace makes you close to God. You see grace when you see people showing God's goodness.

OPTIONS

For Kinesthetic Learners

Give an opportunity for the children to teach the signing for God the Father to the first graders.

WORD OF GOD

I thank God always for the grace he gave you in Christ Jesus.

1 Corinthians 1:4

A Gift of Grace

There are many things to see and hear and smell at a baptism—water, candle, white dress, and oil. But there is one gift you cannot see. It is the gift of God's **grace.**

At baptism, you receive a share in God's own life. You now belong to God. You can call God "Father." God's grace also helps you show his goodness.

As a reminder of God's gift of grace, you can learn how to call God "Father" in American Sign Language.

God

Our

Father

3 Grace in Action
Direct attention to the photos on page 71. Repeat that good actions show God's grace, or God's goodness. Ask the children to turn to one another and tell how the people in the photos are showing grace.

4 Activity
Say that the photos are missing their titles. Ask the children to write them in. The titles should focus on the good actions that are being done.

5 God Our Father
Tell the children that everyone at a baptism prays the Our Father. The people pray to God, the Father, who loves them. They pray so that the baptized person will always depend on God. Lead the children in signing the words, *God the Father.*

Grace in Action

Look at the pictures. The children are showing God's goodness. Write a caption for each picture. Talk about what you write.

VIRTUE FAITH GRACE **VOCABULARY**

Grace God's goodness in you.

Baptism The sacrament that welcomes you into the Church as a child of God. In Baptism God takes away your sins.

You may display vocabulary cards with the words *grace* and *baptism* on them. Before the children leave for home, use the cards for review.

Lesson Plan · Day 4

Write these on the chalkboard and have the children guess the words: *Cr__a__or F__t__e__* Say that the words are names they have learned for God *(Creator, Father).*

❶ God Is Near

Say that Jesus was very close to God, his Father. Jesus called his Father a special name that means loving Father. The name is a word in the language Jesus spoke. Have the children do the coloring activity to discover the name Jesus used *(Abba).* Add the name to the chalkboard.

❷ Shining Light

Talk with the children about light. Remind the children that they have God's grace, or goodness, inside them. Say that Jesus wants them to be like a light and show their goodness. Jesus said, "Your light must shine before others."

TEACHING TIP

Whenever possible, have the children brainstorm ideas with each other. They can quickly turn to the child sitting next to, across from, in front of, or behind. This method will involve the whole class, rather than only the individuals who might otherwise be called upon.

A Loving Father

Jesus was very close to God, his Father. When Jesus prayed to God, Jesus used a special name from the language he spoke. The name is a word for a loving father.

Color the spaces that have either an X or an O. You will see the name Jesus called God.

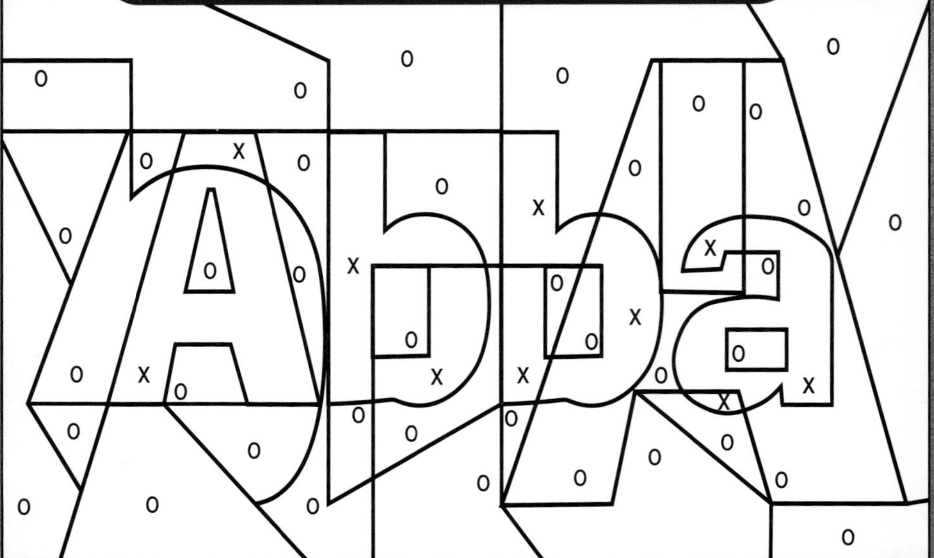

3 Activity
Allow a few moments for the children to tell the child sitting behind how to show goodness. Then give time for the children to write their answers and to color the candles on the page.

SHINING LIGHT

Jesus told his followers, "Let your light shine for all the world to see" *(Matthew 5:16)*. He wanted all God's children to let the grace of their baptisms show in all that they do.

Think of four ways that you can be a shining light—how you can let God's grace show. Write one way on each candle. You can color and decorate the candles, too.

OPTIONS

For Visual-Spatial Learners
You may wish to set up a large sheet of transparent paper or a white bedsheet on a wall in the room. Place a bright light a few feet behind the sheet. Children can stand behind the sheet and act out ways to show goodness.

Prayer

The prayer experience is an essential part of the chapter. This prayer will help the children recall their baptismal promises.

1 Prepare for Prayer

Gather the children around a prayer space. You may choose a prayer leader or take the role yourself. Encourage the children to respond enthusiastically.

2 Profession of Faith

Tell the children that special promises are made at Baptism. When they are baptized as babies their parents and godparents make those promises for them.

This prayer comes from the promises made at Baptism. Have the children stand as they profess their beliefs.

LEARNING TO PRAY

The gesture you use to pray, arms up and palms in, is a traditional way to praise God. If you wish, you may ask the children to create other appropriate gestures to use while praying.

TEACHING TIP

Have the children learn the Our Father. First, say that in the prayer we praise God as most important in our lives. We ask God to give us what we need to be good, to forgive us and to help us forgive others, and to lead us away from what is evil or bad. Second, have the children learn the prayer. Rote is a good method. Singing the words to a melody works very well.

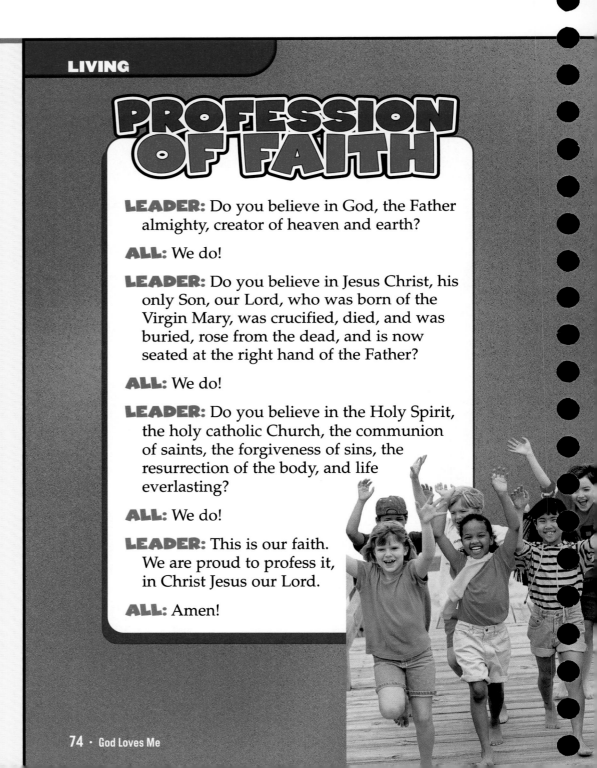

PROFESSION OF FAITH

LEADER: Do you believe in God, the Father almighty, creator of heaven and earth?

ALL: We do!

LEADER: Do you believe in Jesus Christ, his only Son, our Lord, who was born of the Virgin Mary, was crucified, died, and was buried, rose from the dead, and is now seated at the right hand of the Father?

ALL: We do!

LEADER: Do you believe in the Holy Spirit, the holy catholic Church, the communion of saints, the forgiveness of sins, the resurrection of the body, and life everlasting?

ALL: We do!

LEADER: This is our faith. We are proud to profess it, in Christ Jesus our Lord.

ALL: Amen!

1 Know
Direct attention to the Know section. Review that God shows love in the sacrament of Baptism. God's grace, or goodness, helps us know, love, and serve God. Point to the *Do You Know?* question on the chalkboard. Let the children answer it by reading aloud the two statements.

2 Love and Serve
Say that acts of love show God's grace, or goodness. Have the children draw a way they will show love to their families. Then, find an example of a halo in the book and explain its use in art. Use the activities on the page to help the children discover ways they can be holy.

3 God's Friends
Tell the story of Saint Rose, who was given a special name by her family. Ask the children to listen how Rose showed God's goodness. Lead the children to see that Rose used the gifts God gave her.

Know

Baptism

- Grace—new life in Christ
- Membership in the Church

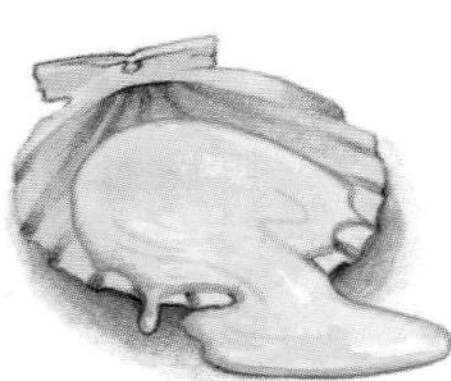

Love

How do you show that you are proud to be a Catholic? In the heart, draw a sign to show how proud you are.

Serve

How can you show the light of Christ to others? List three ways you will show that you are a baptized child of God.

1.

2.

3.

CHAPTER 4
REVIEW and EXPLORE

GOD'S FRIENDS

Saint Rose of Lima

Rose lived in Lima, Peru. Her family called her Rose because she was as pretty as a rose. Rose grew flowers and food. She sold the flowers and gave the money to the poor. She used the plants she grew to help sick people get well. Rose followed the light of Christ all her life.

A Little Catechism

Invite the children to open their religion books to *A Little Catechism.* Choose one or more of the selections below for memory work or reinforcement. You will find your copy of the catechism on pages 23–43 of this Teacher's Edition.

1. Read statement 6 on page 10. Make sure the children begin to understand *grace.*
2. Read about the seven sacraments on page 14.
3. Read Come, Holy Spirit on page 22. Emphasize how Baptism brings the Church Family together.

Know | Love | Serve

Note The activities on this page provide ways for the children to share their learning with their families. The activities are related to the week's theme.

1 Introduce
Tell the children that this is a fun page to do at home. Have them silently read the section titled On Your Own. Ask someone to share what the activity says to do. See if there are any questions. Then do the same with the section titled With Your Family.

2 Pray Together
With hands folded or arms up in praise, pray the prayer in the prayer burst.

Online for Families
Remind the children to check the Benziger Web site this week with their families.
www.benziger.glencoe.com

CHAPTER 4 HOME and FAMILY

Dear Family,

I just finished chapter 4. I learned more about the sacrament of Baptism. I learned that I received a new life of grace. I learned you made a promise of faith for me. Please help me remember that I am a child of God.

On your own

Draw or find two pictures for a family album. One picture can show that you are proud to be a member of your family. The other can show that you are proud to be a member of the Catholic Church.

With your family

At a family meal, light a candle. Or you can light everyone's baptismal candle. Talk about Baptism. Share stories. Talk about how you and your family can show the light of Christ.

Loving Father, by your grace, I am your child!

GO ONLINE!
http://www.benziger.glencoe.com

1 Preparation
Tell the children that there are many ways that people show their love for God. Direct the children's attention to the photos. Talk about the objects, the clothing, and the actions they see. Talk about how the children in the photos use these to show love and respect for God.

2 Project
Ask the children to think about the many ways they show love to God the Father. Then ask them to think of an object or symbol that shows that they are loving children of God. Allow them to draw their sign or symbol in the space.

THE CHURCH TODAY

Look at the pictures on this page. All around the world, God's children try to show how much they love their Father. The children want to let the light of God's grace shine through them.

Talk about the pictures. When you are finished, use the space to design a sign that shows you are a member of the Church. Tape the sign where all can see your shining light.

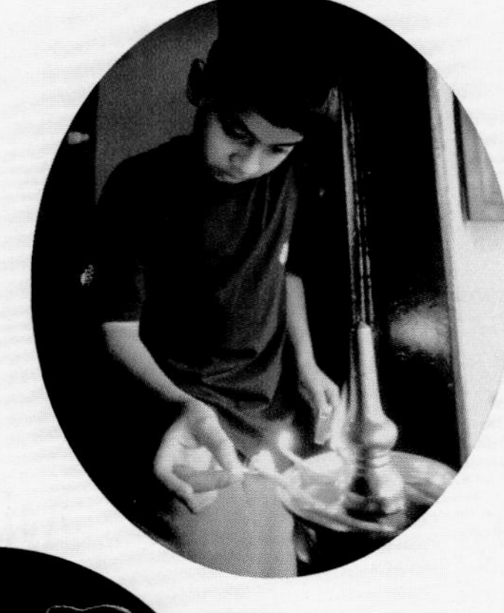

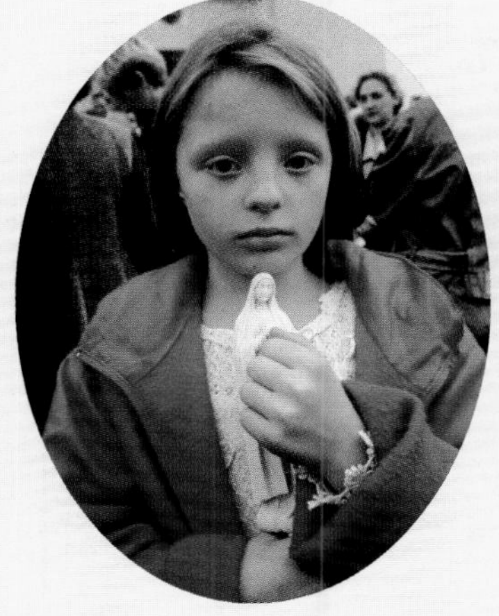

Maryknoll

IDEAS THAT WORK

You may want to set aside a brief time daily for quiet prayer time, such as when the day begins or right after recess. To guide the children, direct them to the prayers in *A Little Catechism.*

ANSWER KEY

This is the answer key for the chapter test on page 117.

A. 1. a 2. a

B. water, holy oil, candle

C. Father, Son, Holy Spirit

Name ____________________

Acts of Love

Families show love in many ways.

Cut out the pieces. Glue them where they are needed. At home you can show love in the same ways.

I can Learn
I can pray.
I can help.
I can help.

Name ____________________

Chapter 4 Test

A. Circle the letter of the words that best finishes each sentence.

1. When you are baptized you become
- **a.** a child of God.
- **b.** a part of creation.

2. When you are baptized you receive God's
- **a.** grace.
- **b.** candle.

B. Circle three signs of God that you see at Baptism.

water   rings   holy oil   candle

C. Fill in the words that are missing. You can pick from the box.

Father / Mary / Son / priest / Holy Spirit

The priest says these words at Baptism. "I baptize you in the name of the ____________________, and of the ____________________, and of the ____________________. Amen."

Strategies for Review

The purpose of the Unit Review is to reinforce concepts presented in this unit. You may wish to assign the Remember and Answer sections for homework. Review these sections with the students so that you can answer any questions they may have. Students may work independently, in small groups, or as a class. Use the method that works best with your group.

1 Remember

Write the sentences on the chalkboard. Read each statement aloud, and have the class repeat it. Erase a key word from each statement. Have volunteers fill in the missing words. Erase a different word from each sentence. Call on other students to fill in the missing words.

2 Answer

Read each statement aloud. Give the students time to circle Yes or No. Then read each statement again. Have everyone who circled Yes stand. Explain any statements that are answered incorrectly.

Unit 1 REVIEW

Remember!

1. God made the world and everything in it.
2. Jesus showed people that God listens, cares, and forgives.
3. The Bible tells about God's love.
4. Jesus is God's Good News.
5. You become part of the Catholic family when you are baptized.

Answer!

1.	Everything God made is good.	Yes!	No
2.	Jesus is God's Son.	Yes!	No
3.	God loves only Jesus.	Yes!	No
4.	You can show God's love to others.	Yes!	No

Do!

Show that you are one of God's children.
Draw a picture.
Share your picture with others.

3 Do
Read aloud the directions for the activity. Share some ideas about how people can show that they are God's children. *(praying, helping others, being kind, forgiving others)* Encourage each child to display his or her picture at home as a reminder to live as God's child.

4 Share
Writing this letter is a prayer activity. Explain to the students that praying is a way for them to keep in touch with God. Consider having the children write their letters in the church or eucharistic chapel. Place a large envelope addressed to Jesus in front of the tabernacle. Invite the children to place their letters in the envelope.

Share!

God sent Jesus to keep in touch with you.
Write a letter to Jesus. Tell Jesus how you are being his good follower.

ANSWER KEY

Answer
1. Yes
2. Yes
3. No
4. Yes

Unit 2

Give to the Lord the glory due his name.

Psalm 29:2

Chapter

Loving God

The STORY KEEPERS

Entry Into Jerusalem
When Jesus entered Jerusalem riding on a donkey, he was hailed as the one who comes in God's name. As Ben explains while telling the story, even though Jesus was not the kind of Messiah people expected, he was revealed as the One who comes in the name of the Lord. View the clip, tell the story, and lead activities suggested in the guide.

Korea  From Maryknoll

TEACHER RESOURCE CENTER

Faith Formation

Keep the Commandments

If you wish to enter into life, keep the commandments.

Matthew 19:17

Most of us are familiar with the Old Testament passage describing Moses on Mt. Sinai receiving the Ten Commandments on stone tablets (*Exodus 20:2–17*). This image expresses the belief that God's laws are literally "written in stone,"and are therefore concrete and absolute. Jesus reminded people of the right way to look at God's laws. For Christians, as for Jews, the Ten Commandments are the very least that can be done to bring about God's kingdom of justice, peace, and love. Jesus says that to seek perfection it is necessary to discover the spirit of the Law, and to "love your neighbor as yourself" *(Matthew 22:39).*

Which of the Ten Commandments is the most difficult for you? Why?

CHECK THE CATECHISM

Section Two of the *Catechism of the Catholic Church* is devoted to coverage of the Ten Commandments. See paragraphs 2052–2074 for further insight into the relationship between the covenant and the Decalogue.

The Decalogue

An ancient word for the Ten Commandments is *Decalogue*, meaning "ten words." When the Israelites were led out of slavery into freedom, the "ten words" provided them with the guidance they needed to keep the covenant with God that was their heritage. The Decalogue showed them the way of life that God willed for them: to live in peace, justice, and harmony, with one another.

How could you go beyond the "letter of the law" to follow Jesus' commandment to love your neighbor as yourself?

Background

Children and Rules

The theme of Unit 2 is love for God. The basis for loving God is the Ten Commandments, summarized in the Great Commandment. Children in second grade seem to want to know two things about rules: Who is the boss and what are the limits? The higher the authority, the more weight the rules seem to have. Still, children often prefer their own rules to those of the person in charge. The natural way for children to learn limits is to test the rules.

The Ten Commandments set limits on behavior. Disobedience, fighting, lying, stealing, and cheating are issues that the children need help understanding as they explore limits on the playground, in the classroom, and at home.

Faith Summary

- **God gave the Ten Commandments.**
- **Loving God is inseparable from loving others.**
- **Jesus gave the new commandment to love God and others.**

Growth and Development

It is helpful to remember two characteristics of second graders as you teach this lesson:

- ***Second graders are beginning to understand concepts and categories.*** Help the children realize that the commandments set standards in two ways. They reveal that certain types of behavior are contrary to the love of God and neighbor. At the same time, the commandments indicate areas of behavior by which people express and develop love.
- ***Second graders are acute observers of the adults around them.*** Jesus declared that people will be judged by how they give love. The children learn about love from Jesus, their parents, and their teachers.

A Teacher's Prayer

God of Moses and God of Miriam, you have written the commandments on my heart. Bless me with vision to see what you have written and to live accordingly. Bless me with passion for sharing with the children what is written on my heart. Bless the children. Amen.

Vocabulary Preview

Ten Commandments
Great Commandment

Scripture

Exodus 19:5–8: God talks to Moses
Exodus 20:1–17: Ten Commandments
John 14:15: Keep my commandments.
Matthew 22:34–40: Great Commandment

Related Resources

Video

"Ten Commandments" (Augsburg/Fortress, 1-800-328-4648 or www.augsburgfortress.org). This series examines the Ten Commandments and their relevance to our lives today. (Children, 45 to 50 minutes each)

Book

Keenan, James F. *Commandments of Compassion* (Sheed & Ward, 1-800-266-5564 or www.sheedandward.com). This book, written in a very engaging fashion, is a thoughtful, insightful, and enriching work on the commandments. (Adult)

TEACHER ORGANIZER

Planning Guide

The basic content for each chapter is divided into four class sessions. There are a number of options for the fifth session. Extension, review, and testing options are described under Day 5 Alternatives. The Quick Check box will help you evaluate the week's lessons.

Chapter Goals

In this chapter, the students will learn about

- ❏ Rules and laws
- ❏ The Ten Commandments
- ❏ The Great Commandment

	DAY 1 · INVITATION	DAY 2 · DISCOVERY	DAY 3 · DISCOVERY
OBJECTIVES	**The students will be able to** • Make discoveries about the importance of rules • Create game rules • Determine rules for fair play	**The students will be able to** • Draw conclusions about God's laws • Recognize the Ten Commandments • Retell the story of Moses on Mount Sinai	**The students will be able to** • Make discoveries about the Great Commandment • Connect loving others with loving God • Recognize the Great Commandment
PREPARATION	• Think of a few ways to make up a board game using a paper clip, a pencil, and student page 83 • Decide how to organize the students into groups	• Make copies of the resource master on page 138 • Read through the Bible story • Be ready to share a few rules of your home or workplace	• Prepare the vocabulary
MATERIALS	• Paper clip and pencil for each student	• Copies of the resource master, pencils	• Pencils, crayons
OPTIONAL ACTIVITIES	• **Ideas That Work** Count off to form groups • **Curriculum Challenge** Draw game boards	• **Resource Masters** Make rules to solve problems • **Ideas That Work** Ten letter or business size envelopes, commandments written out, cut up, and in the appropriate envelopes, a one-minute timer	

Learning Objectives

By the end of this chapter, the students should be able to

- ❑ Explore the purpose of rules and laws
- ❑ See the commandments as ways to love God and others
- ❑ Discover ways to follow the commandments

DAY 4 · LIVING

The students will be able to

- Determine ways to follow a commandment
- Show how a commandment helped them do the right thing
- Pray a prayer of promise to obey

- Tape the paper on the chalkboard
- Think of ways students can personalize the commandements on student page 89

- Long sheet of chart paper
- Drawing supplies or painting supplies
- Masking tape
- Pencils, crayons

DAY 5 · ALTERNATIVES

There are a number of alternatives to help you plan Day 5.

Prayer Experience

Use With Your Help on either Day 4 or Day 5. Try to obtain simple rhythm instruments to accompany the prayer.

Review and Explore

The students will need pencils, slips of paper, and a container labeled "We love God." Consider bringing to class some soothing instrumental music.

Home and Family

Send the page home with the students, or assign one or more of the activities.

The Church Today

The students will make a poster for the Great Commandment. You will need poster board or fabric. (Decorating stores often give away books of sample fabrics.) Consider having stencils of the alphabet, too.

Chapter Test

The chapter test appears as a resource master on page 139.

Quick Check

Do this evaluation as soon as you finish each chapter.

Did I follow my lesson plan?

How can I tell that I met the learning objectives for the lesson?

What activities did the children enjoy most?

How could I improve this lesson?

Benziger on the Web
For more ideas, visit us at **www.benziger.glencoe.com**

Interactive Lesson Planner
Your ILP provides more help in preparing to teach this chapter.

Celebrate
Turn to page 22 of this book. Check for seasonal celebrations.

Lesson Plan · Day 1

Have the children read aloud the chapter title and the chapter's Scripture verse. Pose the Do You Know? question, and accept all reasonable responses. At the end of the week, come back to this question to see how the children's knowledge has developed.

1 Follow Rules

Draw attention to the photograph. Then, let the children talk among themselves about a game they like to play and about two of the game's rules. Next, ask questions like these: How do you feel about rules? What would happen if games did not have rules?

Reiterate that games cannot be played without some rules, and that every game has its own rules. Ask whether baseball can be played with soccer rules. Suggest that certain rules are the same for every game. See who can guess some of those rules.

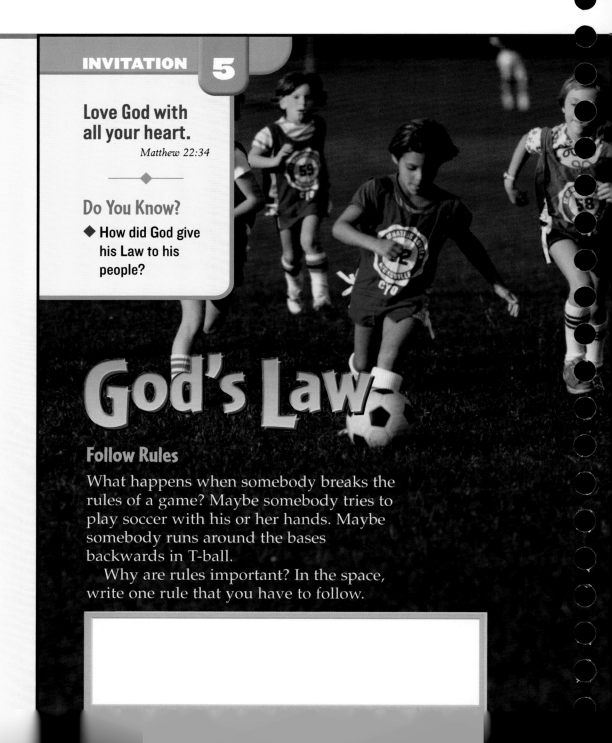

IDEAS THAT WORK

A way to organize the children into groups is to have them use numbers to count off. (For example, if each group will have three members, the children will count off by threes.) You can use any category to count off—letters of the alphabet, colors, planets, states, and so on. You also can use facts you want to review from a certain subject area.

TEACHING TIP

It may be helpful to review the idea of cooperative learning. Before having the children work in small groups, let them share the rules of working with others. You may wish to post a list of the rules somewhere in the classroom. Keep the list simple and short, perhaps totaling three guidelines. As you walk around and visit each group, affirm its efforts by referring to a rule the group is following and saying something like this: "You are doing a great job of listening to one another!"

Love God with all your heart.
Matthew 22:34

Do You Know?

◆ How did God give his Law to his people?

God's Law

Follow Rules

What happens when somebody breaks the rules of a game? Maybe somebody tries to play soccer with his or her hands. Maybe somebody runs around the bases backwards in T-ball.

Why are rules important? In the space, write one rule that you have to follow.

2 Activity
Challenge the children to think of another rule that works for any game. They should write this new rule on the line provided. Invite the children to work as partners if they wish.

3 Rules Help
Call attention to the game board on student page 83, with its space theme. Invite the children to be game makers. They are to make up rules for playing a game using a paper clip and a pencil, along with the game board. The children may work in groups of three or four. They may write the name of their game on the page. After a given time, let the groups tell about their games.

Rules Help

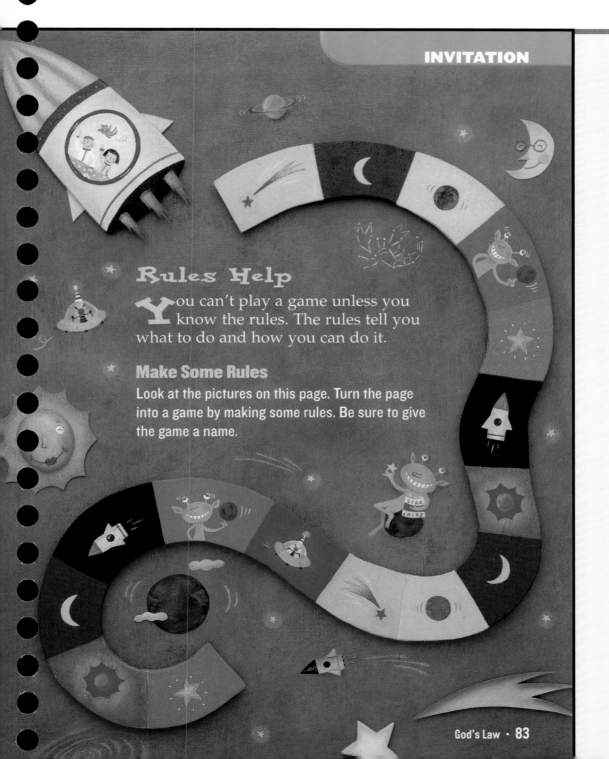

You can't play a game unless you know the rules. The rules tell you what to do and how you can do it.

Make Some Rules

Look at the pictures on this page. Turn the page into a game by making some rules. Be sure to give the game a name.

CURRICULUM CHALLENGE

Children Love Games If the students enjoy this activity, you may wish to use the structure of a game as a way to review concepts or as a way to reinforce good behavior. The children may draw game boards. Give them a few choices of themes. Let the themes reflect what you would like them to learn or review. For example, the game might use the undersea theme you may be studying, or it may have the theme of kindness.

Lesson Plan · Day 2

Tie into the previous session by sharing some rules you have at home or in the workplace.

1 This We Believe

Write the words *Ten Commandments* on the board. Tell the children that these laws are not like other laws. These laws are given by God. Ask them to repeat the name of God's laws after you. Then point out the This We Believe! box. Ask a volunteer to read this to the class, and ask everyone to repeat it.

2 A Gift from God

Tell the children that they will hear a Bible story about God giving the Ten Commandments to a man named Moses. Read aloud the Bible story. The children may wish to discuss the way God's people were feeling before and after God gave his special gift to them. Read the story aloud again, or ask volunteers to take turns reading the story to the class.

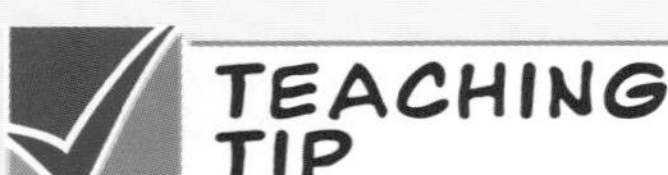

TEACHING TIP

Throughout the year, the children will have opportunities to learn the Ten Commandments and to understand them. After the children have heard the Scriptural language of the commandments, you may wish to display them in wording that is easy to understand, such as the following:

- Love God always, above everyone and everything else.
- Pray to God and honor God's name.
- Keep Sunday holy.
- Obey your parents and others who are in charge.
- Respect yourself and all living things. Do not harm living things.
- Be pure in what you do.
- Do not steal.
- Do not lie or speak meanly of others.
- Be pure in what you think and say.
- Do not be greedy.

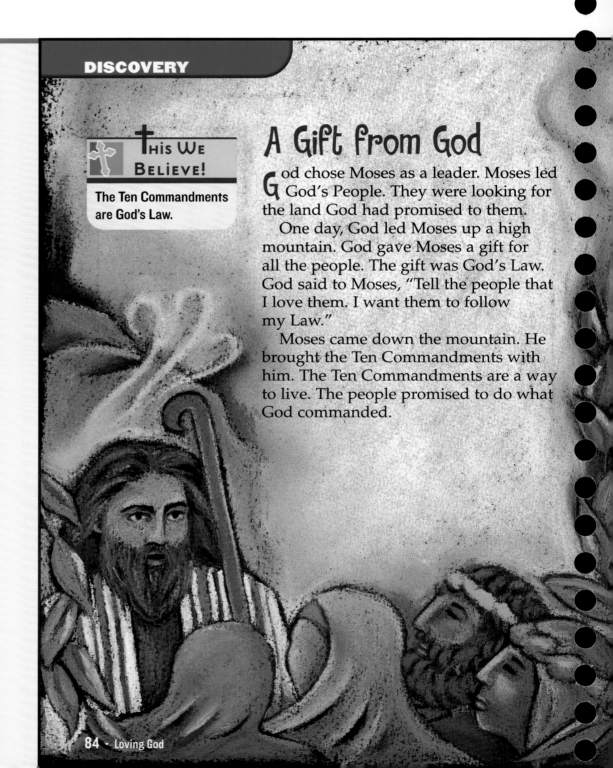

This We Believe!

The Ten Commandments are God's Law.

A Gift from God

God chose Moses as a leader. Moses led God's People. They were looking for the land God had promised to them.

One day, God led Moses up a high mountain. God gave Moses a gift for all the people. The gift was God's Law. God said to Moses, "Tell the people that I love them. I want them to follow my Law."

Moses came down the mountain. He brought the Ten Commandments with him. The Ten Commandments are a way to live. The people promised to do what God commanded.

3 The Ten Commandments

Ask the children to look at student page 85. Give them a few moments to skim the Ten Commandments. Read the Ten Commandments aloud. Ask why they think God gave these laws. Help them see that these laws are a sign of love and a way to help people.

4 Activity

Have the children work in pairs, perhaps on the floor or in a reading corner, to help each other memorize the Ten Commandments. Set a time limit. When all students are back in their places, quiz them by reading the Ten Commandments aloud, omitting key words that the students can fill in as a group.

5 Word of God

Ask a student to read the Scripture verse in the Word of God box. Encourage them to guess about what Jesus means in this verse.

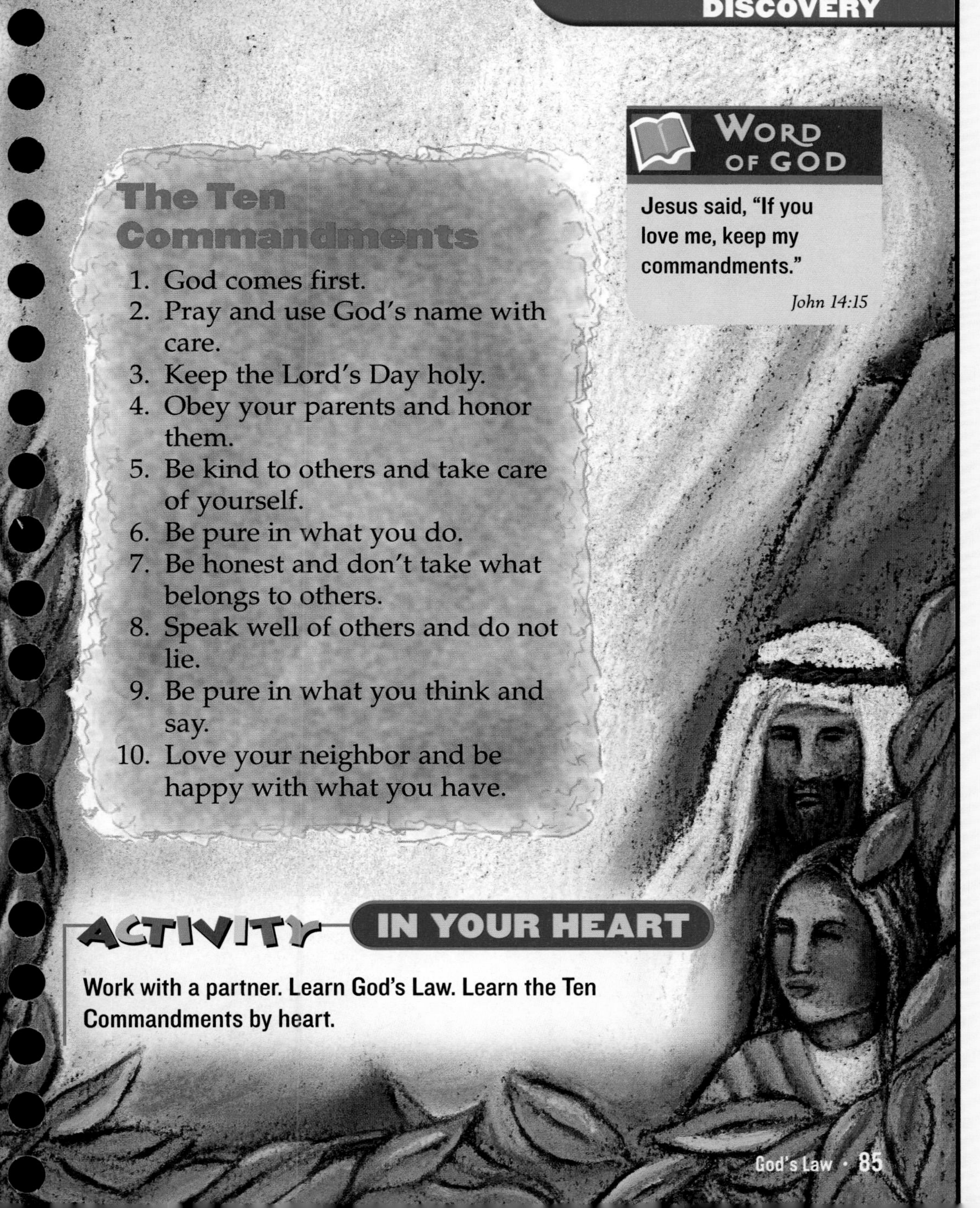

DISCOVERY

The Ten Commandments
1. God comes first.
2. Pray and use God's name with care.
3. Keep the Lord's Day holy.
4. Obey your parents and honor them.
5. Be kind to others and take care of yourself.
6. Be pure in what you do.
7. Be honest and don't take what belongs to others.
8. Speak well of others and do not lie.
9. Be pure in what you think and say.
10. Love your neighbor and be happy with what you have.

WORD OF GOD
Jesus said, "If you love me, keep my commandments."
John 14:15

ACTIVITY IN YOUR HEART
Work with a partner. Learn God's Law. Learn the Ten Commandments by heart.

God's Law · 85

RESOURCE MASTERS

The resource master on page 138 is an activity about making rules to solve problems. Children may work individually or in groups.

IDEAS THAT WORK

Try this fun way to help the children memorize the Ten Commandments. Write each commandment on the front of an envelope. Inside the envelope, enclose the commandment, cut into individual words. With a one-minute timer, the child dumps out the words and starts to recreate the commandment on the outside of the envelope. Make sure that the child correctly reads the commandment before the minute is up.

Lesson Plan · Day 3

Review the Ten Commandments with the children. You may wish to quiz them as a group as you did yesterday.

1 Gather

Build on what the children know. Ask the difference between rules and laws. Ask what word is used to describe God's laws. *(commandment)* Say that God sent Jesus to teach us how to keep the commandments. Ask them which commandment they think is most important. Volunteers may share their answers.

2 The Great Commandment

Read aloud the first paragraph on student page 86. Help the children understand that Jesus is saying that all the commandments are about one thing. Have volunteers guess what that one thing is. *(love)* Ask the children to read the next paragraph. Tell them that the Great Commandment reminds us to love God and others, and the Ten Commandments tell us how to do that.

VIRTUE FAITH GRACE **VOCABULARY**

Ten Commandments God's laws that tell how to love God and others.

The Great Commandment "Love the Lord, your God, with all your heart, with all your soul, and with all your mind. Love your neighbor as yourself."

The Great Commandment

One day, a man asked Jesus, "Teacher, which commandment is the greatest one?"

Jesus answered, "Love God with all your whole heart, with your whole soul, and with your whole mind. This is the greatest commandment. The second one is like it. Love your neighbor as yourself."

Based on *Matthew 22:34–40*

Find the great-commandment path. Trace a path from start to finish. Make sure you can say the words of Jesus by heart.

3 Activity
Read aloud the directions for the activity. Tell the children that they will find the name of Jesus' teaching in this activity. They may write the answer along the bottom of the page. Together, practice saying the Great Commandment.

4 Show Love
Share the information and explain the next activity. Ask the children to draw one of the arrows. Guide the children to see what the arrow means: To love God is to love others. Suggest that with each arrow drawn, the children softly say aloud, "I love God when I love others." Allow time for them to draw a picture in the box.

Show Love

Jesus said that you can show that you love God by showing love to others. Draw lines to connect the pictures with the sign in the center. In the empty frame, draw a picture of one way you can show love.

If you love me, keep my commandments.

John 14:15

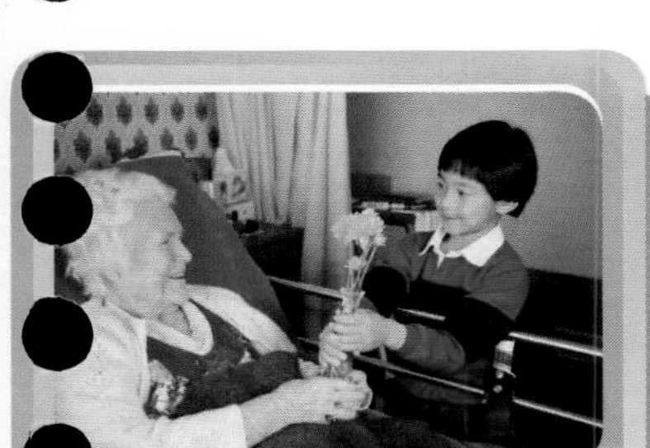

Love God

TEACHING TIP

When you observe situations that need fixing, lead the children to make up a guideline (or rule). Children often respond better to a guideline that they helped create. Give the children practice in making rules. Use situations you have observed (without revealing those involved), or make up scenarios that are common to second-grade children.

Lesson Plan · Day 4

Tell the students that although God gave the Ten Commandments long ago, we still follow them today.

1 The Big Picture

Ask the children to refer to the Ten Commandments on student page 85 or to the list displayed in the room. If you have not posted a rewording of the commandments, give a brief explanation of each commandment (see Teaching Tip on page 128). Have each child choose a commandment. Proceed with the directions in the activity.

LIVING

THE BIG PICTURE

Work together to create a big picture.

1. Tape a big sheet of paper to the chalkboard.
2. Work together or in small teams.
3. Draw a picture that shows people obeying God's Law.
4. Tell about what you are drawing.

❷ Key Words

Now let the children personalize their understanding of the commandments. Read the directions to the class. They may do the page on their own. Offer an opportunity for sharing when most students have completed the activity.

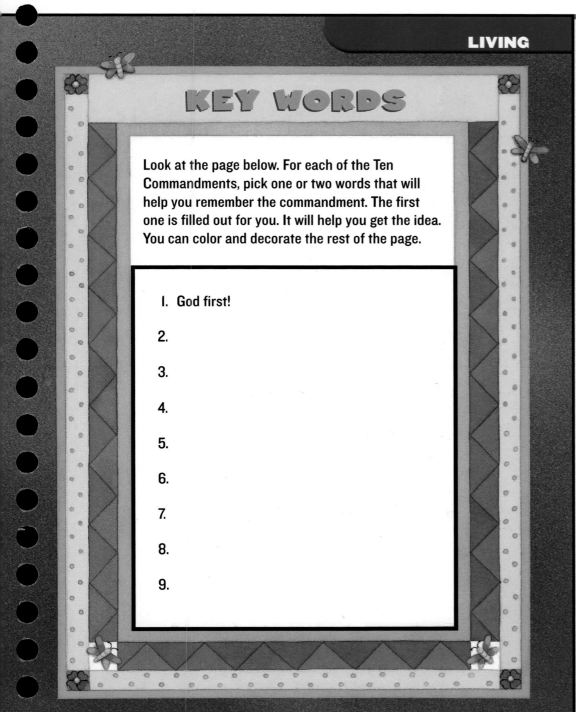

KEY WORDS

Look at the page below. For each of the Ten Commandments, pick one or two words that will help you remember the commandment. The first one is filled out for you. It will help you get the idea. You can color and decorate the rest of the page.

1. God first!
2.
3.
4.
5.
6.
7.
8.
9.

The children may need guidance in completing the activity on student page 89. Think about the commandments that have the most relevance to the children, and focus on them. Relate those commandments to specific situations and list them on the board (wanted to lie, wanted to take something, wanted to miss Mass, wanted to make fun of someone, and so on).

Prayer

This simple prayer service will bring the idea of the Ten Commandments to the hearts of second graders. Encourage them to respond in a way that lets Jesus know that they will try their best to keep their promises.

1 Prepare for Prayer

Ask the children to run their fingers down the page, calling out word clues that relate the prayer to the Ten Commandments. Accept all reasonable responses.

2 With Your Help

Have a practice reading. Ask whether there are any questions about when to speak, or about the meaning of the prayer. Then, gather in the prayer area to pray.

OPTIONS

For Those Who Learn Musically Invite the children to use simple rhythm instruments, such as bells, triangles, and wood blocks to add some background music to the prayer's response.

LEARNING TO PRAY

Because this is a chapter about rules and laws, be sure the children are clear about proper behavior during prayer. They may need a reminder for several weeks. Think of a phrase that you can use to get the children ready to pray. Choose a gentle prompt such as, "Show me that you are ready."

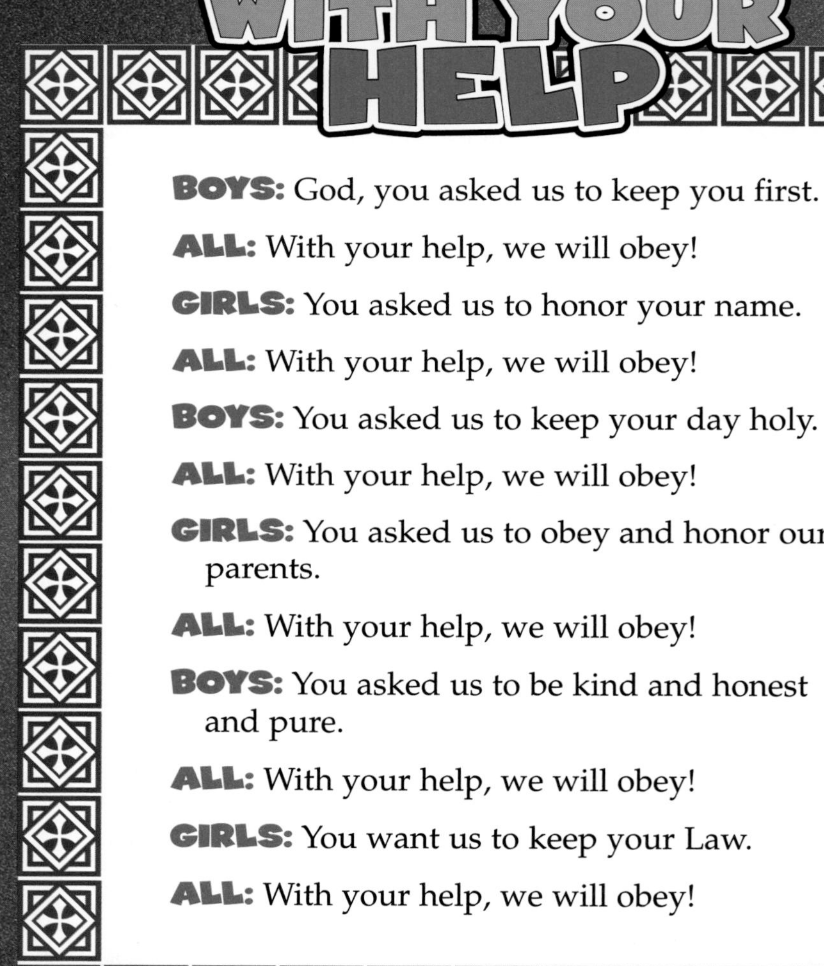

WITH YOUR HELP
BOYS: God, you asked us to keep you first.
ALL: With your help, we will obey!
GIRLS: You asked us to honor your name.
ALL: With your help, we will obey!
BOYS: You asked us to keep your day holy.
ALL: With your help, we will obey!
GIRLS: You asked us to obey and honor our parents.
ALL: With your help, we will obey!
BOYS: You asked us to be kind and honest and pure.
ALL: With your help, we will obey!
GIRLS: You want us to keep your Law.
ALL: With your help, we will obey!

1 Know
Refer the children to the graphic organizer as a guide for reviewing the chapter. Ask volunteers to tell what they know about the Ten Commandments. Give prompts to elicit the three statements in the graphic organizer. List the facts on the board. Then ask volunteers to circle reasons why we keep the commandments.

2 Love and Serve
Help the children brainstorm words that show love, and write the words on the board. Set a time limit for the activity. Then, give the children slips of paper on which they may write the ways they will show love for God. Keep the slips in a special container labeled "We love God." Keep the container available to the children all year.

3 God's Friends
Show the illustration of Saint Benedict, and explain briefly what it means to be a monk. Ask the children to listen for one of Saint Benedict's rules. Read aloud the text about Saint Benedict. Ask the children to share something they heard that surprised them.

CHAPTER 5
REVIEW and EXPLORE

Know

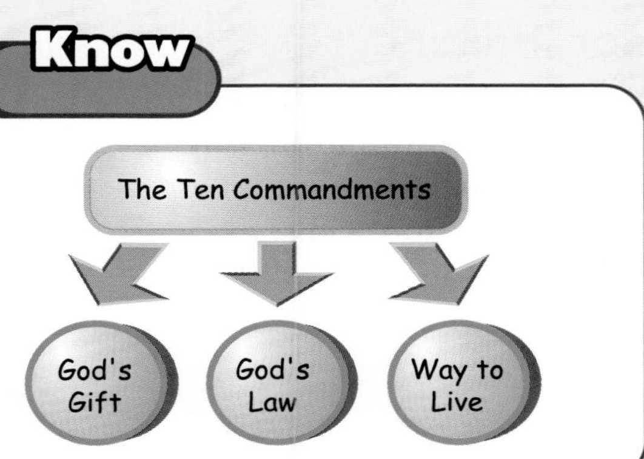

Love

In the space, write a commandment that teaches you how to love others.

Choose one of the commandments. Make a little reminder. Remember that when you obey this commandment, you obey God's Law.

GOD'S FRIENDS

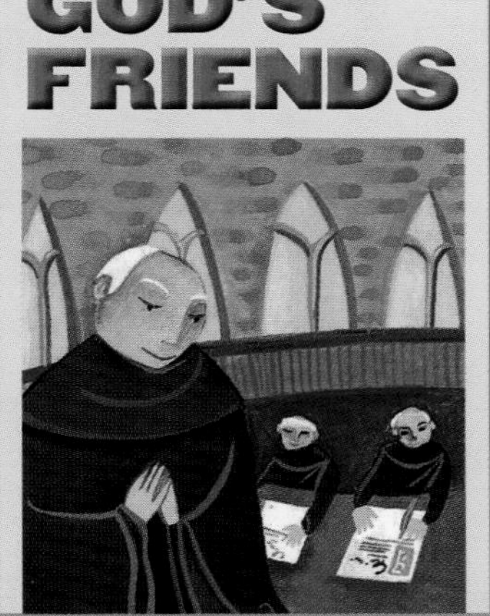

Saint Benedict

Benedict told his monks to work and pray. "That is how we love God," he told them. Benedict and his monks worked hard and prayed all day long. Many men and women follow the Rule of Saint Benedict.

A Little Catechism

Invite the children to open their religion books to *A Little Catechism.* Choose one or more of the selections below for memory work or reinforcement. You will find your copy of the catechism on pages 23–43 of this Teacher's Edition.

1. Locate the Ten Commandments in your little catechism.
2. Review each of the commandments with the children. See how many they can put in their own words.
3. Read question 6 on page 13. Encourage children to memorize the answer.

Know Love Serve

Note The activities on this page provide ways for the children to share their learning with their families. The activities are related to the week's theme.

1 Introduce
Recall that certain rules are good for every game. Ask for opinions: Are certain rules good for every friendship? Have the children silently read the first activity. Ask how many have family rules. Let the children silently read the second activity.

2 Pray Together
Direct attention to the prayer burst. Say that the words are from the Bible. Let the class pray aloud the prayer in the prayer burst.

BIBLE BASICS

Have the children look at the Word of God on page 87. Say that a line from the Bible is called a verse. A part of a poem is also called a verse. Pique the children's curiosity by saying that there is a way to know when a verse comes from the Bible. Have the class read the citation. Say that the name and the numbers have meaning. Using your class Bible, show the location of the Gospel of John, the fourteenth chapter, and verse 15.

Online for Families
Remind the children to check the Benziger Web site this week with their families.
www.benziger.glencoe.com

CHAPTER 5
HOME and FAMILY

Dear Family,

I have just finished chapter 5. I learned that the Ten Commandments are God's Law. They are a gift from God. They are a way to live, too. Help me learn and remember God's Law.

With others

Make up a list of three or four friendship rules. Write one of the rules you make in the space.

FRIENDSHIP RULE

With your family

Talk about the rules your family has. How are these rules a way to live? How are these rules like a gift?

I love you God—with my whole heart.

GO ONLINE!
http://www.benziger.glencoe.com

1 Introduction
Ask the children to picture themselves at Mass. Picture the priest behind the altar. See all the people standing. The priest is blessing everyone. (Now say the words of the final blessing.) Tell the children that the priest stands in place of Jesus. Jesus is blessing the people and asking them to follow him.

2 Project
Recall that the Great Commandment helps us follow Jesus. Have the children work individually or in groups to make a sign for the Great Commandment. Display the signs in the classroom. Several lessons will refer to these signs.

THE CHURCH TODAY

At the end of every Mass, the priest or the deacon says, "Go in peace to love and serve the Lord." How can you do that? You can follow God's Great Commandment.

Find the story of the Great Commandment in your book. Make a sign that shows the Great Commandment. (Hint, the Great Commandment really has two parts.)

You can decorate your sign. Hang your sign where it will remind you and others about the Great Commandment.

IDEAS THAT WORK

The project on this page focuses on the Great Commandment. The signs will serve as visual clues for learning the Great Commandment. You may wish to bring stencils for lettering the words. Using the stencils will help the children develop their fine-muscle control.

ANSWER KEY

This is the answer key for the chapter test on page 139.

A. 1. Moses 2. heart 3. mind 4. yourself

B. 1. a 2. b 3. b

Name ______________________________

Rules Help

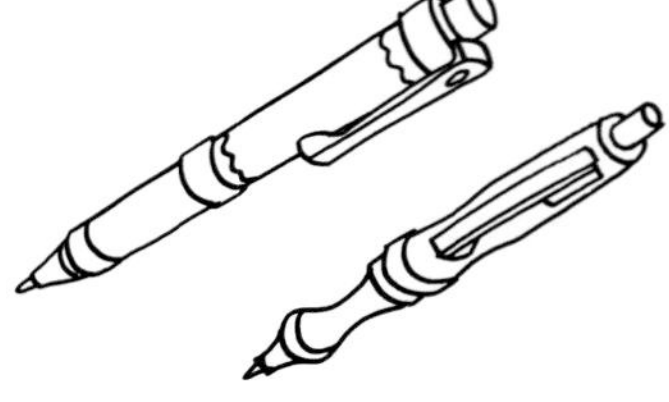

Rules can help solve problems.

Read each problem. Write a rule that may make things better.

1. There is one ball. Four children want to use it.

____

____

2. When Jenny's mom gives her a chore to do, Jenny likes to yell back, "No!"

____

____

3. Somebody keeps taking pencils from the desks.

____

____

4. Somebody wants to be the boss of everything.

____

____

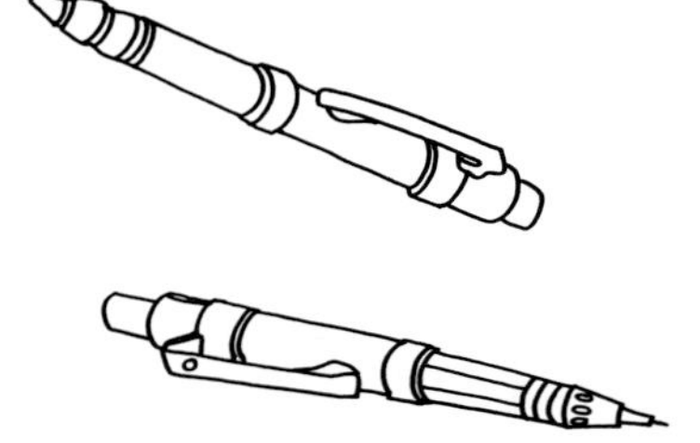

Name ______________________________

Chapter 5 Test

A. Tell about the Commandments. Use words in the box.

Peter / heart / mind / yourself / Moses

1. God gave the Ten Commandments to ________________.

2. Jesus said, "Love the Lord your God with all your

________________,

3. with all your soul, and with all your ________________.

4. Love your neighbor as ________________."

B. Circle the words that best finish each sentence.

1. You follow God's laws
a. to show God love.
b. to stay out of trouble.

2. When you show love to people,
a. you are being silly.
b. you show love to God.

3. The Ten Commandments tell
a. ten things to believe.
b. what is right and wrong.

CHAPTER 6 Trust God

TEACHER RESOURCE CENTER

Faith Formation

CHECK THE CATECHISM

The *Catechism of the Catholic Church* covers the first commandment in paragraphs 2084–2128. See especially the sections on faith, hope, and charity for further understanding.

Serve Him Alone

While Exodus provides the first listing of the Decalogue, the "ten words" that have been translated into a listing of the Ten Commandments, it is in Deuteronomy that we find practical ideas for living out God's Law. The first commandment, "The Lord is our God, the Lord alone" *(Deuteronomy 6:4)*, acknowledges total dependence on God. God is the source of all that is good, and because he loves and protects us, it is possible for us to be free. False gods of idolatry, superstition, and unbelief are cast aside for faith in the one God who saves. We are to worship and serve our one God alone.

What are some "false gods" in your life that sometimes get in the way of following the one God?

The concept of the one God, rather than a multitude of gods, is the foundation of Jewish teaching, on which is built our Christian faith. Deuteronomy further challenges the faithful to love the one God with "all your heart, and with all your soul, and with all your strength," and the Israelites were instructed to "drill [these words] into your children," and to "speak of them at home and abroad" (*Deuteronomy 6:5–7*). These words invite us to look at our lives with a critical eye to find the places that need improvement.

Can you find one or two new and creative ways to speak about your own faith in the one God this week?

Background

Being First

Chapter 6 focuses on the first commandment, which is explained as putting God first. Second graders have clear ideas about what it means to be first. It will not be difficult to connect this concept to the children's experiences. The children will discover ways to follow the first commandment. Prayer is included as one of the ways. Prayer may be a bit challenging to teach, because it is directly tied into the children's natural curiosity about God. They may have questions like these: Is God real? Does God hear me? Does God answer my prayers?

It is important to help children understand prayer as more than asking for things. Let a variety of prayers be part of the children's daily school life. Examine your own attitude toward prayer and your habits of prayer. Speak to the children as one who knows Jesus. Your witness may be the most important aspect of the time you spend with them.

Faith Summary

- We trust God.
- Prayer expresses our trust in God.

Growth and Development

It is helpful to remember two characteristics of second graders as you teach this lesson:

- ***Second graders take generalizations as truth.*** Try to avoid using them, particularly when teaching about prayer. You may say that God listens to all prayer.
- ***Second graders will take you literally.*** Children often expect to get everything they ask for in prayer; they will see prayer as a form of magic. Without going into detail, emphasize prayer as a trust in God to give us what we most need to be better people.

A Teacher's Prayer

Mary, you trusted completely in God's plan for you. Lead me to this same kind of trust with the children who are entrusted to my care. Let God show me the way to be fair, patient, kind, and dependable. Amen.

Vocabulary Preview

trust
prayer

Scripture

Matthew 4:10: Serve God only.
Matthew 6:32–33: Put God first.
Ephesians 6:18: Pray often.
Psalm 146: Trust the Lord.

Related Resources

Video

"Commandments for Young People" (St. Anthony Messenger Press, 1-800-488-0488 or www.AmericanCatholic.org). This series deals creatively with the Ten Commandments. "We Remember" deals with the first three commandments. (Children, 15 minutes each)

Book

Finley, Mitch. *The Ten Commandments: Timeless Challenges for Today* (Liguori Publications, 1-800-325-9521 or www.liguori.org). The first two chapters of this book provide helpful background for teaching the first commandment. (Adult)

TEACHER ORGANIZER

Planning Guide

The basic content for each chapter is divided into four class sessions. There are a number of options for the fifth session. Extension, review, and testing options are described under Day 5 Alternatives. The Quick Check box will help you evaluate the week's lessons.

Chapter Goals

In this chapter, the students will learn about

- ❑ Trust
- ❑ Putting God first
- ❑ Prayer

	DAY 1 · INVITATION	DAY 2 · DISCOVERY	DAY 3 · DISCOVERY
OBJECTIVES	**The students will be able to** • Discern ways they come to trust people • Synthesize information on trust	**The students will be able to** • Apply what they have learned about trust to their relationship with God • Conclude that they are trusted	**The students will be able to** • Recite the first commandment • Discover how much they can trust God
PREPARATION	• Think about what concrete experiences your students have of developing trust	• Know your school policies for reporting child abuse or neglect	• Think about ways you model trust
MATERIALS	• Pencils	• Pencils • Crayons in four different colors for each student	• Crayons, pencils
OPTIONAL ACTIVITIES	• **Vocabulary** Teach the meaning of trust	• **Curriculum Challenge** Add verses to the song, "Oh, I'm a trusted person"	• **Ideas That Work** Record a tape for homebound parishioners

Learning Objectives

By the end of this chapter, the students should be able to

- ❑ See the role of trust in their lives
- ❑ Know the first commandment and ways to follow it
- ❑ Pray in various ways

DAY 4 · LIVING

The students will be able to

- Tell ways to put God first
- Write personal prayers
- Pray and sign a Scripture text from the Psalms

- Practice signing the text from Psalms on student page 102

- Pencils, drawing supplies
- One blank piece of paper, scissors, glue or tape
- Five white cards per student
- Recorded religious music for children

- **Ideas That Work** Use sign language with Scripture verses
- **Curriculum Challenge** Explore ways to speak without words
- **Learning To Pray** Have students make a sign, have children's prayer books available

DAY 5 · ALTERNATIVES

There are a number of alternatives to help you plan Day 5.

Prayer Experience
You may use the Psalm on Day 4 or Day 5.

Review and Explore
Follow the suggestions for teaching the page. The students will need pencils, drawing supplies, and a piece of yarn large enough to tie a knot around a finger. Prepare to teach, or review, the Hail Mary. Make copies of the resource master on page 156.

Home and Family
Send the page home with the students.

The Church Today
If the students will not be doing the project on their own, invite a parish priest and parishioners to class. Or, make arrangements for the students to meet with a priest at the rectory.

Chapter Test
The chapter test appears as a resource master on page 157.

Quick Check

Do this evaluation as soon as you finish each chapter.

Did I follow my lesson plan?

How can I tell that I met the learning objectives for the lesson?

What activities did the children enjoy most?

How could I improve this lesson?

Benziger on the Web
For more ideas, visit us at **www.benziger.glencoe.com**

Interactive Lesson Planner
Your ILP provides more help in preparing to teach this chapter.

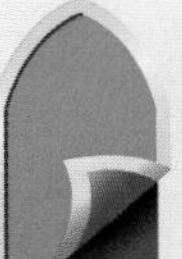

Celebrate
Turn to page 22 of this book. Check for seasonal celebrations.

Lesson Plan · Day 1

Ask the children to read aloud the chapter title and the chapter's Scripture verse. Allow volunteers to tell you the ways they can show love for God. Then ask the children whether they know the meaning of the word worship. Ask for ways they can worship, or honor and praise, God.

1 Do You Know?

Ask a volunteer to write the Do You Know? question on the chalkboard. Discuss the idea of being first. You may ask the children what they like about being first in line, or what it is like to go first when playing a game. At the end of the week, come back to this question to see how the children's knowledge has developed.

2 Hang on, Ben

Ask the children to look at the picture on student page 94. Invite volunteers to talk about what is happening in the picture. Then read the title and discuss the idea of being excited and a little scared when doing something for the first time. Read the story to the children. Invite them to name people who help them when they are scared.

IDEAS THAT WORK

When possible, use peer sharing in your classroom, so that each child has a chance to respond. Have each child share with another child who sits nearby, or use another method to arrange the children in pairs. You may even add a little challenge by asking each child to share with someone with whom he or she has something particular in common. Suggest some possible commonalties—for example, the two may have the same color of hair, or the same kind of pet.

The Lord God will you worship and him alone will you serve.
Matthew 4:10

Do You Know?

◆ How can you keep God first?

Trust God

Hang on, Ben!

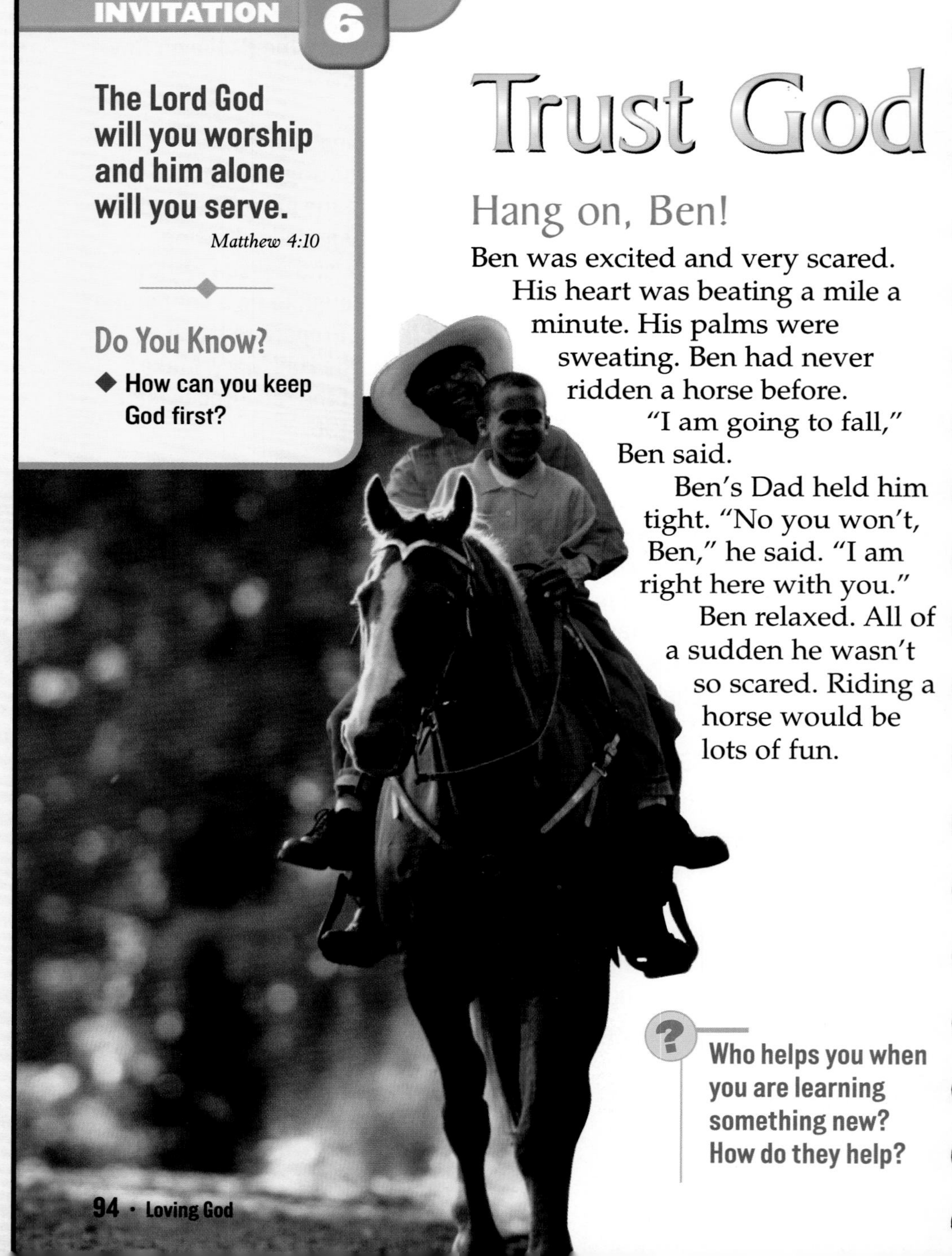

Ben was excited and very scared. His heart was beating a mile a minute. His palms were sweating. Ben had never ridden a horse before.

"I am going to fall," Ben said.

Ben's Dad held him tight. "No you won't, Ben," he said. "I am right here with you."

Ben relaxed. All of a sudden he wasn't so scared. Riding a horse would be lots of fun.

? Who helps you when you are learning something new? How do they help?

3 Help Me

Talk with your students about what it means to depend on someone and about what it means to be dependable. Read the text on student page 95 to the children. Invite them to discuss what is happening in the pictures on the left side of the page, and to work with partners to complete this activity.

Help Me

You need to trust people to help you and keep you safe. You trust the members of your family. You trust teachers and friends.

Help the children in the first column find someone to help in the second column. Draw a line to the person who will help. Talk about the children and about the people they trust.

TEACHING TIP

Religion is made up of many abstract concepts. Second graders think and understand in concrete terms. Therefore, what you do before introducing a religious concept is very important. That is the time to connect to the children's personal experiences as much as possible.

VOCABULARY

Trust To count on or depend on someone or something. Share with the children the ways you trust them. Let them tell how you are trusted.

Lesson Plan · Day 2

Recall yesterday's lesson on depending on others to help. Then read with the children the Scripture verse inside the This We Believe! box.

1 Trust

Read the information on student page 96. Tell the children they are going to make some discoveries about trust. Guide them in writing in the initials of people they trust.

Be sure that each child has crayons in four different colors. Have the children use the crayons to color the lines that connect each outer circle to the center circle. Ask: What do the connections tell you about trust? *(I trust people; people trust me.)* What do you do to show you can be trusted? List responses on the chalkboard under a heading such as *We are trusted.*

TEACHING TIP

During the year, you may come to realize that some of the children may have adults in their lives who cannot be trusted. Some children live in homes where they are abused or neglected. If you ever suspect such circumstances, follow the guidelines established by your school administration.

This We Believe!

God is good and worthy of trust and love.

Who Do You Trust?

Ben felt safe with his dad around. His dad would teach him the right way to ride. Ben trusted his dad.

There are people in your life who keep you safe. There are people who teach you and who guide you. There are people you can be sure of.

Look at the circle of trust. In the small circles, write the initials of four people you trust. Why do you trust each one?

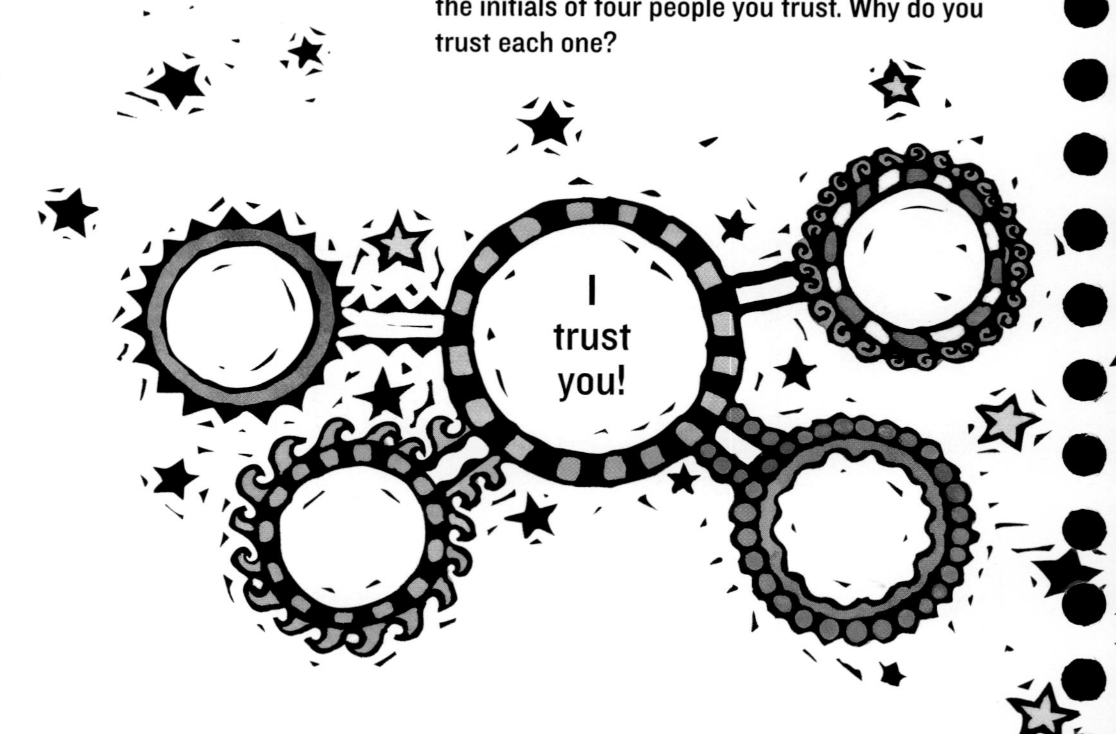

2 A True Friend
Read the text aloud. Let the children tell you what they know about talking to God and about listening to God. Remind them that we call this process prayer. Then invite the children to use their crayons to complete the activity at the bottom of the page.

A True Friend

Jesus showed that everyone can trust God. Jesus showed this by being a good friend.

Jesus met many people and made lots of friends. He showed how much he loved his friends. He took care of sick people and comforted those who were sad.

Jesus forgave people and hugged little children. He prayed and shared meals with his friends.

Jesus was a true friend. He showed that the great and good God is a friend you can always trust.

ACTIVITY **WORDS OF TRUST**

Color the words that tell about trusting God.

Pray Fear
Care
Lie Share
Comfort

CURRICULUM CHALLENGE

Music To connect the abstract concept of trust to the children's experiences, teach this song about trust, sung to the tune of "For He's a Jolly Good Fellow."

Oh, I'm a trusted person.
Yes, I'm a trusted person.
Oh, I'm a trusted person.
You can count on me!

Then, let the children do the connecting. Have them get into groups. Direct each group to come up with a verse that shows a way to trust (for example, "I can keep a secret" or "I do all my chores"). End with all of the groups performing their verses.

Lesson Plan · Day 3

As a review of trust, sing a few rounds of "Oh, I'm a trusted person." See Curriculum Challenge from Day 2.

1 God Is Your Guide

Have the children say the first commandment aloud. Write it on the chalkbaord if necessary. Ask what clues in the commandment say to put God first. Tell the children that when they put their trust in God, God will help and protect them.

TEACHING TIP

A good way to teach trust is to model trust. Make promises that you can keep. Create a warm, welcoming environment in which the children feel free to share. Provide a classroom that is physically and emotionally safe for them. Never make fun of or berate a child, even when your intention is humorous teasing. Be ready and willing to give help.

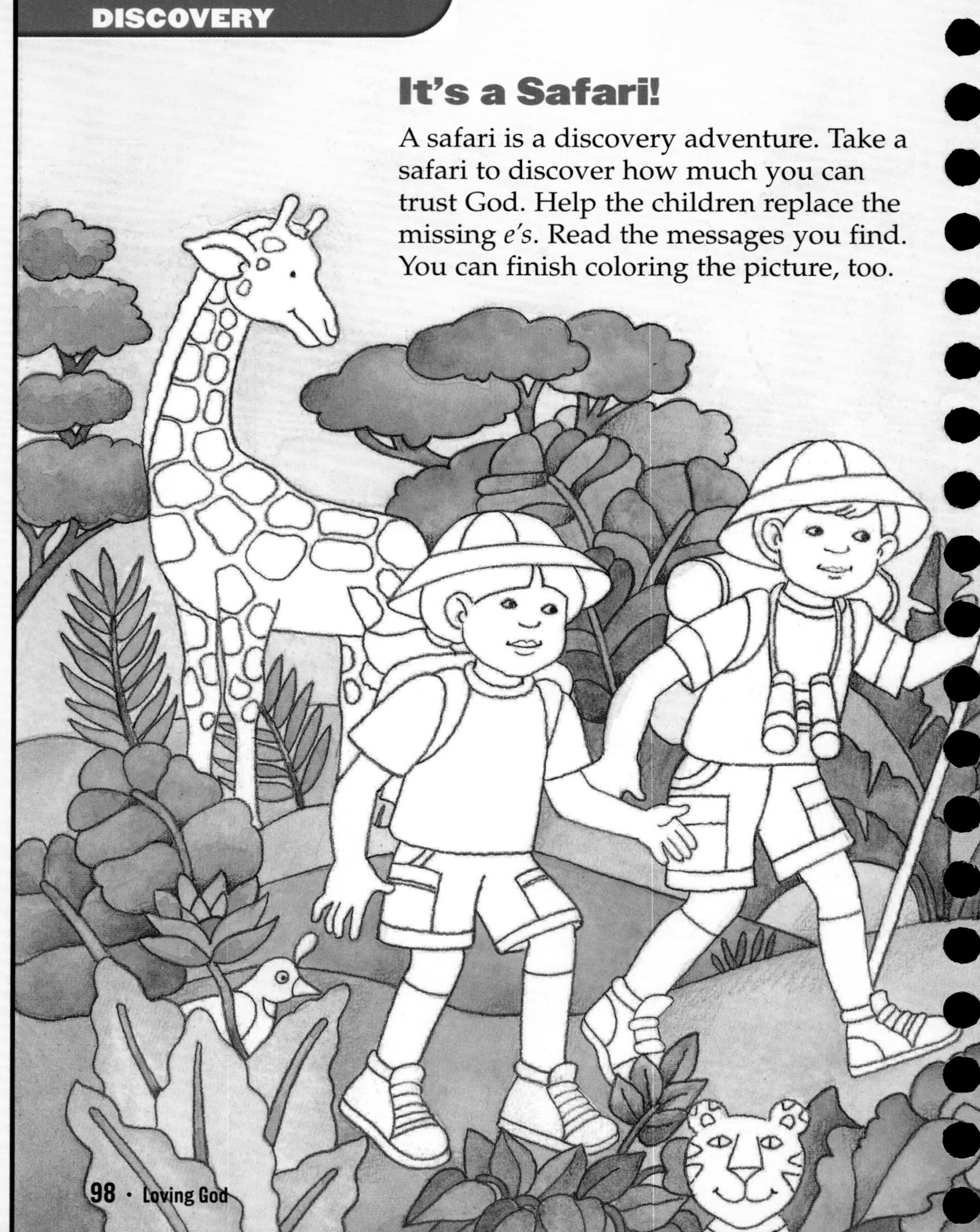

DISCOVERY

It's a Safari!

A safari is a discovery adventure. Take a safari to discover how much you can trust God. Help the children replace the missing *e's*. Read the messages you find. You can finish coloring the picture, too.

98 · Loving God

2 It's a Safari!

Ask the children what they see as they look at student pages 98 and 99. Help them notice that the two children in the picture are on a journey. Invite the children to fill in the missing letters to discover what the animals have to teach them. Encourage the children to color the picture as they think about ways to let God be their guide.

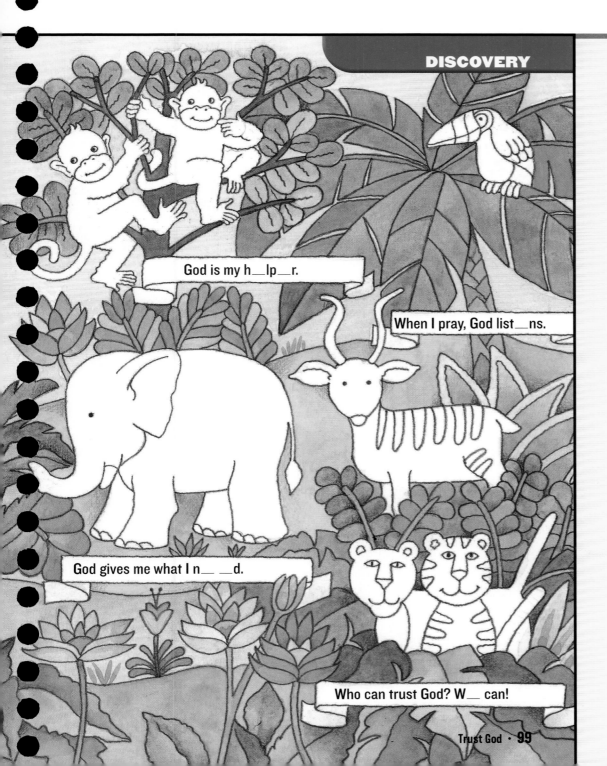

DISCOVERY

God is my h__lp__r.

When I pray, God list__ns.

God gives me what I n__ __d.

Who can trust God? W__ can!

Trust God · 99

IDEAS THAT WORK

Help the children reach out to homebound parishioners. Record the children singing a few rounds of "Oh, I'm a trusted person," but change the words to "You can trust in God." Record the children saying the prayer on student page 102. Give the tape to a Eucharistic minister in charge of home visits, or to a local hospital or care center.

Lesson Plan · Day 4

Have the children read aloud the first commandment. Write it on the chalkboard if needed.

1 Number One

Direct attention to the large numeral on student page 100. Lead the children through the activity on the page. The child who is finished first may draw a large *1* on a blank sheet of paper, and within it write the words: Put God first. The child may cut out the number and glue or tape it to the classroom sign of the first commandment.

LEARNING TO PRAY

Make prayer an integral part of second-grade life. Engage some children to make a sign for the prayer table based on Ephesians 6:18. Have available some richly illustrated, easy-to-read children's prayer books, such as *I'm Thankful Each Day* by P. K. Hallinan and *Thank You for This Day: Action Prayers, Songs, and Blessings* by Debbie Trafton O'Neal. Invite the class to bring in prayer books, and to share ideas for praying.

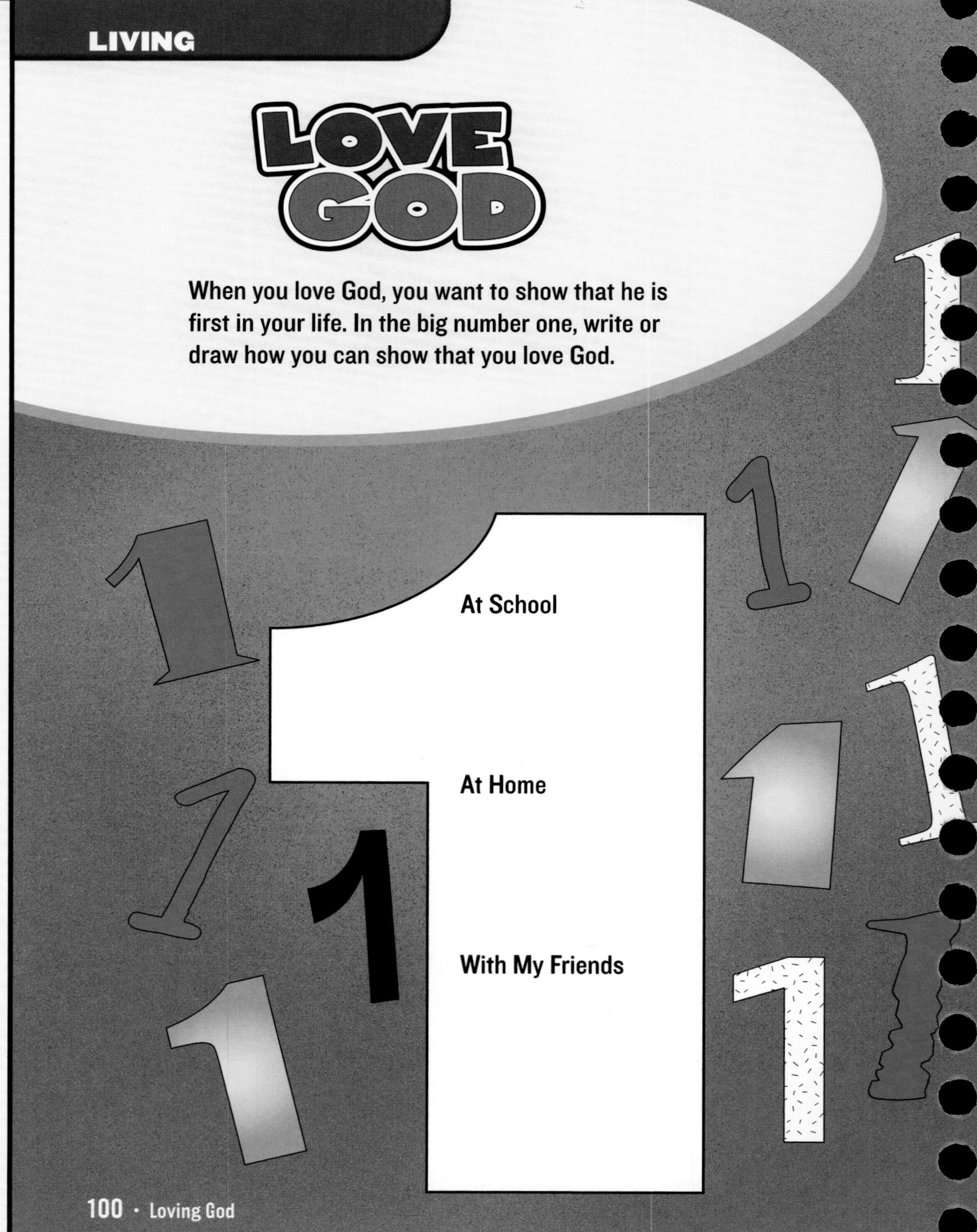

LIVING
LOVE GOD
When you love God, you want to show that he is first in your life. In the big number one, write or draw how you can show that you love God.
At School
At Home
With My Friends
100 · Loving God

2 Prayer Cards

Create a comfortable atmosphere for this activity. Consider letting the children sit wherever they wish in the room. Guide them to quiet themselves and encourage them to think about what they want to say to God. Use the ideas on student page 101 as prompts. Read the suggestions slowly, pausing to give the children time to think. Next, give each child five plain cards, such as half an index card. While the children are writing their prayers, play a recording of religious songs for children. Invite them to decorate their cards.

PRAY ALWAYS

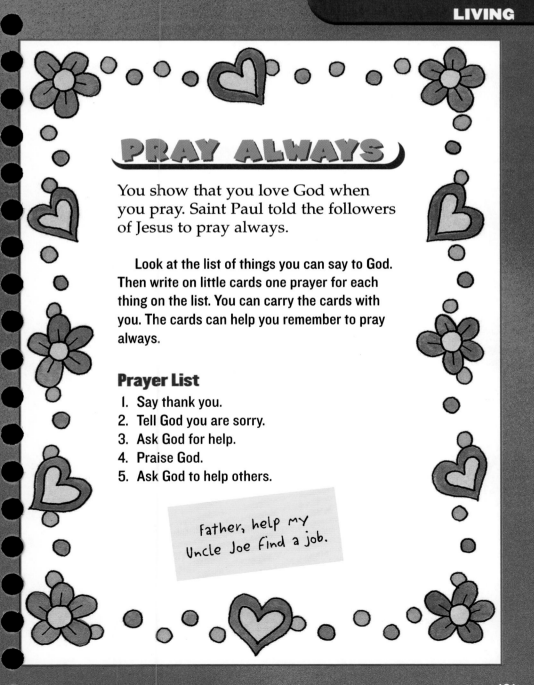

You show that you love God when you pray. Saint Paul told the followers of Jesus to pray always.

Look at the list of things you can say to God. Then write on little cards one prayer for each thing on the list. You can carry the cards with you. The cards can help you remember to pray always.

Prayer List

1. Say thank you.
2. Tell God you are sorry.
3. Ask God for help.
4. Praise God.
5. Ask God to help others.

Father, help my Uncle Joe find a job.

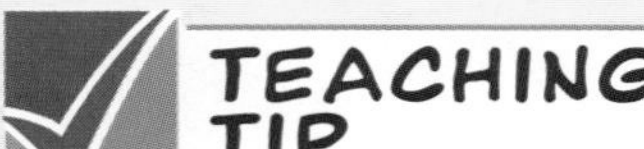

TEACHING TIP

Because the children will learn from your example, it is often helpful for you to do the same activity that they are doing. It could be very effective for you to make a prayer card as the children are making theirs. You may wish to write a prayer for the children and pray it with them.

Prayer

This week's prayer gives you and the children an opportunity to pray for trust together. This would be a good time to look into the resources available to you for learning simple sign language. Your students will delight in the idea that they know a second language!

1 Prepare for Prayer

Divide the class into two groups. Assign a good reader to lead each group through its lines. Then practice the lines said by all.

2 We Trust In You

Gather together in the prayer area. Ask the children to quiet themselves inside and out. Pray together. If you have learned to sign some or all of the words, sign those the second time you pray.

IDEAS THAT WORK

Signing Bible verses is a good way to introduce sign language to children. Signing also presents a common ground for hearing impaired and hearing children.

CURRICULUM CHALLENGE

Social Studies You may provide the opportunity for children to explore ways to speak without words. Some children may discover common gestures used to indicate simple words and phrases, such as *yes, no, what,* and *you're in trouble.*

LIVING
WE TRUST IN YOU
God, you made the heaven and the earth.
We trust in you!
You care for the hungry and for those who are hurt.
We trust in you!
You protect strangers and children.
We trust in you!
You care for us always.
We trust in you!
Based on Psalm 146
102 · Loving God

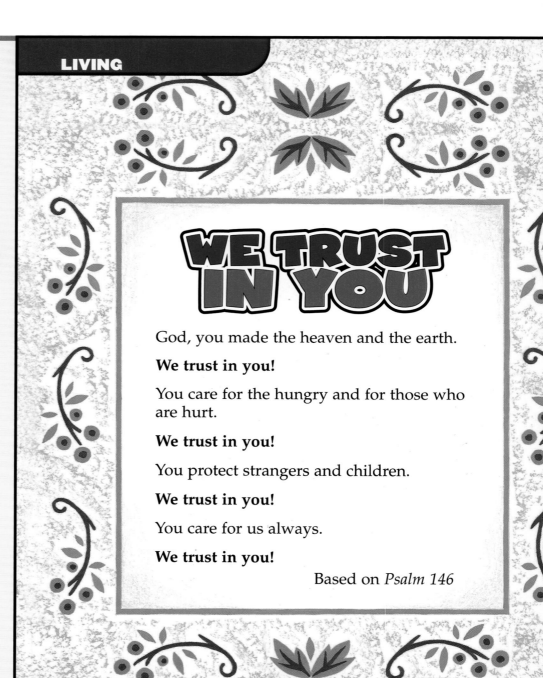

1 Know

Ask the children to say the first commandment. Have each child turn to someone sitting nearby. Ask the pairs to take turns telling a few ways to put God first. Then call attention to the graphic organizer, and read aloud the ways that are listed.

2 Love and Serve

Have the children silently read the Love activity, and write their prayers. Give each of them a piece of yarn. Guide each child to tie the yarn loosely around his or her partner's finger as a reminder to start the day with God. Lead the children through the Serve activity. Give a few moments of thinking time before the writing begins.

3 God's Friends

Show the illustration, and tell the children they are going to hear about the mother of Jesus. Tell or read the story. Say that an angel is a messenger of God. Ask the children how Mary showed trust in God. If time allows, introduce (or review) the Hail Mary. Give the children the resource master, found on page 156, to do now or take home.

Know

1 God is a good friend.

- Trust God.
- Pray often.
- Be a good friend.

Love

In the space, write a short morning prayer that shows how you trust God. Say the prayer every day.

Serve

Write or draw one way you can help others put trust in you!

CHAPTER 6
REVIEW and EXPLORE

GOD'S FRIENDS

The Blessed Mother

God sent the Angel Gabriel to Mary. Gabriel said, "God is with you. God wants you to be the mother of Jesus." Mary was afraid, but she trusted God. Mary said, "Yes. I will do as God wants."

A Little Catechism

Invite the children to open their religion books to *A Little Catechism.* Choose one or more of the selections below for memory work or reinforcement. You will find your copy of the catechism on pages 23–43 of this Teacher's Edition.

1. Read about Psalms and Ashes on page 12. Talk about Ash Wednesday and how ashes remind us to put God first.
2. Refer to Talking to God on page 17. Remind the children that prayer is an opportunity to stay close to God.
3. Read about Mary's Joy on page 27. Remind the children that Mary put her trust in God.

Know Love Serve

Note The activities on this page provide ways for the children to share their learning with their families. The activities are related to the week's theme.

1 Introduce
Ask the children to pair with someone who sits near. One child pretends to be the parent and asks, "What did you learn in religion this week?" The other child answers. The children then reverse roles.

2 Pray Together
Go through the activities with the children. Tell them to think about the different times their family members need help. End the week by praying aloud the prayer in the prayer burst.

Online for Families
Remind the children to check the Benziger Web site this week with their families.
www.benziger.glencoe.com

Dear Family,
I have just finished chapter 6. I learned that God is a good friend. I learned that I can trust in God. Help me by showing me how our family trusts God.

With others
Look through your storybooks, games, and magazines. Find one example of trust. Share the example with a friend or family member.

With your family
Use the sample below to make coupons—one for each member of the family. Give someone in your family a coupon when he or she really needs your help.

I know you need help!
You can count on me!

**Dear God,
I trust in you!**

GO ONLINE!
http://www.benziger.glencoe.com

1 Introduction
On the chalkboard, write *Catholic Church* in large letters. All around the words draw simple church buildings. Label each building with the name of a parish, and include the children's parish, too. Ask the children to come to the chalkboard, and point to the church building that has their parish's name.

2 Activity
The children may do the activity completely on their own. See the Ideas That Work feature for other ways to make discoveries about the parish.

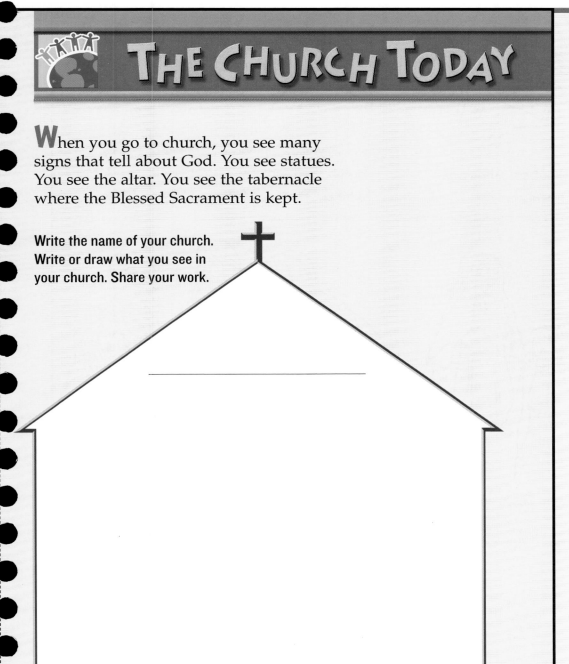

THE CHURCH TODAY

When you go to church, you see many signs that tell about God. You see statues. You see the altar. You see the tabernacle where the Blessed Sacrament is kept.

Write the name of your church. Write or draw what you see in your church. Share your work.

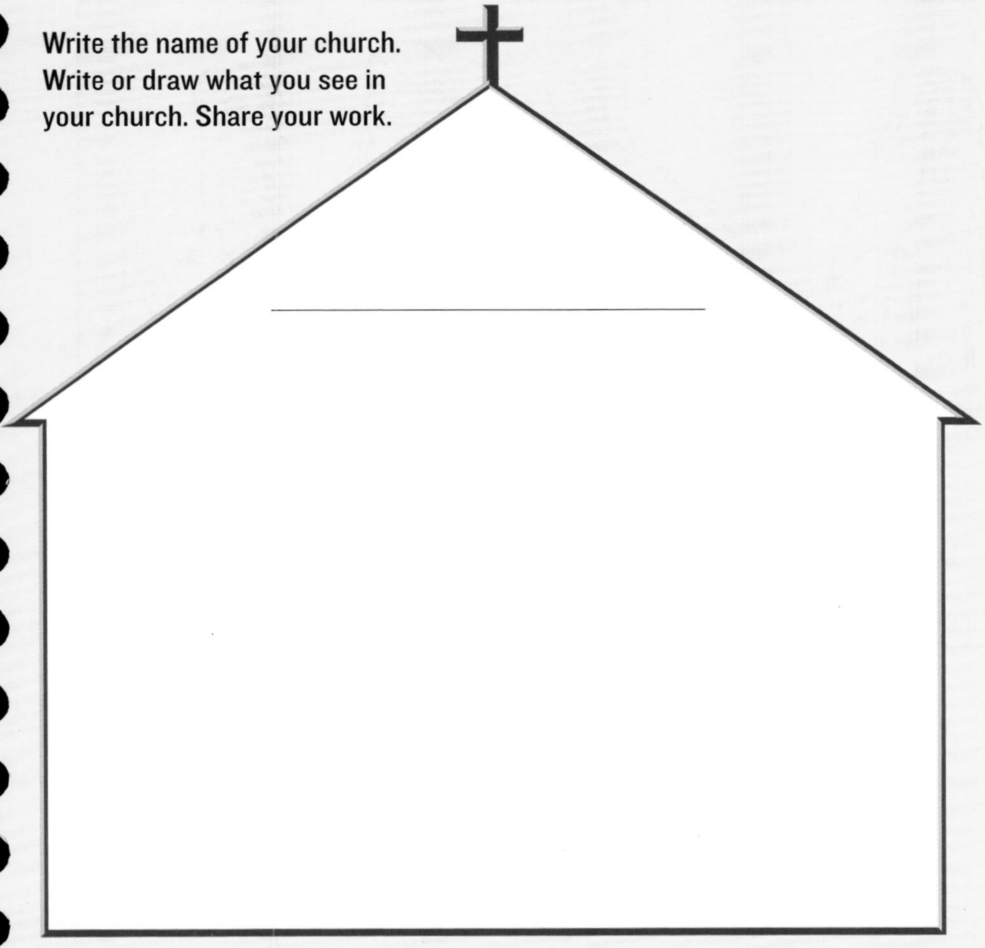

IDEAS THAT WORK

If you wish, invite a parish priest and some parishioners to the class to be interviewed about parish life. They can work with the children in groups. As an alternative, if the church is nearby, walk to the church, notice its sign, and visit the rectory to do the inquiries. This step would require you to make arrangements ahead of time.

ANSWER KEY

This is the answer key for the chapter test on page 157.

A. 1. a 2. b 3. b 4. b

B. 1. God 2. me

C. a, b, d, e

Name ______________________________

Mary

Make this booklet to learn about Mary, the mother of Jesus.

Cut on the solid lines. Put the pictures in order. Staple the pictures together.

Mary was born without sin. Anne and Joachim were Mary's parents.

Mary grew up and was going to marry Joseph. God sent the angel Gabriel to ask Mary to be the mother of Jesus. Mary said, "Yes."

Mary and Joseph loved Jesus and cared for him.

When Jesus grew up, he taught about God. Mary traveled with Jesus as he helped people.

Name ______________________________

Chapter 6 Test

A. Circle the letter of the words that best finish each sentence.

1. To count on someone means that you know how to
a. trust.
b. smile.

2. One way you can show that you trust God is to
a. do what you want.
b. do what Gods wants.

3. You can trust God to do
a. very little.
b. what is best for you.

4. The first commandment says to put God
a. in church.
b. first.

B. Finish the first commandment. Choose two words from the box.

Jesus / God / me / Moses

1. I am the Lord, your ____________________.

2. You shall not have any other god besides ____________________.

C. Draw a line from the word prayer to every sentence that tells about prayer.

Prayer

a. is talking and listening to God.
b. keeps you close to God.
c. works like magic.
d. puts God first in your life.
e. helps you keep God's laws.

CHAPTER 7 God's Name

TEACHER RESOURCE CENTER

Faith Formation

CHECK THE CATECHISM

Paragraphs 2142–2167 of the *Catechism of the Catholic Church* present some of the practical ways in which the second commandment can be followed. Paragraph 2159 is especially eloquent in describing the importance of the Christian name in eternity.

God's Name Is Holy

Mary's Canticle is her hymn of praise following the angel's message that Mary is to become the mother of Jesus. Mary says, "God who is mighty has done great things for me, holy is his name." The second commandment teaches that the name of God is indeed holy, and not to be used without reverence. Respect for God's name is vital. Promises, oaths, and vows that are made in God's name are not to be taken lightly. Using God's name in prayer gives honor and glory to the God "who has done great things" for those who believe.

How do you react when you hear the name of God or of Jesus used inappropriately?

Scripture tells us that God bestowed on Jesus "the name that is above every other name" *(Philippians 2:9)*. Because the name of Jesus is sacred, his followers are called to show reverence for it. To honor the name of Jesus is to honor God's name. Because the name of Jesus Christ is holy, his followers reverence the name of Jesus. The Sign of the Cross is an everyday reminder of the importance of reverencing God's name.

When you were baptized, your own name was made holy. What is the significance of your name in your family?

Background

Honor God's Name

Chapter 7 focuses on the second commandment and using God's name with respect. Children are into names. They enjoy rhyming their names, making up names, calling people names. There are opportunities within the chapter for the children to examine the right and wrong uses of names. The lesson hinges on the fact that using a person's name with respect shows respect for the person.

Once the children understand the significance of how names are used, it is a logical step for them to see that God, who is holy, has a name that is holy. The names of God and Jesus are to be used with honor and respect. The children will discover names the Church uses for God and how these names tell about God. Address God by a variety of names in your classroom prayers so that the children grow in their personal understanding of God.

Faith Summary

- God's name is holy.
- Honor and belief are expressed in God when God's name is respected.
- Holy people, holy places, and holy things are given respect.

Growth and Development

It is helpful to remember two characteristics of second graders as you teach this lesson:

- ***Second graders engage in name-calling.*** It is a common occurrence for children their age.
- ***Second graders are capable of seeing things from another's point of view.*** If there is a problem with name-calling, have students talk about how people feel when they are called names.

A Teacher's Prayer

Triune God—Creator, Redeemer, Sanctifier—you are always with me and mindful of me. You call me by name. Bless me with a kind and patient heart that treats every child with respect. Amen.

Vocabulary Preview

respect
holy

Scripture

Psalm 29:2: Give glory to the Lord.
Psalm 8:1: Glorious is the Lord's name.
Matthew 16:15–18: Jesus renames Simon.

Related Resources

Books

McBride, Alfred. *The Ten Commandments: Covenant of Love* (St. Anthony Messenger Press, 1-800-488-0488 or www.AmericanCatholic.org). Chapter two provides helpful background on the second commandment. (Adult)

Sasso, Sandy Eisenberg. *In God's Name* (Treehaus Communications, 1-800-638-4287 or www.treehaus1.com). This children's book is a spiritual celebration of all the people of the world and their belief in one God. (Children)

TEACHER ORGANIZER

Planning Guide

The basic content for each chapter is divided into four class sessions. There are a number of options for the fifth session. Extension, review, and testing options are described under Day 5 Alternatives. The Quick Check box will help you evaluate the week's lessons.

Chapter Goals

In this chapter, the students will learn about

- ❏ Respectful use of names
- ❏ Respect for God's name
- ❏ The second commandment

	DAY 1 · INVITATION	DAY 2 · DISCOVERY	DAY 3 · DISCOVERY
OBJECTIVES	**The students will be able to** • Share how it feels when their name is used to say something good • Choose a name that describes them	**The students will be able to** • Make the association that using a person's name with respect shows respect for the person • Recognize that God is holy and so is God's name	**The students will be able to** • Name ways to use God's name with respect • Discern ways to follow the second commandment • Discover names used for God
PREPARATION	• Ahead of time, ask those who belong to a team to bring in their team shirts • If needed, make copies of the resource master on page 174	• Read about making Word Webs, page 164 • Write the second commandment on the board	• Prepare the reading of the story • Consider taking the children to church tomorrow to practice prayerful gestures
MATERIALS	• Drawing supplies • Pencils	• Pencils	• Writing paper, a sheet per child • Crayons or markers • Pencils
OPTIONAL ACTIVITIES	• **Curriculum Challenge** Gather drawing paper, markers, scissors, a cord, and clothespins • **Options** For a survey on names, have graph paper	• **Learning To Pray** Use of different names for God • **Teaching Tip** Make a Word Web • **Vocabulary** Create a wall of words	• **Options** Gather a bag of balloons • **Ideas That Work** Consider forming a Welcoming Committee

Learning Objectives

By the end of this chapter, the students should be able to

- ❑ Understand that respect for a name shows respect for a person
- ❑ Recognize the second commandment
- ❑ Determine ways to follow the second commandment

DAY 4 · LIVING	DAY 5 · ALTERNATIVES
The students will be able to • Analyze actions that do and do not show respect for God • Praise the Lord • Use God's name in blessing	**There are a number of alternatives to help you plan Day 5.** **Prayer Experience** Use the Prayer of Praise on Day 4 or Day 5. **Review and Explore** Follow the suggestions that are given in the plans. **Home and Family** Send the page home with the children. **The Church Today** Use this activity to start discussion on people in our lives who show God's goodness to us. **Chapter Test** The chapter test appears as a resource master on page 175.
• Consider the groups you will form and the leaders you will choose	
• Pencils • Sturdy paper, rulers, hole punch, yarn, scissors	
• **Options** Have students ring small bells to accompany the Prayer of Praise	

Quick Check

Do this evaluation as soon as you finish each chapter.

Did I follow my lesson plan?

How can I tell that I met the learning objectives for the lesson?

What activities did the children enjoy most?

How could I improve this lesson?

Benziger on the Web
For more ideas, visit us at www.benziger.glencoe.com

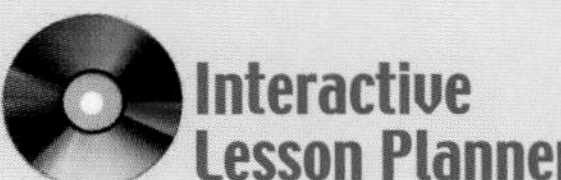

Interactive Lesson Planner
Your ILP provides more help in preparing to teach this chapter.

Celebrate
Turn to page 22 of this book. Check for seasonal celebrations.

Lesson Plan · Day 1

Start this chapter about God's name by saying hello to every child by name. That will get their attention! Then have the children focus on the chapter title and Scripture verse. Call attention to the Do You Know? question.

1 Introduction

Invite the children to look at the picture on student page 106. Ask how many of them belong to a team that has a tee shirt. Encourage the children to tell a little about what it is like to have a team shirt. How do they feel when they hear someone cheer their name?

2 That's My Name!

Read aloud the text. Open discussion to the class. How do you feel when people use your name to say something good? Invite everyone to turn to someone who sits nearby and say something good about that person, using the person's name.

CURRICULUM CHALLENGE

Art Think about using the activity on page 107 as an art project. Have drawing paper, markers, and scissors on hand. Let the children draw and cut out a tee shirt shape, write their new name on it, and decorate it. (If you wish, draw a tee shirt form on a sheet of paper and make copies of it onto drawing paper for the children to cut out.) Bring in cord to string across the room and some clothespins to hang the shirts. Later on in the chapter, the children will discover names for God. Consider having the children draw their new name on one side of the paper shirt, and draw names for God on the other side.

Give to the Lord the glory due his name.

Psalm 29:2

Do You Know?

◆ How do you show respect for God's name?

Why were you given your name?

GOD'S NAME

That's My Name!

You have a name. Your first name tells who you are. Your last name tells that you belong to a family. When you hear your name, your ears perk up. Someone is calling you.

Tom and Terry, Dick and Mary, Bob and Betty, Lynn and Larry all want other people to know and respect their names!

3 Your Name
Have the children try to recall the names of the Seven Dwarfs. *(Sneezy, Sleepy, Doc, Grumpy, Bashful, Happy, Dopey)* Ask why the dwarfs were given those names. *(The names told about their personalities.)* Lead the children into the activity.

4 Activity
Be sure the children have time to think and talk among themselves before they begin the activity. Emphasize that just like the dwarfs' names, their new name is to tell something about them. When they have completed their work, let the children stand and give each other a cheer, using their names.

Tell about You

If your name is Robert, you may like to be called "Bob." If your name is Mary Jane, you might like to be called "M.J."

On the T-shirt, write the name you like to be called. Then draw little pictures on the shirt that will tell about you.

OPTIONS

For Those Who Learn Mathematically These children are logical thinkers who use numbers effectively. They may do a survey on classmates' names and make a graph of their discoveries. For example, the children could graph the first names of their classmates, or graph the ethnic background of the surnames.

Lesson Plan · Day 2

Do a name chant. Make up your own, or follow this pattern. A child calls out his or her name. The class responds. "Hello, Bobby, how are you today?" The child responds, "Very fine, I thank you." The class then says, "Who is next?" Give everyone a chance.

1 Introduction

Ask the children if they have nicknames. What kinds of nicknames do the children have for brothers, sisters, uncles, aunts, and grandparents? Ask: What do those nicknames tell about those people?

2 Many Names

Tell the children that God has special names too. The names tell all about him. Have the class read the paragraphs on page 108. Direct the children's attention to the chart. Read the many names for God. Ask the children to help you think about the meaning behind each one.

TEACHING TIP

As part of the activity on page 111, you can make a Word Web to help the children analyze the names for God. Write the two names on the board and circle them. As the children suggest what the name reveals about God, they draw a line extending from the name. On the line they write what it tells about God. Soon the Word Webs will resemble many-legged spiders.

Many Names for God

WORD OF GOD

O Lord, our Lord, how glorious is your name over all the earth!

Psalm 8:1

You call your family members and your friends by name. There is Uncle Joe and Aunt Tessie. Cousin Fritz is from the country. Grandpa Bill lives in the city. You have special names for those closest to you. Mother, Mommy, Mom, Mama, and Madre are names for a mother. Father, Papa, Daddy, Dad, Padre are names for a father.

God wants you to call him by name. Jesus said to his friends, "When you pray, say 'Our Father.'" Jesus taught his friends to call God "Father."

God has many names. The chart will help you know some of the names for God.

Many Names God The Blessed Trinity Three Persons in One God		
Father Lord Creator Almighty God	**Son** Jesus Christ Savior Master	**Holy Spirit** Comforter Guide Helper
God is love You can call God a friend		

3 Respect
Make up a silly name and ask the children to say it with different feelings (anger, happiness, kindness). After each feeling, ask how that person would feel to hear his name said that way. Say that we all want to have our name used with respect. Read Word of God now or wait until Review and Explore.

4 God's Name
Write the word *respect* on the chalkboard, and ask the children to suggest what it means. Ask: What does respect have to do with the way we use people's names? Have a child or the class read aloud the paragraph on page 109. Ask: How is God's name different from your name? *(God is holy, so God's name is holy. God's name is honored.)*

5 Honor God's Name
Share the information given on the page. Tell the children that the second commandment tells us to use God's name with honor and respect. Ask all to read aloud This We Believe! Give time for the children to do the activity.

Honor God's Name

You want your friends to respect your name. You don't like it when someone says your name in anger or to tease you.

God wants you to honor his name, too. You can use God's name when you pray. You can use God's name when you talk to your friends and family about God. Never use God's name with disrespect or in anger or to show off.

God's name is holy. We must honor God's name.

ACTIVITY BREAK THE CODE

Use the code to find two names for God. Talk about how you can honor God's name.

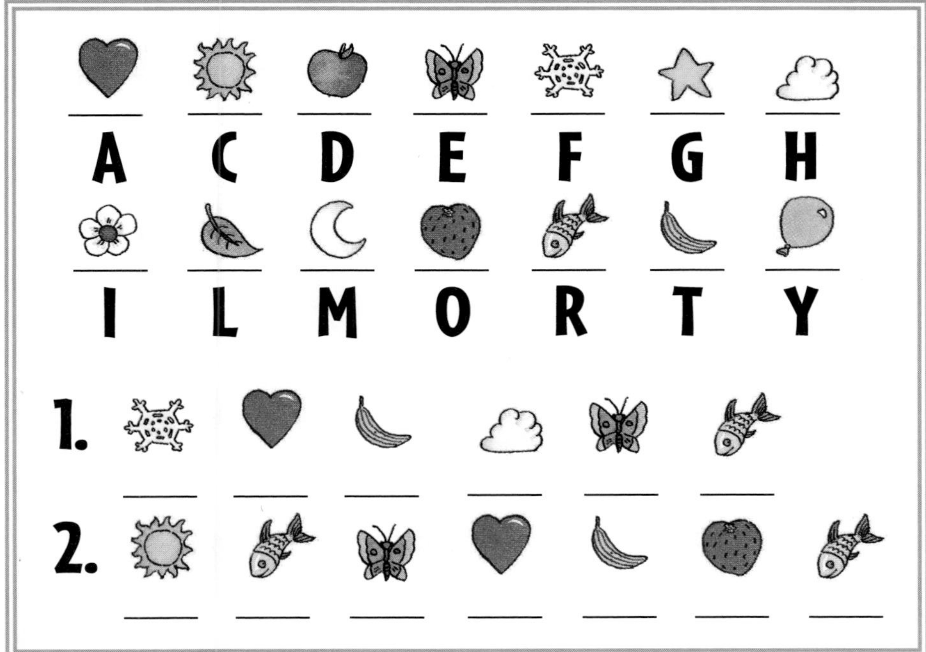

VIRTUE FAITH GRACE VOCABULARY

Respect To treat others the way you want to be treated.

Holy Full of goodness; God is holy and so, God's name is holy.

If you wish, create a display of words that tell how to treat others. So far, your wall would have the words *respect* and *trust* and words you may have introduced in other subject areas. Use the words in writing exercises. You may want to put a photograph of the children on the display. Add a title such as "Treat Us This Way" or "We Treat Others With . . ."

Lesson Plan · Day 3

Connect to yesterday's lesson by asking volunteers to share a time when hearing their name made them feel good.

1 Introduction

Ask the children to pretend they are new on a team, in a school, or in a neighborhood. Some children may share how they would feel. Then, say that you are going to read a story about a boy named Joey who is new in school. Ask the children to listen for ways the people in the story use Joey's name.

2 Joey's Day

Read the story and then ask how Joey's name was used.

LEARNING TO PRAY

Encourage the children to use the names they have learned for God when they pray. Now and then, use the names in class prayers. "Creator God" is particularly appropriate when thanking or praising God for his gifts of creation. "God our Father" is fitting when we pray for our needs and the needs of others.

IDEAS THAT WORK

Engage the children in making your classroom a welcoming place. Creat a Welcoming Committee, and establish some guidelines. How are visitors to the classroom greeted? Who answers the knock on the door? How often are people invited to the room? What are good ways to welcome a new student? If CCD children use the room, how are they welcomed?

The First Day

Joey had butterflies the size of eagles in his stomach. Not only was he going to a new school, he was arriving late—four weeks late. He knew that everybody would have friends. He knew that he would be behind in spelling.

He peeked into Sister Mary Frances's room. "Come on in," the sister said. "We have been waiting for you. Children, this is Joey Antonelli."

The children got out of their seats and surrounded Joey. "Hi!" said one boy. "My name is Stan, but you can call me Red."

"I am Carrie Ann," said one of the girls.

In no time at all, Joey had met everyone in the class. Then Sister said, "Joey, see if you can find the seat we prepared for you."

Joey looked around. On the first seat in the third row was a big red balloon. On the balloon were the words, "Welcome, Joey!"

Joey's butterflies were all gone.

How do you feel when somebody remembers your name?

3 Show Respect
Remind the children that Joey felt much better about being the new kid when he heard his name with a big welcome in front of it! Ask the children to share some of the words of praise that are used along with their names. Read the material on student page 111.

4 Activity
For the activity, tell the children to think of some praise words that they can use along with God's name. Have the children complete the activity.

Show Respect

When the children welcomed Joey, they showed him respect. When you use someone's name with care, you are showing respect, too.

You may have heard people use God's name in anger. You may have heard them use God's name to be mean. If you want to show your love for God, you will always use his name with care. You will use Jesus and Mary's name with care, too.

ACTIVITY SHOW YOU CARE

On the balloons, write or draw three ways you can show respect for God's name.

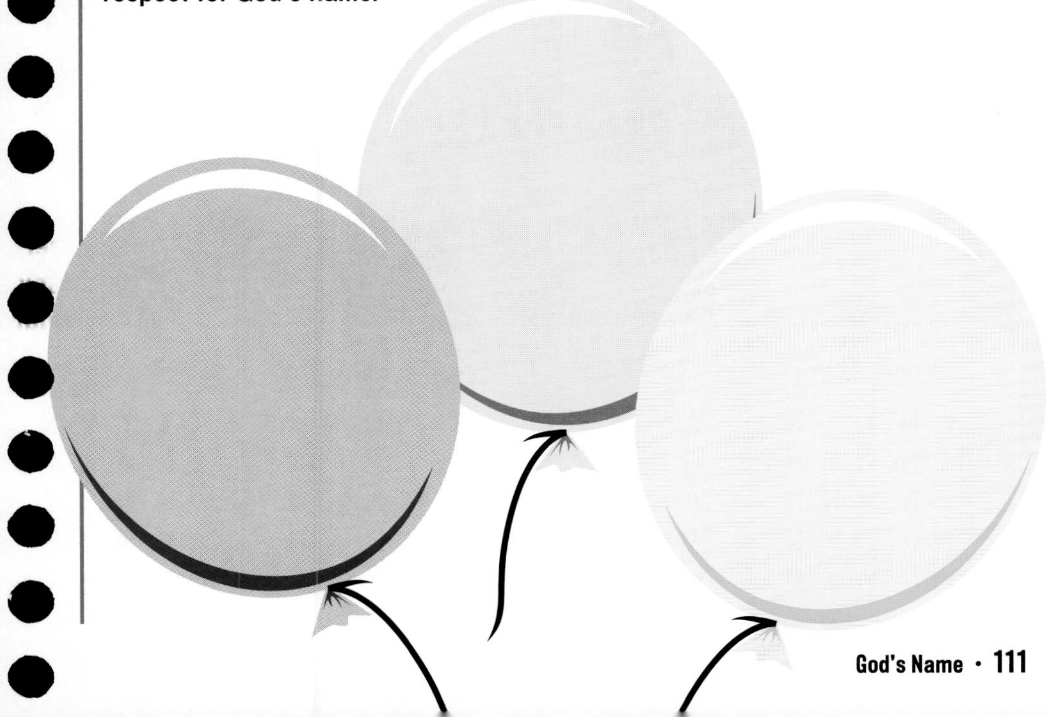

OPTIONS

For Those Who Learn Interpersonally These children work well with others and focus outward to other individuals. Let these children form a group. Give them a bag of balloons. They may use the balloons to surprise another class. Let the group decide how to use the balloons and what to say when they deliver the surprise.

Lesson Plan · Day 4

Let volunteers suggest respectful names they would use when praying to God.

❶ Using God's Name

Call attention to the letter grids on student page 112. Get the children interested in the activity by saying that if they do the activity just right, the grids will form a word. *(holy)* Explain how to do the page. If you wish, let each child decide whether to do the page independently or whether to meet with you and be guided through it.

TEACHING TIP

We retain 70% of what we talk about with others, 80% of what we experience personally, and 90% of what we teach someone else. In step 2 of the plan, set the children up for success. Meet with the leaders of the groups and have them read through the directions. Have them explain how to make the bookmark. Then they will be ready to teach the members of their group.

LIVING

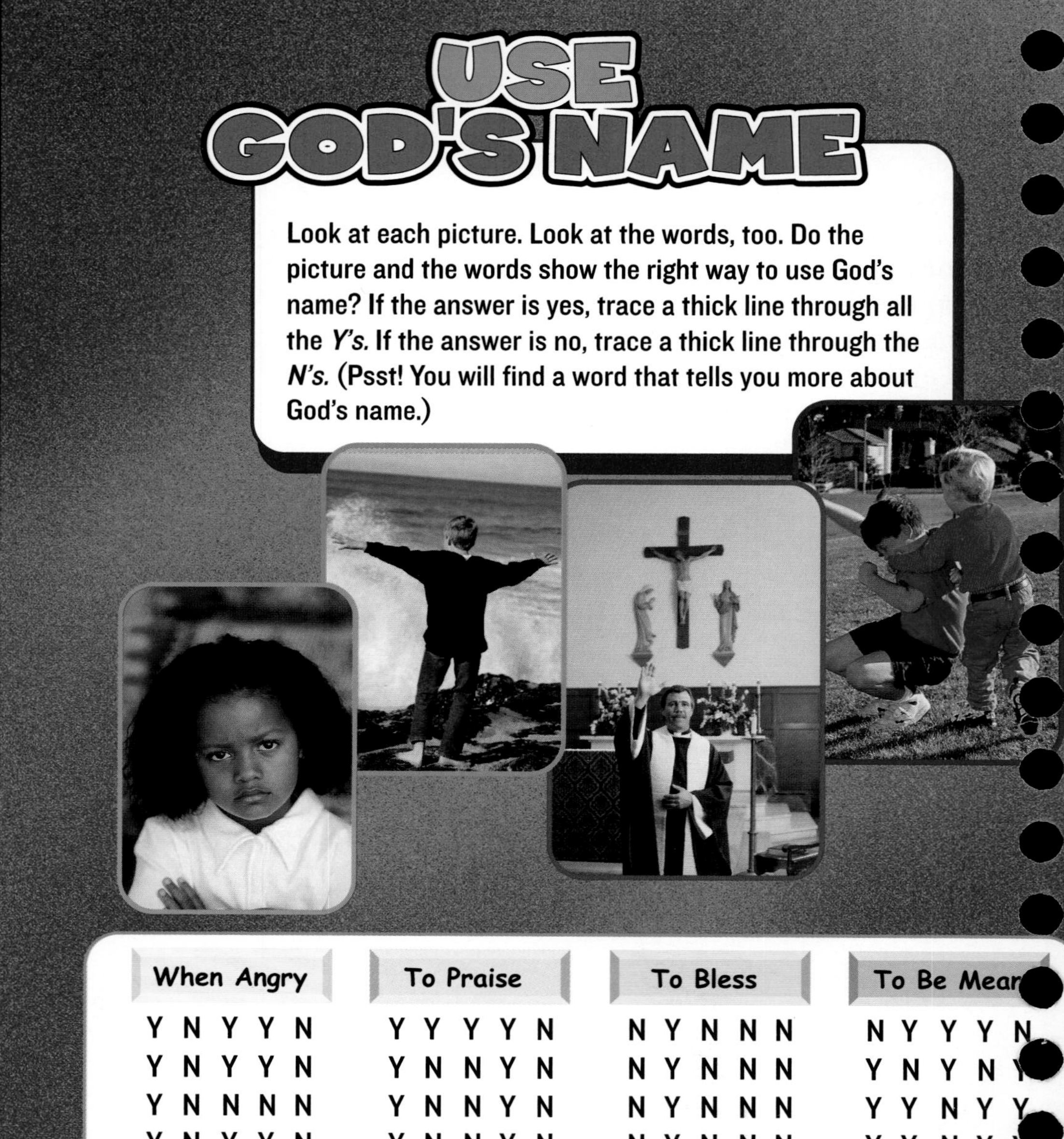

USE GOD'S NAME

Look at each picture. Look at the words, too. Do the picture and the words show the right way to use God's name? If the answer is yes, trace a thick line through all the *Y's.* If the answer is no, trace a thick line through the *N's.* (Psst! You will find a word that tells you more about God's name.)

When Angry	To Praise	To Bless	To Be Mea
Y N Y Y N	Y Y Y Y N	N Y N N N	N Y Y Y N
Y N Y Y N	Y N N Y N	N Y N N N	Y N Y N Y
Y N N N N	Y N N Y N	N Y N N N	Y Y N Y Y
Y N Y Y N	Y N N Y N	N Y N N N	Y Y N Y Y
Y N Y Y N	Y Y Y Y N	N Y Y Y Y	Y Y N Y Y

112 · Loving God

❷ Don't Forget!
Divide the children into groups. Choose a child in each group to distribute the supplies, and choose a leader to explain how to make the bookmark. Sit in on each group and give encouragement and help. When the bookmarks have been made, give the children time to place them in a textbook.

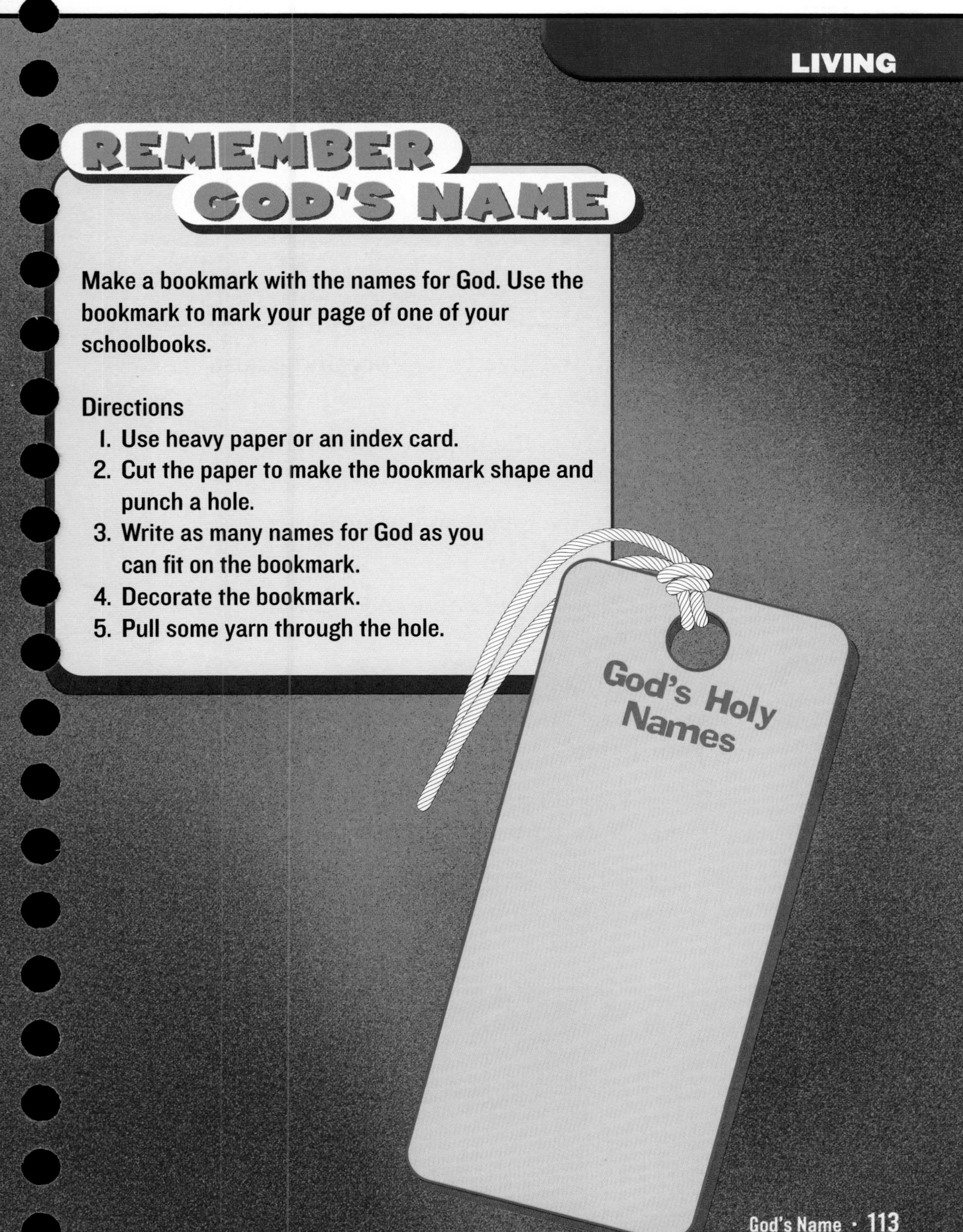

LIVING
REMEMBER GOD'S NAME
Make a bookmark with the names for God. Use the bookmark to mark your page of one of your schoolbooks.
Directions
1. Use heavy paper or an index card.
2. Cut the paper to make the bookmark shape and punch a hole.
3. Write as many names for God as you can fit on the bookmark.
4. Decorate the bookmark.
5. Pull some yarn through the hole.
God's Holy Names
God's Name · 113

IDEAS THAT WORK

It is difficult for the average second grade child to sit more than 15 to 20 minutes for one activity. Incorporate some movement into the day in simple ways. When you read a story, have the children gather near you. When you pray, go to the prayer table or to a religious statue in the school. Have the children move to partner up. Moving around may take a little time, but it is worth the effort. The children will often work better because of it.

3 The Lord

Tell the children that another name often used for God is *Lord.* God is called Lord in the Bible; people pray to the Lord during Mass. The name Lord is a name of respect.

4 A Prayer of Praise

Direct attention to the prayer. Have the children use an index finger to move down the page and find a word that means *praise. (glory)* They should be able to determine the word from the context clues and from their knowledge of the word *praise*. Practice the prayer with enthusiasm. Recall the posture of praise—arms out, palms up. Then, gather to pray. To facilitate use of the prayer posture, say a line of the prayer and have the children repeat it.

LEARNING TO PRAY

For the prayer of praise, focus on how to say the prayer. Ask: What is a good way to praise the Lord? Practice the prayer until it is said with genuine enthusiasm.

OPTIONS

For Those Who Learn Musically The ringing of bells has long been a tradition in the Church. Try to get a collection of small bells donated for your classroom. Children may ring the bells during prayers of praise, much like the bells are rung during the "Gloria" of the Easter Eucharist. Bells may be rung to accompany today's prayer.

WE PRAISE YOUR NAME

ALL: Lord, we give you Glory and praise your name.

BOYS: Holy is the name of God who made the earth and the sky.

ALL: Lord, we give you Glory and praise your name.

GIRLS: Holy is the name of God who made us.

ALL: Lord, we give you Glory and praise your name.

BOYS: We will always honor God's holy name.

ALL: Lord, we give you Glory and praise your name.

1 Know
The children may read Word of God on page 108 aloud. Pose: The Bible says that God's name is glorious. How should we use God's name? Now refer to the graphic. Review how our prayers and actions keep God's name holy. Have a child summarize the second commandment.

2 Love and Serve
Refer the children back to the chart of God's names on student page 108. Ask the children to choose two of God's names that mean the most to them. Ask them to use those two names to write their prayer for the Love activity. Talk to the children about the times that children about the times that God's name might not be used with respect. How can they use God's name with respect? Have the children complete the Serve section.

3 God's Friends
Recall that the children gave themselves new names that told about them. Ask the children to listen to the story of Jesus giving his friend, Simon, a new name. Read the story. Ask: What was Simon's new name? What did Simon's new name tell about him? Show the illustration of Peter.

Know

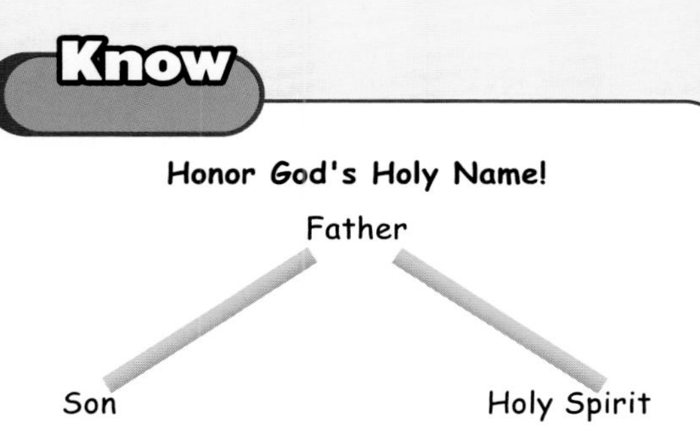

Love

In the space, write a short prayer that uses at least two of God's names.

Serve

Create a plan of action. How will all of you remind one another to honor God's name? Use the space to start your plan.

CHAPTER 7 REVIEW and EXPLORE

GOD'S FRIENDS

Saint Peter

One day Jesus asked his followers, "Who do you say I am?" Simon said, "You are the Son of God." Jesus was happy with Simon's answer. Jesus said, "Simon, your name will now be Peter, which means rock. You will be the leader of my Church."

A Little Catechism

Invite the children to open their religion books to *A Little Catechism.* Choose one or more of the selections below for memory work or reinforcement. You will find your copy of the catechism on pages 23–43 of this Teacher's Edition.

1. Read about the Trinity on page 11. Repeat the last line.
2. Call attention to the Ten Commandments on page 11. Emphasize the second commandment. Repeat it several times.

Know | Love | Serve

Note The activities on this page provide ways for the children to share their learning with their families. The activities are related to the week's theme.

1 Introduce

Briefly explain how to do the two activities. Ask volunteers to share their experiences doing the activities from the previous lesson.

2 Pray Together

Pray the verse in rounds. Let one row of children begin; give each row a signal to start. Repeat the verse until you give a signal to stop. All the voices blending should make a joyful sound of praise.

Online for Families
Remind the children to check the Benziger Web site this week with their families.
www.benziger.glencoe.com

CHAPTER 7
HOME and FAMILY

Dear Family,

I have just finished chapter 7. I have learned that God has many names. God wants us to call him by name. God also wants us to honor his holy name. Help me use God's name with love and respect.

With others

With a friend, make a pact to remind each other to be polite and respectful of others. Try your pact for a week. See what happens.

With your family

As a family, make a report card on using God's name. Talk about how you all use God's name. Do you use it for prayer and praise? Do you ever use it in anger? Do you ever use God's name carelessly?

I praise the name of the Lord.

GO ONLINE!
http://www.benziger.glencoe.com

1 Introduce
Share the information given on student page 117.

2 The Project
Point out the illustrations of church, school and home. Talk with the children about how people in all those places and more can help us see God's goodness. Have the children complete the activity by drawing people who help them learn about God's goodness at church, school and home.

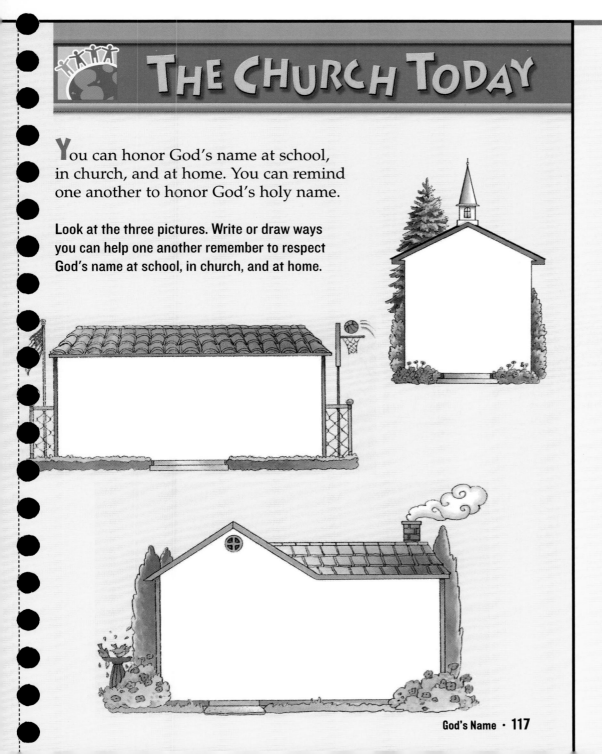

THE CHURCH TODAY

You can honor God's name at school, in church, and at home. You can remind one another to honor God's holy name.

Look at the three pictures. Write or draw ways you can help one another remember to respect God's name at school, in church, and at home.

RESOURCE MASTERS

The resource master on page 174 helps the children identify themselves as Catholics. The children may need help identifying the pope and your bishop. They may question you; or, you may use the opportunity to ask another teacher or school administrator to visit for a few minutes and be interviewed. The children will need pencils.

ANSWER KEY

This is the answer key for the chapter test on page 175.

A. name, vain

B. 1. a 2. a 3. b

C. 1 and 2

D. 1, 4, and 5

Name ______________________________

I Am a Catholic

Fill in each line.

______________________ teaches me about God.

Another Catholic I know is ______________________.

The pope is named ______________________.

The name of our bishop is ______________________.

My favorite saint is ______________________.

A way I treat God's name with respect is ______________________

____

____

____

____

____

____

Name ______________________________

Chapter 7 Test

A. Finish the second commandment. Choose two words from the box.

vain / hand / name / respect

You shall not use the ____________ of the Lord your God in ____________.

B. Circle the words that best finish each sentence.

1. When you respect a person's name, you show
a. respect for the person.
b. you do not care.

2. Jesus said to pray to God as
a. our Father.
b. our Brother.

3. God's name is different from all other names. God's name is
a. hard to say.
b. holy.

C. Put a check by reasons to respect God's name.

_____ **1.** You believe in God.

_____ **2.** You honor God.

_____ **3.** You are angry.

D. Circle three names for God.

1. Father **2.** Joseph **3.** Moses **4.** Creator **5.** Lord

CHAPTER 8 Sunday

TEACHER RESOURCE CENTER

Faith Formation

Give God Thanks and Praise

> ***They devoted themselves to the teaching of the apostles and to the communal life, to the breaking of the bread and to the prayers.***
>
> ***Acts 2:42***

CHECK THE CATECHISM

The *Catechism of the Catholic Church* describes Sunday as "A day of grace and rest from work." More about the third commandment can be found in paragraphs 2168–2195.

Each Sunday, Catholics gather to thank and praise God at Mass. Sunday worship offers "time out" from the hectic pace of everyday life. It is an opportunity to spend time with family and friends praying together as a faith community. Sunday is a day set aside from the rest of the week, designated by Christians as fulfillment of the "Sabbath of solemn rest, holy to the Lord" *(Exodus 20:11).*

What activities or rituals have you developed to make Sunday special?

Keep Holy the Lord's Day

The third commandment presents a challenge for busy people with much to accomplish each week. But it is important to find ways to slow the pace and rest in God's abundant love and to discover the peace that Sunday can bring. Sunday commemorates the day Jesus rose from the dead. Each Sunday can be a "little Easter," full of promise and hope, when time is taken to rest, reflect, and rejoice in God's presence.

How does Sunday Mass help you focus your week?

Background

Sundays and Mass

Chapter 8 ends the unit on love for God. The chapter focuses on the third commandment, keeping Sunday holy. As you will see, the information is given gradually, continually linking the children's experiences to an understanding of the commandment. The children learn that the Mass is the most important way of keeping Sunday holy. Because the children are dependent on adults to help them follow the commandment, it can be frustrating to teach if families are not attending Mass each week.

If you find that the school population is not celebrating Sunday Mass, you may suggest a faculty meeting to address the situation. If your school does not do so, initiate monthly school Masses, with each grade taking the lead in planning.

Faith Summary

- **We honor God by keeping Sunday holy.**
- **The Mass is the most important way to keep Sunday holy.**
- **We have the privilege and obligation to participate in Sunday Mass.**

Growth and Development

It is helpful to remember two characteristics of second graders as you teach this lesson:

- ***Second graders respond to the enthusiasm of adult role models.*** Create in the children an enthusiasm for spending time with God. Share your own joy in the Eucharist; your attitude will be noticed and emulated.
- ***Second graders will learn rituals easily and will want to be contributors to liturgical celebrations.*** Practice the gestures used at Mass so that the children see they are part of a holy and special celebration.

A Teacher's Prayer

I thank you, Lord, for the wonders of creation.
I thank you for new life in Jesus Christ.
Remove from me anxiety and weariness and give me Sunday's holy rest. Bless me as I carry on my vocation to love and serve you. Amen.

Vocabulary Preview

Mass
worship

Scripture

Acts 2:42: All who believed came together to break bread and pray.

Related Resources

Video

"Why Do We Go To Mass On Sunday?" (St. Anthony Messenger Press, 1-800-488-0488 or www.AmericanCatholic.org). This video helps young viewers appreciate the Sunday Eucharist as the source and summit of the faith life. (Children, 13 minutes)

Books

Muller, Wayne. *Sabbath* (Bantam Books, www.bantamdell.com). This book teaches the reader how to use the Sabbath to refresh body, mind, and soul. (Adult)

Osborne, Rick & Bowler, K. Christie. *I Want To Know About The Ten Commandments* (Zondervan 1-800-727-1309 or www.zondervankidz.com). See the section that deals with the third commandment. (Children)

TEACHER ORGANIZER

Planning Guide

The basic content for each chapter is divided into four class sessions. There are a number of options for the fifth session. Extension, review, and testing options are described under Day 5 Alternatives. The Quick Check box will help you evaluate the week's lessons.

Chapter Goals

In this chapter, the students will learn about

- ❑ Sunday as the day to give to God
- ❑ Going to Mass on Sunday
- ❑ The Mass as a celebration

	DAY 1 · INVITATION	DAY 2 · DISCOVERY	DAY 3 · DISCOVERY
OBJECTIVES	**The students will be able to** • Plan a special day for families • See that time spent with families is special	**The students will be able to** • Tell what makes Sunday special to Christians • Talk about reasons for spending time with God • Discover why the Mass is most important to the Church Family	**The students will be able to** • Conclude why the Mass is a celebration • Recognize that going to Mass shows love for God • Discover that sacramentals help us pray
PREPARATION	• Think about what made Sunday special to you as a child • Think about what makes Sunday special to you today	• If needed, make copies of the resource master on page 192 and distribute scissors (you may wish to include glue and sturdy paper)	• Consider using a Venn diagram to teach the Mass as a celebration
MATERIALS	• Pencils	• Pencils	• Pencils
OPTIONAL ACTIVITIES	• **Curriculum Challenge** If the children make plans for a special day, have drawing supplies and scissors on hand	• **Vocabulary** Be sure the children know that Catholics are Christians • **Resource Masters** Puzzle activity about keeping Sunday holy	• **Ideas That Work** Make a Venn diagram comparing and contrasting birthdays and Mass

Learning Objectives

By the end of this chapter, the students should be able to

- ❑ Describe Sunday as a holy day
- ❑ Recognize ways to keep Sunday holy
- ❑ Discover ways to join in the celebration of the Mass

DAY 4 · LIVING

The students will be able to

- Share ways to keep Sunday holy
- Determine ways to participate in Mass
- Celebrate love of God

- Pencils

- **Ideas That Work** Pictures of the different parts of the Mass, strips of paper, an envelope

DAY 5 · ALTERNATIVES

There are a number of alternatives to help you plan Day 5.

Prayer Experience
The prayer experience culminates Unit 2.

Review and Explore
Crayons and pencils are needed. Follow the suggestions on page 189 for teaching the Review and Explore.

Home and Family
Send the page home with the children.

The Church Today
The project involves drawing pictures of ways the children can keep the spirit of the Mass after the celebration is over. See suggestions on page 191.

Chapter Test
The chapter test appears as a resource master on page 193.

Quick Check

Do this evaluation as soon as you finish each chapter.

Did I follow my lesson plan?

How can I tell that I met the learning objectives for the lesson?

What activities did the children enjoy most?

How could I improve this lesson?

Benziger on the Web
For more ideas, visit us at www.benziger.glencoe.com

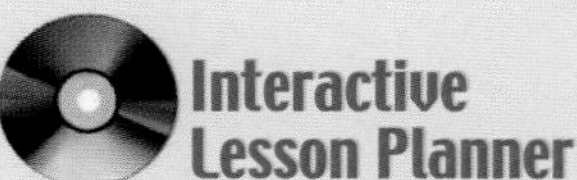

Interactive Lesson Planner
Your ILP provides more help in preparing to teach this chapter.

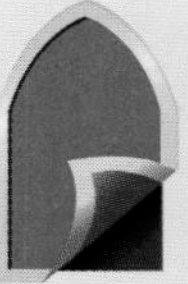

Celebrate
Turn to page 22 of this book. Check for seasonal celebrations.

Lesson Plan · Day 1

Have a brief talk with the children about their favorite day of the week.

1 Being Together

Tell the children they are going to hear a story about the Warner family. Ask them to listen for what makes Sunday a special day for the Warners. Read the story and have volunteers share their responses to the question in the student text on page 118. Then, call attention to the Do You Know? question and ask for more student responses.

Share what made Sundays special to you as a child, or tell some special Sunday routines that you have now, as an adult. The children will appreciate any facts you share. Say that people make days special by doing things together.

TEACHING TIP

When you can, let all children have a chance to share, particularly when the topic may benefit you. The plans the children share in this lesson may give you insights on ways to personalize your teaching. For example, does the sharing seem to indicate that a child is frequently left alone? Does the child's behavior indicate a need for attention?

INVITATION 8

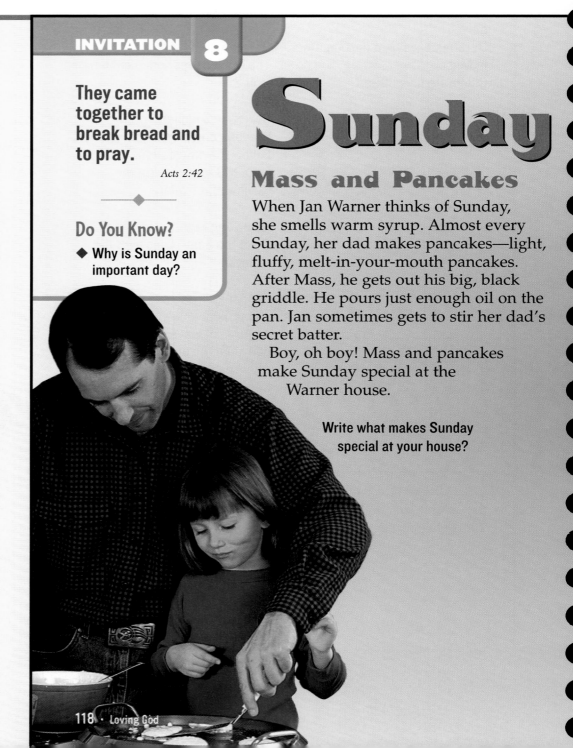

They came together to break bread and to pray.

Acts 2:42

Do You Know?

- Why is Sunday an important day?

Sunday

Mass and Pancakes

When Jan Warner thinks of Sunday, she smells warm syrup. Almost every Sunday, her dad makes pancakes—light, fluffy, melt-in-your-mouth pancakes. After Mass, he gets out his big, black griddle. He pours just enough oil on the pan. Jan sometimes gets to stir her dad's secret batter.

Boy, oh boy! Mass and pancakes make Sunday special at the Warner house.

Write what makes Sunday special at your house?

118 · Loving God

2 Activity
Invite the children to be in charge of planning a special day for their family. Before they write, let the children talk together and get ideas. Encourage the children to make up a name for their special Sunday and to write the name on the page, along with their plan. If time allows, let all of the children tell their plans.

3 Scripture
Invite the children to still themselves. Encourage them to listen as you read Acts 2:42. Explain that this week they will find out more about coming together to celebrate the Sunday Mass.

A Special Day

Is Sunday special at your house? What makes Sunday different from every other day? On the notebook page, write everything that makes Sunday special in your home. Then, write what makes Sunday special for your parish family.

At Home

At the Parish

CURRICULUM CHALLENGE

Art If school Open House or parent-teacher conferences are near, have the children make a display of their plans for a special day. The children may draw a big outline of a shape that suits their plans. Let imaginations flow. The children may then cut out the shape and write their plans on it. The families will enjoy seeing their children's plans and may take them home.

Lesson Plan · Day 2

Review by recalling some of the plans the children created for a special family day.

1 Sunday Celebration

Tell the children that Christians are people who believe in Jesus and follow him. We consider Sunday to be a special day. Read aloud This We Believe! Explain that Sunday is holy because it reminds us that God raised Jesus from the dead. Write on the board: *Sunday is a holy day*. Ask for a show of hands of those who agree that on special days you want to be with people who are special to you. Tell children that on God's special day Christians want to be with God. Talk about the good ways to keep Sunday holy.

Teaching Tip

The children in your classroom probably have a variety of Church experiences. Some may celebrate Mass weekly, while others may not go at all. Some may have good associations with Mass, while others may resent it. Let the children share their feelings and opinions about Mass without fearing your criticism. To help the children understand the Mass as a celebration, set a positive tone. Let your own love of the Eucharist be obvious. Teach the children that each of them is important to the celebration of the Mass. Always bring the Mass to the children's level of understanding, while showing them how to feel a part of the celebration.

This We Believe!

Sunday is a holy day because it reminds us that God raised Jesus from the dead.

Sunday Celebration

Christians gather every Sunday to **worship** God at Mass. They remember the life, death, and rising of Jesus. For Christians, Sunday is no ordinary day. Sunday is a day to celebrate. Sunday is the Lord's Day.

Part of Sunday's celebration is gathering for Mass. Some people go to Mass on Saturday evening. Most people go to Mass on Sunday morning.

When you go to Mass, you sing and pray. Maybe you even get to go to a special room to listen to God's Word with other children. You remember all the wonderful things Jesus did for you. Most of all, you remember that Jesus lived and died for you.

Activity — Sunday Mass

Write or draw what you like best about Sunday Mass at your Church.

2 No Ordinary Day
Say that Catholics believe the best way to be with God is at Mass. Share the information about the Mass on student page 120 and complete the activity.

3 Time Out
Explain to the children that the most important way to keep Sunday holy is to spend time with God at Mass. Tell them they can also keep Sunday holy by what they do with others. Ask for volunteers to tell the class ways they can make Sunday holy by spending time with others. Have the children complete the activity on student page 121.

Time Out

If you get tired while you are playing, what do you say? You say, "Time out." A time out gives you a chance to catch your breath.

Sunday is a time out for Christians. It is a day to pray. But it is also a day to rest. It is a day to be together with family or with friends.

Sunday is a day to have fun, too. It is a good day to take a family walk or have a family talk. It is a good day for games and quiet time, too.

ACTIVITY — FIND THE WORDS

Find and circle the words that tell about Sunday. There are four words to find.

A	P	T	Y	R	N	B	R	C
D	R	E	M	E	M	B	E	R
G	A	T	H	E	R	E	S	F
P	Y	G	R	Y	L	S	T	N

VOCABULARY

Worship To praise and honor God

Mass The celebration of Jesus' gift at the Last Supper

The children may be familiar with the word *Christian*, but it is always good to review who is a Christian. Be sure the children know that Catholics are Christians.

RESOURCE MASTERS

The resource master on page 192 is a puzzle-making activity on how to keep Sunday holy. For easier handling, the children may glue the page to sturdy paper and then cut out the pieces. Scissors are needed.

Lesson Plan · Day 3

Ask: What makes Sunday different from the other days of the week? *(Sunday is a holy day. On Sunday we go to Mass and spend time with God.)*

1 Background

Ask volunteers to tell times members of their family gather together to celebrate. Say that God's Family gathers to celebrate, too. The most important celebration is Sunday Mass.

2 Keep Sunday Holy

Emphasize: The Mass is most important to the Church Family. The Mass is the way we best show love for God. Then explain how to do the page. When all have completed the page, have the children read aloud the sentences about the Mass.

IDEAS THAT WORK

A Venn diagram is a good graphic to use to compare and contrast two items. The diagram is formed by drawing two circles, side-by-side and intersecting. Make a Venn diagram of circles labeled Birthday Celebration and Mass Celebration. Within the birthday circle, list suggestions as to what happens at a birthday celebration that does not happen at Mass. In the Mass circle, list suggestions as to what happens at Mass and not at a birthday celebration. In the area of intersection, list how the two celebrations are alike. You want to use this diagram to help children see the Mass as a celebration, so guide their responses accordingly. For example, the area of intersection may eventually read: gather, gifts, singing, decorations, eating.

Keep Sunday Holy

Every Sunday, Catholics must go to Mass. You go to Mass to show that you love God. You go to Mass to worship together. Look at the three pictures. In the box under each picture tell what you see. How are the people keeping Sunday Holy?

③ What Do You See?
Share: Just like birthday celebrations have special decorations, the church has special things it uses to celebrate the Mass. The things in church are holy because they have been blessed. Direct attention to the illustration on student page 123. Move from one item to the next. Tell the name of the item and its use. Let the children repeat the name after you.

④ This We Believe!
Once again, have the children read aloud This We Believe! on student page 120. Say that Jesus had been put to death. God raised Jesus from the dead on a Sunday. At Sunday Mass, we remember that Jesus was risen from the dead.

What Do You See?

When you go to Sunday Mass, there is much to see. There is much to hear, too. Look at the picture of the people gathered for Sunday Mass. Name what you see in the picture. Can you find these same things in your parish church?

LEARNING TO PRAY

In explaining the holy things used at Mass, focus on their importance, either as a sign of God *(bread and wine)* or as something that helps us pray to God *(crucifix)*.

Lesson Plan · Day 4

Ask the children to name some of the actions or rituals that they remember from Mass.

1 Preparation

See how many actions or rituals of the Mass the children can name. See if they can also name the significance behind them.

2 What Happens at Mass?

Read the directions for the activity. Review each of the statements in the activity. Allow children time to complete the activity. Review the answers in class.

TEACHING TIP

In talking about ways to keep Sunday holy, some children may mention that their family members work on Sundays, or their families shop and do errands on Sundays. Explain that the third commandment asks us not to do any unnecessary work on Sundays. Acknowledge that some families have to work on Sundays and cannot rest and relax. Do not voice judgement on them. Rather, try to lead the children to find simple ways to help their busy families enjoy the day.

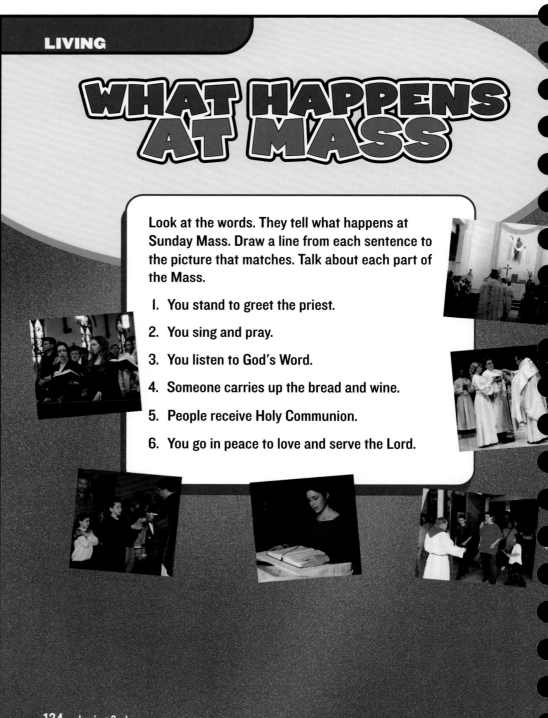

WHAT HAPPENS AT MASS

Look at the words. They tell what happens at Sunday Mass. Draw a line from each sentence to the picture that matches. Talk about each part of the Mass.

1. You stand to greet the priest.
2. You sing and pray.
3. You listen to God's Word.
4. Someone carries up the bread and wine.
5. People receive Holy Communion.
6. You go in peace to love and serve the Lord.

3 Doing Your Part

Tell the children that for the Mass to really mean something to them, they have to play a part, too. Remind the children that everyone has a part to play at Mass. Ask them to share what they think that means.

4 You At Mass

Read the introduction for the activity. Allow the children to complete the activity. You may want the children to work in pairs. After a few minutes, encourage pairs of children to compare their lists with one another. As a class you may want to create a class list with the best ways the children can take part in Mass.

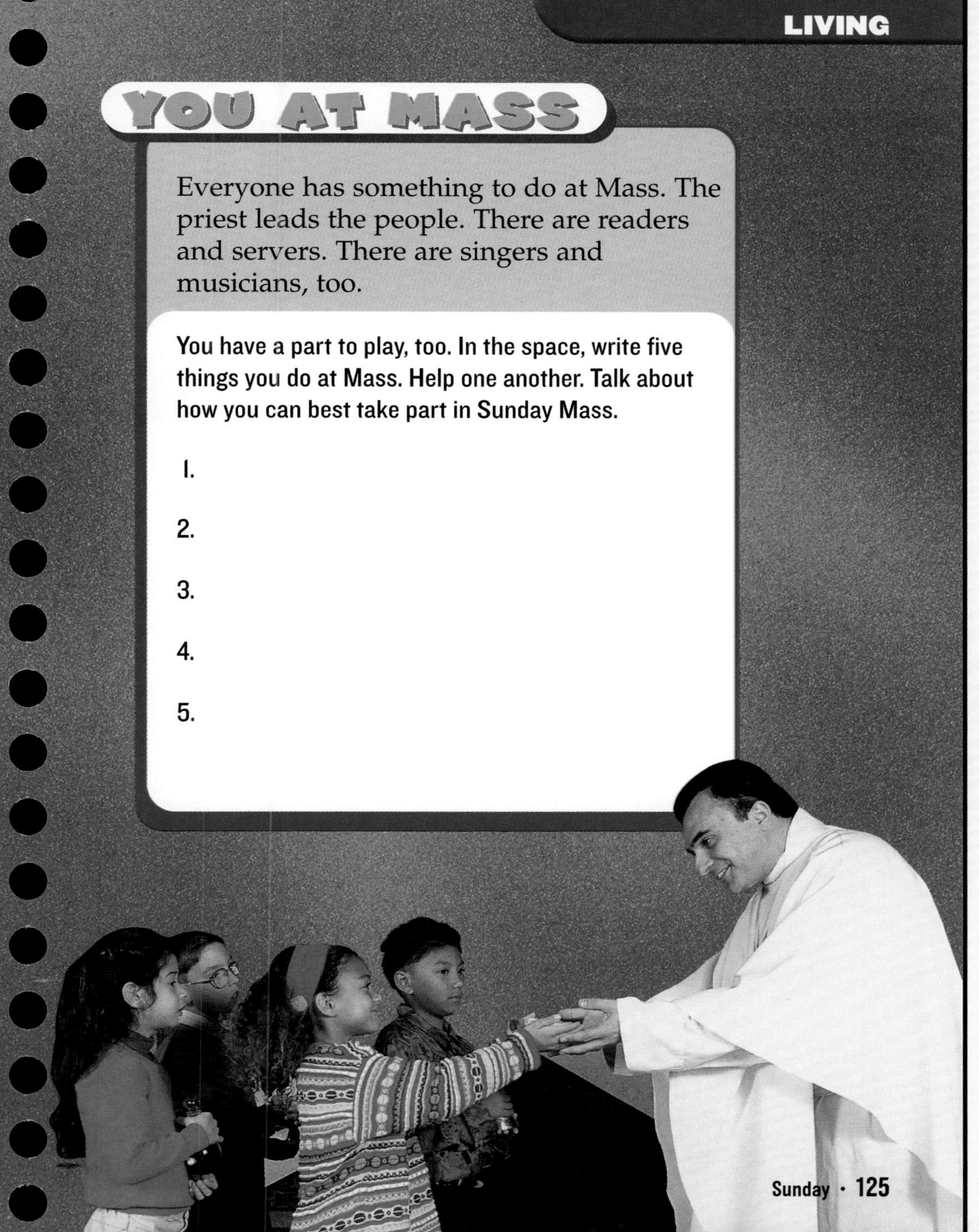

LIVING
YOU AT MASS
Everyone has something to do at Mass. The priest leads the people. There are readers and servers. There are singers and musicians, too.
You have a part to play, too. In the space, write five things you do at Mass. Help one another. Talk about how you can best take part in Sunday Mass.
1.
2.
3.
4.
5.
Sunday · 125

IDEAS THAT WORK

Use a matching activity to help the children identify the parts of the Mass. Cut out pictures of the different parts of the Mass from old textbooks. Write the different parts of the Mass on strips of paper. Keep both in an envelope. The children can match the statements with the pictures. For a little excitement, give them a time limit.

Prayer

Use the prayer on student page 126 for a prayer service with the class.

1 Prepare for Prayer

Gather the children for prayer. Lead the prayer or choose a good reader to lead. Invite the children to reflect on the importance of their participation in Sunday Mass.

2 A Sunday Prayer

Have the children look through the prayer service and highlight their lines. Choose a leader. Gather in the prayer center and begin the prayer.

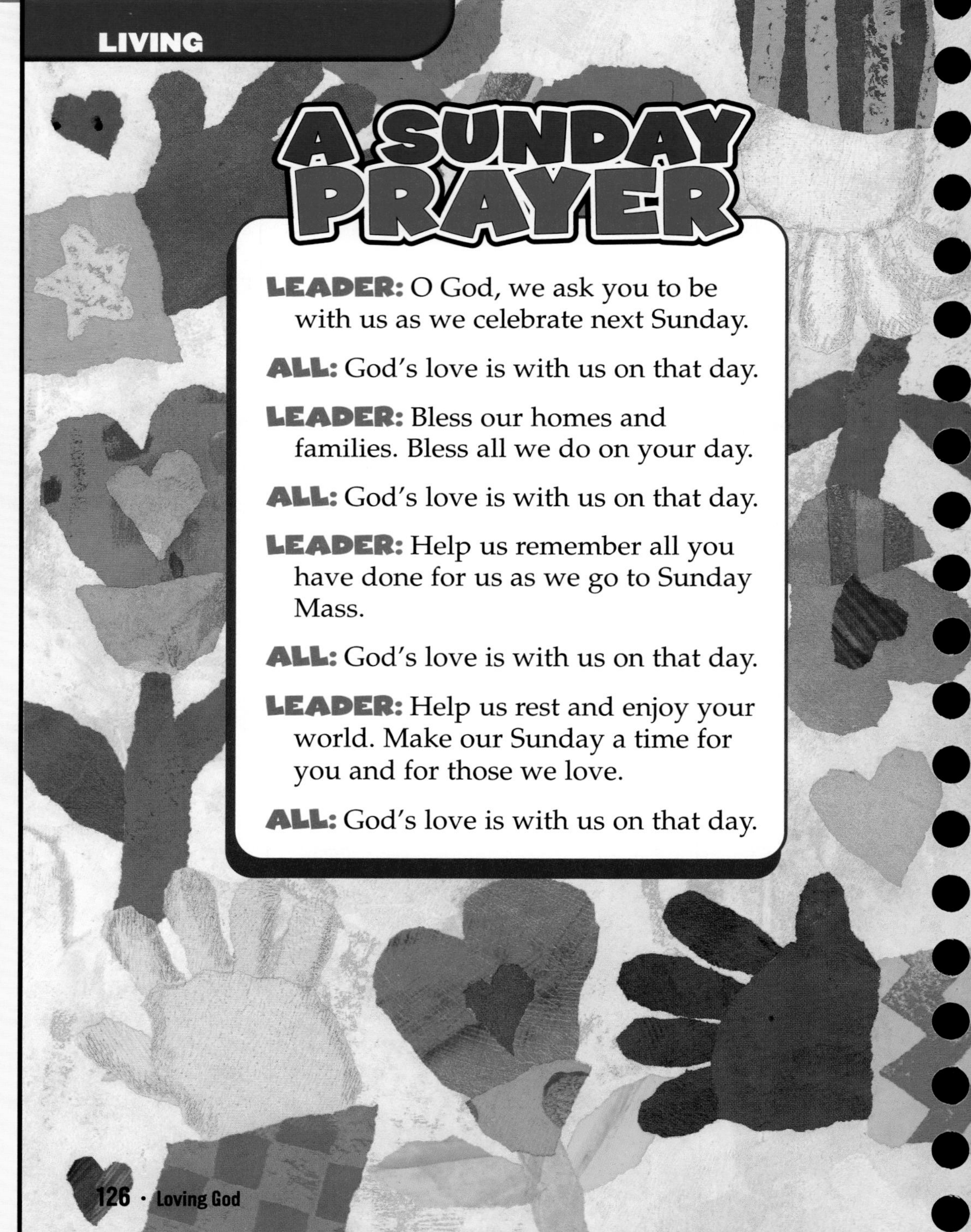

LIVING

A SUNDAY PRAYER

LEADER: O God, we ask you to be with us as we celebrate next Sunday.

ALL: God's love is with us on that day.

LEADER: Bless our homes and families. Bless all we do on your day.

ALL: God's love is with us on that day.

LEADER: Help us remember all you have done for us as we go to Sunday Mass.

ALL: God's love is with us on that day.

LEADER: Help us rest and enjoy your world. Make our Sunday a time for you and for those we love.

ALL: God's love is with us on that day.

126 · Loving God

1 Know
Call attention to the puzzle piece in the center; the other pieces tell ways to keep Sunday holy.

2 Love and Serve
Love: Ask the students to imagine their own homes and think about what is possible for them to do. Serve: Let the children talk about ways they can help others keep Sunday holy.

3 God's Friends
Show the illustration of John XXIII. Say that Pope John had been a pope when the children's grandparents were young. Ask if any of the children have heard the Mass said in another language.

CHAPTER 8
REVIEW and EXPLORE

Know

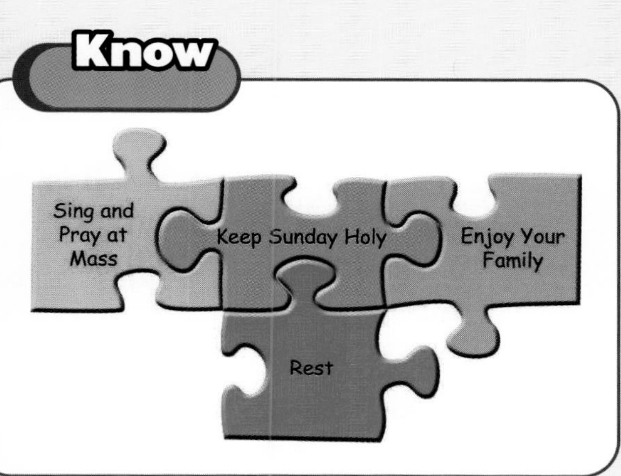
Sing and Pray at Mass
Keep Sunday Holy
Enjoy Your Family
Rest

Love

Write or draw one simple idea to celebrate Sunday in your home.

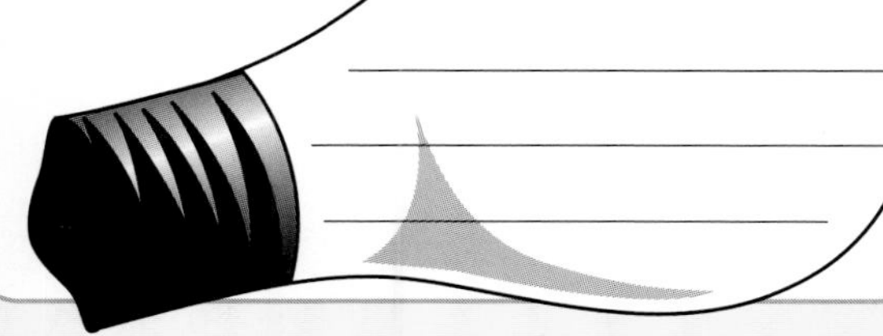

Serve

Write or draw one way you can help someone in your family have a better family celebration.

GOD'S FRIENDS

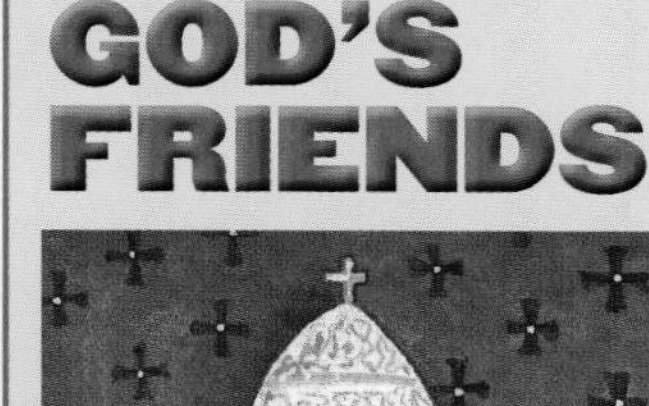

Blessed John XXIII

Pope John wanted everyone to love the Mass. He called a meeting of all the bishops in the world. Pope John and the bishops made changes in the Mass. They made sure you could understand the words. They made sure you would sing and celebrate.

A Little Catechism

Invite the children to open their religion books to *A Little Catechism.* Choose one or more of the selections below for memory work or reinforcement. You will find your copy of the catechism on pages 23–43 of this Teacher's Edition.

1. Review statements 7 and 8 on page 10.
2. Call attention to the third commandment on page 11. Have the children memorize it.
3. Read More About The Mass on page 22. Read, share and remember.

Know Love Serve

Note The activities on this page provide ways for the children to share their learning with their families. The activities are related to the week's theme.

1 Introduce
Recall the signs of God during the Mass—the holy water, the holy oil, the candle. There are signs of God at every Mass. Go through the activity and ask the children to look for the signs when they are in church. Ask if there are any questions.

2 Prayer Burst
Have the children stand to say the prayer.

Online for Families
Remind the children to check the Benziger Web site this week with their families.
www.benziger.glencoe.com

Dear Family,
I have just completed chapter 8. I learned that Sunday is a day to celebrate. It is a day to go to Mass. It is a day to rest and relax. It is the Lord's Day. You can help me by celebrating Sunday with me.

On your own
Make a sign that reminds everyone in the family that Sunday is a day to celebrate.

With your family
Next Sunday, get to church a few minutes early. Greet the other people who are coming to Mass. Sit as close to the altar as you can. Try to remember everything you see and hear. As a family, talk about the Mass. Tell why it is good to go to Mass every Sunday.

Lord, Sunday is your day! Let's celebrate!

GO ONLINE!
http://www.benziger.glencoe.com

1 Prepare
Share the information on the page about things that happen at Sunday Mass.

2 The Project
Crayons and paper circles are needed. Ask the children for ways they can keep the spirit of the Mass even after the celebration is over. Distribute one large paper circle to each child in groups of three. Assign each child in every group a picture to draw showing how they greet, listen, or share a meal during the week. Hang the pictures when they are completed.

THE CHURCH TODAY

You can keep the spirit of Sunday Mass going all week long. The pictures show three things that you do at Mass. Look at the pictures.

We listen.

We greet one another.

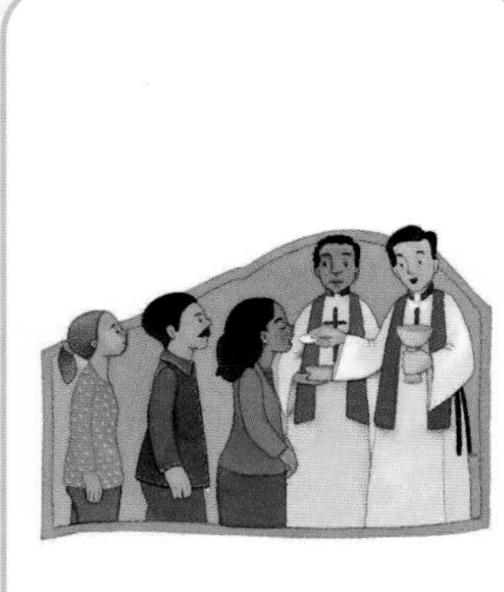

We share a meal.

Make a simple mobile.

1. Cut out three paper shapes.
2. Draw pictures of how you greet people, listen, and share meals.
3. Tape string or yarn to each circle. Tape the string to a stick.
4. Hang the mobile where you will see it every day.

ANSWER KEY

This is the answer key for the chapter test on page 193.

A. Sunday

B. 1. u, a, y 2. o, y 3. o, d 4. a, s

C. 1. b 2. c

Name ____

Keep Sunday Holy

Cut out the puzzle pieces. Put them together to form a message about Sunday.

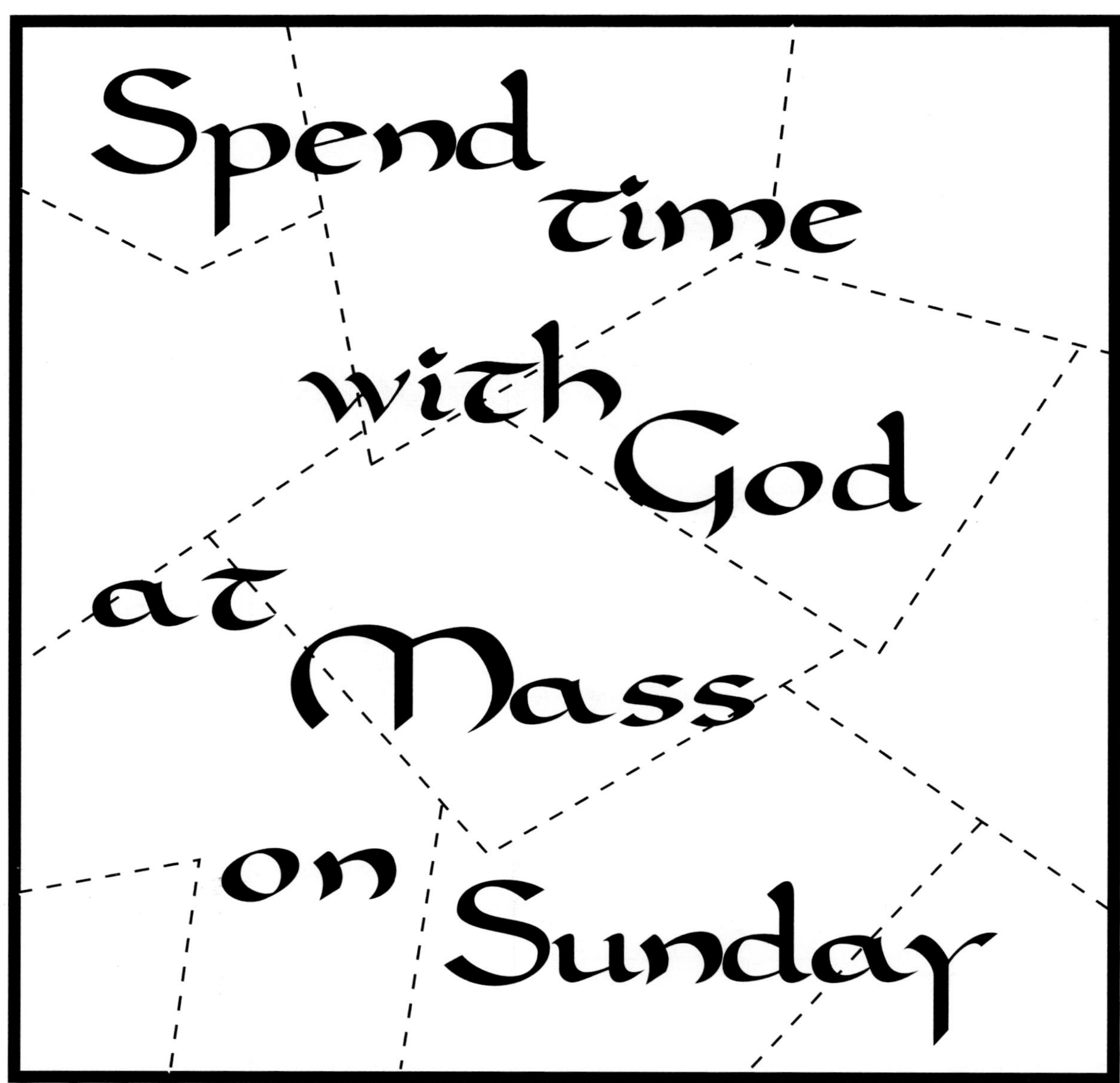

Name ___________________________________

Chapter 8 Test

A. Choose one word from the box to fill in the blank.

good / Sunday / morning

Keep ____________________ holy.

B. Put the letters where they form words.

u y a d o s

1. To Christians S__nd____ is a special day.

2. Sunday is a h__l__ day.

3. Sunday is the day you give to G____.

4. Sunday M__s__ is the most important way to honor God.

C. Circle the word that best completes each sentence.

1. Christians understand Sabbath as

a. Saturday.
b. Sunday.
c. Christmas.

2. Mass is the way to give God honor and

a. fun.
b. song.
c. praise.

UNIT 2 REVIEW

Strategies for Review

The purpose of the Unit Review is to reinforce concepts presented in this unit. You may wish to assign the Remember and Answer sections for homework. Review these sections with the students so that you can answer any questions they may have. Students may work independently, in small groups, or as a class. Use the method that works best with your group.

1 Remember

Invite the students to read each statement aloud with you. After reading each statement, ask whether anyone has questions about it. Check for understanding by turning the statements into simple questions like these: What is God's law for his people? Who is a friend you can always trust?

2 Answer

Give each student an index card containing one of the eight phrases. Ask each of them to find the person who has the matching card. (If you have an odd number of students, give yourself one of the cards.) Gather in a circle, and have the children whose cards match stand side by side. Read the matches aloud. Then have everyone mark the matches in their books on their own.

Unit 2 REVIEW

Remember!

1. The Ten Commandments are God's law for his people.
2. God is a friend you can always trust.
3. God's name is made holy by our prayers and good actions.
4. Sunday is a special day to worship at Mass.

Answer!

Draw lines to match the words in column A to the words in column B.

Column A	Column B
1. Ten Commandments	a. Pray often, trust God
2. Keep God first	b. Pray, rest, celebrate
3. Names for God	c. Rules from God
4. The Lord's Day	d. Father, Creator, Son

Do!

God has many names.
Choose one of God's names.
Make a nametag for God.
Use designs and colors to make it special.

3 Do
Have the students recall names of God. List the names on the chalkboard or a sheet of newsprint. Be sure the children understand what each name means. Provide art materials. After everyone has finished, have each student to share his or her work with a partner. Suggest that the children put God's name tags wherever they need to remember that God is with them.

4 Share
Talk about things that friends do. Help the children recall how God is their friend. Give them time to develop their response. Invite volunteers to share how they will be God's good friends.

Share!
God will always be your friend. How can you be a good friend to God? Use pictures and words to show what you can do.

Friends

ANSWER KEY

Answer
1. c
2. a
3. d
4. b

Unit 3

Do what is pleasing to God.

Romans 12:2

Chapter

Loving Others

The STORY KEEPERS

Good Samaritan
Ephraim is a master storyteller visiting the Christian community in Rome. He meets with the Christians secretly, in the catacombs, and tells how Jesus taught about loving our neighbor in the parable of the good Samaritan. View the clip, tell the story, and lead activities suggested in the guide.

Tanzania From Maryknoll

CHAPTER 9 Home and Family

TEACHER RESOURCE CENTER

Faith Formation

Families Are the "Domestic Church"

In recent Church documents, the family has been referred to as the "domestic Church." This means that it is within the family that persons are called to participate in the work of God on earth. In bringing children into the world and in caring for them, parents reflect God's work of creation. In holy families, children learn about helping the poor, caring for the sick, and reaching out in hospitality to those who have no families. God is indeed present in this "domestic Church."

In what ways does your family resemble the "domestic Church"?

In the fourth commandment, all children are called to respect and honor their parents. However, the intention of the fourth commandment extends beyond obedience. When parents provide examples of forgiveness, compassion, respect, and loving care, children imitate these qualities and honor their parents in return. In caring for elderly parents and family members, adult children also live out the fourth commandment. Society is indeed enhanced by committed and loving families who are strong, faithful, and responsive to God's call to holiness.

How does the fourth commandment challenge you in your relationships with siblings, parents, and children?

CHECK THE CATECHISM

The *Catechism of the Catholic Church* describes the family as a privileged community. It also presents the rights and responsibilities of children and families in following God's will (paragraphs 2206–2233). A very interesting aspect covered in this section on the fourth commandment relates to the duties of citizens and obeying civil authority (paragraphs 2234–2246).

Background

Family Life

Loving others is the theme of Unit 3. The unit opens with a chapter on the basic social structure, the family. Love is first learned in the family, and love is first practiced in family life. No matter what its size or demography, family provides the setting in which children see that the love of God is entwined with love of others. The "others" in their young lives are primarily family.

Secondarily, children learn about love of others in the classroom. You help create a "family" of second graders. By the nature of your profession and through the way you live your faith, you become an important "other" in the children's lives. Your respect and care for the children reflects God's love.

Faith Summary

- **Love of God is love of others. Love of others is love of God.**
- **Children must obey parents and guardians.**
- **Parents must regard and respect their offspring as children of God.**

Growth and Development

It is helpful to remember two characteristics of second graders as you teach this lesson:

- ***Second graders learn respect; it is not an innate trait.*** Chapter 9 covers the fourth commandment, the first dealing with respect for others. Model the behavior by talking with, not at, the children.
- ***Second graders need opportunities to practice their learning.*** Give opportunities for the children to practice caring deeds. Affirm and confirm respectful, caring behavior.

A Teacher's Prayer

Nurturing God, you are the true head of all families. Help me guide the children to see that families are your gift to them. Bless the children with happy families that will nurture and care for them. Shower all families with your love. Amen.

Vocabulary Preview

obey

Scripture

Ephesians 6:1: Obey your parents.

Luke 2:41–52: Jesus in the Temple

Related Resources

Video

"Commandments for Young People" (St. Anthony Messenger Press, 1-800-488-0488 or www.AmericanCatholic.org). "We Honor Parents" covers the fourth commandment. (Children, 15 minutes)

Books

McBride, Alfred. *The Ten Commandments: Covenant of Love* (St. Anthony Messenger Press, 1-800-488-0488 or www.AmericanCatholic.org). Chapter four covers both the fourth commandment and family values. (Adult)

Osborne, Rick and K. Christie Bowler. *I Want to Know About the Ten Commandments* (Zondervan, 1-800-727-1309 or www.zondervankidz.com). See the section that deals with the fourth commandment. (Children)

TEACHER ORGANIZER

Planning Guide

The basic content for each chapter is divided into four class sessions. There are a number of options for the fifth session. Extension, review, and testing options are described under Day 5 Alternatives. The Quick Check box will help you evaluate the week's lessons.

Chapter Goals

In this chapter, the students will learn about

- ❏ Love for God and others
- ❏ Respect for family life
- ❏ Respect for those in charge

	DAY 1 · INVITATION	DAY 2 · DISCOVERY	DAY 3 · DISCOVERY
OBJECTIVES	**The students will be able to** • Propose respectful solutions for problem situations • Identify the home as a place to learn about love	**The students will be able to** • Recognize the fourth commandment • Make concrete the belief that love of God is love for others • Analyze a situation of respect	**The students will be able to** • Broaden their understanding of the fourth commandment to include caregivers • Discover ways to follow the fourth commandment • Tell about the Holy Family
PREPARATION	• Consider having supplies to make simple costumes	• Make copies of the resource master on page 214	• Gather pictures of the Holy Family
MATERIALS	• Student books, pencils	• Crayons, pencils • Copies of the resource master, tape or glue	• Pictures of the Holy Family
OPTIONAL ACTIVITIES	• Curriculum Challenge Make figures of family members	• Ideas That Work Display "Love others" poster • Resource Masters Make a blessing reminder	• Options Make a booklet

Learning Objectives

By the end of this chapter, the students should be able to

- ❑ Demonstrate ways to show respect for family life
- ❑ Recognize the fourth commandment
- ❑ Apply the fourth commandment to daily living
- ❑ Retell a story about the Holy Family

DAY 4 • LIVING

The students will be able to

- Explain ways to show respect in family life
- Demonstrate respect for caregivers
- Understand that they may pray to the Holy Family

- Obtain background music and player

- Background music, player

- **Ideas That Work** Set class goals
- **Ideas That Work** Write thank-you messages

DAY 5 • ALTERNATIVES

There are a number of alternatives to help you plan Day 5.

Prayer Experience
Use the Prayer for the Family prayer service, for either Day 4 or Day 5. The children will need slips of paper and pencils. Add a picture or statue of the Holy Family to your prayer table.

Review and Explore
Pencils are needed. For the optional activity, copies of a simile-writing exercise are needed.

Home and Family
Send the page home with the children, or assign one or more of the activities.

The Church Today
The children prepare a welcome basket for a new family in the parish. You need a basket, a copy of a recent parish bulletin, and art supplies to make a sign and an invitation. Check with the rectory for the name of a newly registered family.

Chapter Test
The chapter test appears as a resource master on page 215.

Quick Check

Do this evaluation as soon as you finish each chapter.

Did I follow my lesson plan?

How can I tell that I met the learning objectives for the lesson?

What activities did the children enjoy most?

How could I improve this lesson?

Benziger on the Web
For more ideas, visit us at www.benziger.glencoe.com

Interactive Lesson Planner
Your ILP provides more help in preparing to teach this chapter.

Celebrate
Turn to page 22 of this book. Check for seasonal celebrations.

Lesson Plan · Day 1

Ask the children to pretend that they are visitors from another planet. You want to know, "What is a family?" Let volunteers give opinions.

1 Scripture

Lead the children to read aloud the chapter title and the chapter's Scripture verse, "Children, obey your parents."

2 Do You Know?

Write the question on the board, and leave it there until the session is over. Children may add answers to it as the session progresses. At the end of the week, come back to this question to see how the children's knowledge has developed.

IDEAS THAT WORK

You may wish to have a costume trunk or box in the classroom. Get donations of items that can make simple costumes. Ties, shoes, jackets, scarves, and hats would be appropriate choices.

TEACHING TIP

This lesson on the fourth commandment offers you a good opportunity to be sensitive to a variety of family situations. Avoid stereotyping a typical family. Help the children understand that there are all kinds of families. Not all families have a father and a mother. Be alert to children who may be teased because of their family situations. Emphasize that God loves all families and that all families are worthy of respect.

INVITATION 9

Children obey your parents.

Ephesians 6:1

Do You Know?

◆ How can you show love to those who care for you?

Home and Family

Learning to Love

Look at the picture. Who will teach the baby how to love others? Who teaches you? Find the hidden words that show where you learn to love.

J	T	H	E
A	B	O	C
T	N	M	Q
M	R	E	U

3 Learning to Love

Direct attention to the text and word search puzzle on student page 134. Read the question aloud. Invite the children to whisper a guess to someone who sits next to them. Then, have the children circle the correct answer. *(the home)*

4 You're in Charge

Read the first paragraph aloud. Invite the children to think about how members of their families share and show kindness. Have volunteers share their responses.

Then, arrange the children in small groups. As the children follow along, read the three situations aloud. Each situation presents a problem that may be found in a home. Have each group pick one situation. Tell group members to make a caring decision that solves the problem. Then have each group act out its chosen situation and the caring decision that was made. You may want to have all of the groups that chose the same situation perform one after another. Lead a discussion about the ways the groups solved the problems.

You're in Charge

Read the three family scenes. Imagine that you can show family love each time. You may act out the scenes, too.

1. The little children are playing. They want to play with the same toy. They pull and argue. You are in charge. What will you do?
2. The family is watching television. Everybody wants to watch a different show at the same time. You are in charge. What will you do?
3. It is a very busy morning. The beds are not made. The cat has not been fed. There is no milk for breakfast. You are in charge. What will you do?

CURRICULUM CHALLENGE

Art This art lesson emphasizes the similarities among the children's families. The children make figures of their family members, using clay. The figures can be glued onto a cardboard base and placed on a long bookshelf or table as part of a display of classroom families.

Lesson Plan · Day 2

Ask the children to say aloud where they first learned about love. *(in their family or in their home)* Then read This We Believe! to the class and point out that Church teaching also knows where love is first learned.

1 Two Sons

Recall that one way we know God's love is through the kind actions of others. Have the children read the story of the two sons. Talk about which son pleased his father more and which son showed respect. Ask the children about the man and his two sons in the picture. Have them describe what is happening in the picture. Ask the children to respond to the question "How do you show God's love to members of your family?"

Share that Jesus knew that families are important. Jesus was born in a family and he shared happy times with families. He wanted families to be happy.

IDEAS THAT WORK

Make a simple poster of these words of Jesus: Jesus says, "Love others as I have loved you" *(John 13:34)*. You can probably find some older children in the school who would enjoy making the poster for you. Perhaps there are children in the parish who are involved in a sacramental program; they may need to do service for others. You may wish to "adopt" one or two children to help you throughout the year with your classroom preparations.

Two Sons

Jesus told a story about a man with two sons. The man asked one son to help work in the field. The son said no. He did not want to go.

Then the man asked the other son to go. Right away the second son said he would go, but he went out to play instead.

Meanwhile, the first son felt sorry about saying no. He went right out to the field and went to work.

Jesus asked his friends, "Which son obeyed his father? Which son showed love for his father?"

? How do you show God's love to members of your family?

2 Love and Respect

Share the information on the page. Write the fourth commandment on the chalkboard. Ask for suggestions as to what the word *honor* may mean in this commandment.

3 Activity

Remind the children that a quilt is made up of many small beautiful pieces. When all these pieces are sewn together, one large guilt is the result. Discuss how a family is like a quilt. *(many loving people make one loving family, it keeps you warm)* Allow the children time to complete the activity. The children can share their answers.

Love and Respect

Children and parents try to make the home a place of love and respect. You can help by listening to and obeying your parents. You can respect and love all those who care for you.

You can show love and respect by helping out at home. You can be kind. You can not talk back.

This We Believe!

The Catholic home is the first place that children learn about God's love.

Look at the quilt. What do you see in the two pictures? In the open spaces, draw more ways you can be a loving member of your home and family.

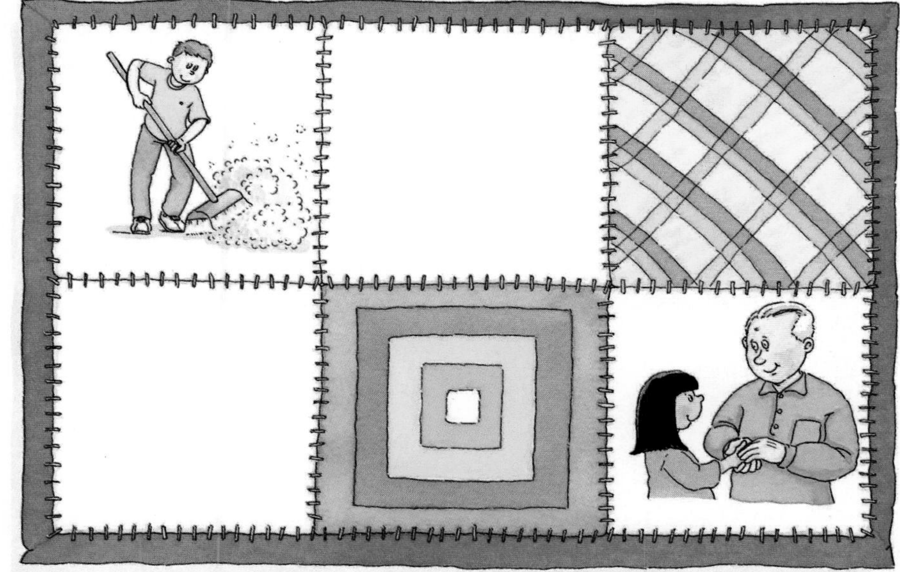

RESOURCE MASTERS

The resource master on page 214 is a craft activity designed to remind the students to say blessings before meals. In making the blessing reminder, the children copy a prayer from their text. They then fold on the dotted lines and overlap the end sections to form a tent shape. Secure with tape or glue. The children take home the blessing reminders to use before meals.

Lesson Plan · Day 3

Ask the children how they feel when they listen to someone who is in charge?

1 No Rain Today?

Invite volunteers to tell about people who guide them, help them, and watch over them. Tell the children that they will read about a boy who was not sure he wanted to take his mother's advice. Read the story. Ask the children to talk about the reasons Masaki did not want to follow his mother's advise. Ask the children to share similar experiences they have had. Allow them to share their responses to the questions at the end of the story.

TEACHING TIP

There are four basic environmental elements to learning: light, temperature, sound, and design. Light: You probably cannot choose a lighting system for your classroom. It is good to know, however, that some poor readers read better in low light, which may cause the words to stand out on the page. Temperature: Cold negatively affects more students than heat. Let the children gauge their own needs when it comes to adding or removing sweaters. Sound: Many young children and many underachievers work well using sound. Make sure some activities involve noise. Design: A large percentage of children work best in an informal environment.

No Rain Today?

Look at the pictures and listen to the story.

Masaki felt grumpy. He did not want to take an umbrella or a raincoat. This was dumb. The sun was high in the sky. The other kids would laugh at him. He was sure of it.

Mom was tapping her toe. That meant she was serious. She was holding the umbrella and the raincoat. "The weather report says there *will* be rain," she said.

Masaki knew he had to do what Mom said. He put on the raincoat and took the umbrella. Then the grumpy boy took off for school.

When he was half way to school, it got very dark. Then it started to rain. It rained hard, but Masaki arrived at school warm and dry.

When he got home that afternoon, his mother had a smile on her face. Masaki smiled right back. He wasn't grumpy anymore.

- How did Masaki's mom show her love?
- How did Masaki show his love?

2 Where is Jesus?
Gather the children, and tell them that you are going to read a Bible story about Jesus and his parents, Mary and Joseph. Say that the story is about a time when Jesus got separated from Mary and Joseph. Ask whether any children have had similar experiences. Focus the children; ask them to try to picture the story in their minds while they are listening. Share the story.

3 Activity
For the retelling of the story, have the children form as many circles as you think will work best. If you wish, give each group a picture of the Holy Family to use as a prompt for remembering the story. The picture can be passed from person to person as the children take turns telling the story.

Where Is Jesus?

When Jesus was twelve years old, he went with his family to Jerusalem for the feast of Passover. When it was time to return home, Joseph and Mary started out with the large group of travelers. But Jesus stayed behind.

Mary and Joseph did not notice that he was missing until the first evening. They were so worried! They hurried back to Jerusalem to find Jesus.

They looked and looked. It took three days to find Jesus. They found him in the Temple. The teachers were asking him questions. They were talking about God's Word. They were surprised that Jesus knew so much about God.

"Son," Mary asked, "why did you do this to us?"

Jesus said, "I was doing my Father's work."

Jesus went back home. He obeyed his parents. He grew in love.

From *Luke 2:41–52*

ACTIVITY — RETELL

Gather in small story circles. Together you can retell the story of Jesus getting lost. Help one another. Talk about the story, too.

OPTIONS

You may wish to have the children write and illustrate a family situation that they experienced. Perhaps a sibling was lost and then found or a family member broke a household item. Compile these stories into a class booklet and discuss how families resolve problematic situations.

Lesson Plan · Day 4
Review by asking the class to share ideas on the purpose of the fourth commandment.

❶ Family Rules
In order for the children to make up three rules for respect in the home, you may have to first lead a general discussion about areas that need respect. *(time, belongings, space)* Keep the discussion general so that information of a personal nature is not revealed. Today's projects work well with some background music.

IDEAS THAT WORK

Children need opportunities to show respect and gratitude.

- After you have read the children's ideas for showing respect to school helpers, choose one and propose that it become a class goal. Write the goal on the chalkboard or on special paper. Until the goal becomes a habit, spend a few moments at the end of each day evaluating how it has been met.
- Plan a simple, fun way to show gratitude to some of the school helpers. The children may blow up balloons and write the words *Thank you* on them. The class could make paper flowers for each helper or a big banner to hang in the hallway.

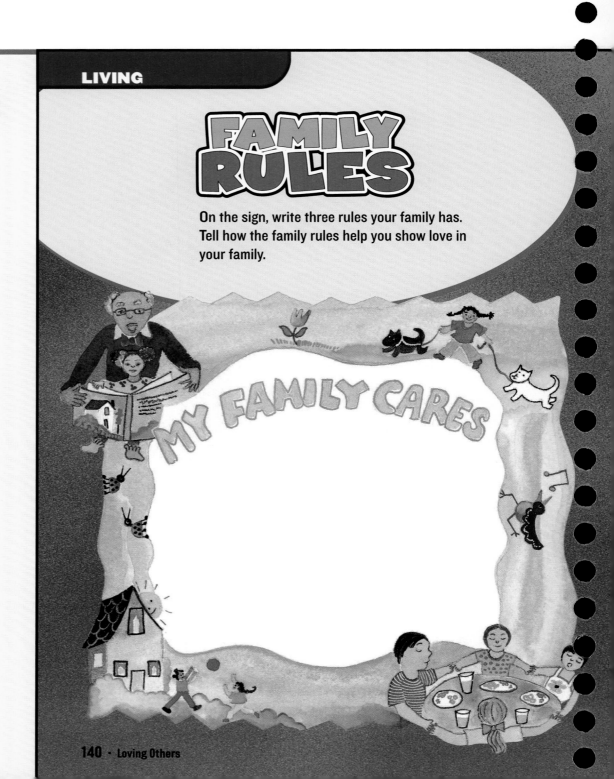

FAMILY RULES

On the sign, write three rules your family has. Tell how the family rules help you show love in your family.

MY FAMILY CARES

❷ Faith at Home

Tell the children that families share many things like love, support, and good times. Ask the children to give other examples of the things that families share. Tell them that families share their faith, too.

Ask the children to think about the many ways that they share their love of God with their families. Read the directions for the activity. Allow volunteers to share their ideas.

FAITH AT HOME

Families share faith, too. On the house, write or draw ways your family shares faith. Draw at least one sign of faith that you find in your home.

Signs of Faith

OPTIONS

For Those Who Learn Intrapersonally These children can examine and express thoughts and feelings. You can count on them to write a good thank-you message to family members. Give the children a focus, such as why they are proud of their families. Provide the quiet time and private place that these children need to reflect and write.

TEACHING TIP

A way to keep a good partnership with the children's families is to recommend good books that they can share with their children. You may want to tell the families about *Serendipity* by Tobi Tobias (Simon and Schuster). The book has charming and fun descriptions of the meaning of serendipity. Looking for life's unexpected blessings is the central theme of the book.

Prayer

This activity will help the children unite their family with the Holy Family in prayer.

1 Prepare for Prayer

Talk about the prayer with the children, emphasizing that inviting Jesus to be with them helps make their families holy. Give each child a slip of paper on which to write his or her family name. Write a slip for yourself, too.

2 Prayer for the Family

Play quiet music. Form a processional line, and place each slip of paper on the prayer table. A child may also carry in a picture or statue of the Holy Family. Begin the prayer service.

LEARNING TO PRAY

Processions are part of the rich prayer tradition that forms the Catholic Church's history. Some processions are Eucharistic, such as those held on the Feast of Corpus Christi. The host is placed in a monstrance and carried by a priest in procession. A benediction follows where Jesus blesses the people. Some processions are devotional, such as the Way of the Cross, a May crowning held to honor Mary, or a procession held in memory of a saint. Some processions are incorporated into marches for a cause, such as a march against abortion. Many cultures include funeral processions as part of their mourning for the dead. Every Mass begins with a gathering procession.

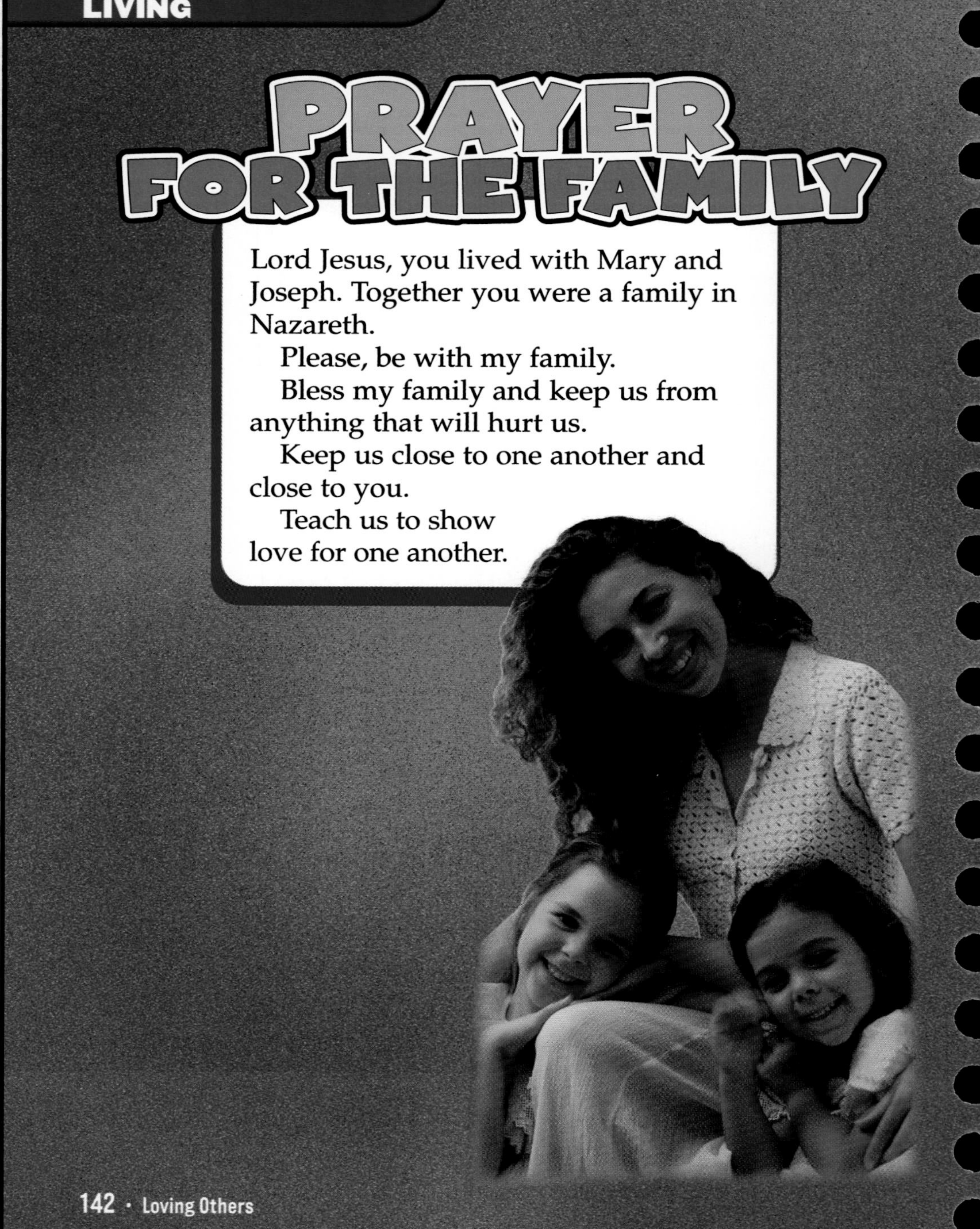

PRAYER FOR THE FAMILY

Lord Jesus, you lived with Mary and Joseph. Together you were a family in Nazareth.

Please, be with my family.

Bless my family and keep us from anything that will hurt us.

Keep us close to one another and close to you.

Teach us to show love for one another.

1 Know
Direct attention to the graphic. Ask the children to silently read the lines. Have the children turn to someone who sits nearby and explain what the graphic means. *(The sentences are ways for loving families to show love for God.)*

2 Love and Serve
Explain the Love activity. Give some time for thinking. Some children may want to think quietly, and others may want to talk about ideas with others. Give time for writing and sharing of ideas. Explain the Serve activity as a time for those who are not members of the family.

3 God's Friends
Show the illustration and share the information. Ask for ways that Giuseppina showed respect for her family. For others? Then have the children tell whether they know anyone like Giuseppina.

CHAPTER 9 REVIEW and EXPLORE

Know

Honor your father and your mother.

Show love for your family.

Respect and obey your parents and those who care for you.

Love

Think about one way that you can be a more loving member of your family. Write it in the space.

Serve

Plan a surprise! Do something for someone who takes care of you. Write or draw what you will do.

GOD'S FRIENDS

Blessed Giuseppina Bonino

When Giuseppina was just a young woman, a priest asked her to care for children who had no family. Giuseppina said that she would.

She spent her whole life taking care of children who had no one to love and care for them. She gave the children a home and a family, too.

A Little Catechism

Invite the children to open their religion books to *A Little Catechism*. Choose one or more of the selections below for memory work or reinforcement. You will find your copy of the catechism on pages 23–43 of this Teacher's Edition.

1. Call attention to the Ten Commandments on page 11. Memorize the fourth commandment.
2. Read about the Holy Family on page 11.
2. Refer the children to the sacraments on page 14. Ask the children to point out the sacraments that have to do with family.

Know Love Serve

Note The activities on this page provide ways for the children to share their learning with their families. The activities are related to the week's theme.

1 Introduce
Arrange the children in pairs. One child pretends to be a parent. The other child tells the parent some things that were learned in religion class in Chapter 9. Then, read aloud the two activities on the page. Ask the children how they will carry them out.

2 Pray Together
The children may quietly pray the prayer in the prayer burst.

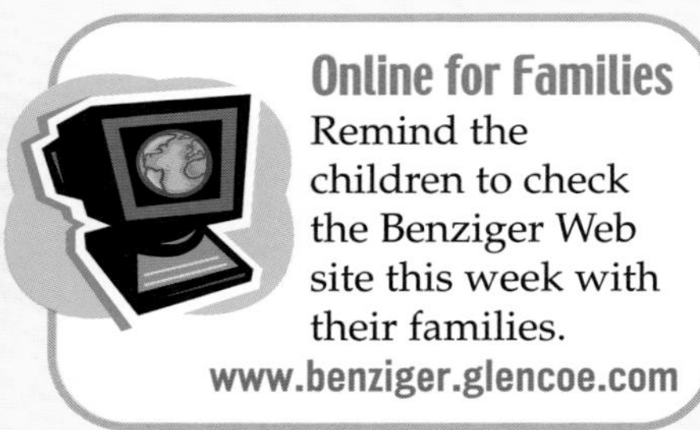

Online for Families
Remind the children to check the Benziger Web site this week with their families.
www.benziger.glencoe.com

Dear Family,

I have just finished chapter 9. I learned that God wants me to obey my parents. He wants me to love and respect my family too. Help me learn how to be a loving and caring member of our family.

On your own

Make a thank-you coupon for someone who cares for you. The coupon can be for something the person wants or needs you to do.

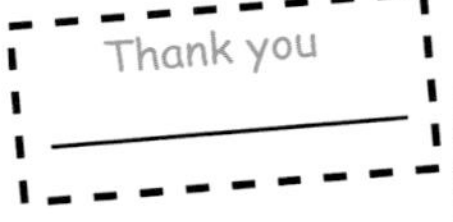

With your family

Watch a family television show together. Talk about the ways the children and grownups treat each other in the show. Do they show love? Do they show respect?

Dear God, help me show love to those who care for me.

GO ONLINE!
http://www.benziger.glencoe.com

1 Prepare
Ask for a show of hands showing who has belonged to your parish since they were babies. Who has moved to this parish? Tell the children that many families move to the parish every year. Jesus said that all are welcome to follow him. All are welcome to join the Church Family. Get the children excited about welcoming a new family to the parish.

2 The Project
Plan the project so that everyone has a part to play. There are suggestions in the book. More items may be added to the basket to allow full participation of the class.

THE CHURCH TODAY

Some homes have a welcome mat. The mat is a sign of **hospitality.** Welcome a new family to your parish. Make a basket or a package.

Here are some suggestions for what you can put in your welcome package.

- A copy of the parish bulletin
- A welcome card
- An invitation to visit the school
- A sign of faith for the family to display in their new home

OPTIONS

For Those Who Learn Musically and Through Nature Children who have musical intelligence may make a tape of songs for the new family. The children can sing songs that they know, or they may take a familiar melody and make up words of welcome. Students who enjoy and understand nature are often good at classifying and collecting. If the weather permits, they may be able to gather and arrange some living things to add to the basket.

ANSWER KEY

This is the answer key for the chapter test on page 215.

A. 1. mother, father (either order) 2. others, loved

B. 1. b 2. c 3. a

C. 2 and 3

Name ____

A Blessing

In the two large spaces, copy a prayer before meals. Then, color the designs. Next, fold the page on the dotted lines. Now, tape or glue the ends.

Name ______________________________

Chapter 9 Test

A. Complete the fourth commandment and the words of Jesus. Use words from the box.

father / parents / mother
others / animals / loved

1. Honor your ____________________ and your

____________________.

2. Jesus said, "Love ____________________ as I have

____________________ you."

B. Draw a line to match the parts that go together.

1. Loving God is	**a.** loving God.
2. Jesus, Mary, and Joseph are	**b.** loving others.
3. Loving others is	**c.** the Holy Family.

C. Put a check by ways to follow the fourth commandment.

_____ **1.** Listen when you want.

_____ **2.** Respect your family.

_____ **3.** Listen to those in charge.

_____ **4.** Help as little as possible.

TEACHER RESOURCE CENTER

Faith Formation

CHECK THE CATECHISM

In paragraphs 2258–2330, the *Catechism of the Catholic Church* presents a comprehensive overview of the fifth commandment. Included are topics such as legitimate defense and avoiding war, abortion, euthanasia, respect for the dead, scientific research, and safeguarding peace.

Called to Peace

Blessed are the Peacemakers . . .
Matthew 5:9

Peacemakers are those who try to avoid violence as a means of resolving conflict. Disciples of Jesus were taught by him to "Love your enemies, do good to those who hate you" *(Luke 6:27).* Jesus asks that the anger and resentment which could lead to violence be replaced by compassion and reconciliation. The fifth commandment also cautions against vengeance, bloodshed, and unjust war. Followers of Jesus are called to find peaceful ways to resolve difficult issues.

How can you be aware of times when you are able to resolve conflict in peaceful ways, resulting in a "peaceful heart"?

All Human Life is Sacred

Because of the belief that all human life comes from God, and all human beings are made in God's image, the Catholic Church has always held the position that all human life is sacred. From conception to death, human life is to be respected, protected, and treated with dignity. The fifth commandment forbids the taking of innocent human life, but it does not end there. Going beyond the command that "you shall not kill" means not only that human life is precious and human dignity is to be upheld, but also that God's people are called to care for the poor, the sick, the hungry, the marginalized, the very young, and the very old.

What could you do this week to help promote the human dignity of each person you encounter?

Background

Peacemakers

The unit's theme of loving others is carried out in Chapter 10. For second-grade students, the primary interpretation of the fifth commandment centers on following the Lord's call to be peacemakers.

The students probably define peacemakers in broad terms, such as those who are involved in stopping wars. For most students, this concept of peace is far removed from their daily experiences. The need for peace is constant, particularly among students who are still in a self-centered age. Your role is to make the students aware of the everyday need for peace.

The students will have a greater role. It will be up to them to evaluate and decide what changes are needed in the classroom, and how they can bring about the changes.

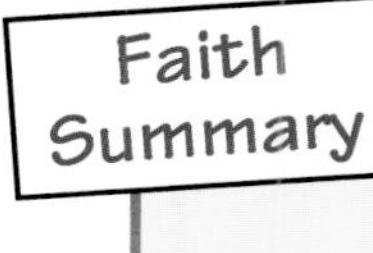

- The Lord calls us to be peacemakers.
- All human life is to be respected.
- Jesus said, "Love your enemies."

Growth and Development

It is helpful to remember two characteristics of second graders as you teach this lesson:

- ***Second graders are developing special friendships, but need guidance in working out conflicts.*** When students are involved in a non-peaceful situation, guide them to express their feelings.
- ***Second graders learn best how to get along with others when adults do not always try to "fix" their disagreements.*** Let peacemakers tell what it feels like to bring peace. Let the students know that forgiveness goes hand in hand with peacemaking—forgiveness of others and of oneself.

A Teacher's Prayer

O God, may peace live among all people of good will. May your peace begin with us in this classroom on this day. May your peace sink deeply into our hearts, and spread throughout the school. I ask you this through Jesus, your Son, who lives in peace and unity with the Holy Spirit, one God, forever and ever. Amen.

Vocabulary Preview

peacemaker

Scripture

Matthew 5:9: Blessed are the peacemakers.

Luke 6:27–37: Love your enemies.

Psalm 1:2: the way to happiness

Related Resources

Video

"Raising Children in a Violent World" (Twenty-Third Publications, 1-800-321-0411 or www.twentythirdpublications.com). This video suggests practical ways for children and parents to counteract violence, starting at home. (Children, 35 minutes)

Book

Christofferson, Hans. *Prayer Service for Peace* (Liguori Publications, 1-800-325-9521 or www.liguori.org). This heart-felt prayer service sets out to disarm violence by revealing its worthlessness and encouraging the dismantling of corruption and oppression. (Children)

TEACHER ORGANIZER

Planning Guide

The basic content for each chapter is divided into four class sessions. There are a number of options for the fifth session. Extension, review, and testing options are described under Day 5 Alternatives. The Quick Check box will help you evaluate the week's lessons.

Chapter Goals

In this chapter, the students will learn about

- ❑ Respect for others
- ❑ Making peace

	DAY 1 · INVITATION	DAY 2 · DISCOVERY	DAY 3 · DISCOVERY
OBJECTIVES	**The students will be able to** • Use the interpretations to draw conclusions about peace	**The students will be able to** • Choose words of Jesus to follow • Discover ways to bring peace	**The students will be able to** • Determine ways to bring peace to specific situations • Evaluate peaceful/non-peaceful choices using cause and effect • Tell what makes a peacemaker
PREPARATION	• Find out how the concepts of bullies and peacemakers are handled in popular children's television programs	• Make copies of the resource master on page 232	• Know where Guatemala is locacted
MATERIALS	• Pencils	• Highlighters • Drawing supplies • Copies of the resource master, pencils • Piece of drawing paper for each student	• World map • Pencils • Drawing supplies
OPTIONAL ACTIVITIES	• **Options** Have available "The Peaceable Kingdom," a painting by Edward Hicks, and *A Peaceable Kingdom: The Shaker Abecedarius* by Alice and Martin Provensen	• **Vocabulary** Add to the World Wall	• **Curriculum Challenge** Create a class poster using self-portraits

Learning Objectives

By the end of this chapter, the students should be able to

- ❑ Evaluate peaceful/non-peaceful situations
- ❑ Determine ways to be a peacemaker

DAY 4 · LIVING

The students will be able to

- Plan a way to be a peacemaker
- Describe traits of a peacemaker
- Pray in song

- Get a copy of a western "Wanted" poster
- Know where El Salvador is located

- Pencils, drawing supplies
- Blue streamer for each child
- Melody for "Peace Is Flowing Like a River" by Carey Landry
- World map

DAY 5 · ALTERNATIVES

There are a number of alternatives to help you plan Day 5.

Prayer Experience
Sing the "Peaceful Heart" prayer experience on either Day 4 or Day 5.

Review and Explore
The students will need pencils. You may choose to use a world map to indicate El Salvador.

Home and Family
Send the page home with the students, or assign one or more of the activities.

The Church Today
Find out how to adopt a needy family. You will need a box or basket to hold supplies for the family.

Chapter Test
The chapter test appears as a resource master on page 233.

Quick Check

Do this evaluation as soon as you finish each chapter.

Did I follow my lesson plan?

How can I tell that I met the learning objectives for the lesson?

What activities did the children enjoy most?

How could I improve this lesson?

Benziger on the Web
For more ideas, visit us at www.benziger.glencoe.com

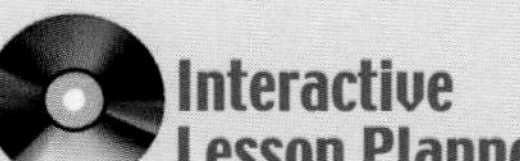

Interactive Lesson Planner
Your ILP provides more help in preparing to teach this chapter.

Celebrate
Turn to page 22 of this book. Check for seasonal celebrations.

Lesson Plan · Day 1

Tell the children that you need their help in figuring out what kind of student would get a "Good Citizen" award. What qualities would that student need to have? How would that student behave towards others? Write their ideas on the board.

You may wish to save the criteria the children just described for your own classroom award program.

1 Do You Know?

Have a volunteer read aloud the chapter title and the chapter's Scripture verse. Pose the Do You Know? feature question. At the end of the week, come back to this question to see how the children's knowledge has developed.

2 The Prize

Ask the children to describe what a peaceful place might be like. Ask: How can people be peaceful? Allow them to give their ideas. Tell them that people who bring peace to others are call *peacemakers.* Tell the children that they will hear a story about a second-grade class that is going to give an award to a peacemaker. Read the story. Talk about children in the story. Who deserves the peacemaker award?

OPTIONS

For Visual Learners Children may want to study the "The Peaceable Kingdom," and learn about the painter, Edward Hicks. You can get versions of the painting in art books or off the Internet. Hicks was a Quaker preacher who was attracted to Isaiah 11:6 by its message of peace. Hicks painted over 100 versions of "The Peaceable Kingdom." Many versions included humans, including a scene of William Penn signing a peace treaty with Indians.

INVITATION 10

Peacemakers will be called God's children.

Matthew 5:9

Do You Know?

◆ Why is it good to be a peacemaker?

Peace

The Prize

Miss Rose was going to give out a peace prize for her second-grade class. The class named three children. They gave a reason why each one should get the prize. Which one do you think deserves the prize? Why do you think so?

1. **Sandy** welcomed the new student, Connie. She played with her. She showed her around, too.
2. **Mike** shared his lunch with Mindy when she forgot hers.
3. **Peter** stopped Juan and Paul from arguing. He asked them to shake hands and be friends.

3 No Bullies Award
Talk about how bullies and their actions make others feel. Ask the children about bullies they have seen in television programs. How did the other characters feel about the bullies? Read the first paragraph aloud.

4 Activity
Review the directions for the activity. Allow the children time to complete the assignment. Ask for volunteers to share their answers with the class. Ask the children to come up with some of their own sentences.

No Bullies Allowed

You know what a bully is, don't you? A bully would never get a peace prize. A bully pushes people around. Jesus does not want his followers to be bullies.

Read the sentences. If the sentence reminds you of a bully, write **B** in the box. If the sentence reminds you a peaceful person, write a **P** in the box.

- ❑ Get out of my way.
- ❑ Do you want to share my lunch?
- ❑ Give me your book right now!
- ❑ Let's play together.
- ❑ Don't feel bad.
- ❑ You did a good job.

BIBLE BASICS

Ask the children to visualize a country where the people do not get along. There is much fighting. The people who are in charge of the country care only about becoming rich. No one helps the poor and needy. There is no justice or peace. A man named Isaiah lives in the country. He tells the people to trust in God. He tells them how to change their lives. Isaiah says:

> The wolf shall be a guest of the lamb
> and the leopard shall lie down with the goat;
> The calf and the young lion shall browse together,
> with a little child to guide them.
>
> *Isaiah 11:6*

Lesson Plan · Day 2

Say that Jesus *was* a peacemaker. He showed people how to get along.

1 Painting Jesus

Ask: If you were going to make a painting of Jesus, what people would you put in it? Lead the responses to be inclusive—people of many cultures, ages, economic backgrounds, and those who are often stereotyped as "bad."

2 Love Your Enemies

Say that Jesus told people how to live peacefully. See the Bible Basics feature. Then, ask the children to follow along while you read Jesus' words. Read aloud the text on student page 148. Have the children highlight the one or two sentences they most want to remember. Ask volunteers to explain their choices.

BIBLE BASICS

Focus the children on the Bible reading by getting them engrossed in the story. Ask them to visualize this scene: Jesus and his apostles are coming down a mountainside. Many of Jesus' followers come to meet him. Large crowds of people from all over the country are there, too. They want Jesus to heal them. They want to hear Jesus speak. They are so very eager to hear what Jesus has to say!

TEACHING TIP

The Scripture reading from Luke is filled with wonderful messages. Using your personal knowledge of the children, focus on the two sentences you find to be most relevant to the class. Lead a discussion about those sentences: How does living this way bring peace? How can we live this way?

Love Your Enemies

One day many people gathered to listen to Jesus. They stood on tiptoes to see. They cupped their hands behind their ears to hear. This is what they heard Jesus say:

Love your enemies, and be good to everyone who hates you.

Ask God to bless anyone who says evil things to you and pray for everyone who is cruel to you.

Give to everyone who asks you. Don't ask people to return what they have taken from you.

Treat others just the way you want to be treated.

Don't judge others. Don't be hard on others, and God will not be hard on you. Forgive others, and God will forgive you.

Based on *Luke 6:27–37*

3 Peaceful People

Ask a volunteer to read aloud This We Believe! Give the children time to talk about situations which need peace. Then, read aloud the text on student page 149. Allow time to do the activity. Let volunteers share their solutions. Ask children to tell how they feel when they make peace.

4 Activity

Guide the children in making two-part drawings. On the left side of their pages, they each draw a child needing care. On the right side of their pages, they each draw themselves showing care. Finally, they each draw an arrow leading from themselves to the child needing care.

Peaceful People

Mary was feeling good. She had a new cap. Bart made fun of Mary's cap. She began to cry. Miguel told Mary not to cry. "It is a very nice cap," he said.

Jesus teaches how to care for others. Jesus teaches how to be a peaceful person. Peaceful people show respect.

Look at the little puzzle. In the blank spaces, draw a way to bring peace.

Do unto others as you would have them do unto you.

VOCABULARY

If you have created a Word Wall of action words *(respect, trust)*, add *make peace* to it.

RESOURCE MASTERS

The resource master on page 232 presents situations that need peace. The children may do the page on their own, or they may brainstorm in groups.

Lesson Plan · Day 3

Ask the children: What would be your wish for the whole world?

1 Sonia's Wish

On a map, show the children where Guatemala is located. Tell them that a girl named Sonia has a very special wish for the world. Read aloud the story. Ask the children to describe the difficulties that Sonia has to deal with *(poverty, she has to care for her brother, she has to work hard).* Write their answers on the board. Direct the children to the photograph. Ask: Does Sonia look like a happy person? What do you think Sonia has that makes her happy?

Allow the children to talk about the things that make them happy. Lead them to focus on special people and attitudes, and away from material things. Then, ask a volunteer to read the Word of God feature.

CURRICULUM CHALLENGE

Social Studies You can easily connect to this chapter's theme throughout the year, and help make your classroom a peaceful place. Ask each child to draw and color a self-portrait. Make one of yourself, too. Each picture is cut out and glued close together on a posterboard. Guide the children in deciding on a good title, such as "The Peaceable Second Grade." Talk about specific ways the class can be peacemakers. Display the poster.

Word of God

Happy are those who follow God's way!

Psalm 1:2

Sonia's Wish

Sonia lives in Guatemala. Sonia's family has to work very, very hard. She does not have any toys. She makes up games with her friends.

Sonia has many chores to do, too. She takes care of her baby brother, Nelson. She makes sure he is happy. Sonia does not fight with her friends because Sonia has a big wish.

Sonia wishes that the whole world would be peaceful and happy. She says that she is sure that her wish will come true. She will start with her own family and friends. She will have peace in her heart and a smile on her face.

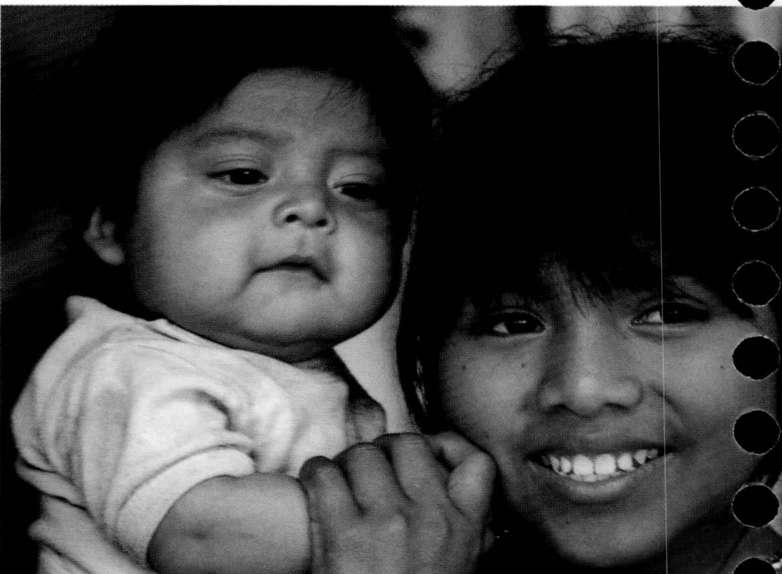

2 Peaceful Hearts
Read aloud the text on student page 151. Allow the children some time to work on the activity independently. Walk around and assist those children who may need help. Reproduce the figures for the activity on the chalkboard. Asking volunteers to share their answers, do the activity as a class.

Peaceful Hearts

Think about peaceful and happy people. You can think about people who are angry and unhappy too.

Look at the diagram. In the oval with the sad face, write words that are not peaceful. In the oval with the smiley face, write words that tell about peace. Use the questions in the boxes to talk about how to have peace in your hearts.

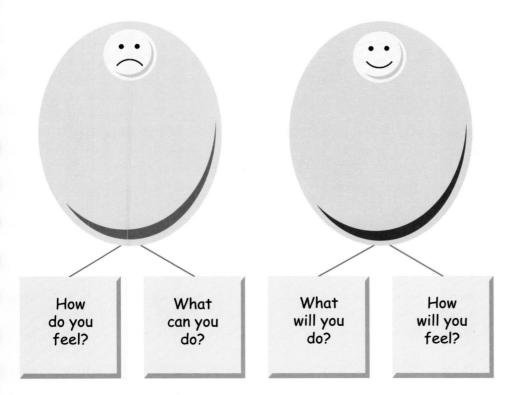

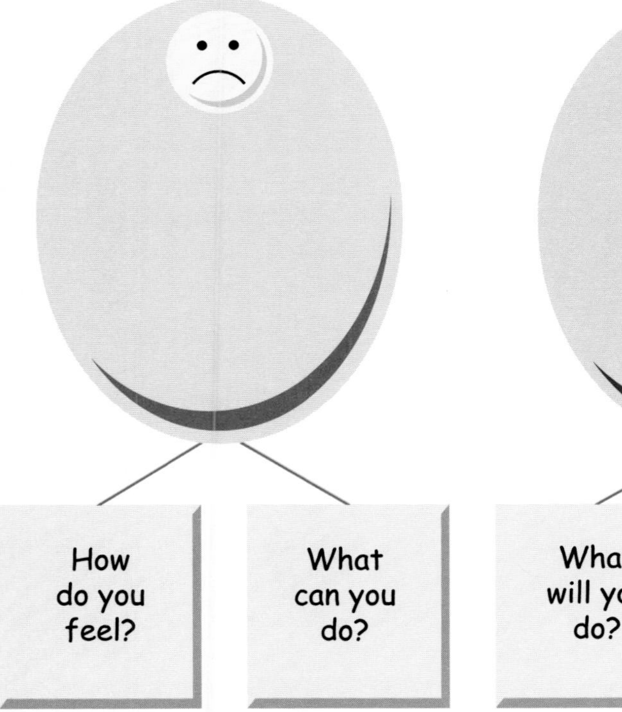

How do you feel?
What can you do?
What will you do?
How will you feel?

TEACHING TIP

A session on peacemaking gives you a good opportunity to learn more about the children. As you observe their writings, drawings, and opinions, you will see ways to help the children follow Jesus. Look for clues: How do the children interpret peace? Where do they need peace in their lives? When do they find peacemaking most difficult? Where do they learn about revenge? Do they forgive themselves?

Lesson Plan · Day 4

Ask: How do you feel when you are a peacemaker?

1 A Peaceful Heart

Remind the children that people need to forgive themselves in order to have peaceful hearts. They can forgive themselves when they know they are trying to be better. Explain the activity on student page 152. Give quiet time for the activity. Lead the children to give specific answers. Play some peaceful background music while the children work. Then, have the children share their work with the class.

IDEAS THAT WORK

You may be able to tie the theme of peacemaking to a school event. Perhaps the school is preparing to celebrate Advent, or it is time for an open house. Look for ways to share the children's work with the rest of the school, or with the parish community.

A PEACEFUL HEART

Color the outline. In the heart, write a one way you can be a peacemaker. Share what you have written with the whole class.

2 God Needs Your Help

Show the sample "Wanted" poster. Ask what kind of information is given. Direct attention to student page 153, and say that the world needs many peacemakers. Explain the activity. Invite the children to complete the poster with the qualities that it takes to be a peacemaker. Their imaginations will be stimulated if the children work in groups. Walk around the room, and give positive feedback.

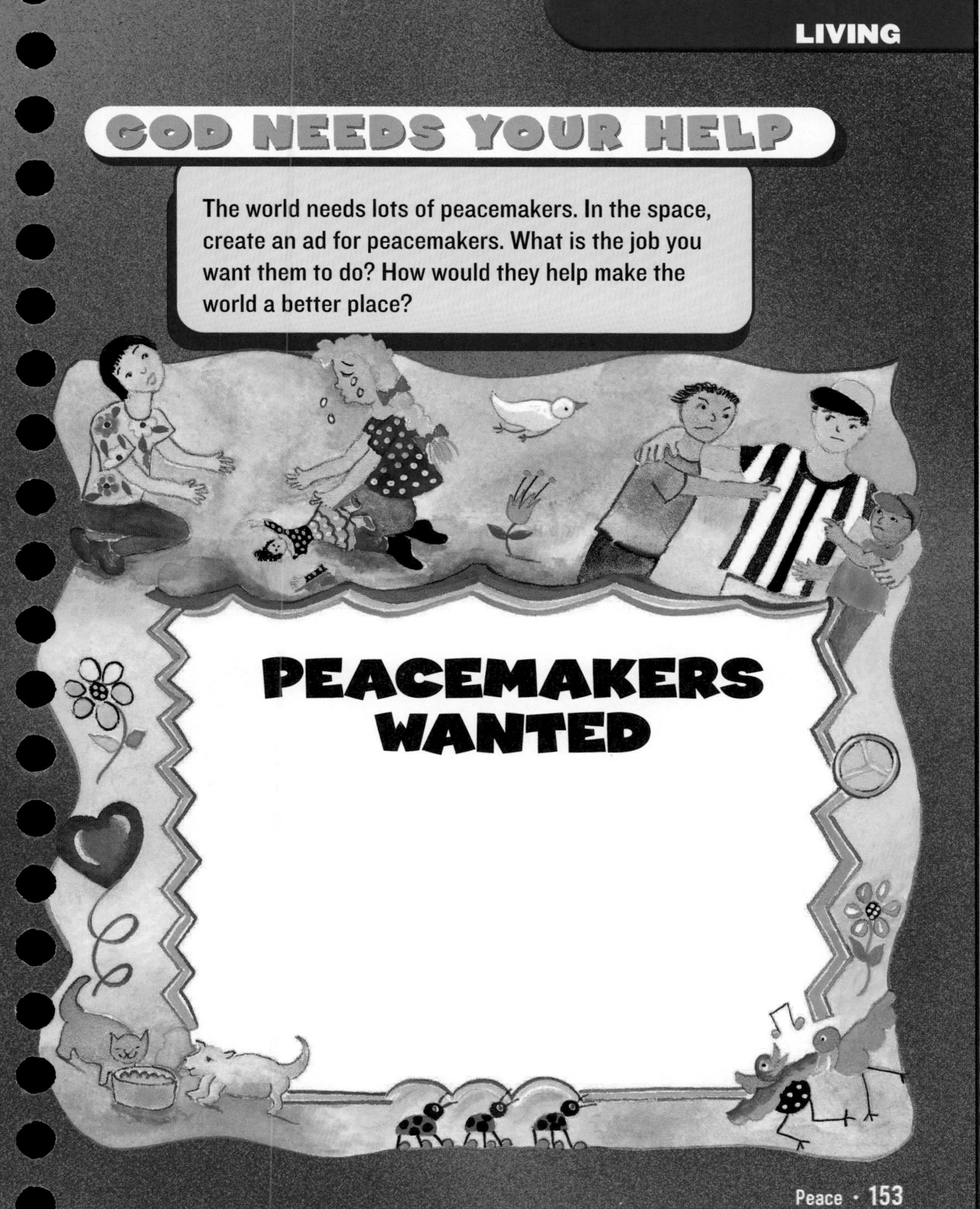

LIVING
GOD NEEDS YOUR HELP
The world needs lots of peacemakers. In the space, create an ad for peacemakers. What is the job you want them to do? How would they help make the world a better place?
PEACEMAKERS
WANTED
Peace · 153

IN THE MEDIA

Chapter 10 gives you the opportunity to help the children evaluate their television viewing. Find out the children's favorite television programs. Let the children tell what they like best about these programs. Guide the children to think about the programs in terms of the ways peace is shown or not shown. The children could evaluate a single episode of one show.

- What was the problem?
- How was the problem solved?
- What are other peaceful ways to solve the problem?

Prayer

Draw a large heart on the chalkboard. Ask volunteers to write words inside the heart that describe a peaceful heart. Be sure that *forgiveness* is one of the words.

1 Prepare to Pray

Have the children sit quietly and comfortably. Lead them in taking several slow, deep breaths. Speak to the children in a quiet voice. Help them feel at peace. Then, practice singing the song together, with gentle voices.

2 A Peace Song

Give each child a blue paper streamer. Ask the children to wave the streamers peacefully. Now sing the song, while waving the streamers. Encourage the children to sway back and forth to the melody.

Movement with prayer is commonplace among many faiths. If movement is new to the children, model the gentle swaying, or ask several children to lead the others.

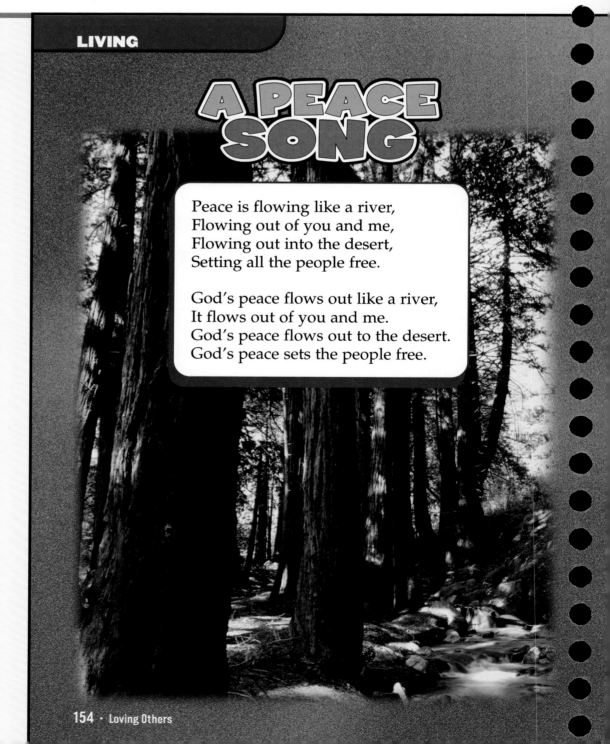

A PEACE SONG

Peace is flowing like a river,
Flowing out of you and me,
Flowing out into the desert,
Setting all the people free.

God's peace flows out like a river,
It flows out of you and me.
God's peace flows out to the desert.
God's peace sets the people free.

1 Know
Direct attention to the graphic organizer, and read it aloud together. Pose the Do You Know? question from student page 146, and see how the children's knowledge has developed.

2 Love and Serve
Remind the children that sometimes it is hard to be a peacemaker. God will help them. Read the Love section. Allow time for the children to write their prayers. Encourage them to pray silently. Consider having the children draw on papers they can take home, so that they may share the focus of today's lesson with their families.

3 God's Friends
If you have a world map, gather the children and show them El Salvador in Central America. Tell about Archbishop Romero. Ask how he was a peacemaker.

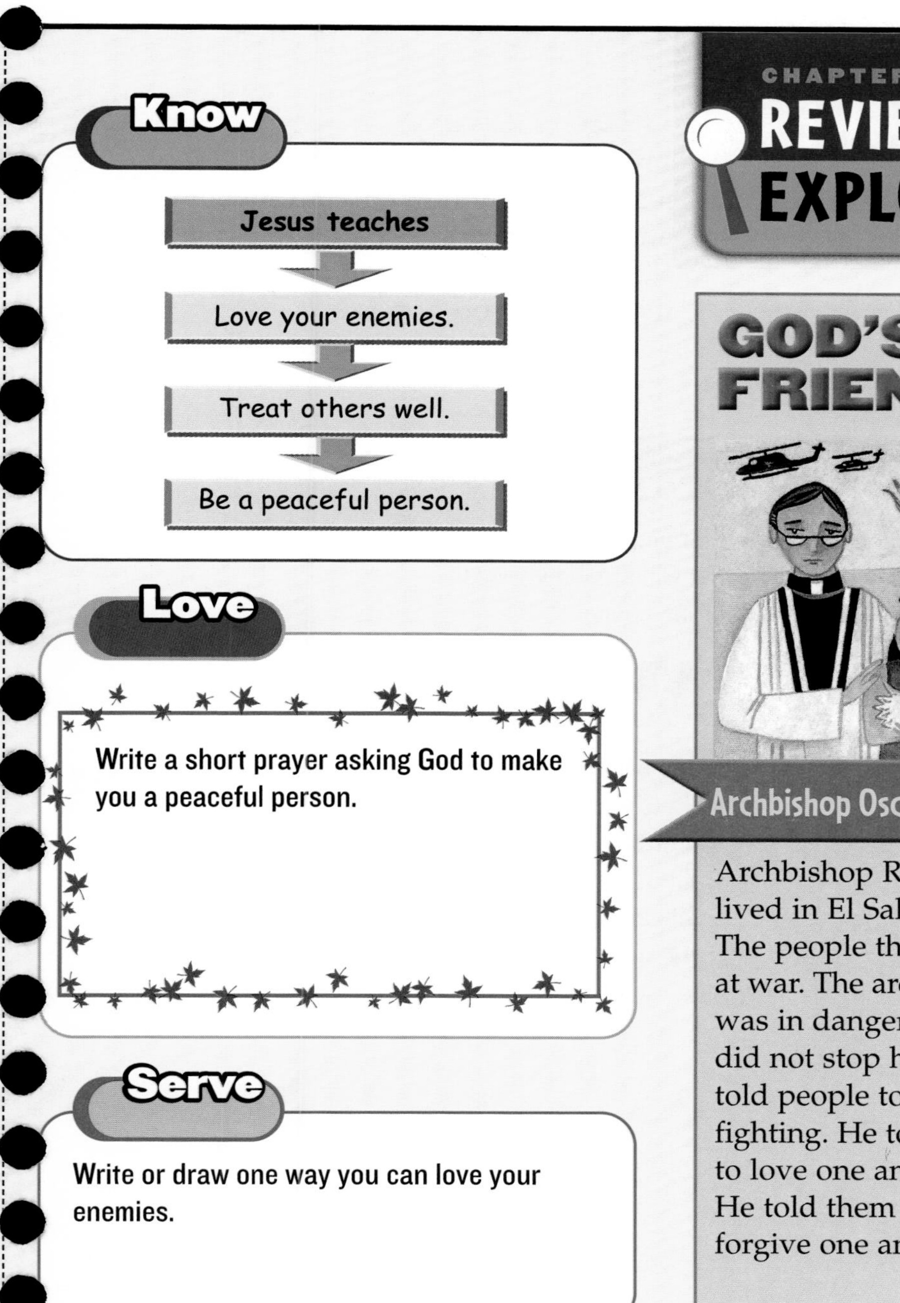

Know

Jesus teaches

Love your enemies.

Treat others well.

Be a peaceful person.

Love

Write a short prayer asking God to make you a peaceful person.

Serve

Write or draw one way you can love your enemies.

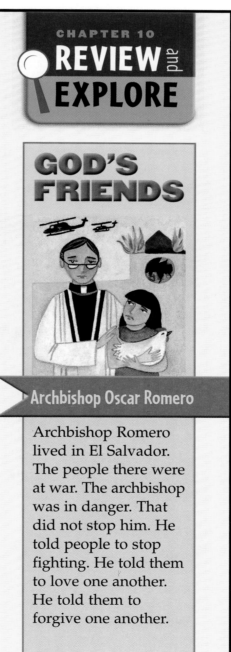

CHAPTER 10 REVIEW and EXPLORE

GOD'S FRIENDS

Archbishop Oscar Romero

Archbishop Romero lived in El Salvador. The people there were at war. The archbishop was in danger. That did not stop him. He told people to stop fighting. He told them to love one another. He told them to forgive one another.

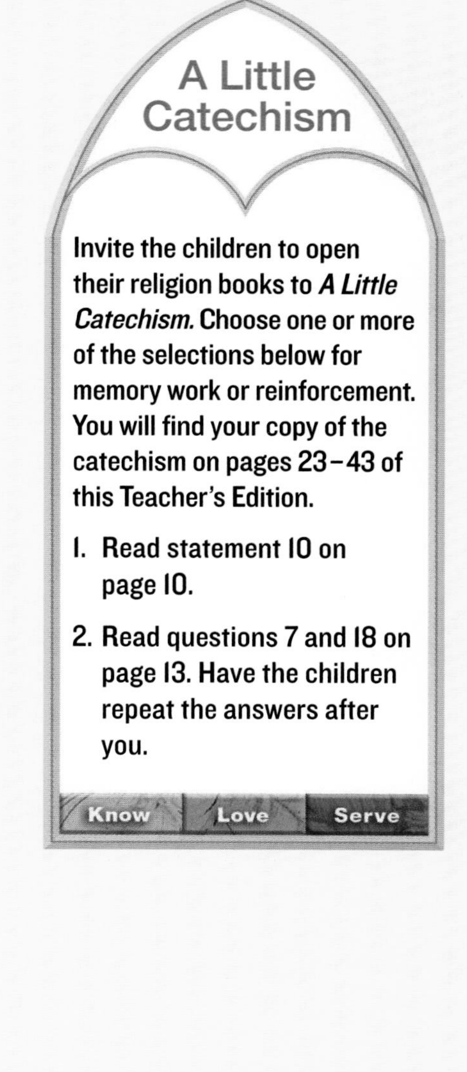

A Little Catechism

Invite the children to open their religion books to *A Little Catechism.* Choose one or more of the selections below for memory work or reinforcement. You will find your copy of the catechism on pages 23–43 of this Teacher's Edition.

1. Read statement 10 on page 10.
2. Read questions 7 and 18 on page 13. Have the children repeat the answers after you.

Know Love Serve

Note The activities on this page provide ways for the children to share their learning with their families. The activities are related to the week's theme.

1 Introduce
Have the children silently read the introduction. With enthusiasm, briefly explain the two suggested activities.

2 Pray Together
Have all pray the prayer in the prayer burst silently. Let all who wish to do so, pray aloud the prayers they wrote as the Love activity on student page 155.

Online for Families
Remind the children to check the Benziger Web site this week with their families.
www.benziger.glencoe.com

Dear Family,

I have just finished chapter 10. I have learned that followers of Jesus love their enemies. They are peacemakers, too. Please help me be kind to others. Help me be a person of peace.

On your own

Make a peace poster for your room. On the poster, write words that will remind you to love your enemies and to bring peace.

With your family

One evening have a peace powwow. Sit in a circle and share ways that the members of your family can love your enemies. Talk about ways you can be a peaceful family. Talk about ways you can settle family arguments without fighting.

Lord, make me a channel of your peace.

GO ONLINE!
http://www.benziger.glencoe.com

1 Prepare
Say that the Church wants to bring peace to the world. In a peaceful world, all people would have the food, clothing, and shelter they need to live. We can bring peace right where we live. Share the information on the page.

2 The Project
Ways to help a needy family are listed on the page. The children will probably have other ideas to add. Do what is most feasible, and what best involves all of the children.

THE CHURCH TODAY

It is very difficult to be peaceful when your life is full of stress. People who are very poor feel the stress of trying to find food, clothing, and shelter.

You can bring peace by helping with some of the service work that is done in your parish. There are many things you can do.

Find out what your parish does to help the needy.

- Collect food for the hungry
- Provide clothing for families in need
- Help people find jobs
- Care for young children so mother can work

As a class, participate in one of the parish activities. Do what you can to make the people who need help feel the gift of Christ's peace.

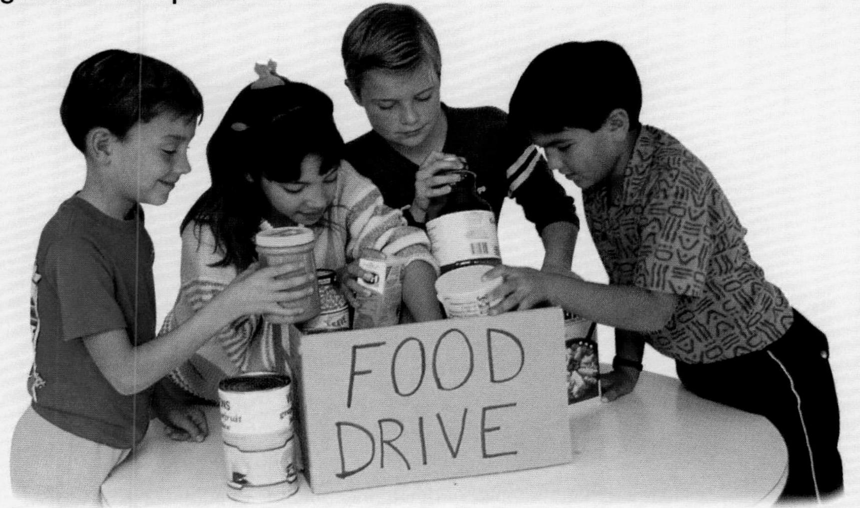

LEARNING TO PRAY

The children are at an age where there is little they can do to bring justice to the world. They are, however, just the right age to do something powerful every day—they can pray, so that people will be moved to help the needy. Pray every day for the family you adopted.

ANSWER KEY

This is the answer key for the chapter test on page 233.

A. 1. Sam 2. Carl 3. Danielle 4. Rosa

B. 1. Be good to everyone

C. 2. Be kind to all living things

Name ___________________________

Peace Needed

You can help make peace.

Finish the sentences by writing what you can do to help make peace. Circle the action you will do.

1. If someone is left out of a game, I can

____

____

_______________________________.

2. If someone in my family is tired, I can

____

_______________________________.

3. If someone is pushing, I can

____

_______________________________.

4. If someone forgot lunch, I can

____

_______________________________.

Name ______________________________

Chapter 10 Test

A. Circle the names of the peacemakers in each sentence.

1. Sam is a friend to all. Samantha likes to tease.

2. When no one looks, Carla cheats. Carl plays fairly, even when he is losing.

3. Danielle lets everyone play. Danny lets the best players play.

4. Rod has to have his way. Rosa gives in now and then.

B. Put a check by the words of Jesus.

_____ **1.** Jesus says, "Be good to everyone, even those who do not like you."

_____ **2.** Jesus says, "Be good to those who treat you best."

C. Write yes by each way to be a peacemaker.

_____ **1.** Hit hard to get your way.

_____ **2.** Be kind to all living things.

_____ **3.** Care for yourself only.

TEACHER RESOURCE CENTER

Faith Formation

CHECK THE CATECHISM

Man is often faced with making difficult moral decisions. He must seriously seek what is right and good. Additional information about making good moral choices and decisions can be found in paragraphs 1776–1802 of the *Catechism of the Catholic Church.*

Turn from Evil and Do Good

It is not always easy to make good moral choices. Forming one's conscience according to the teachings of Jesus and of the Church can be a daunting task. And yet believers are called to take on this task. An informed conscience gives one a clear vision of right and wrong. Living in accord with that same conscience is a challenge that lies at the very heart of Christian life. In order to "turn from evil," one must take an honest look at one's attitudes and behaviors. To "do good" might require one to change some of those same, often deeply imbedded, attitudes and behaviors. It is no small task to follow the call of the Gospel and to love others as Jesus loves us.

When have you found it difficult to accept your own shortcomings and inadequacies?

Conscience Formation

Conscience is one's ability to determine right from wrong. An "informed conscience" looks at Scripture and the faith tradition, listens to the teachings of the Church, consults with others, reflects on life experience, and prays for insight. Then good moral choices and decisions can be made, and it is indeed possible to "turn from evil and do good."

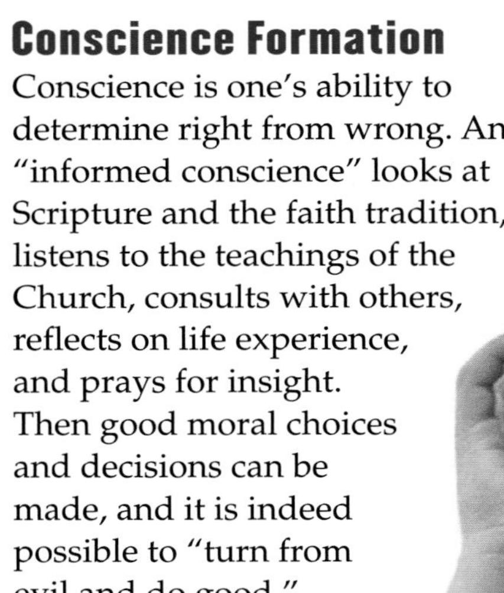

How does your informed conscience help you make good choices?

Background

Making Choices

Second-grade students face choices every day. What may be an easy or unimportant choice for an adult may be seen as a difficult or serious decision for a student.

Chapter 11 helps students understand that some choices are fun and some are tough. Tough choices often involve right and wrong. Recognizing moral choices and using the gift of conscience to help make the right choice are necessary understandings for the reception of the sacrament of Reconciliation.

In the chapter, the students are given three simple steps and a visual prompt for making moral choices. You can use the visual and the steps throughout the year.

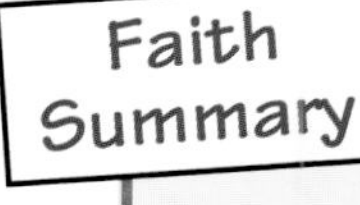

- God gives us free will.
- Our conscience tells us how to make moral choices.
- Our conscience tells us how to follow God's law.

Growth and Development

It is helpful to remember two characteristics of second graders as you teach this lesson:

- ***Second graders can make choices about their behavior.*** Know what kind of choices the students are capable of making and allow them to make those choices. When choices present a moral dilemma, guide them to use the three steps presented in the chapter.
- ***Second graders are developing a sense of responsibility.*** Unless unfitting or dangerous, let the students take responsibility for their choices.

A Teacher's Prayer

God, bless me with grace to model generosity. Replace anger with your peace, lighten sadness with your compassion, ease sorrow with your forgiveness, heal my bruised pride with your understanding, and calm impatience with your serenity. Amen.

Vocabulary Preview

free will
moral choices
conscience

Scripture

Romans 12:2: Do what is pleasing to God.

Related Resources

Books

Duncan, Geoffrey. *600 Blessings and Prayers* (Twenty-Third Publications, 1-800-321-0411 or www.twentythirdpublications.com). A treasury of prayers and blessings. (Children)

Huebsch, Bill. *A New Look At Grace* (Twenty-Third Publications, 1-800-321-0411 or www.twentythirdpublications.com). This book reflects on the meaning of God's grace and challenges the reader to be a gracious receiver of God's gift. (Adult)

Sasso, Sand Eisenberg. *A Prayer For the Earth* (Treehaus Communications, 1-800-638-4287 or www.treehaus1.com). This book, based on the story of Noah, helps children to see how God helps people even in times of great disaster. (Children)

TEACHER ORGANIZER

Planning Guide

The basic content for each chapter is divided into four class sessions. There are a number of options, for the fifth session. Extension, review, and testing options are described under Day 5 Alternatives. The Quick Check box will help you evaluate the week's lessons.

Chapter Goals

In this chapter, the students will learn about

- ❑ Free will
- ❑ Conscience
- ❑ Moral choices

	DAY 1 · INVITATION	DAY 2 · DISCOVERY	DAY 3 · DISCOVERY
OBJECTIVES	**The students will be able to** • Offer advice about a choice made • Self-examine the difficulty of making choices	**The students will be able to** • Evaluate choices they have made • Discover good choices to make • Understand that God helps them make moral choices	**The students will be able to** • Apply steps to making moral decisions • Evaluate the results of making choices • Share how they feel when they make the right choice
PREPARATION	• Think about the decision-making opportunities you give the children	• Think about good choices the students can make	• Make copies of the resource master on page 250 on heavy, light-colored paper
MATERIALS	• One candy per child • Relaxing music	• Pencils	• Pencils • Drawing supplies • Scissors • Hole punch • Yarn or string
OPTIONAL ACTIVITIES	• **Ideas That Work** Distinguish between moral and non-moral choices	• **Options** Act out moral choices • **Curriculum Challenge** Make a list of people who can help make choices	• **Options** Teach a simple song • **Ideas That Work** Make a traffic signal

Learning Objectives

By the end of this chapter, the students should be able to

- ❑ Evaluate choices made
- ❑ Differentiate between moral and non-moral choices
- ❑ Apply three steps to making moral choices

DAY 4 • LIVING

The students will be able to

- Practice making good choices
- Devise a plan for making good choices
- Pray a meditation prayer

- Create a sample of the Activity on student page 164

- Blank paper
- Red, yellow and green crayons
- Pencils

- **Curriculum Challenge** Teach the skill of predicting

DAY 5 • ALTERNATIVES

There are a number of alternatives to help you plan Day 5.

Prayer Experience
Do the prayer experience, "Quiet Time," on either Day 4 or Day 5. You will need a candle and a small bell. Follow the suggestions on page 246 for leading the prayer.

Review and Explore
The children will need pencils.

Home and Family
Send the page home, if possible, or assign one or more of the activities as class work or homework.

The Church Today
This page provides a class project that can be done following the chapter test. Have materials for bar graph available.

Chapter Test
The chapter test appears as a resource master on page 251.

Quick Check

Do this evaluation as soon as you finish each chapter.

Did I follow my lesson plan?

How can I tell that I met the learning objectives for the lesson?

What activities did the children enjoy most?

How could I improve this lesson?

Benziger on the Web
For more ideas, visit us at www.benziger.glencoe.com

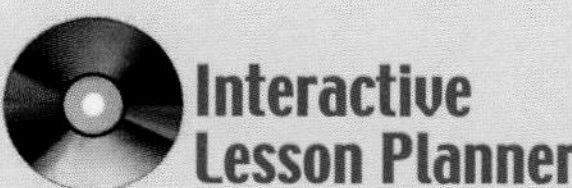

Interactive Lesson Planner
Your ILP provides more help in preparing to teach this chapter.

Celebrate
Turn to page 22 of this book. Check for seasonal celebrations.

Lesson Plan · Day 1
Call attention to the chapter title. Talk about what the chapter may be about. Point out to the children that choosing well requires some thinking as well as some help from those that care about them. At the end of the lesson, come back to the Do You Know? question to see how the children's knowledge has developed.

1 Introduction
Hide a piece of candy in one hand. Let every child guess which hand the candy is in. Give the piece of candy to each child that guesses correctly. Then, go to the children who did not guess correctly. Hold the candy in an open palm. Tell them to choose again.

2 Choose Well
Say that chapter 11 is about making choices that are more important than guessing hands. The children are just the right age for learning how to make important choices. Then, have everyone read aloud the chapter title, Scripture verse, and question. See who can tie the three together. *(We try to make good choices that please God.)*

IDEAS THAT WORK

The lesson will proceed into making moral choices. Perhaps the children are confusing moral and non-moral choices they make every day. If so, divide the children into groups. Let each group have a space at the board. Each group draws and fills in a chart of two columns: Fun Choices; Tough Choices. Afterward ask: What makes the tough choices different from the fun choices? (For example, the children might see that tough choices may have serious consequences; it does not matter what fun choice you make; tough choices may affect someone else.)

Do what is pleasing to God.
Romans 12:2

Do You Know?

◆ Why do you need to make good choices?

CHOOSE WELL

THE BICYCLE MYSTERY

Ricardo knew he wanted to have some "big kid" fun. So, he borrowed his brother's bike. It was a big bike with lots of gears. Ricardo's brother would not be happy if he knew what was happening.

Sure enough, Ricardo crashed the bike. What a mess! His brother was going to be so mad! Ricardo put the bike in the corner of the garage and ran into the house.

A few minutes later, he heard his brother shout, "What happened to my bicycle?"

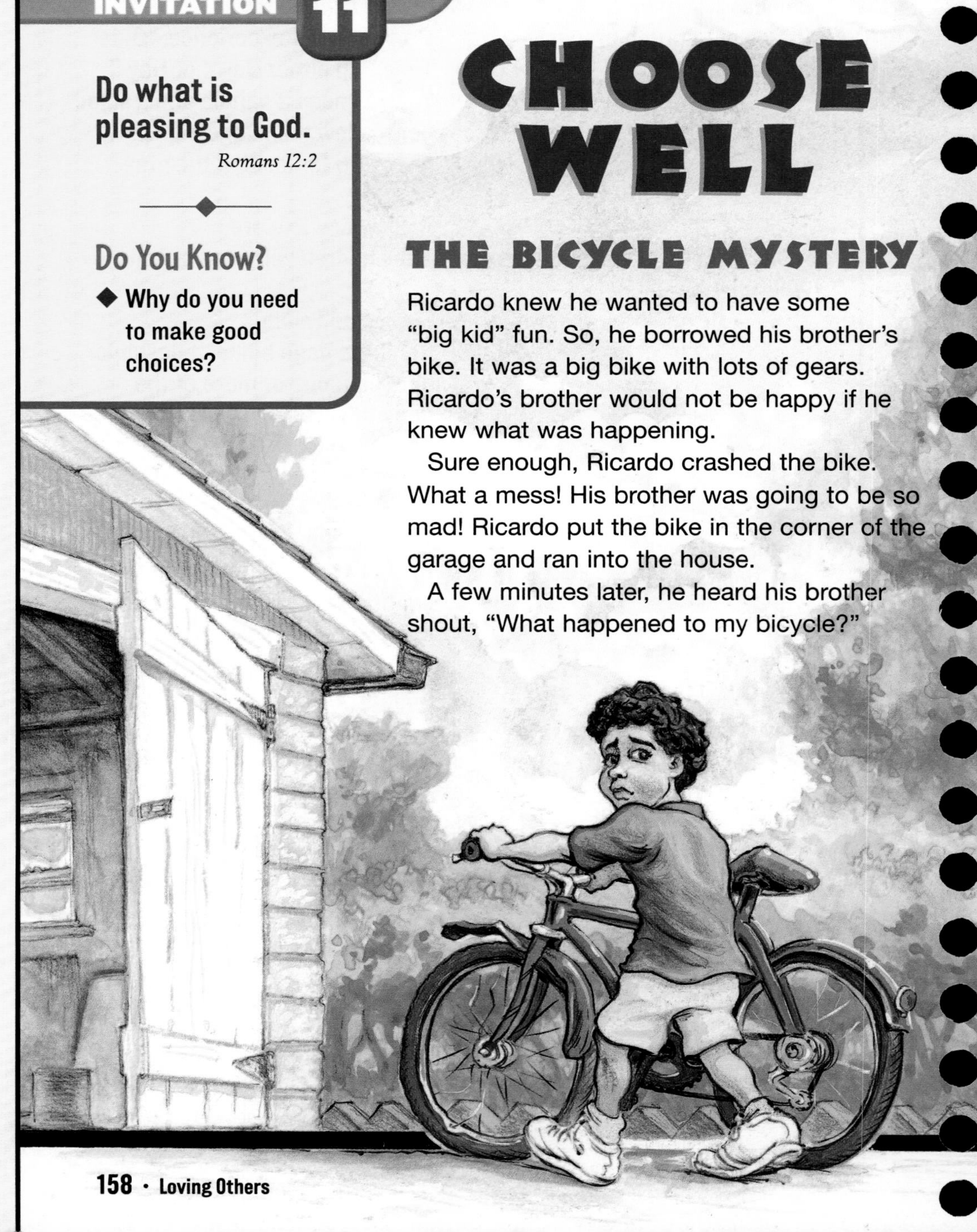

3 The Bicycle Mystery
Read the story. Focus the children on listening for the choice Ricardo made. Ask the children to act out the choice Ricardo should have made.

4 It's Tough
Talk about the choice Ricardo should make. Then, share the information on student page 159. Some children may want to share difficult choices they have to make. Then, play some relaxing music and have the children do the exercise. Emphasize honesty. Say that the answers will be private. You may wish to answer the questions, as well.

IT'S TOUGH

It is not always easy to choose what is right. When Jesus was on earth, he had tough choices to make. Jesus always chose what God wanted him to do.

You can follow Jesus' example. You can try hard to do what God wants you to do.

Read each sentence. Mark the sentence with an *A* if you agree. Mark it with a *D* if you disagree.

_____ It is always easy to choose what is right.

_____ I make all my choices on my own.

_____ I always think about what God wants when I choose.

_____ I know when I have made the right choice.

This chapter on making choices gives you the opportunity to evaluate the role of decision-making in your classroom. Do you allow the children to make some decisions about their behavior? Doing so helps them learn that they are responsible for their own actions. It also minimizes levels of frustration. Rather than making demands, you can offer the children a choice and respect their decision (do this activity or that one; choose one problem to do for homework; decide when you will do the page and turn it in before the day ends).

Lesson Plan · Day 2

Let volunteers tell a choice they made that day. Have everyone call out if the choice was fun or tough.

1 Decisions, Decisions

Introduce the information in the first paragraph. Write *free will* on the chalkboard while explaining the concept. Say that the word *free* means freedom. While explaining *moral choices* write the words on the board. Moral choices are often tough choices. Finish reading aloud student page 160.

2 Question

Emphasize to the children that learning to make good moral choices will help them their whole life. People never stop making moral choices. Then, give the children quiet time to reflect upon the question at the end of student page 160. Make sure they consider a tough choice they recently made.

VIRTUE FAITH GRACE

VOCABULARY

Free will God's gift of freedom to make choices.

Moral choice A choice that involves right and wrong.

Conscience Knowing what is right and what is wrong. Our conscience always tells us to do what is loving and right. Listening to our conscience is listening to God.

OPTIONS

For Children Who Learn Interpersonally These children work well with others. Give them situations of unfairness to act out. Have them determine the right choice that changes the situation. Let the children switch roles until each child plays the person who is treated unfairly. Ask each child to tell how it felt to be treated badly.

God's Word, the Ten Commandments, and the Church teach me how to make moral choices.

Decisions, Decisions

What game will you play? What will you wear? Will you do your homework? Will you finish your chores? Will you play fair? Every day you have more decisions to make.

You have to learn to make decisions because God gave you a gift. The gift is called **free will.** You are free to choose what is right to do or what is wrong to do.

Sometimes you make decisions about playing fair, telling the truth, hurting someone, or obeying your parents. Those kinds of decisions are called **moral choices.**

Think about all the decisions you made today. Were any of those decisions moral choices?

3 Learn to Choose

Say to the children that because God loves them so much, God helps them make good choices. Let volunteers recall people and things that help us live God's way. Then, introduce the word *conscience* and share the information on student page 161. Go back to the story about Ricardo. Ask the children how Ricardo followed his conscience.

4 How to Choose

Say that it is good that God gives each person a conscience. The children will learn three simple steps to follow their conscience. Have the children follow along in their books while you go through each step. Then, have the children say the steps out loud, pointing to each color as they read along.

5 Activity

You may need to give prompts to help the children think of specific good choices. Let the children work independently, and make it clear that they will not have to share their responses.

Learn to Choose

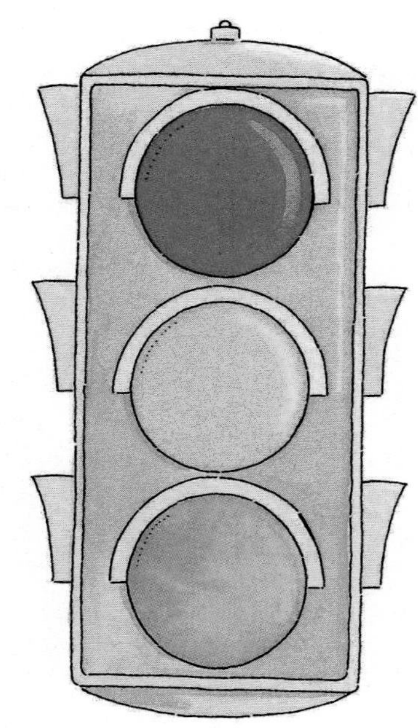

God gave you another gift to help you. That gift is your **conscience.** Your conscience helps you know how to make moral choices.

You learn to make good moral choices. You learn from your family. You learn from God's Word. You learn from the good example of others. When you learn and remember, your conscience will remind you what is right to do.

Three steps will help you get in the habit of listening to your conscience.

1. Stop: Before you make a choice, look at the choices you have to make.
2. Think: What does your conscience tell you about the choice that you have to make? Be honest.
3. Go: Follow your conscience.

ACTIVITY ONE GOOD CHOICE

In the space, write or draw one choice your conscience helps you make.

CURRICULUM CHALLENGE

Social Studies Guide the children to make a list of people who can help them make good moral choices. Ask for the kind of person who would make the list (someone trustworthy, kind, good, smart, holy and so on). The list does not have to be long. It should include family members.

Lesson Plan · Day 3

You may wish to review conscience by having the children sing a simple song. See Options.

1 Learning How

Tell the children that as they grow older they will have harder choices to make. But as they grow, they will also learn more about making good choices. Tell the children that they will read about two children that have some difficult moral choices to make. Use the steps on student page 161 to help the children discover the right thing to do for each situation.

2 Jack and Penny

Slowly lead the children through the three steps while they evaluate Jack and Penny's predicament. STOP: What choices do Jack and Penny have? Write them on the board. THINK: Write the possible consequences under each choice. GO: What do Jack and Penny's consciences tell them to do?

OPTIONS

For Those Who Learn Musically Have these children teach this simple song to the others. The words are sung to "Oh, Dear, What Can the Matter Be?"

I am very confused today.
Tell me, what is the choice
to make.
Oh, my, what does my
conscience say?
It says to do as God asks.

IDEAS THAT WORK

You may want to enlist some help and make a three dimensional traffic light labeled with the three steps for making good moral choices. (Your visual-spatial learners could transform round oatmeal boxes into a display.) Or, make a bulletin board using a traffic light. The more the children are exposed to the three steps, the more apt they will be to use them.

Learning How

As you grow up, you will learn more and more about choosing what is right. When you stop to think, you will discover more and more what to do.

Read the two stories. Talk about what you read. Then use the boxes on the next page to give Penny and Jack some help.

Jack

Patrick heard that Jack was giving a big birthday party. He hinted that he would like to come. Jack didn't want to invite Patrick because the other boys thought that Patrick always acted silly.

Penny

Penny couldn't believe her eyes. A five-dollar bill was lying on the playground. Penny looked around. No one could see. Penny stuffed the money in her pocket. Later, she heard that Vicki was asking if anyone found the five dollars she had lost.

❸ Help Out

Now that the class has used the STOP, THINK, and GO process for Jack and Penny's dilemmas, allow the children to complete the activity on student page 163. Explain that they are also to think of one difficult choice they have had to make. Children are to follow the same process as they did for Jack and Penny. Walk around the room to make sure that children are on task and that they understand the activity. Allow some time for children to share their solutions for Jack and Penny. Ask for volunteers to share personal stories.

Help Out

Use the boxes to help Penny and Jack. When you have finished, make up a story of your own. Then use the last row of boxes to see what you would do.

Jack	Penny	You
What are Jack's choices?	What are Penny's choices?	What are your choices?
What can happen to Jack?	What can happen to Penny?	What can happen to you?
What should Jack do?	What should Penny do?	What should you do?

RESOURCE MASTERS

The resource master on page 250 is a "conscience" visor for the children to make. Make copies of the visor on heavy, light-colored paper. The children will need drawing supplies, scissors, a hole punch, and a 24-inch length of string or yarn. On one side of the visor, the children draw the three lights of the traffic signal from page 161, with the three steps for making a moral choice. On the other side of the visor the children draw how they feel when they follow their conscience.

Lesson Plan · Day 4

Review the steps for making good choices by showing red, yellow, and green circles one at a time.

1 Practice Makes Perfect

Go through the two stories as a class. Then show the red circle and ask all to call out the step. *(stop)* Next, point to a row of children to explain the step. *(Stop and ask what choices you have.)* Repeat with the other two steps.

2 Activity

Distribute paper and red, yellow, and green crayons to children working in pairs. Ask them to draw and color their own "signal": red, yellow, and green on the left side of the paper as a guide. They can label each color. Show your sample. The partners will work on solutions for each story. Walk around and verify that all understand the directions. Finally, let each pair share their solutions.

TEACHING TIP

Some children may approach you about a choice they have to make. Guide them through the three steps they have learned in this chapter. You may also wish to use the steps when you anticipate a time when the children may be challenged to make difficult choices, such as the temptation to make fun of a new student and the temptation to lie rather than get scolded.

LIVING

PRACTICE MAKES PERFECT

Read the two stories. Use the steps you have learned to practice making the right choice.

1. You are kicking your soccer ball down the street. You give it a good whomp! It breaks your neighbor's rose bush. Your neighbor did not see it happen. What is the right choice for you to make?

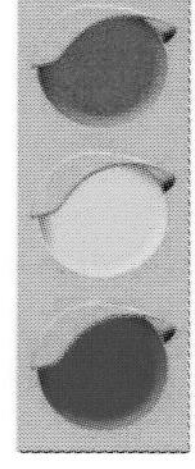

2. You are riding your scooter. Your parents have given you rules to follow. You think it is silly to wear all those pads and to stay on the safe path. What is the right choice for you to make?

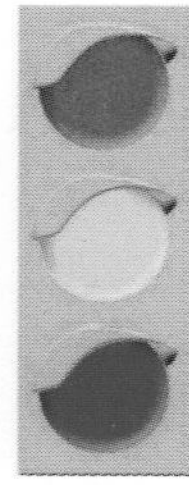

164 · Loving Others

❸ Day After Day

Give the children two or three sheets of sticky notes. Read the introduction to the activity. Allow some quiet thinking time before the children begin the activity. To help the children focus, suggest that they think of a person or situation that forces them to make tough choices.

DAY AFTER DAY

When you follow Jesus, you try to make good choices every day. You will always need to obey God's Law. You will always need to obey your parents and guardians. You will always need to be kind and honest.

Scratch your head and try to remember the past week. On the calendar, write one choice you had to make each day. Did you choose the right thing to do?

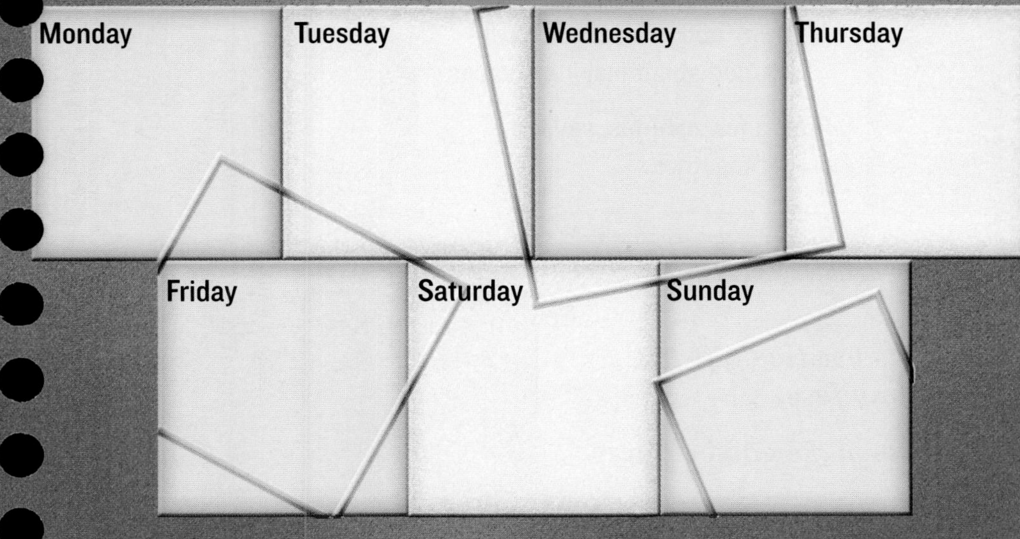

CURRICULUM CHALLENGE

Language Arts Use the three steps for making moral choices to teach children the skill of predicting. With applicable stories, have the readers stop when a character needs to make a choice. Let the readers predict the outcome by going through the three steps from the character's point of view.

Prayer
This prayer experience introduces the children to meditation, an ancient form of prayer. See the Learning to Pray feature below.

1 Prepare For Prayer
Let everyone find a comfortable area to sit. Be sure each child can see the candle. If fire regulations allow, light the candle. Lead everyone in taking three deep breaths to relax. In a quiet voice, tell the children to look at the candle or to close their eyes.

2 Quiet Time
Ring a small bell. Ask the children to think about the times when they chose to do what is right. Read the steps for quiet reflection. (*Pause for at least thirty seconds.*) Then, ring the bell, and tell the children to think about how they feel when they do what is right. (*Pause for another thirty seconds.*) Pray the prayer together.

LEARNING TO PRAY

The prayer experience provides the children some quiet time with God through the use of meditation. You may wish to tell the children that some people spend quiet time every day with God. Some people do not think of anything when they are with God; they use no words to pray.

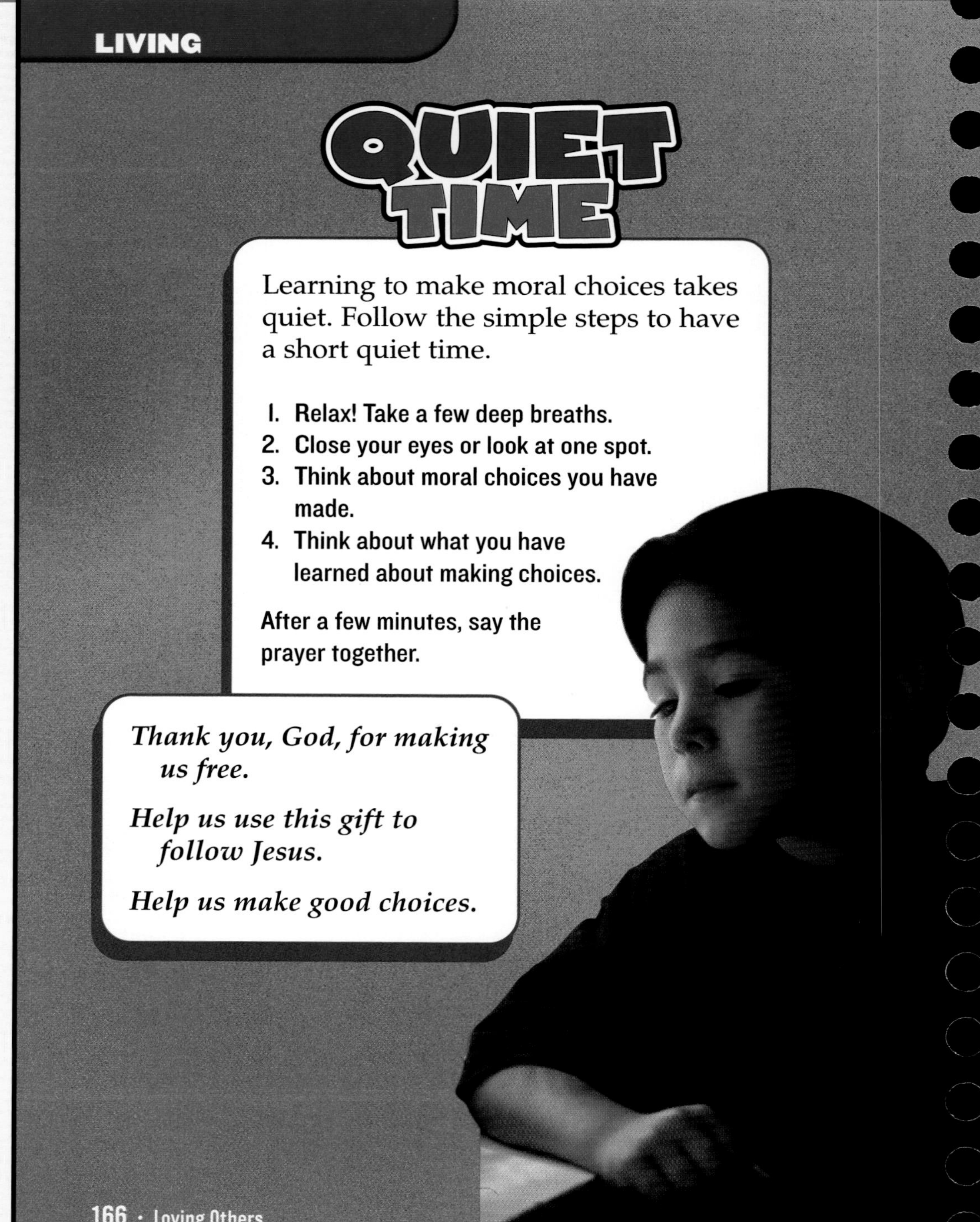

LIVING
QUIET TIME
Learning to make moral choices takes quiet. Follow the simple steps to have a short quiet time.
1. Relax! Take a few deep breaths.
2. Close your eyes or look at one spot.
3. Think about moral choices you have made.
4. Think about what you have learned about making choices.
After a few minutes, say the prayer together.
Thank you, God, for making us free.
Help us use this gift to follow Jesus.
Help us make good choices.
166 · Loving Others

1 Know
Direct attention to the graphic organizer. Review with the class the three steps for making moral choices. Ask the children to discuss how making good choices makes thing better for them and for others. Refer to Do You Know? on student page 158.

2 Love and Serve
Read through the Love and Serve activities. Let the children do them in any order. Invite the children to say their prayer silently at the end of the session or at the completion of the Church Today project.

3 God's Friends
Tell the children they are going to read about a man who went from making wrong choices to making right choices. Share the story in God's Friends. Ask the children how Saint Paul followed his conscience.

Know

Stop to look at the choice.

Think about what is good to do.

Go and follow your conscience.

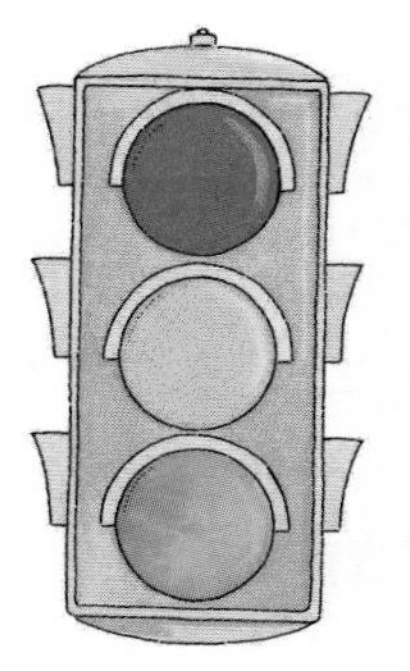

Love

Write a short prayer you can say when you have a moral choice to make.

Serve

In the little boxes, write or draw two ways to help others make good moral choices.

1.	2.

CHAPTER 11 REVIEW and EXPLORE

GOD'S FRIENDS

Paul the Apostle

Saint Paul learned that it was good to follow Jesus. Saint Paul wrote many letters to teach people how to follow Jesus. Learning the words of Saint Paul can help people make good moral choices.

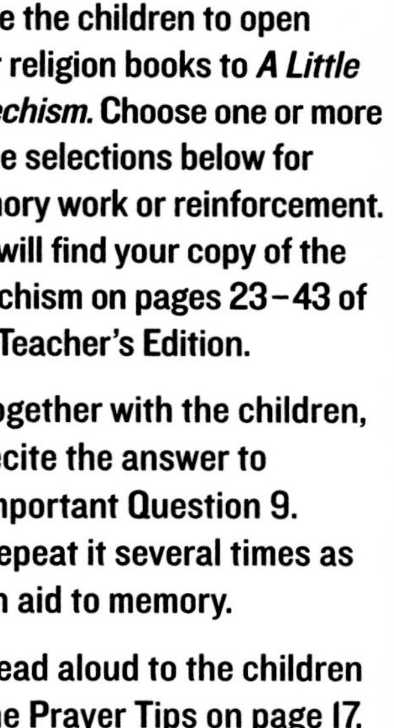

A Little Catechism

Invite the children to open their religion books to *A Little Catechism.* Choose one or more of the selections below for memory work or reinforcement. You will find your copy of the catechism on pages 23–43 of this Teacher's Edition.

1. Together with the children, recite the answer to Important Question 9. Repeat it several times as an aid to memory.
2. Read aloud to the children the Prayer Tips on page 17.
3. As a class, pray the short prayer: Come, Holy Spirit. Repeat it several times, more loudly and then more quietly.

Know Love Serve

Note The activities on this page provide ways for the children to share their learning with their families. The activities are related to the week's theme.

1 Introduce
Working in pairs, have the children pretend to be a parent and child. The child tells the parent what was learned in religion class during the past week. Then, with enthusiasm, briefly explain the two suggested activities.

2 Pray Together
Tell the children that we can pray to the Holy Spirit for help to make good choices. Together, say the prayer in the prayer burst aloud.

Online for Families
Remind the children to check the Benziger Web site this week with their families.
www.benziger.glencoe.com

Dear Family,

I have just finished chapter 11. I learned that I am free to make choices. I learned, too, that I have a conscience to guide me. Please help me when I have moral choices to make.

On your own

Find a small smooth stone. On the stone paint or color a red dot, a yellow dot, and a green dot. Carry the stone in your pocket to help you learn to follow your conscience.

With your family

Talk about the many choices that your family makes. How do members of your family help one another make choices?

Holy Spirit, help me listen to my conscience. Let me do what pleases God.

GO ONLINE!
http://www.benziger.glencoe.com

1 Prepare
Share the background information. Recall that prayer is something everyone can do every day. God is always with us to help us do what is right. Then, give each child a slip of colored paper.

2 The Project
Explain the project. Let one child make the label for the container. You may wish to have the children say the prayers they wrote on student page 167 at the completion of this project.

THE CHURCH TODAY

Making good moral choices can be tough. It is good to pray when you have an important decision to make. You can pray for one another, too.

A Prayer Bowl

Make a prayer bowl to help the whole class remember to pray for the choices you all make.

1. Label a bowl to show that it will contain your prayers.
2. On a slip of paper, write a choice or decision you want some help with.
3. Fold up your paper and tape it shut.
4. Everyone can put his or her paper in the prayer bowl.
5. Place the bowl on the class prayer table.
6. At prayer time, ask God to help you all make good moral choices.

God help us
make good choices

IDEAS THAT WORK

Invite the children to do a survey. Challenge them to ask a few people whom they know to write what they say when they pray for help. The children may make a bar graph to analyze all of the prayers for likes and differences, and they may share the prayers and the results with the class.

ANSWER KEY

This is the answer key for the chapter test on page 251.

A. 1. b 2. a 3. c

B. 1. choices 2. results 3. conscience

C. 1. a 2. a

Name ______________________________

My Visor

On one side draw the three steps for making a moral choice.
On the other side, draw how you feel when you follow your conscience.

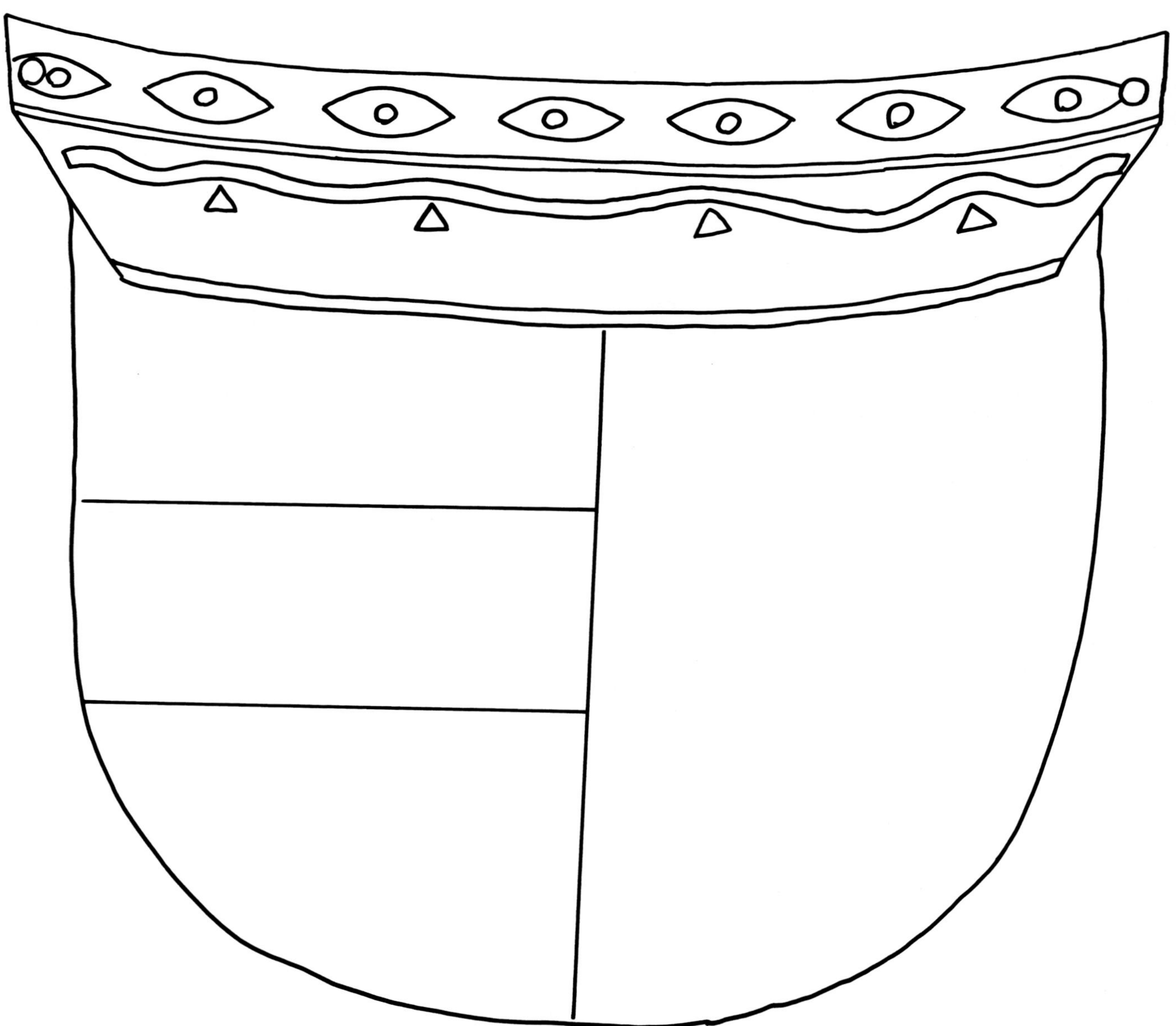

Name ______________________________

Chapter 11 Test

A. Draw a line to match the parts that go together.

1. God gives you free will

2. Moral choices are

3. Listening to your conscience is

a. about right and wrong.

b. to make choices.

c. like listening to God.

B. Write the missing words that tell how to choose.

1. Stop Ask what ________________ you have.

2. Think Think about the ________________ of your choices.

3. Go Go and follow your ________________.

C. Circle your answer to each question.

1. When are moral choices serious?

a. Always.
b. Sometimes.

2. What helps you do what is right?

a. Your conscience.
b. Your ideas.

CHAPTER 12 Do Not Sin

TEACHER RESOURCE CENTER

Faith Formation

Redeemed by Mercy

> *Then the scribes and the Pharisees . . . said to him, "Teacher, this woman was caught in the very act of committing adultery. Now in the law, Moses commanded us to stone such women. So what do you say?"*
>
> *John 8:3–5*

Jesus' answer, "Let the one among you who is without sin be the first to throw a stone at her," illustrates a profound truth: everyone is capable of sinning and chooses to do so at times. Jesus' message to the woman is his message to all sinners: "Neither do I condemn you . . . from now on do not sin any more."

What is your definition of *sin*?

Mortal and Venial Sin

While all sin is serious, mortal sin requires deep and sincere repentance. Mortal sin is deliberately and intentionally choosing to turn away from God's love, in such a way that serious and deadly harm is done. Such sin is rare. Followers of Jesus desire to love God and one another, and try to avoid lesser (venial) sins, as well.

How have you been aware of God's mercy?

CHECK THE CATECHISM

The *Catechism of the Catholic Church* tells in paragraph 1849 how sin is a failure in loving God and neighbor. Much more about the nature of sin can be found in paragraphs 1846–1876.

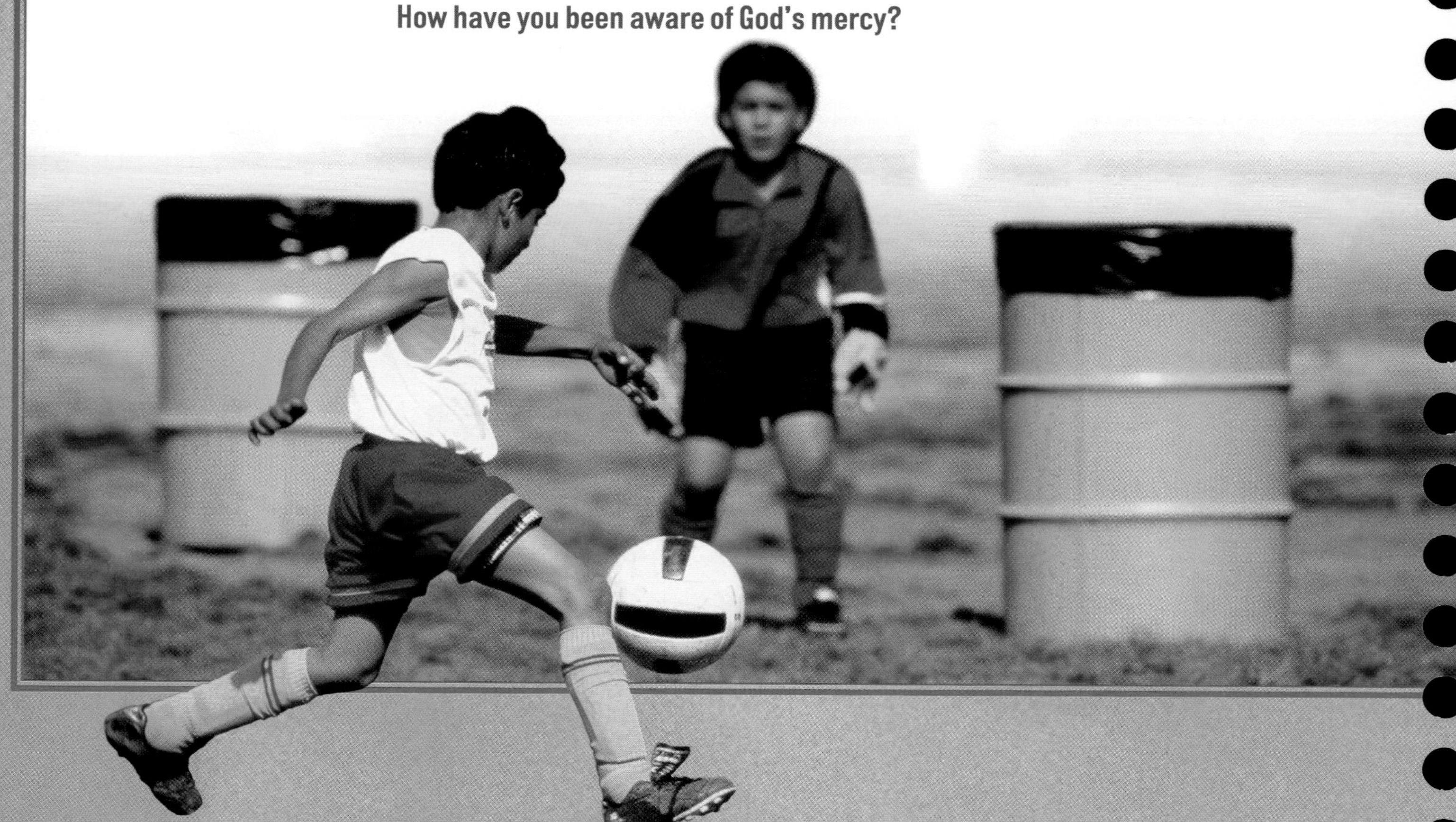

Background

Choices and Consequences

Chapter 12 addresses sin and its consequences. Sin is explained with simple language the students will understand. The students will see that wrong choices have repercussions, for which they must take responsibility.

Students understand there is a difference between saying, "I'm sorry," and feeling sorry for something done. They can say, "I'm sorry" without meaning it, simply to get on with life. But if they feel sorry about something, they want to make up for the hurt they have caused. The difference is a conversion of heart.

Faith Summary

- **Sin is a word, action, or desire that is contrary to God's law.**
- **Mortal sin separates us from God.**
- **Venial sin harms our relationship with God.**

Growth and Development

It is helpful to remember two characteristics of second graders as you teach this lesson:

- ***Second graders are able to understand the feelings of others.*** It will help the students to know that sin is not just rule breaking; sin is hurting others, whether or not this was the intention. The sacrament of Reconciliation will help the students make peace with those they have hurt. It will help them find loving ways to live.
- ***Second graders begin to see consequences for their behavior.*** Moral development, however, may be motivated by a simple desire to avoid punishment. Help the students learn from their mistakes and from criticism. A good way to do so is to ask a question, such as, "What could you do differently next time?"

A Teacher's Prayer

God, you shower me with the gifts of creation, and ask only my love in return. Give me a heart filled with thankfulness, and a spirit eager to serve you. Guide my thoughts to uncover wisdom in the students' hearts and minds. Bolster my strength, that I may cheerfully do all that you ask. Amen.

Vocabulary Preview

sin
mortal sin
venial sin
mercy

Scripture

Romans 12:9: Hate what is evil.
Matthew 5:13–20: salt of the earth
Matthew 5:19: Obey the commandments.
Luke 15:4–7: the lost sheep

Related Resources

Videos

"The Candy Store" (St. Anthony Messenger Press, 1-800-488-0488 or www.AmericanCatholic.org). Encourages children to choose alternatives for living a good life. (Children, 15 minutes)

"Handle With Care" (Oblate Media and Communications, 1-800-233-3629 or www.videoswithvalues.org). Five open-ended moral dilemmas for 2nd–4th graders. (Children, 10 minutes)

Book

McCormick, Patrick. *Sin As Addiction* (Paulist Press, 1-800-218-1903 or www.paulistpress.com). This book explores the addictive nature of sin. (Adult)

TEACHER ORGANIZER

Planning Guide

The basic content for each chapter is divided into four class sessions. There are a number of options for the fifth session. Extension, review, and testing options are described under Day 5 Alternatives. The Quick Check box will help you evaluate the week's lessons.

Chapter Goals

In this chapter, the students will learn about

- ❏ Sin, venial and mortal
- ❏ The consequences of sin
- ❏ God's mercy

	DAY 1 · INVITATION	DAY 2 · DISCOVERY	DAY 3 · DISCOVERY
OBJECTIVES	**The students will be able to** • Understand that some wrong choices are accidents or mistakes • Discover that accidents and mistakes carry the responsibility to apologize	**The students will be able to** • Differentiate sins from accidents and mistakes • Differentiate mortal and venial sins	**The students will be able to** • Conclude that sinful wrongdoing carries responsibilities • Analyze a parable • Discover that God is merciful
PREPARATION	• Review the three steps in making moral choices	• Find the objects that give light	• Prepare to lead a discussion of the symbolism in The Lost Sheep
MATERIALS	• Pencils • The red, yellow, and green circles used in Chapter II	• Pencils • Objects (or pictures of objects) that give light, such as a flashlight, candle, lightbulb	• Pencils • Drawing supplies
OPTIONAL ACTIVITIES		• **Teaching Tip** To explain sin's rippling effect, have a small bowl of water and small objects to toss into it • **Vocabulary** Continue adding to the Word Wall	• **Vocabulary** Continue adding to the Word Wall • **Bible Basics** Make a chart on chalkboard or newsprint

Learning Objectives

By the end of this chapter, the students should be able to

- ❑ Differentiate accidents and mistakes from sins
- ❑ Evaluate the consequences of a wrong choice
- ❑ Conclude that God is merciful and loving

DAY 4 · LIVING

The students will be able to

- List what they know about making choices
- Creatively express the consequences of making a choice

- Pencils
- Drawing supplies
- Copies of the resource master on page 268
- Candle or electric light

- **Curriculum Challenge** Turn the stories into booklets; provide 4 sheets of drawing paper per child, and supplies for matching covers

DAY 5 · ALTERNATIVES

There are a number of alternatives to help you plan Day 5.

Prayer Experience
Use the prayer service, Be Light, on either Day 4 or Day 5.

Review and Explore
The students will need notepaper and sturdy paper button shapes.

Home and Family
Send the page home with the students, or assign one or more of the activities.

The Church Today
The students will make books about choices. Plan how you will organize the activity. Have the necessary supplies—paper, staplers, crayons, markers, magazines, glue. Make arrangements to share the books with the first grade.

Chapter Test
The chapter test appears as a resource master on page 269.

Quick Check

Do this evaluation as soon as you finish each chapter.

Did I follow my lesson plan?

How can I tell that I met the learning objectives for the lesson?

What activities did the children enjoy most?

How could I improve this lesson?

Benziger on the Web
For more ideas, visit us at **www.benziger.glencoe.com**

Interactive Lesson Planner
Your ILP provides more help in preparing to teach this chapter.

Celebrate
Turn to page 22 of this book. Check for seasonal celebrations.

Lesson Plan · Day 1
Review the red, yellow, and green circles from Chapter 11, and ask the children to go through the three steps in making moral choices.

1 Right and Wrong
Ask the children how making choices might go with the title of the chapter. Recall the story of Saint Paul, who traveled to many countries to tell people about living God's way. Ask for a volunteer to read aloud Paul's words in the chapter's Scripture verse. Discuss the Do You Know? question. At the end of the week, come back to this question to see how the children's knowledge has developed.

2 Gotcha!
Invite the children to listen to a story. Focus the children, using the question that follows the story. Then, read or tell the story. Ask for a show of hands: Who thinks that Juan hurt Mike on purpose? Ask why they feel this way. Some children may say that Juan's apology proves that he did not mean to hurt Mike. That could lead to an interesting discussion about the use of the words "I'm sorry."

TEACHING TIP

A great deal of research supports the premise that a read-aloud program, at home and at school, is a major ingredient in creating successful learners. Here are some tips for good storytelling:

- Visualize the details to the story while you are telling it, or reading it.
- Watch the children for reactions.
- Use props, if you are comfortable with them.
- Remember that it is fun to tell a story, and fun to hear one.
- Share tales you know.

INVITATION 12

Hate what is evil, hold on to what is good.
Romans 12:9

Do You Know?
◆ What is a sin?

Do Not Sin

Gotcha!

Mike and Juan had been friends all year. They played on different soccer teams. Today's game was a very important one. The score was tied late in the game.

All at once, Mike was running right at Juan. Juan knew that Mike was the best player on the other team. If he got past Juan, Mike would score, and Juan's team would lose.

Just as Mike was about to pass Juan, Juan stuck out his foot. He tripped Mike. Mike fell down hard. He skidded across the grass. He hurt his knee. He looked at his friend. Juan knew even before he heard the whistle and saw the red card that he had done something very wrong.

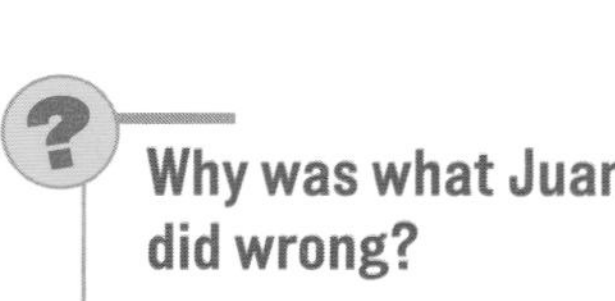

Why was what Juan did wrong?

3 No Mistake
Share the information about accidents and mistakes from student page 171. Emphasize that the person causing the accident, or making the mistake, is still responsible for its consequences. This may be a new concept to the children, and may need further discussion.

4 Activity
Explain how to do the word puzzle. Allow the children time to do the activity. Ask a volunteer to share his or her answer with the class.

No Mistake

You know when you do something by accident. When you bent down to pick up your fork, you knocked over your milk by accident. You tell your mom that you are sorry.

You also know when you do something by mistake. You misspelled the word *donkey* on your spelling test. That was a mistake. You tell your teacher that you will try harder next time.

Sometimes you choose to do something that is not right to do. How do you know that you have done something wrong?

Catholics have a word for choosing to do wrong. You can find that word below. Copy the letters in the yellow squares to the boxes below.

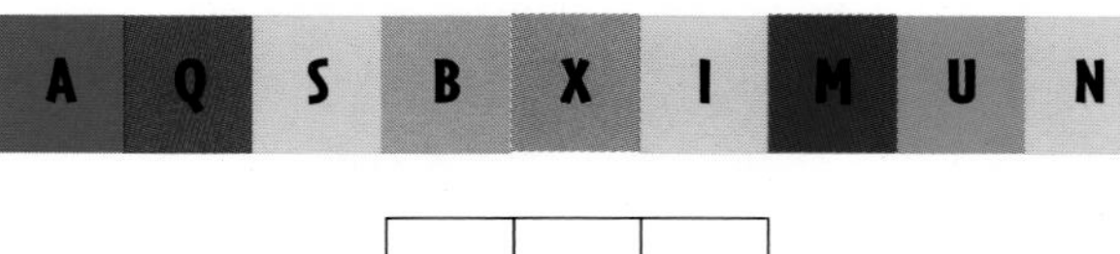

IDEAS THAT WORK

Are the children confused about differentiating accidents and mistakes from wrongdoing? You may wish to use the words "on purpose" to clear things up. Accidents and mistakes are not done on purpose.

Lesson Plan · Day 2

Ask the children to picture what happened to a girl named Toby. See Ideas That Work. Then, ask for a show of hands as to who thinks Toby acted on purpose. How can Toby make up for the trouble she caused? Say that today's lesson is extra important, and all need to listen carefully.

1 Salt of the Earth

Display several different kinds of light-giving objects or pictures of them. Talk about how these objects are helpful to people. Then ask what good is a burned-out lightbulb, or a candle with no wick, or a flashlight with no batteries. Tell the children that Jesus had something to say about being a light for all to see. Read the story.

Ask the children why Jesus said *you* are the light of the world. Ask: If people followed you around all day, what good things would they see you do that bring light into the lives of others? Have a volunteer read aloud the This We Believe! feature on student page 172.

IDEAS THAT WORK

Share "One day Toby woke up in bed, stretched her arms wide, and knocked over a plant, that hit a picture, that fell on the cat, who meowed and screeched, and leaped up on the curtains, that fell to the floor. Oh, my!"

TEACHING TIP

Since the children are concrete learners, you may wish to explain the repercussions of sin in a concrete way. Have on hand a small bowl of water and a few small pebbles, marbles, or any other items which will cause ripples when dropped into the bowl. Gather the children, and mention how calm the water is. Have a shy child drop the objects gently into the water. Ask the children to describe what happened to the water. Say that the pebbles cause quite a change. Sin does that, too. Even sin that seems small can cause big changes in relationships.

This We Believe!

Choosing what is right brings you closer to God. Choosing to do wrong hurts your relationship with God.

Salt of the Earth

One day Jesus was teaching the people. "You are the salt of the earth," he told them. "You are the light of the world, too. Let your light shine so that people will know you are my followers."

Then Jesus went on. "Don't think that I came to take away the law. I want you to obey even the smallest parts of the law. The one who breaks the law will be called least in God's kingdom."

"The one who obeys the law and teaches others to obey the law will be called greatest in God's kingdom. I want you to do what is right."

Based on *Matthew 5:13–20*

How can you be a light for others?

2 Sin
Have a volunteer read aloud the Word of God feature on student page 173. Then, have the children repeat after you the words *venial sins* and *mortal sins.* Lead the children through the explanation of the two types of sins. Ask if there are any questions.

3 Activity
Instruct the students to do the matching activity independently. Allow time to review the answers as a class.

Sin

When you choose to do wrong, you commit a **sin.** A sin is an action against God's Law. When you sin, you are not light for the world. You also hurt your friendship with God.

You cannot commit a sin by mistake or by accident. You have to choose to do wrong. There are two kinds of sin, **mortal sin** and **venial sin.**

1. **Mortal sin** is an action that is very seriously wrong. To commit a mortal sin, you must know an action is wrong. And you must choose to do it anyway.
2. **Venial sin** is less serious sin.

WORD OF GOD

Those who obey the commandments will find God.

Matthew 5:19

ACTIVITY MATCHING

Draw a line from the item in column A with the item in column B that matches it best.

A	B
Mortal sin	Greatest in the kingdom
Venial sin	Very serious
Light for the world	A follower of Jesus
One who obeys God	Less serious

VIRTUE FAITH GRACE VOCABULARY

Sin Choosing to do wrong.

Venial sin Wrong choices that hurt your friendship with God. Most sins are venial.

Mortal sin An action that is seriously wrong. You know that the action is wrong, and you choose to do it anyway.

Consequences The results. You are responsible for the consequences of your sins.

CURRICULUM CHALLENGE

It will help the children to learn that sin is not just rule breaking; sin is hurting others, whether or not this was the intention. Sorrow comes not from breaking rules, but from recognizing that another person has been hurt. The sacrament of Reconciliation will help the children make peace with those they have hurt. It will help them find loving ways to live.

Lesson Plan · Day 3

Tell the children that today they will hear two stories—one about children like them, and another one that Jesus told.

1 Allison's Lie

Share the information on the page, emphasizing that God never stopped loving Allison. Ask the children how that makes them feel. Can Allison and Craig be friends again? How can Allison take responsibility for her lie?

2 Activity

Ask for a show of hands of those who can brush their teeth. Make the analogy: Brushing teeth over and over again becomes a good habit. Making the right choices over and over again forms good habits, too. Ask the children to do the activity in pencil. Allow time for them to share their answers in class.

VIRTUE FAITH GRACE

VOCABULARY

Mercy God's loving forgiveness.

Parable A teaching story. Jesus often told parables. The parable of the lost sheep teaches that God is merciful to sinners who are sorry.

Allison's Lie

Allison and Craig were good buddies. Every day, they would walk to the bus stop together. Every day, they would sit together on the school bus. One day, Tommy asked Craig to sit with him. Craig did. That upset Allison. "I'll show him," she thought.

That day Allison sat with Meg. On the way home, she whispered in Meg's ear. "I saw Craig steal a candy bar out of Billy's desk," she said. It was a lie, and Allison knew it was a lie.

- How did Allison's lie hurt Craig?
- How did the lie hurt Allison?

ACTIVITY THE RIGHT WAY

In the space below, write or draw what you think Allison should do. What should Craig do if he finds out Allison told a lie?

3 God Is Merciful
Lead the children through the introductory paragraph on student page 175. Then, read aloud The Lost Sheep. Ask the children to think of the shepherd as God, and the lost sheep as a sinner who has gone the wrong way, as they hear the story a second time. Reread the story aloud. Discuss the story with the children. See Bible Basics, below, for a suggestion.

4 Activity
The children may complete the activity on their own, and share their answers with someone who sits nearby.

God Shows Mercy

Jesus told many stories about God's love. Jesus knew that all people need God's mercy. They need to know that their sins can be forgiven. There is one special story that Jesus told.

The Lost Sheep

A shepherd has 100 sheep. He loses one of them. So the shepherd leaves the 99 and goes after the lost sheep. When he finds the sheep that was lost, he puts it on his shoulders and carries it home. When he returns home, the shepherd calls together all his friends and neighbors. He says to them, "Be happy with me. I have found my lost sheep."

Based on *Luke 15:4–7*

ACTIVITY — GREAT JOY

In the outline of the lost sheep, write or draw what you learned about God's mercy.

BIBLE BASICS

This Bible story, as a parable, has symbolism. You can help the children understand the symbolism by making a two-column chart of three rows. The left column will have questions about the story's literal meaning. The right column will have questions that help the children interpret the story's meaning. Here is a chart you may use:

Row 1 Do you think the sheep is happy to be back?
Is a sinner happy to be back with God?

Row 2 Why did the shepherd go after the sheep?
How does a sinner get lost?

Row 3 How does the shepherd show that he cares for his sheep?
How does God care for the sinner who is sorry?

Lesson Plan · Day 4

Recall the story of Allison, and ask who Allison hurt with her lie. *(Craig, herself, Meg, and God)* Recall that God gives us free will to make choices. Our conscience tells us the right choice to make. Making the wrong choice on purpose is a sin. God is merciful and welcomes back the sinner who is sorry.

1 Good Habits

Tell the children they are going to take a short trip back in time. Lead them through Unit 3; invite volunteers to call out things they learned. Then, explain the activity on student page 176. Let the children write three good habits for each wrong action. Affirm the children by saying how smart they are, how much they remember, how well they are preparing to receive the sacrament of Reconciliation, and so on. Allow time for the children to share their responses.

OPTIONS

For Intrapersonal Learners

These children are introspective. Adjust the activity on student page 176, so that the children write three things they are proud to know.

Followers of Jesus try to make a habit of good moral choices. They also try to make things right when they do wrong.

Look at the three actions in the first column. In the second column, tell how each person could turn a wrong action into a good habit. You can write or draw.

Wrong Action	Good Habit
Max talked back to his mom.	
Justin took two dollars from his big brother's drawer.	
Patsy hid on the playground during Sunday Mass.	

❷ Cartoon Carnival

Say to the children that they are now going to be artists. Explain the drawing activity on student page 177. The children may work best in groups. Encourage them to brainstorm ideas before beginning to draw.

CARTOON CARNIVAL

Create a cartoon character. In the squares, use the character to tell a story about sin and about God's mercy. Share your cartoon with the class. Share it with your family, too. Be sure to give your character and your story a name.

1

2

3

4

TEACHING TIP

To help the children brainstorm ideas for the activity on student page 177, suggest they draw something that could really happen in everyday life. Try to lead the children away from the very sensational sins they have heard about.

CURRICULUM CHALLENGE

Language Arts You may want to take the story-drawing activity one simple step further. Have the children make booklets of their story frames. Rather than draw in their books, the children may each use four sheets of drawing paper, one sheet per frame. A one- or two-sentence caption may accompany each frame. The children may cover their booklets with fabric, a wallpaper sample, magazine pages, or a large paper folded in half.

Prayer

Today's prayer experience uses the image of light for the world. Have a candle or small electric light on your prayer table, if possible.

1 Prepare for Prayer

Call attention to the leader's line. Choose a leader. Have everyone practice the lines.

2 Be Light

Gather in the prayer area to pray. End with a sign of peace.

The resource master on page 268 is a pencil game about going the right way to God.

LEADER: We are called to be light for the world.

BOYS: When we listen to our families and all who love us, we are light.

GIRLS: When we are peacemakers, we are light.

BOYS: When we follow our consciences, we are light.

GIRLS: When we avoid sin and choose to do what is right, we are light.

ALL: Lord, you will always show us the way. Teach us to be light for the world. Amen.

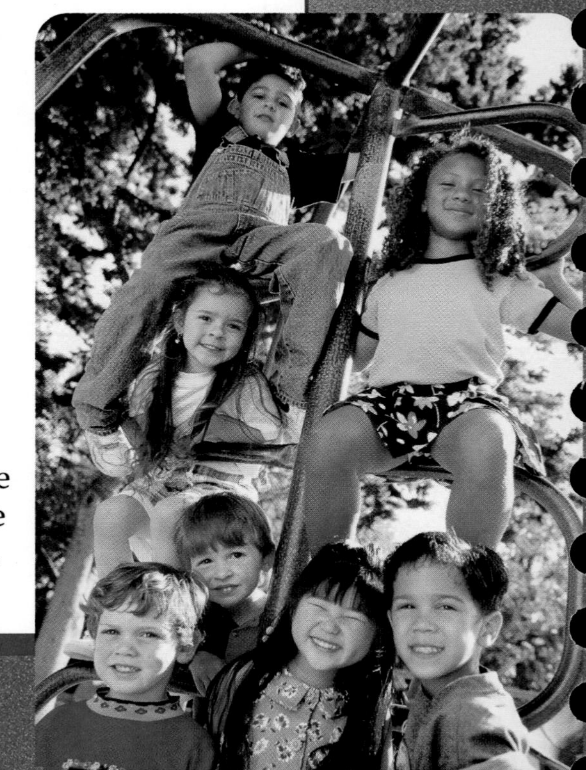

1 Know
Ask the children to turn to someone who sits near, and explain the graphic organizer to each other. Ask whether there are any questions.

2 Love and Serve
Explain the Love and Serve activities. Let each child choose which activity to do first. Set a time limit for completing both Love and Serve. You may give the children notepaper to do the Love activity. Give each child sturdy paper, cut in the shape of a button.

3 God's Friends
Show the illustration. Help the children focus. Share the information about Saint Monica. Ask the children what they can learn from Saint Monica.

CHAPTER 12
REVIEW and EXPLORE

Know

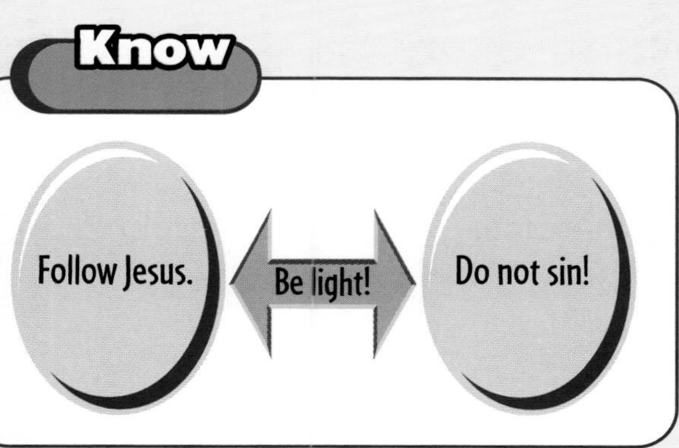
Follow Jesus.
Be light!
Do not sin!

Love

Write one way that you can show light to a friend or a relative.

Serve

Make a button out of cardboard. On the button write "You are light!" Give the button to someone as a reminder.

You are light

GOD'S FRIENDS

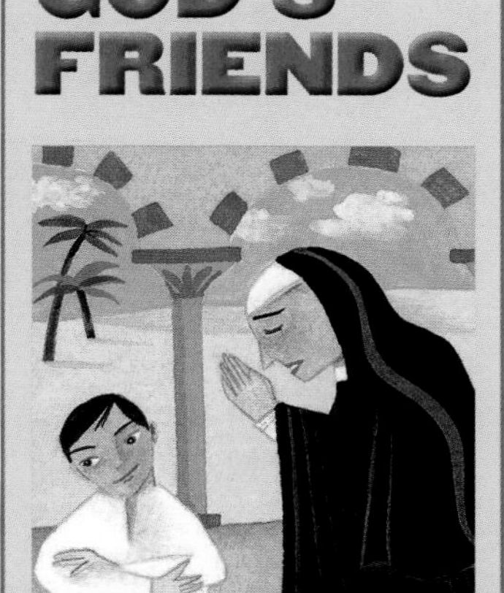

Saint Monica

Monica had a son who chose to sin. Monica worried about her son. She prayed for him, too. She wanted him to change. Finally, her son decided to choose to do good. He followed Jesus. Both Monica and her son became light for the world. Her son is Saint Augustine.

A Little Catechism

Invite the children to open their religion books to *A Little Catechism.* Choose one or more of the selections below for memory work or reinforcement. You will find your copy of the catechism on pages 23–43 of this Teacher's Edition.

1. Review the Act of Contrition on page 16. Have the children begin to learn it by heart.
2. Refer to the sacraments on page 14. Review Reconciliation.

Know | Love | Serve

Note The activities on this page provide ways for the children to share their learning with their families. The activities are related to the week's theme.

1 Introduce
The children may silently read the introduction. With enthusiasm, explain the two activities. Ask how the children will do the activities at home.

2 Pray Together
Have all pray aloud the prayer in the prayer burst.

Online for Families
Remind the children to check the Benziger Web site this week with their families.
www.benziger.glencoe.com

Dear Family,

I have just finished chapter 12. I learned that Jesus wants us to be light for the world. I learned about sin, too. Please help me choose to do what is right and good.

With others

A true friend helps you to be your very best. Talk to one of your friends. Plan to help one another do what is right.

With your family

Choose a story from the Gospel. Read the story together. Talk about the story. How can the story help you follow Jesus and do what is right?

Jesus, Light of the World, help me.

GO ONLINE!
http://www.benziger.glencoe.com

1 Prepare
Share the first paragraph, and say that you know the children can be good teachers. Have the children follow along, while you read about the project. Get their reactions.

2 The Project
Have a serious discussion about choices the children face in school. Let the class decide on several choices. More than one book may be made, ensuring everyone a part to play. If needed, decide on a set number of pages, and put a basic layout plan on the board. See Ideas That Work.

THE CHURCH TODAY

You will have to make good moral choices all your life. Now is a good time for you to get in the habit of doing what is right.

Make a class book of good choices.

1. Talk about your book and plan it together.
2. Talk about some of the choices second graders have to make.
   - Take turns or push and shove
   - Share the ball or hog it all for yourself
   - Do your homework or skip it
   - Let everybody play or leave some out
   - Be patient or use angry words
3. Put a different choice on each page of your book.
4. When the book is finished, put it where all can read it.

IDEAS THAT WORK

You may want to give the children some questions that will help them lay out their pages, and write a coherent story. Tell the children that anyone who reads their book should be able to answer the following questions:

- What is the problem?
- What are the choices?
- What are the results of each choice?
- What is the right choice?

The children may have the tendency to make their story sound like test questions. Show them how to answer the questions using storytelling words.

ANSWER KEY

This is the answer key for the chapter test on page 269.

A. 1. wrong 2. love 3. Mortal 4. Venial 5. closer 6. responsible 7. mercy

B. 1. ✓ 2. ✓ 3. ✓

Name ____________________

Which Way?

Read the choices. Make a line to connect each right choice to the Right Way path. Connect each wrong choice to the Wrong Way path.

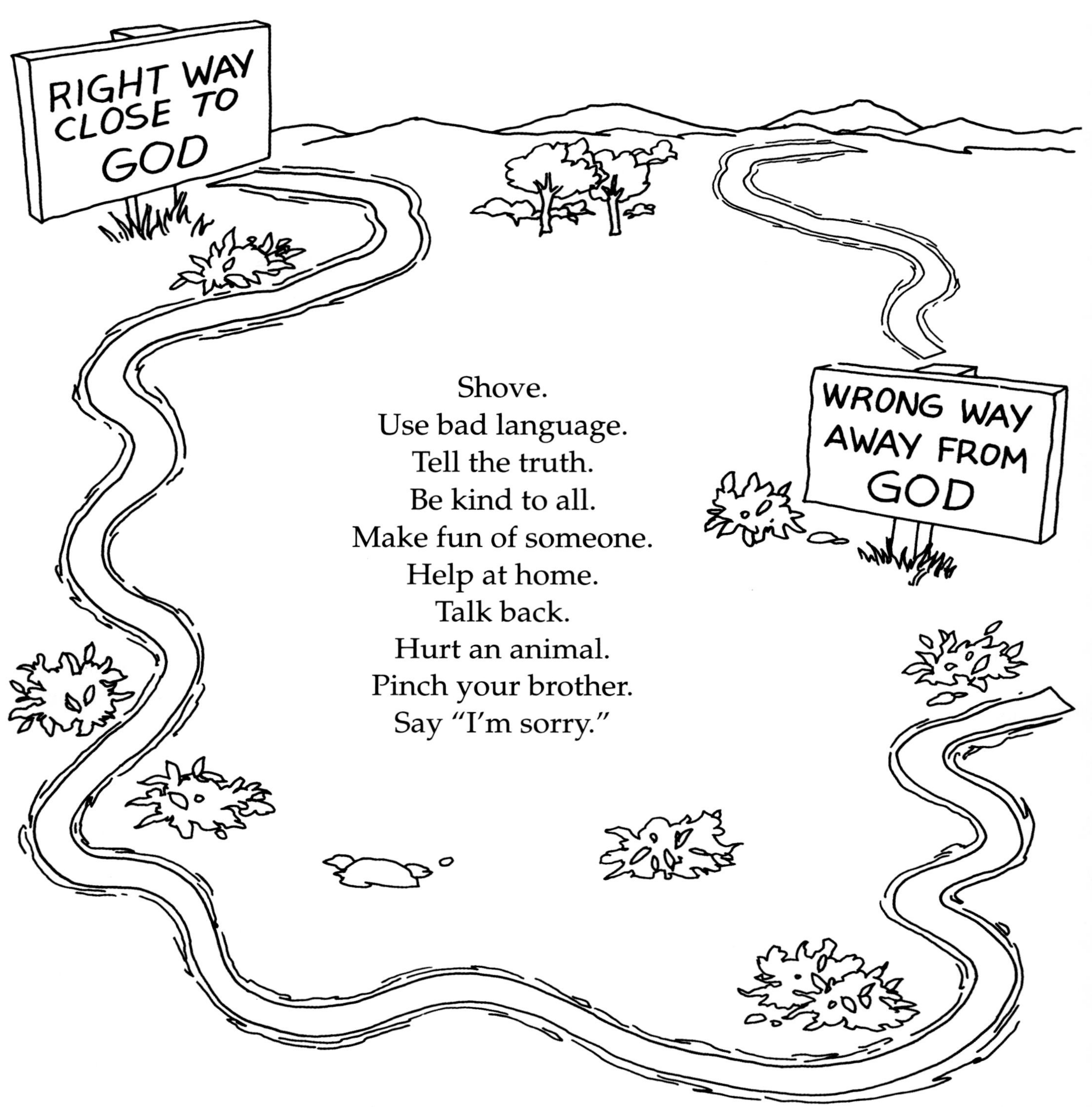

Shove.
Use bad language.
Tell the truth.
Be kind to all.
Make fun of someone.
Help at home.
Talk back.
Hurt an animal.
Pinch your brother.
Say "I'm sorry."

Name ______________________________

Chapter 12 Test

A. Write the word that best finishes each sentence. Use the words in the box.

right / wrong / Mortal / responsible love / closer / away / Venial / mercy

1. Sin is choosing to do what is ______________.

2. Doing what is right shows ______________ for God.

3. ______________ sin is very serious and breaks your friendship with God.

4. ______________ sin hurts your friendship with God.

5. Choosing what is right brings you ______________ to God.

6. You are always ______________ for your choices.

7. God forgives, or shows ______________, to the sinner who is sorry.

B. Check each time you should say you are sorry.

_____ **1.** for accidents

_____ **2.** for mistakes

_____ **3.** for sins

UNIT 3 REVIEW

Strategies for Review

The purpose of the Unit Review is to reinforce concepts presented in this unit. You may wish to assign the Remember and Answer sections for homework. Review these sections with the students so that you can answer any questions they may have. Students may work independently, in small groups, or as a class. Use the method that works best with your group.

1 Remember

Read each statement, and have the students repeat it. To make sure they understand the concepts, invite them to give examples or to explain each statement in their own words.

2 Answer

Point out the word choices at the bottom of the exercise. Go through the answers together. Review any concepts the children seem to have trouble with.

Unit 3 REVIEW

Remember!

1. Your family teaches you about God's love.
2. Peaceful people show respect.
3. You are free to choose what is right and wrong.
4. Your conscience helps you know how to make good moral choices.
5. When you do what is right, you are a light for the world.

Answer!

Complete the sentences with the right words.

1. Children and parents make home a place of love and ________.
2. Jesus teaches you how to show ________ for others.
3. The Ten ____________ can teach you how to make moral choices.
4. You learn from the good ________ of others.
5. Two kinds of sin are venial and ________ sin.

care respect mortal Commandments example

Do!

Cut out a red heart.
Put this special message on it.

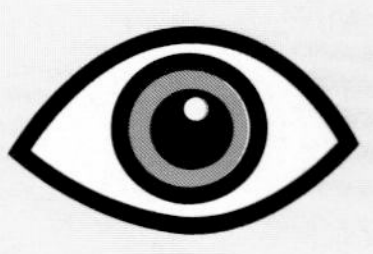  my family!

Put this message where your whole family can see it.

3 Do
Provide paper, markers, scissors, and glue. Suggest that each student write the names of family members on the sign (including his or her own name). Encourage the children to take their signs home and put them where everyone in their families can see them.

4 Share
Share some ideas about what a peacemaker does. To reinforce the concept that this should be an action picture, have each student use scrap paper and a paper fastener to add a movable part to his or her picture. After the children complete the activity, invite them to share how they are peacemakers.

Share!

Jesus says that peacemakers are happy people.
Write the words "I Am a Peacemaker" in the space.
Draw a picture of yourself being a peacemaker.
Share your picture and your idea with the class.

ANSWER KEY

Answer
1. care
2. respect
3. Commandments
4. example
5. mortal

Unit 4

Happy is the person whose sin is taken away.

Psalm 32:1

Chapter

God Heals

The STORY KEEPERS

Father and Two Sons

When the lost son returns home and is forgiven by his father, a great party is held to celebrate. Unfortunately, the elder son refuses to come, even though the father urgently invites him. Helena tells the parable that encourages us all to celebrate forgiveness. View the clip, tell the story, and lead activities suggested in the guide.

Bolivia From Maryknoll

CHAPTER 13 Forgiven

TEACHER RESOURCE CENTER

Faith Formation

CHECK THE CATECHISM

Paragraph 1435 in the *Catechism of the Catholic Church* presents ways in which attitudes of forgiveness and reconciliation can be developed. Paragraph 1439 explains the parable of the prodigal son.

The Need for Forgiveness

The Great Commandment of Jesus is to "Love the Lord your God with your whole heart . . . and . . . your neighbor as yourself" *(Mark 12:30–31).* Often, this is easier said than done. Failures to love are common. Yet Jesus tells his followers that they are called to forgive one another as God forgives them. The gospel story of the Forgiving Father (often referred to as the parable of the prodigal son), found in Luke 15:11–32, and the words of Jesus from the cross, "Father, forgive them" *(Luke 23:34),* speak clearly about the human need to forgive and be forgiven.

Is forgiving others difficult for you? Why or why not?

Seeking God's Forgiveness

All sinners are called to place their trust in God's mercy. When sinners repent and are truly sorry for failing to love, faith in God's mercy and forgiveness brings the assurance that they are reconciled with God and with each other. In the sacrament of Penance, sinners experience the healing presence of God in their lives. The sacrament of Penance is also referred to as "Reconciliation," expressing the idea that a loving relationship with God and neighbor has been restored.

This week, watch for opportunities to make friends again with someone. Reflect on the experience, and discover the joyful heart that comes from the experience of reconciliation.

How does the forgiveness you experience in the sacrament of Reconciliation affect your relationships with others?

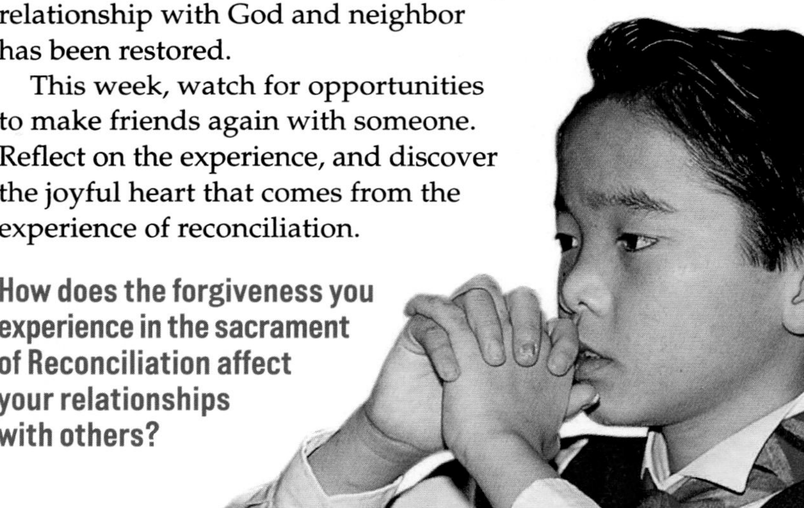

Background

Lost and Found

"God Forgives" is the general theme of Unit 4. Chapter 13 begins the more formal preparation for the reception of Reconciliation.

"Lost and found" is the concept used to help the children understand our need for reconciliation. The children can probably identify with the warmth and comfort of returning home after a trip or the happiness of being reunited with a loved one after even a short separation. By referring to experiences like these, you can help the children connect to Jesus' parables on forgiveness.

In the story of the prodigal son, Jesus focuses on the father's mercy and the joy of reconciliation. The path from isolation to joy leads back home to reconciliation with the father.

Help the children come to know that Jesus says to them, "I see good in you. I see in you the possibility of being the best kind of person." This is something to rejoice over!

Faith Summary

- **God and the Church rejoice when a sinner is sorry.**
- **God forgives the sinner in the sacrament of Reconciliation.**
- **Reconciliation welcomes us back to God and to the Church family.**

Growth and Development

It is helpful to remember two characteristics of second graders as you teach this lesson:

- ***Second graders are quite instinctive.*** They react to hurt and unfairness with strong feelings.
- ***Second graders understand that doing something wrong can cause bad feelings.*** They are eager to change those feelings into good ones again.

A Teacher's Prayer

God, I sing your praises, for you not only forgive me, but you rejoice when I return to you. Let me share with the children how happy you are to welcome them back into your arms when they go astray. Your rejoicing gives us reason to rejoice. Amen.

Vocabulary Preview

forgiveness

Scripture

Psalm 1:1–2: Happy are those who live God's way.

Luke 15:8–10: the parable of the lost coin

Luke 15:11–25: the parable of the lost son

Related Resources

Video

"Pardon and Peace . . . Remembered" (St. Anthony Messenger Press, 1-800-488-0488 or www.AmericanCatholic.org). This video is a moving retelling of the parable of the prodigal son. (Adult, 15 minutes)

Book

Bitney, James. *All Things New: A Celebration of Forgiveness* (St. Anthony Messenger Press, 1-800-488-0488 or www.AmericanCatholic.org). This book helps children understand reconciliation as a celebration of conversion. (Children)

TEACHER ORGANIZER

Planning Guide

The basic content for each chapter is divided into four class sessions. There are a number of options for the fifth session. Extension, review, and testing options are described under Day 5 Alternatives. The Quick Check box will help you evaluate the week's lessons.

Chapter Goals

In this chapter, the students will learn about

❏ Coming back to God
❏ God's merciful forgiveness
❏ Rejoicing in forgiveness

	DAY 1 · INVITATION	DAY 2 · DISCOVERY	DAY 3 · DISCOVERY
OBJECTIVES	**The students will be able to** • Explore feelings about loss • Discuss feelings about finding what was lost	**The students will be able to** • Analyze parables that have the theme of being lost • Expand the meaning of *being lost* to include sin • Share ways of reconciling	**The students will be able to** • Associate forgiveness with a celebration • Tell ways to God's forgiveness • Analyze situations that need reconciling
PREPARATION	• Bring in or make a simple puzzle using a magazine picture or a photograph, and hide one of the puzzle pieces	• Read through Teaching Tip • Make copies of the resource master on page 290 (use heavy paper)	• Prepare questions to prompt discussion
MATERIALS	• Puzzle pieces	• Drawing supplies • Copies of the resource master, crayons or markers, glue, scissors	• Pencils or crayons
OPTIONAL ACTIVITIES	• Ideas That Work Find a partner	• Options Illustrate *lost* using pictures • Resource Masters Complete a picture	• Ideas That Work Make Welcome Back cards

Learning Objectives

By the end of this chapter, the students should be able to

- ❑ Analyze parables to learn about God's mercy
- ❑ Recognize that reconciliation is a celebration of forgiveness
- ❑ Determine ways to reconcile with God and the Church

DAY 4 • LIVING

The students will be able to

- Determine an ending of reconciliation for a story
- Discover words of reconciliation
- Pray for mercy using a traditional Catholic prayer

- Collect examples of "uh-oh" situations

- Pencils

- **Curriculum Challenge** Write reconciliation quotations
- **Options** Learn "I am sorry" in another language

DAY 5 • ALTERNATIVES

There are a number of alternatives to help you plan Day 5.

Prayer Experience
Use the forgiveness prayer experience on Day 4 or Day 5.

Review and Explore
You may wish to incorporate some background music into the lesson.

Home and Family
Send the page home with the students, or assign one or more of the activities.

The Church Today
The children will think about the times that they may feel like acting out in anger and frustration. You may want to have one or two sample situtations ready to begin a discussion that will lead into the activity.

Chapter Test
The chapter test appears as a resource master on page 291.

Quick Check

Do this evaluation as soon as you finish each chapter.

Did I follow my lesson plan?

How can I tell that I met the learning objectives for the lesson?

What activities did the children enjoy most?

How could I improve this lesson?

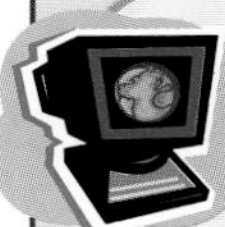

Benziger on the Web
For more ideas, visit us at www.benziger.glencoe.com

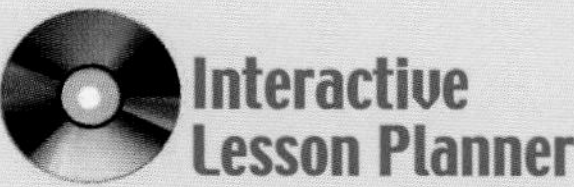

Interactive Lesson Planner
Your ILP provides more help in preparing to teach this chapter.

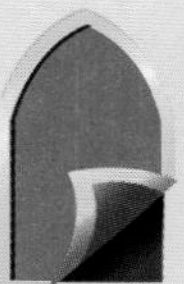

Celebrate
Turn to page 22 of this book. Check for seasonal celebrations.

Lesson Plan · Day 1
Have the children read aloud the title and the chapter's Scripture verse, "Happy are those who follow God's way." Except for one hidden piece, distribute pieces of a puzzle that you made or bought and ask the children to put the puzzle together.

1 The Puzzle
How do the children feel about missing a puzzle piece? Say that the same thing happened to the Leon family one rainy day. Direct attention to the first part of the story. Ask the children to read alternate sentences aloud.

2 Do You Know?
Read aloud the question and have volunteers share their experiences. At the end of the week, come back to this question to see how the children's knowledge has developed.

IDEAS THAT WORK

Here is a way to partner the children for this lesson. Provide enough index cards to equal half the number of children in the classroom. If the total number is uneven, add yourself. Cut each index card into two puzzle pieces. Let each child choose one piece, write his or her name on it, and then find the child who has the piece that fits it. Tape the two puzzle pieces together, and place them along the chalkboard ledge. These student pairs can work together whenever partners are needed in this week's religion classes.

INVITATION 13

Happy are those who follow God's way.
Psalm 1:2

Do You Know?
◆ When do you ask for God's forgiveness?

God Forgives

The Puzzle

The Leon family worked hard on a puzzle. It was all put together. But one piece was missing! Look at the picture and tell what happened next. Tell how the people are feeling.

How do you feel when you find something that you have lost?

3 Found at Last!
Ask the children where the Leons might find the missing puzzle piece. Then, read the text on student page 187. Ask them to share how they feel when they find something that was lost.

4 Activity
Invite the children to look at the puzzle piece. Talk with the children about what could make things right again. Allow time for the children to draw their pictures.

Found At Last!

The Leon family looked everywhere.

They scattered around the house to find the missing puzzle piece. They looked on the floor, and under sofa cushions. The Leon family looked for a long time.

Suddenly, little Carlos held up his sneaker. There, inside his shoe, was the missing puzzle piece!

"Hurray!" they all shouted.

How do you feel when you have found something that you have lost?

Look at the puzzle piece. On the other piece, draw what could make things right again.

Lesson Plan · Day 2

Ask volunteers to share times when they may have been lost and how they felt when they were found.

1 Found!

Tell the children that you are going to share two stories Jesus told about something or someone lost and then found. Have the children follow along as you read aloud The Lost Coin and The Lost Son. Have the children circle what was lost and found. Ask the children how the woman felt when she found the coin. *(happy)* Then ask how the father felt when his son came home. *(happy)*

Tell the children to listen to the parable again, or ask volunteers to mime the stories as you retell them. Point out that Jesus told these stories to help people know that God is happy when we come back to him.

TEACHING TIP

Reading is a constructive activity. Readers construct meaning by comprehending content, understanding symbolic or deeper meanings, and forming opinions about the author's intent. Children need to be shown how to read parables constructively. The Lost Coin is a story about how God rejoices in sinners who return to him. Ask questions that help the children use what they know to figure out the parable's meaning. For example, they might connect to what they know about God's mercy.

As an alternative, ask student partners to retell the story. This time the woman symbolizes God. The coin is the sinner who is first lost and then found. The partners may act out their ideas.

Found!

Jesus called on all people to ask for forgiveness. He told them many stories about God's forgiveness. Jesus said that there is rejoicing when a sinner is sorry.

The Lost Coin

There was once a woman who lost some money. She lit a lamp and searched the whole house until she found the coin. She told her friends and neighbors. They were happy and celebrated together.

The Lost Son

There was once a man who had two sons. The younger son said, "Father, someday you will die. Your money will go to my brother and me. Give me my share now."

The father gave the son his share and the son left home. The son quickly spent all of his money.

He had no home, no food, and no friends. He decided to ask his father to forgive him.

The father had been watching for his son. He saw his son coming and ran to hug him. The son said, "I'm sorry Father. I have sinned against God and you."

The father said, "Welcome home, my son." They were happy and celebrated together.

What was lost and then found in each story?

2 Together Again
Tell the children that there are all kinds of ways to feel lost. Read the first paragraph aloud, and point out that sinners get lost; they go the wrong way, away from God's friendship. Then read the rest of the text aloud.

3 Activity
Explain the activity, and ask the children to take some time to think before they begin drawing. You may need to give some general prompts. Assure the children that their drawings will be private.

Together Again

Sometimes you can be lost. You might not understand your schoolwork. That can make you feel lost. You might have to make a hard decision. That can make you feel lost, too.

When you do what is wrong, you also feel lost. You move away from what is good. You hurt your friendship with God. You can come back to God. The Church family rejoices when someone says, "I am sorry. I made a mistake. I want to be a good friend to God and to everyone."

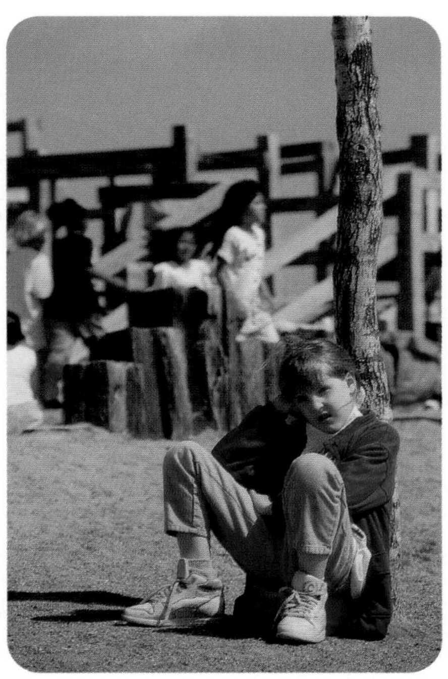

ACTIVITY

Draw a picture about a time you hurt your friendship with God.
Draw a picture of what you did to make things better.

OPTIONS

For Those Who Learn Verbally
These children have a sensitivity to the meaning of words. Encourage the children to explore all the meanings of the word *lost.* They may cut pictures from magazines to illustrate each meaning.

RESOURCE MASTERS

The resource master on page 290 is a craft activity about God welcoming the sinner. You may wish to give the following directions to the children:

- In the doorway draw yourself with God's family.
- Color the church, including the doors.
- Cut out the doors, fold on the lines, and glue the doors on the picture.

Lesson Plan · Day 3

Ask the children to recall what was learned about God in The Lost Coin and The Lost Son. *(God rejoices in the sinner who returns.)*

1 Come Back

Invite the children to tell what they do to ask forgiveness from their families or friends. *(apologize, do something nice)* Ask the children what happens when they ask forgiveness. *(Answers will vary.)* Help the children see that when they ask forgiveness and it is granted, people come back together.

Tell the children that Catholics celebrate God's forgiveness in the sacrament of Reconciliation. Write the word on the board and have the children pronounce it. After telling the meaning of the word, ask the class why *reconciliation* is a good word to describe the sacrament. Have volunteers read the text aloud. Allow time for the children to do the activity.

IDEAS THAT WORK

Just as the lost son was welcomed back by his father, the sinner is welcomed back by God. Give the children the opportunity to be welcoming. Set aside about fifteen minutes for making Welcome Back cards. The cards may be small—the size of a bookmark or holy card. A helper can set some cards on a child's desk after the child has been away.

Sin turns our hearts away from God's love.

Come Back

When you do what is wrong, you can also feel lost. You move away from what is good. You hurt your friendship with God. You can come back to God. The Church family rejoices when someone says, "I am sorry."

ACTIVITY — FOLLOW THE SIGNS

Find your way to God's forgiveness.

2 This We Believe!
Read the statement to the children. Have the children repeat the statement after you. Discuss the relationship between this concept and the maze activity.

3 A Better Way
Have the children read the directions to the activity silently. A volunteer may then explain how to do the page. Allow the children to work on their own. Then hold a class discussion of the solutions possible.

A Better Way

Someone in each story is lost. Draw a line from each story to the best way the person can come back to God.

Cindy broke the flowerpot. Cindy blamed Sue.	Say, "I'm sorry."
Juan hurt Laura's feelings. Laura is very sad.	Tell the truth.
Mike does not know how to add. Mike copies Mary's answers.	Make a better plan.
Bobby does his chores only when he feels like it.	Ask the teacher for help.

VIRTUE FAITH GRACE **VOCABULARY**

Forgive To give up bad feelings toward someone who has hurt you.

You may wish to add the word *forgive* to the classroom Word Wall.

Lesson Plan · Day 4

Find out the many ways the children would complete this sentence: "After I do something wrong, I . . ."

1 The Right Path

Before reading, ask the children to listen for what Tony did that was wrong and what the consequences were. Then read the story aloud and discuss it with the children. Have student partners write endings for the story. If needed, set a minimum number of sentences that should be added. If time permits, have the children share the endings they wrote. This sharing will give you insights into what the children have learned in the chapter.

TEACHING TIP

You may want to make an interactive bulletin board of words that lead back to God and the Church community. Consider displaying cartoons or pictures of children in "uh-oh" situations, such as the one Tony faced on student page 192. Place writing lines with each picture and add a few pencils dangling from yarn. The children can use the pencils to write words that help make up for the wrong done.

THE RIGHT PATH

Read this story.

Tony was doing something that was against the rules. He was bouncing his basketball in the house. As he was bouncing the ball, it got away from him. The ball bounced into the living room. His mother's new lamp crashed to the floor. Tony ran outside.

Mom asked, "Tony, did you break the lamp?"

How can Tony make things right?

Write or draw an ending to the story.

2 Find the Way
After hearing the words Tony used to reconcile in the story endings, the children can explore other words to use. Explain the activity. The right words and their dots lead to the end of the maze. Have partners check each others answers.

FIND THE WAY

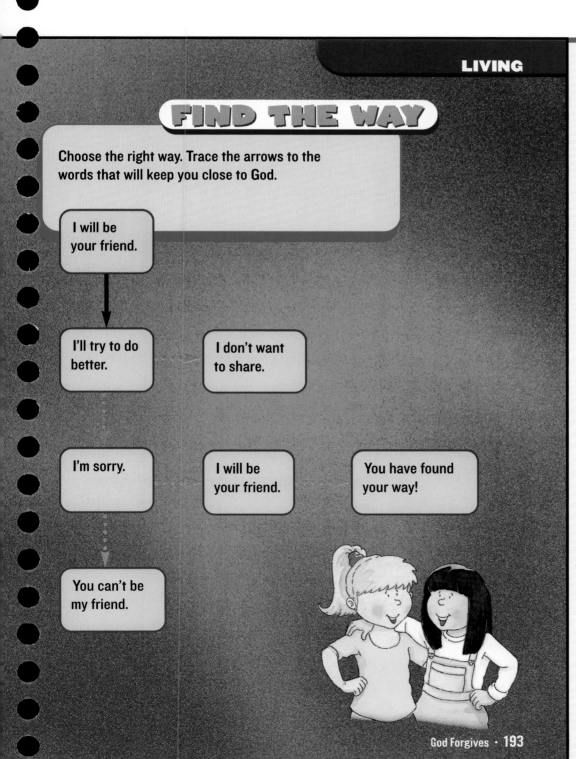

Choose the right way. Trace the arrows to the words that will keep you close to God.

I will be your friend.

I'll try to do better.

I don't want to share.

I'm sorry.

I will be your friend.

You have found your way!

You can't be my friend.

CURRICULUM CHALLENGE

Language Arts The bulletin board suggested in Teaching Tip on page 284 can provide a simple and fun exercise in writing one-sentence quotations. To individualize the activity, make copies of a few pictures onto a page. Add lines for writing, and have the children write an appropriate quote of reconciliation for each picture.

Prayer
This simple prayer is patterned after the Penitential Rite used at Mass. After the prayer, ask the children if they recognize where they have heard it before.

1 Prepare for Prayer
Ask volunteers to recall ways to pray. *(kneeling, thinking, arms held out in praise, singing)* Then, share the introductory information. Model a gentle tapping with the fist. Ask the class why this is a good way to say, "I am sorry."

2 Forgiveness
Gather to pray. As the leader, you may wish to pause for a few seconds before all respond. Doing so will give the children time to think about wrongs done.

LEARNING TO PRAY
The beating of the breast is a traditional way of showing sorrow. Ask the children to look for the action during the Penitential Rite at Mass, when all pray to God for forgiveness for their sins.

OPTIONS
For Auditory Learners Some children in the class may speak more than one language or do not consider English their primary language. If bilingual speakers are in your classroom, ask them to teach the others how to say "I am sorry" in a language other than English. Auditory learners should have little trouble picking up the new sounds and pronunciations.

FORGIVENESS

Make your right hand into a fist and gently tap your heart with it. This action is a way to say, "I'm sorry."

LEADER: For the times we did what was wrong,

ALL: *(Tap your heart.)* Lord, have mercy.

LEADER: For the times we did not forgive,

ALL: *(Tap your heart.)* Christ, have mercy.

LEADER: For the times we did not do what was right,

ALL: *(Tap your heart.)* Lord, have mercy.

1 Know

Refer the children to the graphic organizer as a guide for reviewing the chapter. Emphasize anything that you especially want them to remember. Ask for opinions: Why is this picture of a path a good way to show that God forgives sinners?

2 Love and Serve

Play the background music. Before they do the Love and Serve writing activities, direct the children to first spend a few moments thinking.

3 God's Friends

Show the illustration of Saint Maria Goretti and share the information. Ask whether the children are surprised by her act of forgiveness.

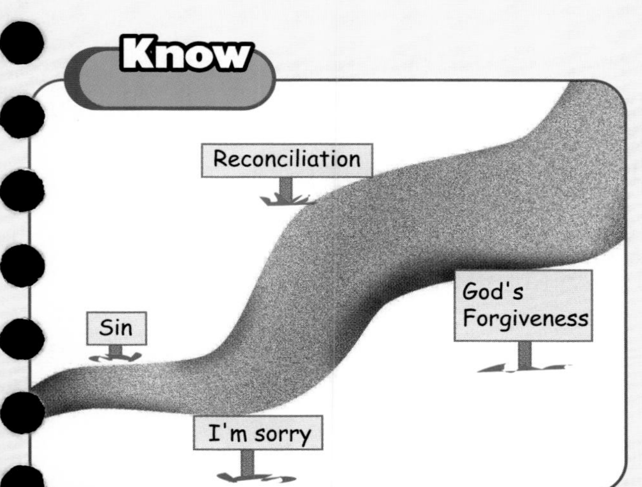

Who does the father in the story remind you of? Use that name to finish this sentence.

______________________ loves me!

Serve

Think about someone whom you need to ask for forgiveness. Finish this sentence.

I will make things good again by

______________________________.

CHAPTER 13 REVIEW and EXPLORE

GOD'S FRIENDS

Saint Maria Goretti

Maria's family was poor. Maria and her family loved God. This made them happy. An angry man attacked Maria. Before she died, Maria forgave the man. In time, the man asked God for forgiveness, too.

A Little Catechism

Invite the children to open their religion books to *A Little Catechism*. Choose one or more of the selections below for memory work or reinforcement. You will find your copy of the catechism on pages 23–43 of this Teacher's Edition.

1. Together with the children, recite the answer to Important Question 4. Encourage the children to memorize this answer.
2. Review the section on the sacraments on student page 14, stressing paragraph 4.
3. As a class, pray the Hail Mary.

Know | Love | Serve

Note The activities on this page provide ways for the children to share their learning with their families. The activities are related to the week's work.

1 Introduce
Have the children read aloud the introductory material. Then, explain the activities.

2 Pray Together
Have all the children pray aloud the prayer in the prayer burst. While praying the prayer, gently tap your heart with a closed fist and ask the children to imitate this gesture.

Online for Families
Remind the children to check the Benziger Web site this week with their families.
www.benziger.glencoe.com

Dear Family,

I have just finished chapter 13. I learned that, when I sin, I hurt my friendship with God and with others.

I can ask for forgiveness. I am welcomed back to God and to my Church family.

On your own

Look at this word: ForGIVEness. What word do you see inside? Forgiveness is about giving love. Have you been a forgiving member of your family? If you need to, make things right.

FORGIVENESS

With your family

At your next family meal, ask someone to light a candle. Each family member can say, "I'm sorry for the ways I've hurt you." Everyone answers, "We forgive you." Let the candle shine to remind everyone about God's forgiveness.

Lamb of God, have mercy on us.

GO ONLINE!
http://www.benziger.glencoe.com

1 Discuss
Begin by asking the students about times they may have felt anger toward others. How did they feel? Did they want to act out? How? Say: "Would acting out your anger make things better or worse?"

2 The Project
Tell the students that sometimes it can be hard to choose the right way, especially when they are feeling sad or angry. Tell them that they will be reading three short stories. They are to write the best way to handle each situation. After the children have completed the assignment, invite sharing.

THE CHURCH TODAY

Sometimes you may want to do things that will turn you away from God. You must be strong and decide to make the right choice.

Read each story. Maybe this has really happened to you. What should you do? Write your answer in the space.

Your friend has broken your favorite toy. You feel angry. You want to break one of your friend's toys.

You should ______________________________

Your mom is angry with you. You did not help around the house. You are punished. You want to get mad too.

You should ______________________________

Your friends took candy from your teacher's desk without asking. You want some candy too.

You should ______________________________

ANSWER KEY

This is the answer key for the chapter test on page 291.

A. 2

B. All sentences should be checked.

C. 1. b 2. c 3. a

Name ________________________________

Rejoice!

When we are sorry for our sins, God welcomes us back again. The Church community welcomes us, too.

In the doorway of the church, draw yourself with God's family. Color the church and the doors. Cut out the doors, fold along the dotted lines, and then glue the doors on either side of the doorway.

Name ______________________________

Chapter 13 Test

A. Bible stories teach you about God. Check the Bible story that shows how God welcomes back a sinner.

_____ **1.** Jesus fed many hungry people.

_____ **2.** The father was happy when his son returned.

B. Check each sentence that tells how you know that God forgives sinners.

_____ **1.** God is present when a sinner wants to come back to him.

_____ **2.** God forgives sinners when they are sorry.

_____ **3.** Jesus told stories that teach about God's mercy.

C. Draw a line to match the parts that go together.

1. God rejoices	**a.** a sinner returns to God and to the Church community.
2. Sin	**b.** when a sinner asks for forgiveness.
3. "I am sorry"	**c.** hurts your friendship with God.

TEACHER RESOURCE CENTER

Faith Formation

Hearing God's Voice

There is a basic conviction in all people of good will that certain behaviors are right or wrong. They search for and promote justice, truth, and fidelity. They refrain from dishonesty, idolatry, and the taking of innocent life. Believers listen to God's voice in determining the rightness or wrongness of their attitudes and behaviors. They recognize that the ability to choose what is right depends on listening carefully to God's voice as God speaks through Scripture, Tradition, Church teaching, life experience, and the examples of the saints and other people of faith.

When have you been conscious of God's voice leading you to do what is right?

CHECK THE CATECHISM

In paragraph 1780, the Catechism of the Catholic Church states that dignity requires the presence of a moral conscience. For more on the judgment of moral conscience, see paragraphs 1776–1802.

Knowledge and Choices

Knowledge is a much greater challenge for us. For humans, determining what is right and what is wrong is a life-long endeavor. As people grow older, they understand that intention, motivation, circumstances, or ignorance affect culpability. People of faith believe that doing only what they know is right will result in the presence of God's peace in their hearts. It is important to periodically take time to reflect on one's attitudes and behaviors and to find ways to grow in God's peace. Following this reflection, we celebrate the acknowledgment of sin and repentance in the sacrament of Reconcilation. This week, take some time to examine your conscience to find what is in your heart that only God knows.

In what ways are you growing in God's peace?

Background

Examining

This chapter covers examination of conscience. The process of reflecting on moral choices is an important step in the preparation for the sacrament of Reconciliation.

In practice, choosing to do what is right and good is often difficult. We can sometimes be selfish and lack good judgment. People of any age are easily swayed by feelings. You may wish to emphasize those points when teaching the children.

Provide a gentle catechesis that helps the children make good moral choices, choices that heal. Acknowledge that sometimes we do the wrong thing. We hurt one another or break promises. Sometimes, even good intentions have harmful results. When this happens, we must start all over again and depend on Jesus' help and strength.

Faith Summary

- The Ten Commandments are a framework for examining the conscience.
- Examination of conscience is a preparation for celebrating Reconciliation.
- Examining conscience includes deciding how to make up for sins.

Growth and Development

It is helpful to remember two characteristics of second graders as you teach this lesson:

- ***Second graders need a framework for examining conscience.*** Give as many opportunities as possible for the children to discover the questions they need to ask.
- ***Second graders can begin to understand their weaknesses and strengths.*** The spiritual habits children form now can help develop a strong adult faith.

A Teacher's Prayer

Compassionate God, help me show the children by my words and attitudes that they can find ways to live as good people. Help me find ways to do likewise. Bless the children and me with the honesty to examine our lives and see how we can come closer to you. Amen.

Vocabulary Preview

examination of conscience

Scripture

Psalm 32:1: Happy is the forgiven sinner.

Psalm 30:11: Have mercy on me.

Related Resources

Video

"Ricky's First Reconciliation" (Twenty-Third Publications, 1-800-321-0411 or www.twentythirdpublications.com). Ricky learns about forgiveness and the steps involved in the sacrament of Reconciliation. (Children, 9 minutes)

Books

Richstatter, Thomas. "Ten Tips for Better Confessions" (*Catholic Update*, St. Anthony Messenger Press, 1-800-488-0488 or www.AmericanCatholic.org). This article offers tips for making confession more meaningful. (Adult)

We Ask Forgiveness: A Young Child's Book of Reconciliation (St. Anthony Messenger, 1-800-488-0488 or www.AmericanCatholic.org). Shares Jesus' message of forgiveness and explains the Rite of Reconciliation. (Children)

TEACHER ORGANIZER

Planning Guide

The basic content for each chapter is divided into four class sessions. There are a number of options for the fifth session. Extension, review, and testing options are described under Day 5 Alternatives. The Quick Check box will help you evaluate the week's lessons.

Chapter Goals

In this chapter, the students will learn about

- ❑ Preparing for Reconciliation
- ❑ Examining the conscience
- ❑ Making up for sins

	DAY 1 · INVITATION	DAY 2 · DISCOVERY	DAY 3 · DISCOVERY
OBJECTIVES	**The students will be able to** • Make a list of questions that look back over the day • See the value of looking back on choices made	**The students will be able to** • Evaluate the choices made by characters in a story • Discover how the characters can take responsibility for their actions	**The students will be able to** • Discuss examining the conscience • Choose a guide for examining our conscience
PREPARATION	• Prepare part of your Lesson Plan book or an organizer	• Prepare to read the story • Analyze the main characters of a story	• Make copies of the resource master on page 308
MATERIALS	• Lesson Plan book or an organizer of some sort	• Something prickly	• Background music • Pencils • Copies of the resource master, pencils
OPTIONAL ACTIVITIES	• Curriculum Challenge Create homework lists	• Curriculum Challenge Analyze the choices of story characters	• Resource Masters Write an examination of conscience

Learning Objectives

By the end of this chapter, the students should be able to

- ❑ Evaluate choices made
- ❑ Make an examination of conscience
- ❑ Determine ways to make up for wrongdoing

DAY 4 • LIVING

The students will be able to

- Discover steps in preparing for Reconciliation
- See the Ten Commandments as a guide for examining the conscience
- Pray for forgiveness

- Prepare to teach a song to the "When the Saints Go Marching in" tune

- Pencils or drawing materials

- Ideas That Work Sing a song
- Curriculum Challenge Make a reminder about preparing for Reconciliation

DAY 5 • ALTERNATIVES

There are a number of alternatives to help you plan Day 5.

Prayer Experience
Use A New Start prayer service on Day 4 or Day 5.

Review and Explore
The students will need pencils. If you have access to a world map, have it handy.

Home and Family
Send the page home with the students, or assign one or more of the activities.

The Church Today
This activity gives the children a fun way to think about making good choices. Necessary supplies are dice and game pieces (paper clips, pennies, pasta, wooden beads, or buttons) to use as markers.

Chapter Test
The chapter test appears as a resource master on page 309.

Quick Check

Do this evaluation as soon as you finish each chapter.

Did I follow my lesson plan?

How can I tell that I met the learning objectives for the lesson?

What activities did the children enjoy most?

How could I improve this lesson?

Benziger on the Web
For more ideas, visit us at www.benziger.glencoe.com

Interactive Lesson Planner
Your ILP provides more help in preparing to teach this chapter.

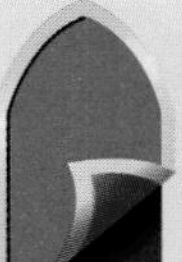

Celebrate
Turn to page 22 of this book. Check for seasonal celebrations.

Lesson Plan · Day 1
Show the class your lesson plan book, particularly where you make lists, or an organizer of some sort. Say that the lists you make help you remember to do what needs to be done.

1 Do You Know?
Have the children read aloud the title and the chapter's Scripture verse, "Happy is the person whose sin is taken away." At the end of the week, come back to this question to see how the children's knowledge has developed.

2 Check List
With pride, tell the children they are old enough and smart enough to make their own lists. Have the list on the page read aloud. Allow time for the children to add what they need to do after they finish their homework. Lists may be shared. Suggest "say prayers," if it has not been listed.

CURRICULUM CHALLENGE

All Subjects Do the children write down their homework before the end of the day? If not, it is a good time to incorporate this habit. Choose a space on the chalkboard for listing the homework. Make sure the space does not change and that everyone can see it. Allow time for the students to copy the list. Suggest that they list their homework in the same notebook every day. Ask the children to make a check next to each item after they have completed it at home. You may want to look at the homework lists daily until you see that the writing and checking have become a routine. The children can quickly show you their lists as they leave the classroom at the end of the day.

Happy is the person whose sin is taken away.

Psalm 32:1

Do You Know?

◆ How do you ask God for forgiveness?

PREPARE

CHECK LIST

Check off the things that you need to remember to do each day.

Finish the list for the rest of your day.

- [ ] Wash up.
- [ ] Get dressed for school.
- [ ] Make your bed.
- [ ] Have breakfast.
- [ ] Go to school.
- [ ] Do your homework.
- [ ] ________________
- [ ] ________________

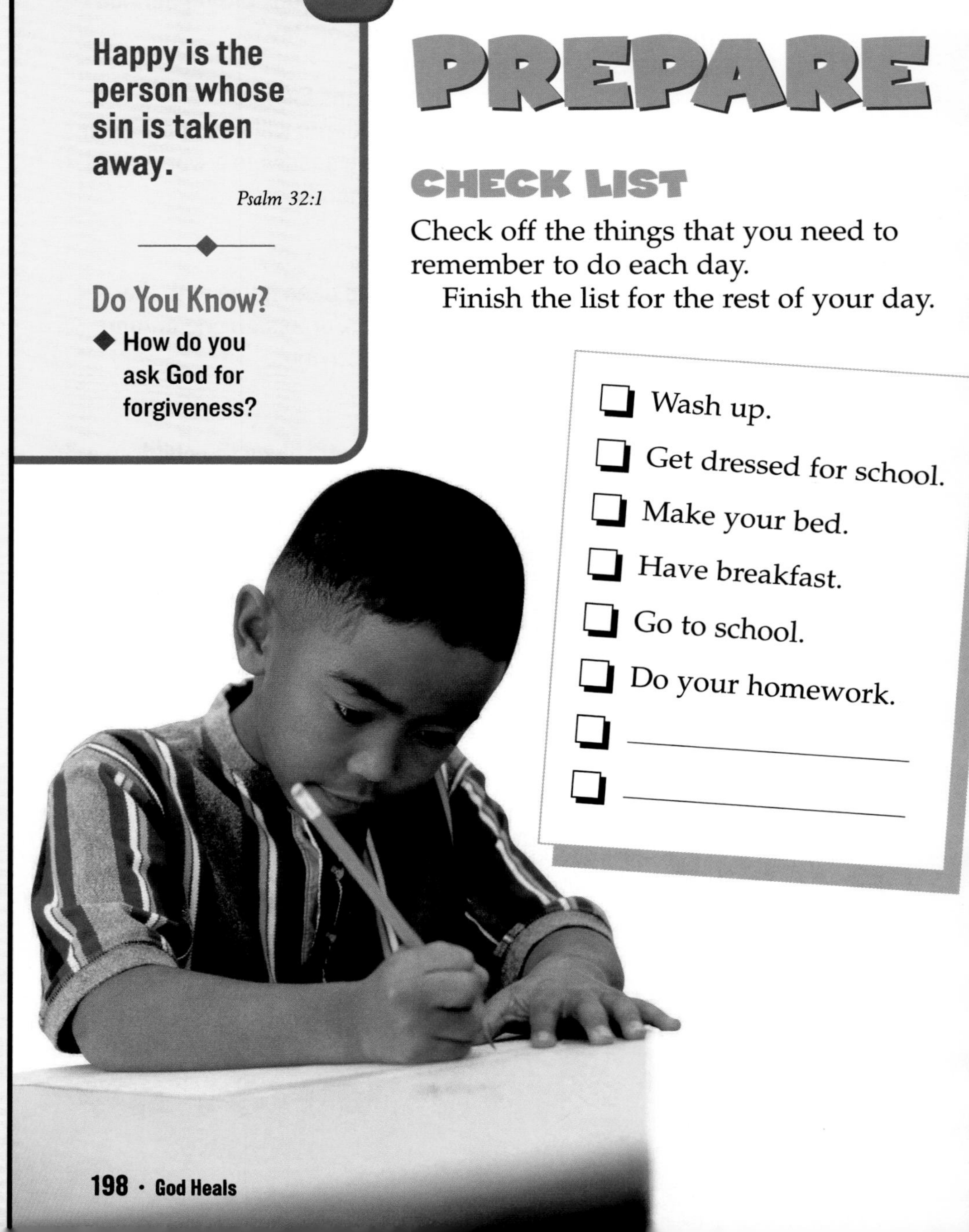

3 What's Next
Ask the children to brainstorm a list that would help with the forgiveness of sins. Record the list on the chalkboard and encourage the class to remember these points as they learn how to prepare for the sacrament of Reconciliation.

4 My Good Day
Encourage the children not to rush into completing the list on student page 199. Each child may either spend quiet time thinking about a good day or spend a few moments brainstorming with a partner. The children may want to copy their checklist and take it home.

WHAT'S NEXT?

Lists can be helpful. They can help you get things done. Lists can also help you to remember.

Here is a list that can help you look back on your day. Add three more things that you need to remember to do each day.

MY GOOD DAY

- ☐ Did I get my chores done?
- ☐ Did I try my best in school?
- ☐ Was I kind to my friends?
- ☐ ____________________
- ☐ ____________________
- ☐ ____________________

TEACHING TIP

Children like lists, and they like checking off the items on lists. Use the method of listing whenever it suits what you are trying to teach. For example, you may want to make lists of vocabulary words and prayers the children need to learn. If any of the children are forgetful, help them make a big reminder list, such as what needs to be taken home every day.

Lesson Plan · Day 2

Ask the children to spend a little quiet time thinking about the choices they made yesterday. Use these questions as a guide: Did I try my best in school? Was I kind to my family? Did I help at home? Did I finish my homework?

1 Introduction

Bring a prickly item to share with the class. Allow for brief discussion about prickly items and their beauty and usefulness. Gather the children close, and tell them that you are going to read a story about squirrels and a porcupine who is very prickly. Ask the children to listen for the choices the animals made.

2 A Prickly Challenge

Have a volunteer read the introduction. Read the story aloud, pausing after Pamela asks the squirrels whether she can go home with them. Ask the children what they would say to Pamela. Discuss the difficulties of being a prickly thing. Have the children speculate what might happen next in the story.

TEACHING TIP

Read the story with expression. Use your voice, your face, and your body. Stress the rhymes while you read. The story has actions to emphasize: "shivered and shook," and "shuddered and trembled." Encourage the children to imitate you.

WORD OF GOD

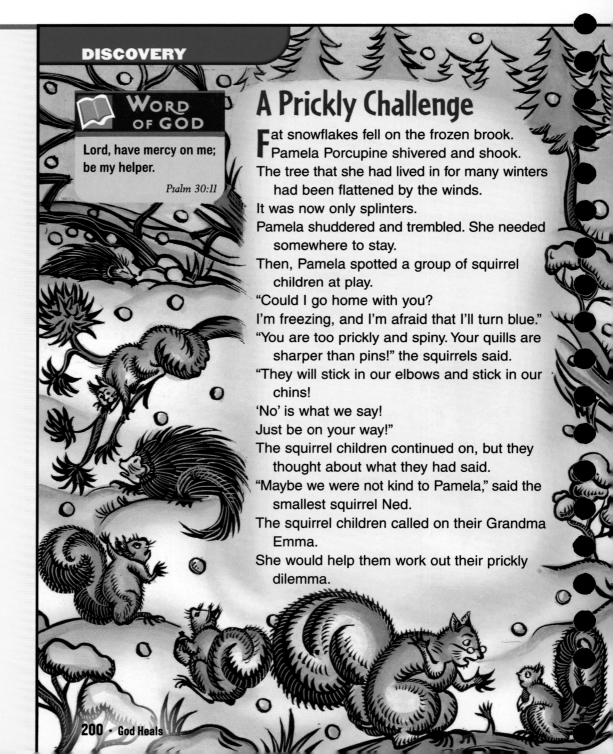

Lord, have mercy on me; be my helper.

Psalm 30:11

A Prickly Challenge

Fat snowflakes fell on the frozen brook.
Pamela Porcupine shivered and shook.
The tree that she had lived in for many winters had been flattened by the winds.
It was now only splinters.
Pamela shuddered and trembled. She needed somewhere to stay.
Then, Pamela spotted a group of squirrel children at play.
"Could I go home with you?
I'm freezing, and I'm afraid that I'll turn blue."
"You are too prickly and spiny. Your quills are sharper than pins!" the squirrels said.
"They will stick in our elbows and stick in our chins!
'No' is what we say!
Just be on your way!"
The squirrel children continued on, but they thought about what they had said.
"Maybe we were not kind to Pamela," said the smallest squirrel Ned.
The squirrel children called on their Grandma Emma.
She would help them work out their prickly dilemma.

3 Story Ending

Finish reading the story. Ask the children why the squirrels said no to Pamela. *(They were afraid she would hurt them.)* Then talk about how the squirrels solved their problem. *(They asked Grandma Emma for help.)* Continue the dicussion with how the squirrels made things right. *(They took Pamela in for protection.)*

Let volunteers tell about prickly problems they face in their lives. *(friends who do not play fair, a brother or sister who teases, parents who are divorced, and so on)* Talk about how the problems can be solved. Keep this discussion simple.

4 Activity

Have all the students read aloud the This We Believe! feature. Ask how the squirrels in the story followed their conscience. Then, explain the activity and direct the children to think of a *specific* way that the squirrels and Pamela could be better friends. Then read the Word of God, encouraging the children to keep this in mind when the examine their conscience.

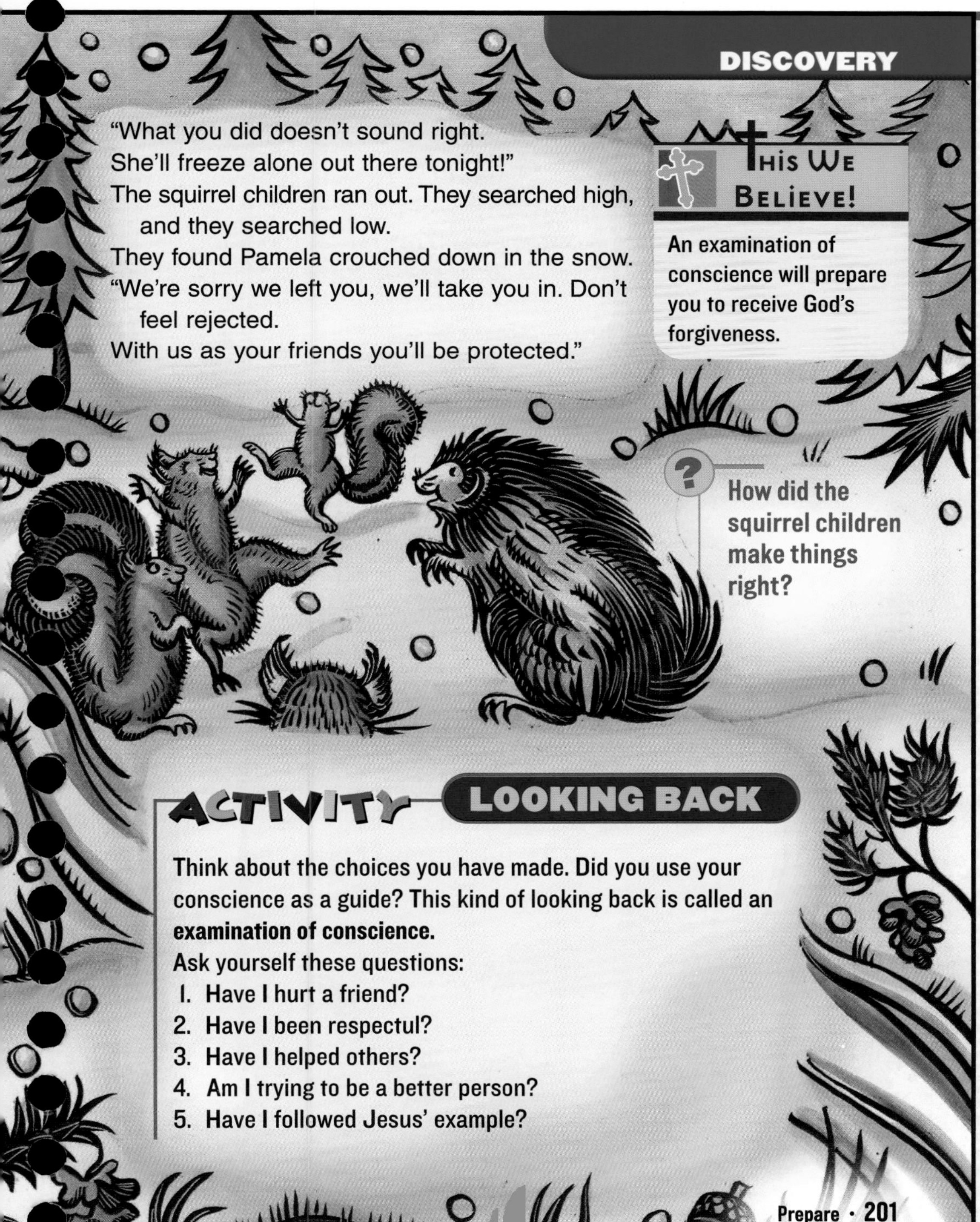

DISCOVERY
"What you did doesn't sound right.
She'll freeze alone out there tonight!"
The squirrel children ran out. They searched high, and they searched low.
They found Pamela crouched down in the snow.
"We're sorry we left you, we'll take you in. Don't feel rejected.
With us as your friends you'll be protected."
THIS WE BELIEVE!
An examination of conscience will prepare you to receive God's forgiveness.
How did the squirrel children make things right?
ACTIVITY
LOOKING BACK
Think about the choices you have made. Did you use your conscience as a guide? This kind of looking back is called an **examination of conscience.**
Ask yourself these questions:
1. Have I hurt a friend?
2. Have I been respectul?
3. Have I helped others?
4. Am I trying to be a better person?
5. Have I followed Jesus' example?
Prepare · 201

CURRICULUM CHALLENGE

Reading Using an appropriate reading story that involves choices or using "A Prickly Challenge," have the children analyze the main characters.

- What moral choices did each make?
- What are two questions that each character could ask to examine his or her conscience?
- How can they make up for their wrong choices?

TEACHING TIP

Remind the children that "A "Prickly Challenge" is a fantasy story. In reality, only human beings have a conscience and make moral choices.

Lesson Plan · Day 3

Play a guessing game with the children. Make ten short lines on the chalkboard, one line for every letter in the word *conscience.* Have the children guess letters until they spell the word. Ask the students how they use their conscience.

❶ Looking Back

Share the introductory material. Write *examination of conscience* on the chalkboard, and have the children pronounce it. See whether they can use their knowledge of the word *examine* to determine what an examination of conscience is.

❷ Examining Conscience

Play some background music softly. Let the children sit wherever they wish. Read the questions on the page, pausing after each to allow time for thought. Ask the children to put a check next to each sentence that tells what they want to do better. Tell them they will not be sharing this examination.

VOCABULARY

Examination of Conscience
To use your conscience to look back at the moral choices you have made.

TEACHING TIP

Respect the children's privacy whenever questions of a moral nature come up, such as those on student page 202. Ask the children to answer the questions silently. Assure the children that no one needs to know their answers. Give the same assurance for the resource master exercise on page 308.

Looking Back

Think about the choices that you have made. Did you use your conscience as your guide? This kind of looking back on the choices you have made is called an **examination of conscience.**

Ask yourself these questions.

1. Have I hurt a friend?
2. Have I been respectful to those who care for me?
3. Have I helped others in need?
4. Have I been respectful in my thoughts, words, and actions?
5. Am I trying to be a better person?
6. Have I followed Jesus' example?

When you think back, see if there's a way that you can do better. You can make up for the wrong choices that you made.

3 How Did I Do?
Stress the importance of examination of conscience. God gives us people and things to guide us in examining our conscience.

4 Activity
Let the children read aloud the guides God gives us. Talk with the children about ways each guide can help. The children then choose one guide and write the appropriate word or words on the lines.

How Did I Do?

Examining your conscience will prepare you for Reconciliation. The questions you ask yourself can also help you see how you can make better choices.

Look at the pictures. Who or what can help you prepare? Use these words. Write the correct word on the line.

parent pray teacher priest Ten Commandments

A ____________________

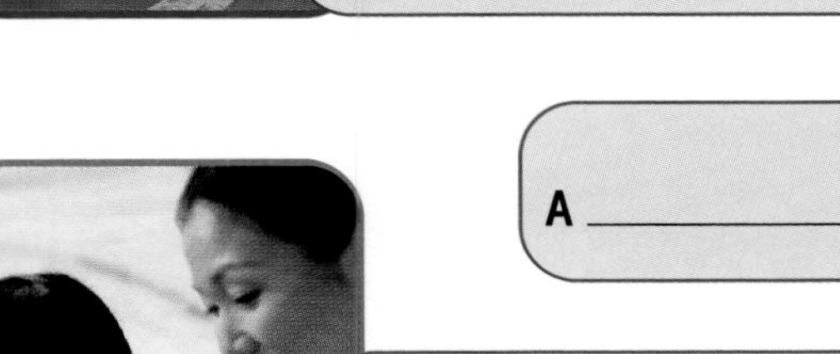

A ____________________

A ____________________

I can ____________________

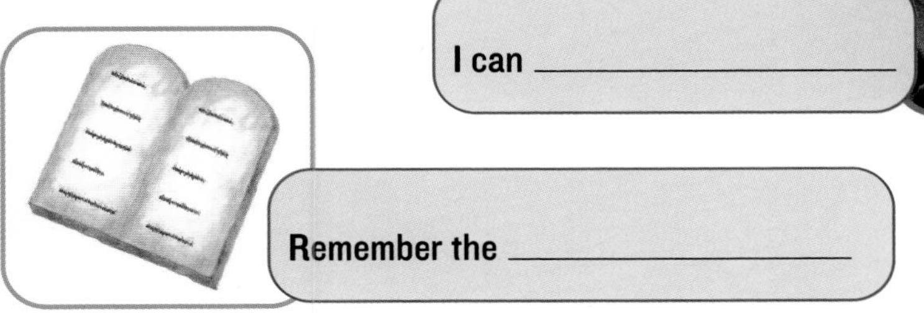

Remember the ____________________

IDEAS THAT WORK

In anticipation of First Reconciliation, you may wish to acquaint the children with the parish priest. Invite him to tell about the importance of examining the conscience. Ask him to talk with the children about simple, practical ways to examine their consciences.

RESOURCE MASTERS

The resource master on page 308 guides the children in writing their own examinations of conscience.

Lesson Plan · Day 4

Sing a simple song together to review examination of conscience. See the Ideas That Work feature below.

1 Better Choices

Talk about "A Prickly Challenge" and how the squirrel children made their choices. Lead the children to discover the best ways they can make choices. Talk about what makes a choice a good choice.

Allow time for the children to draw or write things they can do to make better choices in the circles on student page 204.

Singing helps remembering. Teach this simple song that can be sung to the tune of "When the Saints Go Marching In." For the next few days, sing the song at the beginning or end of class.

How did I do?
How did I do?
What kind of choices did
I make?
Oh, how I want to choose
the right way
And live as Jesus taught.

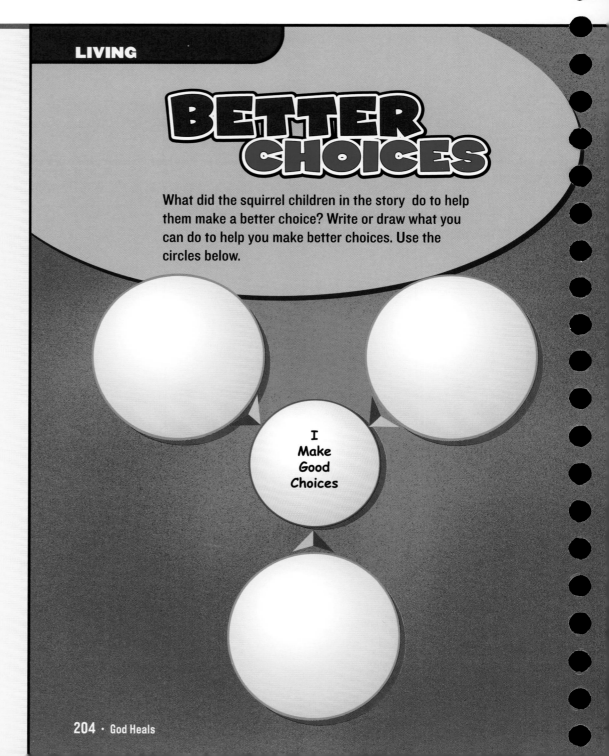

BETTER CHOICES

What did the squirrel children in the story do to help them make a better choice? Write or draw what you can do to help you make better choices. Use the circles below.

I Make Good Choices

❷ How to Prepare

Have the children read the directions silently, and ask a volunteer to explain them aloud. Allow a few minutes for the completion of the activity. Ask everyone to read the sentence aloud. See whether there are any questions about examining the conscience.

HOW TO PREPARE

There are seven words that make a sentence about Reconciliation. The number tells how many words are in that line. Circle the seven words.

Number of words	
3	OZCIUSETHE
1	XGOMTENFPT
1	MCOMMANDMENTSF
2	XGTOEXAMINEOSKM
1	DIJMYOWJ
1	JNFCONSCIENCEOEJNF

Write the sentence.

____

____

____

____

CURRICULUM CHALLENGE

Art This week's art project ties in with the lesson on examination of conscience:

- Make a reminder about preparing for Reconciliation. Give each child a sheet of sturdy paper on which to draw a big, thick check mark. (Or, you can draw such a mark and make a copy of it for each child.)
- Write ways to prepare for Reconciliation on both sides of the check mark.
- Cut out the mark and punch a hole near the top. Tie yarn through it.
- Hang the reminder where the class can use it for reference.

Prayer

This simple prayer can be done on day 4 or day 5 of this session.

1 Prepare for Prayer

Give some time for the children to look over the words they will pray. Allow time for them to examine their conscience. The questions on student page 202 or the questions written on resource master page 308 may be used.

2 A New Start

Begin the prayer service by gathering the group together. Pray the prayer on the page together. Then, join hands and pray the Our Father.

LEARNING TO PRAY

Catholics believe in a merciful God. We ask for forgiveness whenever we gather for the Eucharist. Give each child a copy of the various prayers that form the Penitential Rite. With a partner, have the children circle every word of forgiveness.

Dear God,

We know that we have sinned.

We have hurt you.

We have hurt others.

We open our hearts to you.

Please forgive us and open your arms to us.

LEADER: Let us pray the words that Jesus taught us.

Pray the Lord's Prayer together.

1 Know
Call attention to the graphic organizer that reviews preparation for Reconciliation. Ask the children to check every step that they understand and to ask questions about the steps that are unclear.

2 Love and Serve
The children may need to brainstorm for a short while before feeling ready to write the skinny poem. Walk around and give positive affirmation for the children's loving actions. Guide the children to list specific actions in the Serve activity.

3 God's Friends
Show the illustration. If you have access to a world map, indicate Poland. Share the information about Saint Faustina. Ask the class what they most liked learning about Saint Faustina.

CHAPTER 14
REVIEW and EXPLORE

Know

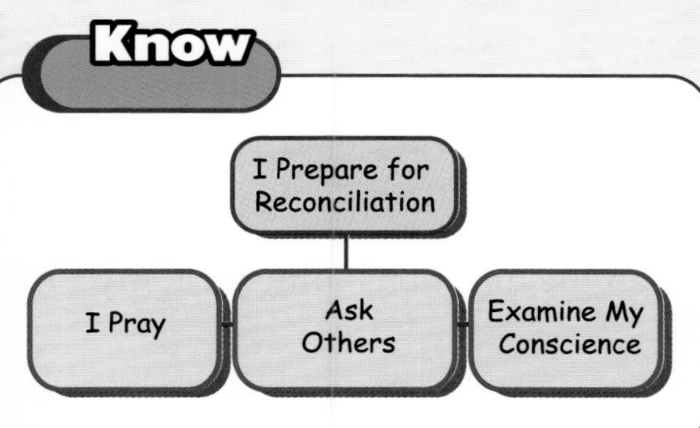

Love

Write a skinny poem. On every line write a word that tells a loving thing that you do.

Me!

Serve

Make a checklist of good things you want to do in the coming week. Do one thing in school, one at home, and one for a friend.

When you do the good thing, be sure to check it off.

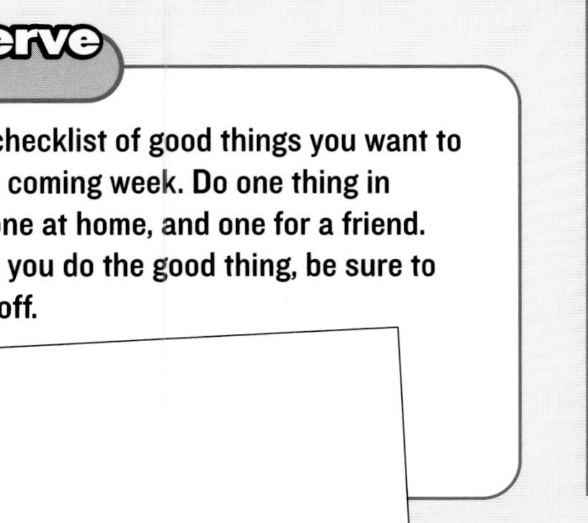

GOD'S FRIENDS

Saint Faustina Kowalska

Faustina was born in Poland. She believed in God's mercy. She spread the word of God's mercy all over the world. Because of Faustina, there is now a special Sunday called Mercy Sunday, which celebrates God's great mercy. She told everyone that God's mercy never ends.

A Little Catechism

Invite the children to open their religion books to *A Little Catechism.* Choose one or more of the selections below for memory work or reinforcement. You will find your copy of the catechism on pages 23–43 of this Teacher's Edition.

1. Together with the children, recite paragraph number 2 on page 10.
2. Review with the children The Ten Commandments on page 11.
3. Ask the children to read aloud Important Question 6 and its answer. Repeat it several times as an aid to memory.

Know | Love | Serve

Note The activities on this page provide ways for the children to share their learning with their families. The activities are related to the week's theme.

1 Introduce
Have the children read the introduction aloud. Explain the activities with enthusiasm.

2 Pray Together
Together, pray the prayer in the prayer burst.

Online for Families
Remind the children to check the Benziger Web site this week with their families.
www.benziger.glencoe.com

Dear Family,

I have just finished chapter 14. I have learned that I can ask God's forgiveness for my sins. To prepare, I must examine my conscience. Help me remember to go through the questions I must ask myself.

With others

With a friend, think of a time you showed forgiveness. How did you feel? Does someone need your forgiveness now?

With your family

Talk about the steps of Reconciliation. Ask questions about things you don't understand. Practice the steps together.

May I open my heart to your forgiveness.

GO ONLINE!
http://www.benziger.glencoe.com

1 Introduce

Go back to the idea that sometimes doing the right thing can be hard. Tell children that sometimes they may not feel like being kind and cheerful. They may be feeling angry, tired, or even a little sad. Remind the children that acts of kindness will not only help them feel better but also bring them closer to God and others. Doing the right thing is always worth the effort.

2 The Project

Divide the children into groups of two or three. Ask them to sit in a way that they can comfortably face one another. Allow them to use floor space, if possible. Distribute one die and game pieces to each group. Emphasize the importance of taking turns. Encourage children to help one another read the words on the game board. Allow enough time for the children to play the game, making sure that each child has had three or four turns around the board. At the end of the game, talk about how kind actions let them move forward and unkind actions had them move back. Talk about how that happens in real life.

THE CHURCH TODAY

Making good choices can be hard. Doing good things will help you be a better follower of Jesus.

Play a game that will help you. Use a penny as a marker. Roll one die. Move your penny. Do what the square tells you to do. Talk together about the actions.

ANSWER KEY

This is the answer key for the chapter test on page 309.

A. I. b 2. a 3. b

B. Accept questions that relate to moral choices.

C. I. and 3.

Name ____________________

How Did I Do?

You will examine your conscience every time you prepare for the sacrament of Reconciliation. You can use the Ten Commandments as a guide. Add some questions to ask yourself.

Love God

- Did I pray?
- Did I use God's name with respect?
- ____________________
- ____________________

Love Others

- Did I hurt anyone's feelings?
- Did I obey my family?
- ____________________
- ____________________
- ____________________

Name ______________________________

Chapter 14 Test

A. Circle the answer for each question.

1. When are you responsible for your choices?
- **a.** sometimes
- **b.** always

2. What is an examination of conscience?
- **a.** looking back at moral choices you made
- **b.** asking for forgiveness

3. What can help you examine your conscience?
- **a.** the Lord's Prayer
- **b.** the Ten Commandments

B. What are three questions you can ask yourself when making an examination of conscience?

____

____

____

____

____

C. Check two reasons why you make an examination of conscience.

_____ **1.** to see what sins I may have committed

_____ **2.** to see if I am feeling good

_____ **3.** to see how I can do better

CHAPTER 15

Signs of Forgiveness

TEACHER RESOURCE CENTER

Faith Formation

Penance and Reconciliation

Before one can be forgiven, one must acknowledge the wrong done to God or to others and be sorry for it. Then comes the hard part for many: asking for forgiveness. The sacrament of Reconciliation offers Catholics a beautiful way of saying "I am sorry" and of experiencing God's forgiveness. God is present in the sacrament of Reconciliation through the priest and the comforting and encouraging words of absolution: "May God give you pardon and peace."

How has the sacrament of Reconciliation been an experience of God's pardon and peace for you?

The Father of Mercies

Confessing one's sins to a priest in the sacrament of Reconciliation is just one aspect of seeking forgiveness. It is also important to heal the people and relationships that have been wounded by one's wrongdoing. We must express a sincere apology to those harmed by our words, actions, or attitudes. We must trust in the grace of forgiveness that God grants all sinners who seek reconciliation with him.

How have you experienced the forgiveness of others?

CHECK THE CATECHISM

In paragraphs 1420–1484, the *Catechism of the Catholic Church* covers in great detail the sacrament of Reconciliation. Look at paragraphs 1446–1449 for an overview of the celebration of the sacrament and the healing words of absolution.

Background

Reconciliation

Loving forgiveness is at the heart of the Gospel. Jesus taught his followers to pray to God as a loving Father rich in mercy and compassion. Reconciliation is about the grace and joy a sinner experiences when reconciled with God. Help the children understand this key idea of Reconciliation with the opening story about Fran and Allie. Love and friendship are renewed by forgiveness.

God is love. When love is shut out, so is God. Help the children see that their choices—good and bad—affect their relationship with God. Reconciliation helps restore and solidify that relationship.

Faith Summary

In Reconciliation we express sorrow for sins and the desire not to sin again.

- **A priest forgives our sins in the name of Jesus Christ.**
- **After Reconciliation we do a penance to show our sorrow.**

Growth and Development

It is helpful to remember two characteristics of second graders as you teach this lesson:

- ***Second graders may have some misconceptions about reconciling.*** For example, they may think that forgiveness is cowardly. Guide the children to see that requesting forgiveness and offering forgiveness take courage.
- ***Second graders may think that Reconciliation is scary.*** Emphasize that God's forgiveness is a healing process, not a compiling of faults.

A Teacher's Prayer

God of goodness and mercy, let the children recognize in me your warmth and compassion. Help them ask forgiveness when they hurt others. Let them be comfortable with the sacrament of Reconciliation so that they may feel the healing peace of your embrace. Amen.

Vocabulary Preview

Reconciliation
examination of conscience
penance
Act of Contrition
absolution

Scripture

Matthew 9:2: Your sins are forgiven.

Luke 7:36–50: Jesus forgives a sinner.

Colossians 3:13: Forgive others as I forgive you.

Related Resources

Video

"The Angel's First Reconciliation Lesson" (Twenty-Third Publications, 1-800-321-0411 or www.twentythirdpublications.com). This video offers information about forgiveness and Reconciliation. (Children, 11 minutes)

Book

Hamrogue, John M. *Forgive and Be Forgiven* (Liguori Publications, 1-800-325-9521 or www.liguori.org). This book helps children grasp the need to forgive others. (Children)

TEACHER ORGANIZER

Planning Guide

The basic content for each chapter is divided into four class sessions. There are a number of options for the fifth session. Extension, review, and testing options are described under Day 5 Alternatives. The Quick Check box will help you evaluate the week's lessons.

Chapter Goals

In this chapter, the students will learn about

- ❑ The steps in Reconciliation
- ❑ Jesus' teachings about forgiveness
- ❑ An Act of Contrition

	DAY 1 · INVITATION	DAY 2 · DISCOVERY	DAY 3 · DISCOVERY
OBJECTIVES	**The students will be able to** • Analyze how to reconcile a wrongdoing • Determine ways to handle anger and make peace	**The students will be able to** • Recognize the five steps in Reconciliation	**The students will be able to** • Conclude that Jesus teaches about forgiveness • Determine words of forgiveness in the Our Father • Discover the elements of an Act of Contrition
PREPARATION	• Ahead of time, ask two girls to act out a short scene that fits the story on student page 210 • Think of a personal story of forgiveness to share	• Make five flash cards of the steps in Reconciliation • Make copies of the resource master on page 326	• Reflect on why the Sacrament of Reconciliation is important to you
MATERIALS	• Pencils	• Flash cards: small pieces of poster board, markers • Copies of the resource master, pencils, scissors, glue	• Flash cards • Pencils
OPTIONAL ACTIVITIES	• Ideas That Work Partner children using the alphabet and numerals	• Ideas That Work Visit the church to view the Reconciliation space • Resource Masters Cut out and glue in the steps in Reconciliation	• Ideas That Work Play a game to retell a Bible story

Learning Objectives

By the end of this chapter, the students should be able to

- ❑ Recognize the steps in Reconciliation
- ❑ Analyze a Bible story to see what Jesus teaches about forgiveness
- ❑ Begin to learn an Act of Contrition

DAY 4 · LIVING

The students will be able to

- Make up actions that show forgiveness
- Discover positive associations with Reconciliation
- Pray an Act of Contrition

- Prepare an explanation of the Act of Contrition

- Drawing materials
- Pencils

- **Options** Perform a scene about forgiveness

DAY 5 · ALTERNATIVES

There are a number of alternatives to help you plan Day 5.

Prayer Experience
Use An Act of Contrition prayer service, on Day 4 or Day 5. If the books are not taken home, make copies of the prayer so the students' families may help them learn it.

Review and Explore
The students need pencils and, if you choose to make puppets, art supplies. If you have a world map, indicate France.

Home and Family
Send the page home with the students, or assign one or more of the activities.

The Church Today
The students will make a cover for the classroom prayer table. Determine what supplies you will need.

Chapter Test
The chapter test appears as a resource master on page 327.

Quick Check

Do this evaluation as soon as you finish each chapter.

Did I follow my lesson plan?

How can I tell that I met the learning objectives for the lesson?

What activities did the children enjoy most?

How could I improve this lesson?

Benziger on the Web
For more ideas, visit us at www.benziger.glencoe.com

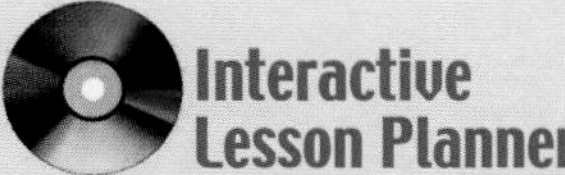

Interactive Lesson Planner
Your ILP provides more help in preparing to teach this chapter.

Celebrate
Turn to page 22 of this book. Check for seasonal celebrations.

Lesson Plan · Day 1

Share a time you had an argument or misunderstanding with a friend or family member. Details are not needed. Focus on your reconciliation with that person.

1 A Bad Time

Have two girls act out the story on student page 210. Then introduce them to the class as Fran and Allie. To promote class discussion, ask why Fran felt bad, too. Ask whether anyone has had a time like this with a friend.

Ask volunteers to whisper suggestions to "Fran" and "Allie" of what they could say to each other. The girls may repeat the suggestions they feel are best. The girls then tell how they feel after making up. Guide them to be specific. Then ask the class what Fran and Allie can do to *show* they are sorry.

IDEAS THAT WORK

Here is another way to partner children. Print the entire alphabet and as many numerals as needed to equal the number of children in the class. Cut each letter and number separately. The children choose one and pair up with the letter or number that adjoins. For example, A goes with B; C goes with D; 1 goes with 2; 3 goes with 4.

Courage, child, your sins are forgiven.

Matthew 9:2

Do You Know?

- How do you prepare to receive the sacrament of Reconciliation?

Signs of Forgiveness

A Bad Time

Fran and Allie were playing after school. Fran made fun of Allie. "You're dumb," Fran said. Then Fran started calling Allie names. Allie began to cry. Allie felt bad. Fran felt bad too.

?
- What could Fran and Allie say to each other?
- How would both girls feel now?

2 Do You Know?
Call attention to the word *forgive(ness)* in the title, Scripture verse, and question. Have the children look ahead through the chapter's pages. With a sense of enthusiasm, indicate that this chapter will show how to receive the sacrament of Reconciliation. At the end of the week, come back to this question to see how the children's knowledge has developed.

3 Hard Words
Let the children share what is difficult about saying "I am sorry." Talk, too, about why the words are important. *(They are the first step in making things better.)*

4 Activity
Have the children get a partner. Read aloud the three scenarios with a tone of belligerence. Tell the partners to choose two of the stories and figure out some good advice for doing what is right. Each group may act out or share its advice for one story. Encourage the rest of the class to give good comments in response. See the Teaching Tip feature below.

Hard Words

Saying "I'm sorry" can be hard to do. Maybe you are too angry to say, "I'm sorry." Things don't get better until someone says, "I'm sorry."

Pretend that other children in your class come to you for help. This is what they tell you. What will you tell them to do?

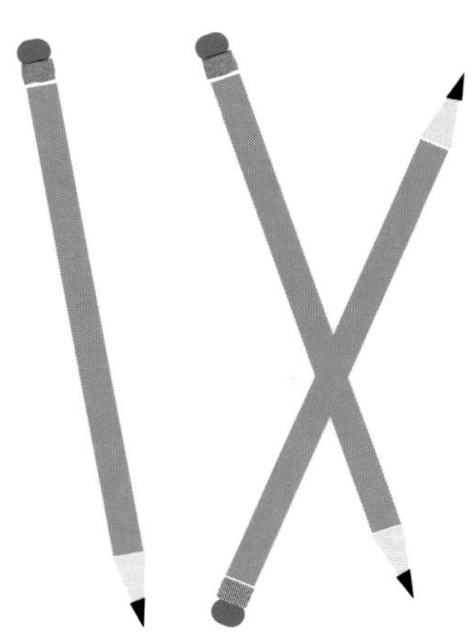

Kate cut in front of me in line. It is my turn to be line leader. I pushed Kate and she fell. We are both mad. What should I do?

____

____

____

____

____

____

Benny and I ran a race. I say I won. Benny says he won. Benny is a cheater. He makes me so mad! What should I do?

____

____

____

____

____

____

I lost my new markers. I think Jenny took them. Jenny got mad when I told her that I thought she had them. Now she is mad at me. What should I do?

____

____

____

____

____

The children may need guidance in giving positive criticism. Give prompts, such as these, that elicit good comments: "What is real about this advice?" "Why would this advice work?" "Why is this good advice?" "Why would you follow this advice?"

Lesson Plan · Day 2

With enthusiasm remind the children that soon they will receive the sacrament of Reconciliation. Today and tomorrow they will learn how!

1 Steps to Forgiveness

Indicate to the class that no one sits at a computer and automatically gets work done. There are steps to using a computer: turn on the machine, read the menu, open a file and so on. There are also important steps to follow in receiving the sacrament of Reconciliation. Then read aloud the introduction and This We Believe!

2 Steps 1, 2, 3

Show a flash card of step one, read it, and have the children repeat it. Tell about the step in simple words. Tape the card to the chalkboard.

Continue in the same way with step 2 and step 3. Arrange the flash cards to ascend like steps from the previous cards.

VIRTUE FAITH GRACE VOCABULARY

Absolution God's forgiveness of sins through the words and actions of a priest.

Act of Contrition A prayer that says you are sorry for your sins and you want to make the right choices.

Penance A prayer or action that shows you are sorry for your sins.

IDEAS THAT WORK

Most children look forward to receiving Reconciliation but some may be a bit anxious. Helping the children learn the Act of Contrition and the steps of the sacrament will add to their confidence. If the children are worried about forgetting what to do or say, assure them that the priest will help them. Explain that the priest will never tell other people what is said in confession. Schedule a time with the parish priest, or without, to view the areas of the church that will be used for Reconciliation.

This We Believe!

In Reconciliation, God forgives us and brings us back to him and to the Church.

Steps to Forgiveness

Catholics have a special way of celebrating forgiveness. It is called the sacrament of **Reconciliation** or **Penance.** The word *reconciliation* means, "bringing back together."

1. To prepare, for the sacrament of Reconciliation **examine your conscience**. You can use the Ten Commandments as a guide.

2. You tell your sins to the priest. The priest forgives your sins in Jesus' name. He tells you how to be more like Jesus.

3. The priest asks you to say some prayers or to do some actions to make up for your sins. This is called a **penance**. You do the penance to show that you are sorry and that you want to make better choices.

3 Steps 4 and 5

Repeat the process with the fourth flash card. Explain that this is the step in which you tell God you are sorry for your sins. Show the class the Act of Contrition on student page 218. Continue with the fifth flash card. Demonstrate the sign of blessing for the children.

4 Activity

Take down the cards. Direct the children to complete the activity. Then put the cards back on the chalkboard to allow the children to check their answers.

4. You pray the **Act of Contrition**. You say you are truly sorry for your sins.

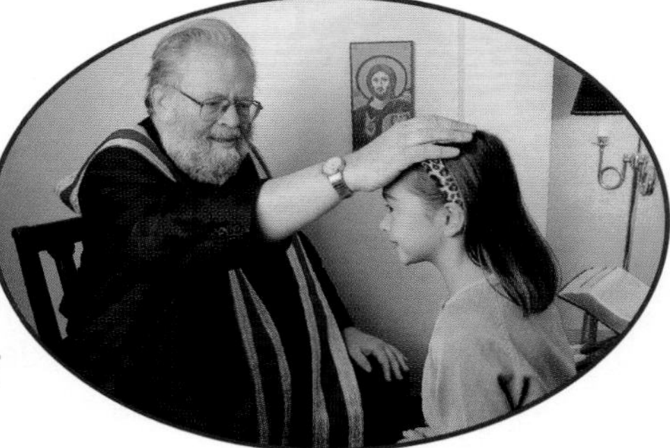

5. The priest blesses you and says the words of **absolution.** The priest stretches out his hand and says, "I absolve you from your sins in the name of the Father, and of the Son, and of the Holy Spirit."

ACTIVITY THE RIGHT STEPS

Number each of the steps for the sacrament of Reconciliation in the right order.

☐ Receive absolution

☐ Accept penance

☐ Say Act of Contrition

☐ Confess sins

TEACHING TIP

Transfer the flash cards of the steps in Reconciliation to a poster and keep on display.

Assure the children that they will go over the steps many times before they receive the sacrament of Reconciliation.

RESOURCE MASTERS

Use the resource master on page 326 for a review of the steps in Reconciliation.

Lesson Plan · Day 3

Have the children turn to someone who sits near and briefly review the five steps in Reconciliation. Ask if there are questions; write them on the chalkboard. Volunteers may help answer them.

1 Jesus Shows Forgiveness

Gather the children close. Tell them that you want to share a story about Jesus showing forgiveness. Ask the children to listen for Jesus' words of forgiveness. Get the children ready to listen. See the Bible Basics feature below. Then, share the Bible story.

2 Discuss

Ask the questions on the bottom of the page. Sum up by restating that the woman washed Jesus' feet to show that she was sorry for her sins. Jesus forgave her. Be sure the children see the most important aspect of the story—the woman was sorry for her sins. Share how wonderful it is that Jesus continues to show forgiveness in the sacrament of Reconciliation.

BIBLE BASICS

Get the children ready to hear the Bible story by setting the mood. Ask the children to imagine the following: "It is evening. A man named Simon asks Jesus to his house for dinner. Jesus is wearing sandals on his feet. He walks along a dusty road to get to Simon's house. Jesus and other guests are having a good time. Suddenly a woman appears."

TEACHING TIP

The children may wonder about Simon's attitude in the Bible story. Explain that Jesus preached about love and forgiveness. Love and forgiveness were new ideas. People had thought that sinners should not be forgiven, no matter how sorry they were. Jesus knew how sorry the woman was for her sins. He knew that she was trying to be better. Jesus showed God's mercy.

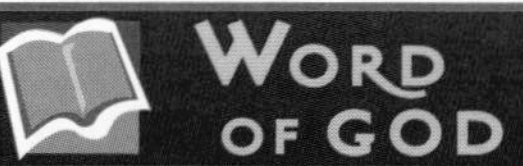

You must forgive each other, as God forgives you.

Colossians 3:13

Jesus Shows Forgiveness

A man named Simon invited Jesus to dinner. A woman came into the room and stood at Jesus' feet.

This woman had done many wrong things. She was crying many tears. She was really sorry. She washed Jesus' feet with her tears and dried them with her long hair. Then she rubbed his feet with oil.

Simon looked at her and thought, "If Jesus were really holy, he would not let this sinner touch him."

Jesus said to Simon, "This woman is sorry. All of her sins are forgiven."

Then Jesus spoke to the woman. "Your faith has saved you. Your sins are forgiven. Go in peace."

Based on *Luke 7:36–50*

?

- Do Jesus' actions surprise you?
- What does Jesus teach you about forgiveness?

3 Pray for Forgiveness
Recall that prayer is talking and listening to God. Share the information in the opening paragraphs on student page 215. Then add that the Act of Contrition is one way to ask God for forgiveness. Direct attention to the activity. The children may help each other fill in the blanks to form the prayer. You may wish to pray the prayer at the end of the day.

4 Activity
Discuss the question at the bottom of the page. Have a volunteer answer the question. Repeat the words as a class.

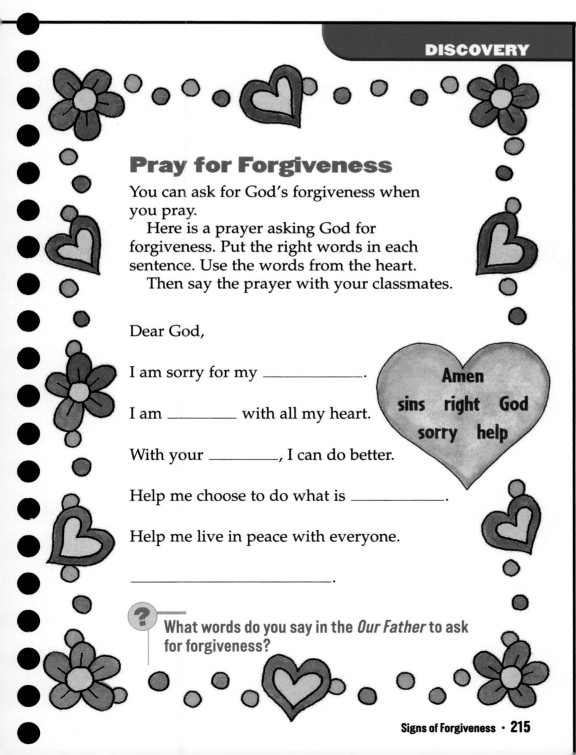

Pray for Forgiveness

You can ask for God's forgiveness when you pray.

Here is a prayer asking God for forgiveness. Put the right words in each sentence. Use the words from the heart.

Then say the prayer with your classmates.

Dear God,

I am sorry for my ____________.

I am ________ with all my heart.

With your ________, I can do better.

Help me choose to do what is ____________.

Help me live in peace with everyone.

________________________.

Amen
sins right God
sorry help

? What words do you say in the *Our Father* to ask for forgiveness?

IDEAS THAT WORK

Involve all of the children in recalling Bible stories. Have on hand beach balls or other safe, lightweight balls that are easy to catch. Oraganize the children into small groups and have a ball for each group. Invite the class to sit on the floor, or to stand, in circles. One person has the ball and tells the beginning of the Bible story. A sentence or two is plenty. That child tosses the ball to another child who then continues the story. Groups should try to give every child a chance to catch the ball and add to the story.

Lesson Plan · Day 4

Review that saying "I am sorry" is an important step in making things good again.

1 Showing Sorrow

Recall that sometimes it is hard to apologize. Ask the children if apologizing is ever easy to do. Let the children talk about this concept with someone who sits near. Volunteers may share their conclusions.

2 Activity

If you have a costume box, dig into it. All of the scenes involve one or two people. Let the children choose if they want to act alone or with a partner. Some children may prefer drawing their response. Let all share an idea. This will allow the children to learn from one another.

OPTIONS

For Those Who Learn Interpersonally You may want to adjust the activity on student page 216. Let these children perform a whole scene that includes the wrongdoing and the making up.

SHOWING SORROW

The children in the stories can say they are sorry. What can they do to *show* they are sorry?

Pick one story and act out a way that the child can show that he or she is sorry.
In the space, you can draw a child showing a way he or she is sorry.

1. Mary played with her sister's doll and the arm came off. What should Mary do?
2. Tanner took money from his sister's piggy bank. What should Tanner do?
3. Chris took his brother's bike without asking and left it at a friend's house. What should Chris do?
4. Jessica laughed at Mrs. Reyes, who walks with a cane. What should Jessica do?

❸ Make It Better

Tell the children to raise their hands every time you say a word that tells about something good. Read the list of words. Ask the children to write the words in the puzzle. They may check their answers with each other.

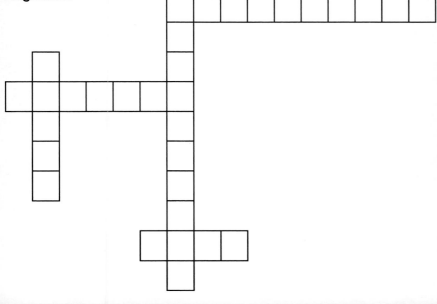

MAKE IT BETTER

Look at the words below. They tell about Reconciliation. Count the number of letters in each word. Put them in the right space.

Peace
Rejoice
Gift
Friendship
Forgiveness

Often times, the words *I'm sorry* are an easy and automatic response to a situation. Children may blurt out the words, without knowing what harm had been done. Or, they may use the words as a magic formula that erases guilt and blame. Help the children see the connection between the apology and the action. When a child says "I'm sorry," ask the child why he or she is sorry. Gently lead the child to say "I'm sorry for. . . ." Using the word *for* will make for a truer apology and will help the child see a connection to the wrongdoing.

Prayer

The prayer experience is an essential part of this chapter's theme development.

1 Prepare for Prayer

Look back at the five steps in Reconciliation on the chalkboard and call attention to the Act of Contrition. Then, go slowly through the prayer on student page 218. Help the children understand the lines and see the beauty of the words.

2 An Act of Contrition

Gather the children together for prayer. Allow time for them to examine their conscience. Then, lead the class in the Act of Contrition. Close with the Sign of the Cross.

Learning to Pray

If you wish, show the children a traditional posture for praying a prayer of sorrow. Have the children cross their arms over their heart and bow their heads. They may repeat the lines of the Act of Contrition after you.

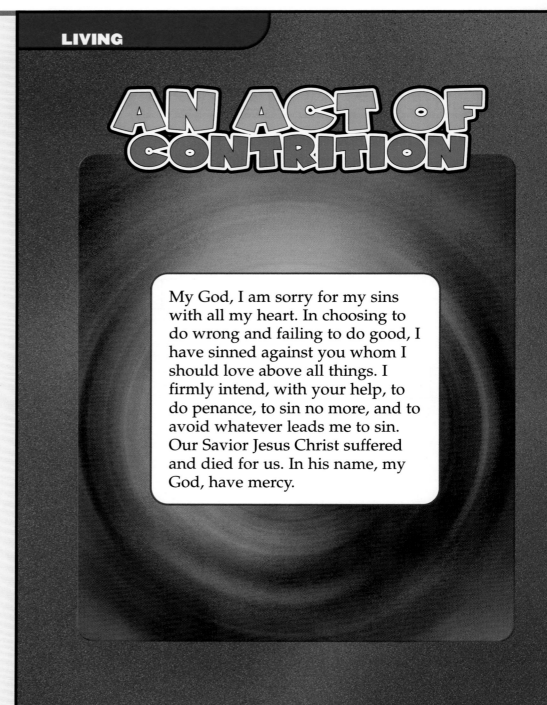

An Act of Contrition

My God, I am sorry for my sins with all my heart. In choosing to do wrong and failing to do good, I have sinned against you whom I should love above all things. I firmly intend, with your help, to do penance, to sin no more, and to avoid whatever leads me to sin. Our Savior Jesus Christ suffered and died for us. In his name, my God, have mercy.

1 Know

Direct attention to the graphic organizer. Ask the children to go through each step with a partner. Have the children place a checkmark next to every step that they understand and can explain. Be ready to review the steps that are not checked.

2 Love and Serve

Take the time needed, now or later, to make the Love activity beneficial to your class. You may wish to use the Serve puppet-making activity as an art lesson. If the art activity is postponed, be sure to give the children the opportunity to present scenes of forgiveness.

3 God's Friends

If you have a world map, find France. Get the children's attention by having them imagine the setting of Ars. Show the illustration of John Vianney and tell about him. Ask the class what is the best thing that they heard about Saint John.

Know

Steps to Forgiveness

- Absolution
- Act of Contrition
- Penance
- Confession
- Examination of Conscience

Love

Finish this sentence. Don't use a word, draw a picture.

When God forgives me, I feel

Serve

Think of a time when forgiveness is needed at home or at school. Work with some friends. Make some puppets to act out your story. Share your story with the class.

CHAPTER 15
REVIEW and EXPLORE

GOD'S FRIENDS

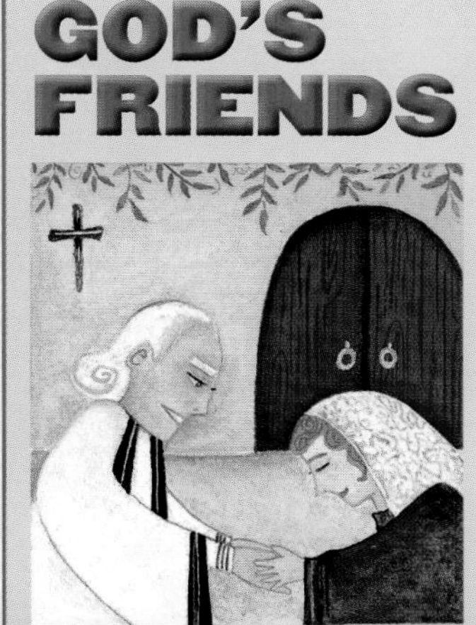

Saint John Vianney

It was easy to find Father John in the French village of Ars. All you had to do was look for a long line of people. They would wait for hours to talk with Father John in confession. He helped people know and trust that God forgave them.

A Little Catechism

Invite the children to open their religion books to *A Little Catechism.* Choose one or more of the selections below for memory work or reinforcement. You will find your copy of the catechism on pages 23–43 of this Teacher's Edition.

1. Review The Act of Contrition with the children. Pray it together as a class.
2. Read aloud to the children the section on the Trinity. Ask the children to repeat each sentence after you.
3. Encourage the children to memorize the answers to Important Questions 2 and 3.

Know Love Serve

Note The activities on this page provide ways for the children to share their learning with their families. The activities are related to the week's theme.

1 Introduce
Have the children follow along while you read the letter aloud. If time allows, the children may pair up, pretending to be a parent and child. The parent may ask the child two questions about what was learned in religion class during the week. Then roles may be reversed.

2 Pray Together
Pray with joy the prayer in the prayer burst.

Online for Families
Remind the children to check the Benziger Web site this week with their families.
www.benziger.glencoe.com

Dear Family,

I have just finished chapter 15. I have learned that, in the sacrament of Reconciliation, the priest gives me absolution for my sins. I can do penance to show that I am sorry for my sins. God forgives me, and I am called back to my Church family.

On your own

Use the code. Learn what Jesus says about forgiving others.

1 = A 2 = E 3 = F 4 = G 5 = H 6 = I 7 = O
8 = R 9 = S 10 = T 11 = U 12 = V 13 = Y

"3__ 7__ 8__ 4__ 6__ 12__ 2__
7__ 10__ 5__ 2__ 8__ 9__ 1__ 9__ 6__
3__ 7__ 8__ 4__ 6__ 12__ 2__
13__ 7__ 11__ "

Based on *Colossians 3:13*

With your family

Ask members of your family to help you learn the Act of Contrition.

Happy are we for our sins are forgiven!

GO ONLINE!
http://www.benziger.glencoe.com

1 Introduce
Show the altar cloths or show some in a catalogue. Call attention to the signs and briefly describe what they symbolize. Let volunteers tell why they think altar cloths are important.

2 Project
Suggest that the children make a new cover for the classroom prayer table. Let them brainstorm for appropriate signs of happiness and hope. Perhaps the children will want to make the cloth reflect the two sacraments they will receive. Have the class figure out a role everyone can play in making the cloth.

THE CHURCH TODAY

Jesus taught that when you show love to others, you show love for God. Forgiving others is one way to show love for God.

As a class, make a special cover for your prayer table. Look through old magazines and find pictures that show love and forgiveness. Cut them out. Glue them to your prayer table cover. Your prayer space will remind you to offer love when someone hurts you.

IDEAS THAT WORK

Perhaps it is difficult for you to schedule a block of time to make the prayer table cloth. You may want to have the children play smaller roles for short periods of time. If so, have the children list the tasks needed to make the cloth *(think of the designs, draw sample designs, make the designs, apply the designs, and so on)*. A small group of children may volunteer for each task. Set a time limit to get each task done.

TEACHING TIP

Perhaps your parish has an Altar Society. A member may wish to visit the class, show some altar cloths, and tell how they care for them.

ANSWER KEY

This is the answer key for the chapter test on page 327.

A. 1. and 2.

B. 1. a 2. b 3. a 4. a

Name ______________________________

Celebrate God's Forgiveness

Find your way to forgiveness by completing the maze. Cut out and glue the name of each step in the Sacrament of Reconciliation. Put the steps on the maze in the correct order.

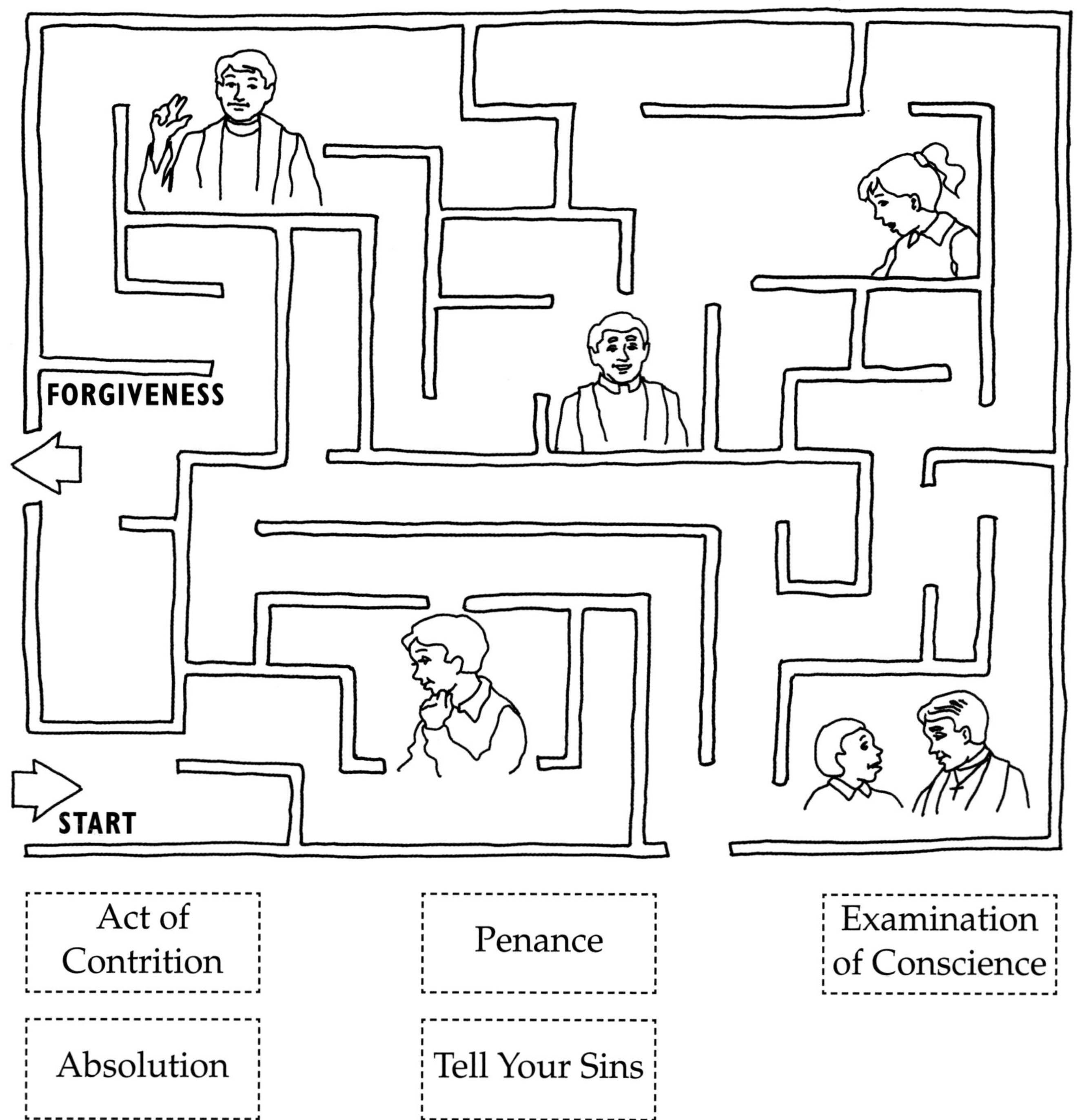

Act of Contrition	Penance	Examination of Conscience
Absolution	Tell Your Sins	

Name ______________________________

Chapter 15 Test

A. Jesus forgave the woman who was sorry for her sins. Circle the two messages of the Bible story.

1. You should forgive others.

2. God loves you even if you sin.

3. God gets angry at sinners.

B. Circle what is true about each step in Reconciliation.

1. You tell your sins to the priest

a. because he is there in place of Jesus.
b. so that he can anoint you with oil.

2. The priest gives you a penance

a. so that you suffer for your sins.
b. so that you show you are sorry.

3. You say an Act of Contrition

a. because you are sorry for your sins and want to do better.
b. because you want to praise God for creation.

4. The priest gives you absolution

a. because God forgives your sins.
b. because you remembered the steps.

Healing Signs

TEACHER RESOURCE CENTER

Faith Formation

CHECK THE CATECHISM

Illness often provokes a search for God. Information about the relationship of illness to faith, forgiveness, and the sacrament of Anointing of the Sick is found in the *Catechism of the Catholic Church,* in paragraphs 1499–1532. Note especially the connection with the previous section, paragraphs 1420–1498, which covers the sacrament of Penance.

The Lord Heals Us

> *Is anyone among you suffering? He should pray. Is anyone in good spirits? He should sing praise. Is anyone among you sick? He should summon the presbyters of the church, and they should pray over him and anoint [him] with oil in the name of the Lord, and the prayer of faith will save the sick person, and the Lord will raise him up. If he has committed any sins, he will be forgiven.*
>
> *James 5:13–15*

There is a clear relationship between the sacrament of Penance and the sacrament of Anointing of the Sick. Penance heals people from sin; Anointing of the Sick brings spiritual healing to those who are elderly, close to death, or seriously ill. Forgiveness of sin is included in both sacraments. These "sacraments of healing" are signs of God's compassion and mercy, lived out in the sacramental life of the Catholic Church.

How important are the sacraments of healing in your own life?

Anointing of the Sick

From the earliest times, the church has been committed to caring for the sick. Sacred scripture is full of examples of Jesus healing the lepers, the lame, the crippled, and the blind. The tradition of caring for the sick, as well as the sinner, is a mark of the Catholic Church to this day.

How is the tradition of caring for the sick a visible ministry in your parish?

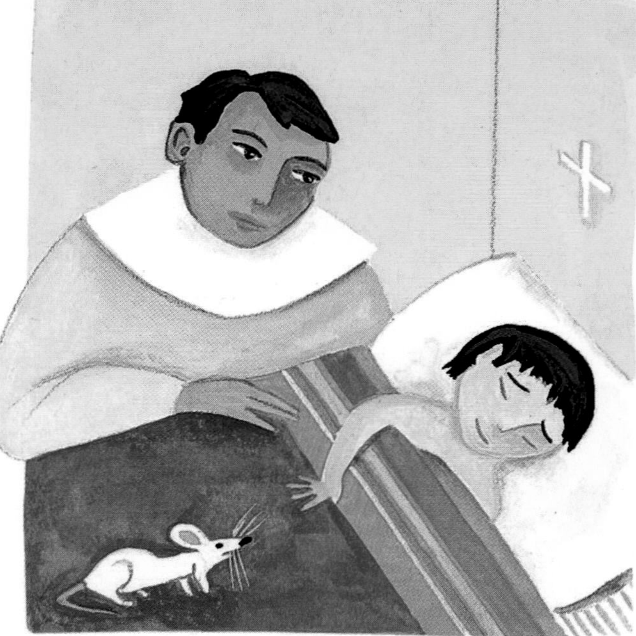

Background

Healing

The focus of chapter 16 is healing. The students will hear that Jesus gave a directive to "Heal the sick." They will learn that the Church today is called to continue healing and forgiveness.

Students associate healing with doctors and parents and medicines—someone or something bigger than themselves. Students usually associate healing with physical problems and pain. You will lead the students to identify different needs for healing and different forms of healing. You will also lead the students to a wonderful discovery. They can be healers. They can help people feel better.

Faith Summary

- **Reconciliation and Anointing of the Sick are sacraments of healing.**
- **Jesus cares about the sick, and has the power to heal them.**
- **The Church answers Jesus' call to heal the sick.**

Growth and Development

It is helpful to remember two characteristics of second graders as you teach this lesson:

- ***Second graders are beginning to understand the needs of others.*** You empower the students when you lead them to an awareness of people's needs. Help them discover ways to bring comfort and care.
- ***Second graders can make conscious choices about reaching out to others who are in need.*** Chapter 16 builds on the concepts of choice that were previously introduced. This chapter directly links making the choice to heal with responding to Jesus' call.

A Teacher's Prayer

Jesus, you were moved with pity and compassion by people in need. I place my faith and trust in you. Keep me alert to the needs of the students. Open my eyes to those who long for a healing voice, a healing smile, a healing heart. Amen.

Vocabulary Preview

Anointing of the Sick
anoints

Scripture

Jeremiah 17:14: Heal me, Lord.
Matthew 10:8, 12: Heal the sick.
Mark 5:22–24, 39–43: Jesus heals Jairus' daughter.
Mark 16:18: laying on of hands

Related Resources

Books

Huebsch, Bill. *Rethinking Sacraments: Holy Moments in Daily Living* (Twenty-Third Publications, 1-800-321-0411 or www.twentythirdpublications.com). This book provides an easy-to-understand treatment of the sacraments. (Adult)

Richstatter, Thomas. "Anointing of the Sick: A Parish Sacrament" *(Catholic Update,* St. Anthony Messenger Press, 1-800-488-0488 or www.AmericanCatholic.org). This article examines our growing understanding of this sacrament, and provides a brief summary of its history. (Adult)

TEACHER ORGANIZER

Planning Guide

The basic content for each chapter is divided into four class sessions. There are a number of options for the fifth session. Extension, review, and testing options are described under Day 5 Alternatives. The Quick Check box will help you evaluate the week's lessons.

Chapter Goals

In this chapter, the students will learn about

- ❑ Jesus' power to heal
- ❑ The sacrament of Anointing of the Sick
- ❑ The Church's mission to heal

	DAY 1 · INVITATION	DAY 2 · DISCOVERY	DAY 3 · DISCOVERY
OBJECTIVES	**The students will be able to** • Understand that the body and spirit may need healing • Suggest ways to make someone feel better	**The students will be able to** • Explain a way Jesus healed • Discover words that heal	**The students will be able to** • Recognize the Anointing of the Sick • Classify signs of the sacraments of healing
PREPARATION	• Think of ways to help Sally feel better	• Make copies of the resource master on page 344	• Review the words and signs of Baptism, Reconciliation, and Anointing of the Sick
MATERIALS	• One nametag per child • Pencils	• Pencils • Crayons or colored markers	• Pencils
OPTIONAL ACTIVITIES	• Curriculum Challenge Talk about ways to stay healthy	• Teaching Tip Talk about situations in need of healing • Resource Masters Use a coloring activity about hurtful or healing situations	• Vocabulary Teach key words from this lesson • Curriculum Challenge Review sequential paragraphs

Learning Objectives

By the end of this chapter, the students should be able to

- ❑ Determine ways they can heal—make people feel better
- ❑ Recognize the sacrament of Anointing of the Sick
- ❑ Do actions that heal

DAY 4 · LIVING	DAY 5 · ALTERNATIVES
The students will be able to • Answer Jesus' call to heal the sick • Determine ways to heal people's spirits • Creatively express a healing message • Promise to try to heal, not hurt	**There are a number of alternatives to help you plan Day 5.** **Prayer Experience** Pray Celebrate Healing on either Day 4 or Day 5. You may wish to add a familiar hymn about healing or reconciliation. **Review and Explore** You will need pencils, notepaper, and prayer cards. Be ready to point out Lima, Peru on a world map. **Home and Family** Send the page home with the students, or assign one or more of the activities. **The Church Today** The students will remember those who need prayers. Index cards, drawing supplies, and pencils are needed. **Chapter Test** The chapter test appears as a resource master on page 345.
• Think of a personal experience when someone helped you feel better • Locate a familiar hymn about healing or reconciliation	
• Construction paper, stickers, glue sticks, scissors, crayons or colored markers • Pencils	
• **Ideas That Work** Use a cardmaking activity • **Vocabulary** Review vocabulary with flashcards	

Quick Check

Do this evaluation as soon as you finish each chapter.

Did I follow my lesson plan?

How can I tell that I met the learning objectives for the lesson?

What activities did the children enjoy most?

How could I improve this lesson?

Benziger on the Web
For more ideas, visit us at www.benziger.glencoe.com

Interactive Lesson Planner
Your ILP provides more help in preparing to teach this chapter.

Celebrate
Turn to page 22 of this book. Check for seasonal celebrations.

Lesson Plan · Day 1
Give each child a nametag to wear. Ask them to print their own name and the word "doctor" on it. Tell the children that today you will be talking about healing.

1 Healing Signs
Write the word *heal* on the board. Talk about the meaning of the word (to make better). Ask the children to notice all the times the word is used in today's lesson. Have a volunteer read aloud the chapter title and the chapter's Scripture verse.

2 A Bad Time
Ask the children to look at the picture on student page 222, and talk about what is happening. Then, read the text aloud to the children. Invite individuals to suggest what each girl needs to feel better.

Heal me, Lord, so I may be healed; save me so that I may be saved.
Jeremiah 17:14

Do You Know?

◆ How does the Church bring healing and peace to others?

Healing Signs

Ouch!

Poor Sue. She has a sore throat and a scraped knee.

Molly feels bad, too. Someone made fun of her new haircut.

- What does Sue need to help her feel better?
- What does Molly need to help her feel better?

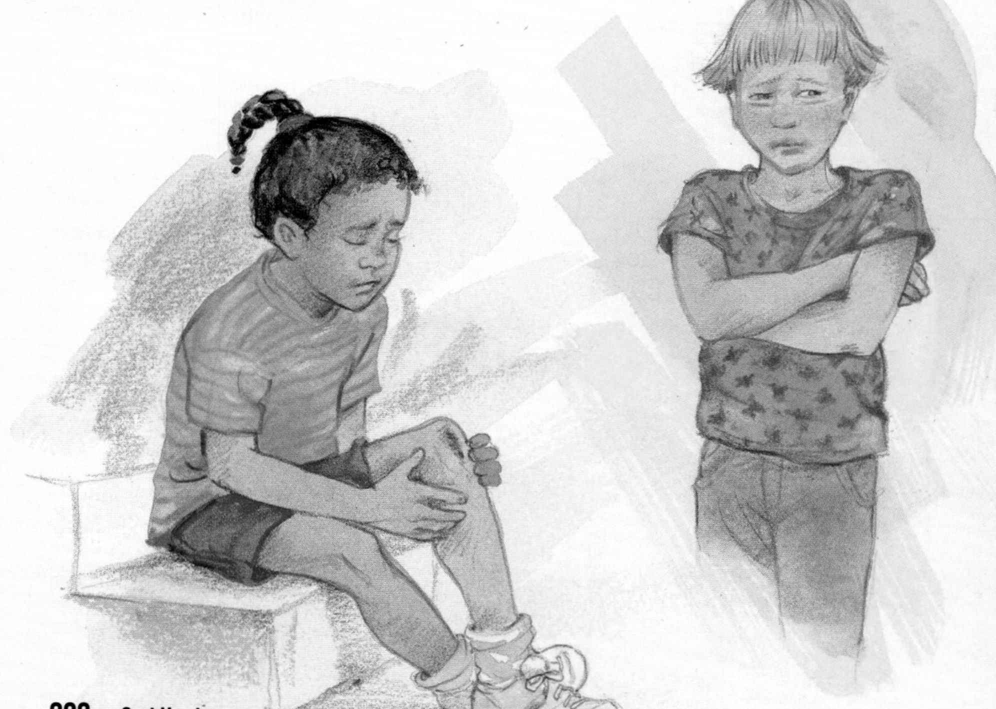

3 Activity
Read the text on student page 223. Emphasize that sometimes we need healing both inside and outside. Talk about the illustration. Talk about Sally's sad situations. Call attention to the children's nametags. Invite them to write prescriptions for Sally.

4 Do You Know?
Read the Do You Know? question on student page 222 to the children. Note their responses. At the end of the week, come back to this question to see how the children's knowledge has developed.

Healing Touch

Sometimes your body may hurt. Sometimes you feel sad or upset on the inside.

Look at Sad Sally. She needs healing on the inside and the outside.

Tell what Sad Sally needs to feel better.

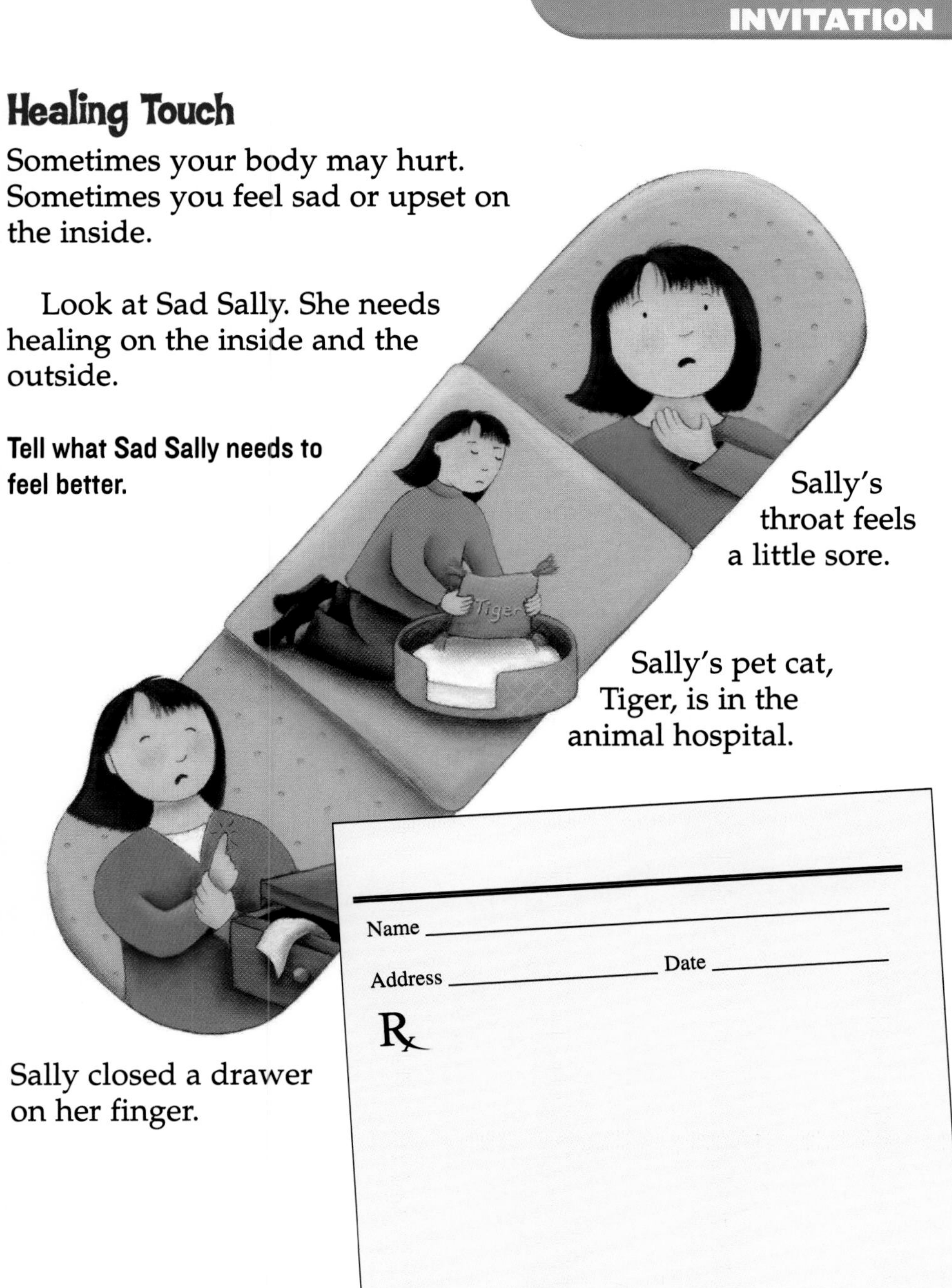

Sally's throat feels a little sore.
Tiger
Sally's pet cat, Tiger, is in the animal hospital.
Name
Address
Date
℞
Sally closed a drawer on her finger.

CURRICULUM CHALLENGE

Health Say that God wants us to take good care of our bodies. Talk about good ways to respect the body and stay healthy.

- Exercise (play) every day.
- Eat foods that help you grow strong.
- Get plenty of sleep.
- Wash your hands often.
- Brush your teeth twice a day.
- Cover your mouth when you sneeze or cough.
- Tell when you are worried, scared, or bothered.
- Tell a parent or adult when you do not feel well.

Lesson Plan · Day 2

Use these situations to review yesterday's lesson. Billy broke his arm. How does he feel? What can help him feel better? Manny yelled at his mom. How does he feel? What can help him feel better?

1 Heal the Sick

Ask the children to read the title. Tell the children that these are the words of Jesus. Call attention to the illustration, and say that it shows a time when Jesus healed a little girl. Share the information in the introduction. Say that Christians follow Jesus. Christians try to heal the sick by helping them feel better.

2 Bible Story

Gather the children, and ask them to listen to the ways Jesus healed. Set the story's mood. See Bible Basics. Then, share the story. At the end of the reading, elicit the reaction of the children to the story, by asking them about the feelings and actions of Jairus, Jesus, and Jairus' daughter.

BIBLE BASICS

The children will better understand the Bible story if you begin this way: "Picture Jesus in a boat. He is talking to the people on the shore of a lake. Suddenly a man named Jairus pushes his way through the crowd. He is a dad. He looks very worried."

Anointing of the Sick gives peace, strength and courage to people who are very sick.

Heal the Sick

Jesus knew that sickness and sadness make life hard. Before Jesus' friends went out to spread the Good News, he said to his followers, "Heal the sick. As you enter a house, wish it peace."

Matthew 10:8,12

To heal is to make better. People need healing on the inside and on the outside.

One day a man named Jairus came to Jesus. He believed in all that Jesus was teaching.

"Jesus, help me. My daughter is dying. Please lay your hands on her so that she may get well and live."

Jesus and his followers went with the man to his house.

3 This We Believe!
Ask a volunteer to read aloud This We Believe! on student page 224.

4 Activity
Direct attention to the illustrations of people who need to hear words that heal. Explain the directions to the children. The children may check their answers with a partner.

Jesus went into the house. Everyone was sad. Jesus walked over to the little girl. He took her by the hand and said to her, "Little girl, I say to you arise!" The girl arose immediately and walked around.

Based on *Mark 5:22–24* and *39–43*

ACTIVITY HEALING WORDS

Words can help you feel better too. Draw a line to match the pictures with the words.

"Would you like to play, too?"

"Would you like to hear a funny story?"

"I brought you these flowers."

TEACHING TIP

Bring the activity on student page 225 into the children's experiences. Give simple examples of times you have observed a need for healing. Keep the examples general, so that no one feels singled out. Do not use names. (Someone is sad because her snack is gone.) After each example, ask, "Is there a Christian in the house?" Let volunteers suggest words that heal.

RESOURCE MASTERS

The resource master on page 344 is a coloring activity about hurtful and healing situations. The children will need crayons or markers.

Lesson Plan · Day 3

Ask the children what are some things Jesus wants Christians to do. Accept all reasonable answers. Remind the children that Christians are called to heal.

1 Getting Better

Read the text aloud to the children. Emphasize that Reconciliation is a sacrament of healing and forgiveness.

Direct the children's attention to the photos of an anointing. Point out the actions of the priest as he celebrates the sacrament.

VIRTUE FAITH GRACE **VOCABULARY**

Anoint means to bless with holy oil to show that God is present.

Anointing of the Sick is the sacrament that answers Jesus' call to heal the sick. The sick and dying are blessed with God's grace, and have their sins forgiven.

WORD OF GOD

In my name, they will lay their hands on the sick and they will recover.

Mark 16:18

Getting Better

In Reconciliation, you celebrate God's forgiveness. You are given a chance to do better. The Church has other ways to help people who need to feel better.

The Church cares and prays for those who are sick and dying. The Church helps these people stay close to God.

The Church celebrates a sacrament with those who are very sick. This sacrament is the **Anointing of the Sick**. The priest blesses, or **anoints**, the person with holy oil. He makes crosses of oil on the person's forehead and hands.

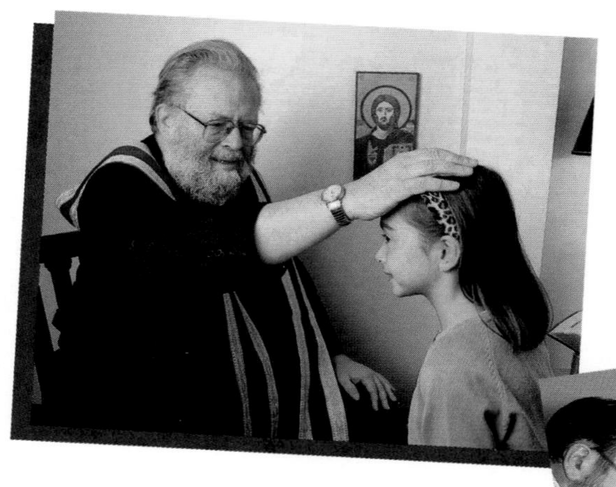

❷ Activity
Tell the children that every sacrament uses words and signs to show that God is present. Recall with them the words and signs of baptism *(water, oil, "I baptize you")*. Direct the children's attention to the word search. Allow time to complete the activity. Some children may need your help in doing the activity.

❸ Word of God
Demonstrate the gesture of laying on of hands. Explain that the priest lays hands on the sick when he celebrates the sacrament of Anointing of the Sick. Read the Word of God, and have the children repeat it after you.

The Holy Spirit gives the person strength, courage, and peace. That is what sick people need.

ACTIVITY

Find the following healing words: oil, anoint, penance, and forgive.

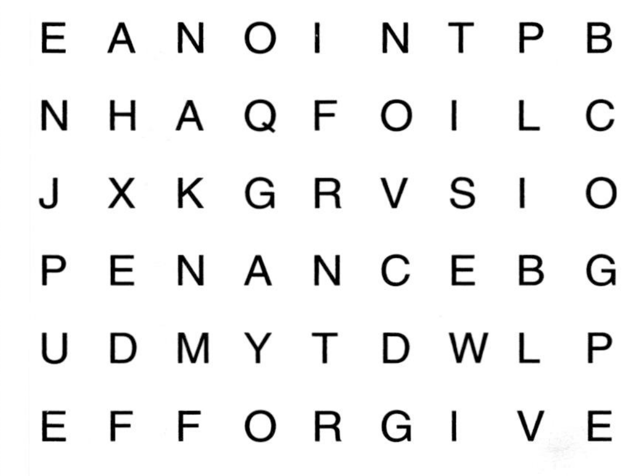

E	A	N	O	I	N	T	P	B
N	H	A	Q	F	O	I	L	C
J	X	K	G	R	V	S	I	O
P	E	N	A	N	C	E	B	G
U	D	M	Y	T	D	W	L	P
E	F	F	O	R	G	I	V	E

CURRICULUM CHALLENGE

Language Arts Use the lesson on healing to teach, or review, sequential paragraphs. Give each child a sheet of writing paper that has the skeleton of a sequential paragraph in place: A topic sentence that tells the name of a person and the healing needed. Following the topic sentence are the words *First, Next,* and *Finally,* with a writing line separating each word. The children may work alone, or with a partner, to write the sentences on the writing lines.

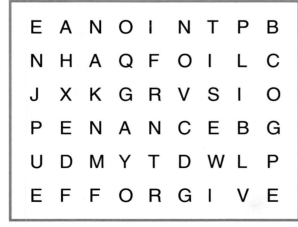

Lesson Plan · Day 4

Share a special way someone helps you feel better when you are ill. Or, share a memory from childhood of something done for you to make you feel better.

❶ Help Others

Have the children repeat after you: "Is there a Christian in the house?" Tell the children that today is a good day to answer Jesus' call to heal the sick. Tell about the cardmaking activity. Have the children read through the suggestions, and then brainstorm among themselves for other ideas. Allow time to complete the activity.

IDEAS THAT WORK

Ahead of time, consider what supplies to have on hand for the cardmaking activity. Show the supplies, and generate ideas as to how they may be used. Children will probably add to the suggestions. You may want to separate the supplies into categories, with each type of supply in its own box. Ask the children to set some guidelines for using the supplies.

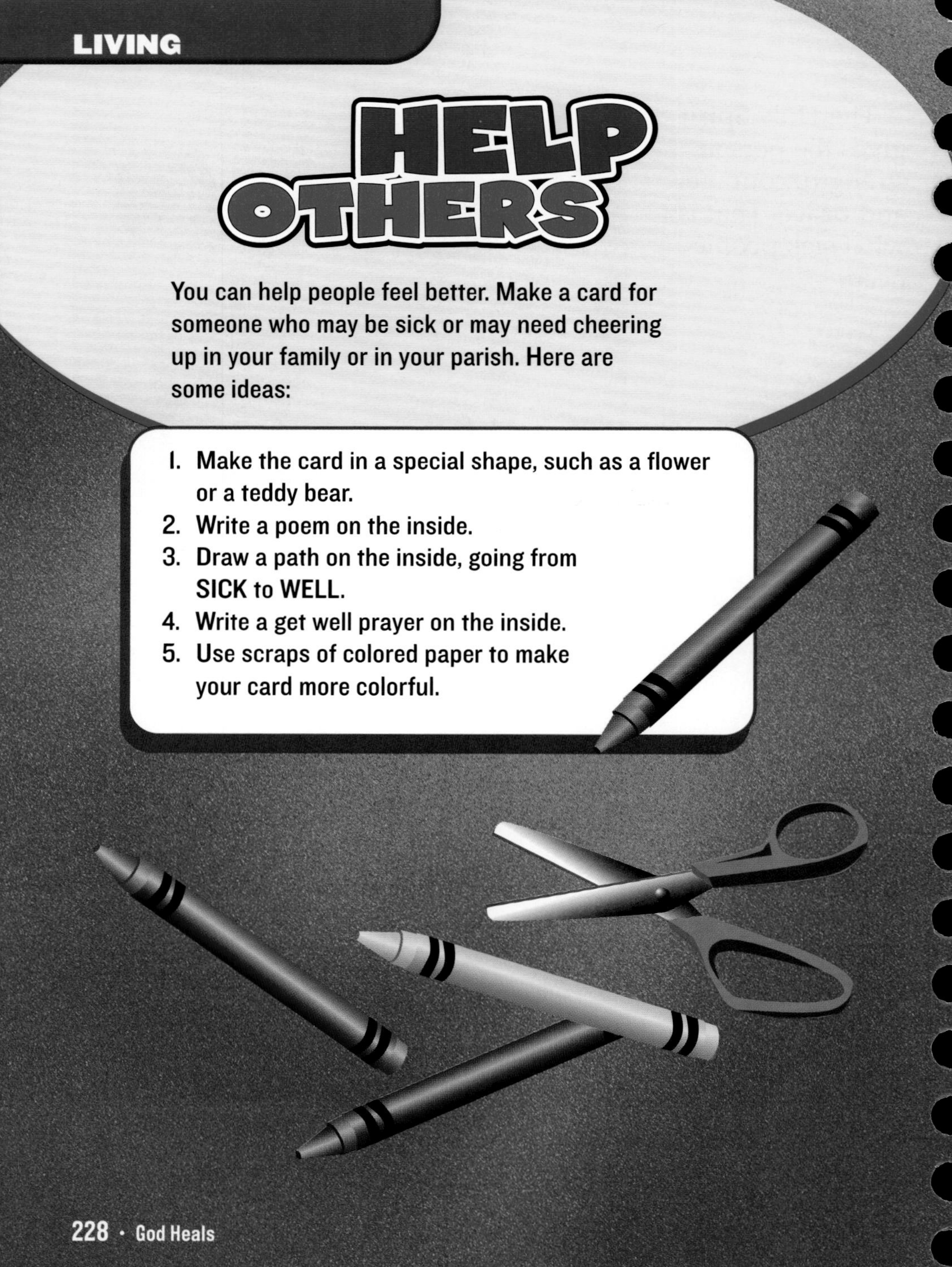
LIVING
HELP OTHERS
You can help people feel better. Make a card for someone who may be sick or may need cheering up in your family or in your parish. Here are some ideas:
1. Make the card in a special shape, such as a flower or a teddy bear.
2. Write a poem on the inside.
3. Draw a path on the inside, going from SICK to WELL.
4. Write a get well prayer on the inside.
5. Use scraps of colored paper to make your card more colorful.
228 · God Heals

❷ Make it Better
Mention that it is good to notice the people we are with every day, to see if they need to feel better. See if any of the children recently made such observations. Direct the children's attention to the people in need on student page 229. Explain the directions. Remind the children to spend a little time thinking, before writing.

❸ Share
Allow time for sharing of the card-making and idea-writing projects. Each child may choose to share either the card or one written action. Give a class cheer after all have shared.

MAKE IT BETTER

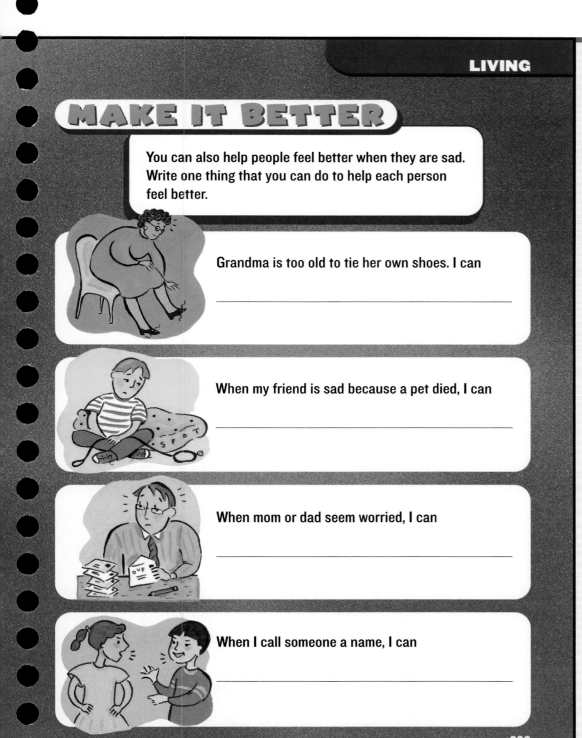

You can also help people feel better when they are sad. Write one thing that you can do to help each person feel better.

Grandma is too old to tie her own shoes. I can

____

When my friend is sad because a pet died, I can

____

When mom or dad seem worried, I can

____

When I call someone a name, I can

____

VIRTUE FAITH GRACE VOCABULARY

At this time of the school year, you may wish to review some of the religious vocabulary that has been introduced. Choose the words, and write each on a flash card. Play a guessing game. Hold a vocabulary word over a child's head. The other children give clues to its meaning.

Prayer

This week's prayer service gives children the opportunity to promise to do healing things.

1 Prepare for Prayer

Gather in the prayer area. Have the class join hands in a circle. Lead the children in prayer.

2 Celebrate Healing

Lead the children through the words of the prayer service. Ask what the promises mean to them.

LEARNING TO PRAY

You may wish to end the prayer experience by singing a familiar hymn about healing or Reconciliation.

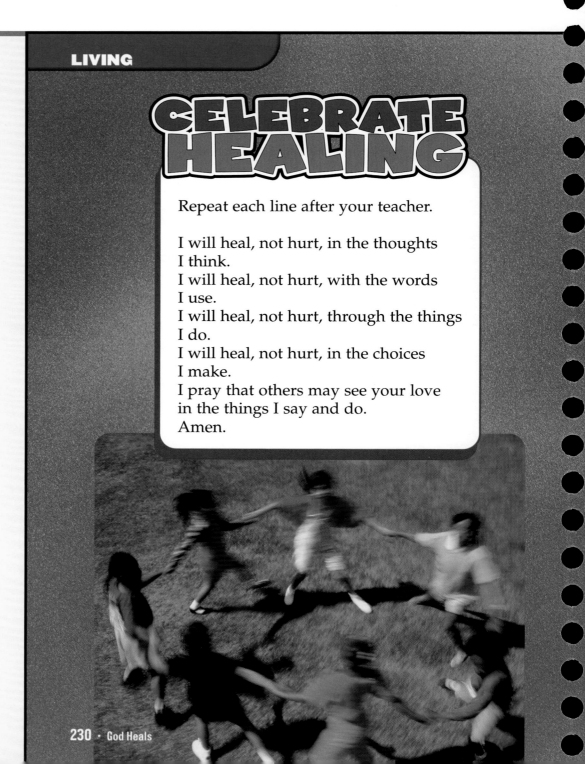

CELEBRATE HEALING

Repeat each line after your teacher.

I will heal, not hurt, in the thoughts
I think.
I will heal, not hurt, with the words
I use.
I will heal, not hurt, through the things
I do.
I will heal, not hurt, in the choices
I make.
I pray that others may see your love
in the things I say and do.
Amen.

1 Know
Call attention to the graphic organizer. Explain how the section in the middle is common to both areas. Pose the Do You Know? question from student page 125, and see how the children's knowledge has developed.

2 Love and Serve
You may wish to take ten minutes for the children to make cards or notes today. Explain the Love and Serve activities. A child can volunteer to be the one who surprises the returning child. Have a few volunteers organize the prayer basket. You may wish to initiate the prayer writing.

3 God's Friends
Point out Lima, Peru on a world map. Focus the children on Saint Martin. Then, share the information on Saint Martin. Ask: How did Saint Martin heal?

CHAPTER 16 REVIEW and EXPLORE

Know

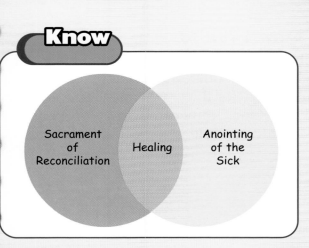

Sacrament of Reconciliation	Healing	Anointing of the Sick

Love

When someone from your class has returned from being sick, send a "Welcome Back" note. Say that you are glad that he or she is feeling better.

Serve

Find a special basket or container for your prayer area. Have a pile of paper cards and a pencil nearby. Whenever you know of someone who needs prayers, write the person's name on a card. A name can be picked whenever you meet there.

GOD'S FRIENDS

Saint Martin de Porres

The sick of Lima, Peru, would wait outside Martin's gates. They knew this kind man would help them get better. There were so many sick children that Martin made a hospital just for them.

A Little Catechism

Invite the children to open their religion books to *A Little Catechism.* Choose one or more of the selections below for memory work or reinforcement. You will find your copy of the catechism on pages 23–43 of this Teacher's Edition.

1. On page 14, have the children memorize the description of Anointing of the Sick.

Know | Love | Serve

Note The activities on this page provide ways for the children to share their learning with their families. The activities are related to the week's theme.

1 Introduce
Explain the two activities. Ask if anyone has anything to report about last week's family activities.

2 Pray Together
Pray the prayer in the prayer burst aloud. Let the girls say it first, then the boys.

Online for Families
Remind the children to check the Benziger Web site this week with their families.
www.benziger.glencoe.com

Dear Family,

I have just finished chapter 16. I have learned that our Church family cares and prays for those who are sick and dying. Our family can help by praying for all the people who need to feel better.

On your own

Think about ways you can help someone feel better. Can you make a phone call? Can you ask, "What's the matter?" Can you give a hug and a smile? Write your idea here:

____

____

____

____

During the week, try to make your idea happen.

With your family

Ask someone in your family to read you a Bible story about Jesus healing someone. Share the story at mealtime. Talk about how you and your family can help someone that is not feeling well.

Loving God, keep me under your care. Strengthen me with your love.

GO ONLINE!
http://www.benziger.glencoe.com

1 Introduce
Introduce the lesson by asking the children whom they would like to remember during prayer times. Allow the children to give responses. Tell the children that everyone has someone that they want to remember in prayer. Say that there is power in numbers, and that the whole class can pray in one voice.

2 The Project
Ask the children to think about a person who needs prayers. Explain the directions. Allow them time to write and decorate their cards. As the children place the cards on the prayer table, ask them to say, "I would like our class to pray for ____________." Do this until all the children have had a turn.

Pick two or three names from the stack at prayer time. Continue this procedure every time the class gathers to pray.

THE CHURCH TODAY

During Mass, the Church remembers all those who need prayers. The people pray for those who are sick. They pray for those who have died.

You can pray for people who may need God's care during the week.

- Think of someone who needs prayers.
- Draw a picture of them on one side of an index card. On the other side, write their name and why you want them remembered.
- Place these prayer cards on your prayer table. Remember one of these people each time your class prays together.

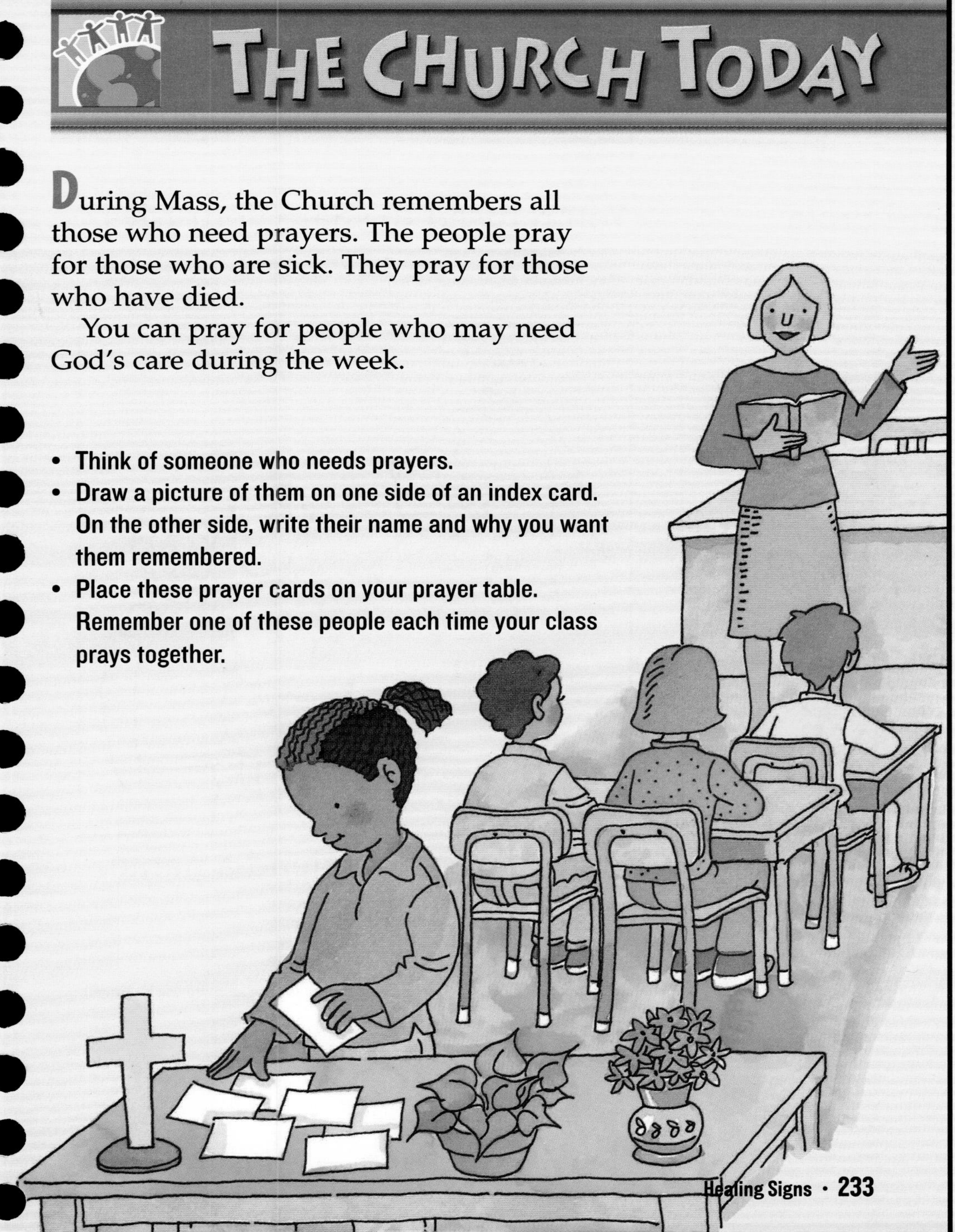

ANSWER KEY

This is the answer key for the chapter test on page 345.

A. 1. a 2. b 3. b 4. a

Name ___________________________________

Healing Needed

Look at each story below. Color the picture that shows how you can heal.

You were angry and broke your mom's vase.

You refused to share your toys.

You took a candy bar from the store without paying for it.

You called your friend a name.

Name ______________________________

Chapter 16 Test

A. Read the sentences and put a circle around the words that best finish each sentence.

1. In Reconciliation and Anointing of the Sick, the Church answers Jesus' call to

a. "Heal the sick." **b.** "Baptize all nations."

2. The sacrament that gives grace to the very sick and to the dying is

a. Reconciliation. **b.** Anointing of the Sick.

3. A priest anoints with

a. holy water. **b.** holy oil.

4. In Anointing of the Sick, a person receives

a. strength, peace, and courage. **b.** baptism with holy water.

UNIT 4 REVIEW

Strategies for Review

The purpose of the Unit Review is to reinforce concepts presented in this unit. You may wish to assign the Remember and Answer sections for homework. Review these sections with the students so that you can answer any questions they may have. Students may work independently, in small groups, or as a class. Use the method that works best with your group.

1 Remember

Write the sentences on the chalkboard. Read each statement aloud, and have the class repeat it. Erase a key word from each statement. Have volunteers fill in the missing words. Erase a different word from each sentence. Call on other children to fill in the missing words.

2 Answer

Read each statement, and give the students time to circle T or N. Then ask volunteers to explain their answers.

Unit 4 REVIEW

Remember!

1. Sin turns your heart away from God's love.
2. You can come back to God when you say, "I'm sorry."
3. Examining your conscience can help you make good choices.
4. In the sacrament of Reconciliation you celebrate God's forgiveness.
5. The Anointing of the Sick gives sick people courage and peace.

Answer!

If the words are true, circle the T.
If the words are not true, circle the N.

1. Jesus wants you to be a better person. T N
2. God forgives you when you are sorry. T N
3. Jesus did not heal sick people. T N
4. The Church Family is happy when someone says, "I'm sorry." T N
5. It feels good to be forgiven. T N

Do!

Praise God for his forgiveness.
Make up a prayer of praise to God.
End your prayer with the word "Alleluia!"
Say your prayer tonight.

3 Do

Help the students recall what it means to praise God. Remind them that *Alleluia* is a joyful word used to praise God. Encourage them to take time each night to examine their consciences, to tell God they are sorry for any wrongs they have done, and to pray their prayers of praise.

4 Share

You may wish to tell the students a short story from your own experience. Give them time to write or draw their own stories. Gather the students in a circle. Invite the children to share their stories of friendship and forgiveness.

Share!

Tell about a time you had trouble getting along with a friend.
How did you show you were sorry?
Write or draw your answer in the friendship circle below.

ANSWER KEY

Answer

1. T
2. T
3. N
4. T
5. T

Unit 5

Whenever you eat this bread and drink this cup, I will be with you.

1 Corinthians 11:26

Chapter

The Holy Eucharist

The Story Keepers

The Last Supper
The Eucharistic Prayer includes an abbreviated recital of the story of Jesus' Last Supper with his disciples before his crucifixion. In the cave where the Christians are hiding, Ben tells the story. View the clip, tell the story, and lead activities suggested in the guide.

Chile From Maryknoll

CHAPTER 17 Gathering

TEACHER RESOURCE CENTER

Faith Formation

CHECK THE CATECHISM

The long section on liturgy in the *Catechism of the Catholic Church* (Section 1, Part Two) provides great insight into many aspects of liturgical celebration. See especially paragraphs 1077–1162.

We Gather in Faith

Cardinal Roger Mahony of Los Angeles recently issued a pastoral letter on the Mass, "Gather Faithfully Together." God's people are indeed called to gather in faith, and to celebrate Sunday liturgy with full, active, and conscious participation. Once a week, the parish community comes together as a family, to express their thanks and praise to God, in the words, music, actions, and gestures that express their faith. While each parish has its own personality, and style of worship, the main focus of the Mass is always to "give God thanks and praise."

What makes Sunday Mass important to you?

The Role of the Parish Community

Everyone is invited to participate fully in the Mass. The priest-presider calls the assembly to worship, and leads the prayer. Many others represent the parish community as greeters, sacristans, readers, altar servers, or Eucharistic ministers. The gifts of each member of the assembly are most evident at Mass when a spirit of generosity, welcoming, and hospitality prevails. When the parish family is "gathered faithfully," no one remains a stranger. This week at Mass, introduce yourself to someone you do not know, and note your response and theirs.

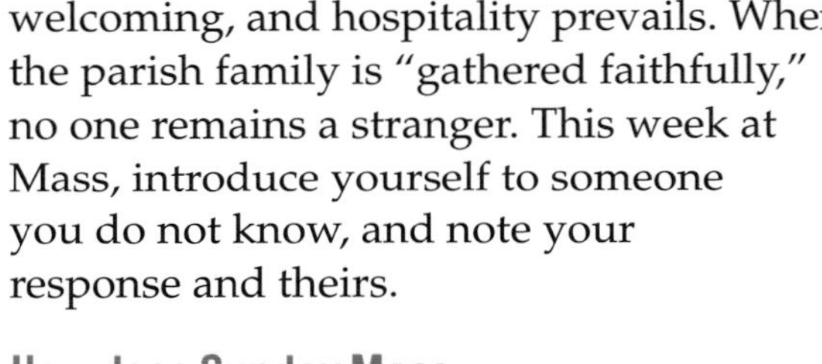

How does Sunday Mass express your faith and the faith of your parish?

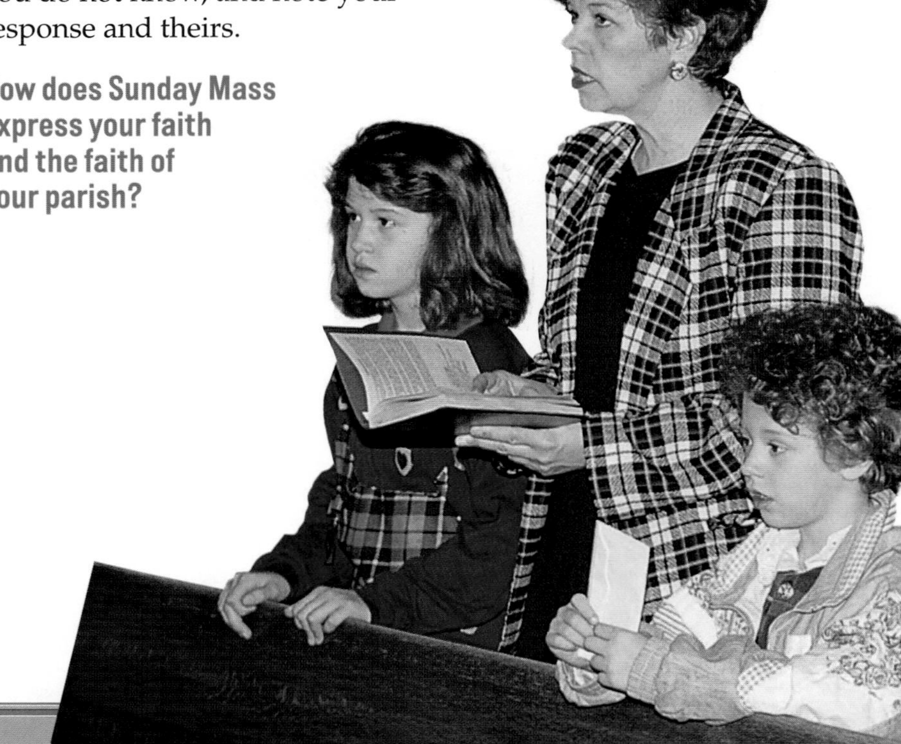

Background

Gathering

Unit 5 has the theme "We Celebrate," and covers the parts of the Mass in sequential order. Chapter 17 focuses on the Gathering.

The chapter begins with a joyful focus on God's blessings. Help the students explore the blessings in their lives. If possible, take them outside to see, hear, smell, and touch God's gifts of creation.

The Mass is introduced as a gathering of praise, to celebrate all God's blessings. The students have some understanding of and experience with gathering. No matter where their families gather, there are usually common elements—a reason for coming together, a sense of oneness, and, often, something to eat. The session on the Gathering of the Mass ties into the students' experiences of family gatherings.

Faith Summary

- God is the source of blessings.
- Jesus gathers us at Mass.
- At Mass, we celebrate God's blessings.

Growth and Development

It is helpful to remember two characteristics of second graders as you teach this lesson:

- ***Second graders want to feel important.*** The Mass is a place where students are important. They are needed, they are wanted, they are called.
- ***Second graders want to be involved in what is going on around them.*** Turn the room into a worship space. Let the students act out each part of the Gathering, with songs, responses, and actions. Gradually, the students will learn to take part in the celebration of Mass fully, actively, and consciously.

A Teacher's Prayer

Creator God, you created all people to be one human family. Bless me as I gather with the students, and with our school family. Let your presence be felt. Bless the students to know how good it is to learn and share together. Amen.

Vocabulary Preview

blessing
Mass
gathering

Scripture

Matthew 18:20: Where two or three are gathered . . .
John 2:1–11: the wedding at Cana
Joel 2:21–24, 26–27: the earth rejoices
Psalm 115:14: Psalm of blessing

Related Resources

Videos

"The Angel's Mass Lesson." (Twenty-Third Publications, 1-800-321-0411 or www.twentythirdpublications.com). This video gives students a deeper understanding and appreciation of the Eucharistic mystery, and its importance in their lives. (Children, 11 minutes)

"The Roman Catholic Mass Today: An Introduction and Overview." (Liturgy Training Publications, 1-800-933-1800 or www.ltp.org). Available in English and Spanish, this video spotlights four diverse parishes, to present a look at contemporary Sunday Eucharist. (Adult, 30 minutes)

TEACHER ORGANIZER

Planning Guide

The basic content for each chapter is divided into four class sessions. There are a number of options for the fifth session. Extension, review, and testing options are described under Day 5 Alternatives. The Quick Check box will help you evaluate the week's lessons.

Chapter Goals

In this chapter, the students will learn about
- ❏ God's blessings
- ❏ The Gathering at Mass
- ❏ Prayers and actions of the Gathering

	DAY 1 · INVITATION	DAY 2 · DISCOVERY	DAY 3 · DISCOVERY
OBJECTIVES	**The students will be able to** • Associate God as the giver of blessings • Discover ways one is blessed • Name personal blessings	**The students will be able to** • Retell a Bible story about the wedding in Cana • Analyze a Bible story to learn about Jesus • Tell about a personal, special gathering	**The students will be able to** • Associate the Mass with reasons for celebrating God's blessings • Say responses from the Gathering • Act out the parts of the Gathering
PREPARATION	• Prepare to sing the simple song, "The More We Get Together" • Reflect on times you use the words bless or blessing	• Prepare to read the Bible story • If needed, make copies of the resource master on page 366	• Think through how you will present the pages • rearrange the room • Choose a gathering hymn to sing, or use the suggested verse
MATERIALS	• Pencils	• Copies of the resource master • Pencils, drawing supplies	• Pencils, drawing supplies • Bowl with holy water • Bible or a Book of Gospels • Two candles
OPTIONAL ACTIVITIES	• **Ideas That Work** Teach a gathering song • **Vocabulary** Continue teaching the vocabulary words • **Options** Make blessing books, using heavy paper and drawing supplies, pictures cut from magazines, and glue	• **Bible Basics** Have volunteers share about weddings, and set the scene for the story • **Teaching Tip** Have the children reenact the story • **Resource Masters** Color and tell stories about gathering	• **Ideas That Work** Turn the classroom into a worship space • **Vocabulary** Continue teaching the vocubulary words

Learning Objectives

By the end of this chapter, the students should be able to

- ❏ Name blessings from God
- ❏ Recognize parts of the Gathering at Mass
- ❏ Say responses from the Gathering

DAY 4 · LIVING

The students will be able to

- Determine ways to be part of the celebration of Mass
- Understand the Mass as a gathering of one Catholic Church family
- Praise God for blessings

- Decide how you will form groups

- Pencils

- **Ideas That Work** Sing "He's Got the Whole World in His Hands," and create new verses
- **Options** Have some students make dioramas, using shoe boxes, glue, and a variety of items such as spools and pipe cleaners

DAY 5 · ALTERNATIVES

There are a number of alternatives to help you plan Day 5.

Prayer Experience
Use the Rejoice prayer service on Day 4 or Day 5. If books of blessings were made, they may be used with the prayer.

Review and Explore
Play some familiar hymns or children's hymns while the students work. The students need pencils, black crayons, scissors, colored paper, and glue.

Home and Family
Send the page home with the students, or assign one or more of the activities.

The Church Today
The students will make puzzles of sacramentals used at Mass. They need heavy paper, drawing supplies, and scissors. Find examples of the items in the students' text or in a religious supply catalogue.

Chapter Test
The chapter test appears as a resource master on page 367.

Quick Check

Do this evaluation as soon as you finish each chapter.

Did I follow my lesson plan?

How can I tell that I met the learning objectives for the lesson?

What activities did the children enjoy most?

How could I improve this lesson?

Benziger on the Web
For more ideas, visit us at **www.benziger.glencoe.com**

Interactive Lesson Planner
Your ILP provides more help in preparing to teach this chapter.

Celebrate
Turn to page 22 of this book. Check for seasonal celebrations.

Lesson Plan · Day 1

Begin today's session by singing "The More we Get Together." (See Ideas That Work.) Tell the children that this week they will be learning about what happens when Catholics get together at Mass.

1 Do You Know?

Point out the chapter title. Ask the children the Do You Know? question about why Catholics come together on Sunday. List their answers on the chalkboard. At the end of the week, come back to this question to see how the children's knowledge has developed.

2 I Am Blessed

Read the text aloud to the children. Ask then to share times when they have used or heard others use the words *bless* or *blessing*. *(when someone sneezes; when a baby is born)* Tell them times when you use those words. Have the children finish the sentence on student page 238.

IDEAS THAT WORK

Here is a verse to sing to the melody of "Did You Ever See a Lassie?" Have everyone stand, and move about the room as they sing.

The more we get together,
Together,
Together.

The more we get together,
The happier we'll be.
We go this way (smile and shake hands),
And that way (now do so to someone new),
And this way (now do so to someone new),
And that way (now do so to someone new).

The more we get together,
The happier we'll be.

TEACHING TIP

Unit 5 covers the Mass in age-appropriate details for second graders. Keep in mind that some of the children do not have weekly Mass experiences. Adjust the lessons as needed.

Where two or three are gathered in my name, I am with them.

Matthew 18:20

Do You Know?

◆ Why do Catholics get together on Sunday?

Gathering

I Am Blessed

A **blessing** is a gift from God. Your life is filled with blessings! What a reason to be glad!

Finish the sentence.

God blesses me with ________________.

3 Activity
Help the children to recall some of the blessings in their lives. Then, ask them to fill in the sentences on student page 239. Remind them to think for a few minutes before they begin to write.

4 Share
After the children have completed the page, let them read the sentences aloud, saying the words they inserted. Respond to each sentence with a joyful exclamation, such as "Praise God!," "Glory to God!," or "Glory Alleluia!"

5 Scripture
Read the chapter's Scripture verse with the children, to conclude today's lesson.

Blessings Everywhere!

Look around you! There are many reasons to thank and praise God.

Finish the sentences below.

1. I am blessed with life. I can think, play, feel, and ______________________.

2. I am blessed with creation. There are playful puppies, tall trees, and ______________________.

3. I am blessed with people who keep me close to God. Their names are ______________________.

4. I am blessed with Jesus who ______________________.

5. I am blessed with the Holy Spirit who fills me with goodness and ______________________.

VOCABULARY

Blessing A gift of life and happiness from God.

OPTIONS

The whole of God's work is a blessing. Have the children make blessing books, which can be used with the prayer experience on student page 246. Using drawing supplies or pictures cut from magazines, the children can make pages showing blessings they receive from God. To connect to the Mass, the children can write on the first or last page: *Blessed be God.*

Lesson Plan · Day 2

Begin by helping the children recall what a blessing is. Have volunteers share some blessings they are glad about.

1 A Special Gathering

Say that people come together to celebrate God's blessings. Ask the children to share some happy times when people gather to celebrate. Direct the children's attention to the illustration on student page 240. Ask the children what is happening in the picture.

Read the story of the wedding feast. Pause at the two questions in paragraph three. Ask the children what they think will happen. Then, read the next paragraph, and ask Jesus' question. Do not be surprised if children suggest that Jesus go to the store to buy wine. Explain that in those days people did not buy wine; they made it. Finish reading the story.

BIBLE BASICS

Let a few volunteers briefly share their experiences at weddings. Then, bring the children's experiences into the Bible story, by saying, "Picture the party that follows a wedding. There are lots of happy people. They are talking at tables. They are dancing to music. They are eating good food, and drinking good wine. Children are giggling, while they run and slide on the slippery floor."

TEACHING TIP

Have the children personalize the Bible story. Let them form groups of threes, and reenact the story. Let the children use their own words, so that you can see whether they have a basic understanding of the story.

A Special Gathering

One day, Jesus was invited to a wedding. The wedding was in the town of Cana The bride's friends were coming. The groom's friends were coming, too.

Jesus was at the wedding with his mother and some good friends. There was food to eat and wine to drink. Everyone was having a very good time.

Then something happened. There was no more wine. What would the family do? What would the people drink?

Mary, the mother of Jesus, talked to her son. "They have no more wine," she said. Jesus smiled and said, "What do you want me to do?"

Jesus talked to the helpers. He asked them to pour water into six big jugs. They did. "Take it to the man in charge," said Jesus.

② Discuss
Lead the children in a discussion about what Jesus did. Ask them how the bride and groom felt about running out of wine. What did Jesus do? Why do they think Jesus made more wine? *(He cared about the bride and groom.)*

③ Activity
Prepare the children to do the activity. Walk around, and give positive feedback about the wonderful occasions the children have celebrated. After the activity is completed, give the children time to share these experiences with someone who sits nearby.

The man took a drink. He was so surprised. "This wine is better than the other wine we had," he said.

Jesus' friends saw this and they began to believe in him. "What a wonderful gathering this was!"

Based on *John 2:1–11*

YOUR TURN

In the space, draw a picture or write a short story about a special gathering you have had.

RESOURCE MASTERS

The resource master on page 366 is a combination coloring/storytelling activity about the concept of gathering. The children need crayons. Call attention to the details that help define a gathering—people talking, sharing, and eating. Allow the children time to tell their story to a friend.

Lesson Plan · Day 3

Remind the children that people gather to celebrate. Tell them that today they are going to learn about what Catholics do at the beginning of Mass.

1 Jesus Gathers Us

Recall *blessings* and say that Catholics are so grateful for God's blessings that they gather *every Sunday* to praise and thank God. Read the first paragraph aloud to the children.

Share the information in the second paragraph. Invite the children to circle, or underline, the last line. Say that men, women, and children all play a part in celebrating the Mass. At the bottom of student page 242, have the children draw a picture of themselves at Mass.

IDEAS THAT WORK

Turn the classroom into a worship space, to help the children understand their role in the Gathering. The classroom door becomes the door to the church. Near it, place a bowl of holy water. Choose children to play the roles of priest, servers, and ministers. Give the servers a candle, and the priest the Bible. Designate an aisle for the entrance procession. Put the prayer table in a central area, and use it as the altar. Determine an area of pews.

VOCABULARY

Mass The celebration of the Eucharist.

Gathering Jesus brings us together to worship at the Mass.

The Church is a community of people gathered by God to follow Jesus.

Sunday Mass

Every Sunday Catholics come together to celebrate God's blessings. Catholics show that they are a community of men, women, and children who believe in God. That celebration is called the **Mass.** Everyone at Mass has a part to play.

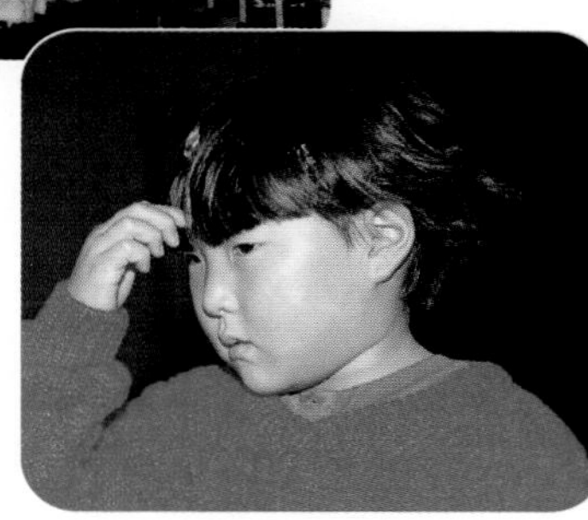

When you worship at Mass you use words and actions. When you enter church, you show that you are a follower of Jesus. You use holy water to bless yourself with the sign of the cross.

2 The Gathering

Explain each part of the Gathering. Help the children with the sequencing activity. Have all read aloud the This We Believe! feature. Ask whether there are any questions. Read aloud the text on student page 243 slowly once. Then, tell the children that you will take the part of the priest, and they will take the part of the people.

3 Activity

Use the suggestion from Ideas That Work on page 358. Have the children enter through the church door, using holy water to make the sign of the cross. Then, they can stand at the pews for the entrance procession, singing the line: "We gather together to sing of God's blessings." Have them make the sign of the cross. Greet the children, and go through the responses.

The Mass Begins

You are ready to worship God. The music plays. You stand and sing.

You make the sign of the cross. Then, the priest opens his arms and greets everyone. He tells you that God is with you. The priest says, "The Lord be with you." You say, "And also with you."

Then, all the people pray, "Lord, have mercy."

On most Sundays, you sing a song of praise. Everyone says or sings "Glory to God in the highest!"

This is the end of the gathering time at Mass. You sit down to listen. You are ready to hear the Word of God

ACTIVITY — WHAT COMES FIRST?

Number the sentences in the order in which they happen at Mass.

_______ You bless yourself with the sign of the cross.

_______ You pray "Lord have mercy."

_______ You pray "Glory to God in the highest."

_______ The priest greets you.

TEACHING TIP

In general we learn:
10% of what we read.
20% of what we hear.
30% of what we see.
50% of what we both see and hear.

Throughout Unit 5, you are given suggestions for making the learning of the Mass as effective as possible. Knowing the children as you do, continually add your own visual and audio ideas.

IDEAS THAT WORK

Children sometimes do not feel connected to the unfamiliar adult language and symbolic actions of the Mass. Emphasize that everyone is important to this celebration! (The theme of inclusion, all having a part to play, has been stressed since Chapter 1.) Let the children feel the deep meaning in the words and gestures they are learning.

Lesson Plan · Day 4

Recall the Gathering of the Mass.

1 We Are One

Make a large *1* on the chalkboard. Say that a *one* can mean "we are together, we are united." Talk with the children about ways the second grade is one. Draw a large circle, and write their ideas in it. *(Learn the same things, meet in the same place, work and play together, and so on.)*

2 Activity

Say that at Mass, the people say the words, and do the actions, together. Explain that these words and actions show that they are one in their belief in God. Let the children talk about ways the people in the photos show they are one. Invite the children to fill in the blanks independently.

TEACHING TIP

The children may need a little structure to do the activity on page 245. After explaining the activity, review the guidelines for working in a group. Recall that everyone is important in a group, because all opinions are important. Choose a leader for each group, someone who can keep focused. Choose someone to jot down the ideas as words or phrases. You may also wish to have a timekeeper for each group.

IDEAS THAT WORK

To expand on the idea that people are one, sing "He's Got the Whole World in His Hands." After singing the first verse, the children can add refrains that mention people in various cities or countries. For example, they can sing, "He's got the people in Mexico in his hands."

WE ARE ONE

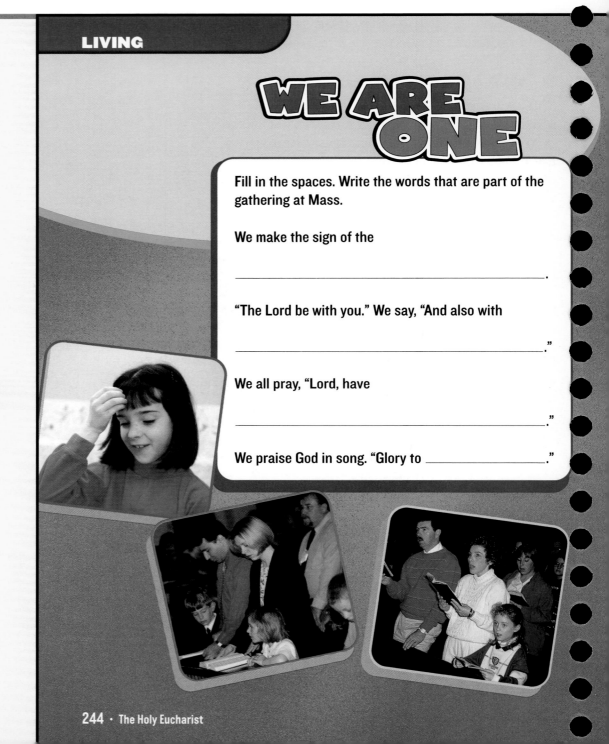

Fill in the spaces. Write the words that are part of the gathering at Mass.

We make the sign of the

______________________________.

"The Lord be with you." We say, "And also with

______________________________."

We all pray, "Lord, have

______________________________."

We praise God in song. "Glory to ______________."

❸ How to Celebrate

Remind the children that they help form the one Catholic Church family. The prayers they say, and the actions they do, show that they are one. Explain the activity. Give the children examples. Have the children work in groups to complete the activity. Walk around the room to help the children, as they do the activity. Then, have a volunteer from each group share one of their answers with the class.

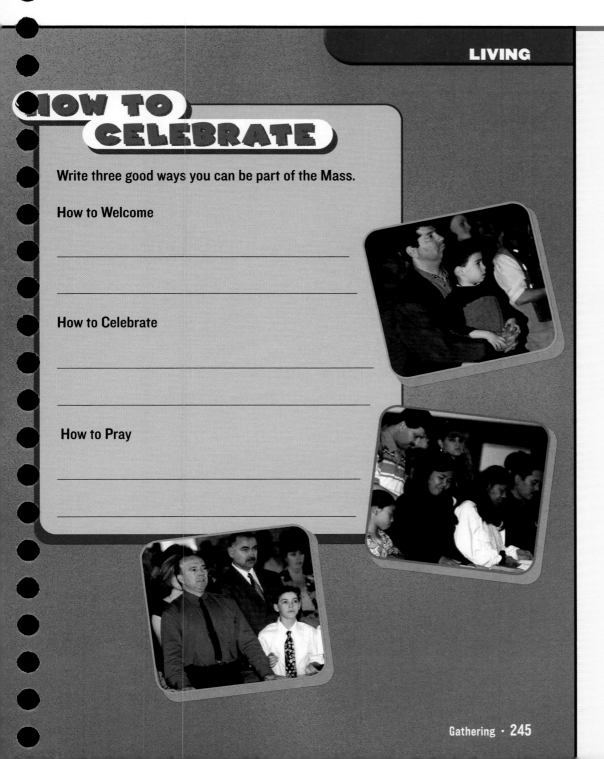

HOW TO CELEBRATE

Write three good ways you can be part of the Mass.

How to Welcome

____

____

How to Celebrate

____

____

How to Pray

____

____

OPTIONS

For the Visual-Spatial Learners These children are able to represent visual and spatial ideas. You may wish to have them create dioramas of the inside of a church, in place of one of the Living writing activities. They will need a box to represent the church, and items such as spools and pipe cleaners to make the interior. When they have finished, the children can form groups. One child from each group will use the diorama to explain what is inside a church.

Prayer
The prayer experience in an integral part of this chapter.

❶ Prepare for Prayer
Guide the children to call out blessings from God while you read the prayer. *(animals, green fields, ripe trees and vines, and so on)* Emphasize Joel's message. We are thankful to God in good times and bad times.

❷ Rejoice
If weather permits, gather outdoors to pray. Otherwise, invite the children to imagine each of these blessings as they are prayed.

LEARNING TO PRAY
If the children made books of blessings, you may wish to use them with this prayer experience. At the end of the prayer, each child may show and describe one page from his or her book. Doing so will help the children connect prayer to their lives. If the children have not made books, you can be the first to say a spontaneous prayer that praises God for his blessings, such as "Rejoice! God has blessed us with friends."

REJOICE!

Earth, rejoice!

God has done great things!
Rejoice all animals!

God has made all the fields green.
The trees and the vines are ripe.

Children, rejoice in God!
God has blessed you and the land.

You shall have much to eat.
You shall give God thanks.

See how good God is!
Give thanks and rejoice in God.

From *Joel 2:21–24, 26–27*

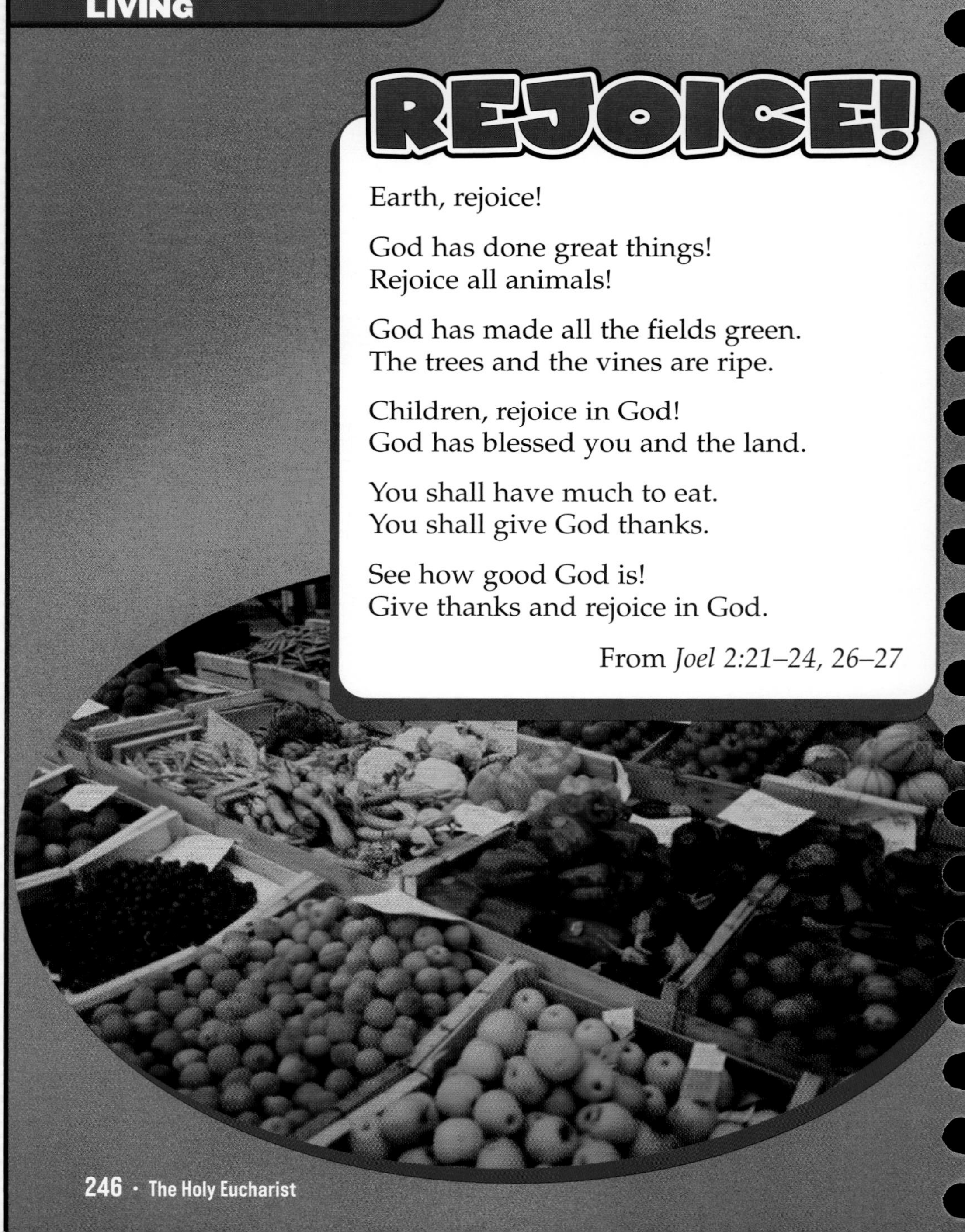

1 Know

Invite the children to tell what they think makes the beginning of Mass a gathering. Expect simple responses. *(the people meet in church, they sing together, they pray aloud together)* Then, direct attention to the graphic organizer on the page.

2 Love and Serve

Read aloud the directions for the Love activity. Explain to the children that they will be making a picture called a mosaic. Remind them that the stained glass windows in their church may resemble this design. Encourage the children to think of a beautiful blessing for which they are thankful. Conclude the session by allowing the children to bless each other, as described in the Serve activity.

3 God's Friends

Explain that we know about important things that happened long ago, because people wrote them down. We know how the first followers of Jesus celebrated the Mass, because a man named Justin wrote it down. Show the illustration, and share the information.

CHAPTER 17

REVIEW and EXPLORE

Know

Gathering

You make the sign of the cross.
You say you are sorry for your sins.
You praise God.

Love

With a pencil, draw a picture of something from nature that you are thankful for. Trace the lines with a black crayon. Fill in the spaces with bits of colored paper. Remember to thank God for that blessing at Mass.

Serve

Place your hand gently on the head of a friend. Say, "May the Lord bless you more and more" *(Psalm 115:14)*.

GOD'S FRIENDS

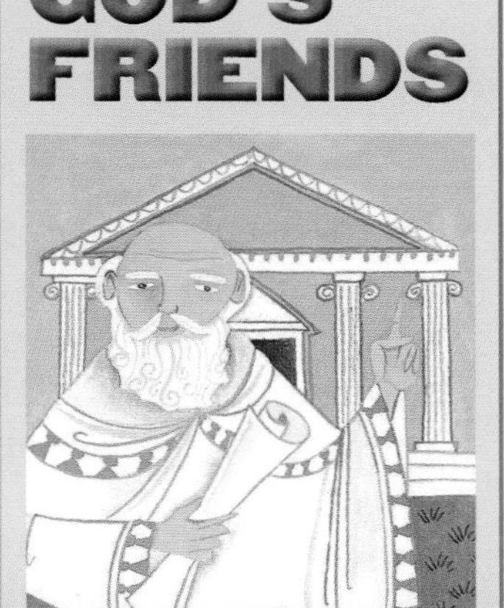

Saint Justin

Justin lived about 100 years after Jesus died. The followers of Jesus gathered every Sunday to remember him. Justin wrote down the things that they did to celebrate. Today, we celebrate the sacrament of Eucharist in the same ways.

A Little Catechism

Invite the children to open their religion books to *A Little Catechism.* Choose one or more of the selections below for memory work or reinforcement. You will find your copy of the catechism on pages 23–43 of this Teacher's Edition.

1. Locate the Ten Commandments in the catechism.
2. Refer the children to the third commandment.
3. Explain that one way Catholics obey God's command to keep holy the sabbath is by gathering to celebrate the Mass. Have the children repeat this commandment several times.

Note The activities on this page provide ways for the children to share their learning with their families. The activities are related to the week's theme.

1 Introduce
Have the children read aloud the letter to their families. Explain the first activity, and talk about simple ways people greet one another. Explain the second activity.

2 Pray Together
All together, say or sing the line from the "Gloria." Ask the children to look for all they have learned about the Gathering, when they are at Mass on Sunday.

Online for Families
Remind the children to check the Benziger Web site this week with their families.
www.benziger.glencoe.com

Dear Family,

I have just finished chapter 17. I have learned that on Sundays I gather with my Church Family to thank God for his blessings. I pray and sing songs of glory to God.

With others

In many parishes, when Mass begins the people greet one another. They do this to show that they all belong to God's family. How do you greet people? At the beginning of each school day, greet your teacher and friends. You are all part of the same school family.

With your family

On the way to Sunday Mass, talk about how important it is to welcome others. How do you feel when you are welcomed? Think about a family that you see at church. Before or after Mass, introduce yourselves to that family.

Glory to God and peace to his people on earth.

GO ONLINE!
http://www.benziger.glencoe.com

❶ Introduce

Recall that special words and actions are part of celebrating the Mass. Say that there are also special objects that are used at Mass. These special objects are holy, because they tell us that God is present. Some holy objects help us pray.

❷ The Project

Introduce the items the children are to draw. If possible, have pictures of them. Then, distribute the drawing paper and supplies. You may want to set a time limit for drawing, and a time for the exchanging of puzzles. Some children may need to keep their puzzle pieces separate. Have envelopes or paper clips available.

THE CHURCH TODAY

Some things in church help us to pray. Some things are holy and are used in every Catholic Church around the world. The holy things show that God is there in the church.

Draw pictures of holy things used at Mass. Draw an altar, a crucifix, a host, a chalice, and the Book of Gospels. Use heavy drawing paper.

Make some puzzles. Cut each picture into three pieces.

Trade your puzzles. Now put them together.

TEACHING TIP

You should be able to find examples of an altar, a crucifix, a host, a chalice, and a Book of Gospels in the children's text. Find them ahead of time, and mark them for quick and easy sharing. Or, ask someone in the rectory to lend you a catalogue from a store that sells religious supplies.

ANSWER KEY

This is the answer key for the chapter test on page 367.

A. 1. b 2. c 3. a

B. 1. X 2. X 3. X 4. X 5. X

Name ____

A Family Gathering

Color the picture. Tell someone a story about this family gathering.

Name ______________________________

Chapter 17 Test

A. Match Up. Draw a line from the priest's words to your response.

1. The Lord be with you.

2. In the name of the Father, and of the Son, and of the Holy Spirit.

3. Lord, have mercy.

a. Lord, have mercy.

b. And also with you.

c. Amen.

B. Mark an *X* next to the actions of the Gathering at Mass.

1. _____ The priest, servers, and a reader come down the aisle.

2. _____ The priest opens his arms to greet you.

3. _____ You listen to a Gospel story.

4. _____ You say "I'm sorry" aloud to God.

5. _____ You receive Jesus.

CHAPTER 18 Listen

TEACHER RESOURCE CENTER

Faith Formation

The Liturgy of the Word

The readings from Scripture proclaimed during the Liturgy of the Word are contained in the Lectionary for Mass. Over the course of three years, the lectionary cycles through a selection of passages from the Old Testament and the Gospels and epistles of the New Testament. At each Sunday Mass, the liturgical year is reflected in the proclamation of three Scripture passages and a sung psalm response. In the course of each liturgical year the Liturgy of the Word presents the entire story of salvation history, from Creation to the Israelites to Jesus to the establishment of Christianity and the Church.

How do you prepare to hear the Scripture at Mass each week?

The Presence of Jesus

Contemporary Church teaching emphasizes the four ways in which Jesus is present at Mass. Jesus is present in the Eucharist, the priest, the community of the faithful, and the Word of God proclaimed at Mass. It is therefore vital that the Word is well proclaimed and that the homily clearly presents the meaning and significance of the Scripture readings.

What helps you to experience the presence of Jesus in the Sunday readings?

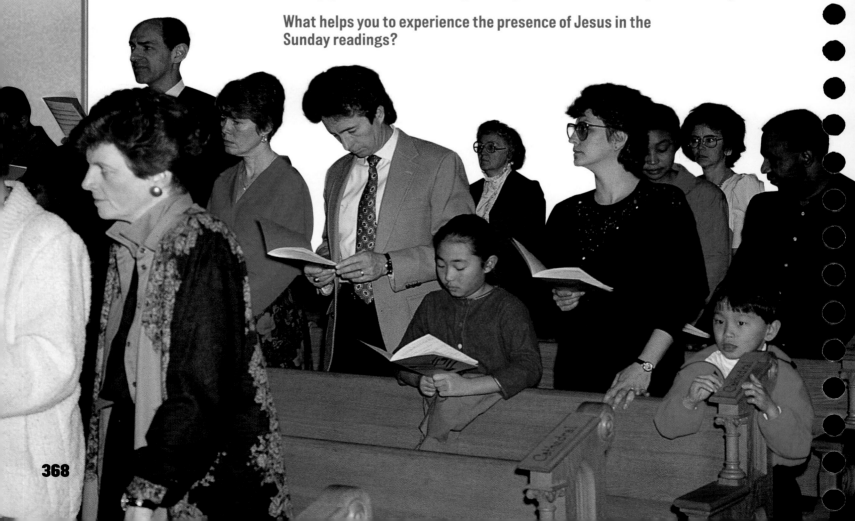

CHECK THE CATECHISM

The *Catechism of the Catholic Church* refers to the Word of God in the liturgy in paragraphs 1100–1102. See also paragraphs 1088–1089 for more about the presence of Jesus in the liturgy.

Background

Listening

Chapter 18 continues the focus on the Mass. The children discover how to listen and respond to the Word of God.

Sometimes the hardest part of listening is quieting oneself. Children, like adults, need to get beyond the background noise in their heads before they can open their minds and hearts to the Scriptures.

The story Jesus told about the good ground is one children can easily visualize. They have already unlocked metaphors (for one, they imagined an old woman as God and a coin as a sinner). In this lesson you will lead them carefully through the metaphor Jesus used when he compared good soil with good listening.

Faith Summary

- **During the Liturgy of the Word we listen and respond to God's Word.**
- **The homily invites us to accept God's Word.**
- **In the Creed we profess our belief in a triune God.**

Growth and Development

It is helpful to remember two characteristics of second graders as you teach this lesson:

- ***Second graders are capable listeners.*** Help the children realize that the good listening skills they practice in school and at home are the same kind of listening needed during Mass.
- ***Second graders respond well to repetition and established patterns.*** In class, they listen to stories, hear them read in depth, and then respond—the same pattern they experience in the Liturgy of the Word.

A Teacher's Prayer

Thank you, Redeemer, for your presence in our lives and for giving us stories to inspire and guide us. Help me tell your stories to the children in a way that brings them closer to you. Let them open their hearts and minds to the messages you have to tell. Amen.

Vocabulary Preview

Liturgy of the Word
homily
Creed

Scripture

Luke 11:28: Hear and obey God's Word.
Mathew 13:1–9: The Good Ground
Psalm 119:89: You Word, Lord, stands forever.

Related Resources

Video

"Mass for Young Children" (St. Anthony Messenger Press, 1-800-488-0488 or www.AmericanCatholic.org). In simple language, this two video set provides a clear explanation of the Mass. (Children, 10 minutes each)

Book

DiGidio, Sandra. *How All of Us Celebrate the Mass* (*Catholic Update,* St. Anthony Messenger Press, 1-800-488-0488 or www.AmericanCatholic.org). This article focuses on the celebrating community as one of the most important elements of the Eucharistic celebration. (Adult)

TEACHER ORGANIZER

Planning Guide

The basic content for each chapter is divided into four class sessions. There are a number of options for the fifth session. Extension, review, and testing options are described under Day 5 Alternatives. The Quick Check box will help you evaluate the week's lessons.

Chapter Goals

In this chapter, the students will learn about

- ❑ The Liturgy of the Word
- ❑ The Word of God
- ❑ Prayer of the Faithful

	DAY 1 · INVITATION	DAY 2 · DISCOVERY	DAY 3 · DISCOVERY
OBJECTIVES	**The students will be able to** • Recall favorite stories • Determine what makes a good listener	**The students will be able to** • Discover the message of a Bible story • Discover the meaning of an analogy in a Bible story • Tell how to listen to God's Word	**The students will be able to** • Recognize the Liturgy of the Word • Tell how to listen to the readings at Mass • Respond to the Word of God
PREPARATION	• Think of examples of various kinds of stories	• Have student drawings ready in advance • Practice the Scripture reading	• Think through your presentation of the Liturgy of the Word • Make copies of the suggested Scripture verses for readers • Make copies of the resource master on page 384
MATERIALS	• Several items that make noise • Student books • Poster board, art materials, tape	• Bowl of big seeds • Pot or bowl of soil • Pencils • Drawing paper, art supplies	• Two candles • Bible or Book of Gospels • Tape and scissors
OPTIONAL ACTIVITIES	• Teaching Tip Create poster with ways to listen • Ideas That Work Discuss how to listen	• Options Tell the Bible story using simple visuals • Ideas That Work Use seeds to dramatize the Scripture reading	• Vocabulary Liturgy of the Word, homily, creed

Learning Objectives

By the end of this chapter, the students should be able to

- ❑ Define the Liturgy of the Word as a time to listen to God's Word
- ❑ Describe the parts of the Liturgy of the Word
- ❑ Describe ways that they can take part in the Liturgy of the Word

DAY 4 · LIVING

The students will be able to

- Creatively retell a favorite Bible story
- Make up a Prayer of the Faithful
- Respond to God's Word in prayer

- Make plans with the first or third grade to eat lunch together (to share Bible story booklets)

- Drawing paper and supplies to make four-page books
- Pencils
- Staplers

- **Resource Master** Cut and fold activity
- **Ideas That Work** Teach a preparation song for listening to Bible stories

DAY 5 · ALTERNATIVES

There are a number of alternatives to help you plan Day 5.

Prayer Experience
Use the Prayer for God's People on Day 4 or Day 5.

Review and Explore
Prepare a students' version of the Gospel reading for the coming Sunday. The students need sturdy paper and drawing supplies to make a bookmark. They can add yarn tassels, too.

Home and Family
Send the page home with the students, or assign one or more of the activities.

The Church Today
The students plant promise seeds and need paper cups, soil, newspapers, and easy-to-grow seeds, such as lima beans or pumpkin seeds. Have water on hand for watering the seeds.

Chapter Test
The chapter test appears as a resource master on page 385.

Quick Check

Do this evaluation as soon as you finish each chapter.

Did I follow my lesson plan?

How can I tell that I met the learning objectives for the lesson?

What activities did the children enjoy most?

How could I improve this lesson?

Benziger on the Web
For more ideas, visit us at www.benziger.glencoe.com

Interactive Lesson Planner
Your ILP provides more help in preparing to teach this chapter.

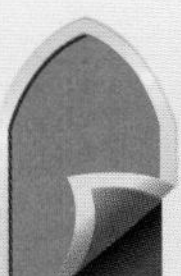

Celebrate
Turn to page 22 of this book. Check for seasonal celebrations.

Lesson Plan · Day 1
As the children are getting settled for religion class, use the noisemakers you brought. Make the sounds in decreasing volume, loudest first.

1 Listen
When the sounds get soft, ask: How can you best hear quiet sounds? *(Focus, concentrate, be quiet.)* Have the children read the chapter title. Say that you wonder what listening has to do with the Mass. Ask the children for their ideas on what they think listening may have to do with the Mass. Then, read together the Scripture verse, which has the answer.

2 Do You Know?
Tell the children that the Liturgy of the Word is the part of the Mass where the lectors and priest read the Scripture. Then ask the question. List their answers. At the end of the week, come back to this question to see how the children's knowledge has developed.

INVITATION 18

Blessed are they who hear the Word of God and obey it.
Luke 11:28

Do You Know?

◆ How do you take part in the Liturgy of the Word?

Listen

Story Time

Miss Todd tells us stories. She's our very favorite. She told of a golden egg, and the old goose that laid it. We sit and we listen when we hear the story bell chime. We can't wait for the words "Once upon a time."

What stories do you like to hear over and over again?

3 Story Time

Ask how many enjoy listening to a story. Read the poem about Miss Todd. Let the children share the names of their favorite stories. Ask the children about the people who tell them stories.

4 Something for You

Share the information on student page 251. If possible, give an example of different kinds of stories. Use stories from the children's readers or stories that have been read to the children. Discuss how important good listening is to the enjoyment of a story. Allow children time to complete the list.

Something for You

Every story you hear has something for you. Some stories will make you laugh. Some stories will make you think. Some stories teach a lesson. All you have to do is listen.

How can you be a good listener?

Complete the list below.

- Look at the person who is speaking.

- Try to picture what you hear.
- ______________________

TEACHING TIP

Take the list of listening traits on student page 251 one step further and make it useful to the class. Let the children share their ideas. Have the class agree on two or three ways to be a good listener. *(Do not interrupt. Show respect. Ask questions.)* Have a child draw a large ear on poster board. Within the ear write the ways to listen. Post where all can see. Refer to the poster when needed.

IDEAS THAT WORK

Good listening is a skill people need their whole lives through. Lead the children through a discussion about listening. What are their favorite sounds? Least favorite? What words do they like to hear? When is it easy to listen? When it is difficult to listen? End by asking the children to listen very carefully. Say: God loves second graders!

Lesson Plan · Day 2

Ask everyone to start talking to one another. Stand at the front of the room and with great drama, say something very important in your usual speaking voice. Stop the talking and ask what you said. Help the children understand that we cannot hear if we do not listen.

1 A Way to Listen

Say that Jesus knew the importance of listening. Jesus was a good listener and a wonderful storyteller. Once upon a time Jesus told a story about how to listen to God. Gather the children close and ask all to listen carefully.

2 Good Ground

Tell the story, integrating visuals, if possible. Sprinkle seeds as you tell the story when you tell every scene of the story. See Ideas that Work. Show the seeds and soil.

OPTIONS

For Those Who Learn Visually

Young children, in general, are high visual learners. It would benefit the whole class if the Bible story were told with simple visuals. Have the visuals in the room so that the children could tell the story over and over again. Ahead of time, ask four children to each draw a scene: (1) Wild birds (2) Lots of rocks (3) Lots of weeds (4) Some wheat.

VOCABULARY

The **Liturgy of the Word** is the part of Mass when the Gospel is read.

A **Homily** is an address or sermon given after the Gospel during Mass.

The **Creed** is a statement of Christian beliefs.

A Way to Listen

One day Jesus was sitting beside the Sea of Galilee. Many people came to see him. The crowd was so large that Jesus had to sit in a boat. The people stood on the shore and listened to Jesus speak. Jesus told a story about a farmer and some seeds. The story is all about listening to the Word of God.

Good Ground

Jesus said, "A farmer went out to plant his seeds. Some seeds fell along a path. Wild birds ate them up.

"Some other seeds fell on rocky ground. These seeds grew a little. But the soil wasn't deep enough. The plants wilted and died.

"Other seeds fell among thorny weeds. The weeds took up all the space and the farmer's seeds could not grow.

"But some seeds fell on good ground. They sprouted and bloomed into big heads of wheat."

Based on *Matthew 13:1–9*

3 God Speaks
Read the final paragraph aloud to the children. Tell the children that they are good ground waiting for God's Word to be planted in their hearts. Ask the children to name some good ways to listen to God.

4 Activity
Explain the activity. Invite the children to work independently. Then let the children read the completed sentences together.

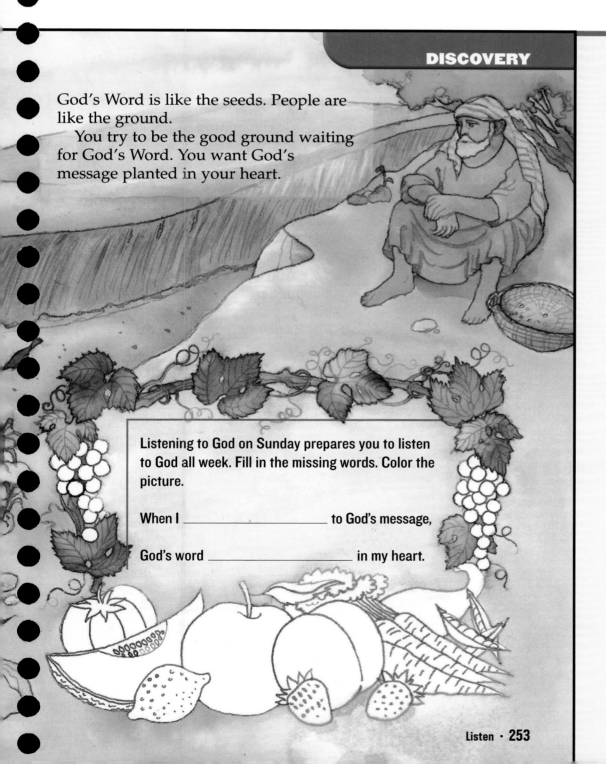

God's Word is like the seeds. People are like the ground.

You try to be the good ground waiting for God's Word. You want God's message planted in your heart.

Listening to God on Sunday prepares you to listen to God all week. Fill in the missing words. Color the picture.

When I ______________ to God's message,

God's word ______________ in my heart.

IDEAS THAT WORK

When you share the first sentence of the story, let big seeds sprinkle from your hand. If the children have done the optional activity on page 375, the wild birds the children have drawn can appear to eat them.

Show the drawing of rocks and sprinkle the seeds by it, saying that the rocks took up too much soil. The plants got dry and died.

Show the weeds and sprinkle seeds among the picture, telling how the weeds choked the seeds so that they could not grow.

Sprinkle some seeds. Say that the seeds went into good ground. There were no rocks, no weeds, no wild birds. The seeds grew into big heads of healthy wheat.

Lesson Plan · Day 3

Ask volunteers to share something they learned because they were good listeners.

1 God's Word

Recall the Gathering at Mass, which is a time for getting ready. Write *Liturgy of the Word* on the chalkboard for all to repeat. Explain that the Liturgy of the Word is a time for listening. Circle *Word* and ask about whose Word is listened to at Mass. Read aloud the material on student pages 254–255.

2 Learn by Doing

Prepare the children to enact the Liturgy of the Word by reviewing each part in turn and working with the children on the correct responses. Use the information on student pages 254–255 as a guide. Choose children to act as readers and a priest.

Lead the children through the Liturgy of the Word. Have the readers and priest read the lines suggested in "Bible Basics."

TEACHING TIP

Here is a summary of steps to enact The Liturgy of the Word:

- Sit ready to listen. Reader reads First Reading. All respond, "Thanks be to God." All say the Psalm.
- Reader reads Second Reading. All respond.
- Priest reads Gospel. All respond, "Praise to you, Lord Jesus Christ."
- Priest gives homily.
- All stand and say, "We believe in God the Father, the Son, and the Holy Spirit."
- All say, "For those who are hungry, so they may be helped. We pray to the Lord. Lord, hear our prayer."

Your Word, Lord, stands forever.

Psalm 119:89

God's Word

People liked listening to the stories Jesus told. You listen to Jesus, too. Every week you hear God's Word when you celebrate Mass. This time of listening to God is called the **Liturgy of the Word**.

You sit, ready to listen. You hear a Bible story about God's love for you. A second Bible reading tells you how to love God.

The reader says, "The Word of the Lord." Everyone is happy to listen to God. Everyone responds, "Thanks be to God."

Next, a story about Jesus is read from the Book of Gospels. The people get ready to listen by singing "Alleluia."

The priest reads a story about Jesus and says, "The gospel of the Lord." We thank Jesus for showing us how to love God. We say, "Praise to you, Lord Jesus Christ."

The priest helps everyone to understand the message of God's word. This is called the **homily**.

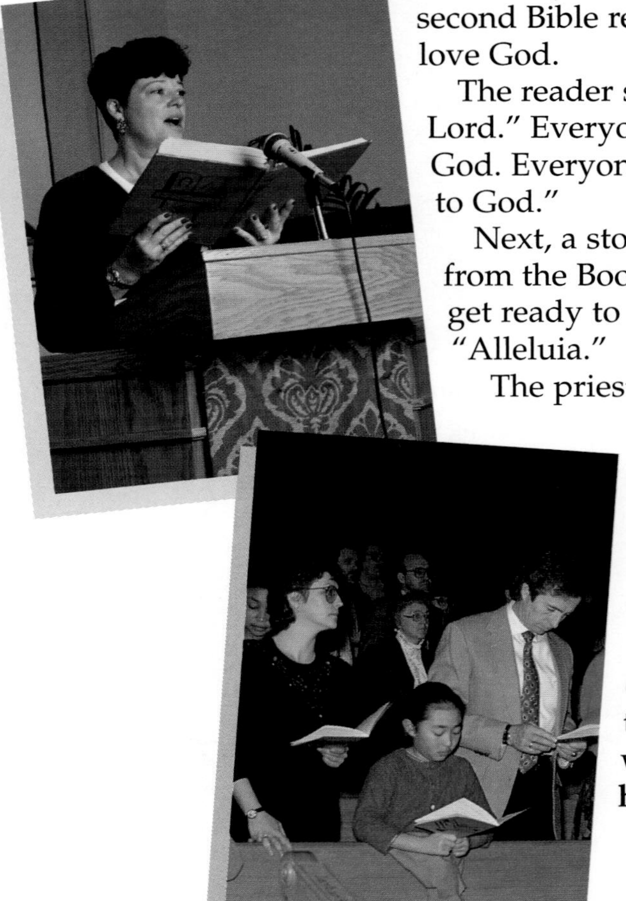

3 Activity
Read the directions. Allow the children to write the correct word in the correct space. Conclude by reading the Word of God and This We Believe!

After the homily, the people stand and say the **Creed**. The Creed says that God's people believe in God the Father, the Son, and the Holy Spirit.

The people respond to God's Word by praying for the Church and for all people. You say, "Lord, hear our prayer."

Now the altar is prepared for Communion. The Liturgy of the Eucharist begins.

God speaks to us at Mass. We listen and respond.

ACTIVITY

Look at the pictures. Use the words to tell what you do in the Liturgy of the Word.

Listen Pray

I ____________________

I ____________________

BIBLE BASICS

Use these lines adapted from Scripture as practice for enacting the Liturgy of the Word.

First Reading God gave us Jesus who showed us God's love. *(Acts 2:22) The Word of the Lord.*

Psalm Keep me safe, O God, you are my hope. *(Psalm 16)*

Second Reading Whenever we are in need, we should come bravely to our merciful God. God will treat us with kindness. *(Hebrews 4:16) The Word of the Lord.*

Gospel Jesus said, "Go and tell people everything I have told you. I will always be with you." *(Matthew 28:20) The Gospel of the Lord.*

Homily Tell others about God's love.

Lesson Plan · Day 4

Ask students to recall the main focus during the Liturgy of the Word. (*listening to God's Word being read*)

1 Tell a Story

Share the introductory paragraph. With enthusiasm, talk about some of the Bible stories the children have heard. They may want to flip back through the pages and call out their favorites. Make a list on the board.

Explain the bookmaking activity. Say that the books will be shared with another grade. Show how to plan the four pages. On the chalkboard, draw a chart like the one on the page. Fill it in, using one of the listed stories. Distribute supplies. Let each child decide whether to work alone or with a partner. Set a time limit.

RESOURCE MASTERS

The resource master on page 384 is a cut and fold activity that summarizes the parts of the Liturgy of the Word.

LIVING

TELL A STORY

You listen to God's Word, or the Bible, at Mass. You also hear Bible stories in class. What are some stories you know about Jesus?

Pick your favorite Bible story about Jesus. Tell the story in a four-page book. Save room on each page for a drawing.

To make the book, you need two sheets of paper. Fold the sheets in half. Tuck one sheet inside the other. Staple the pages together.

Share your Bible story. You will spread the Word of God!

❷ We Pray

Tell the children they have a very important job today. They are going to write a Prayer of the Faithful like that said during the Liturgy of the Word at Mass. Do the activity as a class. Explain that the name *Lord* is another name for God. Make copies of the finalized prayers and use them as a class prayer now and then.

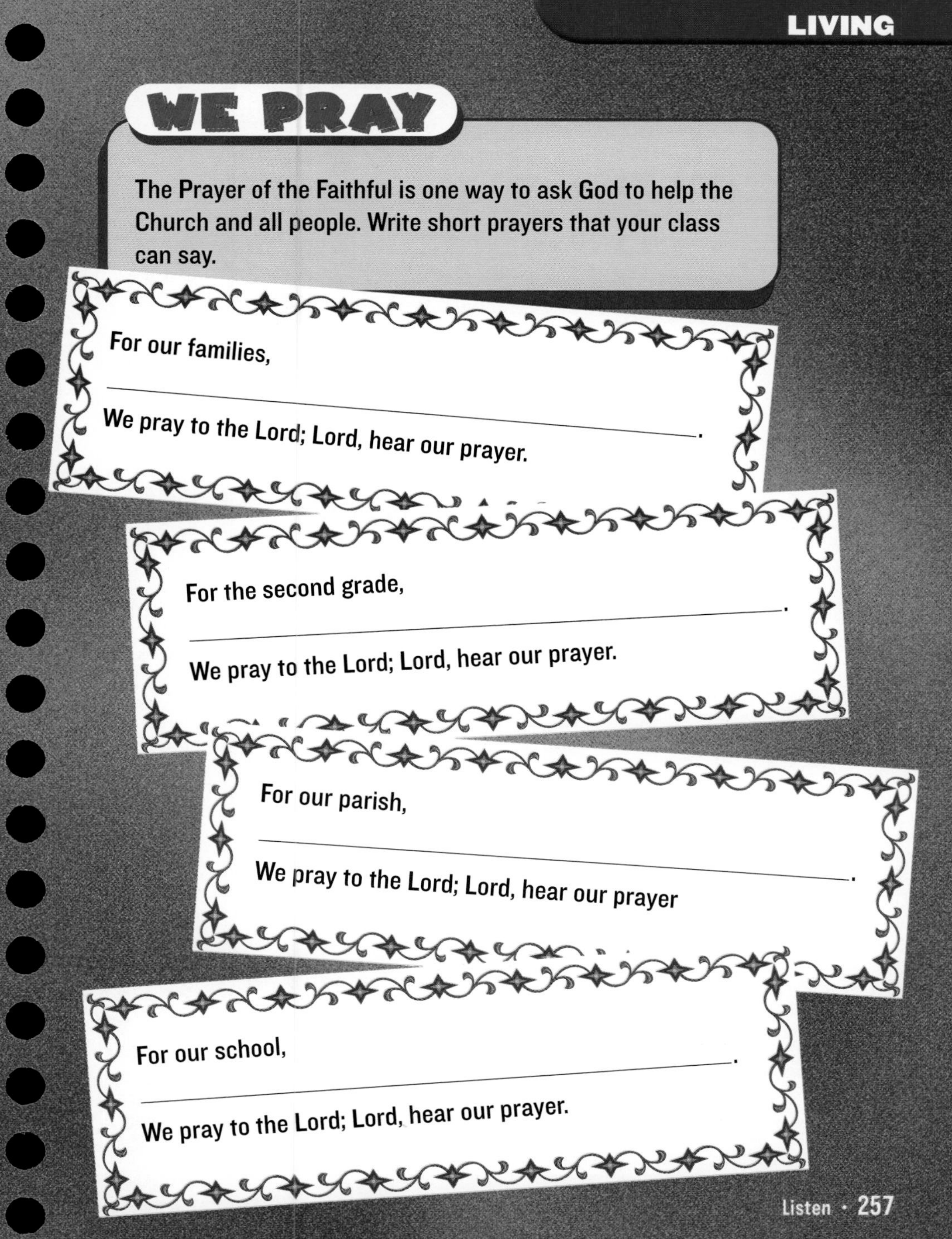

LIVING
WE PRAY
The Prayer of the Faithful is one way to ask God to help the Church and all people. Write short prayers that your class can say.
For our families,
We pray to the Lord; Lord, hear our prayer.
For the second grade,
We pray to the Lord; Lord, hear our prayer.
For our parish,
We pray to the Lord; Lord, hear our prayer
For our school,
We pray to the Lord; Lord, hear our prayer.
Listen · 257

LEARNING TO PRAY

The liturgy is the Church's public prayer. Participation in the Eucharistic liturgy is the Church's greatest communal prayer. The Prayer of the Faithful is a prayer of petition that focuses on human needs.

Prayer
This prayer experience focuses on praying for the needs of others.

1 Prayer
Tell the children that they are going to say a Prayer of the Faithful like that said during the Liturgy of the Word at Mass.

2 Prayer for God's People
Gather the children into a circle and pray the prayer. Pause after each petition to allow the children to name what they would like to pray for.

IDEAS THAT WORK

You may wish to show that Bible story time is a very special time. Just before you share a Bible story, sing this song to the melody for Frère Jacques (Are You Sleeping?).

Listen closely, listen closely
To God's Word, to God's Word.
Come and gather near me.
God is talking to you.
Hear God speak.
Hear God speak.

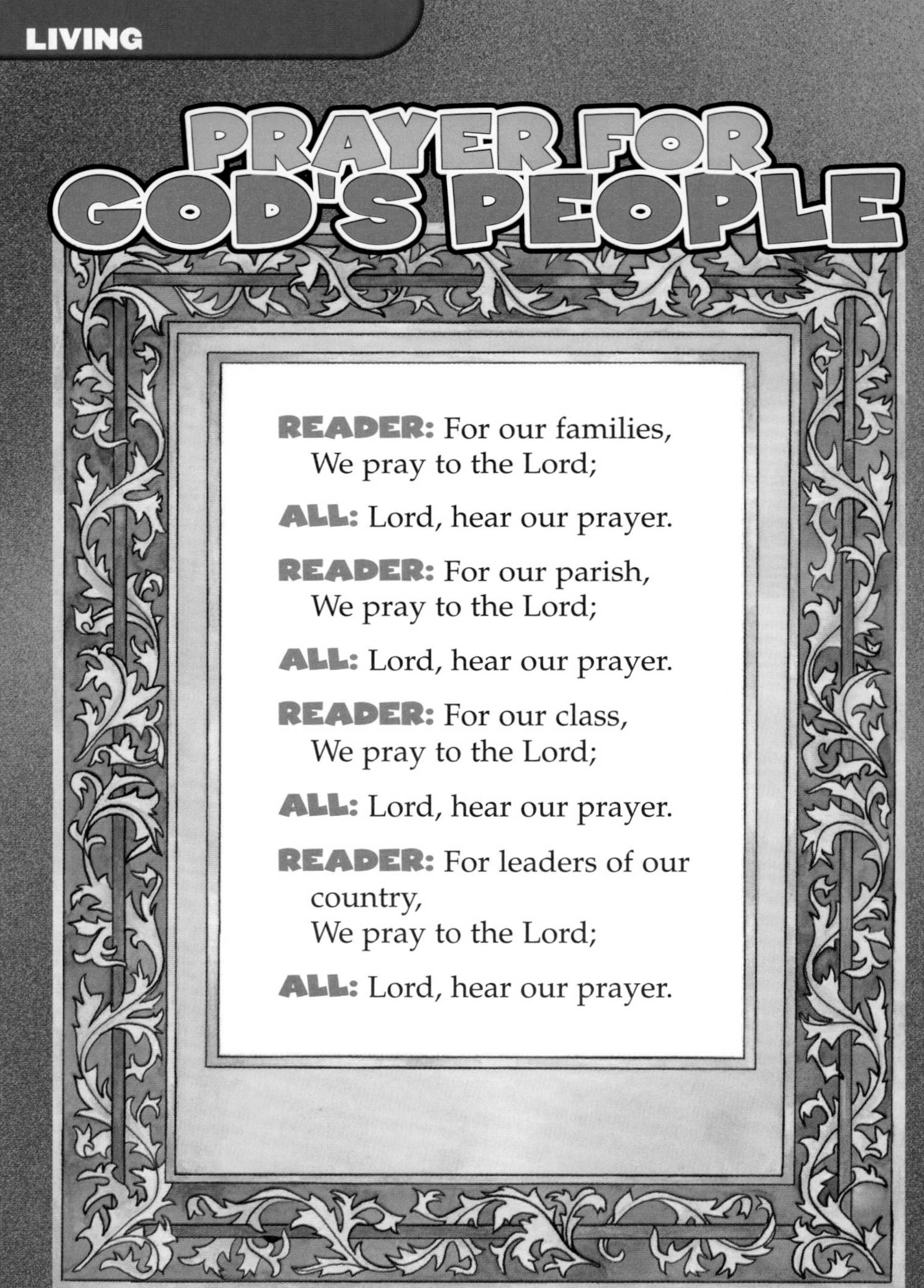
PRAYER FOR GOD'S PEOPLE
READER: For our families,
We pray to the Lord;
ALL: Lord, hear our prayer.
READER: For our parish,
We pray to the Lord;
ALL: Lord, hear our prayer.
READER: For our class,
We pray to the Lord;
ALL: Lord, hear our prayer.
READER: For leaders of our country,
We pray to the Lord;
ALL: Lord, hear our prayer.

1 Know
Call attention to the graphic organizer. Review the important points.

2 Love and Serve
Ask the children to listen carefully to the Gospel you are going to read. Talk together about its message. Then, talk about the Psalm in the Serve section. Have a discussion about how God's Word is like a light. Give time to make the bookmarks.

3 God's Friends
Ask the children to imagine a time when children did not get to hear about God. Then tell about Saint Charles. See if anyone knows a child who goes to the parish religious education sessions.

CHAPTER 18
REVIEW and EXPLORE

Know

Liturgy of the Word

You listen.
You say "I believe".
You pray for others.

Love

Find out what the Gospel reading for the week is. Talk about its message. Write a sentence or draw a picture about what God's message says to you.

Serve

Make a bookmark that says something about God's Word. Give your bookmark to a friend as a reminder of God's Good News. Use these words:

God's Word is a lamp for my feet, a light for my path.

Psalm 119:105

GOD'S FRIENDS

Saint Charles Borromeo

"Come to class, children," said Father Charles. Five hundred years ago, children in many parishes did not get to hear God's Word. Father Charles started religion classes for them. Today, parishes still hold religion classes for children.

A Little Catechism

Invite the children to open their religion books to *A Little Catechism.* Choose one or more of the selections below for memory work or reinforcement. You will find your copy of the catechism on pages 23–43 of this Teacher's Edition.

1. Ask the children to begin the section "More about the Mass." Read with them the two introductory sentences.
2. Have the children read and reread the first three of the bulleted items on the list, until they can complete the last words in each item from memory.

Know | Love | Serve

Note The activities on this page provide ways for the children to share their learning with their families. The activities are related to the week's theme.

1 Introduce
Have all read aloud the letter. If time allows, have volunteers tell about doing last week's activities with their families. Briefly tell about the two activities.

2 Pray Together
Before you say the prayer in the prayer burst with the class, show the children the action that goes with the prayer. Close the fingers of the right hand into the palm. As the words are prayed, use the thumb to make a cross on the forehead, the lips, and the heart.

Online for Families
Remind the children to check the Benziger Web site this week with their families.
www.benziger.glencoe.com

Dear Family,
I have just finished chapter 18. I have learned that God has a special message for me. I hear God's Word at Mass. It is called the Liturgy of the Word. You can help by talking to me about God's special message after Mass each Sunday.

With others

Jesus sent the followers to spread the Word of God. You are also one of Jesus' followers. Tell someone about Jesus and some of the things that he did.

With your family

People pray "Prayers of the Faithful" during Sunday Mass. Everyone responds, "Lord, hear our prayer." Write some prayers like these for your family.

May the Word of God be in my mind, on my lips, and in my heart.

GO ONLINE!
http://www.benziger.glencoe.com

1 Discuss
Tell the introduction to the children. As you mention each suggestion, pause briefly to let the children think about what was said. Ask the children to think of a way to come closer to God. The way will be secret.

2 The Project
Have the seed planting supplies set up. Let the children suggest good guidelines to do the activity. Give basic instructions for planting seeds.

3 Pray
Bring this week to a close by having the children recite the Word of God on student page 254.

THE CHURCH TODAY

Think about a way that you can grow closer to God. Maybe you want to stop teasing your little brother or sister. Maybe you want to stop lying when it's easier than telling the truth. Make a promise that is just right for you.

Plant a Promise

Get some seeds, soil, and a cup. Carefully plant the seeds. The seeds are like the promise you made to God.

Water the seeds and give them sunlight. Keep track of their growth. Keep track of yourself, too. See if you are keeping your promise and are growing closer to God.

TEACHING TIP

If the room is arranged in tables, give each table the needed supplies. If the children sit in rows of desks, have the supplies available in various parts of the room. Let all the children place newspapers on the workspace and on the floor.

ANSWER KEY

This is the answer key for the chapter test on page 385.

A. 1.

B. 1. Word 2. song 3. Bible 4. Gospel 5. homily 6. Creed 7. everyone

Name ______________________________

Liturgy of the Word

Learn about the Liturgy of the Word. First, cut the two strips. Next, tape the strips together in the right order. Finally, fold the strip back and forth on the dotted lines.

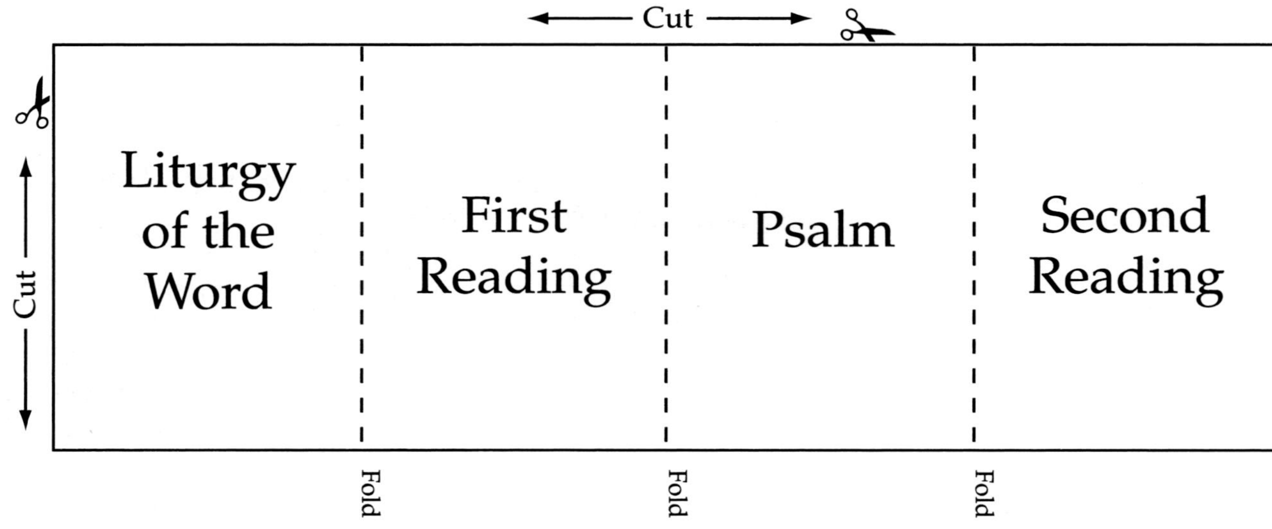

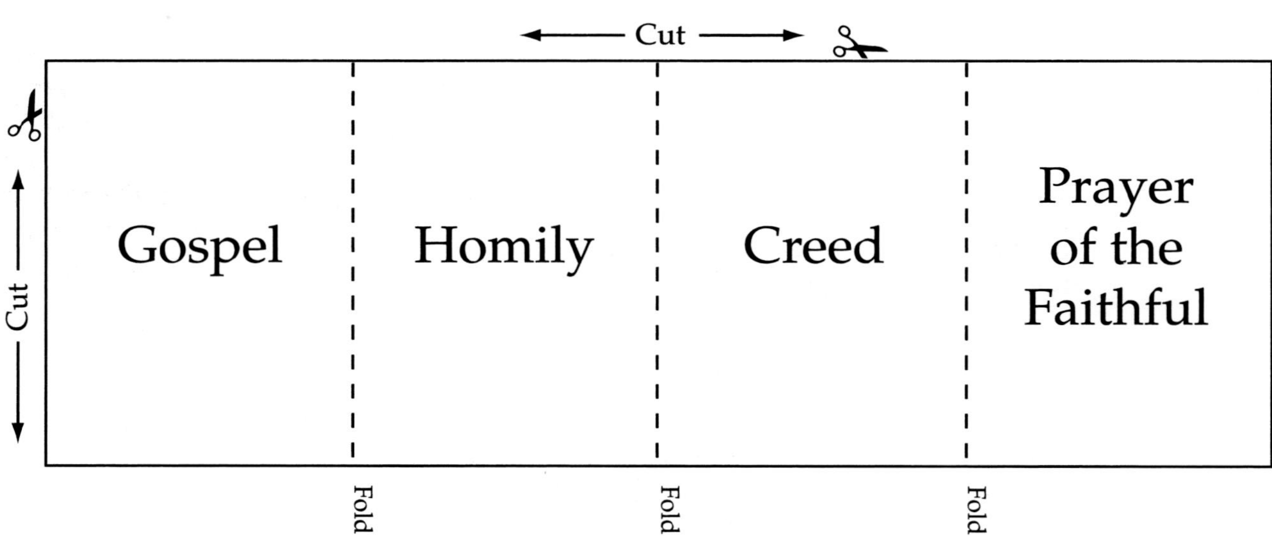

Name ______________________________

Chapter 18 Test

A. Find the Message

Jesus told a story about a farmer planting seeds.

The seeds in good ground grew into wheat.

Circle one message.

1. You can let God's Word grow in your heart.

2. You can forgive those who are sorry.

3. You can help those who need you.

B. Fill in the words that tell about the Liturgy of the Word. Use the words in the box.

song / Gospel / homily / everyone pray / Bible / Creed / Word

1. You listen to the ________________ of God.

2. You sing a psalm, or ________________, from the Bible.

3. You listen to a second ________________ story.

4. You stand and listen to a ________________, the Good News of Jesus.

5. You listen to the priest give a ________________ to help you understand the Bible readings.

6. You stand and say the ________________ to show that you believe in God.

7. You ask God's help for ________________.

TEACHER RESOURCE CENTER

Faith Formation

Remembering Jesus' Selfless Love

Do this in memory of me.

from the Eucharistic Prayers of the Mass

The Eucharistic Prayer retells the story of Jesus' last meal, his suffering, and his death. Every Mass is an opportunity to hear the story again and to remember what Jesus' example of selfless love means in the lives of his followers. Throughout the centuries, Catholics have faithfully celebrated the Eucharist, and received the Body and Blood of Jesus. They continue to live out God's will, as they heed the command of Jesus to "do this in memory of me."

What parts of the Eucharistic Prayer are the most meaningful for you?

The Liturgy of the Eucharist

The Liturgy of the Eucharist celebrates both the sacrifice of Jesus and the nourishment of his Body and Blood. Believers are challenged to live lives of sacrifice, caring for the needs of others before their own. They are nourished in this task by the Eucharist, as the life of Jesus within themgives them strength, peace, and joyful hope.

How does the Liturgy of the Eucharist remind you of a family meal? A sacrifice?

CHECK THE CATECHISM

For more about the command of Jesus to "Do this in memory of me," see paragraphs 1341–1344 of the *Catechism of the Catholic Church*. The Liturgy of the Eucharist is covered in paragraphs 1345–1347.

Background

Remembering

Chapters 19 and 20 cover the Liturgy of the Eucharist. Chapter 19 ends with the memorial acclamation. Chapter 19 connects with the children's experiences, using stories as a way of remembering special people and events. The tradition of storytelling bridges the gap between today's children and those of Jesus' time. A present-day story shows the children how people are remembered and recognized in stories. A Bible story shows them that Christians remember Jesus through stories. The story of the road to Emmaus helps the children discover how Jesus was recognized and known.

Jesus blessed the bread, broke it, and shared it. How awesome that you can help the children know Jesus in the breaking of the bread at Mass!

Faith Summary

- **The Mass is a remembrance of Jesus.**
- **The central prayer of the Mass is the Eucharistic Prayer.**
- **In the Eucharist, the bread and wine become the Body and Blood of Jesus.**

Growth and Development

It is helpful to remember two characteristics of second graders as you teach this lesson:

- ***Second graders have a deep capacity for spirituality.*** They long for intimacy with God. They are just the right age to develop a deeper awareness of the Eucharist.
- ***Second graders understand the power of a good story.*** This is an ability that many adults have lost. In this chapter, you will help these children to recognize the Eucharistic Prayer as the story of Jesus.

A Teacher's Prayer

Jesus, walk with me on the road to Emmaus. Slow me down, so that I can listen to the children, and to your Word. Help me to appreciate all that the children teach me about you. Help me to see you, and know you, in each of them. Amen.

Vocabulary Preview

Eucharist

Scripture

1 Corinthians 11:25: "Do this in remembrance of me."
Luke 24:29–33: the road to Emmaus

Related Resources

Videos

"Apple" (St. Anthony Messenger Press, 1-800-488-0488 or www.AmericanCatholic.org). The story in this video is a Eucharistic parable. (Children, 12 minutes)

"Grandma's Bread" (St. Anthony Messenger Press, 1-800-488-0488 or www.AmericanCatholic.org). A family prepares a special Easter bread for a First Communion celebration. Available in English and Spanish. (Children, 17 minutes)

Book

Von Lehmen, Jeffrey. "Real Presence in the Eucharist" (*Catholic Update*, St. Anthony Messenger Press, 1-800-488-0488 or www.AmericanCatholic.org). A four page essay that explains in simple language the meaning of real presence. (Adults)

TEACHER ORGANIZER

Planning Guide

The basic content for each chapter is divided into four class sessions. There are a number of options for the fifth session. Extension, review, and testing options are described under Day 5 Alternatives. The Quick Check box will help you evaluate the week's lessons.

Chapter Goals

In this chapter, the students will learn about

- ❑ The Liturgy of the Eucharist
- ❑ The Eucharistic Prayer
- ❑ The Consecration

	DAY 1 · INVITATION	DAY 2 · DISCOVERY	DAY 3 · DISCOVERY
OBJECTIVES	**The students will be able to** • Determine that stories help them remember people • Discover the importance of family memories	**The students will be able to** • Realize that Christians have stories that remind them of Jesus • Analyze a Bible story to see how Jesus is present • Discover that Jesus is known in the breaking of bread	**The students will be able to** • Recognize the Liturgy of the Eucharist • Realize that Jesus is present in the breaking of the bread at Mass
PREPARATION	• Bring an item that is a reminder of someone (letter, photo, keepsake) • Prepare to tell a little story about the person	• Prepare your reading of the Bible story • Decide which cartoon character or superhero you will discuss	• Arrange the room for enacting the Eucharistic Prayer • Collect items to represent the cruets holding water and wine, chalice, hosts, and money
MATERIALS	• Item of remembrance • Pencils • Drawing supplies	• Pencils • Highlighters	• Items to represent the gifts brought during the presentation of gifts • Pencils
OPTIONAL ACTIVITIES	• Curriculum Challenge Collect family stories for display in the classroom or make them into a book	• Teaching Tip Answer questions about the Bible story	• Vocabulary Continue teaching the vocabulary words

Learning Objectives

By the end of this chapter, the students should be able to

- ❑ Understand some ways people recognize and remember one another
- ❑ Discover that Jesus is known in the breaking of the bread
- ❑ Realize that Jesus is truly present in the breaking of the bread at Mass

DAY 4 • LIVING

The students will be able to

- Recognize the Mass as a meal
- Discover ways to offer themselves to God at Mass
- Remember the Last Supper in prayer

- Make copies of the resource master on page 402

- Table cloth, cups, food, drinks
- Butcher block paper, tape
- Copies of the resource master, pencils, crayons
- Cards, string, glue, paper

- **Ideas That Work** Make arrangements to visit the church
- **Resource Masters** Discover how we offer ourselves to God during Mass
- **Curriculum Challenge** Create gratitude windsocks

DAY 5 • ALTERNATIVES

There are a number of alternatives to help you plan Day 5.

Prayer Experience
Use the Sign of Love prayer service on either Day 4 or Day 5. A long piece of butcher-block paper is needed.

Review and Explore
The students need pencils to do the activities. If possible, ask someone to share with the class some Mass responses in another language.

Home and Family
Send the page home with the students, or assign one or more of the activities.

The Church Today
You may wish to prepare the students for The Church Today activity by reading the story "Stone Soup" by Marcia Brown.

Chapter Test
The chapter test appears as a resource master on page 403.

Quick Check

Do this evaluation as soon as you finish each chapter.

Did I follow my lesson plan?

How can I tell that I met the learning objectives for the lesson?

What activities did the children enjoy most?

How could I improve this lesson?

Benziger on the Web
For more ideas, visit us at www.benziger.glencoe.com

Your ILP provides more help in preparing to teach this chapter.

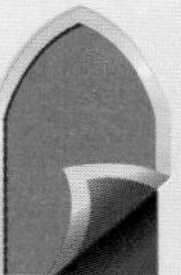

Celebrate
Turn to page 22 of this book. Check for seasonal celebrations.

Lesson Plan · Day 1

Call attention to the chapter title and the chapter's Scripture verse. Say that there is a time at Mass for remembering Jesus.

1 Remember

Show the item you brought that is a reminder of someone (letter, photo, keepsake). Tell a little story about the person. Volunteers may wish to tell about reminders they have of people. Ask the children why it is good to have things that remind us of people.

2 Family Stories

Gather the children, and tell them to listen closely to a story about three girls and their Uncle Billy. Read aloud the story.

What reminded the girls about Uncle Billy? What is a silly remembrance about Uncle Billy? Why did the girls enjoy the story? Talk about the importance of family stories. Review the last line of the story to prepare for Holy Communion.

TEACHING TIP

Children who have endured divorce, separation, or death may want to tell about their mementos of people they have lost. Be sensitive to their need to talk about their experience.

IDEAS THAT WORK

Involve the children in the story by asking three girls to say the lines of Maggie, Molly, and Mary. Each line is easy to remember. Tell the girls their lines, and say that you will nod to them when it is their time to speak.

Do this in remembrance of me.

1 Corinthians 11:25

Do You Know?

◆ What do you remember at the Liturgy of the Eucharist?

Remember

Family Stories

When Maggie, Mary, and Molly got home from school, their mom greeted them with the news, "We got a letter from Uncle Billy."

"Where is Uncle Billy now?" asked Molly.

"The army sent him to Germany," Mom answered. "I miss him," said Maggie.

"Mom," the girls asked together, "tell us that story about Uncle Billy."

? What is your favorite family story?

3 Activity
Let the children share family stories, either with the class or with a group. Then, let the children go back to their desks to write and illustrate a family story.

4 Do You Know?
Ask the children the Do You Know? question: What do you remember at the Liturgy of the Eucharist? At the end of the week, come back to this question to see how the children's knowledge has developed.

Billy Don't!

Mom smiled and waved her hand. She had told the story so many times she didn't have to think anymore. "Uncle Billy was always getting into trouble. Your grandma would wag her finger at him and say, 'Billy, don't.'"

"One day Uncle Billy got lost at the shopping mall. When the guard asked, 'You're Billy Johnson aren't you?', your Uncle Billy looked the guard right in the eye and said, 'Nope, my name is Billy Don't!'"

The girls all laughed. It seemed like Uncle Billy was right in the room with them.

Think of a story that helps your remember someone or something special. Write the story.

Draw a picture of who or what you remember when you hear the story.

CURRICULUM CHALLENGE

Language Arts You may wish to do the activity as a writing lesson. The children may use writing paper. You can guide them through the steps of writing their family story. The children should include an illustration. Display all of the stories, or make them into a book: *Our Family Stories.*

Lesson Plan · Day 2

Recall yesterday's story writing activity. Have a few volunteers tell the name of the person they wrote about. Say that family stories help us remember people.

1 Remembering Jesus

Add that Christians have stories that help us remember Jesus. Ask: When your friend phones you, how do you know it is your friend? *(recognize the voice or a way of talking)*

Name a cartoon character or superhero that is familiar to the children, and help them discover how they recognize that person. *(clothing, mannerisms)* Say that you are going to read a Bible story about Jesus. You want the children to listen to how Jesus was recognized.

BIBLE BASICS

Help bring the presence of Jesus to the children by beginning the Bible story this way: "Picture a dusty road that leads to town. Two men are walking down the road. They are busy talking. They are very sad. Their friend, Jesus, has been put to death on a cross. They had thought God sent Jesus to save them from sin. Now they are confused."

On the Road

It was the Sunday after Jesus died. Two of his followers were walking to a town called Emmaus.

Jesus walked up to them. They did not recognize him.

"What are you talking about?" he asked.

"We were talking about Jesus. My friend and I are his followers.

"We thought he was the Savior that God promised to send. But he was crucified three days ago. Now some women say that his tomb is empty. We don't know what to think!" Jesus shook his head. "You are slow to understand and to believe the Word of God," Jesus said. "The Scriptures say that the Savior would die and then rise again."

2 On the Road

See the Bible Basics feature. Then, read the story with feeling, so that the children hear frustration or sadness in the followers' voices, and hear the followers' surprise and happiness at the end. To help the children comprehend the story, pause occasionally while reading. See the Teaching Tip feature.

3 Break Bread

Have the children go back to their desks and have them highlight the sentence that tells how the men recognized Jesus. Make the connection: Jesus broke bread and shared it—the same action Jesus did at the Last Supper with the Apostles, the same action that happens at Mass. When the bread is broken and shared, we know that Jesus is there with us.

Jesus kept walking to Emmaus with the two followers.

On the way, Jesus explained many of the things from Scripture that were written about the Savior.

Jesus and the two men went to an inn and sat down together for supper.

But the two men still did not recognize Jesus.

Then Jesus took the bread.

He broke it, blessed it, and shared it with them. At that moment the two men recognized Jesus.

Then suddenly Jesus was gone.

"That was Jesus!" said Cleopas. "We must go back and tell the others this good news."

And they left at once for Jerusalem.

Based on *Luke 24:29–33*

- When did Jesus' followers recognize him?
- Why did they go back to Jerusalem?

TEACHING TIP

Here are questions that will help the children better understand the Bible story:

- Read the section up until Jesus speaks, and then ask, "Why were the men sad and confused?"
- Read Jesus' words about the Scriptures, and retell them, such as "Believe the Word of God. The Bible said that the Savior would die, and then would rise from the dead."
- Read the next paragraph. Ask if the men recognized Jesus. Then read about their arrival at an inn.
- Complete the reading. Ask: What did Jesus do that helped the men to recognize him? Why did the men go back to Jerusalem?

Lesson Plan · Day 3

Have the children look at student page 265. Read aloud the highlighted sentence that tells how the men recognized Jesus.

1 Remembering Jesus

Write *Liturgy of the Eucharist* on the chalkboard. Have all pronounce it. Say it is the second part of the Mass, when we remember and receive Jesus. Say that we offer ourselves to Jesus, as we offer the gifts. (Show the gifts.) The bread and wine will become Jesus' Body and Blood. The money helps the parish, and those in need. Read aloud the text on student pages 266–267.

2 Eucharist

Tell the children that today they will reenact the Liturgy of the Eucharist. See the Ideas That Work feature. Have the children bring the gifts to the priest. Say that the priest spreads his arms and prays over the bread and wine, while giving thanks for all God's blessings. (All respond, "Blessed be God forever.") The priest asks the Holy Spirit to change the bread and wine to Jesus.

IDEAS THAT WORK

Create an aisle in the room for the presentation of gifts and a space for an altar. Choose five children to bring up the gifts, and a child to be the priest. Let children bring up items that represent the cruets, chalice, hosts, and money. Establish a reverential tone. Emphasize the importance of this part of the Mass—Jesus actually comes to us. Before you begin leading the children through the Liturgy of the Eucharist, let them suggest ways they should behave.

Remembering Jesus

The **Eucharist** is a way to remember Jesus. Gifts of bread and wine are brought to the altar. These gifts are a reminder of all of God's blessings. The bread and wine will become the Body and Blood of Jesus. The priest prays over the bread and wine. The people say, "Blessed be God forever."

During the Eucharistic Prayer the priest does as Jesus did at the Last Supper. The priest holds up the bread for all to see. He says the words Jesus said. "Take this all of you and eat it: this is my body which will be given up for you."

Then, the priest says and does what Jesus did at the Last Supper. (Have the priest hold up the bread, while you say the words of Jesus. Then, do the same with the cup.) Something wonderful happens. The bread and wine are Jesus. (All stand and say: "Christ has died. Christ has risen. Christ will come again.")

3 Activity

Do the activity as a class or independently. Ask: How do we give thanks to God at Mass? Together; read aloud the This We Believe! feature.

The priest holds up the cup of wine and says what Jesus said.

"Take this, all of you and drink from it: this is the cup of my blood, the blood of the new and everlasting covenant. It will be shed for you and for all so that sins may be forgiven. Do this in memory of me."

The people remember Jesus' sacrifice by saying, "Christ has died, Christ has risen, Christ will come again."

THIS WE BELIEVE!

The Eucharist is a sacrifice of thanksgiving to God the Father.

ACTIVITY

What does the word Eucharist mean? Change every red letter to the letter that comes after it in the alphabet. Put the new letters on the lines.

S G A M K R F I U H M G

___ ___ ___ ___ ___ ___ ___ ___ ___ ___ ___ ___

BIBLE BASICS

You may want to talk about the Last Supper, so that the children understand that Jesus' words and actions are remembered at Mass. They will also realize how Jesus' actions of breaking, blessing, and sharing bread were what helped the men to recognize him at Emmaus.

VIRTUE FAITH GRACE VOCABULARY

Liturgy of the Eucharist The Liturgy of the Eucharist is the second part of the Mass when the bread and wine become the Body and Blood of Jesus and you receive Jesus in Holy Communion.

Christ is a name for Jesus that means the "one chosen by God."

Lesson Plan · Day 4

Ask the children to talk with a friend: How do we recognize Jesus at Mass? (*The words and actions of the Last Supper are said and done. The bread and wine become Jesus.*)

❶ A Special Meal

Tell the children you want to have a special meal with them. Ask what is needed. A table! Set up a table. A cloth! Add a cloth. Food! Have children help you set out food and drinks. Say that something very important is still missing. See if anyone guesses that people are needed.

❷ The Table of the Lord

Invite the children to the table, with their books and pencils. Recall the Last Supper. What did Jesus do with the bread and wine? (*He blessed them and shared them. He asked his followers to do the same.*) Say: Think of the altar as a table. What happens at the altar? (*Food is brought, blessed, and shared.*)

IDEAS THAT WORK

If possible, make arrangements to take the children into church, to see the chalice, hosts, cruets, and plate up close. This will help the children to experience a sense of reverence, and to feel more connected to what happens during Mass.

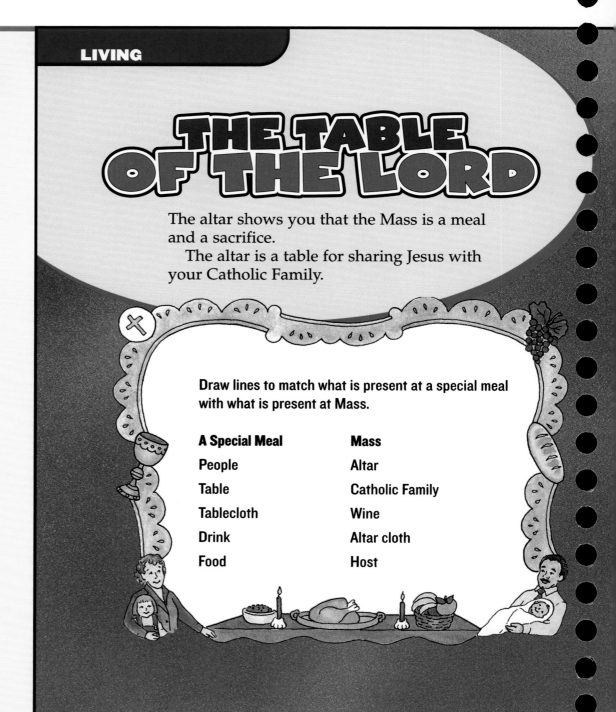

THE TABLE OF THE LORD

The altar shows you that the Mass is a meal and a sacrifice.

The altar is a table for sharing Jesus with your Catholic Family.

Draw lines to match what is present at a special meal with what is present at Mass.

A Special Meal	Mass
People	Altar
Table	Catholic Family
Tablecloth	Wine
Drink	Altar cloth
Food	Host

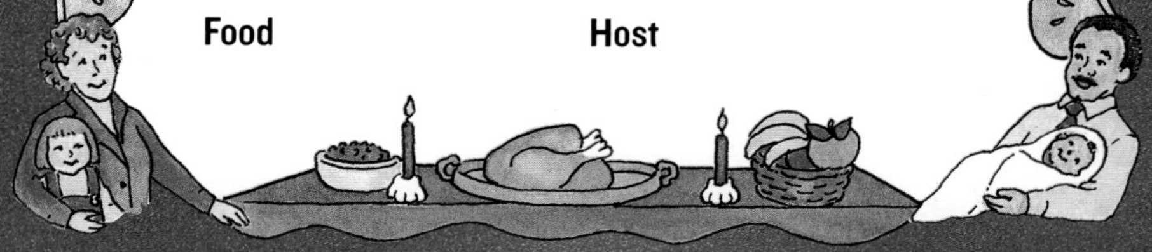

3 Activity
Say that a table is a place where a family shares food. The altar is a table where the Family of God shares Jesus. Have the children do the matching exercise. Then, enjoy the treats together.

4 I Give Myself
Talk about how a table is prepared at home for a meal. Recall how the altar is prepared with gifts of bread and wine at Mass. If you wish, have the children complete the resource master. The resource master will prepare the children to select a personal gift to give God. Lead the children through the directions on student page 269. Allow time to complete the activity.

I GIVE MYSELF

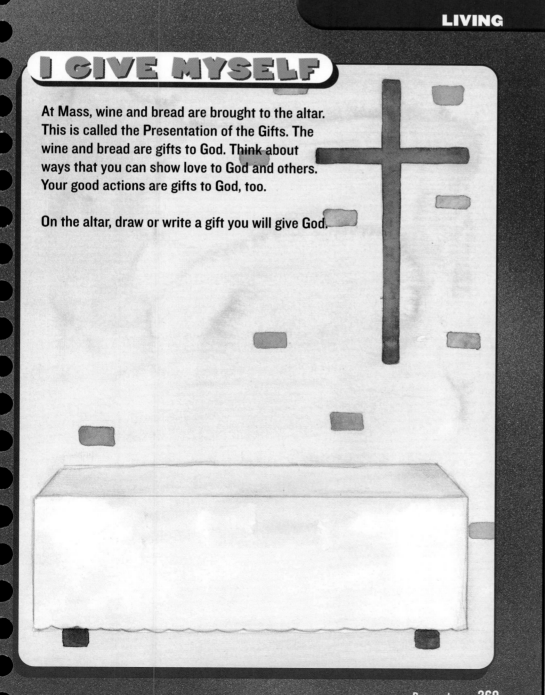

At Mass, wine and bread are brought to the altar. This is called the Presentation of the Gifts. The wine and bread are gifts to God. Think about ways that you can show love to God and others. Your good actions are gifts to God, too.

On the altar, draw or write a gift you will give God.

The resource master on page 402 is an activity that helps the children discover how they offer themselves to God during Mass. The children will need pencils and crayons.

Prayer
The prayer experience is an important part of the week's lesson. This prayer will remind the children of Jesus and the Last Supper.

1 Prepare for Prayer
Tape a sheet of butcher-block paper to the floor. Use a sheet long enough for all to sit around. Have a child write the name Jesus at one space. Gather all to remember Jesus and the Last Supper. Assign the children to side one or side two.

2 Sign of Love
When all are ready, pray together.

CURRICULUM CHALLENGE
Art Giving thanks to God at Mass prepares you to give thanks every day of the week. The children can make a windsock of things they are thankful for.

- Start with a small card. On it write: Thank you, God. Punch a hole in the center near the top, and a hole near both bottom corners.
- On a second card, draw or write things you are thankful for. Punch two holes at the top, to match the placement of the two holes on the bottom of the first card.
- String the two cards together.
- Glue a long sheet of tissue paper to the bottom card. Cut the tissue paper into strips. Do not cut all the way to the card.

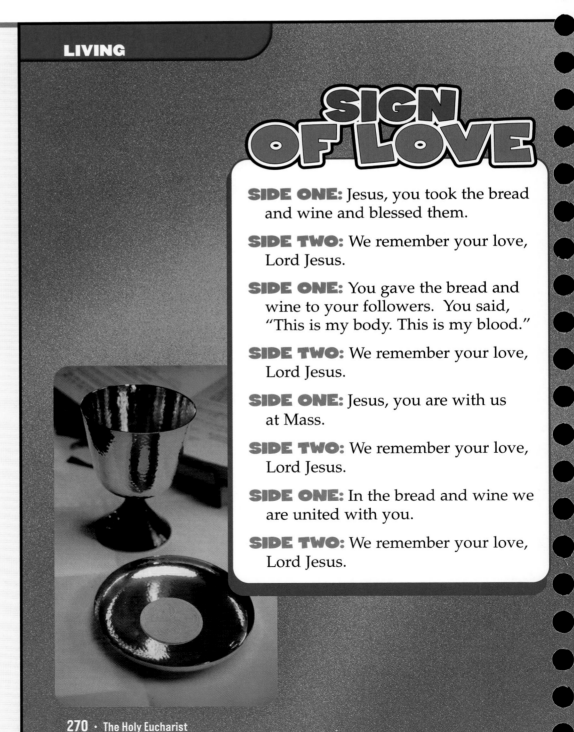

SIGN OF LOVE

SIDE ONE: Jesus, you took the bread and wine and blessed them.

SIDE TWO: We remember your love, Lord Jesus.

SIDE ONE: You gave the bread and wine to your followers. You said, "This is my body. This is my blood."

SIDE TWO: We remember your love, Lord Jesus.

SIDE ONE: Jesus, you are with us at Mass.

SIDE TWO: We remember your love, Lord Jesus.

SIDE ONE: In the bread and wine we are united with you.

SIDE TWO: We remember your love, Lord Jesus.

1 Know
Have the children point to the graphic organizer and, with a partner, slowly go through each step of the Liturgy of the Eucharist. Then, review the parts as a class.

2 Love and Serve
Love: Review the different parts of the Mass with the children to assist them with this activity. Serve: Give time for thinking and for writing. Let the children see you write, too.

3 God's Friends
Show the illustration, and share the information on Saint Dominic Savio. Then, ask the children to pretend that Saint Dominic will visit them. Ask them what questions they would ask Saint Dominic.

CHAPTER 19 REVIEW and EXPLORE

Know

Liturgy of the Eucharist

You give God thanks and praise.
You remember the Last Supper.
Jesus is present in the bread and wine.

Love

Write two things you do or say at Mass to help you remember what Jesus did.

____

____

Serve

Finish these sentences.
At play, I can show thanks to Jesus by

______________________.

At school, I can show thanks to Jesus by

______________________.

GOD'S FRIENDS

Saint Dominic

Dominic learned to serve Mass when he was five years old. When Dominic made his First Holy Communion, he wrote rules for himself that he tried to keep. Later, Dominic became a priest. Dominic had a special devotion to the Eucharist.

A Little Catechism

Invite the children to open their religion books to *A Little Catechism.* Choose one or more of the selections below for memory work or reinforcement. You will find your copy of the catechism on pages 23–43 of this Teacher's Edition.

1. Read to the children the two introductory sentences from page 22, "More about the Mass." Now read the first three items about the Mass—but allow the children to complete each sentence verbally.
2. Ask the children to open their books to page 22. Read and reread the next three items with them until they can complete each sentence by heart. Remember to make this fun!

Know Love Serve

Note The activities on this page provide ways for the children to share their learning with their families. The activities are related to the week's theme.

1 Introduce

Have the children read the letter aloud. They may then read the activities silently, and share ways they think they will do the activities with their families.

2 Pray Together

Recall that the words in the prayer burst are said at Mass. Stand and say or sing the words together. If you sing the acclimation, do so three times.

Online for Families
Remind the children to check the Benziger Web site this week with their families.
www.benziger.glencoe.com

Dear Family,

I have just finished chapter 19. I have learned that at Mass I remember Jesus in a special way. The gifts of bread and wine become Jesus' Body and Blood.

With others

Ask a grandparent or an older friend to help you learn some of the prayers that you say at Mass. Maybe you can learn the "Holy, Holy, Holy." This is a joyful prayer that praises God.

With your family

Remembering is important in families. Remembering helps bring people together. Ask your family to tell you some of your favorite family stories.

Christ has died. Christ is risen. Christ will come again.

GO ONLINE!
http://www.benziger.glencoe.com

1 Introduce
Gather the children for story time. Read the story "Stone Soup" by Marcia Brown. Tell the children that when people come together to work together, good things can happen. Ask them to recall how that happened in the story. Introduce the word *unity.* Tell the children that they will be putting together the ingredients to make a special stew.

2 The Project
Talk about all the flavors that come together to make a good stew (vegetables, spices, meat). Each ingredient has its own taste, but together they combine to make one great taste! The same is true in the world. We all have our own special gifts and talents. When we put all of our gifts together, we can make a world of peace and harmony.

THE CHURCH TODAY

The Eucharist brings God's people together to receive the gift of Jesus. In return, Jesus wants you to live with others in peace and unity.

Make some unity stew.
What are the ingredients for unity stew?
What are the things that bring people together?
Write them in the pot.

Get ready to bring all the ingredients together to make one great stew!

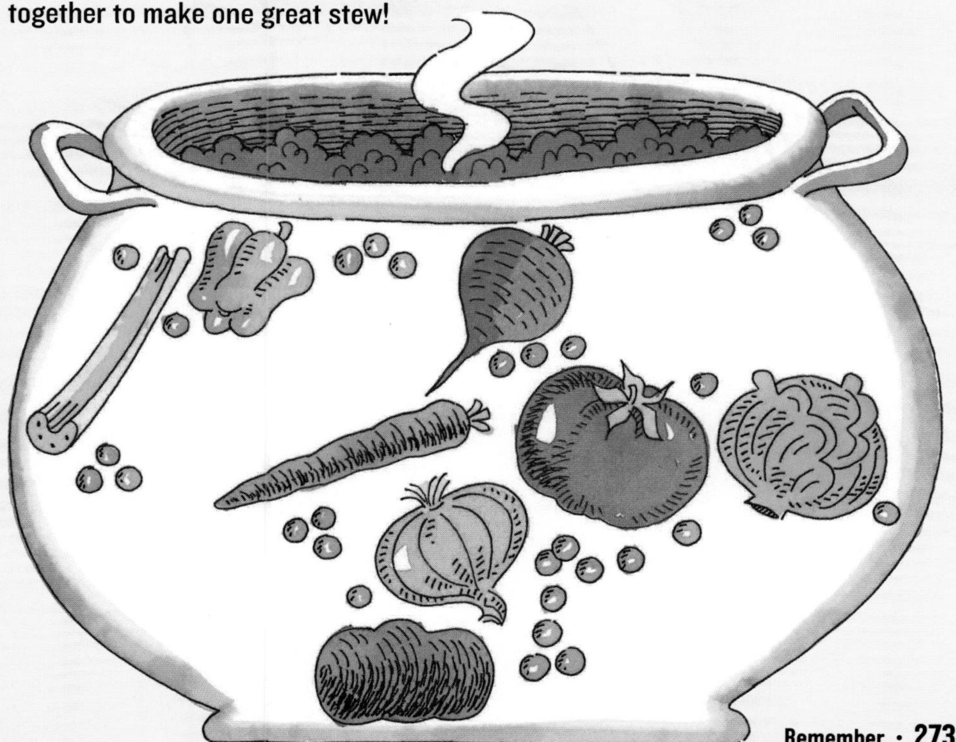

ANSWER KEY

This is the answer key for the chapter test on page 403.

A. followers; bread; wine; body; blood; memory; me; shared; blessed; Jesus

Name ______________________________

I Offer Myself

At Mass, we give gifts to God. You can give yourself. You can do good things that show you love God.

Circle what you will offer. Color the picture.

Say the prayers

Sing the songs

Give thanks to God

Listen carefully

Show respect

Do the actions

Name ______________________________

Chapter 19 Test

A. Show how Jesus is remembered at Mass. Use the words from the box.

bread /	Jesus /	wine /	memory /	blessed
me /	shared /	followers /	body /	blood

Jesus shared his Last Supper with his ______________.
He blessed ______________, broke it, and shared it. He took ______________, blessed it, and shared it. He said that the bread was his ______________ and the wine was his ______________. He told his friends, "Do this in ______________ of ______________."

The Last Supper is remembered at Mass. The preist says the words of Jesus. At Mass the bread is blessed, broken, and ______________. The wine is ______________ and shared. The bread and wine become ______________.

TEACHER RESOURCE CENTER

Faith Formation

CHECK THE CATECHISM

In paragraph 1324, the *Catechism of the Catholic Church* quotes the Vatican II document *Lumen Gentium,* describing Eucharist as "the source and summit of the Christian life." For further insight, see paragraphs 1328–1344.

At Supper with Jesus

The cup of blessing that we bless, is it not a participation in the blood of Christ? The bread that we break, is it not a participation in the Body of Christ? Because the loaf of bread is one, we, though many, are one body, for we all partake of the one loaf.

1 Corinthians 10:16–17

The Eucharistic Prayers of the Mass include the invitation to believers from Jesus to take and eat and become one with his Body. Jesus invited his friends to be united with him in Holy Communion. This is a profound invitation. However it is also a challenging invitation because it implies change and transformation of communities and individuals. In the letter to the Corinthians, Paul is not expounding piety as he uses the image of one loaf. No, he is challenging the community at Corinth to take a look at some of the behaviors and attitudes that they are developing. Communion is food for the journey. It nourishes us for mission. It strengthens us to do the deeds and preach the words of Christ.

How does the Eucharist nourish you?

I Do Believe

When they receive Holy Communion, Catholics respond to the statement, "The Body (or Blood) of Christ" with a clear "Amen", meaning, "Yes, I do believe." Jesus' very life is present in both or either the consecrated bread and the consecrated wine. This official Church doctrine is central to the faith of Catholics, and is a continuing source of joy, comfort, and hope.

When you receive the Eucharist, what does your "Amen" mean for your day-to-day life?

Background

A Generous Heart

Chapter 20 continues the explanation of the Liturgy of the Eucharist, from the Lord's Prayer through the reception of Holy Communion. The chapter's theme is sharing.

The children will enjoy the story of Even Steven, especially his dilemma about giving away the bigger piece. Most second graders do not like the thought of giving away the bigger piece. Learning to share comes gradually. Generous hearts are grown and nurtured by other generous hearts. Children learn to share by observing others share and by being the recipients of generosity.

Children do not need theological discourses on the Eucharist. They will intuitively understand the gift of Jesus sharing himself with them through his life and death and in Holy Communion. They will also comprehend what a gift that is.

Faith Summary

- The Eucharist unites us with Jesus.
- The Mass is a meal in which we share the Body and Blood of Jesus.
- In Eucharist Jesus shares himself, soul and divinity.

Growth and Development

It is helpful to remember two characteristics of second graders as you teach this lesson:

- ***Second graders are learning to share.*** This is perhaps the single most important task in becoming mature human beings. As you teach the chapter, you can help them grow into more loving persons.
- ***Second graders thrive in an environment of sharing.*** They respond to kindness by becoming kind. Make your classroom a laboratory for practicing this virtue on a daily basis.

A Teacher's Prayer

Loving Lord, you are eager to share your life with the children and with me. Bless me with a generous heart like yours. Let me give of myself so that the children experience your generosity. Bless them with generous hearts, too. Help us all to understand that generosity helps build your kingdom on earth. Amen.

Vocabulary Preview

Holy Communion
Communion

Scripture

1 Corinthians 11:26: I am with you.
John 6:33: bread from heaven

Related Resources

Video

"The Table of the Lord" (St. Anthony Messenger Press, 1-800-488-0488 or www.AmericanCatholic.org). This series of four videos helps prepare young students and their parents for the child's First Eucharist. (Children, 20 minutes each)

Books

Luebering, Carol. "First Communion: Joining the Family Table," (*Catholic Update,* St. Anthony Messenger Press, 1-800-488-0488 or www.AmericanCatholic.org). A good four-page explanation of First Communion. (Adults)

"We Say Thanks: A Young Child's Book for Eucharist" (St. Anthony Messenger Press, 1-800-488-0488 or www.AmericanCatholic.org). This book explains the parts of the Mass in simple language. (Children)

TEACHER ORGANIZER

Planning Guide

The basic content for each chapter is divided into four class sessions. There are a number of options for the fifth session. Extension, review, and testing options are described under Day 5 Alternatives. The Quick Check box will help you evaluate the week's lessons.

Chapter Goals

In this chapter, the students will learn about

- ❑ Jesus, the Bread of Life
- ❑ Holy Communion
- ❑ Receiving Holy Communion

	DAY 1 · INVITATION	DAY 2 · DISCOVERY	DAY 3 · DISCOVERY
OBJECTIVES	**The students will be able to** • Discover the importance of sharing • Associate sharing with a generous heart	**The students will be able to** • Call Jesus the Bread of Life • Find meaning in a Bible story	**The students will be able to** • Discover how to prepare at Mass to receive Jesus • Share a sign of peace • Show how to receive the host and cup
PREPARATION	• Make a large question mark that reads: What is very special about this week?	• Prepare copies of the resource master on page 420	• If possible, invite older children to speak about their experience of the Eucharist • Invite eucharistic minister from parish or other adult volunteer to assist
MATERIALS	• Platter of graham crackers to be shared • Paper, pencils or markers	• A variety of breads and bread products • Pencils or highlighters • Copies of the resource master plus art materials	• Unconsecrated hosts, grape juice, plate, cup, small cloth • Paper, pencils
OPTIONAL ACTIVITIES	• **Ideas That Work** Make Y and N signs to talk about sharing • **Options** Generate list of things to share at school	• **Resource Masters** Solve a word puzzle	• **Ideas That Work** Practice receiving the Eucharist • **Vocabulary** Write some thoughts using religious vocabulary words

Learning Objectives

By the end of this chapter, the students should be able to

- ❑ Discover a basic understanding of Jesus as the Bread of Life
- ❑ Discuss ways to prepare for Communion
- ❑ Identify the different ways to receive Holy Communion

DAY 4 • LIVING

The students will be able to

- Determine the roles of those who help them prepare for Holy Communion
- Give thanks to Jesus
- Identify actions that show Communion is a holy time

- Pencils
- Candle and matches, if allowed
- Cassette or CD of Communion hymns
- Crayons, markers, paper

- **Teaching Tip** Act out reverential responses
- **Curriculum Challenge** Draw host and cup, write reflections

DAY 5 • ALTERNATIVES

There are a number of alternatives to help you plan Day 5.

Prayer Experience
You may do the A Quiet Time prayer experience on either Day 4 or Day 5. Play some soft music and, if allowed, light a candle during silent prayer.

Review and Explore
The students need pencils to do the activities. If you wish, look through a diocesan newspaper for a picture of the present pope.

Home and Family
Send the page home or assign one or more of the activities as class work or homework.

The Church Today
The students learn the signs of Eucharist and use them in creating a Eucharistic banner. Decide how to organize the activity. Use whatever supplies are available, including a means for displaying the banner.

Chapter Test
The chapter test appears as a resource master on page 421.

Quick Check

Do this evaluation as soon as you finish each chapter.

Did I follow my lesson plan?

How can I tell that I met the learning objectives for the lesson?

What activities did the children enjoy most?

How could I improve this lesson?

Benziger on the Web
For more ideas, visit us at **www.benziger.glencoe.com**

Interactive Lesson Planner
Your ILP provides more help in preparing to teach this chapter.

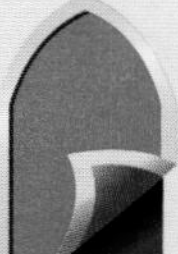

Celebrate
Turn to page 22 of this book. Check for seasonal celebrations.

Lesson Plan · Day 1

Display a sign of a big question mark that reads something like this: What is very special about this week?

1 Share

Call attention to the title and ask for suggestions as to how it connects to the Mass. Give special significance to the words of Jesus and then, ask all to read them aloud. Now, pass around a platter of graham crackers (the kind that can be broken into sections). Be sure there are not enough crackers for everyone.

When the children notice that more crackers are needed, say that there are not anymore. Ask what should be done. When the children suggest sharing, affirm them. Say that they are ready for the special week. They are ready to learn about Holy Communion, a time when Jesus shares himself.

TEACHING TIP

Religion lessons give endless opportunities to ask questions. Here are some reasons why asking questions is a powerful teaching tool:

- Questions stimulate thinking.
- They give valuable information.
- They get children to open up.
- They lead to focused listening.

Always be open to the asking of questions. Asking questions puts children in control and helps them persuade themselves.

Whenever you eat this bread and drink this cup, I will be with you.

From *1 Corinthians 11:26*

Do You Know?

- What do you receive in Holy Communion?

Share

Even Steven

Hi! My name is Steven. My parents are always telling me to share. They always say, "Be *even*, Steven." I don't always like to share.

My dad says that sharing is the most important thing. He says that when things aren't even, I should give the bigger part away. That doesn't sound very even to me.

2 Even Steven
Ask the children what they know about sharing. Prepare the children to listen for what Even Steven was taught about sharing. Read the story. Ask the children whether they agree with Steven's dad that sharing is important. Ask the children whether they agree with Steven that sharing can be hard.

3 Should I?
Focus the children to listen for the message about sharing. Read the poem with a sense of delight. Share your own answers to the questions, then, ask the children to share with a partner. Ask the children whether it's easier to share with some people than with others.

4 Activity
Explain that the activity is a good way to see how to be better. Let the children fill in the chart privately and independently. Let them see you do the chart in your book. You may want to talk a little about good things that can be shared that are not seen or touched. *(love, care, happiness)*

Should I?

I should, I shouldn't
Sometimes it's hard,
To share the things I want to guard.
But way down deep inside I know,
That when I share, in love I grow.

- What things are easy to share?
- What things are harder to share?

Put an X in the square that best tells how well you share.

What to Share	Great	So-So	Badly
A Treat	☐	☐	☐
A New Toy	☐	☐	☐
Happy Story	☐	☐	☐
Bad mood	☐	☐	☐

IDEAS THAT WORK

Engage all of the children in answering the questions in a quick and simple way. Have the children tear a sheet of paper in half and write an *N*, for no, on one piece and a *Y*, for yes, on the other.

OPTIONS

For Those with Verbal Abilities Ask these children to make a list of things that can be shared at school. Challenge them to think broadly—pencils, smiles, happiness can all be shared. Ask the group to make the list as long as they can.

Lesson Plan · Day 2

Pose a riddle: I am a food that is eaten by people all around the world. I come in different shapes. I smell good. What am I? *(bread)*

Show the breads you brought or have the children talk about different types of bread they eat. See how many eat some form of bread every day. Make a list on the chalkboard of the good things about bread.

1 Prepare

Recall that we can share many things, things we can see and things we cannot see also. Say that Jesus promised to share a very special gift—himself! Jesus promised to share himself as food. Jesus gives himself as Bread in the Eucharist. This Bread is not like any other bread in the whole world.

TEACHING TIP

Use the pictures in the story to help the children note that the people chose to walk away from Jesus.

Read up to Person 3
Ask: How did Jesus help the hungry people? Circle the sentence that tells a different kind of food people need.

Read up to Person 1 What is God's work? What do people have to do to get life from God? What do we call God's life in us (grace)?

Read up to Person 4 Will people have to eat Jesus? Circle the words that explain the Bread of Life. Say that being happy with God forever is called heaven.

RESOURCE MASTERS

The resource master on page 420 is a quick word game that reviews beliefs about Holy Communion.

Jesus Makes a Promise

Jesus promised to share a very special gift—himself! People receive Jesus, the Bread of Life, at Mass.

Act out this play about the Bread of Life.

SPEAKER: After Jesus fed all of the people with the five loaves and two fish, he went away. People looked for Jesus.

PEOPLE: Let's go find Jesus.

PERSON 1: Look, there he is!

JESUS: You are looking for me because I fed you when you were hungry. But you need another kind of food.

PERSON 2: What kind of food do we need?

JESUS: You need food from God. This food lasts forever. If you do God's work, you will have this kind of food.

PERSON 3: What is God's work?

JESUS: You do God's work when you believe in me. Believe in me and you will receive bread from heaven. This bread gives life to the world.

PERSON 4: Please, give us this bread.

② Jesus Makes a Promise

Gather the children with their books and pencils or highlighters. Direct attention to student page 276 and have the children circle the words Bread of Life. Say that this is a name Jesus gives himself. The children will read a play that explains why Jesus is the Bread of Life.

Have the children do guided reading of the play, circling or highlighting while they read. (See Teaching Tip.) Choose children to read the parts; have all read aloud the words of Jesus. Briefly tell about the time Jesus fed a large crowd of people, and then, read.

Ask the children why the people left Jesus. What was too hard for them to do? *(believe in God, live God's way)* Tell them that they will soon become one with Jesus when they receive Jesus in Holy Communion. Holy Communion is also called Eucharist.

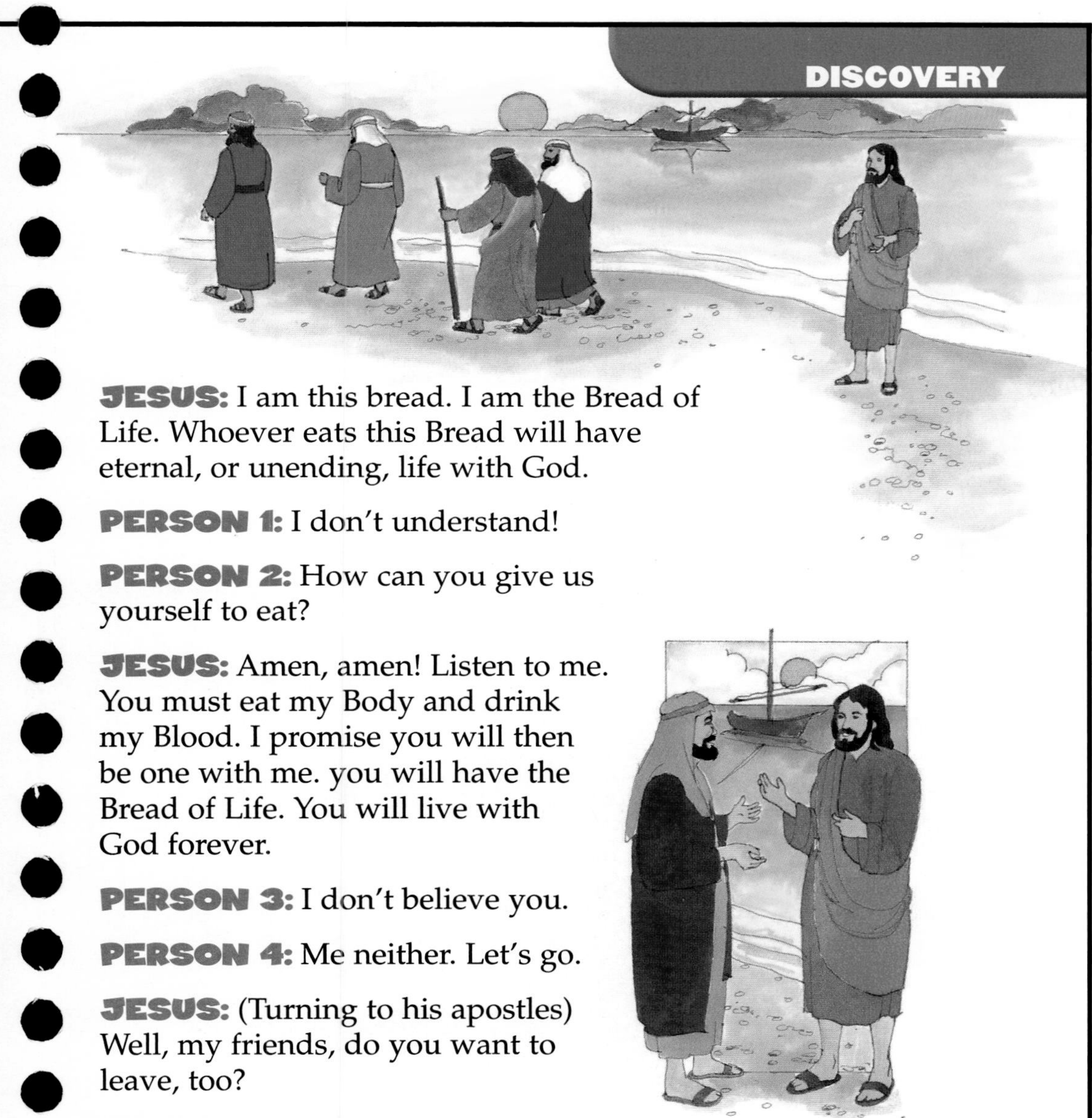

JESUS: I am this bread. I am the Bread of Life. Whoever eats this Bread will have eternal, or unending, life with God.

PERSON 1: I don't understand!

PERSON 2: How can you give us yourself to eat?

JESUS: Amen, amen! Listen to me. You must eat my Body and drink my Blood. I promise you will then be one with me. you will have the Bread of Life. You will live with God forever.

PERSON 3: I don't believe you.

PERSON 4: Me neither. Let's go.

JESUS: (Turning to his apostles) Well, my friends, do you want to leave, too?

PETER: Where would we go? You are the Christ, the Holy One sent by God. We believe in you.

Based on *John 6:24–69*

Lesson Plan · Day 3

If possible, invite older children as guest speakers to talk about their First Holy Communion.

1 Prepare

Recall that we can share many things. Say that Jesus promised to share a very special gift—himself! Jesus promised to share himself as food. Jesus gives himself as Bread in the Eucharist. This Bread is not like any other bread in the whole world.

2 Holy Communion

Remind the children that at Mass the bread and wine become the Body and Blood of Jesus. Read the first two paragraphs in the student text aloud to the children. Then tell the children they are going to do two things that we do at Mass to prepare to receive Jesus.

IDEAS THAT WORK

Make an aisle in the room that leads to the altar. Portray the priest yourself. If possible, ask a Eucharistic minister to serve the cup. Have unconsecrated hosts or flat candies on hand, along with a handsome cup with grape juice, and a beautiful cloth for wiping the cup.

OPTIONS

Have copies available of *The Lord's Prayer* by Tim Ladwig, *I Can Pray to Jesus!* by Debbie Trafton O'Neal, or *The Tortilla Factory* by Gary Paulsen (also available as La Tortilleria)

WORD OF GOD

I will give you bread from heaven to eat.

John 6:33

Holy Communion

Jesus shared a special meal with his friends. It was the Last Supper. During Holy Communion everyone shares the Body and Blood of Jesus.

To get ready to receive Jesus, you stand and say the prayer Jesus taught his followers. You say the Lord's Prayer as part of the family of God.

The priest then prays that God will give all his people peace. You turn to the people around you and share a sign of peace.

How do the Lord's Prayer and the sign of peace prepare you to receive Jesus?

Ask the children to stand and join hands and say or sing the Our Father. Use gestures (either hold hands or invite the children to extend their hands out with palms up). Then enact the Sign of Peace with them.

Conclude by asking: "How do these prayers prepare you to receive Communion?

3 Receiving Jesus

Read the material on student page 153. Expand on the two ways that the children can receive the host. See Ideas That Work for tips on how to enact the ritual.

4 Activity

The children draw the cross on the host. Ask the children why they think the host has a cross on it. Read together the This We Believe! feature.

Read aloud the Do You Know? question. At the end of the week, come back to the question to see how the children's knowledge has developed.

Receiving Jesus

At Holy Communion you are ready to receive Jesus. The word **Communion** means "one with."

You can receive the host in your hand or on your tongue. The priest or minister says, "The Body of Christ." You say, "Amen." You may be offered the cup. The priest or minister says, "The Blood of Christ." You say, "Amen."

You return to your seat. You can say a thank-you prayer.

Jesus is truly present in Holy Communion. Receiving Jesus makes us one with him and with the Church.

ACTIVITY IN YOUR HANDS

The hands are ready to receive Jesus. Draw a host in the hand. Put a cross on the host.

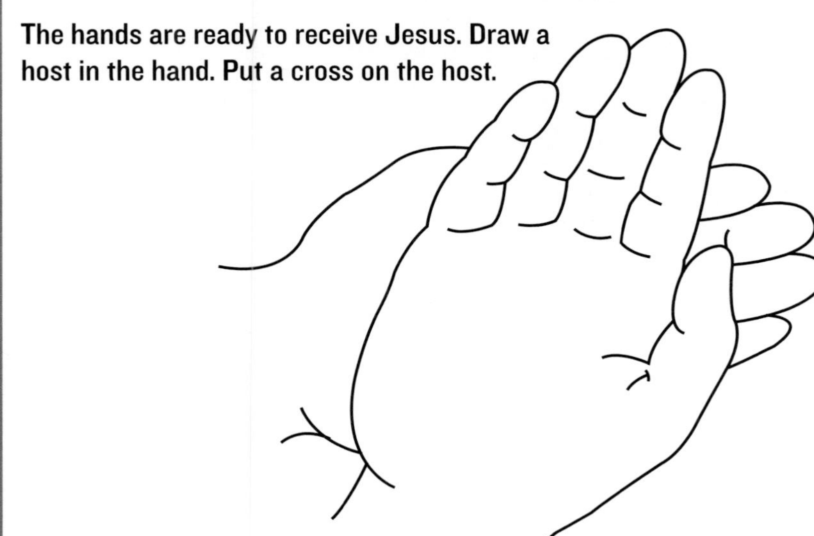

TEACHING TIP

You may wish to practice both in the classroom and also at church. Have each child practice how to approach the priest and how to respond. In receiving the host, show the placement of hands and the extension of the tongue. Explain how to step aside and chew the host. Show how to sip from the cup. Show the reverential way to return to the pew.

VOCABULARY

Communion Holy Communion you become one with Jesus and one with God's Family.

Holy Communion Receiving Jesus' Body and Blood in the form of bread and wine.

The children have learned a lot of religious vocabulary words. Ask the children to write some facts or words about Eucharist that they are proud to know.

Lesson Plan · Day 4

Direct attention to the photos and say that because receiving Holy Communion is such an important time, there are people who help you prepare. Ask volunteers to share their personal experiences with helpers.

1 Helpers

Ask the children to think about the ways they may need to prepare for Holy Communion. *(learn prayers, learn procedures and gestures)* Ask the children to imagine how each person in the pictures is being a helper. Ask the children to identify the people that will be helping them prepare for this important event.

TEACHING TIP

Have the children share their responses regarding Communion as a holy time by acting them out. This will be good practice for developing a reverential attitude in church.

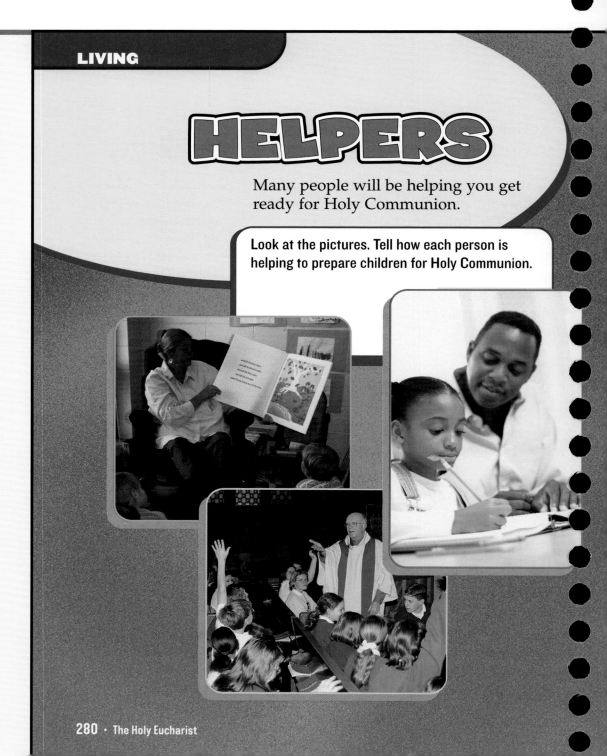

HELPERS

Many people will be helping you get ready for Holy Communion.

Look at the pictures. Tell how each person is helping to prepare children for Holy Communion.

2 A Holy Time
Direct attention to student page 281 and ask the children to fill in the lines in the first part. After some sharing of responses, ask the children to think about the ways they will show that Communion is a holy time. Share responses again.

A HOLY TIME

Write your own ideas.
How do you know that receiving Jesus is a holy time?

- People fold their hands.
- People walk in a line.
- People look straight ahead, at the priest.
- ______________________________

How do you show that Communion is a holy time?

- ______________________________

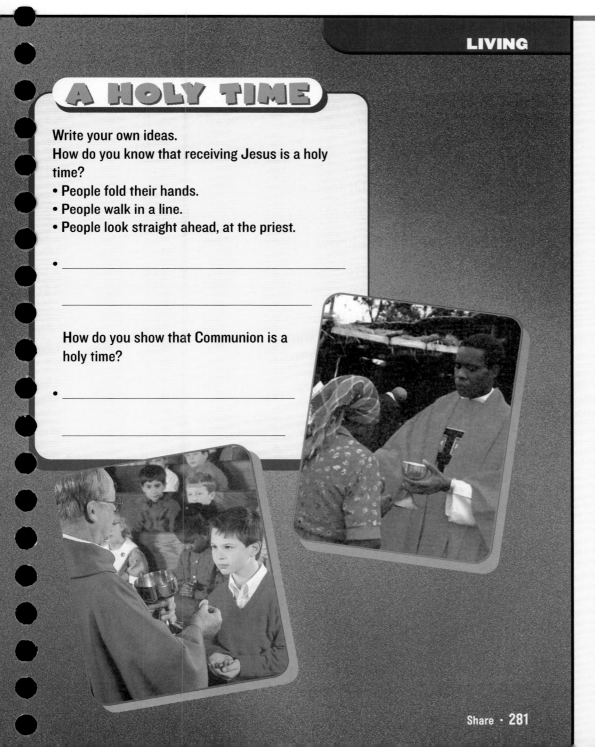

IDEAS THAT WORK

Familiarize the children with hymns for Communion time by playing some as background music while they do student page 281.

CURRICULUM CHALLENGE

Language Arts You may wish to have the children draw a large host and a large cup on plain paper. They can use the shapes to write their thoughts about Holy Communion.

Prayer
Tell the children that when they go to Mass and receive Holy Communion they celebrate the sacrament of Eucharist. The word Eucharist means "thanksgiving." After receiving Jesus you spend some quiet time in thanksgiving.

1 Prepare
Gather the children on a rug or in the prayer area. Play some quiet background music and light a candle, if permitted.

2 A Quiet Time
Let the children get comfortable and spend some quiet minutes praying to Jesus. Then, ask the children to quietly pray the prayer on the page.

LEARNING TO PRAY

If you have not done so, this is a good time to introduce the children to prayers of thanksgiving. Once children are in the habit of saying thanks in their prayers, they will find even after the most boring and difficult days, there is almost always something to be thankful for.

A QUIET TIME

Dear Jesus,

Thank you for being with me.

I know you are with me.

Help me to see you in the people who love me.

Help me to go in peace to love and serve you so that others will know you through my actions.

Amen.

1 Know
Have the children look at the graphic organizer and read the summary statements aloud. Ask how the Lord's Prayer and the sign of peace help people prepare to receive Jesus.

2 Love and Serve
Love: Ask the children to be sure to circle an action they can do and will do. Serve: First, talk about gifts people have. Without using names, you can mention some gifts you have noticed in the children. After the activity is completed have the children stand and give themselves a cheer.

3 God's Friends
Give a brief introduction to popes. Write the name of the present day pope. Show the illustration of Pope Pius X and share the information about him.

Know

Holy Communion

You gather at the altar with your parish family.
You share the Body and Blood of Jesus.

Love

Write one way that you will remember that Jesus is always with you.

____

Serve

Jesus shared a special gift. What gift of yourself can you share with others?

____

CHAPTER 20 REVIEW and EXPLORE

GOD'S FRIENDS

Pope Pius X

Pope Pius knew how much Jesus loves children. And he knew that children love Jesus, too. Pope Pius X said that people should receive Jesus often. Children can receive Jesus, too.

A Little Catechism

Invite the children to open their religion books to *A Little Catechism.* Choose one or more of the selections below for memory work or reinforcement. You will find your copy of the catechism on pages 23–43 of this Teacher's Edition.

1. Ask the children to turn to Important Questions on student page 12. Tell them this section is about the most important questions they can ask.
2. Call their attention to questions 12, 13 and 14 on student page 13. Have the children repeat these questions and answers about the Eucharist until they know them by heart.

Know Love Serve

Note The activities on this page provide ways for the children to share their learning with their families. The activities are related to the week's theme.

1 Introduce
Explain the activities. Have volunteers tell whom they may ask to help them practice receiving Communion.

2 Pray Together
Say the prayer in the prayer burst together. Suggest that the children quietly say the prayer while they walk to the priest to receive Jesus.

Online for Families
Remind the children to check the Benziger Web site this week with their families.
www.benziger.glencoe.com

Dear Family,

I have just completed chapter 20. I have learned that Jesus shares a special gift with me. Jesus shares the gift of his Body and Blood through Holy Communion. You can help by reminding me to bring the gift of myself to Mass.

With others

Ask someone to help you practice receiving Communion. What will you say after the priest says, "The Body of Christ."?

With your family

Talk about the gift that each member of the family can offer to God on Sunday. How will they share that gift with others during the week?

Come to us, Lord Jesus, so that we may be more like you.

GO ONLINE!
http://www.benziger.glencoe.com

1 Discuss
Review the Last Supper. Include the words of Jesus, too. Share the introductory information on the page.

2 Project
A banner will be a beautiful announcement of the important event the children are preparing for. Plan the making of the banner so that all children have a part to play.

3 Pray
Conclude this session by inviting the children to repeat these words: Thank You, God, for Jesus, the Bread of Life.

THE CHURCH TODAY

Think about the Last Supper. What did Jesus offer to his Apostles? The Church uses bread and grapes as signs of the Eucharist. These signs decorate altar cloths and banners. Sometimes, you see the signs on the clothing the priest wears to say Mass.

A Holy Communion Banner

Make a holy communion banner for your classroom. You can use pieces of cloth. Use the cloth to make the signs of the Eucharist. You can use colored paper or glitter.

Hang the banner outside your classroom.

Everyone will know that Jesus will be sharing a special gift with you.

TEACHING TIP

Plan the banner-making project so that it best suits the circumstances of your class. The size and details involved should depend on how you will get everyone involved. If you wish, the children can work in groups, one at a time, while other independent activity is going on.

ANSWER KEY

This is the answer key for the chapter test on page 421.

A. 1. a 2. a 3. b

B. 1. amen 2. hand 3. tongue 4. Christ 5. amen 6. hands 7. Jesus

Name ____

Receiving Jesus

Read each sentence.

Put the boxed letter on the line for that sentence.

What word did you spell?

___	___	___	___	___	___	___	___	___
1	**2**	**3**	**4**	**5**	**6**	**7**	**8**	**9**

1. It gives gra[c]e.

2. It means [o]ne with.

3. It is a sacra[m]ent.

4. It is a holy [m]eal.

5. It joins o[u]r Catholic family together.

6. It is a celebratio[n].

7. It uses bread and w[i]ne.

8. It is the B[o]dy and Blood of Jesus.

9. It joins us in the death and resurrectio[n] of Jesus.

Name ______________________________

Chapter 20 Test

A. Circle the answer that best finishes each sentence.

1. You become one with Jesus when you receive him in
a. Holy Communion.
b. Reconciliation.

2. Jesus called himself
a. the Bread of Life.
b. the follower of the Lord.

3. Before you receive Jesus, you share
a. an Act of Contrition.
b. a sign of peace.

B. Write how to receive Holy Communion.

The priest holds the host and says, "Body of Christ."

1. You say, "____________________."

2. You take the host in your ____________________

3. or on your ____________________.

The priest or minister holds the cup of wine.

4. The person says, "Blood of ____________________."

5. You say, "____________________."

You take a sip.

6. You fold your ____________________ and walk back to your pew.

7. There you talk to ____________________.

UNIT 5 REVIEW

Strategies for Review

The purpose of the Unit Review is to reinforce concepts presented in this unit. You may wish to assign the Remember and Answer sections for homework. Review these sections with the students so that you can answer any questions they may have. Students may work independently, in small groups, or as a class. Use the method that works best with your group.

1 Remember

Put the names of the students in a hat. Draw the name of one child. Have that child read the statement. Draw another child's name. Ask that child to state or explain the concept in his or her own words.

2 Answer

Divide the class into small groups. Ask each group to decide which answers are correct. Then ask each group to think of *another* correct answer for each question. *(Possible answers: 1. Singing, praying with others 2. with love and respect, as you would listen to Jesus 3. his life, his love)* Invite each group to share its answers with the class.

Unit 5 REVIEW

Remember!

1. At Sunday Mass, Catholics gather to worship, celebrate, and remember.
2. God's Word is the story of God's love for you.
3. The Eucharist is a way to remember Jesus.
4. Jesus shares the gift of himself at Holy Communion.
5. Everyone at Mass has a part to play.

Answer!

Circle the best answer.

1. How do you worship at Mass?
   a. by not paying attention
   b. with words and actions
2. How should you listen to the Word of God?
   a. by thinking about dinner
   b. with an open heart
3. What does Jesus share with you at Holy Communion?
   a. his Body and Blood
   b. his shoes

Do!

When you sing and pray at Mass, it shows that you belong.
Tell about the things that people do at Mass.
How do they show that they belong to God's Family?

3 Do

Have the students remain in their small groups. Ask each group to act out something people do at Mass. After the class identifies a group's action, talk about how this action shows that the students belong to God's Family.

4 Share

Read the text and have the children complete the thank-you sentence. Suggest that they use bright markers to color each space that has a dot. Hang the completed pictures in your prayer area. Gather to pray a class litany using the prayers the children wrote.

Share!

Saying Amen is a way to say that you are part of God's Family.
Take turns completing this sentence:
"Thank you God for ____________."
Everyone answer "Amen!"
Color each space that has a dot.
What word do you see?

ANSWER KEY

Answer

1. b
2. b
3. a

Unit 6

Never give up, follow the Holy Spirit, and serve the Lord.

Romans 12:11

Chapter

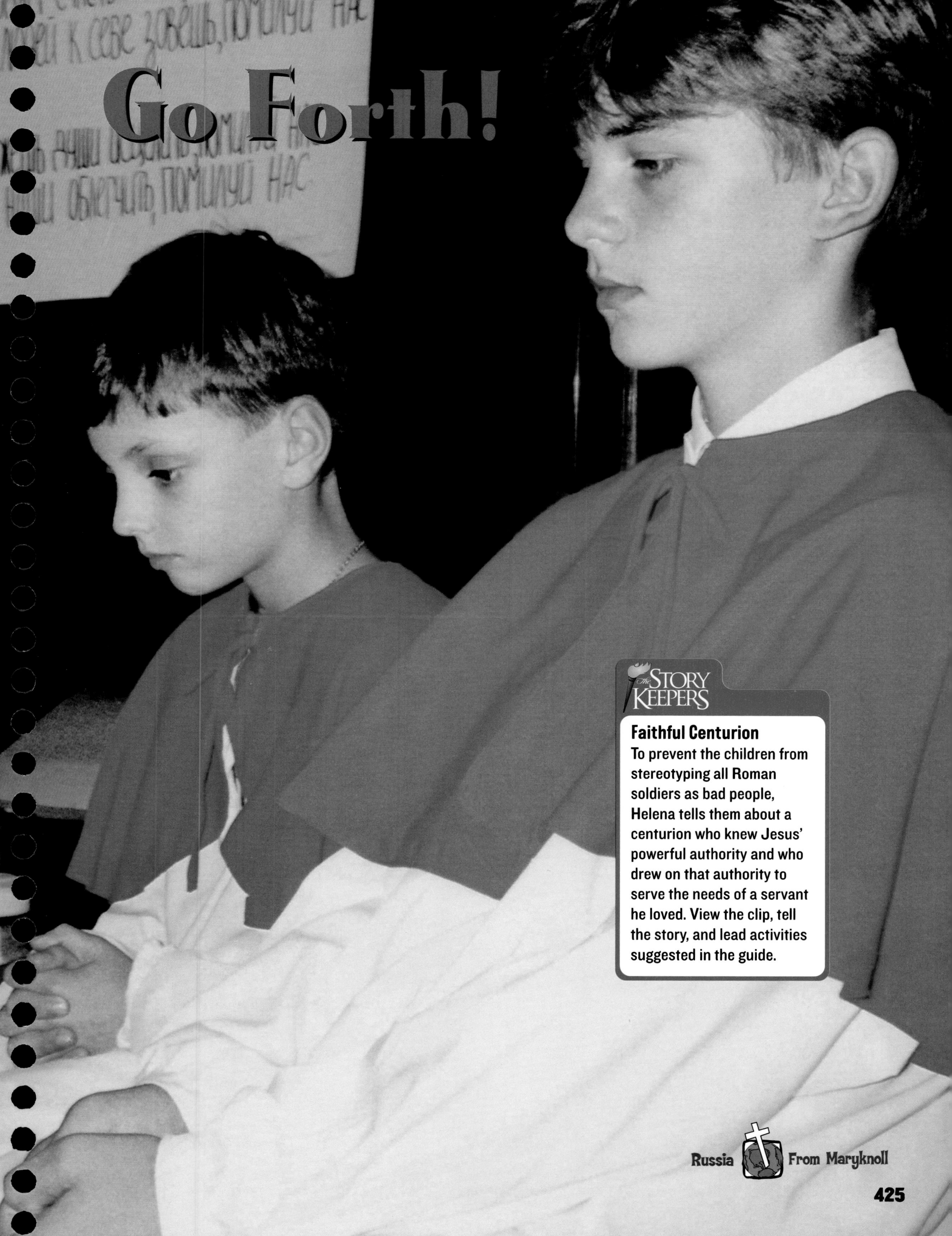

Go Forth!

The STORY KEEPERS

Faithful Centurion

To prevent the children from stereotyping all Roman soldiers as bad people, Helena tells them about a centurion who knew Jesus' powerful authority and who drew on that authority to serve the needs of a servant he loved. View the clip, tell the story, and lead activities suggested in the guide.

CHAPTER 21 One Family

TEACHER RESOURCE CENTER

Faith Formation

CHECK THE CATECHISM

Paragraphs 849–860 of the *Catechism of the Catholic Church* explore the Church's summons to proclaim the Word to the entire world. These paragraphs discuss the origin, purpose, and motivation for the missionary work of the apostolic Church.

Go and Tell

Jesus sent out these twelve after instructing them thus, "Do not go into pagan territory or enter a Samaritan town. Go rather to the sheep of the house of Israel. As you go, make this proclamation: 'The kingdom of heaven is at hand.'"

Matthew 10:5–7

How do your words and actions proclaim that the kingdom of heaven is at hand?

Beginning Here, Now

When Jesus commissioned the Twelve, he did not just fling them out to the four winds. He asked them to travel light, to stay with the local population, to proclaim that the kingdom was near to hand, and to spread peace. As we know, the presence and message of the Twelve spread eventually to the very ends of the earth, transcending mountains and crossing oceans. The message of salvation was so attractive and so compelling, there was no need for doodads and techniques and bells and whistles. You are those apostles today. You are sent to carry the same Good News. You are among those faith-filled, hopeful, and loving persons who today stand for the Good News of God's saving presence in one specific place and time—a second grade classroom in the dawning years of a new millennium.

In what ways does your joy in service to the kingdom of heaven offer powerful witness to your children?

Background

Teaching about One Family

Second graders imitate what they consistently see and hear. How wonderful, then, when the words they hear match the actions they see. Missionary activity is not merely a proclamation; it is a way of life. The witness of honorable, loving, faith-filled people must accompany any proclamation of Good News. Without this witness, words are lifeless and powerless. This chapter explores the power of Christian witness in the person of missionaries who bring Good News, peace, and unity. The children will learn about those who are sent forth, of their message, and of their example. They will learn how they too can participate in the missionary work of the Church by helping those who are sent and by being good witnesses right where they are.

Faith Summary

- **All baptized Catholics are called to share in the missionary work of the Church.**
- **By their presence and words, missionaries proclaim the Good News.**
- **Helping the poor and needy is essential work of missionaries.**

Growth and Development

It is helpful to remember two characteristics of second graders as you teach this lesson:

- ***Second graders want to help.*** Young children are empathetic. Their generosity outstrips their capability to help. They need appropriate, supervised experiences in serving others.
- ***Second graders want to belong.*** Make a special effort to include the shy child. Find a way to include the child whose behavior seems anti-social. Keep in mind that this child needs help learning appropriate ways to work with others.

A Teacher's Prayer

Risen Lord, you are our Good News. We pray that our actions and words are Good News for one another. May the simple faith of these children enliven my faith. May my faith be a strong witness to them. May we merrily work and pray together, and may our classroom resemble a little, low heaven—just for now. Amen.

Vocabulary Preview

missionaries

Scripture

Luke 5:11: The Twelve are commissioned.

Related Resources

Books

Hest, Amy. *When Jessie Came Across the Sea* (Candlewick Press, 1997). This story of a child coming to a new land can help the children appreciate the challenging adjustments people such as immigrants and missionaries face. (Children)

Dulles, Avery. *Models of the Church: Expanded Edition* (Doubleday, New York, 1987). See specifically chapter 5, "The Church as Herald," which discusses proclaiming the Word. For a complete view of these models, see also chapter 12, "The Evaluation of Models." (Adult)

TEACHER ORGANIZER

Planning Guide

The basic content for each chapter is divided into four class sessions. There are a number of options for the fifth session. Extension, review, and testing options are described under Day 5 Alternatives. The Quick Check box will help you evaluate the week's lessons.

Chapter Goals

In this chapter, the students will learn about

- ❑ Their call to share in the missionary work of the Church
- ❑ The ways missionaries proclaim the Good News
- ❑ Helping the needy and poor as an essential work of missionaries

	DAY 1 · INVITATION	DAY 2 · DISCOVERY	DAY 3 · DISCOVERY
OBJECTIVES	**The students will be able to** • Define the word ***missionary*** • Identify the work of missionaries	**The students will be able to** • Describe the ways missionaries do God's work • Trace the Gospel and the Eucharist to the first disciples	**The students will be able to** • Describe the ways missionaries do God's work today • Identify ways they can care for others
PREPARATION	• Get addresses of missioners • Gather arts and crafts from local church missioners • Get a book of saints • Gather instruments and recordings of worldwide music	• Preview adapting "Go Tell It on the Mountain" • Practice telling a story based on Acts	• Gather props • Make up riddles as examples
MATERIALS	• Paper, pencils • Anthology of saints • Recordings and player • Arts and crafts from local church missioners	• Writing materials • Bible • Crayons • Sheet music or recording and player	• Writing materials • Bibles • Props
OPTIONAL ACTIVITIES	• **Options** Write a class letter • **Ideas That Work** Research and report on Saint Therese of Lisieux • **Curriculum Challenge** Learn about music of many lands • **Ideas That Work** Learn about missioners' arts and crafts	• **Options** Adapt lyrics of a spiritual • **Bible Basics** Retell a story from Acts • **Teaching Tip** Relate disciples' experiences to the Eucharist	• **Bible Basics** Dramatize Jesus' calling disciples • **Ideas That Work** Create riddles

Learning Objectives

By the end of this chapter, the students should be able to

- ❑ Name the varied good works that missionaries do
- ❑ Commit themselves to doing God's work
- ❑ Choose ways to support missionary activity

DAY 4 • LIVING

The students will be able to

- Tell the work of missionary societies
- Choose ways to help missioners
- Commit themselves to do God's work at home

- Reserve a computer
- Gather information about Maryknoll
- Make copies of the resource master on page 442

- Globe or wall map
- Writing and drawing materials
- Basket
- Computer
- Make copies of the resource master on page 442

- Resource Masters Play a board game
- Teaching Tip Learn about Maryknoll

DAY 5 • ALTERNATIVES

There are a number of alternatives to help you plan Day 5.

Prayer Experience
Use the prayer experience on either Day 4 or Day 5. Follow the suggestions on page 438 for leading the prayer.

Review and Explore
Follow the suggestions on page 439 for teaching the page. If you will give the chapter test on Day 5, assign this page as homework the night before.

Home and Family
Send this page home, if possible. You may also assign one or more activities as class work or homework.

The Church Today
This page provides a class or group project that may be started in class following the chapter test.

Chapter Test
The chapter test appears as a resource master on page 443.

Quick Check

Do this evaluation as soon as you finish each chapter.

Did I follow my lesson plan?

How can I tell that I met the learning objectives for the lesson?

What activities did the children enjoy most?

How could I improve this lesson?

Benziger on the Web
For more ideas, visit us at www.benziger.glencoe.com

Interactive Lesson Planner
Your ILP provides more help in preparing to teach this chapter.

Celebrate
Turn to page 22 of this book. Check for seasonal celebrations.

Lesson Plan · Day 1

Ask the students if they have ever gone to a far away place for vacation. Ask what they found new and exciting. Ask if they missed anything or anyone from home. Explain that today they will learn about people who work for God in far away lands.

1 Introduction

Read the chapter's Scripture verse aloud. Ask the children to name some of Jesus' followers. Ask if they think of themselves as Jesus' followers.

2 Do You Know?

Read the question and ask the children to explain the meaning of *missionary.* Have them look it up in the glossary. Focus on the root meaning—"to send." List the children's ideas about what "God's work" is. Keep the list for later reference. At the end of the week, come back to this question to see how the children's knowledge has developed.

OPTIONS

For the Linguistic Learner
Invite the students to write a class letter to their parish or diocesan missions telling the missioners of their interest and assuring them of their prayers.

IDEAS THAT WORK

Tell the students that Saint Therese of Lisieux is the patron saint of missioners. Have a volunteer team look up the life of Saint Therese and prepare to tell the class about her.

They became Jesus' followers.

Luke 5:11

Do You Know?

◆ How do missionaries do God's work?

One Family

A New Life

Paul and Ana moved from their home in the United States to a new home in Venezuela. Their parents are **missionaries.** Their work is to teach and help the poor all over the world.

At first it was hard. Paul and Ana missed their old life. But things are different now. Paul and Ana have learned to speak Spanish. They have new friends. They know more about helping and sharing.

From your friends at Maryknoll

③ A New Life

Focus the children's attention on the photos and introduce Paul and Ana. Ask for clues of their new life as a missionary family. Then, have the children read the first paragraph to learn about Paul and Ana's new life. Have the children read the second paragraph to discover what Paul and Ana learned.

④ Little Missionaries

Ask the children to look at the picture of the child dancing. See if any of them can demonstrate dance steps they learned from another culture. Ask the students to read about Sarah and Maza to find out what they learned in this new land.

⑤ Activity

Read the directions. Give the students time to show their work and tell how they would help.

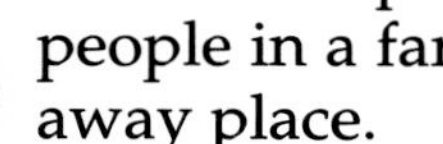

Little Missionaries

Sarah and Maza live in Venezuela too. These little missionaries are learning about caring and giving just like Paul and Ana. They have also learned to speak Spanish. They have learned about music and dance from the children in Venezuela. They have learned to spread God's love to people in a far away place.

Pretend that you are a little missionary. Where would you go? How would you help? Draw a picture.

CURRICULUM CHALLENGE

Tell the children that music is a language everyone understands. Check with the music teacher and gather instruments, such as pipes or flutes, tambourines, drums, rattles and the like. Play recordings such as these CDs: *World Voices* (Hearts of Space, P.O. Box 31321, San Francisco, CA 94131) or *Intiraymi: Traditional Music from the Andes* (Dr. Carmen A. Chuquin, 644 State Street, Madison, WI 53703).

IDEAS THAT WORK

Gather information about a mission. Locate the mission on a map. Invite the students to imagine themselves as missionaries. Write two columns on the board. Write "Good Stuff" and "Tough Stuff" at the head of the columns. Have the students think of five items under each column head. Offer an idea for each, such as: "You are doing God's work" and "It is tough to learn a new language."

Lesson Plan · Day 2

Invite the students to think of news that is too good to keep. Have them gather in a circle and ask a volunteer to whisper the news to the child to the right, who will pass it on to the child to the right. When the message gets to you, make a formal announcement: "(Child's) good news is. . . ." Play this game with other good news.

1 Love God

Direct the students to the picture and ask who is giving and who is receiving news. Then, have the students read the story to find out what the news was. Ask the children to identify some of the good work Jesus did. *(healed, forgave, offered peace)*

2 Activity

Give the students time to discover the hidden word. To connect it with the word mission, challenge them to use both words in a single sentence. *(For example: Jesus sent his disciples on a mission to spread good news.)*

OPTIONS

For the Musical Learner

Invite the students to create lyrics and adapt the spiritual for Christmas, "Go Tell It on the Mountain." Have them sing the song announcing Jesus' birth. Then invite them to create their own lyrics, such as: Jesus Christ is Lord; . . . is the Word; . . . is here; . . . is Savior; and the like.

LOVE GOD

People who love God want others to know God, too. Good news needs to be spread.

When Jesus was with his followers for the last time, he sent them on a **mission,** or assignment, to do God's work.

Jesus said, "Tell everyone about me. Teach them to do as I have done."

From *Matthew 28:19–20*

ACTIVITY FIND THE FOLLOWER

Find out what a follower of Jesus is called. Color the spaces that have a cross in them.

3 The Church Grows

Ask the students to tell a story based on the picture on this page. Look for an awareness of proclaiming, or telling, good news. Focus their attention on the expressions of the listeners. Comment that after the sharing of the Good News, Jesus' disciples shared something else too. Have them read to discover what they shared. *(They shared in communion and in the breaking of the bread.)* Give the students time to draw people to the picture.

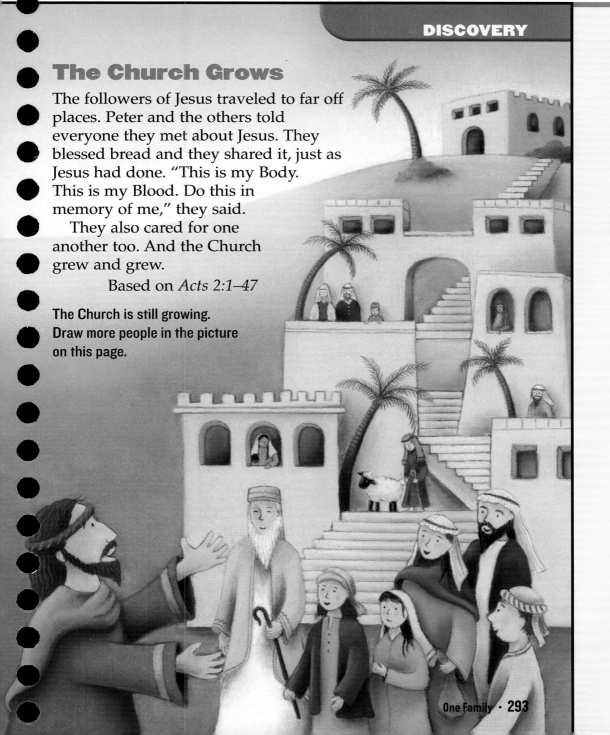

The Church Grows

The followers of Jesus traveled to far off places. Peter and the others told everyone they met about Jesus. They blessed bread and they shared it, just as Jesus had done. "This is my Body. This is my Blood. Do this in memory of me," they said.

They also cared for one another too. And the Church grew and grew.

Based on *Acts 2:1–47*

The Church is still growing. Draw more people in the picture on this page.

BIBLE BASICS

Tell in your own words the story of the first Christian communities from Acts 4:32–34 and 9:31. Ask the students why the behavior of the first Christians drew many people to join them.

TEACHING TIP

Liturgy Connection Treat student pages 292 and 293 as two parts of a whole. Point out that the proclamation of the first followers of Jesus and the sharing in the Body and Blood of the Lord match the two parts of the Mass. The proclamation of the Good News is called the Liturgy of the Word, and the sharing in the breaking of the bread and communion is called the Liturgy of the Eucharist. Connect this to the children's Sunday experience, especially their First Communion day.

Lesson Plan · Day 3
Read the opening sentence. Say the names of the missionaries and have the students repeat the names after you. Explain that these people are today's missionaries and that they are like the first disciples of Jesus.

1 Blessed Elias Del Socorro Nieves
Locate Mexico on the map. Challenge the students to read about him and tell how the people helped him and how he helped them. Compare the parish-building work of Blessed Elias with ministries in their parish.

2 Jean Donovan
Locate El Salvador and Ohio. Ask the students to read silently to discover what kind of missionary work Jean did. Ask them if they know anybody who helps in the way Jean did in El Salvador.

BIBLE BASICS

Retell the story of Jesus' calling of four of the Apostles away from their work of fishing (Luke 5:1–11) to their new work of fishing for people to follow Jesus. Ask how the missionaries are "fishers" today. Invite students to act out the play. Pick students to play the roles of Jesus, Peter, Andrew, James, and John.

HELPING HANDS

Missionaries travel far to spread God's love.

Blessed Elias Del Socorro Nieves

Elias was a priest that worked hard to serve the people of his parishes. He was sent to be a pastor of a very poor parish in Mexico. Very few people lived there. He helped the people build their church and their parish.

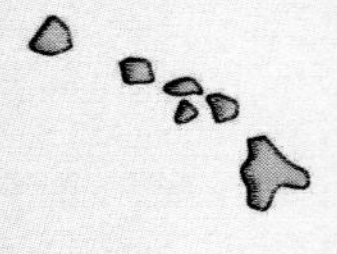

Jean Donovan

Jean Donovan was a very smart businesswoman. She left her home in Ohio to go to El Salvador. There was a terrible war in El Salvador. No one was safe, not even the children. Jean showed her love. She ran a home for the hungry and the sick.

3 Father Damien
Invite the children to share their ideas about being left out or chosen last. Direct their attention to the picture of Father Damien and locate the Hawaiian Islands. Simply explain that the people were alone because they had a disease others were afraid they would catch. Ask the students to read to discover how Father Damien helped them.

4 This We Believe!
Read the statement. Ask how the three missionaries answered God's call.

5 Activity
Have the students complete the first activity. Give them time to choose the missionary they would like to help and to gather their ideas about why they made the choices they did.

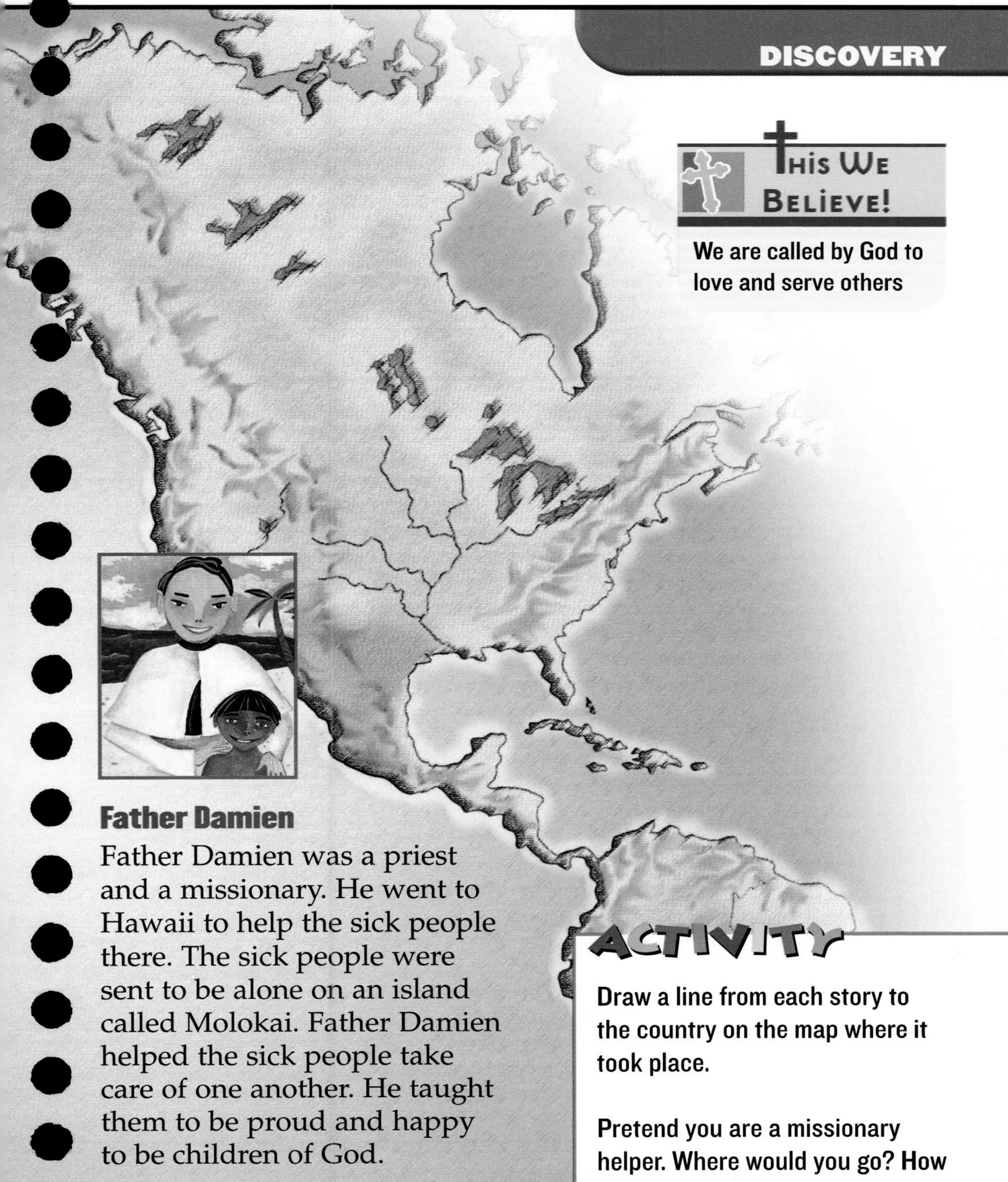

This We Believe!

We are called by God to love and serve others

Father Damien

Father Damien was a priest and a missionary. He went to Hawaii to help the sick people there. The sick people were sent to be alone on an island called Molokai. Father Damien helped the sick people take care of one another. He taught them to be proud and happy to be children of God.

ACTIVITY

Draw a line from each story to the country on the map where it took place.

Pretend you are a missionary helper. Where would you go? How would you help?

IDEAS THAT WORK

Invite the children to make up riddles about the three missionaries following these guidelines: Give two facts about the missionary. End your riddle with "Who am I?" Tell the children that the first child to guess correctly gets to read his or her riddle next. Expand and deepen this exploration to include disciples such as Peter, Andrew, James, and John, as well as people everyone in the class knows or can be expected to know who do the Lord's work at home as well as abroad.

Lesson Plan · Day 4

Ask the students to tell about a time when working or playing together was better than being alone. Explain that today they will learn that Jesus' followers liked being together as they helped one another do God's missionary work.

1 Reaching Out

Read the introductory paragraph to the children. Ask if they know people who do this work today. Challenge them to think locally as well as globally.

2 Africa, United States, Latin America

Use a globe or wall map to locate Africa, the United States, and South America. Also, identify your town on the map. Read about the missionary work in each place. Have the students color the pictures. Discuss the similarities and differences they observe among the three missionaries in these three different places.

Tell the students about the Maryknoll order. Use these facts as a basis. Maryknoll is a short name for the Catholic Foreign Missionary Society of America. This society is based in the United States. It was founded in 1911. Members of Maryknoll are priests, brothers, and sisters. Today, about 400 lay missioners are part of the Lay Mission Program, founded in 1994. Contact Maryknoll at www.maryknoll.com for extensive information about the society.

REACHING OUT

Maryknoll Missionaries help people all over the world. They help the sick, orphans, the elderly, and people who have been hurt by war.

Read about how Maryknoll Missionaries help people in these countries. Color the pictures.

Africa

Maryknoll Missionaries make sure that children have places to go to get medicine when they are sick. Missionaries teach and help people learn to take care of themselves.

United States

Maryknoll Missionaries bring the Good News of Jesus to the poor and suffering in the United States.

3 What Can You Do?

Read and talk about each point and guide the students to agree on one activity they can do as a class. Ask for other ideas as well.

Latin America

Maryknoll Missionaries work in schools, and hospitals. They teach children and grown-ups about God. They help people feel better about themselves.

What Can You Do?

Can you do something to help? Here are some ideas:

- Write a prayer for the people that Maryknoll Missionaries help.
- Write a prayer for Maryknoll Missionaries.
- Save a few cents and send them to help the Maryknoll Missonaries help others. Your teacher can help you.

RESOURCE MASTERS

The resource master on page 442 is a game board. The children can play this game alone or with a partner. Each child will need a place marker.

Prayer

The prayer experience is part of every chapter. This activity provides opportunities for the students to witness and to pray as they do God's work.

1 Prepare for Prayer

Comment that Jesus came to show and teach his followers how to be like him. Ask for their ideas about imitating Jesus in thought, word, and deed. Emphasize that all of these actions are missionary actions; they are God's work.

2 Answer the Call

Say that prayer helps missionaries do God's work. Invite the students to read the prayer silently to discover what they are asking of Jesus. *(to answer his call; to trust; to show love to all)* You may be the leader, or choose a volunteer leader. Gather in the prayer area to pray.

TEACHING TIP

Ask the children to name the ways missionaries do God's work. Be sure they include themselves. Help the children see that caring for the outer (the poor, hungry, ill-housed) and inner needs (sense of worth, well-being, community) are all ways of doing God's work.

LEARNING TO PRAY

In the prayer service, build in an opportunity for the children to make a commitment to use their skills and abilities to do God's work. Provide small slips of paper and pens and have them write their commitment and fold the paper. Collect the commitments in a basket after the last "Leader" part of the prayer. Give clear directions so the children know what to do.

ANSWER THE CALL

LEADER: Dear Jesus, you came to tell us about the kingdom of God. Help us to live as you ask.

ALL: Dear Jesus, help us answer your call.

LEADER: Help us to trust in you as we do your work.

ALL: Dear Jesus, help us answer your call.

LEADER: Dear Jesus, we know that you love us. Help us to show this love to others near and far.

ALL: Dear Jesus, help us to answer your call.

Amen!

1 Know
Read the description of the work of missionaries. Ask the children to name missionaries they learned about today and to tell how these missionaries did God's work.

2 Love and Serve
For the serve activity, after the children have written down their ideas, invite them to pair off and act out their missionary roles. Next, have the pairs meet with another pair or two to act out their ideas for a larger audience. Pool the children's ideas and find one way they can do God's work as a class.

3 God's Friends
Read about Saint John Eudes. Ask the children if they know any one who does God's work as a teacher of others. Talk about ways their words and actions teach others. Invite examples, such as: obeying parents, stopping to help a smaller child, caring for a pet, standing up for a friend in trouble, and the like.

Know

Missionaries

Help the poor all over the world.

Love

Pretend you are a missionary helper. Write three things you would teach another child about Jesus.

Serve

Your parish does many things to serve others in other countries. Your class members can serve, too. Write one way that you can help someone in another country. Put all of your ideas together. Talk about one thing you can do now.

CHAPTER 21
REVIEW and EXPLORE

GOD'S FRIENDS

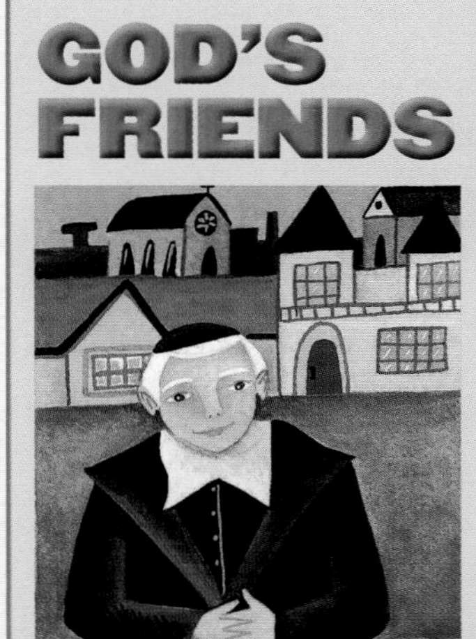

Saint John Eudes

Father John believed that priests were shepherds to God's people. He traveled all over to teach priests how to better care for people in need. Father John believed that caring for others was the best way to serve God.

A Little Catechism

Invite the children to open their religion books to *A Little Catechism.* Choose one or more of the selections below for memory work or reinforcement. You will find your copy of the catechism on pages 23–43 of this Teacher's Edition.

1. Read about signs and symbols on page 12. Have the children think of a symbol or sign that will remind them of the work that missionaries do for others around the world.
2. Read questions number 5 and 15 on pages 12 and 13. Invite the children to read the answers with spirit and enthusiasm.

Know Love Serve

Note The activities on this page provide ways for the children to share their learning with their families. The activities are related to the week's theme.

1 Introduce
Invite the children to tell how they can do God's work in their families and work with their families to help missionaries in far away places. Invite the children to pool their ideas to make up a class prayer for children everywhere. Urge the children to pray this prayer with their families.

2 Pray Together
Retell the story of Jesus' calling his friends to become fishers of all people. *(Luke 5:1–11)* Pray the prayer in the prayer burst to bring the class to an end.

Online for Families
Remind the children to check the Benziger Web site this week with their families.
www.benziger.glencoe.com

Dear Family,

I have just finished chapter 21. I have learned that missionaries help the poor all over the world. I have learned that I can help too. I can start by helping those around me. You can help by finding ways that our family can help others in far away places.

On your own

Write a prayer to remember the poor children in other lands. Say this prayer in the morning or before you go to bed.

With your family

At your grace before meals, remember those who are hungry all over the world.

Help me to accept my mission from Jesus.

1 Discuss
Direct the students' attention to the illustration at the bottom of the page. Ask for their comments. Explain that they will make a large mural like it. Read the directions aloud and discuss each item.

2 Project
Make sure that the students understand the nature of this long-term project. Focus on the first part of the project: showing and telling how the Good News is spread all over the world. Brainstorm more ideas that they can illustrate. Have the children choose something from the list to add to the mural.

3 Pray
Gather the children in the prayer area and invite them to sing a hymn that reflects the work of Jesus' followers, such as "He's Got the Whole World in His Hands," "Let There Be Peace on Earth," "Go Tell It on the Mountain," and the like.

THE CHURCH TODAY

Get a big space ready in your classroom. Get the longest piece of paper you can find. Make a class mural.

You will work on this project until school ends for the year.

In big letters, give the mural a title. You can use: We Are Sent!

The mural will have three parts. This week you will work on the first part.

In the first area of the mural, share what you know about how others share the Good News of God's love to people all over the world. You can work by yourself or with a partner. Paint, draw, or write. Use pictures or words. There are all kinds of ways to tell others about God.

ANSWER KEY

This is the answer key for the chapter test on page 443.

A. 1. Missionaries 2. Damien 3. Followers 4. Jesus

B.–C. Accept all reasonable responses.

Name ______________________________

Do God's Work

Cut out the numbered squares.
Turn them over and mix them up.
Use a button or a penny as a marker.
Put your marker at "Start."
Pick one of the numbered squares.
Move your marker the number of spaces it shows.
When you land on a space, do what the words tell you.

 **START** 

Tell how you can share your toys.
Move ahead 1 space.

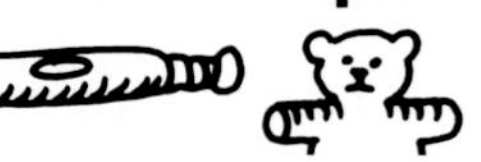

Print the name of one missionary here:

____

____

Move ahead 1 space.

What chore can you do without being asked?

____

Move ahead 1 space.

Who teaches you about God's love?

____

Move ahead 2 spaces.

Who calls you to serve?

____

Move ahead 1 space.

How can you cheer up a friend who is sad?

____

Move ahead 1 space.

How can you do something nice for another?

____

Move ahead 1 space.

How can you take care of your neighborhood?

____

Move ahead 1 space.

"They became Jesus' followers"
Luke 5:11

Name ______________________________

Chapter 21 Test

A. Write the missing words in the sentences. Choose words from the word list.

Missionaries / Jesus / Damien / Followers

1. ____________________ teach and help the poor all over the world.

2. Father ____________________ taught sick people to be proud and happy to be God's children.

3. Jesus asked his ____________________ to do God's work.

4. Missionaries and all helpers do the work of

____________________.

B. Make up a prayer asking God's help for missionaries.

____

____

____

____

C. Draw a picture showing how you can do God's work today.

TEACHER RESOURCE CENTER

Faith Formation

One in Peace

I, then, a prisoner for the Lord, urge you to live in a manner worthy of the call you have received, with all humility and gentleness, with patience, bearing with one another through love, striving to preserve the unity of the Spirit through the bond of peace: one body and one Spirit, as you were also called to the one hope of your call; one Lord, one faith, one baptism; one God and Father of all, who is over all and through all in all.

Ephesians 4:1–6

As a member of your parish, how do you preserve and promote peace and unity?

CHECK THE CATECHISM

Christ himself is the source of ministry in the Church. Christ gave those who are invested with a sacred power the task of promoting the interests of their people so that all that belong to the People of God may gain salvation. The *Catechism of the Catholic Church* examines ministry in paragraphs 874–879. For more information about the parish community see also paragraph 2179.

God's Holy People

One of the major insights of the Second Vatican Council (1962–1965) was an understanding of the Church as the People of God. This means that all Catholics are called to participate fully in the life of the Church. The parish provides the setting where this happens. The parish is the gathering of the faith-filled Resurrection community. Members gather also to hear and live the Word, to serve, and to celebrate. These great ministries of gathering, proclaiming, serving, and celebrating are everybody's responsibility and privilege. One can see the outlines of the parish in the Acts of the Apostles, where believers gathered to witness the Resurrection in their attitudes, words, and actions.

What ministry in your parish are you most proud of? Why are you proud of this ministry?

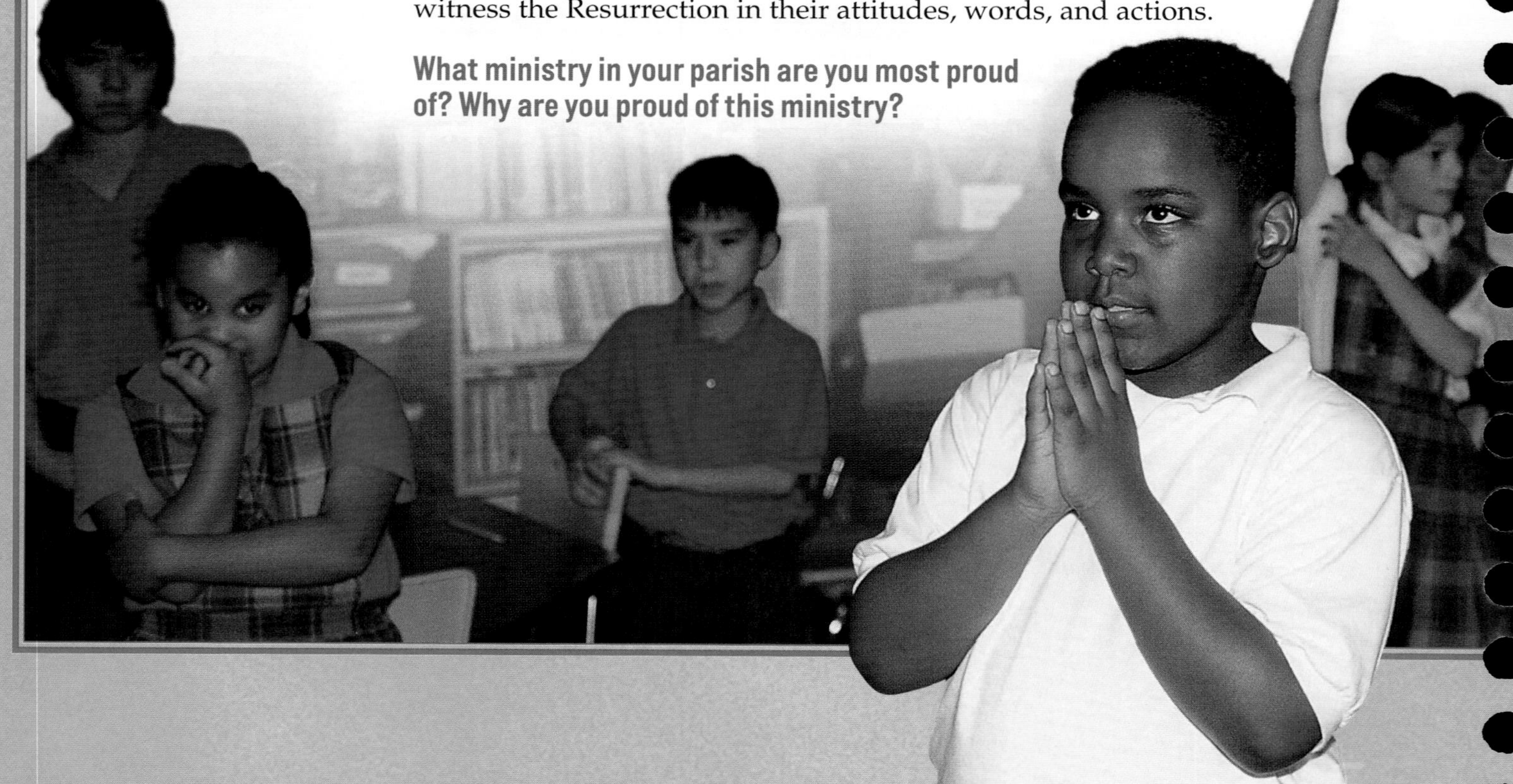

Background

Teaching about the Parish

Second graders have immediate experience of their local parishes. The celebration of their First Communion welcomes them to full participation in the Eucharist. The parish religious education program gathers them to learn the Gospel message. The parish gathers its people to serve and reach out to those in need. The parish is a place of festivals and fun. The students bring all of these concrete experiences to their exploration of the parish. In this lesson, they are invited to contribute to the life of the parish so that it is truly a live-giving Resurrection community, a presence of Christ in the world today.

Faith Summary

- The parish is a living community of faith.
- The parish serves those in need.
- The parish gathers to celebrate and proclaim the Gospel.

Growth and Development

It is helpful to remember two characteristics of second graders as you teach this lesson:

- ***Second graders want to contribute.*** To help the students understand their value in the parish, ask adult supervisors to enlist the students' help in simple, necessary tasks such as stacking food shelves, running errands, passing out bulletins before Mass, and the like.
- ***Second graders need concrete examples of abstract concepts such as the idea of community.*** Invite the students to assemble a puzzle to show the idea that all members of the parish community are needed, and each member plays a different role.

A Teacher's Prayer

O Lord, you gathered a people to yourself. May we hear and heed your holy Word. Grant us a spirit of community, service, and celebration. Help the students realize that their hope, youth, and enthusiasm are blessings to the parish community and a reminder that the Church is ever new. Amen.

Vocabulary Preview

parish

Scripture

Acts 2:44: the ideal Resurrection community

Related Resources

Video

"My Father's House" (St. Anthony Messenger Press, 1-800-488-0488 or www.AmericanCatholic.org). A seven-year-old girl explores her Catholic parish church and recalls what she has been taught about the liturgy. (Children, 10 minutes)

Books

Bausch, William. *The Parish of the Next Millennium* (Twenty-Third Publications, 1-800-321-0411 or www.twentythirdpublications.com). This book takes a look at the challenges facing the parish church and offers hope. (Adult)

Wilkes, Paul. *Excellent Catholic Parishes: The Guide to Best Places and Practices* (New York: Paulist Press, 2001). In this representative sampling of excellent parishes, you will find many solid ideas to help make your parish more effective. (Adult)

TEACHER ORGANIZER

Planning Guide

The basic content for each chapter is divided into four class sessions. There are a number of options for the fifth session. Extension, review, and testing options are described under Day 5 Alternatives. The Quick Check box will help you evaluate the week's lessons.

Chapter Goals

In this chapter, the students will learn about

- ❑ Their parish as a living community of faith
- ❑ How their parish serves those in need
- ❑ How their parish gathers to celebrate and proclaim the Gospel

	DAY 1 · INVITATION	DAY 2 · DISCOVERY	DAY 3 · DISCOVERY
OBJECTIVES	**The students will be able to** • Identify ministries in their parish • Describe their parish as a gathering of faithful people	**The students will be able to** • Describe ministries in the parish • Name contributions they can make to the parish	**The students will be able to** • Describe how the Church gathers God's People • Explain how the Church sponsors and nurtures growth in faith • Identify Baptism as a sacrament of welcome
PREPARATION	• Prepare for a visit with parish historian or archivist • Gather information and items about the parish patron	• Get small prizes • Provide cards and envelopes	• Make plans to go to the parish church • Gather art materials
MATERIALS	• Pencils • Colored chalk, colored pens • Photos and objects about parish history	• Writing materials • Prizes • Art materials • Cards and envelopes	• Writing materials • Art materials
OPTIONAL ACTIVITIES	• **Teaching Tip** Motivate to increase student involvement • **Options** Pantomime parish activities and ministries • **Vocabulary** Discuss the meaning of "parish" • **Ideas That Work** Welcome a guest speaker	• **Options** Make ministry armbands • **Ideas That Work** Play a memorization game • **Options** Write thank-you cards to parishioners	• **Options** Sketch the church from different perspectives • **Ideas That Work** Frame and display children's work • **Learning To Pray** Share in prayer service

Learning Objectives

By the end of this chapter, the students should be able to

- ❑ Identify the ministries in their parish
- ❑ Choose ways they can contribute to the ministries of their parish
- ❑ Ask God to guide their parish life and ministry

DAY 4 · LIVING

The students will be able to

- Tell how the parish gathers for prayer and service
- Pray that Jesus guides them in their ministry in the parish church

- Gather logos of familiar groups
- Practice gestures to accompany prayer
- Make copies of the resource master on page 460

- Art material
- Copies of the resource master, pencils

- **Options** Create a parish logo
- **Vocabulary** Learn names of items and places in a church
- **Resource Masters** Decide on ways to minister

DAY 5 · ALTERNATIVES

There are a number of alternatives to help you plan Day 5.

Prayer Experience
Use A Parish Prayer on either Day 4 or Day 5. Follow the suggestions on page 456 for leading the prayer.

Review and Explore
Follow the suggestions on page 457 for teaching the page. If you will give the chapter test on Day 5, assign this page as homework the night before.

Home and Family
Send this page home, if possible. You may also assign one or more activities as class work or homework.

The Church Today
This page provides a class or group project that may be started in class following the chapter test and completed outside of class.

Chapter Test
The chapter test appears as a resource master on page 461.

Quick Check

Do this evaluation as soon as you finish each chapter.

Did I follow my lesson plan?

How can I tell that I met the learning objectives for the lesson?

What activities did the children enjoy most?

How could I improve this lesson?

Benziger on the Web
For more ideas, visit us at www.benziger.glencoe.com

Interactive Lesson Planner
Your ILP provides more help in preparing to teach this chapter.

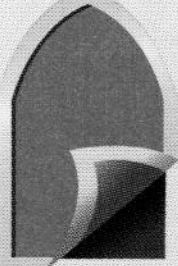

Celebrate
Turn to page 22 of this book. Check for seasonal celebrations.

Lesson Plan · Day 1
Draw a large simple outline resembling your parish church. Label the drawing with the name of your parish. Invite the children to write their names inside the drawing.

1 Introduce
Read the chapter's Scripture verse aloud. Tell the children that this verse tells about the first followers of Jesus. Point out that they gathered and shared their goods.

2 Do You Know?
Read the question. Using the parish name, write this incomplete sentence on the chalkboard: *"(Parish name) is a place where . . ."* Ask the students to come to the board and write an ending for the sentence-starter. You might suggest an ending, such as "people pray." Save the list the children generate for future reference.

TEACHING TIP
Children will more readily contribute their ideas for the add-on activity if you provide colored chalk (or colored pens). Invite them to come forward in pairs to write their ideas.

OPTIONS
For the Active Learner
Invite volunteers to mime parish activities, such as prayer, service, celebrations. Have the child who guesses correctly be next. Allow them to mime in pairs. For example, service activities may require more than one child.

VIRTUE FAITH GRACE **VOCABULARY**
Parish Make sure the children understand that the word "parish" means the same as *faith community.* Make it clear that their parish is a gathering of faithful people in a certain location. They might be interested to learn that many parishes together make up a diocese.

All who believed were together and had all things in common.
Acts 2:44

Do You Know?
◆ How do parishes serve others?

A Parish

Saint Angela's

The school playground looked different. There were tables of clean clothes all over the basketball court. Boxes of books covered the lunch tables. People were filling paper bags with things to buy. The parish would make a lot of money to buy pillows and blankets for the city's poor.

What could you do to help?

3 Saint Angela's
Invite the children to picture the setting described as you read the story. Ask them how Saint Angela's parish is helping the poor. Use the illustration to generate discussion. Challenge the children to identify the many ways people helped organize the Saint Angela fundraiser. Use the question to gather ideas about how the children might help.

4 Activity
Ask the children to close their eyes. Lead a small imaginary journey to inventory some logical places at home such as the children's bedroom, the attic, a storage room, or the garage. Pause periodically and ask them to call out items they could contribute from each room. Give the students time to complete the activity and show what they have drawn.

The people of Saint Angela's parish worked hard. Everyone pitched in. Some people brought things to be sold. Other people put things in neat piles. Everyone did their part.

In the bag, draw something you could bring to the yard sale that someone else could buy.

TEACHING TIP

Throughout this chapter continue to stress that a parish is all of the people who form it. Many children tend to think that a parish is the church building. Some think that the truly important people in a parish are the ordained ministers. Take every opportunity to point out concrete examples of the contributions of all members of the parish.

IDEAS THAT WORK

Gather information about the parish's name. Explain to the children that parishes are named after persons *(Saint Patrick, Holy Spirit)*; holy days *(Assumption, Ascension)*; or a holy object *(Blessed Sacrament)*. Consult a parish member who seems to act as an unofficial archivist to discover interesting facts about the founding of your parish. Invite him or her to speak to your class. Be sure to have plenty of photos and historical objects at hand.

Lesson Plan · Day 2

Invite the children to tell about their favorite parish event. Encourage them to think broadly—from sacramental celebrations to parish festivals. Ask why they favor the event they name.

1 Busy Parishes

Refer to the many ideas the children contributed to the sentence: *(Parish name) is a place where.* Ask for a show of hands if they think their parish is a busy one. Read the opening sentence. Ask the children to identify the activities in the two photos on student page 304. Then ask two children to read the text. Ask for examples of people who *hear* God's Word at Mass and *do* God's work.

Now focus students on the photos on student page 305 to identify other parish ministries. Read the first caption. Connect the work of Mrs. Miller to the parish religion program the children participate in. After reading the second caption, ask the children to tell about festivals in your parish or other parishes. Ask why parishes have festivals. *(for community-building, for fun, for money)*

OPTIONS

For the Artistic Child Invite the children to make an armband with their name and a title that tells how they contribute to the life and work of the parish. Tell them your idea for your armband: *(Your name) the fixer-upper.* Tell about your skill and how you contribute it to the parish. Encourage the children to draw pictures on their armbands as well. After they complete their work, secure their armbands with masking tape and let the children wear them for the rest of class time.

IDEAS THAT WORK

To aid memorization, play a game. Write out the This We Believe! statement in large words. Make copies and cut the words apart. Put the words in envelopes and give each envelope to a small group. Have them assemble the words to make the belief statement. Accept the ministries in any order. Give simple gifts to the winners.

This We Believe!

A parish brings people together to pray, celebrate, and do good works.

Busy Parishes

A parish is a church community. A parish can do many things. Look at what a parish can do.

Saint Mary's parish prays together at Mass. The people remember what Jesus said and did.

Hungry people will get food from Saint Anthony's Parish. Parish members share God's love with others.

❷ What's Going On?

Gather a list of parish events. Invite the children to add their ideas. Include sacramental celebrations, anniversaries (of the parish, of patron saints), as well as parish festivals. Set aside time for the children to show their artwork and tell about it.

❸ This We Believe!

Have the children pair off to memorize the statement.

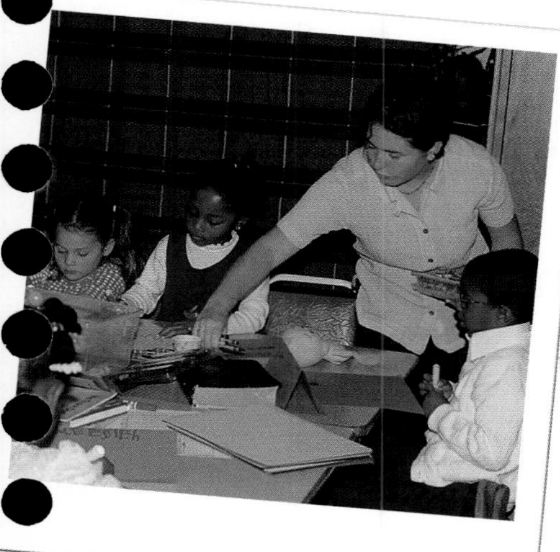

Mrs. Miller teaches the second grade children of Saint Clare's Parish about Jesus.

It's time for fun at the Holy Cross Parish festival. Parish members will share happy times with one another.

ACTIVITY WHAT'S GOING ON?

What's happening at your parish? Draw a picture.

OPTIONS

For the Writer Invite the children to think of people in the parish who work hard and contribute their time and talent. Brainstorm a list of names. Add names of your own, keeping in mind the unsung members of the parish, such as the secretary or janitor, a devoted usher, the person who makes bouquets for the sanctuary, and the like. Have the children make a thank-you card for these people. You may have so many unsung heroes in your parish that one child will need to make more than one card. Be sure they are delivered!

Lesson Plan · Day 3

Invite the students to name the groups to which they belong. *(family, school, teams, church)* Ask them to tell what they like best about each group. *(for example: Saturday night supper, recess, winning, special holy days)*

1 A Church Community

Read the introductory sentences aloud. Invite the children to name parish events that draw people together. Ask them to refer to their own parish experience and to study student pages 304 and 305 to refresh their memory. Ask children who are new to the parish to tell about events in their former parish. Give the students time to draw their view of the parish church and to share their drawings.

OPTIONS

For the Artistic Learner

Invite the students to do sketches of the church from whatever external perspective they choose. Within reason, have them scatter around the outside of the church building and draw what they see from that perspective. Consider providing a new medium such as high grade paper and charcoal or soft-lead pencils or crayons.

IDEAS THAT WORK

Students appreciate it when you make their artwork special by displaying it in an attractive way. Construction paper frames highlight their work and bring colors in bold relief.

A Church Community

A church is a place where the people of God come together.

The people in a parish go to the same church.

Draw a picture of your parish church.

The name of my parish church is

_______________________________.

2 Grow in Faith
Ask a volunteer to tell what is happening in the picture. Identify the minister of Baptism *(a deacon)*, the parents and the godparents. Read the story about growing in faith. Note that Baptism is the beginning of the newly baptized person's life of faith. Ask the children to tell how they have grown in faith. Ask them to tell how they can help another person grow in their faith. *(Teach a younger sibling; set a good example; cooperate with people who help them grow in faith.)*

3 Activity
Give the students time to complete this activity. As they name the people who help them grow in faith, ask them to write the names of these people in the church outline.

Grow in Faith

People in your parish come together to celebrate.

They share God's love with each other. Members of your parish help you grow in faith too. They help you believe in God and trust in God's love.

See how your parish helps you grow in faith.

ACTIVITY

Write the names of two people in your parish that teach about Jesus' love for you.

____

____

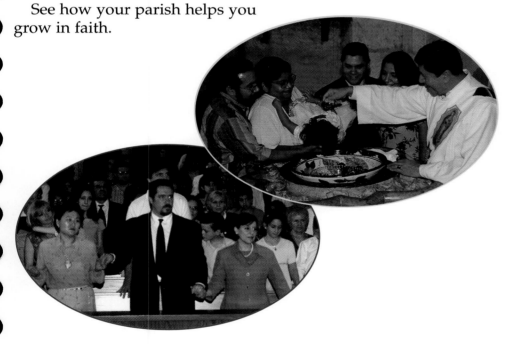

LEARNING TO PRAY

The Rite of Baptism teaches that the faith community is called do its part to help the newly baptized grow in faith. Lead the children in this prayer service:

Leader: What do you ask for this child?
Parents: We want our child to receive the grace of Christ in the Church.

Leader: Will you help the parents teach their child to grow in faith?
All: Yes, we will!

Leader: The Christian community welcomes you with joy in the name of the Father, the Son, and the Holy Spirit.
All: Amen. Alleluia!

Leader: Dear brothers and sisters, we ask that the Lord Jesus bless this child and the parents and godparents and the whole Church.
All: Amen. Alleluia!

Lesson Plan · Day 4

Invite the children to brainstorm ways that the parish church helps others.

1 Working Together

Read the directions and the three ways all parishes help others. Ask for specific examples of each. *(religion class; remembering the sick and dead at Mass; weddings and First Communion day)* Ask the children to look at the ideas they generated about the parish as a helping community. Have the children print these ideas as well as ideas of their own on the remaining spokes. Provide time to discuss their work.

OPTIONS

For the Artistic Learner

Talk with the children about logos that identify groups and organizations. Show them a number of logos, such as those familiar to them: the Red Cross; cars; boy scouts and girl scouts; school symbols, or logos. Ask the children to develop a logo, or symbol, to be a hubcap for the wheel on this page. If your parish has a symbol, or logo, show it to the children. Give them time to describe and explain their artwork.

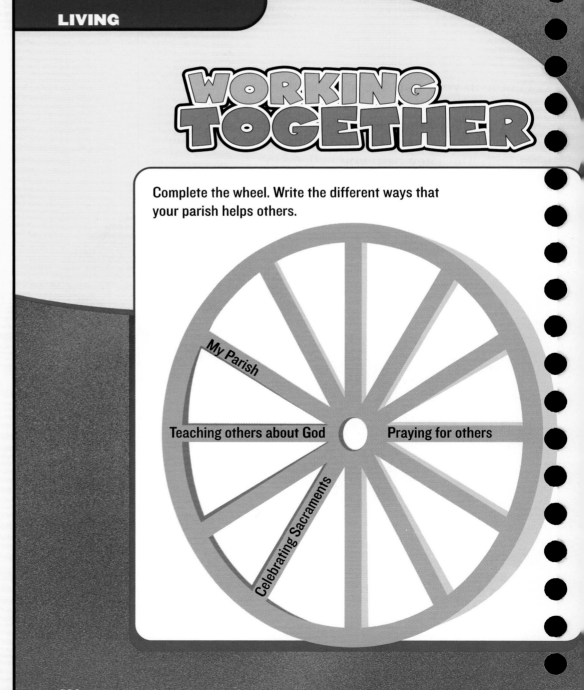

WORKING TOGETHER

Complete the wheel. Write the different ways that your parish helps others.

My Parish

Teaching others about God

Praying for others

Celebrating Sacraments

❷ Your Parish

Read the opening question and ask the students to call out their responses. Go through the four items and check to see that the children understand each one. Note that the second sentence refers to items in the church. You might tell them your favorite item. After they complete their work, have the students gather in small groups and share their work. Gather the children and ask volunteers to share their ideas.

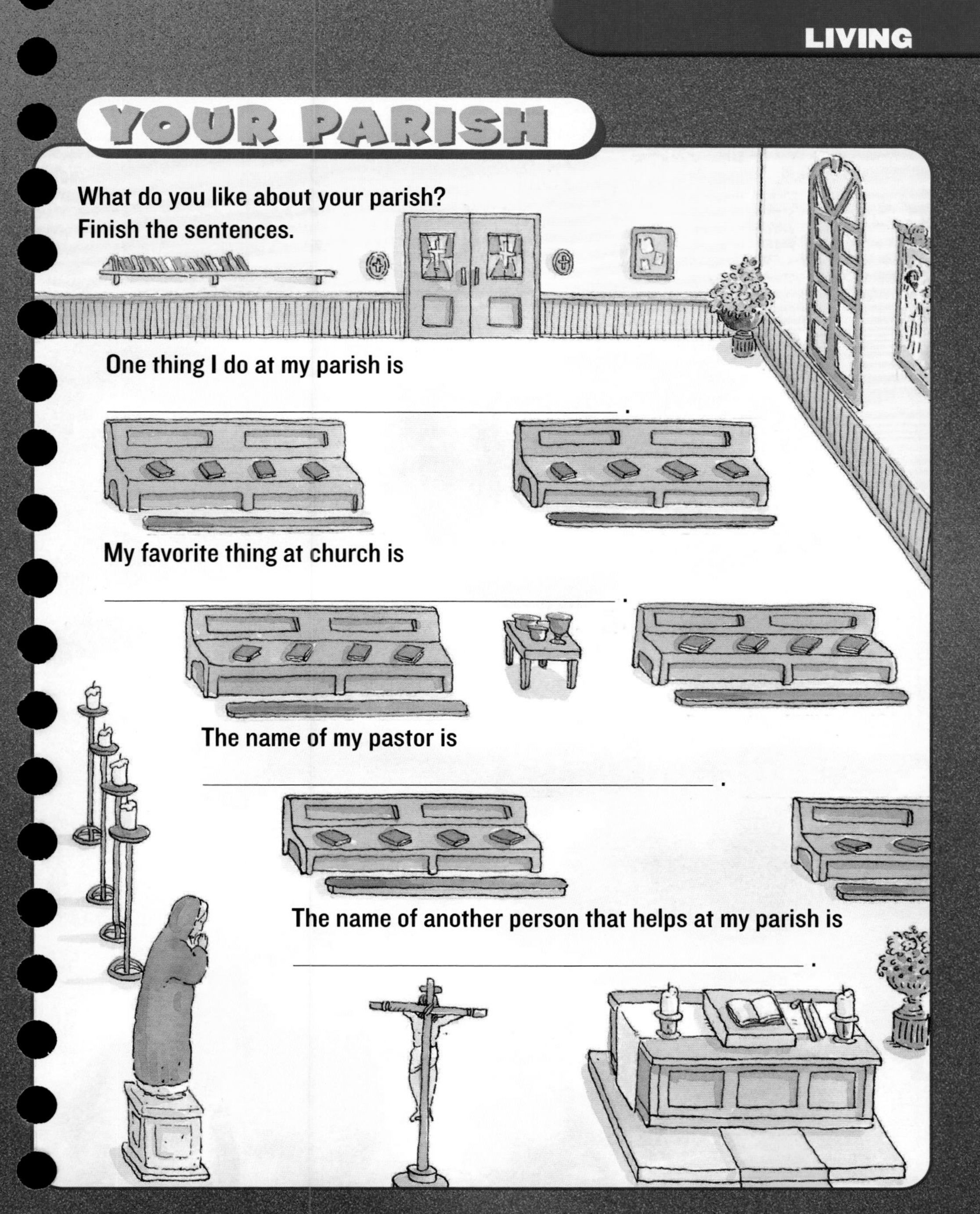

LIVING
YOUR PARISH
What do you like about your parish?
Finish the sentences.
One thing I do at my parish is ______.
My favorite thing at church is ______.
The name of my pastor is ______.
The name of another person that helps at my parish is ______.
A Parish · 309

VIRTUE FAITH GRACE VOCABULARY

Take this opportunity to introduce the students to words for various items in a typical Catholic church. Teach them to identify the following, moving from the back to the front of the church: holy water fonts, pews, kneelers, and offertory gifts. Point out that the area where the altar is located is called the *sanctuary*. Add that it is separate from the main body of the church. The book on the altar is called the *sacramentary*. The cross and corpus is called a *crucifix*. The place where the Gospel is proclaimed is called the *ambo*.

Other items of devotion are the *stations of the cross* (along the outer wall) and *statues*. Compare these pictured items to their counterparts in the parish church.

Prayer

The prayer experience is part of every chapter. This activity provides opportunities for the students to make their petitions for Jesus' presence in the Church's ministries.

1 Prepare for Prayer

Read the first line of the prayer. Say that this is a prayer asking Jesus to be with the parish in all its work.

Ask four volunteers to read each of the petitions beginning with "When." Practice reading the first and last parts of the prayer in unison.

2 A Parish Prayer

Gather in the prayer corner. When all are attentive and ready, pray the parish prayer together.

LEARNING TO PRAY

Add gestures to the parish prayer. Invite the students to suggest gestures to show prayer, helping, having fun, learning, community. If they are unfamiliar with gestures as part of prayer, consider providing these gestures and having them imitate you. This will take a little practice, but if you begin simply, they will readily follow and finally add ideas of their own.

RESOURCE MASTERS

The resource master on page 460 challenges the children to find ways to contribute to their parish life. They may complete this activity alone, in groups, or at home.

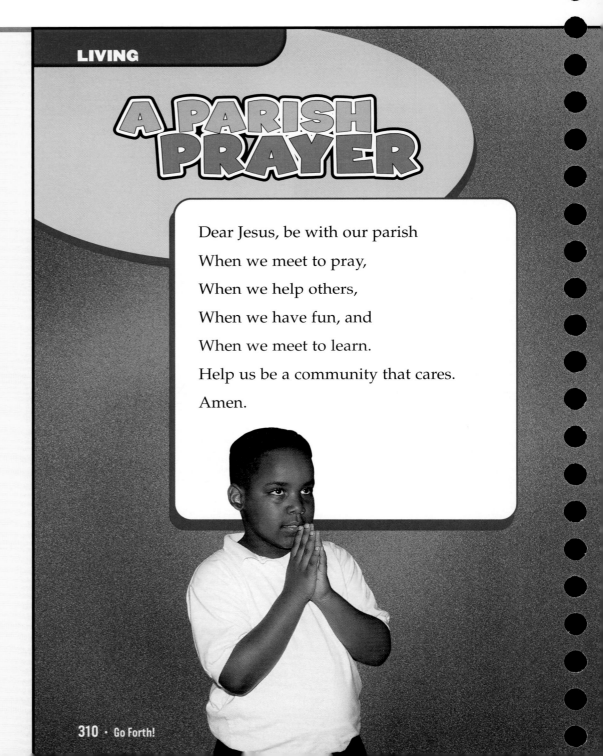

A PARISH PRAYER

Dear Jesus, be with our parish
When we meet to pray,
When we help others,
When we have fun, and
When we meet to learn.
Help us be a community that cares.
Amen.

1 Know
Ask the children to tell ways that their parish prays, celebrates, and serves. Challenge them to say how they contribute to these parish ministries.

2 Love and Serve
Have enough supplies at hand so that the children can make as many shamrocks as they wish. For the Serve activity, enlist the children's help to plan out a place and time to report back on the ways they helped in the parish. Be ready to guide the children to choose to help in ways that are appropriate for them.

3 God's Friends
Read about Blessed Vicente Villar. Ask the children how Blessed Vicente carried out Jesus' words, ". . . whatever you did for one of these least brothers of mine, you did for me" *(Matthew 25:40)*. Ask them if they know anybody like Blessed Vicente.

Know

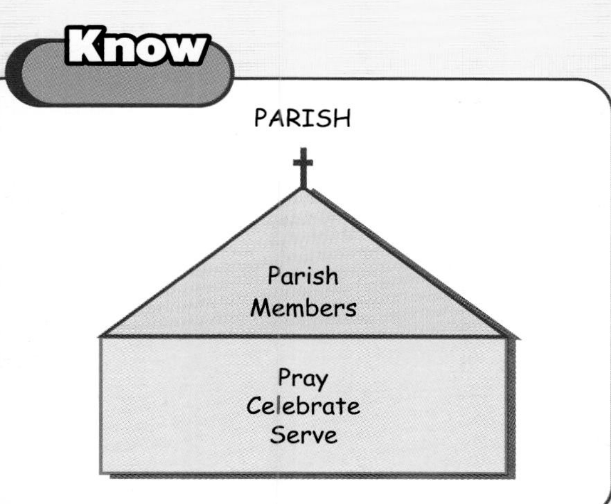

Love

Cut out a shamrock. On the shamrock, write the words, *We are lucky to have you.* Give your shamrock to a parish helper.

Serve

Your parish does many things to serve others. Write down one way you can help. Put everyone's ideas in a basket on the prayer table. Pray that God will help you. Check back in a week. Did you do your part?

GOD'S FRIENDS

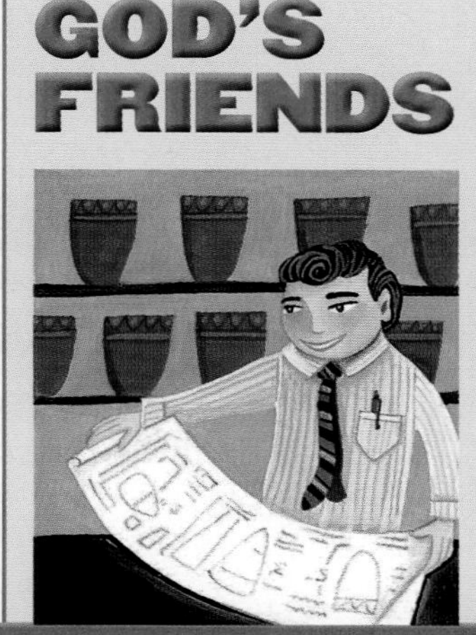

Blessed Vicente Villar

Vicente worked in his family's ceramic shop in Spain. But he still made time to serve others. He helped the poor. He helped in his parish. Vicente taught that to serve others was to serve God.

A Little Catechism

Invite the children to open their religion books to *A Little Catechism.* Choose one or more of the selections below for memory work or reinforcement. You will find your copy of the catechism on pages 23–43 of this Teacher's Edition.

1. Read about the Holy Spirit on page 22. Help the children find the sentences that tell how the Holy Spirit is with their parish family.
2. Read the story of The Boy and the Buffalo on page 25. Ask the children to find the sentences that tell how the Ting Vi's village is like a parish family.

Know Love Serve

Note The activities on this page provide ways for the children to share their learning with their families. The activities are related to the week's theme.

1 Introduce
Invite the children to tell how they do or can contribute to the parish as a family. Urge them to discuss the part of parish life their families like best. Suggest that perhaps the family can offer their services in the areas of prayer and service they most enjoy. Invite the children to consider how they can be cheerful and generous givers at home.

2 Pray Together
Ask the children to add their ideas about ways they can become caring members of their parish. After they have offered their ideas, close by praying the prayer in the prayer burst.

Online for Families
Remind the children to check the Benziger Web site this week with their families.
www.benziger.glencoe.com

Dear Family,

I have just finished chapter 22. I have learned that my parish comes together to pray and serve others. I can help too. You can help by making sure that our family serves as part of our parish family.

On your own

Serving others begins at home. Think of a job that needs to be done in your house, such as putting away the dishes or the groceries. How can you help?

With your family

Talk about how long your family has been in your parish. Talk about what your family likes best about your parish.

Dear God, help me to be a caring member of my parish.

GO ONLINE!
http://www.benziger.glencoe.com

❶ Discuss
Refer to the mural that the children have already started. Recall the ideas about missionaries they illustrated in the first panel.

❷ Project
Brainstorm more ideas than they can illustrate about their family ministry in the parish today. Have the children choose something from the list to add to the mural.

❸ Pray
Gather the children in the prayer area and invite them to pray the parish prayer on page 310 in their texts. Provide an opportunity for them to state the ways they plan to participate in the ministry of the Church today.

THE CHURCH TODAY

Remember the mural you began in chapter 21?

The mural you're making is about being sent to know, love, and serve God.

In the first part of the mural, you showed that people are sent all over the world to tell others about Jesus.

Now it's time to make the second part. Draw a picture of how you or your family serve in your parish. Add these pictures to your mural. You have shown how people serve around the world and in your parish.

ANSWER KEY

This is the answer key for the chapter test on page 461.

A. 1. c 2. a 3. b

B. 1. no 2. yes 3. no 4. yes 5. yes

Name ______________________________

How I Can Help

How can you serve others?

Match each need with a way to help. Read each sentence. In the box, put the letter of the way to help. Then, circle the letter of a way you can help today.

Need	Ways I Can Help
☐ **1.** Mrs. Jones has to walk a long way to get to Mass.	**a.** I can rake and bag leaves and pick up junk.
☐ **2.** Our classroom is a mess after religion class.	**b.** I can put cans in neat rows on the food shelf.
☐ **3.** Our parish wants to have a children's choir.	**c.** I can sing, and I like to.
☐ **4.** Bags of canned food were left at the church door.	**d.** I can ask our family to give free rides.
☐ **5.** Father O'Malley says that Sunday Mass is special.	**e.** I can help clean up the classroom.
☐ **6.** Monday is the day to take care of the lawns and gardens at the parish.	**f.** I can wear my best clean clothes.

Name ______________________________

Chapter 22 Test

A. Draw a line to match the parts that go together.

1. Parish members come together to

2. A parish is a

3. When you pray and do good works

a. Church community.

b. Jesus is with you.

c. pray, celebrate, and do good works.

B. Draw a circle around Yes if the sentence is true. Draw a circle around No if the sentence is not true.

1. Second graders are not old enough to share in parish prayer and work. Yes No

2. Parish members share God's love with others. Yes No

3. Parish members never have fun. Yes No

4. The first followers of Jesus helped others. Yes No

5. Prayer helps us remember that Jesus is with us. Yes No

CHAPTER 23 Do God's Work

TEACHER RESOURCE CENTER

Faith Formation

Let Your Actions Speak

Be doers of the word and not hearers only, deluding yourselves. For if anyone is a hearer of the word and not a doer, he is like a man who looks at his own face in a mirror. He sees himself, then goes off and promptly forgets what he looked like. But the one who peers into the perfect law of freedom and perseveres, and is not a hearer who forgets but a doer who acts, such a one shall be blessed in what he does.

James 1:22–25

What helps you remember that you are called to do God's work?

CHECK THE CATECHISM

It is necessary for the People of God to participate in promoting the common good for the good of others and of society.

The *Catechism of the Catholic Church* examines ministry in paragraphs 874 to 879. Also see paragraphs 1878–1880 and 1913–1916 for a fuller development of the responsibilities of ministry.

Witness Through Service

The letter of James recalls the value of doing God's work rather than simply talking about it. The familiar phrase of "talking the talk" summarizes the idea adequately. The Concluding Rite of the Eucharist reminds us that we are sent out to "love and serve the Lord." Our response to this, interestingly, is "Thanks be to God!" We take leave of the assembly on Sunday grateful for the opportunity to live out our baptismal commitment to ministry. As members of the Body of Christ, we are called to share the joys and sorrows of all humankind. Endless opportunities call to us to risk using our skills and talents for others. Serving God in one another is our privilege and a task. "Thanks be to God" is an appropriate response to the commission we are given weekly.

What need do you see around you that you think you are equipped to respond to but are a little shy about?

Background

Doing God's Work

The second graders have been exploring their responsibility to contribute to the life of the parish. They are eager to share in ministries provided by parish organizations as well as individuals. The parish that is committed to service is truly a life-giving Resurrection community, a presence of Christ in the world today. And a ministering community is also a powerful witness for young children. This lesson reminds us of Jesus' word and example. The children will see how his example and message is lived out in the Church who loves and serves the Lord. They will learn how they can carry forth Jesus' work, which is God's work on earth.

Faith Summary

- **The baptized are sent to love and serve the Lord.**
- **Jesus showed his followers how to serve.**
- **In serving others, Christians serve Jesus himself.**

Growth and Development

It is helpful to remember two characteristics of second graders as you teach this lesson:

- ***Second graders learn by example how to reach out to others.*** Take every opportunity to include the children in well-supervised, limited, effective parish ministry.
- ***Second graders thrive on being involved in meaningful projects.*** When including children in parish ministries, provide ways for them to see the effects of their efforts. For example, if they helped prepare for a parish festival or stocked food shelves, have them greet and welcome the clients or participants.

A Teacher's Prayer

Lord, you told the Apostles that those who are called to lead must be servants of all. Then, you humbly washed the Apostles' feet. Bless me with a servant heart. Provide me with all I need to model your leadership. When I grow weary in service, strengthen me again and again. Amen.

Vocabulary Preview

service

Scripture

John 13:15: imitating Jesus' service

Luke 22:27: Jesus is a servant leader.

Related Resources

Video

"Beatitudes for Young People" (St. Anthony Messenger Press, 1-800-488-0488 or www.AmericanCatholic.org). This three-video set helps young children see ways of being and serving that relate to the Beatitudes. (Children, 15 minutes each)

Books

Crosby, Michael. *House Disciples* (Orbis Press, 1-800-258-5388 or www.videoswithvalues.org). This book offers an excellent treatment of the theme of discipleship and Church. (Adult)

Wilkes, Paul. *Excellent Catholic Parishes: The Guide to Best Places and Practices* (New York: Paulist Press, 2001) This book provides summaries of the many parishes that carry on the work of gathering, celebrating, proclaiming, and serving. (Adult)

TEACHER ORGANIZER

Planning Guide

The basic content for each chapter is divided into four class sessions. There are a number of options for the fifth session. Extension, review, and testing options are described under Day 5 Alternatives. The Quick Check box will help you evaluate the week's lessons.

Chapter Goals

In this chapter, the students will learn about

- ❑ Their baptismal call to love and serve the Lord
- ❑ The words and actions of Jesus as a servant leader
- ❑ Ways that Christians serve Jesus in others

	DAY 1 · INVITATION	DAY 2 · DISCOVERY	DAY 3 · DISCOVERY
OBJECTIVES	**The students will be able to** • Identify their gifts • Evaluate their service to others • Choose a way to share their gifts	**The students will be able to** • Describe the value of examples of service • Share in a prayer leading to a commitment	**The students will be able to** • Connect service with the Concluding Rite of the Mass • Describe how they are ready to serve
PREPARATION	• Practice telling the story from John 13:1–9 • Gather ideas for the self-test grid	• Make a rebus about yourself • Practice leading a guided meditation • Choose recorded music	• Gather ideas for service • Make up prayers for a litany
MATERIALS	• Writing materials • Bible • Props	• Art materials • Prizes • Recorded music and player	• Writing materials
OPTIONAL ACTIVITIES	• Options Dramatize Jesus' example of servant leadership • Ideas That Work Evaluate ways to share gifts	• Options Create rebuses • Learning To Pray Follow a guided meditation	• Options Dramatize the Concluding Rite at Mass • Learning To Pray Create a litany prayer

Learning Objectives

By the end of this chapter, the students should be able to

- ❏ Identify the words that sent them to love and serve the Lord
- ❏ Describe how Jesus showed his followers to serve
- ❏ Choose ways to be of service to others

DAY 4 · LIVING	DAY 5 · ALTERNATIVES
The students will be able to • Name the ways Jesus served and called others to serve • Choose ways they can serve others at home • Express in prayer their willingness to serve	**There are a number of alternatives to help you plan Day 5.** **Prayer Experience** Use the prayer service on either Day 4 or Day 5. Follow the suggestions on page 474 for leading the prayer. **Review and Explore** Follow the suggestions on page 475 for teaching the page. If you will give the chapter test on Day 5, assign this page as homework the night before. **Home and Family** Send this page home, if possible. You may also assign one or more activities as class work or homework. **The Church Today** This page provides a class or group project that may be started in class following the chapter test and completed outside of class. **Chapter Test** The chapter test appears as a resource master on page 479.
• Make and post a paper tree trunk and branches • Print children's names on their page of compliments • Make copies of the resource master on page 478	
• Colored chalk or markers • Writing materials • Art materials • Copies of the resource master	
• **Ideas That Work** Create a tree of knowledge and participate in a compliment circle • **Resource Masters** Decide on ways to serve	

Quick Check

Do this evaluation as soon as you finish each chapter.

Did I follow my lesson plan?

How can I tell that I met the learning objectives for the lesson?

What activities did the children enjoy most?

How could I improve this lesson?

Benziger on the Web
For more ideas, visit us at **www.benziger.glencoe.com**

Interactive Lesson Planner
Your ILP provides more help in preparing to teach this chapter.

Celebrate
Turn to page 22 of this book. Check for seasonal celebrations.

Lesson Plan · Day 1
Ask the students to compare their level of capability to younger and older children. Ask them what jobs and chores they can do that smaller children cannot. Ask how their growing skills and accomplishments make them feel.

1 Introduce
Read the chapter's Scripture verse and ask the children what actions they think Jesus might be referring to. Read or tell the story based on John 13:1–9.

2 Do You Know?
Read the question and ask the children if they can recall where they have heard the words "love and serve the Lord." Ask them to share ways they can love and serve the Lord. At the end of the week, return to this question to see how the children's knowledge has developed.

OPTIONS

For the Visual Learner Have the children act out the story of Jesus' washing the feet of his disciples. (see *John 13:1–9*) Provide props. You might want to prepare them for the story by explaining that washing the feet of others was a lowly, messy chore nobody wanted to do. Emphasize that Jesus was willing to do this lowly job for others.

INVITATION 23

What I have done, so you must do.

John 13:15

Do You Know?

◆ What are some ways that you can "love and serve the Lord?"

Do God's Work

Pick Me!

Mr. McCarthy, the teacher, needs some help. Who will pass out the papers? Who wants to lead the prayer? Who can be in charge of the play equipment?

Circle the word that tells how you feel when you have a job to do.

Happy **Proud** **Important**

? What's a job you like to do in school?

3 Pick Me!

Read the selection on student page 314 aloud. Ask the children about some of the tasks that need to be done in religion class. Use the question to discover how they help in their schools. Give them time to circle their responses. Note that when they help others, they feel happy, proud, and important. Ask for other ideas about how they feel when they accomplish something good.

4 Gifts to Give

Say that God has blessed each of them with gifts they should be proud of and happy to share with others. Read the stories on this page. Then ask them to look at the pictures and also to think of other ways that Thomas and Samantha can share their gifts. You may want to suggest a few more typical situations before the children determine their own gifts and how to share them.

Ask the students to tell what they do well. If this question puzzles them, suggest a gift you have especially appreciated this year. After they illustrate how they can use their gifts for others, have them gather in small groups to show and discuss their work.

Gifts to Give

Thomas is very good with puzzles. His younger sister thinks that puzzles are hard! Thomas likes to help his sister put puzzles together.

Samantha is very patient with animals. She takes care of the new puppies right after they are born. Her job is to teach others how to take care of the puppies.

What do you do well?

____

____

Draw a picture of how you help others with your special gift.

IDEAS THAT WORK

On the board, make a grid listing serving actions. Write a few of your own in the first column, such as: *I share what I have. I play fair. I spend time with others.* Ask the students to suggest other ideas. Write the words *Never, Sometimes, Always* across the top of the chalkboard. Ask the students to take a small self-test to determine what kind of helpers they are. Ask them to circle one kind of service they could improve on.

Lesson Plan · Day 2

Ask the children to tell why following the example of others is a good way to learn. Have them give examples about how they learned to weave a potholder, build a birdhouse, shoot a basket, and the like.

1 Jesus Shows You

Comment that this story will be familiar to them. Study the key and be sure that the children understand what the pictures stand for. Invite the students to pair off and read the rebus story.

Afterward, read it aloud pausing at each rebus while the children call out the correct word. Ask the children about the decision Jesus made to teach by showing, rather than just telling.

OPTIONS

For the Artistic Learner Invite the students to create a rebus story about themselves and their gifts. Ask them to create a rebus illustrating the following: themselves, their gifts, and how they share their gifts. Show a rebus about yourself to help them understand the task. Ask them to keep their rebus secret. Collect the rebuses and display them on the wall. Have the children guess the author, gift, and service of their classmates. For fun, you might want to give small prizes.

Jesus Shows You

Jesus

Apostles

Peter

At the Last Supper, Jesus showed how to do God's work.

One  and his  ate a special meal. 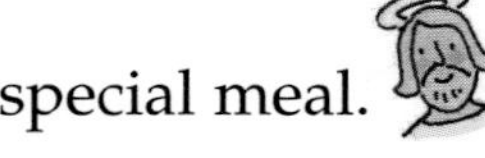 got a  and some 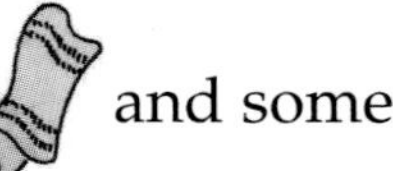. He began to wash the Apostles' . They all wore . The  was dusty. Their 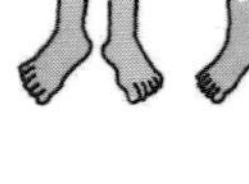 were  clean.  did not want Jesus to act like a servant.  asked  to . But  washed the feet of all the . Then Jesus said, "What  have done, so must you do."  was telling us  serve others.

From *John 13:1–15*

❷ You Can Serve
Read the first directions and each sentence about Jesus. Check to be sure that they understand that the first statement means that Jesus cared for all people, not just important or famous people. Give the children quiet time to think about and check the following three statements and evaluate themselves.

❸ Activity
Invite volunteers to show their drawings and tell how they feel they can serve as Jesus showed them.

You Can Serve

What does the Bible tell you about Jesus? Look back at the story. Find facts that show which of the sentences below are true.

Jesus treated all people the same.
Jesus showed love.
Jesus did what was needed.

Make a ✔ next to each sentence that tells how you can be like Jesus.

- ☐ Be kind to those who are different from you.
- ☐ Show love in the ways you can.
- ☐ Look for ways to help.

ACTIVITY A SPECIAL VISITOR

Pretend that Jesus is visiting your classroom. Draw a picture of how Jesus can show you how to serve others.

LEARNING TO PRAY

Before doing the activity, guide the children in a brief meditation. Make the room as conducive to reflection as possible. Ask the children sit with their backs straight so that they can breathe evenly and deeply. Provide quiet recorded music. Have them close their eyes and wait until they seem to be quiet inside. Describe Jesus coming to the classroom, stopping by them and speaking to them. Pause briefly. To bring the guided meditation to a close, describe Jesus saying good-bye and leaving the room. Ask them to open their eyes, and turn off the music. Then quietly move into the activity.

Lesson Plan · Day 3
Make up some tasks that need volunteers—jobs that would interest the children (taking a message to the principal's office, feeding the gerbils). Select a few students to do these tasks. Or, take time to review the tasks that the students regularly perform. Thank them for their help and comment that they are generous and are following Jesus' example of service.

1 Go and Serve
In pairs, invite the children to take turns reading each paragraph of this section to find out about service as a Christian ministry. Challenge them to tell the words that open and close each Mass and to explain what Catholics are sent out to do after each Mass.

2 Question
Ask a volunteer to identify how the children in the photo show that they love and serve the Lord. Invite the children to make a list of ways they can love and serve the Lord. Use the This We Believe! feature as a summary of the main idea of this page.

OPTIONS

For the Active Child Choose a child to play the priest. Ask the rest of the class to be the assembly. Direct the child to stand in front and say the words of welcome and of dismissal. Encourage the children in the assembly to respond clearly and firmly.

This We Believe!

The Mass sends us out to love and serve others.

Go and Serve

Mass begins with a sign of the cross. As Mass ends, the priest blesses you in the name of the Father and of the Son and of the Holy Spirit. The priest or deacon then says, "Go in peace to love and serve the Lord."

With these words you know that the Mass has ended. Your work to love and serve others has just begun.

Every week, Jesus sends you to do God's work. Jesus is saying. "I want you to tell others about God. Love one another. Serve others."

What good thing can you do as a member of God's Church?

3 Are You Ready?
To prepare the children for this activity, suggest familiar situations that require preparation. For example, you might have the children demonstrate how they are ready to begin a race, to share a meal, to dive off a diving board, to sing the national anthem. Then read the section and the directions. After the children have completed their work, give them time to share their ideas.

4 Word of God
Read the statement aloud and ask: Are you ready? Wait for an enthusiastic response, "Yes!" If their response is tepid, read the statement and question a second time and ask for a more enthusiastic response.

Are You Ready?

When you leave church you do not leave God behind. God is always with you. You have work to do! Your home, your school, and your neighborhood need you.

A helping attitude begins at home.

Word of God

I am among you as the one who serves.

Luke 22:27

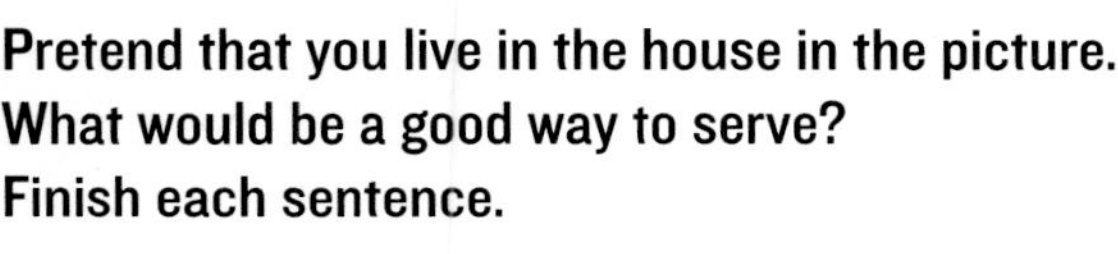

Pretend that you live in the house in the picture. What would be a good way to serve? Finish each sentence.

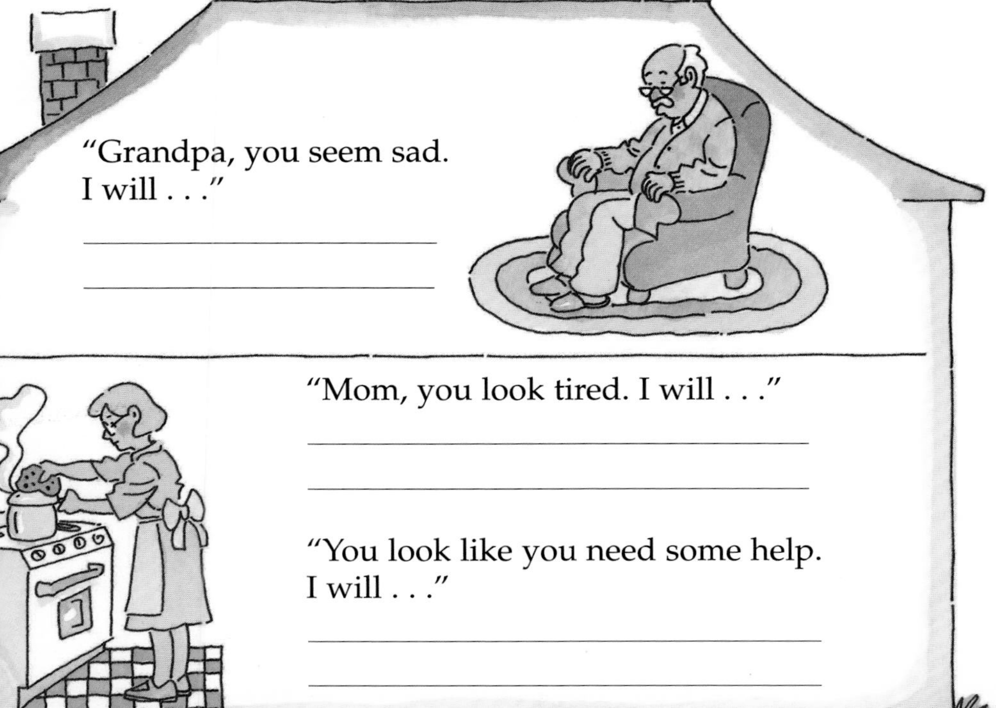

"Grandpa, you seem sad.
I will . . ."
"Mom, you look tired. I will . . ."
"You look like you need some help.
I will . . ."

LEARNING TO PRAY

Turn the children's responses from the activity into a litany. Follow this outline:

Jesus: I am among you as one who serves. Are you ready?

Student 1: I am ready! I will . . .

Jesus: I am among you as one who serves. Are you ready?

Student 2: I am ready! I will . . .

Lesson Plan · Day 4

Draw a very large sprawling outline on the chalkboard to act as a kind of graffiti wall. Print *Jesus* at the top. Ask the children to come forward in pairs or triads to print short phrases about Jesus' message and ministry. You might begin by choosing colored chalk or marker and printing, *likes children.* Then call on children to add their phrases.

1 Tree of Knowledge

Read the directions and ask the students to think of ways they can tell about Jesus. Remind them that actions as well as words can give others messages about Jesus. Invite them to share their ideas in small groups of about four. Encourage them to add the ideas they learned from others.

IDEAS THAT WORK

Have the children cut out leaves of any shape. Cut out a large free-hand trunk and branches and mount it on the wall. Have the children draw on the ideas they generated and add as many leaves as they can—the more the better.

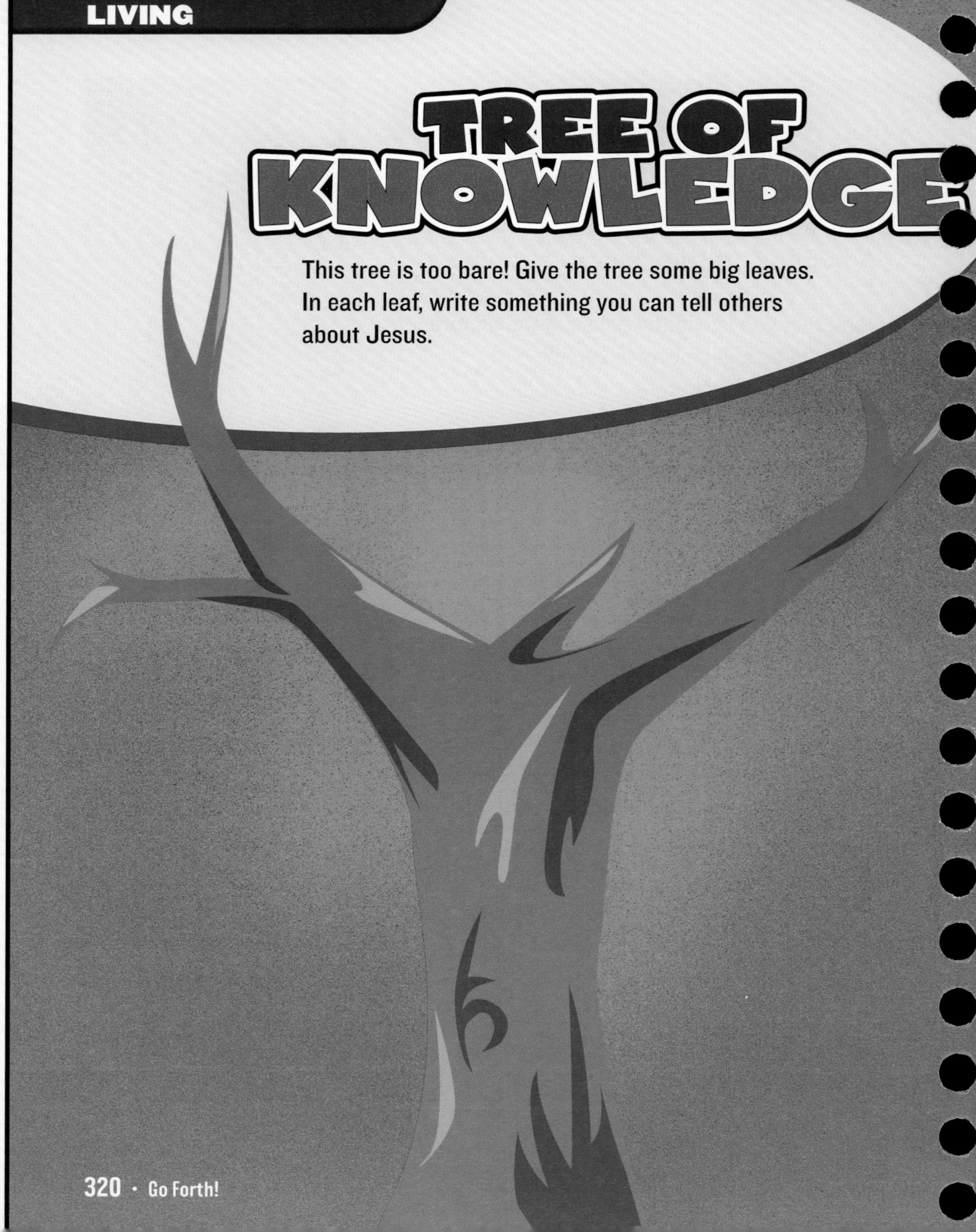

LIVING
TREE OF KNOWLEDGE
This tree is too bare! Give the tree some big leaves. In each leaf, write something you can tell others about Jesus.
320 · Go Forth!

2 Serving at Home

Read the directions, and ask the children to give examples of ways they serve by helping without being asked, listening, and saying "thank you." Give them time to draw or print ideas in the two empty boxes. Have them share their ideas by miming them while their classmates guess or by simply talking about their ideas.

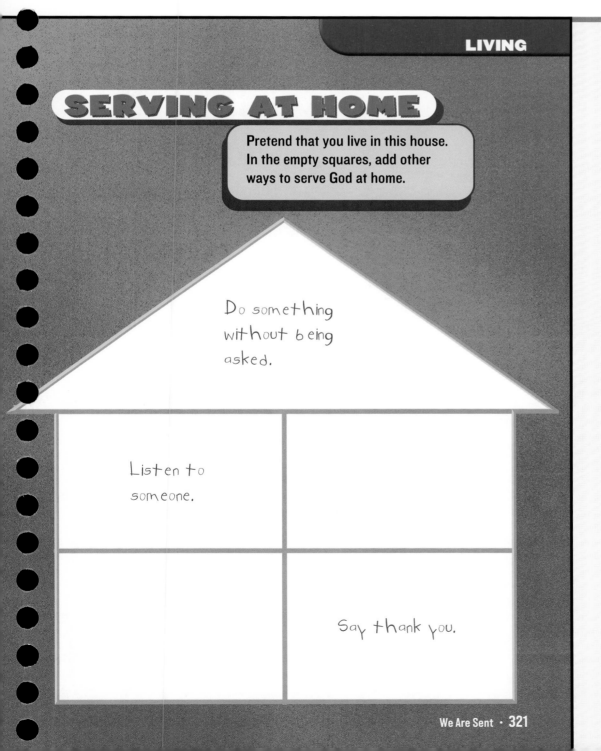

SERVING AT HOME

Pretend that you live in this house. In the empty squares, add other ways to serve God at home.

Do something without being asked.

Listen to someone.

Say thank you.

IDEAS THAT WORK

Ask the students to gather in groups of about six. Give each child a sheet of paper with his or her name on the top. Join one of the groups and demonstrate this procedure: At the bottom of the sheet of paper of the child to your right, print a good characteristic (for example, *a good helper*) and fold the paper up to cover your printing. Have all the children in each group pass their named papers to the right for another child to write a complimentary characteristic. When their paper returns to them, the children should have five complimentary characteristics. This is a real day brightener that helps children acknowledge their skills and qualities. Lead a discussion about how they can use their good qualities and skills for others.

Prayer

The prayer experience is part of every chapter. This activity provides opportunities for the students to make to ask God to help them be ready and willing servants.

1 Prepare for Prayer

Have the children glance through the prayer. Then practice the repeated "All" response and the longer ending response. Get the children in the spirit of the prayer by asking how they act when they know an answer and want to be called. Divide the class in half and identify them as sides 1 and 2.

2 Send Me!

Gather in the prayer corner. Practice a familiar hymn that has a servant theme. You might want to use "Peace Prayer" (based on the prayer of Saint Francis of Assisi) or music recommended for the Evening Mass of the Lord's Supper (Holy Thursday), such as "Where Charity and Love Are Found."

The resource master on page 478 challenges the children to find ways to be of loving service. They may complete this activity alone, in groups, or at home.

SEND ME!

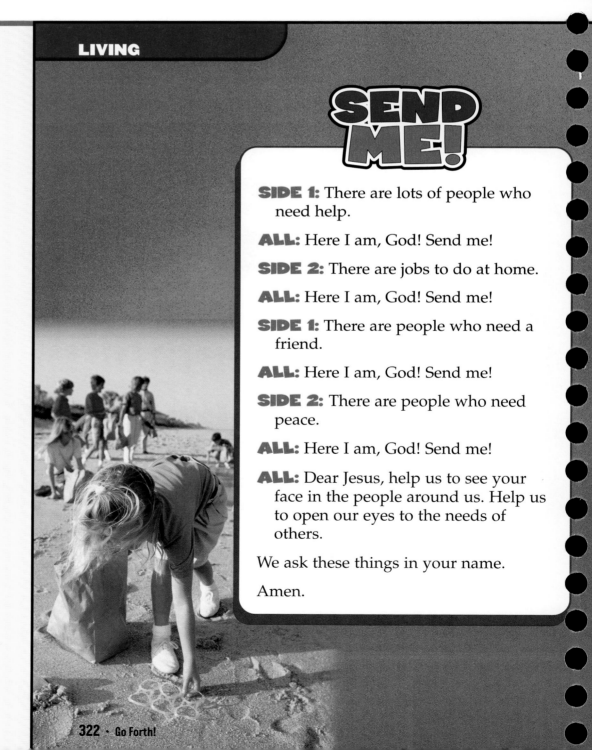

SIDE 1: There are lots of people who need help.

ALL: Here I am, God! Send me!

SIDE 2: There are jobs to do at home.

ALL: Here I am, God! Send me!

SIDE 1: There are people who need a friend.

ALL: Here I am, God! Send me!

SIDE 2: There are people who need peace.

ALL: Here I am, God! Send me!

ALL: Dear Jesus, help us to see your face in the people around us. Help us to open our eyes to the needs of others.

We ask these things in your name.

Amen.

1 Know

Discuss the three ways the children and the rest of their parish can fulfill their commission to serve. Set a one-minute timer and invite the students to call out as many ideas as they can in that time.

2 Love and Serve

Invite the students to share the results of their work on the Love section. Give them time to complete the Serve section. Ask volunteers to share their ideas, but allow the children to pass if they want to. Put a sticker, preferably a smiling face one, on their forehead, cheek, or hand, or use a rubber stamp on the top of their hand as a reminder to carry out the service they chose.

3 God's Friends

Read about Saint Margaret of Scotland. Use a globe or wall map and ask if the children can find Scotland. Ask if they would expect a queen to care for the poorest of all. Connect the service of Saint Margaret with Jesus' service.

Know

To Love God and others

I AM SENT

To tell others about God

To serve God

Love

You can show love for others with a smile or a kind word. Between the faces, write a kind thing you can say to change a sad face to a happy face.

Serve

Think of something that you do everyday, like having lunch or doing classwork. Write one way that you can help someone during that time.

CHAPTER 23
REVIEW and EXPLORE

GOD'S FRIENDS

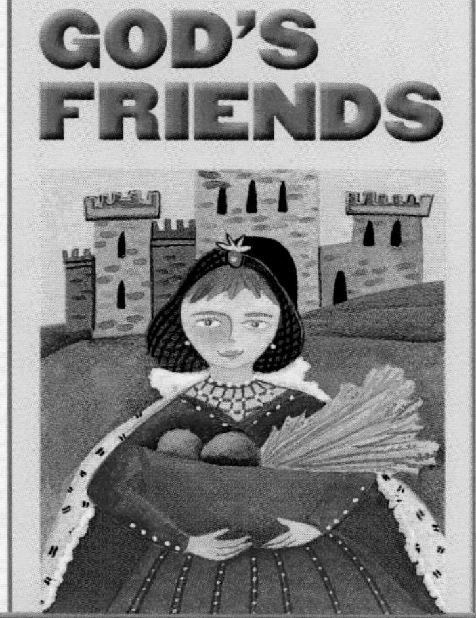

Saint Margaret

Queen Margaret of Scotland walked through the dark streets. She saw poor homeless people. Margaret knelt down and washed their feet. Then she slipped coins into their hands. Margaret always served those who most needed help.

A Little Catechism

Invite the children to open their religion books to *A Little Catechism*. Choose one or more of the selections below for memory work or reinforcement. You will find your copy of the catechism on pages 23–43 of this Teacher's Edition.

1. Read the scripture story from Matthew on page 23. Ask: What does Jesus mean when he says, "If you want to be number one, you must serve others"?
2. Read the story of Katherine Drexel on page 24. Have a discussion about how Katherine listened to God's message to serve others.

Note The activities on this page provide ways for the children to share their learning with their families. The activities are related to the week's theme.

1 Introduce
Invite the children to tell how they hear and heed the commission to be of loving service. Help the children begin designing their postcards. In case of accidents, have extra index cards at hand. Discuss ideas the children could include on their postcards. Connect the postcard activity with a family discussion about spreading the message of loving service everywhere.

2 Pray Together
Read this prayer aloud. Ask the children to add their ideas about ways they can be cheerful givers. You might want to adapt a happy psalm such as the short and joyful Psalm 100.

Online for Families
Remind the children to check the Benziger Web site this week with their families.
www.benziger.glencoe.com

Dear Family,

I have just finished chapter 23. I have learned that each week I am sent out to do God's work. I do God's work by loving and serving others. You can help by reminding me that I can do God's work at home.

With others

Ask someone to help you make a postcard. You will need a stamp and an index card. Draw a picture on one side of the index card. On the other side write one thing that you learned about Jesus this week. Send the card to someone you know.

With your family

Ask your family to think of one way that everyone can spread the message of God's love this week.

God, help me to serve you with gladness.

GO ONLINE!
http://www.benziger.glencoe.com

1 Discuss
Refer to the mural the students began. Recall the ideas about missionaries they illustrated in the first panel and family ministry in the parish in the second panel.

2 Project
Brainstorm other ideas they can illustrate focusing on service to their family. Encourage them to be specific. Also, suggest that the children think of family members who are at school or in military service as well as grandparents, aunts and uncles, and friends whom the children think of as family.

3 Pray
Invite the children to quietly pray for their families as you pause after each of the phrases in this prayer:
Father in heaven, you are the creator of all. Bless everyone in our family. *(pause)* Help us to live in peace and love. *(pause)* Watch over us at home and away from home. *(pause)* May we all share life with you and your Son, Jesus, with the Holy Spirit now and forever. Amen.

THE CHURCH TODAY

It's time to do the third part of your class mural.
You know that service begins at home.

Draw a picture of something you do at home to help your family. Add your picture to the others about helping.
See the many ways that you can serve God by serving others!

ANSWER KEY

This is the answer key for the chapter test on page 479.

A. 1. b 2. b

B. 1. yes 2. no 3. yes

C. Accept all reasonable responses.

Name ______________________________

I Can Serve

Look at each picture. In the box beside it, draw how you can serve.

Name ________________________________

Chapter 23 Test

A. Circle the word that best completes the sentence.

1. Jesus showed his followers that he is a leader who

a. wins. **b.** serves. **c.** scolds.

2. As Mass ends, you are sent out to

a. do your homework. **b.** love and serve the Lord.

c. work for money.

B. Circle yes if the sentence is true. Circle no if the sentence is false.

1. Jesus said, "I am among you as one who serves."	yes	no
2. You are only called to serve people who are nice to you.	yes	no
3. God has given you skills and gifts to share with others.	yes	no

C. Draw a way that you can use your gifts to help others.

CHAPTER 24 Know, Love, and Serve

TEACHER RESOURCE CENTER

Faith Formation

Joy-filled Ministry

Do not be afraid! I know that you are seeking Jesus the crucified. He is not here, for he has been raised just as he said. Come and see the place where he lay. Then go quickly and tell his disciples, "He has been raised from the dead, and he is going before you to Galilee; there you will see him. Behold I have told you." Then they went away quickly from the tomb, fearful yet overjoyed, and ran to announce this to his disciples.

Matthew 28:5–8

CHECK THE CATECHISM

The *Catechism of the Catholic Church* brings new insight into Christian holiness in paragraphs 2006–2016. The mission of the Church is set forth in paragraphs 849–857.

Joy in the Resurrection runs deep. It is not the same as feeling good. It is more than having been blessed with a sunny disposition. The kind of joy the first witnesses experienced existed with palpable fear and bewilderment. Joy based on faith runs deep. The joy of the Resurrection is nourished by the Spirit. A faithful community sustains it. Joy is manifest in enthusiastic service, in running quickly to announce the good news of the Resurrection, and in anticipating the presence of the Risen Lord among us. Faith-filled people find their joy in knowing and loving. They express their joy in service.

As you reflect on this school year, when has the Risen Lord been most clearly with you and the students? What are those moments of felt joy?

Be filled with Joy

In this unit, the second graders have been studying their call to serve others. This final lesson of the year helps them to see that knowledge of God includes love and service. The children will learn that this three-fold vocation of knowing, loving, and serving begins and ends in joy. They will be invited to consider the joy of the first disciples that attracted others. People understand the kind of joy expressed in generous service.

How do you witness to and announce the joyful news of the Resurrection to others?

Background

Knowing, Loving, and Serving

The students have been studying their call to serve others. This final lesson of the year helps them to see that knowledge of God includes love and service. The children will learn that this three-fold vocation of knowing, loving, and serving begins and ends in joy. They will be invited to consider the joy of the first disciples whose very joy attracted others. Everyone, including second graders, needs tangible, consistent models of Christian joy. They can see how joy looks when they see the cheerful giving, generous service, and loving attitude of today's Easter People among whom they are numbered. Enjoy one another today. Send the children out in peace to love and serve the Lord all summer long!

Faith Summary

- Christians rejoice in the Resurrection.
- Followers of Jesus are called to know, love, and serve God.
- The Holy Spirit helps followers of Jesus.

Growth and Development

It is helpful to remember two characteristics of second graders as you teach this lesson:

- ***Second graders aim to please.*** Appeal to the children's natural desire to please. Help them to do what is good and right by setting an example and by inviting them to share in generous work.
- ***Second graders need affirmation from adults.*** Everyone needs to be proud of his or her accomplishments. Keep an eye out for their efforts and successes. Also, help them to learn when they fall short or appear disappointed with the results of their efforts.

A Teacher's Prayer

Holy Spirit, you were sent by God to be with us and to help us understand all that Jesus said and did. Be with me as I try to teach and explain the grand and wonderful things of God. Fill my heart with joy. Bless the children with joyful hearts, too. Amen.

Vocabulary Preview

know
love
serve

Scripture

Luke 1:14: a promise of joy
Acts 2:37–47: the ideal Christian community
John 14:6: Jesus as the way, the truth, and the life

Related Resources

Books

Lionni, Leo. *Matthew's Dream* (New York: Scholastic, Inc., 1991). Matthew the mouse finds his vocation. He discovers how to paint with colors of joy. (Children)

Murphy, Elspeth Campbell. *Where Are You, God? Psalm 130 for Children* (David C. Cook Publishing Co., 1980). A good way to pray as you send the children to enjoy their summer. (Children)

Zannoni, Arthur E. *Jesus of the Gospels: Teacher, Storyteller, Friend, Messiah* (Cincinnati, OH: St. Anthony Messenger Press). The last chapter in this book deals with the biblical roots of discipleship and the challenges of Jesus to his disciples as presented in the Gospels. (Adult)

TEACHER ORGANIZER

Planning Guide

The basic content for each chapter is divided into four class sessions. There are a number of options for the fifth session. Extension, review, and testing options are described under Day 5 Alternatives. The Quick Check box will help you evaluate the week's lessons.

Chapter Goals

In this chapter, the students will learn about

- ❑ The joy of the first Christians
- ❑ Their call to know, love, and serve God
- ❑ The guidance of the Holy Spirit

	DAY 1 · INVITATION	DAY 2 · DISCOVERY	DAY 3 · DISCOVERY
OBJECTIVES	**The students will be able to** • Identify ways to bring joy • Connect service and joy	**The students will be able to** • Identify actions of joyful Christians • Describe ways they can show their joy as Christians • Connect the Mass to joyful service	**The students will be able to** • Show ways they can live as joyful Christians • Write sentences expressing love to God and others
PREPARATION	• Practice telling the story of John the Baptizer's mission • Cut out circles for faces	• Make and label slips • Gather ideas to role play	• Prepare gestures for Mary's prayer
MATERIALS	• Writing materials • Bible • Props • Art materials	• Sad and glad faces • Art materials • Labeled slips, container	• Writing materials • Art materials • Bible
OPTIONAL ACTIVITIES	• **Ideas That Work** Make sad and glad faces	• **Options** Role-play with sad and glad faces • **Teaching Tip** Discuss the Eucharist and service	• **Options** Dramatize ways joy is expressed • **Learning To Pray** Memorize and pray Mary's prayer of Joy

Learning Objectives

By the end of this chapter, the students should be able to
- ❑ Tell how they can be joyful witnesses
- ❑ Name ways to love and serve God
- ❑ Pray to the Holy Spirit for help and guidance

DAY 4 · LIVING

The students will be able to
- Identify ways to love and serve the Lord
- Pray for the guidance of the Holy Spirit

- Practice guiding meditative prayer
- Wrap a gift box with a large mirror inside
- Make copies of the resource master on page 496

- Writing materials
- Gift box, mirror
- Recorded music and player
- Copies of the resource master

- **Learning To Pray** Lead a meditation prayer
- **Ideas That Work** Pass around a gift box surprise
- **Resource Masters** Make plans to share joy

DAY 5 · ALTERNATIVES

There are a number of alternatives to help you plan Day 5.

Prayer Experience
Use the prayer on either Day 4 or Day 5. Follow the suggestions on page 492 for leading the prayer.

Review and Explore
Follow the suggestions on page 493 for teaching the page. If you will give the chapter test on Day 5, assign this page as homework the night before.

Home and Family
Send this page home, if possible. You may also assign one or more activities as class work or homework.

The Church Today
This page provides a class or group project that may be started in class following the chapter test and completed outside of class.

Chapter Test
The chapter test appears as a resource master on page 496.

Quick Check

Do this evaluation as soon as you finish each chapter.

Did I follow my lesson plan?

How can I tell that I met the learning objectives for the lesson?

What activities did the children enjoy most?

How could I improve this lesson?

Benziger on the Web
For more ideas, visit us at **www.benziger.glencoe.com**

Interactive Lesson Planner
Your ILP provides more help in preparing to teach this chapter.

Celebrate
Turn to page 22 of this book. Check for seasonal celebrations.

Lesson Plan · Day 1
Recall the words of dismissal at Mass and recall that the children have learned how to be of loving service at home and in the parish. Tell the children that they have been called to be of service. Encourage an enthusiastic response such as, "Yes we're ready!"

1 Introduction
Read the Scripture verse. Tell the children the story from Luke 1:1–15. Explain that an angel told of the birth of a John the Baptizer whose joy and gladness was to say, "Jesus is here!"

2 Do You Know?
Read the question and ask the children to tell of their experiences of joyful sharing of God's love. Be alert to their understanding of the signs of joy. *(people were generous, pleasant, smiling, gentle, peaceful)* To jog their memories, recall that they have studied ways people serve in their home and parish. Also, offer an idea of your own.

INVITATION 24

You will have joy and gladness.

Luke 1:14

Do You Know?

◆ How do you share the joy of God's love?

Know, Love, *and* Serve

A Good Place

For a long time, a place called Gladd Street was known as "Sad Street." Hardly anyone wanted to live there. Then things changed. Neighbors helped neighbors. People from other neighborhoods came to help out. Sad Street became Gladd Street again!

Look at the picture. How did people make "Sad Street" into Gladd Street?

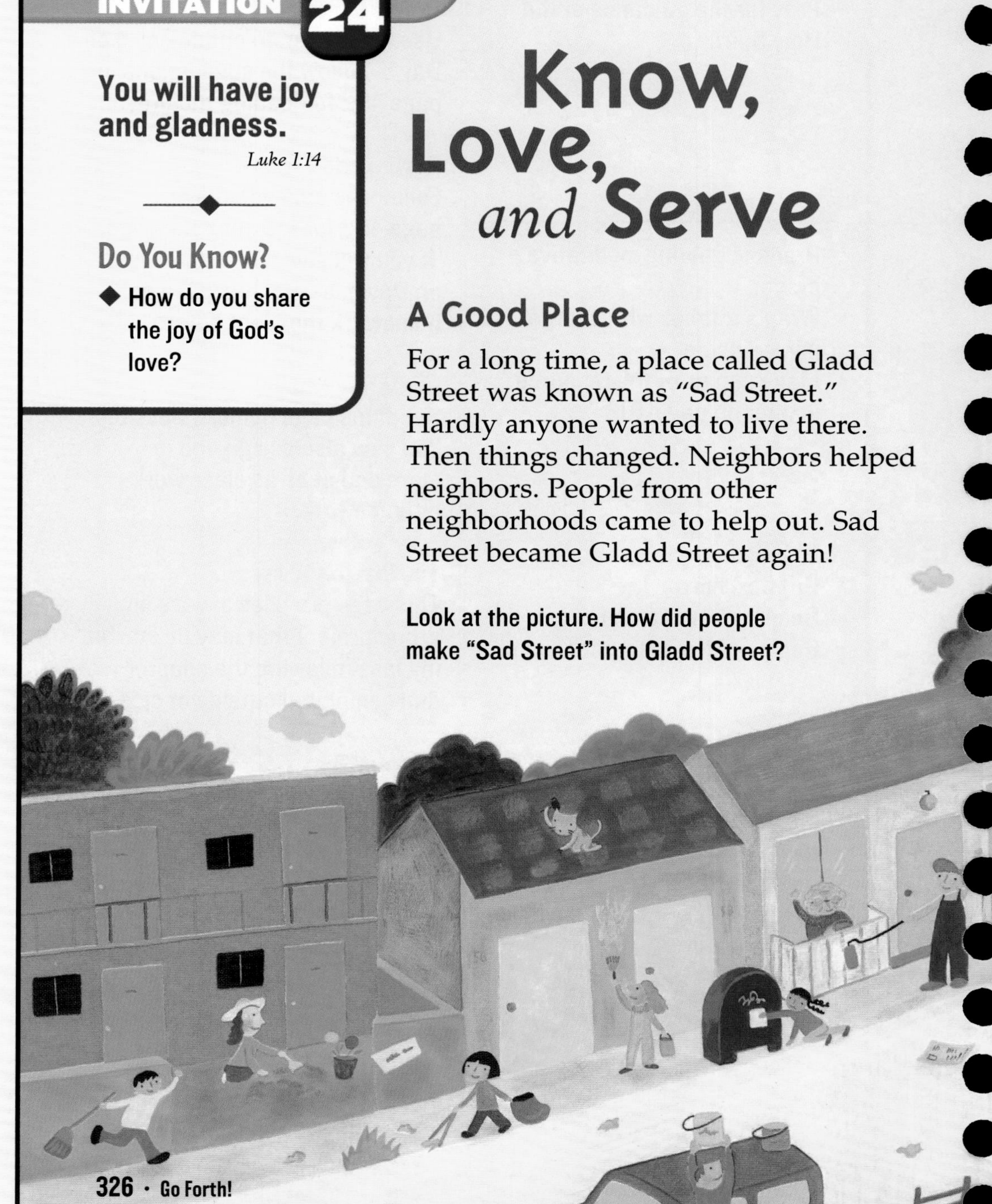

3 A Good Place

Ask the children to imagine the opposite of joy and to think about what a place like Sadd Street might be like. Ask some volunteers to put on a sad face and walk in a way that people who live on Sadd Street might walk. Invite the children to read the story aloud to find out what happened on Sadd Street.

Focus the children's attention on the illustration. Ask them to point out the many good things they see happening to turn Sadd Street into Gladd Street.

4 Good Ideas

Ask the children to put themselves on Sadd Street. Ask them to share some ideas on how they could help. After they have called out some ideas, allow the children some time to complete the activity.

Draw yourself and others helping out on Gladd Street. How can you make Gladd Street a better place?

IDEAS THAT WORK

Have the children draw a happy face on one side of their drawing paper and a sad face on the other. Ask them to display the face in response to the following statements: School children throw cans and bottles on the lawn with the For Sale sign on it. The Johnson family babysat for the Kelly's. The Kelly family helped the Wong family move in. The Lopez family waved and smiled to welcome the new family. Ask the children to continue this story by making up small scenes of their own that call for a sad or glad response.

Lesson Plan · Day 2

Ask the children to identify people who seem to be cheerful as they help others. Expect responses from the store clerk to the pastoral minister. Ask them why these people seem happy to help. Explain that today they will learn about happy helpers.

1 Service with a Smile

Have the children look at the picture and tell about what is happening. After reading the story, ask if and why they would like to be with these people. Ask what the community did to help others. *(shared their meals with joy; praised God)* Ask the children to tell how a stranger might feel in the company of the people in the story.

2 Activity

Set the children to work coloring the banner. Invite them to make up a litany using the brief prayer, "Come, Holy Spirit," as a response. Offer ideas of your own such as: When I see someone who needs my help. When I have a good idea. When I am afraid.

OPTIONS

For the Active Learner Provide small stories related to the service shown in the illustration on this page. Ask volunteers to role-play ways to serve with joy. The children can use their sad and glad faces for the role-playing activity. Consider using these ideas: Your little sister is afraid of the dark. A friend forgot his lunch box on the bus. Your friend's pet rabbit is sick. Your elderly neighbor is not strong enough to spade her garden. Your brother's team lost the championship baseball game.

Together

On the day that Holy Spirit came, Peter spoke to all the people.

"Join us," Peter said, "and be baptized in the name of Jesus. You will receive the Holy Spirit too."

Many, many people were baptized that day.

All who believed shared everything they had. They prayed in the Temple, and they broke bread in their homes. They ate their meals with joy, and praising God. Everyday more and more people joined them.

Based on *Acts 2:37–47*

Color the Holy Spirit prayer.

COME, HOLY SPIRIT!

3 Joy

Divide the class in half and ask them to stand facing each other. Direct one half of the class to read the words in regular type beginning with "God's People . . ." Have the other half read the lines written in boldface type. Point out that the first lines tell about the celebration of the Eucharist and the boldface lines describe how Catholics carry out their ministries in their world.

Joy

God wants you to be happy now and forever. Review what you have learned about happiness and joy.

God's People come together to celebrate.

They help one another and pray together, too.

Joy *is gathering.*

God's Family listens to stories about Jesus.

They listen to stories about Jesus.

Joy *is remembering.*

God's Family celebrates the Eucharist.

The Eucharist is an offering to God.
The Euchartist reminds people of Jesus' death and resurrection.

Joy *is thanking.*

TEACHING TIP

To explore the connection between the celebration of the Eucharist and joyful service, talk about the connection between the events in each set:

God's people come together to celebrate—Introductory, or Welcoming, Rite.

God's Family listens to stories about Jesus—Liturgy of the Word.

God's Family celebrates the Eucharist—Liturgy of the Eucharist; especially, the Eucharistic Prayer.

Jesus shares himself with his friends—Communion Rite.

Invite the children to show or demonstrate the words and gestures of each part of the Mass.

Lesson Plan · Day 3

Recall the five ways followers of Jesus can be happy and bring happiness to others right now. If the children need help, refer them to the five joy words on student pages 329 and 330 in their books. *(sharing, remembering, caring, thanking, gathering)*

1 Show Your Love

Read the directions. Allow the children to work independently or with partners.

LEARNING TO PRAY

Tell the children the story of Mary's visitation to Elizabeth based on Luke 1:39–49. To prepare them to hear the story, explain the following: Mary knew she was to be the Mother of Jesus. Mary went to help Elizabeth who was waiting for the birth of her own baby. Elizabeth knew that Mary was going to be the Mother of Jesus. Mary said a prayer of joy at Elizabeth's house. Have the children memorize this prayer based on Luke 1:46–47: "My soul sings of the greatness of the Lord. My spirit rejoices in God my savior." Also, enlist their help to incorporate gestures as they say the prayer.

Jesus shared himself with his friends.

Jesus gave his Body and his Blood in the forms of bread and wine.

Joy *is sharing.*

Jesus rose from the dead.

He showed his friends that he would never leave them alone.

Joy *is caring.*

❷ Activity
Give the children time to complete this exercise. Invite them to share their sentences.

Show Your Love

Find the joy words in this puzzle.

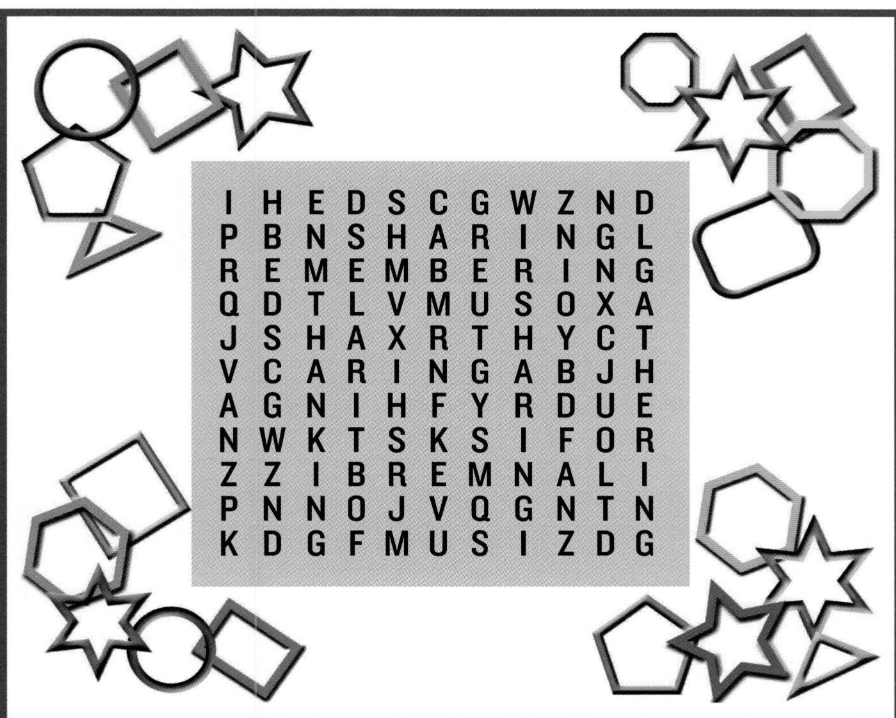

ACTIVITY WITH JOYFUL WORDS

Pick one of the joy words. Use it in a sentence.
Tell how much you love God and one another.

OPTIONS

For the Active Learner Divide the class into groups of two or three. Give each group one of the following topics: *gathering, remembering, thanking, sharing,* and *caring.* Have each group put on a skit to demonstrate the word it drew. Help the groups that have trouble getting started. Allow a few minutes for the children to practice. Then, after reading each section of the text, have the appropriate group put on its skit. As an option, you may also have the children illustrate their topic by drawing a picture.

Lesson Plan · Day 4

Gather the children in the prayer corner and ask them to trace a cross on the part of their body you mention: *Receive the sign of the cross on your ears: Hear the ways the Lord calls you. Receive the sign of the cross on your eyes: See where God is present. Receive the sign of the cross on your lips: Speak the Word of God. Receive the sign of the cross on your hands: Reach out to others. Receive the sign of the cross on your feet: Walk in the way of the Lord. Amen.*

1 What Can You Do?

Read the sentence starter in the first box. Then give the children time to read each labeled box. Point out that their Baptism prepared them to follow Jesus in the way only they can. Give them time to complete the exercise. Afterward, have the children gather in small groups to share their ideas.

LEARNING TO PRAY

Make this part of the lesson a kind of meditation. Prepare the room to make it conducive to reflection. Have music ready to play. Ask the students to be quiet inside and out. Use the opening blessing to guide their prayer. Quietly begin the meditation by saying, "May we hear (see, speak, reach out to, walk toward) you in these ways . . ." After each invocation, pause briefly to give the children time to pray quietly.

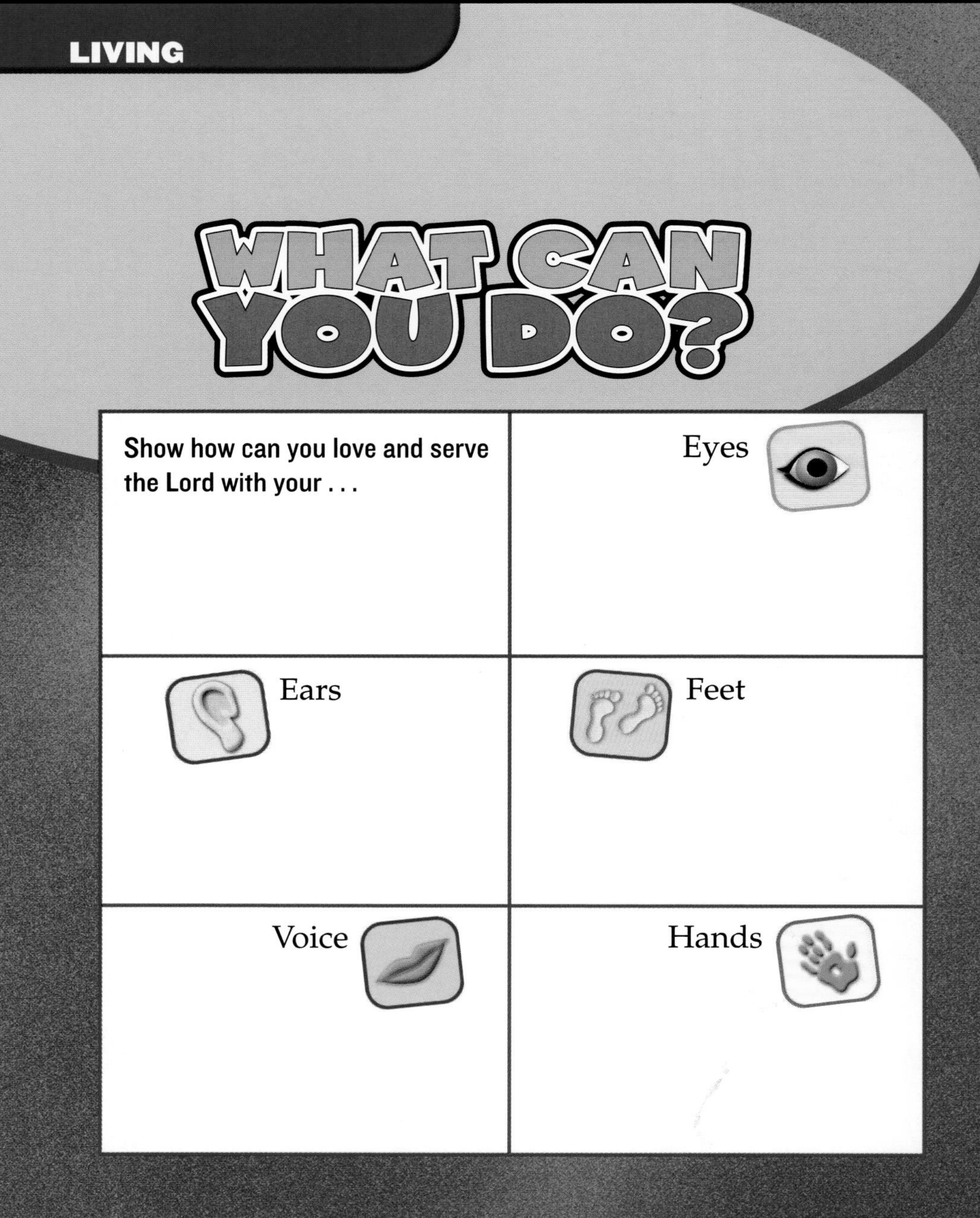

LIVING
WHAT CAN YOU DO?
Show how can you love and serve the Lord with your . . .
Eyes
Ears
Feet
Voice
Hands
332 · Go Forth!

2 A Promise

Read the directions. See if the children recall the rainbow as God's promise to Noah to care for all creatures. Suggest that the children draw on what they have learned to help them decide how they can best know, love, and serve God. Invite them to complete the sentences in the rainbow. Talk about how they concretely serve God in these ways.

LIVING

A PROMISE

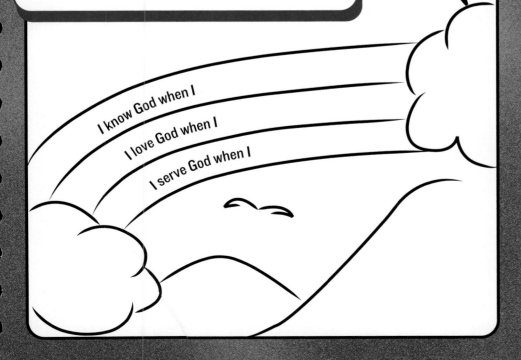

You have learned many things this year. You have learned about knowing, loving, and serving God.

A rainbow is a sign that God will always love and care for you. How will you know, love, and serve God? Finish each sentence in the rainbow. Color the picture.

I know God when I

I love God when I

I serve God when I

IDEAS THAT WORK

Tell the children that God has given them gifts to help them know, love, and serve him as they joyfully minister to others. Then, show the children a covered, gift-wrapped box. Tell them that you have a gift from God in the box. Ask the children to sit in a circle at an arm's length from each other. Tell them to keep their discovery a secret. After the last child has looked into the box with the mirror inside, ask if they were surprised to learn that *they* are God's gifts to the world. Tell them specific ways they are gifts of God for you. Note their enthusiasm, their cooperation, their liveliness, their good ideas, and so on. Ask them to name a way they can continue to be gifts of God to and for others.

Prayer
The prayer experience is part of every chapter. In this service, the children pray for the guidance of the Holy Spirit.

1 Prepare for Prayer
Direct the children's attention to the photo. Ask the children if the Holy Spirit is at work in this group of children. How can they tell? Point out the presence of the Holy Spirit. Compare this awareness of the guidance and help of the Holy Spirit to the story, "Together," on student page 328.

2 Come, Holy Spirit
Gather in the prayer corner. Practice singing the familiar hymn, "Come, Holy Spirit." Divide the class in two groups and have each group face each other on either side of the enthroned Bible opened to the Book of Acts. Have them practice praying alternate lines. Close with the song to the Holy Spirit.

The resource master on page 496 challenges the children to find ways to gather, remember, thank, share, and care this summer. Ask them to complete this activity alone, in groups, or at home.

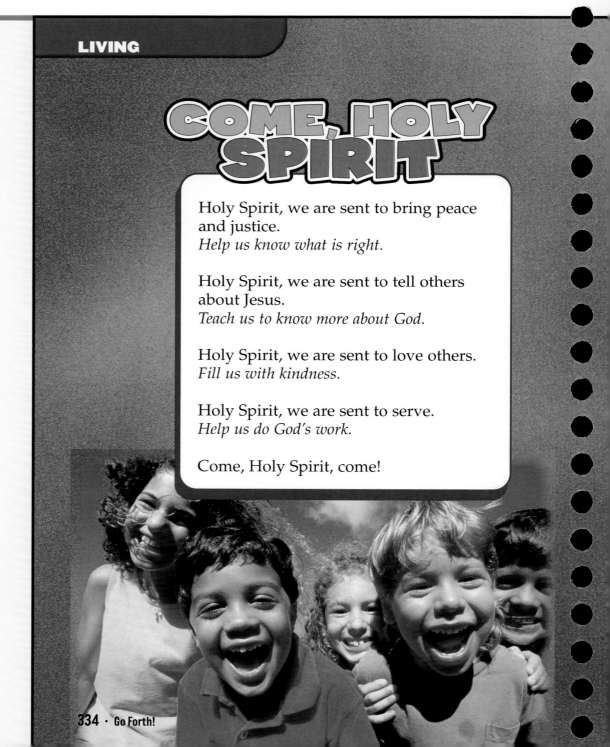

Come, Holy Spirit

Holy Spirit, we are sent to bring peace and justice.
Help us know what is right.

Holy Spirit, we are sent to tell others about Jesus.
Teach us to know more about God.

Holy Spirit, we are sent to love others.
Fill us with kindness.

Holy Spirit, we are sent to serve.
Help us do God's work.

Come, Holy Spirit, come!

1 Know
Discuss the three ways the children can show that they know, love, and serve God.

2 Love and Serve
In working with the children on the Love section, help them to understand that feelings can include a sense of pride and accomplishment, and relief, as well as the more obvious signs, such as a big smile. Ask volunteers for their ideas about ways to follow Jesus today.

3 God's Friends
Ask the children to read about Saint Maria Venegas to find out how she brought help and happiness to others. Ask the children to look up the other God's Friends sections in their texts to gather the names of saints and good people who know, love, and serve God.

CHAPTER 24

REVIEW and EXPLORE

Know

Know, Love, and Serve God
Follow Jesus
Serve Others
Love Others

Love

Remember a time when you were a good Christian. Fill in the chart.

What I Did	How I Felt

Serve

Think of two ways you can be a good follower of Jesus. Write your ideas on a footprint. Put the footprints near the prayer area.

GOD'S FRIENDS

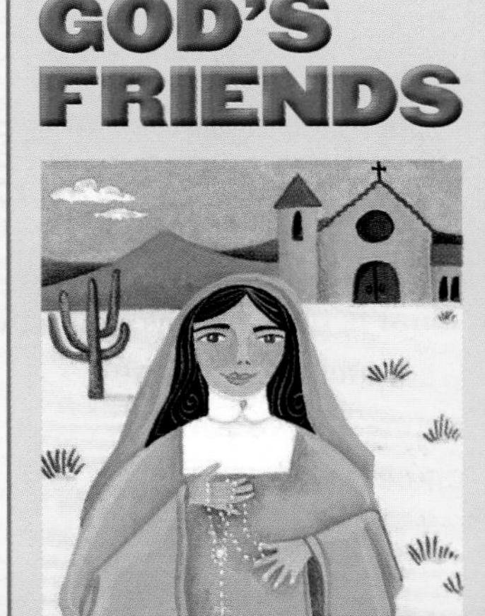

Saint Maria Venegas

Maria grew up serving others. She helped her family and the people in her parish. Maria then spent many years working in a hospital caring for the sick. Maria then became the first female saint of Mexico.

A Little Catechism

Invite the children to open their religion books to *A Little Catechism.* Choose one or more of the selections below for memory work or reinforcement. You will find your copy of the catechism on pages 23–43 of this Teacher's Edition.

1. Read aloud statements 9 and 10 on page 10. Repeat them several times as an aid to memory.
2. Review Talking to God on page 17. Remind the children that prayer is an aid in finding happiness in the presence of God.
3. As a class, pray the Glory be to the Father.

Note The activities on this page provide ways for the children to share their learning with their families. The activities are related to the week's theme.

1 Introduce
Invite volunteers to tell one way their actions make others happy. Talk about things the children do at home or at school.

2 Pray Together
Have a child read the adapted Scripture on student page 328. Conclude by praying the prayer in the prayer burst.

Online for Families
Remind the children to check the Benziger Web site this week with their families.
www.benziger.glencoe.com

Dear Family,

I have just finished chapter 24. I have learned that God wants me to spread the word about his love. I can do this by sharing and caring. God wants everyone to know how much he loves us.

On your own

Picture yourself on the way to school. What is one thing you can do that would make someone happy? Write your choice in the smile.

With your family

Pray for the people who spread the Word of God, both near and far.

Holy Spirit, fill my heart with joy!

GO ONLINE!
http://www.benziger.glencoe.com

1 Discuss
Invite the children to recall the many things they learned during the school year. You may use the end of the year review on pages 500–501 to guide your discussion.

2 Project
Discuss ideas on what the children can include in their postcards. Discuss the many ways that the children can show that they know, love, and serve God even during vacation time. Have extra post cards available in case the students want to send more than two.

3 Pray
If permitted, make the end of the year prayer special by lighting votive candles. Gather the children in the prayer corner. After the first part of the prayer, allow the children to share their special intentions.

THE CHURCH TODAY

What a good year you had! Gather and pray.

Thank you, God, for the second-grade class and for the friends we made.
Thank you, Jesus, for showing us the way to God.
Thank you, Holy Spirit, for filling us with love.

Now, get two postcards ready for mail. Put your teacher's name on one card. You can send your teacher's postcard to your school. Fill out the other card for a second-grader.

Send the cards this summer. On each card tell something you're doing to know, love, and serve God.

ANSWER KEY

This is the answer key for the chapter test on page 497.

A. 1. know 2. gather 3. serve 4. Holy Spirit 5. joy

B.–C. Accept all reasonable responses.

Name ____________________

Good Old Summertime!

Read each question. Think of how you can bring joy as you serve others this summer. Write down your idea. Share it with others.

How can I be a person who gathers others?

How can I remember God's goodness?

How can I thank God and others?

How can I praise God and others?

How can I share?

How can I care?

Name ____

Chapter 24 Test

A. Write the missing words in the sentences. Choose words from the word list.

serve / Holy Spirit / gather / know / joy

1. Listening to the Gospel on Sunday is a way that I can ____________________ God.

2. Catholics ____________________ to celebrate the Eucharist.

3. You can ____________________ God and others by sharing your gifts.

4. The ____________________ guides you to do God's work.

5. Praising God is a way of sharing your ____________________.

B. Pick one of these ways to share your joy: gathering, sharing, remembering, thanking, caring. Tell how you share your joy.

____

____

____

C. Draw a picture of a person whose words or actions show you how to know, love, and serve God. Share your picture and tell a story about this person.

Strategies for Review

The purpose of the Unit Review is to reinforce concepts presented in this unit. Review these sections with the students so that you can answer any questions they may have. Students may work independently, in small groups, or as a class. Use the method that works best with your group.

1 Remember

Go through each statement to make sure the students understand the concepts. Divide the class into small groups, and assign each group one of the statements. Have each group decide what its statement means and then act out its meaning for the class.

2 Answer

Explain the directions. Read each statement aloud, and allow time for the children to color the appropriate faces. Ask several volunteers to explain their answers.

Remember!

1. Missionaries help the poor all over the world.
2. People in a parish come together to pray and to serve.
3. Members of your parish help you grow in faith.
4. Jesus sends you to do God's work.
5. God wants you to be happy now and forever.

Answer!

Color the happy face if the answer is yes.
Color the sad face if the answer is no.

1. Can missionaries help people where you live?

2. Do people in a parish share God's love with each other?

3. Does God want you to serve only people you know?

Do!

Make some magic eyes.
Put on your magic eyes.
Look all around the room.
How can you help?
Do the helpful thing.

❸ Do

Provide materials, and tell the students how much time they will have to make their magic eyes. You can help by prearranging some things that need to be done in the classroom. Afterward, thank them and talk about how they helped. Ask the children where else they could wear their magic eyes. *(at home, on the playground)*

❹ Share

Get the students on the right track by talking about how they helped in the classroom. Encourage them to draw new ideas for their classmates to guess. Give them time to develop their ideas. Have them gather in small groups so that each child can present his or her drawing.

Share!

Finish this Helper Hat.
On the hat, draw something that you use when you help others.
Share your picture with your class.
Can your friends guess how you help?

ANSWER KEY

Answer

1. yes
2. yes
3. no

Strategies for Review

The end of the year review is meant to give the students an opportunity to view and to review the content of the entire year.

❶ Remember

Invite the students to look at the visuals on both pages. Ask each child to choose a visual from one of his or her favorite chapters. Then invite volunteers to share the visuals they chose and to tell the class what they remember about the related chapters. After each student shares, ask the other children what they remember from the related chapter.

❷ Answer

Choose statements from the pages that will be easy for the students to complete in one or two words. For example: "God is a friend you can always ________." *(trust)* Read the statement, and have the students volunteer their answers.

End-of-Year Review

1. God's Gifts

- God created the world and everything in it.

- God gave you the gift of his Son, Jesus.

2. Prayer and Praise

- The Bible is God's message of love for you.

- You gather to pray, worship, and celebrate at Mass.

3. Love and Care

- God is a friend you can always trust.

- Peacemakers care for others by showing love and respect.

3 Do

Have the students choose one of the six unit titles on the two review pages. Invite them to turn to that unit in the student book and review the pictures and activities in the four chapters. Then have them close their books. Distribute drawing materials, and invite each student to draw a picture about one of the stories in that unit.

4 Share

Display the students' drawings in your prayer center, and gather the students there. Conclude the review by asking the students to join hands and pray the Our Father.

4. Welcome

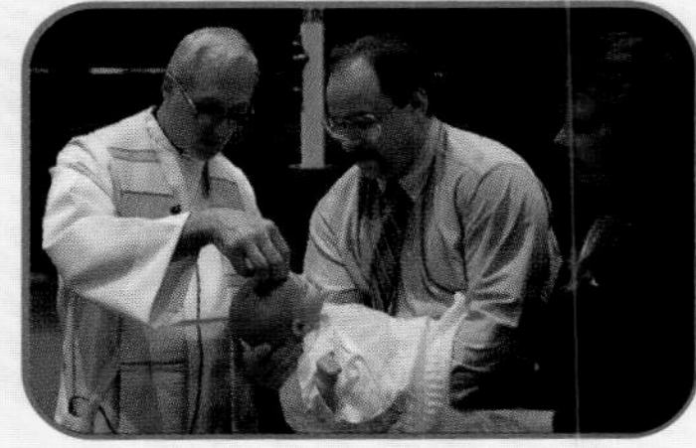

- Baptism welcomes you into the Church community.

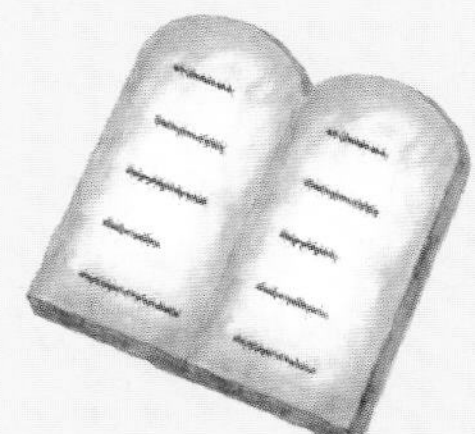

- God gave you the Ten Commandments to help show you the way.

5. Celebration

- Everything God made is good.

- God forgives you when you are sorry.

6. Giving

- People of God pray and show God's love to others.

- You are sent to love and serve others.

ENGLISH

Absolution The prayer of forgiveness, prayed by a priest, in the sacrament of Reconciliation.

Advent The days before Christmas when Christians wait and prepare to celebrate the coming of the Savior, Jesus Christ.

Altar The table used for the celebration of the Eucharist.

Angel A messenger from God.

Anoint To make the sign of the cross with holy oil on the body of someone.

Anointing of the Sick A sacrament of healing through which the sick and the dying receive the care of the Church and the grace of God's healing love.

Apostles The twelve first followers of Jesus. Jesus sent the Apostles to spread the Good News.

SPANISH

Absolución La oración del perdón que reza un sacerdote en el sacramento de la reconciliación.

Adviento Los días anteriores a la Navidad, cuando esperamos la venida de Jesús y nos preparamos para ella.

Altar La mesa que se usa para la celebración de la Eucaristía.

Ángel Un mensajero de Dios.

Ungir Hacer la señal de la cruz sobre el cuerpo de alguien con los santos óleos o aceite sagrado.

Unción de los enfermos Un sacramento de curación por medio del cual los enfermos y los moribundos reciben la gracia del amor sanador de Dios.

Apóstoles Los primeros seguidores de Jesús. Jesús envió a los Apóstoles a difundir la Buena Nueva.

Baptism The sacrament, or celebration, that frees you from sin and welcomes you to the Family of God, the Church.

Bible The book of God's Word.

Bautismo El sacramento, o celebración, que te libera del pecado y te da la bienvenida en la familia de Dios, la Iglesia.

Biblia El libro de la Palabra de Dios.

Bishop The leader or shepherd of Catholics in a group of parishes called a diocese.

Obispo El líder de los católicos de un grupo de parroquias llamado diócesis.

Blessed Sacrament Jesus present in the Eucharist under the form of bread and wine.

Santísimo Sacramento Jesús presente en la Eucaristía bajo la forma de pan y vino.

Blessed Trinity The three Persons in one God—God the Father, the Son, and the Holy Spirit.

Santísima Trinidad Las Tres Personas en un solo Dios: Dios Padre, Hijo y Espíritu Santo.

Body of Christ The bread that is Jesus; Holy Communion.

Cuerpo de Cristo Jesús hecho pan; la Sagrada Comunión.

Catholic A member of the Church is called a Catholic. Catholics are also called Christians.

Católico(a) Se llama católico(a) a un miembro de la Iglesia. Los catóIicccs tambiién se llaman cristianos.

Child of God Someone who believes in God and tries to follow his Word.

Hijo(a) de Dios Alguien que cree en Dios y trata de seguir su palabra.

Christian Everyone who believes in Jesus, is baptized, and tries to follow the teachings of Jesus.

Cristiano(a) Son cristianos todos los que creen en Jesús, están bautizados y tratan de seguir a Jesús.

Christmas The day on which the Church celebrates and remembers the birth of Jesus.

Navidad El día en el que la Iglesia celebra y recuerda el nacimiento de Jesús.

Church Family of people joined together by faith in Jesus and by Baptism. Church is also the building where Christians gather for common prayer and Mass.

Iglesia Una familia unida por fe en Jesús y en el bautismo. La iglesia es también el edificio donde los cristianos se reúnen para la oración en común y la misa.

Confession Telling sins to the priest in the sacrament of Penance, or Reconciliation.

Conscience Knowing what is right and what is wrong.

Contrition Being sincerely sorry for your sins.

Creation Everything God made—the universe and all its creatures.

Confesión Contar los pecados al sacerdote en el sacramento de la reconciliación.

Conciencia Saber lo que está bien y lo que está mal.

Contrición Arrepentirte de tus pecados.

Creación Todo lo que Dios hizo: el universo y todas sus criaturas.

Creed A prayer that sums up what Christians believe about their faith. At Mass, the Family of God prays the Nicene Creed.

Easter The day on which the Church celebrates and remembers that Jesus was raised from the dead.

Eucharist The sacrament in which you

Credo Una oración que resume todas nuestras creencias. En la misa rezamos el Credo de Nicea-Constantinopla.

Pascua Día en el que la Iglesia celebra que Jesús resucitó o volvió a la vida de entre los muertos.

Eucaristía Sacramento en el que recibes el

receive the Body and Blood of Jesus; another name for the Mass.

Cuerpo y la Sangre de Cristo; otro nombre para la misa.

Examination of conscience Thinking about your words and actions in the light of the Gospel to see how you may have sinned; a way to prepare for the sacrament of Penance, or Reconciliation.

Examen de conciencia Pensar en tus palabras y tus acciones a la luz del Evangelio para ver cómo puedes haber pecado; una forma de prepararte para el sacramento de la reconciliación.

Faith Believing in God with all your mind and all your heart.

Fe Creer en Dios con todo tu mente y con todo tu corazón.

Family of God Members of the Church who share God's love and keep his Law.

Familia de Dios Miembros de la Iglesia que comparten el amor de Dios y obedecen su ley.

Free will The ability God gives you to choose an action—to choose either right or wrong.

Libre albedrío La capacidad que Dios te da para elegir lo que está bien o lo que está mal.

Gather To come together in order to form a community for prayer and good works. Your parish gathers for Mass on Sundays.

Congregarse Reunirse para formar una comunidad para la oración y las buenas obras. Tu parroquia se congrega en la misa los domingos.

Good News What Jesus told the people—the Good News of God's saving love; another name for the Gospel.

Buena Nueva Lo que Jesús contó a la gente: la Buena Nueva del amor de Dios para todos los hombres y las mujeres.

Gospels The four books at the beginning of the New Testament, which tell the story of Jesus and his teachings.

Evangelios Los cuatro libros que aparecen al comienzo del Nuevo Testamento que cuentan la historia de Jesús.

Grace The love God gives you to be a child of God; God's life within you.

Heaven Being happy with God forever.

Holy Communion The Body and Blood of Christ, which you receive at Mass.

Holy Family Jesus, Mary, and Joseph.

Gracia El amor que Dios te da para ser un hijo o hija de Dios; la vida de Dios dentro de ti.

Cielo Ser feliz para siempre con Dios.

Sagrada Comunión El Cuerpo y la Sangre de Cristo que recibes en la misa.

Sagrada Familia Jesús, María y José.

Holy Spirit The Helper promised by Jesus.

Homily A special talk given by the priest at Mass which helps you apply the Word of God to your everyday life.

Image of God The call to be like God; the desire to be united with God. All people are created in the image of God.

Jesus Christ God's Son and your Savior. Jesus was born of the Virgin Mary.

Kingdom of God The People of God who live God's way and will be with God forever.

Last Supper Jesus' last meal with his friends.

Espíritu Santo El Ayudante que Jesús prometió.

Homilía Un sermón o plática especial que el sacerdote dice en la misa para ayudarte a aplicar la Palabra de Dios en tu vida.

Imagen de Dios Ser como Dios y desear estar en unión con Dios. Todas las personas son creadas a imagen de Dios.

Jesu Cristo El Hijo de Dios y tu salvador. Jesús nació de la Virgen María.

Reino de Dios El Pueblo de Dios que vive según el plan de Dios y que estará con Dios para siempre.

Última Cena La última comida de Jesús con sus amigos.

Lent The time before Easter to pray and to do good.

Cuaresma Los días anteriores a la Pascua, para rezar y hacer el bien.

Liturgy of the Eucharist The part of the Mass for remembering, giving thanks, and taking part in the death and resurrection of Jesus. It includes the Eucharistic Prayer and Holy Communion.

Liturgia Eucarística Parte de la misa para recordar, agradecer y compartir la muerte y resurrección o vuelta a la vida de Jesús. Incluye la Oración Eucarística y la Sagrada Comunión.

Liturgy of the Word The part of the Mass during which the Scripture readings, homily, Creed, and prayer of the faithful take place.

Liturgia de la Palabra La parte de la misa en la que tienen lugar la lectura de las Escrituras, la homilía, el Credo y la Oración de los Fieles.

Lord's Prayer The prayer Jesus taught his followers.

Oración del Señor La oración que Jesús nos enseñó.

Mary The mother of Jesus and your mother, too.

María La Madre de Jesús y también nuestra madre.

Mercy An action that shows loving care and forgiveness.

Misericordia Bondad que se demuestra al que ofende.

Mission The work a person is called to do. The mission of the Church is to spread the Word of God.

Misión El trabajo que se manda hacer a una persona. La misión de la Iglesia es difundir el Evangelio.

Moral choices The decisions you make about how to treat yourself, other people, and the rest of creation.

Parable A story that has a special meaning or a lesson to teach. When Jesus was teaching his followers, he used many parables.

Parish A community of Catholics who pray, learn, celebrate, and serve together.

Elecciones morales Decisiones que tomas sobre cómo te tratas a ti mismo, y cómo tratas a los demás y el resto de la creación.

Parábola Una narración que tiene un significado especial o una lección que enseñar. Jesús enseñaba con parábolas.

Parroquia Una comunidad de católicos que rezan, aprenden y sirven juntos.

Pastor The priest who is the leader of your parish.

Penance The sacrament that celebrates God's loving forgiveness. Penance is also a prayer or action that shows you are truly sorry for your sins.

Pope The leader of the Catholic Church and the bishop of Rome.

Prayer The raising of the mind and heart to God.

Pastor El sacerdote que es el líder de tu parroquia.

Penitencia El sacramento que celebra el perdón de Dios. También, una oración o acción que demuestra que estás verdaderamente arrepentido de tus pecados.

Papa El líder de la Iglesia católica y el obispo de Roma.

Oración La elevación de la mente y el corazón a Dios.

Reconciliation Another name for the sacrament of Penance.

Sabbath A day of rest, prayer, and worship. Christians celebrate Sunday as a Sabbath day, or the Lord's Day.

Sacramentals Objects and actions that remind you of God. A crucifix is a sacramental.

Reconciliación Otro nombre para el sacramento de penitencia.

Sabbat Un día para el descanso y el culto u homenaje a Dios. Los cristianos celebran el domingo como día sabático, o día del Señor.

Sacramentales Objetos y gestos que te recuerdan a Dios. Un crucifijo es un sacramental.

Sacraments Signs of God's life and love. The sacraments help the Family of God celebrate special times. There are seven sacraments.

Saints Holy people who love Jesus and who help others follow him are called saints. Saints receive the reward of eternal life with God. These saints are the heroes of the Family of God.

Sacramentos Signos o representaciones y celebraciones especiales de la vida y el amor de Dios.

Santos(as) Se llama santos(as) a las personas puras que amaron a Jesús y que ayudan a los demás a seguirlo. Los(as) santos(as) reciben la recompensa de la vida eterna junto a Dios.

Sin A word, action, or desire against the Law of God.

Pecado Una palabra, acción, o deseo contra la ley de Dios.

Tabernacle The special box in which the Blessed Sacrament is kept after Mass.

Ten Commandments God's rules of love that show people how to follow God's will.

Tabernáculo La caja especial donde se guarda el Santísimo Sacramento después de la misa.

Diez Mandamientos Las reglas del amor de Dios que muestran cómo vivir según el plan de Dios.

Trust To place your faith and hope in someone.

Witness To show that you believe in Jesus by what you say and do.

Word of God Another name for the Bible.

Confiar Depositar tu fe y tu esperanza en alguien.

Dar testimonio Mostrar lo que crees por medio de lo que dices y haces.

Palabra de Dios Otro nombre para la Biblia.

Index

All numbers indicate student page numbers unless otherwise noted.

ACKNOWLEDGMENTS

Illustrations Winky Adam 39, 76; Martha Aviles: 86, 89, 129; Pearl Beach: 191, 200–201; Karen Stormer Brooks: 314; Nan Brooks: 88, 98–99; Annette Cable: 20–21; Tom Chalkley: 54, 158–159; Peter Church: 44–45, 58–59; Ande Cook: 39, 51, 63, 75, 91, 103, 115, 127,143, 155, 167, 179, 195, 207, 219, 231, 247, 259, 271, 283, 295, 299, 311, 323, 335; Carolyn Croll: 139, 148, 175; Renee Dailey: 138; Eldon Doty: 209; Rusty Fletcher: 274–275, 285; Claudine Gevry: 32–33, 53, 164, 187, 223, 292–293; Carol Haag, Icon Courtesy: 27; Laurie Harden: 23, 66; Amanda Harvey: 60–61; Dennis Hockerman: 36; Nicole in den Bosch: 30–31, 56–57, 62; Susan Jaekel: 117; Judy Jarrett: 140, 153; Anthony Lewis: 41, 95, 110, 302–303, 309; Christi Payne: 10–13, 15–17; Mick Reid: 136–137, 146–147, 161, 193; Jaclyn Scardova: 252–253; Stacey Schuett: 162, 261–263; Susan Simon: 67; Susan Spellman: 70, 75, 174, 188, 222; Judy Stead: 229, 238–239; Mary Thelen: 126; George Ulrich: 42, 135, 190, 197, 221, 233, 249, 273, 301, 313, 316, 319, 325; Paula Wiggins: 84–85, 192, 224–225; Sachiko Yoshikawa: 83, 326–327

Photographs AJA Productions/ImageBank: 203; Bob Borton/ Courtesy of the Sisters of the Blessed Sacrament: 25; Boyana Church National Museum, Sofia, Bulgaria/SuperStock International: 47; Bro. Joe Brunner, MM./Maryknoll Photo: 80–81; Myrleen Ferguson Cate/PhotoEdit: 125, 157; Dennie Cody/FPG International: 87; W. Perry Conway/Corbis/LA: 34; Steve Jay Crise/Corbis/LA: 20; Adam Crowley/PhotoDisc: 160; Jim Cummings/FPG International: 198; Bruce Curtis/ Stock Imagery: 82; Electra Vision/PictureQuest: 173; EyeWire Collection/EyeWire: 203, 280; Lourdes Fernandez, MM./ Maryknoll Photo: 28–29; Finnabarra/Maryknoll Photo: 26; Frank Lane Picture Agency/Corbis/LA: 35; Tony Freeman/ PhotoEdit: 23; Tony Freeman/PhotoEdit/PictureQuest: 166; Mark E. Gibson/Corbis/LA: 55, 106; Rob Goldman/FPG International: 318; Rick Gomez/Stock Market: 334; Philip Gould/Corbis/LA: 11; Spencer Grant/Art Directors & Tripp Photo Library: 112; Jeff Greenberg/PhotoEdit: 304; Jeff Greenberg/PictureQuest: 280; David Hanover/Tony Stone Images: 178; Gary Holscher/Tony Stone Images: 258; Richard Hutchings/PictureQuest; 225; SK Jold/The Image Works: 18; Rob Lewine/Stock Market: 93; Stuart McClymont/Tony Stone Images: 225; Albert Michini/Courtesy of the Sisters of the Blessed Sacrament: 25; Robert Milazzo/Maryknoll Photo: 184–185; Mug Shots/Corbis/Stock Market: 94; Nature Scenes CD/PhotoDisc Vol 36: 108; Richard Nowitz/PictureQuest: 250; O'Brien Productions/Corbis/LA: 8; Gene Plaisted/Crosiers: 68; Pat Powers and Cherryl Schater/PhotoDisc: 112; R.B Studio/Stock Market: 74; Steve Raymer/Corbis/LA: 251; Reporters Press Agency/PictureQuest: 225; Carl Schnider/ FPG International: 170–171; James L. Shaffer/Shaffer Photography: 194, 206, 226–227, 242–243, 254–255, 266–267, 270, 278–279, 307, 310; Nancy Sheehan/PhotoEdit: 118; Stephen Simpson/FPG International: 230; Adam Smith/ Corbis/LA: 121; Sean Sprague/Maryknoll Photo: 290; Sutherland Photo: 21, 124; SW Productions/Index Stock Images: 251; Mark Swisher: 213–214, 226–227; Liba Taylor/ Corbis/LA: 14; Arthur Tilley/FPG International: 136, 322; Jerome Tisne/Tony Stone Images: 112; Steve Vidler/ PictureQuest: 246; John Wang/PhotoDisc: 154; Weekend Living CD: 305; Eric Wheater/Maryknoll Photo: 236–237; Ross Whitaker/Image Bank: 176; Bill Wittman: 69, 120, 242–243, 266–267, 282, 298; Xavier Photographs/Courtesy of the Sisters of the Blessed Sacrament: 25; David Young-Wolff/ Tony Stone Images: 134

0-07-821721-0 0-07-821730-X 0-07-821739-3 0-07-821748-2 0-07-821757-1 0-07-821766-0

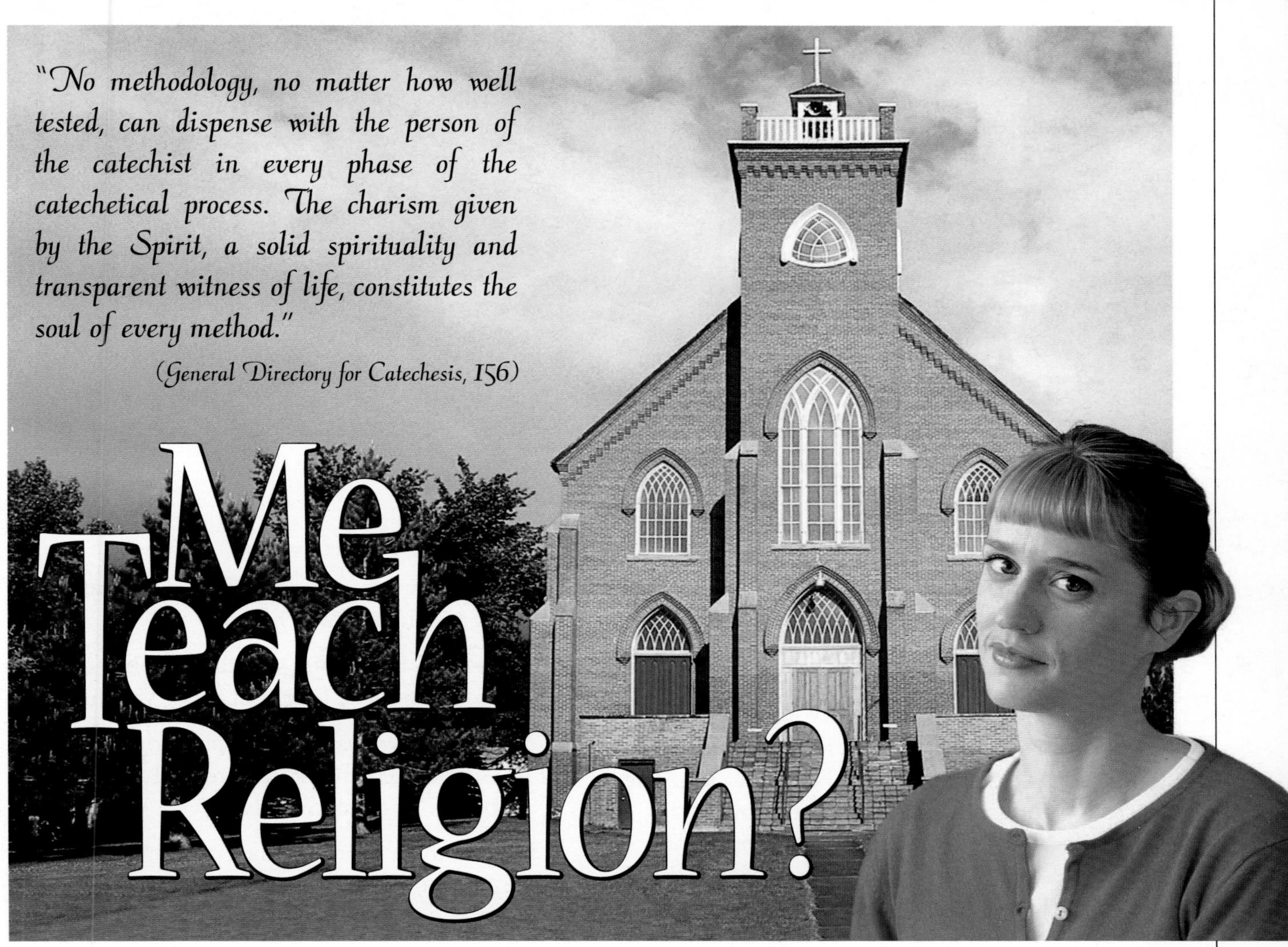

"No methodology, no matter how well tested, can dispense with the person of the catechist in every phase of the catechetical process. The charism given by the Spirit, a solid spirituality and transparent witness of life, constitutes the soul of every method."
(General Directory for Catechesis, 156)

Me Teach Religion?

It was a typical Sunday in so many ways. As she gathered with the other men and women on the church steps, Miriam wondered about her place there. "Am I qualified for this?" she thought.

Miriam knew she was here because of her daughter's questions about Jesus. Elizabeth was only eight, but she was certainly able to think. "Mommy, why did Jesus have to die?" "Why do we ask God to 'lead us not into temptation'?" Miriam was constantly challenged by Elizabeth's questions, and she had actually learned much about her own faith in an effort to find the proper answers for her precocious daughter.

Miriam felt that if her children were to love God, they would learn this primarily at home. So she showered them with love and encouragement. She spoke often of God's love and kindness. She had, however, left the children's formal religious formation to the parish catechists.

At Mass on the third Sunday in August, Father Frank spoke of the importance of Christian witness. As he ended the homily, Father Frank mentioned that parishioners were needed as teachers in the parish's religious education program. Miriam wondered if God was calling her to continue with other children the work she had already begun with Elizabeth and her other children. Later that afternoon, reality set in. "Me, a teacher?" Miriam thought, "No way."

Now, here she was ready to be commissioned as a catechist for the parish. She wasn't sure whether to be happy or panic.

Whether you are an experienced or first-time catechist, or a teacher in the parish school, you may feel a bit nervous about the role of sharing your faith.

- **What do you think will help you be a successful catechist?**
- **How are you supported as a catechist by your parish? Your family, friends, and other teachers?**
- **What hopes do you have as you begin this new year?**

The Role of the Catechist

A Catechist's Spirit

The fundamental task you have as a catechist is to proclaim Christ's message, to join in the effort to develop the Christian community, to lead people to worship and prayer, and to motivate your learners to serve others. Wow! That is a tall order for anybody. But if you look at what you do merely as a task, you are doomed to fail. The necessary underpinning of that monumental task is the catechetical spirit. That spirit is not fully developed in anybody who attempts the catechetical task. As the General Directory for Catechesis (and almost every other document written on the subject of catechetics) has pointed out, this spirit is an ideal, and it is a challenge. But every element of the ideal is attainable.

The following are suggestions to further your own growth as a catechist.

1. Be real. Base your spirituality on the real world and the world of those you teach.
2. Ground yourself in Sacred Scripture. Be the Gospel for others. Believe in the Gospel's power to transform lives.
3. Become a more Eucharistic person—more gracious and more grateful.
4. Recognize that Christian spirituality—ministerial spirituality—without community is a contradiction in terms.

Catechist or Teacher?

Do you see yourself as a catechist or as a teacher of religion? While often used synonymously, the words do have different meanings. Generally speaking, all catechists are teachers of religion, but not all teachers of religion are catechists.

Whether you are a teacher in a Catholic school or in a parish School of Religion, if your goal is the faith growth of the children, then you are a catechist.

The Person of the Catechist

You have answered a call from Christ and from the Church to be a catechist. By answering the call, you have expressed a willingness to help others grow in faith and a willingness to be open to growth yourself.

5. Realize that you do not teach your own ideas, but you need to be filled with the grace of God and the truth of the Faith. Teach Jesus.
6. Become a more welcoming person. In your catechetical ministry invite people into the family—to stay.
7. Wake up the need for the habit of prayer—everyday prayer.
8. Meet the enemy of sin—forgiveness. And in that meeting, discover that reconciliation is basic equipment for those who would spread Good News.
9. Know that the earth needs you. Creation is a gift to be cherished and handled with care. See that the Gospel is laced with the call to justice and the promise of peace.
10. Be a joyful Christian.

How Do You Rate Yourself as a Catechist?

The following personal traits are essential to the role of the catechist. On a scale from 1 to 10, with 10 being the best, rate how well you fulfill these traits?

The catechist has:

- ☐ an active faith life expressed in the worshiping community.
- ☐ a willingness and ability to be a witness to the Gospel.
- ☐ an interest and concern about people's growth in faith.
- ☐ an ability to relate well with others.
- ☐ an integration of prayer into her or his personal life.
- ☐ a willingness to be of service to the Church.
- ☐ a loyalty and faithfulness to the Church and its teaching.
- ☐ a sense of humor and the flexibility to adapt to learning situations.
- ☐ a willingness to learn, grow, and change.

In what areas are you the strongest? In what areas do you need to improve?

Prayer of Joy

Get into the habit of turning to God with sentiments of happiness. Prayers of thanksgiving and of praise spring easily to the lips of a joyful person. You might also memorize the short prayer below. Having these words in your heart can put words in your mouth when you are sincerely happy.

Blessed are you, O Lord,
blessed are you!
In your generosity, you have done
great things for me,
and holy is your name.
Let my life shine with the happiness
you have shared with me.

Family and Parish

> *"Parents receive in the sacrament of Matrimony 'the grace and the ministry of the Christian education of their children', to whom they transmit and bear witness to human and religious values. This educational activity which is both human and religious is 'a true ministry', through which the Gospel is transmitted and radiated so that family life is transformed into a journey of faith and the school of Christian life."*
>
> *(General Directory for Catechesis, 227)*

General Observations About the Family

The family is the first catechist. What happens at home is a sharing of faith that fits into the rhythm of family life as it is lived—hectic, disorganized, even messy. The family models faith without incense, vestments, or liturgical music.

As a catechist, you relate not only to the children but to their families as well. If you keep the information provided here in mind, you will relate well to the families and will also support the faith sharing that goes on in the home.

There is no perfect family. While *Christ Jesus, the Way* promotes and supports an intact family with two parents in a permanent relationship, fewer and fewer families fit that profile. Make sure that you never refer to such a family as ideal, better, best, typical, more faithful, or use any similar terms. In the same vein, never refer to families that do not fit the profile as broken, fragmented, or bad. When you are with the children, keep any judgments you have about their families to yourself.

Not all families are happy. *Christ Jesus, the Way* points to a family life that is positive, wholesome, and happy. No family has all those qualities all the time. Some families are miserable places to be. This unhappiness may reveal itself in discussions. Do not draw attention to it. Avoid comments such as "That's so sad!" or "How horrible for you!"

Some families have problems. Alcoholism, gambling, abuse, and other problems may be present in the families of the children you teach. You are not a family therapist. If you suspect problems that pose a real danger to the child, inform your director or principal. Your director, principal, or the pastor is trained to deal with these situations.

Do not become a surrogate parent. Maintain a physical and emotional distance from the children you minister to. Signs of affection should always be *group* signs. Do not single any child out for your special care.

Maintain contact with the families. Call each family during the year. You can get feedback and encourage participation. Establish communication and a relationship with the family early on thereby opening the doors to continuing dialog and partnership.

"Catechesis is a responsibility of the entire Christian community. Christian initiation, indeed, "should not be the work of catechists and priests alone, but of the whole community of the faithful."

(General Directory for Catechesis, 220)

The Parish's Responsibility for Catechesis

Responsibility for catechesis belongs to the entire parish. A responsible parish community is a network of people working together to catechize and be catechized. Activities which foster this vision are:

1. **Publicity** Display the children's work wherever possible. Request the prayers of the community for children preparing for sacraments. Let the parish know when children are involved in Christian service.
2. **Invitation** Invite parish ministers as guest speakers to witness first hand to the children about their call and involvement in church ministry. Invite parishioners to special liturgical celebrations your class or school is having.
3. **Support** Encourage the children and their families to take an active part in parish activities. Perhaps your class can volunteer to help with some parish activity.
4. **Liturgy** Everything that is done in the class with the children should lead them to a fuller participation in the Sunday liturgy. Liturgical catechesis is an aim of *Christ Jesus, the Way* through instruction about the liturgical life of the Church, and through the children's participation in the liturgical celebrations found in *Celebrate*.

Lesson Planning

Planning the Lesson

The importance of lesson planning cannot be overstated. A good day in the classroom begins with an effective lesson plan. A well thought out plan can help you accomplish your learning goals while keeping the children excited about the topic. The better your planning, the less likely the children will become bored and disrupt the class, and the more likely you will feel calm and in control. A carefully planned lesson will benefit both you and the children.

Benefits for the catechist:

- Gives you a feeling of control, confidence and security.
- Keeps you focused.
- Helps you transition smoothly through the various activities within the lesson.
- Helps you accomplish the lesson goals.

Benefits for the children:

- Attracts and maintains the attention of the children.
- Maximizes the use of time and minimizes confusion and disruptions.
- Promotes and facilitates learning.
- Gives the children clear expectations.
- Gives the children clear goals—children will be aware of exactly what they need to know or do.
- Gives the children a purpose "I know why I am here."

Getting Started

1. Look through your religion textbook, and get an overview of the year. What is the general topic or theme for the year? How are the lessons arranged?
2. Create flexible and adaptable timelines, and set your overall learning goals.
3. Make a planning calendar of the year.
   - How long is your lesson time?
   - How many sessions will you have?
4. Plan for special events.

   Check for special events that will preempt your class and that may be incorporated into your lesson plan. These might include holidays, sacramental celebrations, and holy days. Make sure you check the *Celebrate* book for prayer services that are seasonally appropriate or will reinforce a particular theme or concept the children are exploring.

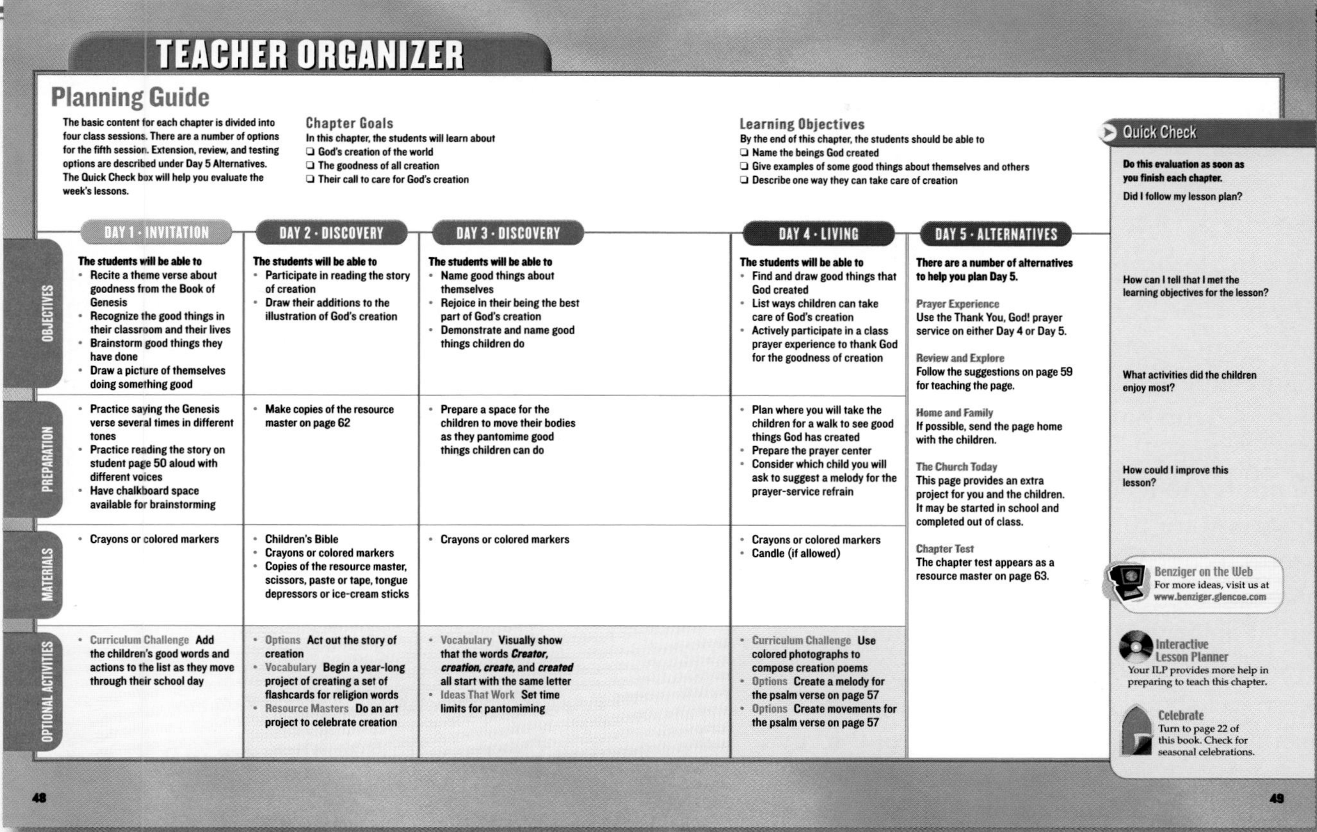

TEACHER ORGANIZER

Planning Guide

The basic content for each chapter is divided into four class sessions. There are a number of options for the fifth session. Extension, review, and testing options are described under Day 5 Alternatives. The Quick Check box will help you evaluate the week's lessons.

Chapter Goals
In this chapter, the students will learn about
- ❑ God's creation of the world
- ❑ The goodness of all creation
- ❑ Their call to care for God's creation

Learning Objectives
By the end of this chapter, the students should be able to
- ❑ Name the beings God created
- ❑ Give examples of some good things about themselves and others
- ❑ Describe one way they can take care of creation

	DAY 1 · INVITATION	DAY 2 · DISCOVERY	DAY 3 · DISCOVERY	DAY 4 · LIVING
OBJECTIVES	**The students will be able to** • Recite a theme verse about goodness from the Book of Genesis • Recognize the good things in their classroom and their lives • Brainstorm good things they have done • Draw a picture of themselves doing something good	**The students will be able to** • Participate in reading the story of creation • Draw their additions to the illustration of God's creation	**The students will be able to** • Name good things about themselves • Rejoice in their being the best part of God's creation • Demonstrate and name good things children do	**The students will be able to** • Find and draw good things that God created • List ways children can take care of God's creation • Actively participate in a class prayer experience to thank God for the goodness of creation
PREPARATION	• Practice saying the Genesis verse several times in different tones • Practice reading the story on student page 50 aloud with different voices • Have chalkboard space available for brainstorming	• Make copies of the resource master on page 62	• Prepare a space for the children to move their bodies as they pantomime good things children can do	• Plan where you will take the children for a walk to see good things God has created • Prepare the prayer center • Consider which child you will ask to suggest a melody for the prayer-service refrain
MATERIALS	• Crayons or colored markers	• Children's Bible • Crayons or colored markers • Copies of the resource master, scissors, paste or tape, tongue depressors or ice-cream sticks	• Crayons or colored markers	• Crayons or colored markers • Candle (if allowed)
OPTIONAL ACTIVITIES	• Curriculum Challenge Add the children's good words and actions to the list as they move through their school day	• Options Act out the story of creation • Vocabulary Begin a year-long project of creating a set of flashcards for religion words • Resource Masters Do an art project to celebrate creation	• Vocabulary Visually show that the words ***Creator, creation, create,*** and ***created*** all start with the same letter • Ideas That Work Set time limits for pantomiming	• Curriculum Challenge Use colored photographs to compose creation poems • Options Create a melody for the psalm verse on page 57 • Options Create movements for the psalm verse on page 57

DAY 5 · ALTERNATIVES

There are a number of alternatives to help you plan Day 5.

Prayer Experience
Use the Thank You, God! prayer service on either Day 4 or Day 5.

Review and Explore
Follow the suggestions on page 59 for teaching the page.

Home and Family
If possible, send the page home with the children.

The Church Today
This page provides an extra project for you and the children. It may be started in school and completed out of class.

Chapter Test
The chapter test appears as a resource master on page 63.

Quick Check

Do this evaluation as soon as you finish each chapter.

Did I follow my lesson plan?

How can I tell that I met the learning objectives for the lesson?

What activities did the children enjoy most?

How could I improve this lesson?

Benziger on the Web
For more ideas, visit us at www.benziger.glencoe.com

Interactive Lesson Planner
Your ILP provides more help in preparing to teach this chapter.

Celebrate
Turn to page 22 of this book. Check for seasonal celebrations.

48 49

Weekly Lesson Planning

1. Read the entire lesson to get its overall content, design and spirit. Highlight or underline parts of the lesson you deem most important.
2. Read the catechist background pages for the lesson.
3. Identify your objectives.

   What do you want the children to learn?
4. Formulate the lesson plan. Use the catechist/teacher planner page to assist you.

   How will you teach your lesson?

   What activities will you use?

   What materials will you need?

   What materials will the children need?

   What can you accomplish within your time frame?

   How will you know what the children have learned?

Materials

Remember to plan for and anticipate the materials and resources you will be using for each lesson. If you have materials readily accessible, you will have a smooth transition between activities. Instructional resources can include:

- Activity resource pages in your Catechist edition and other print materials.
- Visuals such as: illustrations, photographs, flash cards, charts, maps, posters, exhibits, bulletin boards, and transparencies.
- Audiovisual materials: TV clips, videotapes, films, filmstrips or CD-roms.
- Music tapes and CDs.
- Human resources such as parents, parish personnel and community persons.

Classroom Dynamics

Teaching Methods

Common sense is the best possible guideline for any teacher-learner interaction. You will grow in your mastery of teaching skills with time and experience, but here are some hints from those who have been active in catechetics for a long time:

- Do not try to teach too much. It is more important for the children to grasp the essential concepts and to have a chance to integrate the messages into their own lives than it is for you to cover every bit of information in the lesson plan.
- Learn to listen. Listen to questions, remembering that any question is important to the person asking it. Listen between the lines, to tone of voice and body language.
- Encourage the children to think. Ask questions, and answer questions with more questions. (Note how often Jesus does this in the Gospels!) The most lasting lessons are discovered, like buried treasure.
- Respect individual learning styles. It will not take long for you to note which children are most articulate, but you need to spend more time drawing out the shyer children, whose insights may be equally worthwhile. Without quashing enthusiasm, work for a balance in which everyone's gifts are respected.

Environment

Children learn from everything around them. The colors, shapes, lighting, and sounds that make up the environment can engage and encourage learning. Maintain a pleasant, clean, and creative atmosphere.

Children respond to beauty and order, so use visuals that are colorful and bright. Pictures, posters, banners, and children's art all tend to make religion class a pleasant place to be. Use symbols that represent the spirit of who we are as a people of God. Use music often.

Set up a prayer table and make it a focal point of the room. Cover the table with fabric, changing it according to the seasons of the Church year. A pillar candle, wooden cross, plant, and a Bible or Children's Lectionary are other items that can be placed on the table. Use statues, images or icons, and flowers to represent the saints and feasts celebrated during the liturgical year. Encourage the children to create a prayer table for their families at home.

Classroom Management

Children learn best when they are in a safe, well-ordered and non-distracting environment. It is always important to keep things moving during the session. Today's children have been reared on sound bites and brief television episodes. They have difficulty concentrating for too long on one thing.

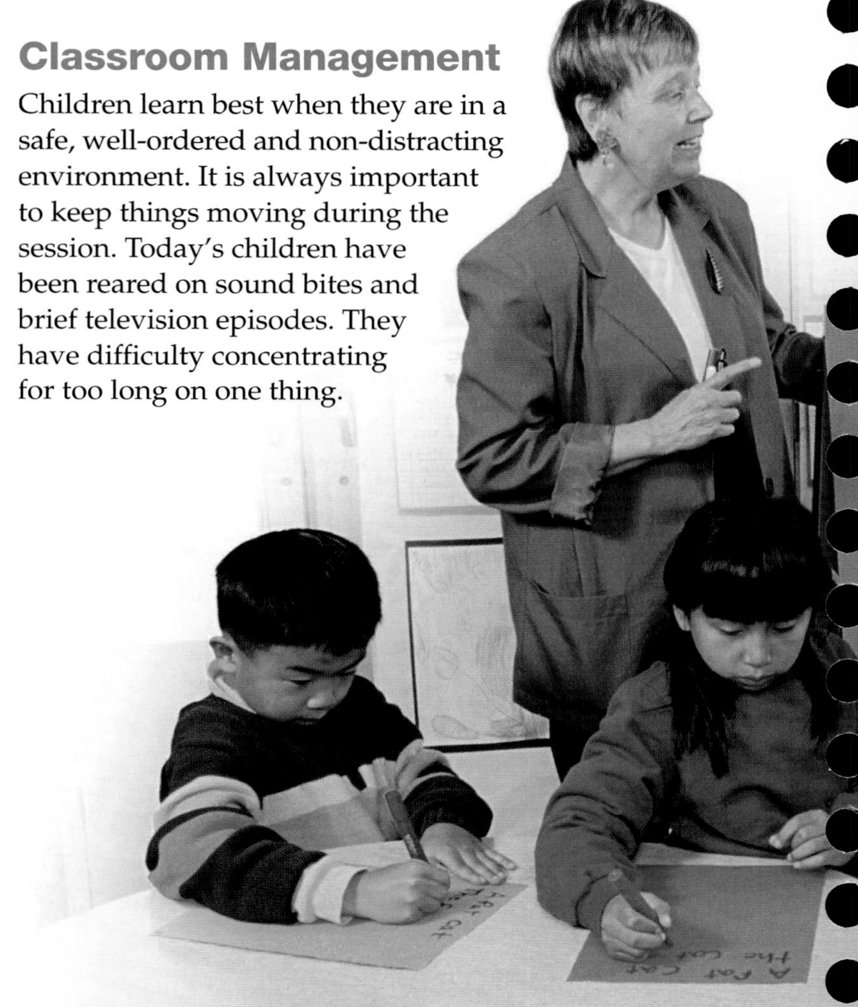

Tips on peaceful and practical management:

- Begin with ground rules established for the class. Discuss the need for rules with the children. Invite the children to help draw up rules. This emphasizes to the children that what happens in class depends on cooperation and shared responsibility.
- Always follow through with what you say you will do. Let the children know the consequences of their actions.
- Remember the purpose of your class—to share the Good News of Jesus and his kingdom. Affirm your children often.

Questioning Techniques

The art of questioning is a skill catechists need to develop. The following types of questions will help you achieve greater student participation.

- **Boomerang questions** can be used to turn a student's question into opportunities for class participation. "That's an interesting question, John. Does anyone have a possible answer?"
- **Comparison questions** develop critical thinking skills: "How would you compare the story of the Good Samaritan to situations you have experienced?"

- **Application questions** allow the children to solve problems based on what they have learned: "Can you give me an example of how you could show more kindness to your brothers and sisters?" These questions also provide measurable evidence of what the children have learned.
- **Recall questions** reveal what the children remember: "Which book in the New Testament gives a description of life in the early Church?
- **Opinion questions** are appropriate at the beginning or middle of a discussion: "Why do you think the Samaritan stopped to help the man lying at the side of the road?"
- **Opinion surveys** identify what the class is thinking: "One at a time, tell me which commandment you think is most important."
- **Pull-in questions** are simply a way to include other children in a response: "Can anyone add to that point? Does anyone think differently?"
- **Evaluation questions** call for the student to make a judgment: "What other ways could Jim and Joe have found to settle their differences?"
- **Repetition** of questions in a lesson is a good way to drill for understanding. Ask the "Do You Know?" question again during the review.
- **Review questions** reveal whether your children learned the major points of a previous lesson.

A Cooperative Spirit

Create an atmosphere in which the success of one increases the success of all. The Church Today projects are one way to encourage group cooperation and learning but there are many other opportunities as well. In general:

- Choose an appropriate task.
- Identify, define, and model specific cooperative behaviors that you want the children to use.
- Use small groups of two or three children to start with. Build toward larger teams.
- Make sure everyone on the team has a role to play.
- Encourage positive interdependence.
- Keep competitiveness out of the cooperative team effort.
- After the task is completed, make time for whole class sharing.

Teaching Techniques

Jesus was not a theologian.
He was God who told stories
—Madeleine L'Engle.

Storytelling

Storytelling is an important tool for the catechist. Throughout history, stories have helped people understand themselves. Much of biblical literature is in story form. The Israelites used stories to convey God's love for them. Jesus did much of his teaching in the form of stories. Stories are important for children because:

- Stories allow the children to feel, to empathize, and to be compassionate toward others.
- Stories create memories.
- Stories are entertaining and engage the imagination.
- Stories encourage reflection and allow the children to see life in a new light. Stories help the children discover their own beliefs.
- Stories unlock experiences.
- Stories help build community.
- Stories allow the children to see the consequences of an action.
- Stories teach the children about heroes, heroines, and saints and allow them to experience adventure, expand their cultural understanding, and see common experiences.
- Stories can be a key in helping the children to pray. After hearing a story that has touched their hearts, they can be led to articulate in prayer the emotions that have been experienced.
- Stories can address a number of environmental and peace issues.
- Folk tales expose the children to various cultures and ways of living and thinking.

Storytelling Techniques

- Create a good listening environment. Make sure you have everyone's attention before beginning. Allow a hushed silence of expectation to develop.
- Be a storyteller, not a story reader. Pause to add details. Give the children a chance to respond.
- Make eye contact with the children.
- Tell the story as if you were really experiencing the events. Use facial expressions, gestures, tone of voice, and volume to add interest. Use direct quotes to make the story come alive. "Jesus said, 'Lazarus! COME OUT!!!!'" has more impact than saying, "Then Jesus told Lazarus to come out of the tomb."
- Tell the story slowly, and show pictures when possible. Build up to the climax.
- Encourage children to chime in with a familiar phrase. Occasionally let the children finish a predictable sentence.
- After a story is told, encourage the children to draw their favorite part of the story.
- Tie things together. There is no harm in letting the class in on why you are telling the story. Ask the children to tell what they learned from the story.
- Don't over analyze the story. Trust the story.

Storytelling Props

- Flannel board
- Sound effects
- Transparencies
- Movement and gestures
- Puppets
- Music
- Chalkboard

Drama

Drama-based activities personally involve the children in the lesson, and allow them to experience what it is like to "be" a particular character in a given situation.

The word "drama" means "doing." Drama is the art of bringing a story to life. In making themselves part of a story, the children will make the story their own.

Use the following techniques to help children become involved in role-playing and drama:

- Select a passage or story that is movement-oriented and has action potential.
- Choose methods such as "theater in the round" or puppet theater to involve shy children.
- Read the passage and discuss it before acting it out. But do not over-analyze; it takes the freshness and spontaneity out of the children's interpretation.
- Avoid typecasting. Let the children experience the whole range of role-playing possibilities. Primary children especially enjoy personifying animals or natural objects such as trees and rocks.
- Rewrite a scripture story (or have the children rewrite) into a modern day setting.
- Experiment with styles. In a time-limited situation, you may want the quickness and flexibility of improvised skits without costumes or sets. Other circumstances may call for elaborate pageants. Keep the goal of the activity—a memorable religious experience, not a Broadway or Hollywood extravaganza—clearly in mind.

Music

Music engages the person—body, mind, and spirit. Music can calm or inspire. It can bring back memories of people and events. Music can even challenge.

You hear music throughout your day. You take in its spirit and it finds a place within you.

- How is music a part of your life?
- How does your attitude about music affect the way you participate in song?
- How does your attitude about music or song impact how you use music with the children?

Music in Class

Use music for listening and music for singing. Make music an essential and regular part of your class time. Play quiet background music while the children are working individually or as a group. Choose a class song. Sing something simple to start your class time as part of your ritual opening prayer. Choose a song to end your time together. Remember: repetition is okay. If it is good music, it will take root within and lead to prayer, meditation and learning.

Music in Teaching

Find music to sing together or to listen to that supports and expands the topic and spirit of the lessons. Benziger offers a music CD for use in the classroom. The songs have been carefully chosen to complement the lessons and to enrich liturgical experiences. The music CD includes songs and hymns for prayer and celebration. Repeated use of music in the classroom will encourage the children to participate more fully in the Sunday liturgy.

Music in Prayer

There are many languages or expressive elements that are prayer, not just words. Song expresses what words alone cannot reach. Whenever at prayer, all present need to be invited into song. If it enables greater confidence and participation, use the recording offered with this series as accompaniment to your song.

Scripture, Prayer, and Social Justice

Using Scripture With Children

An important mission of the catechist is to cultivate in the children a love of Sacred Scripture—especially the Gospels. *Christ Jesus, the Way* is filled with Scripture passages or stories based on the Scriptures. Here are some suggestions for making the Scriptures come alive for the children:

- Present the narrative material from the Bible in story form.
- When using Bible stories, assign characters and parts of the narration to different children.
- Invite the children to act out a Bible passage through mime, role play or using their own words.
- Ask the children to draw a picture or make some creative project that expresses one aspect of the story's significance.
- Children can make simple puppets of the characters in the story by drawing the face of a character on a paper plate and using that plate-face as the character when they say their lines.
- Scripture can become more relevant for the intermediate age children if it is related to other subjects they study. Maps and timelines give an idea of major historical events in relation to major biblical events.
- Give some background information on the culture at the time the story takes place.

Create a simple but elegant enthronement of the Bible. Have a procession with the Bible being carried high, and place the Bible on your prayer table. When reading from the Scripture for prayer, always reverence the Bible making a slight bow before picking it up from the prayer table. By giving the Bible a place of honor in the classroom, the children will begin to give the Bible a place of honor in their lives.

Seeking Justice and Peace

It is important for Catholics to understand that a concern for justice and peace is essential to an authentic Christian faith-life.

Education for justice should occur at every age. Justice cannot be taught in a single lesson; it should permeate the catechatical environment. Although specific issues have changed over the centuries, seven foundational principles characterize the Church's teaching about justice:

1. Every human person possesses a basic dignity that comes from God.
2. Each person has basic rights and responsibilities that flow from his or her God-given dignity.
3. Each person has been called to support the family, form community, and participate in the life of society.

4. Work is part of the human condition; there is a dignity to work, and workers have rights.
5. In all cases, people are to be guided by a fundamental option for the poor and vulnerable.
6. As a goal, Catholics are to work for solidarity with the human family in search of world peace, global development, environmental protection, and safeguarding international human rights.
7. The goods of this world are intended by God for the benefit of all. Everyone is called to exercise responsible stewardship of creation.

The Catholic social justice tradition has continued to our own day through many encyclicals and Church teachings and is based on the Gospel call to love. Like love, social justice is at the very heart of Christian living.

Non-Violent Problem Solving

Teaching peaceful ways of dealing with conflicts promotes non-violent responses. Help the children focus on these ways by working with them to:

- Identify the problem or conflict.
- Name alternative solutions.
- Make a plan of action.
    - Evaluate the effectiveness of the plan.
        - Redesign, continue or discontinue the plan according to its effectiveness.

Promoting Justice

Children in primary grades are highly impressionable. The goal is to lead the children to adopt certain styles of behavior that prepare the way for justice later on.

- Focus on positive values such as peace and caring.
- Foster attitudes of respect, acceptance, and sharing.
- Review your teaching techniques. Balance cooperative learning methods with competitive ones.
- Use rivalries and moments of conflict among the children as opportunities for teaching methods of nonviolent problem solving.

Classroom Prayer and Celebration

Prayer is an integral part of the catechetical endeavor. Pray with the children, and build in them a sense of wonder for the sacred. Help them to recognize God's living presence in every moment of their lives.

- The act of prayer should be an integral part of every lesson, not something merely tacked on to the beginning or end.
- Prayer must be experienced. Meaningful prayer experiences will have far more impact than any memorization or discussion.
- Do not limit the children to just one form. Music, dance, and other forms of artistic expression can be powerful forms of prayer.
- Repetition is necessary for people to grow comfortable with a prayer form. The prayer services in *Celebrate* follow the more formal format of public worship. Familiarizing the children with the order, ritual, responses, and reflection, will lead them to a more active participation in the Sunday Liturgy.

Media Literacy

Media Literacy

In America, the media are everywhere and constant. Every piece of media arbitrates attitudes, values, behavior, culture, and morality. There is no doubt that the media are a dominant and influential force in the lives of children.

Basic Media Literacy

Media can be an effective teaching tool. However, catechists have an obligation to use the media responsibly and critically.

- Media should be used to support a lesson. Talk about the message of the media. Use Christian moral values as a point of comparison.
- Do your homework. Review any media that you wish to use with the class for language, violence, and any negative messages.
- Use a segment of a current TV series or movie to make a value statement. If a show, game, or lyrics are violent, abusive, selfish, suggestive, or even immoral, make sure that the judgment is clear. Hold it up to the light of a Christian response.
- Set a good example. Talk to the children about what you watch, read, and listen to. Children can learn to form good judgments through the example of those that they respect.
- Learn about the movies, video and computer games, and music that are popular and available to children.
- Listen to the children and ask questions. They will not be shy about telling you what is important in media and in pop culture.
- Ask yourself if a piece of media encourages positive reflection, exploration, research, or further action. If so, it can be a valuable tool for teaching.

Cultural Awareness

Parishes across the United States are welcoming Catholics from an increasingly wide range of cultural and racial backgrounds. Communication among diverse peoples needs to be encouraged if our children are to grow in their vision of the kingdom. As a catechist, you model and set the tone for acceptance and understanding of a culturally diverse people.

The following strategies will help work with culturally and ethnically diverse children:

- Incorporate home culture. Learn about the children's home and community culture to better understand the children's behavior in and out of class. Ask the children about the religious and other traditions that they practice at home and invite them to share their experiences with the class.
- Encourage the active participation of parents and guardians. Remind the parents about the importance of talking to their children, reading to them, and sharing personal and family histories andtraditions with them.

- Use culturally relevant materials. *Christ Jesus, the Way* shows diversity through the photos and illustrations, through the stories, and through life examples. Use materials and examples of your own that recognize, incorporate, and reflect the children's racial heritage.
- Identify and dispel stereotypes. Use language and resources that are non-sexist, non-racist, and non-ethnocentric. Dispel stereotypes that the children may experience in the media or in their everyday lives.
- Encourage group activities. This increases the likelihood of inter-ethnic friendships and improved attitudes and behaviors toward classmates of different backgrounds.
- A few words in a foriegn language is no substitute for global and cultural awareness.

Multiple Intelligences

In the religious education class, the goal is to actively engage the children in the sharing of faith. Not all children are engaged in the learning process in the same way. According to the Theory of Multiple Intelligences, every person has abilities in at least eight different areas. Tapping into those areas by the way the class is structured, and the activities that are chosen will produce better results in the children's response to the topic.

The following is a list of the eight intelligences and their definitions along with some ideas to stimulate your thinking as far as planning for various activities that can be used in religious education.

- **Linguistic intelligence** is the ability to understand the meaning and order of words. Word games, puzzles, scripture stories, saint stories, prayer journals, oral presentations, poetry, and Bible activities are all examples of enabling learning through the use of language.
- **Musical intelligence** manifests itself in sensitivity to pitch, melody, rhythm and tone. Create occasions for using song, liturgical hymns and responses, or song as prayer.
- **Logical-mathematical intelligence** is the ability to use numbers effectively and use logic to solve problems. Religious significance of certain numbers 40, 3, 12, number games, graphs, time-lines, sequencing events and stories are of interest to children who have a mathematical ability.
- **Bodily-kinesthetic intelligence** uses the body skillfully. Gestures with song and prayer, drama, crafts, dance help the children who prefer movement.
- **Spatial intelligence** is the ability to think in images and pictures. Maps and models, geography of the Holy Land, church architecture, the use of scenery to depict an event or period appeals to this type of learner.
- **Naturalistic intelligence** recognizes plants, animals, and other parts of the natural environment as important. Nurturing plants and animals in the classroom, creating a nature area, using the outdoors for part of a class or for prayer, emphasizing the goodness of creation, praying the psalms are all ways to engage this type of learner.
- **Interpersonal intelligence** is the ability to understand the feelings and moods of others. Group projects, peer tutoring, and games are this type of learner's preferred style.
- **Intrapersonal intelligence** is understanding one's own strength and weaknesses. Reflection time, journal writing, personal prayer, and examination of conscience are all ways to engage this learner.

Being aware of the needs of the children will go a long way to creating an environment where sharing faith is exciting and meaningful.

Arts and Crafts

Arts and Crafts activities are very important for religious education. Children express and develop creativity in many ways—painting, cutting, pasting, drawing and coloring, pounding and forming clay, working with puppets, and playing games. These activities allow for self-expression, and they foster creativity and sharing.

Make a clear connection between the lesson and the craft or art project. Will it help the children remember the lesson? Will working on the craft or project offer opportunities for cooperation and Christian service?

Catechist Tips

- Make sure the craft or art project is age-appropriate.
- Keep an art supply box. Fill the box with the necessities such as markers, crayons, scissors, glue, construction paper, yarn or ribbon, and a ruler. Add seasonal items when called for.
- Keep projects simple.
- Make a sample.
- Save scraps: tissue paper, construction paper, cloth, etc.
- Maintain a costume box. Include old robes, yardage, fabric scraps, sashes, ropes, Christmas garland, scarves, and the like.
- Keep art and craft activities as natural, spontaneous, free, and enjoyable as possible.

Projects

The following are suggestions for arts and crafts projects:

Paper art
- Collages
- Mosaics
- Texture rubbing
- Tissue paper
- Paper weaving
- Mobiles
- Origami
- Newspaper art
- Dioramas
- Foil paper

Paper mâché
- Masks
- Piñatas

Puppetry
- Finger puppets
- Paper plate puppets
- Spoon puppets
- Paper bag puppets
- Stick puppets
- Sock puppets

Clay
- Pottery
- Sculpture

Paint
- Sponge paint
- Paper batik
- Finger paint
- Straw blowing pictures

Yarn
- Ojos de Dios (Eye of God)